Chauceer's *Knight's Tale*

AN ANNOTATED BIBLIOGRAPHY 1900 TO 1985

As the first of the *Canterbury Tales*, the *Knight's Tale* attracts special attention, particularly in relation to the overall structure of the work and to the other tales. It has been the subject of a vast body of comment by scholars and lay readers. Monica McAlpine provides access to this material in the first of the Chaucer Bibliographies series to deal with a narrative portion of that author's best-known work.

McAlpine includes book-length and chapter-length studies, portions of books and chapters, articles and portions of articles, notes, substantive commentary in editions, study guides, and a few allusions previously unnoticed. Unpublished dissertations are included on a selective basis. Reviews that reflect scholarly debate on the *Knight's Tale* have also been annotated.

The first section of the bibliography covers the various editions and translations of the work published between 1900 and 1985. The second includes backgrounds and general studies, and the third deals with the three major sources. The fourth section provides a chronologically ordered survey of material on the Knight in the General Prologue and the Links. The final section, also chronologically divided, discusses works on the *Knight's Tale* itself.

MONICA E. McALPINE is Professor of English, University of Massachusetts, Boston.

The Chaucer Bibliographies

Chaucer's *Knight's Tale*

AN ANNOTATED BIBLIOGRAPHY

1900 TO 1985

Monica E. McAlpine

Published in association with the University of Rochester by

UNIVERSITY OF TORONTO PRESS

Toronto Buffalo London

Toronto Buffalo London
www.utppublishing.com

ISBN 978-0-8020-5913-0 (cloth)
ISBN 978-1-4426-1485-7 (paper)

Canadian Cataloguing in Publication Data

McAlpine, Monica E., 1940–
Chaucer's Knight's tale:
an annotated bibliography 1900–1985

(The Chaucer bibliographies; 4)
Includes index.
ISBN 978-0-8020-5913-0 (bound). ISBN 978-1-4426-1485-7 (pbk.)

I. Chaucer, Geoffrey, d. 1400. Knight's Tale – Bibliography. I. Title.
II. Series.

28164.M22 1991 016.821'1 C91-093646-3

For Bob Hinman
in gratitude for his teaching and example

Contents

General Editor's Preface

The Chaucer Bibliographies will encompass, in a series of sixteen volumes, a complete listing and assessment of scholarship and criticism on the writings of Geoffrey Chaucer, and on his life, times, and historical context. Three volumes – on Chaucer's lyrics and *Anelida and Arcite*, on the translations, scientific works, and apocrypha, and on the *General Prologue* to the *Canterbury Tales* – have already appeared. The present volume, on the *Knight's Tale*, continues work on the *Canterbury Tales*, and will be followed by other volumes on the *Tales*, though publication of volumes on Chaucer's other poetry will appear in the next years as well. Each volume will center on a particular work, or a connected group of works; most contain material on backgrounds or related writings, and several will be topical in their coverage (music, visual arts, rhetoric, the life of Chaucer, and so on). Like all bibliographical projects, the series places unswerving emphasis on accuracy and comprehensiveness; yet the distinctive feature of the Chaucer Bibliographies, as this and the earlier volumes make clear, is the fullness and particularity of the annotations provided for each entry.

The individual volumes in the Chaucer Bibliographies series do not therefore constitute a reference work in the ordinary sense of that term. While they will enumerate virtually every publication on Chaucer worthy of notice, and give complete coverage to materials from the twentieth century, they go far beyond the usual compilation, bibliographic manual, or guide to research. The bibliographies are not mechanical or machine-produced lists. Each volume makes use of the intellectual engagement, learning, and discretion of a scholar actively at work on Chaucer. The series therefore serves not simply as the collection of all relevant titles on a subject, but as a companion and reliable guide to the reading and study of Chaucer's poetry. In this, the Chaucer Bibliographies represent an innovative and penetrating access to what Chaucer means, and has meant, to his readers. The project offers the full richness and detail of Chaucer's thought and world to a much wider audience than these have, even after one hundred years of energetic scholarship, ever before reached.

Before all else, then, the series provides a means of making practical headway in the study of earlier literature in English and its cultural context. These volumes will make the writing of Chaucer – the earliest figure in the canon of great writers in the English language – more immediate and more directly accessible to all readers. Although readers for six centuries have often praised Chaucer as a moving, superb, complex writer, even teachers of his writing sometimes feel less than fully informed. Moreover, despite his canonical stature, Chaucer has often remained unread or not fully appreciated because of the obstacles of language and historical distance. The goal of this project, at its first level, is to increase the numbers of those who read with understanding and pleasure by increasing the kinds of things that can be readily known about Chaucer. The Bibliographies will effect a major change in how Chaucer gets read, at what levels, and by whom.

The Chaucer Bibliographies seek to intensify the comprehension and enjoyment of beginning readers in university, college, and high school classrooms, presenting themselves as tools to both students and teachers. The series will move undergraduates more quickly from the generalizations and observations of textbooks and instructors to a direct access to the richness and variety of Chaucer's writing, and to its connections with medieval realities and modern understandings. For graduate students, the books will constitute a crucial resource for course work, exam preparation, and research. For non-specialist teachers of Chaucer in survey, masterpiece, and special topic courses, the series offers the means to a broader base of knowledge and to a more intense and shapely preparation than instructors, given the constraints of their work time, were previously able to manage. By clarifying and connecting both recent and long-available materials, and by making them readily accessible, the Chaucer Bibliographies can renew the teaching and reading of Chaucer, and enable the development of alternative approaches to understanding his writing.

The series promises still more for specialist readers. The fullness and detail of the annotations in each volume serve, in the first instance, as a check against duplication and redundancy; scholars and editors will be able to chart the place of new or proposed work quickly. Likewise, Chaucerians engaged with a topic or set of issues will be able to advance or situate their work more quickly by reference to the materials in the appropriate volumes in the series. In consolidating the massive work that has been done in the last century or so in medieval studies, and particularly on Chaucer, the Bibliographies provide the ground on which new work in Chaucer can build. Their presence will encourage more efficient research on minute as well as expansive topics, and will likewise facilitate work on the larger patterns and themes of Chaucer criticism, and on the ways in which institutions have fostered and used the reading and study of his writing.

In addition to Chaucerians, the Bibliographies benefit other specialists in medieval literature in offering ready access to publications on Chaucer that take up a variety of materials relevant to other fields. Whatever use the materials gathered in these volumes have for particular queries or problems, they will also address the interests of a range of scholars whose expertise extends to Chaucer, but whose contributions to Chaucer studies have been inhibited by the daunting mass of Chaucer scholarship. The Bibliographies place interdisciplinary research by Chaucerians at the disposal of scholars in history, art history, and other related areas, and so make multidisciplinary, collaborative work more possible and even more likely. In short, this massive effort to bring knowledge about Chaucer together strives to open up, rather than to close off, further innovative work on pre-modern culture.

The first four volumes in the series have analyzed, on average, some eight hundred items each. These include editions of Chaucer's writing, studies of language, manuscripts, and audiences, his sources and their contexts and intellectual connections, directly relevant background materials (eg, estates satire, medieval science, chivalry, the tradition of Boethius, the influence of Italian writers), and all publications (in whatever language) bearing directly on Chaucer's poetry. The early volumes have thoroughly fulfilled the promise of the series to sort out and make accessible materials that are confused or obscure, including early philological publications in German and Scandinavian languages, privately printed or scarce volumes, and recent work in Australia and Japan. But even more strikingly, in bringing together all the materials on specific poems and subjects, these volumes have given new definition to the boundaries of Chaucer studies. Rather than working as a mopping-up operation, telling readers what they already knew, these volumes have taken their place in the new flourishing of Chaucer research and criticism, enabling and even inspiring fresh and solidly grounded interrogations of the poetry. They stand not simply as the summation of a great tradition, but as an impetus for more intense and expansive understandings of Chaucer. The sweeping vision of late medieval writing offered in each volume represents a reconfiguration of knowledge that justifies and encourages work by an expanded community of scholars, of whom Chaucerians form merely the core.

In producing volumes that record all relevant titles and that specify – and, in effect, assess – the content and interconnections of Chaucerian criticism, the Chaucer Bibliographies define a new space for themselves in their own field, and perhaps more widely among other reference tools as well. The volumes, published and projected, differ markedly in purpose and use from other introductory bibliographies and cumulative listings. Those unmarked, or minimally annotated listings are in essence on-going reviews of research, and as such they offer limited help to the specialist, and still less orientation or access to the uninitiated. Volumes in the Chaucer Bibliographies project take these publications as a base of information (and make reference to them), but the aim of each volume is to offer in-depth coverage of the work(s) at hand. Contributors initially review annual and collected listings, but acquired learning, developed instincts, and the extensive reading demanded for the preparation of each volume together provide titles and leads that complete the search. The series as a whole seeks to stand as a definitive companion to the study of Chaucer, a starting point from which future work on the poet will proceed. It addresses itself to an audience beyond the community of professional Chaucerians, inviting non-Chaucerian scholars and non-specialist teachers and students to take part in the continuous process of understanding Chaucer.

The series achieves this inclusiveness through exhaustive itemization, full and strategic commentary, attention to backgrounds and corollary issues, demonstration of interrelationships and connected themes through annotation, cross-referencing, and indices, and the report of significant reviews. Its design entails an examination of every relevant published item, in all foreign languages, though contributors will trust their own expertise and discretion in determining the choice and extent of annotations. Information on a 'ghost' or an inaccessible but useless item may prove as valuable to users of these volumes as careful assessments of central books in the field; contributors have consequently taken special pains not to pass over inadvertently or to deliberately omit any 'trivial' writings. The specification of items in these volumes should obviate the need for many pointless struggles with the trammels of scholarship as readers of Chaucer pursue their special interests.

The Chaucer Bibliographies have been produced through the work of a diverse and distinguished array of experts. Such a format –

where the individual efforts of autonomous scholars take their place within the well articulated, coherent framework of a single project – represents in a peculiarly appropriate way a project like this, with its broad base and wide appeal. The authors of individual volumes include both distinguished and younger Chaucerians, all of whom have demonstrated their learning and their engagement with the project. The expansive work for each volume has been carried out over a period of years by an individual scholar or a team in close collaboration, conceiving each volume as a single, coherent intellectual project giving access to Chaucer's poetry. Having a collective of two dozen Chaucerians actively engaged in the same project has already led to a more thorough cross-checking, a richer array of suggestions and shared information, and a larger number of surprising finds – some obscure, some obvious – than any individual or more limited collaborative effort could produce.

Since materials for the entire series will be on magnetic tape, floppy disks, or hard disks, it will be possible for the University of Toronto Press to issue revised editions of volumes, or to provide updated versions of the Bibliographies. It will also be possible to issue a general index to all sixteen books, though at present no decision has been made on this. The comprehensive and accessible character of the materials gathered for this entire project makes them the possible substance of a Chaucer data base. Although the production of an on-line data base is not a feature of the Chaucer Bibliographies project, several scholars have expressed interest in this further use for the work of the series. Inquiries and suggestions on this possibility will be welcomed by the General Editor and the University of Toronto Press.

The Chaucer Bibliographies as a project, and its individual volumes, have demanded extraordinary commitments of time and of intellectual and financial support. Brian J. Thompson, Provost of the University of Rochester, provided initial and continuing assistance towards realizing the project's goals. Since August 1989, the Project has been supported in large part by a grant through the Division of Research Programs of the National Endowment for the Humanities (USA). Prudence Tracy, the series' Editor at the University of Toronto Press, has carefully seen the volumes through production. Individual authors and the Editorial Board have made this a genuinely collaborative project; among the latter, John Leyerle has been especially active and effective in forwarding the work of the Bibliographies. Susan Sandell Draper, as Editorial Assistant to the Project, prepared the initial copy for the present volume; John G. Roberts III has produced the final copy, and in the course of his work he has solved many compositional problems, headed off even more, and made technical and substantive contributions to the excellence of this volume.

Thomas Hahn
Rochester, NY
12 June 1990

Preface

The *Knight's Tale* has been so frequently a subject of comment by both scholars and common readers that it is virtually impossible to collect all discussions of it. If I were to add to discussions of the Tale all the references to the Knight's portrait, I could probably fill yet another half-volume with annotations. These observations are not intended to justify any deficiencies in this bibliography, but rather to recognize that the materials collected here exist in a still broader context of comment and allusion which testifies to the important place the Knight and his Tale have long held in the mental world of many readers of English literature.

While acknowledging this significant limitation, my aim is to be, in the ordinary scholarly sense, 'exhaustive' in my coverage of commentary on the *Knight's Tale*. This volume includes book-length and chapter-length studies, portions of books and chapters, articles and sometimes portions of articles, notes, substantive commentary in editions, study guides, and a few allusions not previously noticed. Unpublished dissertations are included on a selective basis. Reviews that address substantive problems in the *Knight's Tale* have also been annotated. As with the other volumes in this series, the chronological point of departure is 1900, taken as defining the era of scholarship inaugurated by Skeat's edition in 1894 (see **3**), but I have also included some earlier materials of special interest.

As the first of the *Canterbury Tales*, the *Knight's Tale* attracts a special kind of attention, particularly in relation to the overall structure of the work and to other specific tales, most notably the *Parson's Tale*, the *Man of Law's Tale*, the *Monk's Tale*, and *Melibee*. Of special significance is its position in Fragment I and its web of interconnections with the *Miller's Tale*, *Reeve's Tale*, and *Cook's Tale*. The annotations frequently present with considerable fullness critical formulations that compare and contrast tales, especially within Fragment I, rather than attempting to isolate comments on the *Knight's Tale* in an artificial manner that would ultimately obscure their significance. A second issue concerns the narrator of the Tale and the Knight of the *General Prologue*. Many critics, though certainly not all, have regarded the narrator of the Tale as the Knight himself, rather than the poet. Studies of the Knight's performance as narrator are treated in the section on the Tale; when a critic gives extended attention to the Knight's portrait and to his role as narrator, the item is annotated in both of the relevant sections of this volume.

The entries on the Knight and on the Tale are organized in a way that compromises between alphabetical and chronological principles of order: ie, within each of five chronological divisions, items are presented in alphabetical order according to the author's last name, with several items by an individual author being presented in chronological order. I have reasoned that in a volume organized in a strictly alphabetical fashion, there would be no convenient way for a reader to reconstruct any even rough chronological sequence for the commentary, but there would be two largely duplicative alphabetical orderings in the main body of annotations and in the index. Under the system I have chosen, the work of a few scholars is disposed over two or more sections; all the work of any one scholar can be easily recovered, however, through use of the index. A common objection to chronological schemes is that scholarly discussion does not evolve in any strict temporal order but often involves unpredictable leaps and linkages. These relationships can be readily recovered, though, through the system of cross-references within the annotations as well as through the index, where for each item, both main entries and cross-references are given and distinguished from each other.

Within the annotations, I have attempted to record the full range of interpretations of frequently treated passages and issues. At the same time, I have tried to cite even brief discussions of seldom treated lines and topics, especially where the author's treatment of familiar topics was more commonplace. Regrettably, it has not been possible to note, or even sometimes to signal the presence of, all the valuable materials that a student of the *Knight's Tale* and its contexts might want to know about; the scholarly sources are simply too rich to permit it. At the extremes of brevity and extension, the length of the annotations does usually reflect my judgment of the value of the items, but in the broad middle range, many different considerations affect length: eg, it is very difficult to suggest the substance of a stylistic analysis in brief compass.

Throughout the volume, but especially in the central section on the *Knight's Tale*, I have used somewhat frequent and sometimes extended direct quotation. Since the Tale's interpreters deal so frequently with the same subjects, it would often have been difficult to bring out their distinctive contributions through the instrumentality of my own homogenizing prose. My own words would to a degree misrepresent the eloquent formulations of many critics. Even where the authors' words may inspire reactions other than admiration, they will enable the reader of this volume, I hope, to experience something of the passion, variety of intellectual styles, humor, contentiousness, subtlety, and humanity of these ninety years of debate. I have, of course, made a particular effort to quote those frequently cited critical formulations that make up a now traditional body of glosses for the Tale.

The list of editions, presented in chronological order according to the general format for this bibliographical series, is selective and yet designed to represent as fully as possible the varied aspects of the history of the Tale's presentation. It includes all editions of the Middle English text of any critical value, and those whose introductions, notes, glossaries, or bibliographies are noteworthy. All separate editions of the *Knight's Tale* have been included. Attention has been paid to such practices as excerpting, illustrating, and censoring. The list of translations, though much more selective, has been chosen on similar principles.

Despite the crucial importance of Boethius' *Consolation of Philosophy* to the *Knight's Tale*, the *Consolation* is not included in my section on sources because of the thoroughly detailed treatment of Chaucer's *Boece*, of Boethius, and of Boethian influence on Chaucer in Russell A. Peck's volume in this series: *Chaucer's 'Romaunt of the Rose' and 'Boece' ... 1900 to 1985* (1988). My treatment of the scholarship on the *Teseida*, the *Thebaid*, and the *Roman de Thèbes* is highly selective, emphasizing works in English and works already singled out for attention by Chaucerians. Within the sections on sources, editions and translations are listed in chronological order; all other items, in alphabetical order.

The topical subdivision of the section on 'Backgrounds and General Studies' reflects the emphases I have found in Chaucerian scholarship, and will help readers, it is hoped, to locate items of interest more rapidly while mitigating the dizzying sense of miscellaneity often experienced in consulting such lists.

My inclusion of an exhaustive section on the Knight's portrait in the *General Prologue* reflects three realities. For eight hundred years knights have had an important cultural significance (by contrast with, say, summoners), and for many of those years, Chaucer's Knight has played a prominent role in shaping perceptions of knighthood, especially among general readers and cultural commentators. Most importantly, interpretations of the portrait have, arguably at least, had an impact on readings of the Tale, an impact that can now be explored in some detail. My treatment of the Knight's portrait goes beyond the kind of attention it was possible to give to any one pilgrim in Caroline Eckhardt's volume on the *General Prologue* in this series (1990).

On certain technical points: Within each annotation, I have preserved the author's spellings (eg, 'Emelye' / 'Emily') and manner of treating terms (whether underlined or placed in quotation marks). Where I have supplied line references, they have been given as in Robinson's second edition (**39**), and where an author has used a different form of reference, both lineations have been given. Material in brackets always represents terms or information supplied by me. I have used ellipses only to indicate omissions within quotations, and I have adjusted end punctuation to fit my own prose context.

Other scholarly works that an author discusses in a prominent way are cross-referenced by number (in boldface) in the body of the annotation. At the end of the annotation, cross reference numbers direct the reader to other entries in which the work just annotated is cited. Cross references for corrigenda, however, usually appear at the appropriate place in the body of the annotation. I have sometimes provided cross references to related materials in this volume.

I wish to express my gratitude to A.J. Colaianne, one of the original General Editors, who invited me to participate in the Chaucer Bibliographies project. Thomas Hahn, current General Editor, has overseen the production of this volume with tact, kindliness, and good sense. The standard of work set by Russell Peck, in the first two volumes of the series, has been a source of constant instruction and inspiration. I profited from Thomas Ross' early draft of material for the *Miller's Tale* volume, and I derived much help from materials prepared by Caroline Eckhardt for her volume on the *General Prologue* and from correspondence with her. Howell Chickering provided generous assistance with the scholarship on chivalry, and Janet Smarr responded to questions on Boccaccian scholarship. For a careful reading of the manuscript at an intermediate stage, I am indebted to Alan Gaylord. Of course, I alone remain responsible for any deficiencies in the work.

I am happy to record my very special thanks to Hildegarde von Laue, librarian at the Healey Library of the University of Massachusetts at Boston, now retired. Without her dedicated service, this work could not have been completed. The entire library staff has been consistently helpful. I was also fortunate to have the expert services of Sarah Boslaugh and Mary Ann Boelcskevy, graduate students in the English Department of UMass–Boston, in translating German scholarship. I am equally indebted to Maureen Ryberg, who carried the burden of Italian translation, with assistance from Sandra Gregoli. John Roberts, of the English Department at the University of Rochester, scripted the text on computer and led me gracefully through the stages of preparing final copy.

The work on this volume was supported in part by a Faculty Development grant from the College of Arts and Sciences at UMass–Boston, which provided a course reduction. Additional grants from Educational Needs funds supported reproduction and other costs.

Finally, I am grateful to my son, Andrew McAlpine Crossley, for bringing so much of the world, so joyfully, into my life, day by day. And to my husband, Bob Crossley, I am grateful for his usual, immense patience and generosity, shown in so many ways but not least in sharing space on the hard disc.

Abbreviations

LITERARY WORKS CITED

Aen	*Aeneid* (Vergil)
Anel	*Anelida and Arcite*
Ariadne	*The Legend of Ariadne*
Astr	*A Treatise on the Astrolabe*
BD	*Book of the Duchess*
Bo	*Boece*
CA	*Confessio Amantis* (Gower)
ClT	*Clerk's Tale*
CkP	*Cook's Prologue*
CkT	*Cook's Tale*
Consol	*The Consolation of Philosophy* (Boethius)
CT	*Canterbury Tales*
CYT	*Canon's Yeoman's Tale*
De Casibus	*De Casibus Virorum Illustrium* (Boccaccio)
Dec	*Decameron* (Boccaccio)
Div Com	*The Divine Comedy* (Dante)
Equat	*Equatorie of the Planetis*
Fables	*Fables Ancient and Modern* (Dryden)
Filos	*Il Filostrato* (Boccaccio)
FQ	*Faerie Queene* (Spenser)
FranT	*Franklin's Tale*
FrT	*Friar's Tale*
GP	*General Prologue*
HF	*House of Fame*
Hypermnestra	*The Legend of Hypermnestra*
Inf	*Inferno* (Dante)
KQ	*Kingis Quair* (James I of Scotland?)
KnT	*Knight's Tale*
LGW	*The Legend of Good Women*
ManT	*Manciple's Tale*

Mars	*The Complaint of Mars*
Mel	*Tale of Melibee*
MerT	*Merchant's Tale*
Met	*Metamorphoses* (Ovid)
MilT	*Miller's Tale*
MLT	*Man of Law's Tale*
MkP	*Monk's Prologue*
MkT	*Monk's Tale*
MND	*A Midsummer Night's Dream* (Shakespeare)
NPP	*Nun's Priest's Prologue*
NPT	*Nun's Priest's Tale*
P&A	*Palamon and Arcite* (Chaucer's early version of *KnT*)
Pal	*Palamon and Arcite* (Dryden's translation of *KnT*)
Par	*Paradiso* (Dante)
PardT	*Pardoner's Tale*
ParsT	*Parson's Tale*
Partenopeu	*Partenopeu de Blois* (anonymous French Romance)
Partonope	*Partonope of Blois* (anonymous English romance)
PF	*Parliament of Fowls*
PhyT	*Physician's Tale*
Phyllis	*The Legend of Phyllis*
Piers	*Piers Plowman* (Langland)
Pity	*The Complaint unto Pity*
PrT	*Prioress' Tale*
Purg	*Purgatorio* (Dante)
Ret	*Chaucer's Retractation*
RTh	*Roman de Thèbes* (anonymous)
Rom	*The Romaunt of the Rose*
RR	*Le Roman de la Rose* (G. de Lorris & Jean de Meun)
RvT	*Reeve's Tale*
SGGK	*Sir Gawain and the Green Knight* (anonymous)
ShT	*Shipman's Tale*
Siege	*The Siege of Thebes* (Lydgate)
SNT	*Second Nun's Tale*
SqT	*Squire's Tale*
SumT	*Summoner's Tale*
TC	*Troilus and Criseyde*
Tes	*Il Teseida* (Boccaccio)
Thop	*Tale of Sir Thopas*
Theb	*Thebaid* (Statius)
TNK	*The Two Noble Kinsmen* (Shakespeare & J. Fletcher)
Truth	*Truth: Balade de Bon Conseyl*

WBP	*Wife of Bath's Prologue*
WBT	*Wife of Bath's Tale*

JOURNALS AND REFERENCE WORKS CITED

Ang	*Anglia*
AnM	*Annuale Mediaevale*
AN&Q	*American Notes and Queries*
BlakeS	*Blake Studies*
CE	*College English*
ChauR	*Chaucer Review*
CL	*Comparative Literature*
CR	*Critical Review*
DAI	*Dissertation Abstracts International*
DQR	*Dutch Quarterly Review*
E&S	*Essays and Studies*
EIC	*Essays in Criticism*
EJ	*The English Journal*
ELH	*English Literary History*
ELN	*English Language Notes*
EM	*English Miscellany*
EngR	*English Record*
ES	*English Studies*
Expl	*Explicator*
FCS	*Fifteenth-Century Studies*
JEGP	*Journal of English and Germanic Philology*
LeedsSE	*Leeds Studies in English*
M&H	*Medievalia et Humanistica*
MA	*Le Moyen Âge*
MÆ	*Medium Ævum*
MED	*Middle English Dictionary*
MichA	*Michigan Academician*
MLN	*Modern Language Notes*
MLQ	*Modern Language Quarterly*
MLR	*Modern Language Review*
MP	*Modern Philology*
MS	*Mediaeval Studies*
N&Q	*Notes and Queries*
Neophil	*Neophilologus*
NM	*Neuphilologische Mitteilungen*
OED	*Oxford English Dictionary*
PLL	*Papers on Language and Literature*

PMLA	*Publications of the Modern Language Association*
PQ	*Philological Quarterly*
REL	*Review of English Literature*
RES	*Review of English Studies*
RomR	*Romanic Review*
RPh	*Romance Philology*
SAC	*Studies in the Age of Chaucer*
SAQ	*South Atlantic Quarterly*
SBoc	*Studi sul Boccaccio*
SMC	*Studies in Medieval Culture*
SP	*Studies in Philology*
Spec	*Speculum*
TCAAS	*Transactions of the Connecticut Academy of Arts and Sciences*
TLS	*London Times Literary Supplement*
TSLL	*Texas Studies in Language and Literature*
UTQ	*University of Toronto Quarterly*
YES	*Yearbook of English Studies*
YFS	*Yale French Studies*

Introduction

Composition and Revision of the *Knight's Tale*

The question, when was the *Knight's Tale* composed, is really three questions in one: when was the work known as *Palamon and Arcite* composed, when did that work become the *Knight's Tale*, and in what ways was *Palamon and Arcite* revised in the process of becoming the *Knight's Tale*? The external evidence for the existence of a work known as *Palamon and Arcite* and for a date of composition in or before the mid-1380s is the reference in the F version (lines 420–1 cf G 408–9) of the Prologue to the *Legend of Good Women* (dated 1386–8). Brink **529**, who originated the theory that the *Palamon* was an abandoned work in seven-line stanzas, parts of which Chaucer later used in *Anelida* and *Troilus*, dated the original work in 1372–6. His theory and date were successfully opposed by Pollard **7** and Tatlock **632**, who, however, preferred a late date of 1391. The *Anelida* is now regarded as Chaucer's first attempt (1372–80) to adapt Boccaccio's *Teseida*, rather than as a remnant of the *Palamon*. The relation of the *Knight's Tale* to *Troilus* has long been a puzzle (see Lowes **596**, Mather **607**, Tatlock **632**). Robinson **751** regarded the matter as unsettled but dated the *Knight's Tale* 1382 and *Troilus* 1386. Stephen Barney has recently suggested that Chaucer worked simultaneously on these two poems and *Boece*.[1]

Arguments from internal evidence have focused on the relation of dates in the text to actual fourteenth-century calendars, on astrological references, and on alleged historical allusions. The calendar method made perhaps unwarranted assumptions about Chaucer's poetic intentions and failed to establish the date of composition

1 *The Riverside Chaucer*, ed. Larry D. Benson [Boston: Houghton Mifflin, 1987], p 1021. On the *LGW* see M.C.E. Shaner and A.S.G. Edwards, p 1060.

definitively (see Skeat **625**, Manly **605a**, Mather **607**). North **874** thinks Chaucer began work on the Tale in 1387, partly on the basis of Saturn's position in Leo (I.2462). None of the proposed historical references can be regarded as secure (see Cook **537**, Hinckley **576**, Lowes **595**, Parr **737-8**, Pratt **744**).

The question of what revisions the *Knight's Tale* may have undergone is probably unresolvable. In reaction against Brink's elaborate theory, the scholarly consensus has admitted only lines I.875–92 and 3107–8 as adaptations to the Canterbury context, and line 1201, with its reference to a written work, is sometimes cited as evidence that Chaucer did not fine-tune his text to a pilgrim-narrator. Earlier scholars tended to see Chaucer as a poet who did little revising in general. Manly and Rickert claimed, on the basis of manuscript evidence, that Chaucer did sometimes revise his texts, including the last 300 lines of the *Knight's Tale*, rather minutely, but their treatment of authorial revision has been stringently criticized by Kane (see **42R** and **717**). David **936** regards incorporation of the *Palamon* into the *Canterbury Tales* as itself a major transformation, and Owen **733** characterizes the construction of Fragment I as Chaucer's last great poetic work.

Early Appreciation of the *Knight's Tale*

For over two hundred years after its composition, appreciation of the *Knight's Tale* took as one of its forms creative adaptation by other artists, including Clanvowe, Lydgate, James I, the author of *Partonope of Blois*, Douglas, and Spenser. In the late sixteenth and early seventeenth centuries the Tale enjoyed a flurry of popularity as a source for plays: lost plays by R. Edwardes (1566) and Philip Henslowe (1594), *Midsummer Night's Dream* (1595/6) and *Two Noble Kinsmen* (c 1613). The Theseus of *Midsummer Night's Dream* is viewed as one of Shakespeare's most important debts to Chaucer. Although echoes of the Tale have been found in Milton (**1114**) and Keats (**747**), the Renaissance stage career of the *Knight's Tale* seems to mark the end of one era in its appreciation.

In this same early period, allusions to the *Knight's Tale* are rather frequent. John Shirley prefixed an 'advertisement' to the Tale in MS Harley 7333, promising 'disporte and leornyng of all [th]oo that beon gentile of birthe or of condicions' (1450).[2] Wyatt (1542; Spurgeon

2 Derek Brewer, ed. *Chaucer: The Critical Heritage* (London: Routledge and Kegan Paul, 1978), Volume 1, 65. All further references to this two-volume work will appear in the text.

629, 1:83–4) criticized those who preferred *Thopas* to the *Knight's Tale*, and Sir Francis Beaumont appealed to decorum (1597; Spurgeon, 1:146) to justify such different sorts of tales as the Miller's and the Knight's. For the seventeenth century, described by Spurgeon as 'the time of gloom and neglect' (1:xxxvii) and by Brewer, as 'the pause in appreciation of Chaucer' (1:13), only a very few allusions, reflecting mostly antiquarian interests, have been identified. The *Knight's Tale* was not a special victim of neglect; on the contrary, it is the second most frequently cited Canterbury tale before 1700 (after the *Nun's Priest's Tale*), and the most frequently cited tale from 1700 to 1800, as well as the most frequently cited tale overall from the beginning to 1800 (Spurgeon, 1:lxxix).

A principal cause of the Tale's high visibility after 1700 was the publication in that year of Dryden's version in his *Fables Ancient and Modern*, and his praise of Chaucer's work in his famous Preface as a poem 'of the *Epique* kind' 'perhaps not much inferiour' to the *Iliad* or the *Aeneid*. He found the *Knight's Tale* equal to the ancient texts in learning, diction, manners, and disposition (or construction); deficient only in Aristotelian unity of time; and superior in having a 'more pleasing' story, presumably because of its more prominent love interest. Dryden might have assessed Chaucer's epic intentions differently if he had been familiar with the *Teseida* and Chaucer's reworking of it, or if he had weighed the retrospective lights thrown on the *Knight's Tale* by the *Miller's Tale*, but this style of reading was not yet practiced.

More revealing than his generic classification of the Tale was Dryden's stylistic transformation of it in his version. He made the Tale more dramatic by rounding out the characters and defining the time and space in which they act (Middleton **863**), and he burnished the Tale's already considerable visual appeal by the use of painterly pictorialism (Doederlin **1085**). He streamlined the narrative by dividing it into three parts and introducing new symmetrical elements (Miner **865**, Milne **1003**). Many of Dryden's changes made Chaucer's tale more homogeneous in tone and more straightforward in its implications. He devised a neat formula linking Arcite's love and his repentance; eliminated all 'trivial' elements, such as Arcite's mouse (I.1261) and Mars' child-devouring sow and cook's ladle (I.2019–20); and dropped the narrator. The humor, the philosophical complexities, and the variousness of matter and style in Chaucer's work were sacrificed in favor of sobriety, certainty, and a general elevation of theme and treatment (see esp. Middleton).

In the eighteenth century, John Dart, author of the Life of Chaucer in Urry's edition of the *Works* (1721), followed Dryden in praising the *Knight's Tale* as 'the best of [Chaucer's] Performances, ... a finished Epick Poem' (Spurgeon, 1:360). Many commentators throughout the century agreed, though Samuel Johnson, one of several Neo-classical critics who had little enthusiasm for Chaucer (Brewer, 1:13), objected both to Dryden's 'hyperbolical commendation' and to the anachronism of the Tale's setting (Spurgeon, 1:456). Dryden's version of the Tale was reprinted in both Thomas Morell's edition of the *General Prologue* and *Knight's Tale* (1727), and in George Ogle's volume of modernizations (1741). Later, both Thomas Gray (1760) and Thomas Warton (1774) praised what Gray called the 'grave and stately' meter of the *Knight's Tale* (Spurgeon, 1:420).

Throughout the century, the humorous Chaucer was especially valued, with one versifier presenting a 'gay Chaucer' as a Knight accompanied by his Squire, 'Humour' (1782; Spurgeon, 1:466). *Thopas* was highly esteemed, as by Hurd (1762; Spurgeon, 1:421–2), prompting Joseph Warton to admonish his readers that 'it is a common mistake that Chaucer's excellence lay in his manner of treating light and ridiculous subjects; for whoever will attentively consider the noble poem of Palamon and Arcite will be convinced that he equally excels in the pathetic and sublime' (1782).[3] An anonymous commentator, in a set of notes on Dryden's version (1785; Spurgeon, 1:480–1), shows a striking degree of ambivalence about the humor of the *Knight's Tale.* Aptly describing the Tale as being 'of a mixt nature,' he notes Chaucer's fondness for 'jests and dashes of satire'; yet he finds the lament of the Athenian women a 'miserable jest' and the tree nymphs an incongruous bit of burlesque. He concludes uncertainly that Dryden should 'perhaps' be praised for preserving Chaucer's 'satirical pleasantries.' J. H. Mortimer's illustration of Palamon and Arcite fighting (1779) was planned as part of a series of illustrations favoring comical Chaucerian subjects (Spurgeon, 1:447), but in Mortimer's depiction of Emelye for Bell's edition of Chaucer (1782–3), Miskimin **1004** finds a sign of the transition from Chaucer the witty satirist to Chaucer the melancholy poet.

As the nineteenth century opened, Dorothy Wordsworth (1803) was reading the *Knight's Tale* with 'exquisite delight' (Spurgeon, 2:14). Although it is impossible to surmise confidently the source of her

3 J.A. Burrow, ed., *Geoffrey Chaucer: A Critical Anthology* (Baltimore: Penguin, 1969), p 77.

delight (she also read the *Miller's Tale*: 2:3), William Godwin was at the same time describing the *Knight's Tale* as the most 'powerful portrait of chivalry that was perhaps ever delineated' (*Life of Chaucer* [1804], p 193). Scott fostered this view by using three passages from Dryden's version as epigraphs to chapters of *Ivanhoe* (1819), including the famous chapter on the tournament of Ashby-de-la-Zouche. The Tale was sufficiently popular at this time to inspire a new modernization in verse by Lord Thurlow (1822; Spurgeon, 2:140), and it was 're-done' four more times during the century. Nevertheless, just as some in the eighteenth century had preferred *Thopas* to the *Knight's Tale*, so some like George Frederick Nott (1815–6) now favored the *Squire's Tale*, with its unity of subject, figures, ideas, and machinery, as a noble 'specimen of romantic imagination' over the *Knight's Tale* with its troubling incongruities (Spurgeon, 2:79–80). Nott praises Chaucer, however, for his delineation of character, finding 'shades of difference' worthy of Homer in the heroic figures of the Knight, the Squire, Palamon, Arcite, Emetrius, and Lygurge. Blake's engraving of the Canterbury pilgrims (1809), as well as his celebration of them in the Descriptive Catalogue as 'lineaments of universal human life,' had given a powerful new impulse to the appreciation of character. Later, however, the *Knight's Tale* would begin to lose its claim to this kind of interest; Furnivall (1873) classified the Tale as early work of Chaucer's on the ground of its weak characterization: 'Who knows which is Palamon and which is Arcite?' (Brewer, 2:174).

More durable for the *Knight's Tale* would be the emphasis on Chaucer's realism, conceived not as the social satire appreciated from the sixteenth century on but as a non-rhetorical immediacy of style. 'His words point as an index to the objects, like the eye or finger. There [are] ... no borrowed roseate tints.' So says Hazlitt (1818; **572**) while commending several passages in the *Knight's Tale*, including the descriptions of Emelye in the garden, Palamon in his cell, and the temple of Mars. Hunt (1855; **579**) makes a similar point in his comment on the implied comparison of Emelye with the sun: 'The poet lets nature speak for herself. He points to the two beautiful objects before us, and is content simply hailing them in their combination.' Chaucer's descriptions of nature were admired throughout the century, but 'Matthew Browne' (William Brightly Rands, 1869; **531**) warned minds formed on Wordsworthian poetry that Chaucer's Nature is God's Vicar, 'an obedient worker,' not a source of revelation. The passage on the busy lark (I.1491–2) is 'beautiful ... but ...

all homely; it is all the *face* of nature; ... there is no undercurrent.' Browne did not consider this difference a deficiency in Chaucer.

Perhaps a Wordsworthian influence can also be traced in the emphasis on a topic Dryden had introduced, Chaucer's pathos. Several of the passages cited by Hazlitt are notable for their pathos, and Swinburne (1880) later praised Chaucer for combining the 'great gift of specially English humour' with 'the inseparable twin-born gift of peculiarly English pathos. In the figures of Arcite and Grisilde, he has actually outdone Boccaccio's very self for pathos' (Brewer, 2:223). One of the things that had been substantially lost since Dryden, and the replacement of *Troilus and Criseyde* by the *Canterbury Tales* as Chaucer's premier work, was an appreciation of Chaucer as love poet. In 1877 William Cyples **545** explained Chaucerian 'usages' in love in patient detail, with frequent reference to the *Knight's Tale*. At the same time, the century's appreciation of the Middle Ages was reaching a new stage in the glamorization of things medieval by the pre-Raphaelites. The *Kelmscott Chaucer* (1896) enshrines a poet of pathos, love, and romantic pastness. Yet the *Knight's Tale* has qualities — variousness, humor, realism, rhetorical density, detachment — that resist the 'Romantic "medieval" frisson' (Brewer, 2:21), and these same qualities may have disqualified it for Arnold's accolade (1880) of 'high seriousness.' The *Knight's Tale* is not mentioned in the great Victorian's famous essay (on 'The Study of Poetry').

Modern Criticism of the *Knight's Tale*

In the period between Skeat's edition (1894, **3**) and Robinson's (1933, **39**), Chaucer's stylistic achievement, especially in descriptions, was widely appreciated, sometimes being cited as the Tale's greatest strength. The list of admired passages — eg, Theseus' homecoming, Emelye in the garden, the princes' meeting in the wood, the theater, Lygurge and Emetrius, the tournament, Arcite's death-bed scene — was often repeated, with pre-eminence being granted to the descriptions of the temples. This sense of the Tale is embodied in Root's famous phrase, 'a web of splendidly pictured tapestry' (**619**) and in the early practice of presenting the Tale in selections (**13**, **22**, **29**, **32**; cf **62**).

A strong consensus found characterization an undeveloped aspect of the Tale, even its chief weakness. Nevertheless, some readers found a significant distinction between Palamon and Arcite; Root touched lightly upon an antithesis between acting and dreaming which was developed more insistently by Fairchild **557** as an antithesis between an 'active' Arcite and a 'contemplative' Palamon. Still, readers were unable to agree on who was the ethically superior or more sympathetic prince. Emelye was appreciated as an embodiment of feminine beauty whose restricted role was necessary to that status. Theseus was seen by a few critics as Chaucer's strongest character, even as a spokesman for the poet; Brink **530** offered an original characterization of the Duke as 'a sort of earthly Providence' (cf Mather's 'smiling providence of the romance' [**606**]), a view that would not find an echo until the studies of Frost **684** and Muscatine **726**.

The solution of the most famous crux in the *Knight's Tale*, Lowes' demonstration (**599**) that *hereos* (I.1374) is a technical term for a mental condition arising from passion, helped to clarify the place of courtly love in the poem. Dodd **548** provided a useful overview of the traditional elements, and Hulbert **578** described the operation of the *demande d'amour*. Some commentators (eg, Getty **560**) believed Chaucer was satirizing the courtly tradition. By contrast, the theme of male friendship inspired an enthusiastic response (eg, Cowling **540**, Mather **606**) which is also mirrored in illustrations (**23**, **38**) highlighting the meeting of the princes in the wood.

The historicity of the Tale was understood to lie in its allusions to contemporary events (Hinckley **576**) and in its mirroring of contemporary military and chivalric realities (S. Robertson **616**). Chaucer's concern with philosophical issues was also recognized, as by Stewart **630**, yet Jefferson's survey of Boethian borrowings (**582**) did not inspire new interpretations, possibly because the philosophical passages were sometimes seen as detachable, even objectionable, digressions. The first approaches to the thought of the Tale were made through astrology, first by Grimm **565** and then by Curry **543**, who in the last three pages of his study linked the Tale's astrology with a Boethian system of cosmic governance. Patch **611** and Baum **653** both commented on the unusual combination of philosophical concerns and humor.

In fact, Patch identified 'the tone of something rather like levity' as the 'most surprising' element in the Tale. Frequently noticed, the Tale's humor was variously associated with lack of seriousness, worldly wisdom, or satiric intent. Getty **560** was unusual in appreciating humor as one aspect of a complex Chaucerian attitude. Still, humor conflicted with expectations aroused by the Tale's genre. Emphasizing its idealism and lack of realistic characterization and action, Root **619** urged readers to give themselves up to the 'spirit of romance'; and Ker **98** proclaimed the Tale 'a complete and perfect version of a medieval romance.' But Patch and others objected to the classification, partly because of the Tale's humor.

In the period between Robinson's first and second editions (1933–1957), there were echoes and extensions of this earlier work, as in Kane's emphasis on the Tale's stylistic brilliance (**702**); Marckwardt's study of characterization (**718**), reversing Fairchild's thesis; and Ham's reiteration of the importance of courtliness (**692**). A major departure in the criticism of this period was new and sophisticated attention to the verbal and structural aspects of the work. Speirs **766** demonstrated the New Criticism in an analysis of the description of Mars which established the crucial importance of that passage. Everett's important address on 'Chaucer's "Art Poetical"' (**680**), reflecting scholarly advances in the understanding of medieval rhetoric, described the parallelism in the Tale's structure and claimed for it the power to embody theme. Specific rhetorical devices such as puns (Kökeritz **706**, Baum **651**) and types of narrative (Schaar **756**) soon began to receive attention. In a second departure, critics began to view the *Knight's Tale* not just as a story with philosophical digressions but as a philosophical narrative. Wilson **787** stressed an implied reconciliation of human and divine love; Whittock **785** saw the conflict between chivalric ideals and Fortune as representative of all human experience. Both reinterpreted the Tale's humor as a way of capturing profound realities – 'the comic ironies of life' (Wilson) or 'the terrible irreconcilabilities inherent in life' (Whittock).

This was the context in which the two most important articles of this period appeared, articles whose influence was to extend over thirty years, those by Frost (1949, **684**) and Muscatine (1950, **726**).

Frost began by opposing the only dissent from the strengthening chorus of praise for Theseus, Webb's treatment of the Duke as a cruel tyrant (**779**). Frost's main concern, however, was to challenge the long-standing views of the Tale as a 'splendidly pictured tapestry' and as a mere *collage* of rhetorical, chivalric, and philosophic elements. Concentrating on the character and action Root had disparaged, Frost described three concentric circles of emotional, ethical, and theological interests, linked together by the Tale's rhetorical parallelism and 'formal regularity of design.' His argument for Palamon as the more idealistic prince was the most 'old-fashioned' aspect of his presentation. More revisionist was his characterization of Theseus as 'the executant of destiny' and his attention to the gods as representatives of destiny (Venus, Diana, Mars, Saturn) and providence (Jupiter). He saw the 'idealized aristocratic universe' of the Tale as contested by tragic elements; a principle of divine order was only suggested, by the gods and by Theseus' final speech. Frost did not treat the Tale's structure as symbolic but only as a source of beauty fittingly reflecting the Knight-narrator.

Unlike Frost, Muscatine commended Root's focus on style but found the treatment superficial. He supported Root's caveat about emphasizing characterization, arguing against defining differences, particularly of an evaluative kind, between Palamon and Arcite. The princes are equally representative of the noble life and of the relation of human beings to the universe; Theseus' role is central in a work concerned with providential order. De-emphasizing narrative, Muscatine analyzed the structure of the Tale, which he regarded as symbolic of the noble life, a life that was itself symbolic of cosmic order. It is these symbolical relationships that distinguish Muscatine's interpretation from Frost's and from all earlier readings. Because his primary concern was with style, Muscatine developed the first of these relationships more fully than the second, and only briefly noticed the 'formidably antagonistic element' of chaos which threatened the noble life, and the 'tension' between the Tale's orderly structure and the 'violent ups-and-downs' of its narrative. These less developed areas of his argument were to attract extensive critical response.

... and Boethius' *Consolation of Philosophy* ...

In the mid-1950s, in a development consistent with the new emphases established by Frost and Muscatine, the long delayed examination of the Tale's Boethianism began in earnest. In line with his dramatic theory, Lumiansky (1952/1955, **713**) underlined the suitability of a Boethian narrative to the wise Knight. Ruggiers (1956, **752**) treated the Tale as 'a Boethian test case' exploring philosophical as opposed to religious insight, and Kaske (1957, **703**) used Boethian ideas of good and evil fortune to explain the relationship of the *Knight's Tale* to the *Monk's Tale*. Since Lumiansky has the honor of presenting the first full-scale Boethian reading of the Tale, it is appropriate to use his argument as the starting point for an overview of this important chapter in the history of the *Knight's Tale*.

Lumiansky laid out several positions that have attracted wide agreement: he associated Palamon and Arcite with the Boethian persona; he saw Theseus as a man of insight who understands God's providential plan; he regarded Theseus' final speech as a successful statement of that plan; and he addressed the question of the Tale's final impact, balancing tragical elements with philosophical consolation. On the other hand, Lumiansky regarded Arcite as more enlightened than Palamon, a view echoed among Boethian readings of the Tale only by Schmidt (1969, **886**) and Payne (1981, **1116**). Most critics have seen the princes as alike in their subjection to appetite and their misunderstanding of Fortune and Providence, freedom and fate (eg, Huppé **844**, Hatton **965**). Halverson went beyond Lumiansky in associating Theseus directly with Philosophy herself, but this view did not become common. Instead, a revisionist trend depicted Theseus as only gradually acquiring a Boethian outlook (eg, Bartholomew **795**, Reidy **1014**), or as limited in his grasp of the Boethian vision (eg, Gaylord **955**).

Although Lumiansky devoted only one sentence to Theseus' final speech, it has since become the crucial text for an assessment of the Tale's Boethianism. Salter (1962, **883**) objected to Theseus' attempts to attribute the actions of the gods to the First Mover. Underwood (1959, **776**) began the analysis of discrepancies between Boethius' arguments and Theseus'; Westlund (**896**) joined in, emphasizing the unChristian nature of the speech. Kean (**984**) made a strong defense of its philosophical coherence, and yet observed that it could not silence the voices of pain in the Tale. A turning point had clearly been reached by 1977 when Burlin **928** declared, 'the limitations of Theseus' speech are serious.' Burlin himself extended the critiques of Theseus' Boethianism, and further attacks followed (eg, Aers **904**). The analysis of the gap between Theseus' speech and the *Consolation* has become so detailed that it seems impossible the speech can ever recover the aura of authority it once enjoyed. This situation may be reflected in Harder's suggestion (**1099**) that the Knight, not Theseus, provides a Boethian ending, and in Schweitzer's view (**1122**) that the audience is meant to supply a corrective Boethian vision.

Answering to this controversy over Theseus, another question which did not trouble Lumiansky has arisen: how Chaucer *meant* to use Boethian philosophy in the Tale. Pearsall (1970, **875**; cf 1985, **1117**) suggested that Chaucer may originally have intended to compose a demonstration of the errors of passion and dependence on Fortune but failed because of the unexpected force he gave to depictions of human pain and divine malice. Another approach holds that the limits of the Tale's philosophical outlook are part of a deliberate Chaucerian strategy – either to depict an admirable pagan philosophy showing the heights reason can achieve without revelation (eg, Van **1050**), or to depict a deficient pagan philosophy showing the great need of Christian revelation (eg, Westlund). The problem of confining the poem's Boethian dilemmas to pagan times was pinpointed by

Salter (1983, **1120**), however; Chaucer seems to have used a pagan setting to acquire the imaginative space for the depiction of timeless problems (Kean **984**).

The possibility that the *Consolation* itself may be criticized by the Tale is implied in the way Salter set the authority of Chaucer's plot against the authority of the *Consolation* in her discussion of the 'test case' of Palamon's lament (I.1303–33). Justman (**983**) argued that Chaucer meant to expose the discrepancies between actual experience and the paradigms assumed in Boethius' arguments. Elbow (**942**), on the other hand, saw Chaucer as learning from Boethius how both to affirm the truth of opposite propositions and to transcend the contradiction. Payne (**1116**) characterized both the *Consolation* and the Tale as Menippean satires with dialogic structures. The Tale parodies the aspirations of philosophy, as in the application of the comment on destiny (I.1663–72) to an extremely improbable coincidence. Despite differences of opinion and emphasis, criticism has been increasingly successful in showing how Chaucer read the *Consolation* as a poet, attending not just to the conclusions of the argument but also to the various voices to be heard and the various visions to be confronted in the course of its unfolding.

... Modern Criticism (continued) ...

The reverberations of the critical developments at mid-century were long and richly diverse. Frost's preference for Palamon inspired a spate of articles (Lloyd **710**, Delasanta **821**, Schmidt **886**); yet, though critics continue to distinguish differences between the princes, Muscatine's insistence on their equal worth has generally prevailed. Much more important were the extensions of the arguments Frost and Muscatine had in common. R.H. Green **690** supported the central role granted to Theseus by invoking a tradition in which the Athenian represents the rational soul; both Palamon and Arcite were proportionally demoted, as representatives of irrationality. Halverson **691** distinguished three kinds of order – natural, social, and cosmic – and linked them to the Tale's settings. He was the first, it appears, to interpret the marriage of Palamon and Emelye as a symbol of cosmic order. Applying his powerful new exegetical method, D.W. Robertson **879** saw Theseus as an iconographic figure representing the New Law, as well as rationality, and invoked the tradition of the two Venuses to condemn Arcite and to celebrate the cosmic significance of Palamon's marriage. Haller **831** argued the special appropriateness of the epic genre, modelled on Statius, to express the relationship of the noble life to social and cosmic order.

Support for Muscatine's thesis concerning symbolic form came from Jordan's exposition (1967, **846**) of 'inorganic structure,' a distinctively medieval rhetoric that aims to represent values such as rationality rather than to develop character or action. Jordan provided a refined analysis of the Tale's symmetries, distinguishing the audience's reactions to the fictional and structural elements at key points. In this reading, the poem's form directly symbolizes cosmic order (without the intermediary of the noble life emphasized by Muscatine) and, broadly, the human capacity to construct, especially in art. This approach allows Jordan to acknowledge inconsistencies in point of view and tone, which he takes to be Chaucer's way of exposing the limitations of his own fiction and of human capacities in general.

Throughout the late fifties and the sixties there was also spirited opposition to the theses of Frost and Muscatine. In two revisionist readings, Underwood **776** pointed to Theseus' role in creating disorder as well as order, while Westlund **896** assigned more weight than Muscatine to the element of chaos and took a darker view of the gods than Frost, arguing that the Tale's paganism was meant to suggest the need for pilgrimage and Christian faith. In opposition, Neuse **871** characterized Theseus as a 'political opportunist' and presented the Knight-narrator as having a superior comic vision that recognizes the Duke's distortion of lordship as well as the princes' distortion of love. Salter **883** identified divergent 'languages' and 'voices' in the Tale, suggesting that the story line was not appropriate to the exploration of suffering into which Chaucer was drawn. She was perhaps the first to interpret Arcite's death-bed magnanimity not just as the zenith of male friendship but as a contrast to the malice of the gods. She objected to Muscatine's identification of rhetorical order with imaginative ordering, and regarded Theseus' final speech as the crux of the Tale's artistic problems.

Many of the other studies of the sixties might be seen as divergently nuanced accounts of how the cosmic order of the Tale is experienced by both the characters and the audience. Pratt **745** accommodated some of the seeming contradictions under the formula 'joye after wo,' a cycle of experience occurring within a clearly providential order. Donaldson **675** took a fideistic position, emphasizing the different conclusions proposed by reason and faith. Corsa **815** thought the Tale enacted distributive justice, but found the underlying philosophy thin, the outlook of a sentimental Knight-narrator. Harrington **833**, on the other hand, believed that Chaucer had turned what might have been only an entertaining *demande* into a satisfying philosophical demonstration. Huppé **844** interpreted the Tale as a 'high comedy' in which moral values are unquestionably clear while the divine plan can only be glimpsed in emblems such as Theseus' activities. Spearing **888** seems to have been the first to study the animal and prison imagery, which he saw as embodying the pessimistic vision of a world ruled by arbitrary Fortune and cruel gods.

Something of the Tale's continuing capacity to escape definition may be reflected in Ruggiers' divergent readings. In 1959 (**753**) Ruggiers described a fictional world in which all the extra-human forces are manifestations of the First Mover, all the joys and sorrows are directed by universal love, and God's will is declared and explained by his spokesman, Theseus. In 1965 (**881**) Ruggiers described the Tale as an experiment, a puzzling work neither comic nor tragic, which supports the idea of providential order while denying us, through irony, the satisfaction of any unqualified affirmations. Perhaps the most determined attempt to tame the Tale's puzzles was Thurston's study (1968, **891**) of the Tale's 'artistic ambivalence.' Read one way, the *Knight's Tale* celebrates chivalry, Thurston argued; read another way, it satirizes, playfully, chivalry and the literary forms in which it is expressed, though the ideals that chivalry represents remain untouched. Thurston's work is notable for its attention to the Tale's problematic humor, but its concept of a satiric text whose surface meaning is reversed by a second level of implied meaning has been generally regarded as too rigid and simple.

In the nineteen seventies, renewed attention was paid to the Tale's astrology and depiction of the gods. North **873** suggested that Chaucer may have believed in astrological determinism, and Smyser **152** associated what he regarded as the gods' decisive role in the action with Chaucer's deep interest in astrology in the 1380s. Wood **902**, on the other hand, argued for a Chaucerian emphasis on freedom, with Palamon, Arcite, and Emelye allying themselves with the destructive aspects of the gods, and Theseus allying himself with their positive aspects. Brooks and Fowler **807** portrayed the gods as representing stages of human development from youthful Venerian interests to middle-aged Martian functions to mature Saturnian wisdom. A more static conception of the gods as representing the various aspects of the ideally balanced personality was advanced by McCall **998**.

Of special concern was Saturn, the god Chaucer added to Boccaccio's story. Wood regarded Saturn as wholly destructive; I.

Robinson **1018** portrayed the god's inimicability to significance in human life, and Blodgett **918** characterized the god as a figure of death. Gaylord **955** neutralized Saturn, so to speak, by characterizing him as 'a kind of baleful summary of the implications in the infatuate desires of the lovers.' In the schemes of Brooks and Fowler and of McCall, Saturn is almost wholly a positive force. The most learned argument for a Saturn of healthful influence is Kean's (**984**); but appeals to pre-existing traditions seem unlikely to defuse the power of the poetry in which Chaucer presents his destructive god.

A second prominent concern of criticism in the nineteen seventies was the character of Theseus. New information was supplied by Scheps **1031**, who studied the hero's treatment in Plutarch, Ovid, Statius, and Boccaccio; by Reidy **1014**, who compared the Duke's behavior with the laws of medieval warfare explicated by Keen (**190**); and by Burnley **209**, who compiled the medieval terminology associated with tyranny and found Theseus to be an anti-type of the tyrant. A major trend treated Theseus not as an embodiment or agent of destiny or providence, as he had appeared in the nineteen fifties, but as a fully human figure who undergoes an education. Bartholomew **795** was apparently the first to advance such an argument, portraying Theseus as moving from the control of Fortune to a reverence for Natura. Fifield **824** studied Theseus' gradual acceptance of fallibility and mutability. Brooks and Fowler saw Theseus as approaching but not fully attaining Saturnian wisdom; McCall, by contrast, believed that the Duke achieves Saturnian wisdom, as seen in his responses to Arcite's death. That death is also the crucial event for Reidy **1014**, who presented Theseus as achieving deeper Boethian vision. Van **1050** identified the scene in the grove as the turning point in Theseus' maturation as a Boethian governor. Crampton **935** treated Theseus as a man of action motivated by illusions who through both the encounter in the grove and Arcite's death arrives at a truer but still imperfect vision. Emphasizing the same events, Lawler (**994**) described the Duke as a man who acquires crucial 'experience' on which depends the 'auctoritee' of his final speech.

Theseus' moral superiority to Palamon and Arcite had been emphatically developed by several critics (eg, Bolton **803**) in the nineteen sixties, but in the seventies, the relationship was often seen as more subtle. Burrow **929** regarded Theseus' wise 'middle-aged' perspective as the dominant one, but insisted that our sympathies for Palamon and Arcite are preserved. Elbow **942** based his argument for Theseus' superiority on the Duke's combination of the princes' virtues – Arcite's 'gift for detachment' and Palamon's 'gift for involvement.' Similarly, Lawler **994** saw Theseus as combining in an ideal fashion the 'auctoritee' represented by Egeus and the 'experience' represented by the princes. A new instability in the perception of Theseus is suggested by the contrast between Kean's view of him (**984**) and Burlin's (**928**). Kean praised Theseus' vision but saw his actions as constrained by the imperfect world in which he must act; Burlin thought the pagan Duke's vision flawed but found his actions a saving evocation of Christian ethics. As Theseus himself has become a more imperfect, often ambivalent figure, the contributions the other characters make to Chaucer's broad, and comprehensively sympathetic, depiction of the human condition are being once again appreciated.

Interpretations of Emelye have, to a degree, followed dominant critical trends. Halverson's treatment of her as the May Queen symbolizing natural order (1960, **691**) was expanded by Cameron (1968, **808**), who asserted that she also embodies the aristocratic ideal (social order) and represents Fortune (cosmic order). These three categories embrace much of the subsequent criticism. I. Robinson **1018** suggested, however, that Chaucer uses Emelye to show the limitations of the chivalric ideal; Thurston **891** cited her lack of power as disqualifying her for the courtly role; and Weissman **1052** saw her impotence as part of Chaucer's critique of the role itself. Minnis **1112** interpreted her passivity before Fortune as virtuous pagan fatalism, while Harrison **1100** saw Diana and Emelye as representing the carnality and mutability of all humans. A few critics treated Emelye as a negative exemplar: of irrational Amazonian disorder (Allen and Moritz **1064**); of self-indulgence (Wood **902**); or of failure to order the appetites (Gardner **954**). Brooks and Fowler **807** presented her as undergoing an education – moving from allegiance to Diana to the company of Venus. Kolve assimilated Emelye to the prison motif, eg, as an image of the freedom the princes have lost. Despite these efforts, Emelye still seems resistant to confident interpretation. Her characterization is one of the points at which Chaucer refused to compose a conventional romance; at the same time, she has not proved easy to assimilate to the philosophical readings of the Tale.

In the nineteen seventies, the Knight-narrator made a new claim on critical attention. Earlier critics had drawn admiring portraits of a humorous, philosophical, idealistic, or stoic Knight, though Penninger **876** and Foster **826** had gently faulted the Knight's exaggerated faith in chivalry. Meier (1969, **862**) seems to have been the first to devote an entire article to the Knight as narrator, finding in the Tale's use of *occupatio* and humor signs of the Knight's grim pessimism. In the animal imagery Helterman (1971, **466**; cf **969**) saw a reflection of the Knight's paradoxical involvement with violence, and in his use of *occupatio*, a refusal to face the collapse of Theseus' quest for order and a failure to perceive the need for an ideal of life superior to chivalry. Fyler (1979, **952**) stressed the likenesses in outlook between the Knight and his surrogate, Theseus, and compared the Knight's efforts to achieve artistic order with the Duke's efforts to secure social order. Watson (1980, **1051**), focusing on contradictions between narrative detail and auctorial commentary, defined the Knight as an 'enlightened pragmatist' like Theseus whose search for order is a spur and a guide to our own while it offers no solutions.

Yet several critics in this period objected to identifying the Knight with the narrator of the Tale (eg, Howard **974**; cf Brewer **1001**). In his study of the narrator's two styles, Stephen Knight **989** treated the narrator not as an 'organic personality' but as a 'tool of the author.' The current critique of dramatic readings of the *Canterbury Tales*, as formulated by Lawton **1106**, for example, strengthens this view. Still, the *Tales* vary in the relations they establish between tale and teller, and the problem remains of placing the *Knight's Tale* on this spectrum. Many readers would agree that the narrative voice is an important aspect of the Tale; but whether Chaucer intended readers to identify that voice with the Knight of the *General Prologue*, or meant it to impersonate a 'knightly mentality,' as Howard seems to suggest, or perhaps a particular but common human outlook only plausibly attached to a knight, and exactly how the voice affects the meaning of the Tale as a whole – all these are issues requiring further debate.

Muscatine's classic study continued to evoke responses in the seventies. In dissent, K. Blake **916** defined the noble life as a purely arbitrary human creation having no connection with cosmic order; she re-interpreted the Tale's balanced rhetoric as suggesting futility and questioned the identification of Theseus with destiny in readings of a passage (I.1663–74) that has become something of a crux. David **936** seconded both Muscatine's analysis of structure and Salter's analysis of voice, concluding that the Tale does not so much celebrate an existing order as express a nostalgic wish for order. Raising new questions about how to define order, Blodgett **918** stressed the 'negative states' of imprisonment and exile and reached a conclusion directly contrary to Muscatine's, that the *Knight's Tale* enacts a breakdown of anagogic relations. In the absence of strong new support, the trend seemed to be toward a gradual dismantling of many aspects of Muscatine's reading. The most positive development was Herzman's insightful treatment of the paradoxical relation of ends and means in a reading (**970**) that linked Muscatine's emphasis on chivalry with Jordan's emphasis on art. From another perspective, Herzman's focus on paradox associated him with several critics who were making new attempts to capture the Tale's ambivalences. Elbow **942** explored the possibility that the Tale exhibits the structure of a *demande*, and Fichte **947** saw the *Knight's Tale* as a model of Chaucer's *ars poetica*, a Nominalist art that eschues *ex cathedra* propositions (cf Gardner **954**). At the same time, Kean characterized the Tale very differently, as a 'morality play,' and Burlin called it, perhaps more accurately, a 'philosophical parable.'

... and Boccaccio's *Teseida* ...

An important development in this period was the appearance of Boitani's monograph (1977, **922**) on Chaucer and Boccaccio, superseding Cummings' early study (1916, **541**). Boitani extended Cummings' quantification of Chaucer's debts, from elements of plot, characterization, and setting to such matters as structure, iconography, and style. Much more importantly, however, Boitani constructed a sense of Chaucer as a reader of Boccaccio, presenting the English poet as a mature artist who re-casts the young Italian's *avant garde* work in the terms of a conservative medieval culture. The ground had been well prepared by Pratt's analysis (**743**) of how Chaucer learned from and surpassed Boccaccio, and by J.A.W. Bennett's studies (**656**, **914**) of how Chaucer's uses of the *Teseida* were affected by his reading of Dante.

The nature of specific comparisons between the *Knight's Tale* and the *Teseida* has tended to reflect the preoccupations of Chaucerian criticism. In the early period, none was more important than characterization. Early critics disagreed as to whether Chaucer introduced new distinctions between Palamon and Arcite or made them more alike, but since mid-century there has been general agreement, reflecting the view of the Tale as a philosophical work, that Chaucer introduced a new equality between the princes as a means of exploring issues such as cosmic justice. Chaucer's Theseus has been appreciated as being a more multi-faceted character than Boccaccio's Teseo (eg, Mather **606**, Bennett **657**; but cf Boitani and Wright **790**), though Theseus's greater severity toward Thebes and the princely prisoners has been cited in the many indictments of the Duke (Webb **779**, Van **1050**, Kolve **1105**). On the other hand, Hanning **962** has criticized Teseo as a superficial figure whose actions in establishing order, a key theme of Chaucerians since mid-century, have not the ethical significance of Theseus'. Dodd **548**, looking for the satisfactions to be derived from rounded characterization, argued for Emilia's superiority to Emelye. Approaching the heroine from a rhetorical perspective, Brewer **665** defended Chaucer's omission of physical detail as necessary to constituting Emelye as the projection of an ideal. Reflecting a third, feminist perspective, Weissman **1052** argued that Chaucer restricts Emelye's action and consciousness in order to make explicit Boccaccio's implicit confinement of the court lady in a male sphere.

Similarly, early critics focused on changes to the plot, as in Palamon's seeing Emelye first (Mather **606**); but later critics emphasized differences in theme, as in Chaucer's greater concern with the relations of humans and gods (Salter **883**, **1120**). Chaucer's excision of Arcite's ascent to the spheres has attracted comment in all periods, but early readers speculated on Chaucer's own religious outlook (Lounsbury **594**) while later ones attempted to define the vision projected by the Tale as a whole (Westlund **896**). Only since mid-century have Chaucer's additions of Saturn (K. Blake **916**) and of the building of the theater (Van **1050**), elements associated with cosmic and social order, assumed special significance. Early critics saw Chaucer as turning a pseudo-classical epic into a romance (Ker **583**) with a greater emphasis on courtly love (Ham **692**). Later critics saw Chaucer as turning the Italian epic into a philosophical allegory (Branch **923**) with a greater emphasis on destiny and providence (Bennett **657**). Fyler **952**, Hanning **962**, and Payne **1116** have spotlighted Chaucer's use of the Knight-narrator as a transforming factor.

In the last twenty years the *Teseida* itself has received renewed attention from Boccaccio scholars. Hollander (1977, **230**) attributed to Boccaccio, even in his early works, a Christian approach to love centered on the values of marriage. His reading of the *Teseida*, which draws on the tradition of the two Venuses and asserts the importance of Boccaccio's glosses, has been supported by Smarr's astrological studies (**252**, **253**) and Kirkham's numerological analysis (**246**). These interpretations have a good deal in common with Robertson's exegetical criticism, and partly because the high-water mark of Robertsonianism has passed, seem unlikely to affect deeply interpretation of the *Knight's Tale*. Interestingly, Boitani read the *Teseida* not as a seamless moral parable but as a work structured by 'knots' of contradictory purposes never fully resolved by Boccaccio. New attempts to conceptualize Chaucer's relationship to the *Teseida* in broad terms would be welcome; David Wallace **234**, who studies Boccaccio and Chaucer as pioneers in combining popular and illustrious literary traditions, has not yet given the *Teseida* and *Knight's Tale* extended treatment. Two overlapping studies, by Branch **242** and Ginsberg **243**, on Boccaccio's use of the argument *in utramque partem* may prove useful in discriminating the nature of Chaucer's interest in the *demande*.

... Modern Criticism (continued) ...

In 1980 there appeared what seem to be the last two studies (in the period covered by this volume) to present themselves as direct responses to Muscatine's thesis. Aers **904**, inverting the thesis, argued that Chaucer condemns through Theseus certain forms of social order and their tendency to exploit theodicies for their own ends. Describing Theseus' immersion in a life of violence that subsumes both his compassionate impulses and his ideas of love, Aers interpreted Arcite's death-bed magnanimity as a sign of the humanity crushed by Theseus' order. Proposing only to revise Muscatine's thesis, Hanning **962** identified the use of a story-telling knight as Chaucer's most original contribution to the literature treating Thebes and the theme of order. The theater represents the highest achievement of both the Knight's art and Theseus' politics, but Arcite's death is a defeat that is not convincingly overcome. The Tale studies the tension between idealism and violence in the experience of a typical late medieval knight.

These two studies agree in seeing the *Knight's Tale* as concerned with medieval ideologies and institutions; at the same time they treat enduring themes, and in Hanning's case, sympathy for the Knight and for Theseus is maintained. Thus they contrast with Jones' narrower characterization of the Tale, also in 1980, as 'a hymn to tyranny' (**981**). The Knight is portrayed as dealing with literary materials whose ideals he neither understands nor values. The contrast between the matter and the manner of narration, along with allusions to contemporary Italian tyrants, reveals the Knight's own corruption and, by extension, the fall of late medieval knighthood from earlier chivalric ideals. Jones' reading of the Tale is a pendant to his main project, a reinterpretation of the Knight of the *General Prologue* as a 'shabby mercenary,' and is driven by the same interpretative model, a contrast between surface and sub-surface meaning.

... and the Knight's Portrait ...

While by 1980 the *Knight's Tale* had attracted a diverse body of commentary testifying to its variousness, its profundity, its imperfection (perhaps) and its medieval alterity (certainly), the tradition of commentary on the Knight's portrait had been much more homogeneous, one factor, perhaps, in making it an inviting target. There appear to have been only two phases in the early modern interpretation of the portrait, with Robinson's first edition (1933) marking the turning point. In the first phase, the Knight was admired as the ideal English gentleman, an instance of the late Victorian reinterpretation of chivalry documented by Girouard **160**. Particular attention was paid, for example, to the suggestion (I.69–71) of the Knight's admirable condescension to his social inferiors (eg, **340**, **390**), and it is possible that readers at the turn of the century appreciated some authentic nuances of the portrait which cannot now be so keenly felt. The Knight's military career received so little attention that Manly **335** was led to 'revive' the portrait by showing that the list of battles was not fanciful but realistic, a possible career in the late fourteenth century. Manly was misunderstood, however, as attempting to find one living model for the Knight (**336**). Robinson rejected such an approach, emphasizing the literary nature, and again, the ideality of the Knight (**388**).

In the second phase of commentary, critics celebrated the Knight's spiritual excellence and social utility rather than his class status while glancing at the contrastive degeneration, actual or alleged, of late medieval knighthood. Although Morgan **480** saw the details of the portrait as intended only to develop the ideal concept, more critics understood them as intended to create the illusion of individuality, as summed up in Moorman's phrasing, 'an idealized reality ... a realized ideal' (**430**; cf Owen **482**). Again the list of battles was important, being often cited as an individualizing touch supporting the ideal conception by 'lashing [it] to reality' (Badendyck, **401**). Every line of the portrait attracted extensive commentary, with the list of the Knight's virtues (I.45–6) and the stain on his *gypon* (I.75–6) being registered as especially powerful. The strength of this idealized view of the Knight can be estimated from the fact that line I.72, 'He was a verray, parfit gentil knyght,' was often said to be the best known line in Chaucer.

Yet several studies questioned this consensus, finding the Knight to be in some sense unworthy (eg, Helterman **466**), or limited (eg, Malone **379**, Courtney **408**), or obsolescent if admirable (eg, Howard

468). By far the most negative of these, before Jones, is Mitchell's (**429**); the most important, perhaps, is Mann's (**474**), which supplies the context of estates literature and brings the portrait within the circle of the methods and themes of the rest of the *Prologue* by describing the Knight as a 'professional specialist.' Interestingly, Jones' analysis of the actual history of the Knight's battles is generally thought to be the strongest part of his argument; though his own treatment of them and of medieval attitudes toward war appears one-sided, he has exposed an area of neglect by literary scholars.

It seems premature, however, to attempt to define a new phase in this body of criticism. Many of the authors of skeptical readings of the portrait would not want to associate themselves with Jones' position, and many of these readings have depended too narrowly on a belief in Chaucerian irony. This formalist approach not only requires review on its own terms, but needs to be supplemented by new explorations of Chaucer's philosophical and historical vision. Jones' flawed but probing and detailed critique continues to direct critical efforts on a smaller scale; perhaps a new consensus will emerge when his work receives the full and thoughtful response it deserves.

... Modern Criticism (continued) ...

One of the issues Jones' work highlights is the need for continuing study of the relation of both portrait and Tale to their historical context. R. Loomis suggested early on that the portrait expresses sympathy with the Wycliffite position on war (1940, **374**). Hatton's argument (1968, **417**) connecting the portrait with the crusading program of Philippe de Mézières has only recently (1983) received support from Keen **504** and Porter **514**. Cowgill **934** cited Hatton's work, however, in interpreting the Tale as a protest against the Hundred Years' War (cf Olson **1009**). Of course, many of the familiar readings of the Tale have political implications; in *Poetry and Crisis* (1972), Muscatine made explicit the Chaucerian position on royal power which is implicit in his original study (**1005**). Only a few critics (Blamires **917**, Schaefer **1029**) have attempted direct political analyses of the Tale, however. In one of the most promising of these, Herz (1964, **834**), with the aid of Huizinga **188**, analyzed the mentality of Froissart's *Chronicles* (**183**) and compared it with that of the Tale. Recently, Middleton (1985, **1111**), drawing on new critical perspectives on Huizinga's work and on new concepts, in Renaissance scholarship, of the relation between social appearances and social reality, has portrayed Theseus as the ideal prince envisaged by Philippe, one who rules most effectively through ceremonies like the tournament. More needs to be done to bring this kind of study to maturity and to fit the results into the wider question of how Chaucer's art is related to his era.

In the nineteen eighties, seeking alternatives to the dramatic approach to the *Canterbury Tales* which emphasizes the relation of tale to teller, some critics focused on the exposition, across tales, of thematic issues or on the interaction of generic visions. These approaches have brought new attention to marriage in the *Knight's Tale*. Presenting the *Tales* as collectively offering a normative definition of human society, Allen and Moritz (1981, **1064**) treated Theseus as a *pater familias* whose rule of his family is the model for his rule of society. Cooper (1981, **1082**) studied the treatment of marriage in two romances and two fabliau, reaffirming its status as an emblem of providential order. In their emphases on social and cosmic order, these two studies sum up the positive interpretations that have been offered since Green (**690**), Halverson (**691**), and Robertson (**879**) first focused attention on the topic. In the interim, objections have been raised based on the political motive for the marriage of Palamon and Emelye, the philosophical difficulties in the way of seeing the marriage as a reward, and the challenge to the symbolic status of marriage offered by the other tales of Fragment I. Opinion is so polarized that Blodgett **918** can see the marriage as an 'anti-climactic arrangement' while Boheemen **919** can see it as the 'grete effect' toward which the Tale moves. The marriage has probably been asked to bear a greater weight of symbolic meaning than it can sustain, as reflected in the suggestions of Burlin **928** and Harder **1099** that Theseus himself does not understand the significance of the marriage he arranges and that only the Knight and the audience do.

In another new approach to the *Canterbury Tales*, Kolve (1984, **1105**) studied central narrative images that combine mimetic and iconographic significances, focusing in the *Knight's Tale* on settings. The prison is at once a literal place, a metaphor for love, and an image of the world; the theater is an image of human life in that world, its rationality, passion, and 'epistemological and teleological darkness.' Kolve contrasts the prison with the garden, while several critics have discussed the tension between the prison and some other motif: pilgrimage, feasting, the concepts of play-space and ordered cosmos. Although the temples, when considered alone, are usually interpreted negatively as representing carnality and irrationality (eg, Gaylord **955**), when the theater is considered as a whole, the interpretation is usually positive, as in the astrological interpretations of McCall **998** and Brooks and Fowler **807**. Jordan cited the way the theater is described, according to Gothic principles of structure, as evidence for its being an emblem of the human capacity for noble achievement. Hanning **962** and Herzman **970** characterized the theater as representing the aims, or the highest achievements, of art and chivalry, language and government. Rowe **1021** and Cooper **1083**, however, saw the theater as an image of disorder which must be corrected or overcome by the final events of the Tale. Van **1150** took a middle way by seeing it as an emblem of personal and social disorder deliberately so designed by Theseus in order to educate the princes. The attention to the theater, at least since Jordan's work (1967), contrasts with the emphasis on the tournament early in the century and is another evidence of the shift in interest from plot to theme, and of the redefinition of a courtly romance as a philosophical romance.

Kolve's discussion of narrative images supported his characterization of the world of the Tale as a distinctively pagan one. In the same year (1984), Spearing **1128** praised Chaucer's attempt to depict sympathetically a historical pagan past as one of his greatest achievements. In the major study of this topic, Minnis argued (1983, **139**, **1112**) that late medieval thought credited pagans with anticipating the Christian notion of providence and asserted the possibility of heathens being saved, and that Chaucer's interest in paganism was historical, not moral. Minnis interpreted the Tale as condemning paganism while treating pagans sympathetically. Emelye and the princes are morally superior to their gods, and Theseus is an exemplary monotheist possessed of a superior understanding of necessity. Somewhat surprisingly, Minnis found Theseus' final speech deficient, from a Christian point of view, only in its praise of fame. Critics have divided on whether the Tale's paganism suggests Christianity in the main positively, by anticipation (eg, Benson **799**, Burlin **928**), or mostly negatively, by deficiency (Burnley **209**, Westlund **896**, Thundy **1042**). Readings emphasizing an idealized noble life or a traditional Boethianism presented the world of the Tale as Christian in essence if not in name; critical consensus on the paganism of that world might result in a significant shift. Spearing (1985, **1130**) has recently warned against seeing that world as merely pagan, however, rather than representative of a general human condition.

The persistency of certain problems in the reading of the *Knight's Tale* is nowhere better illustrated than in the question of its humor.

Patch's puzzlement (above, xxxi) returned in Howard's declaration (1976, **974**) that its humor is the Tale's 'most controversial aspect.' Meier **862** pointed out that the humor displayed in the narration, pre-eminently in the *demande* (I.1347–54), the comment on Arcite's fatal illness (I.2759–60), and the comment on his soul (I.2809–15), is associated with instances of suffering, and interpreted it as an aspect of the Knight's pessimistic stoicism. Foster **826** saw the Knight as unaware of the comic effects of his own narration, which Chaucer manipulates to qualify the Knight's idealism. Salter **883** characterized the Knight's joviality as incomprehension of the pain revealed by his narrative, and evidence of Chaucer's inability to achieve a unified vision. Howard insisted, however, that the humor is not part of any portrayal of a Knight-narrator but is evidence of the poet's characteristically ironic attitudes. Similarly, David **936** paired the sense of the ridiculous in the Tale with the sense of evil as part of Chaucer's vision of order. Burrow **929**, on the other hand, linked Theseus' humor with the Knight's and with Chaucer's as part of a philosophical attitude of acceptance shared by the poet and his characters and much 'Ricardian' literature. R. H. Green **690** recognized that the Tale's amused, sardonic, flippant tone qualifies in hard to define ways the schematic significances suggested by traditions of classical fable, and Wood **901** made a similar observation about the relation of the 'slippery' tone to traditions of astrological imagery. Many critics are agreed that it is a mistake to turn the humor into a blunt instrument in the service of systematic satire. Interestingly, all the work reviewed here was published before Howard's declaration on the controversy; few recent critics have addressed this largely unresolved problem.

Finally, the generic identity of the *Knight's Tale* has continued to tease critics. It has been called a 'chivalric romance,' a 'didactic romance,' a 'social romance,' and most commonly, a 'philosophical romance.' The list of its characteristics said by Chaucerians to be unusual in romance is long: its philosophical questioning, its interest in good rulership, its use of allegory, its realism, its special uses of language, its humor, satire, and amused tone, and its tragic elements. Yet, students of the genre regard several of these characteristics as typical of the romance (cf **92**, **101**, **1035**). Cooper **1083** has proposed that the Tale's romance vision is challenged from within by tragic vision even as it is challenged from without by fabliau vision. Jordan's study of Chaucer's habits of narrative composition (**97**), presented as a challenge to the use of the label 'romance,' is a valuable exposition of Chaucerian style in general, but does not focus on those elements of a work that, shaping audience expectations, define the partly public entity that is a genre. Blamires' argument (**917**) that Chaucer had a distaste for prowess exemplifies current critical interest in defining Chaucer's attitudes toward romance, and Spearing's study (**1128**) of the greater unfriendliness of Lydgate toward romance should help to place Chaucer accurately on the spectrum. Romance is receiving special attention from theorists like Jauss (**96**; cf **91**), and new approaches to the *Knight's Tale* informed by developments in genre theory can be expected.

... and Statius' *Thebaid* ...

Although the belief that Chaucer transformed Boccaccio's epic into a romance was long a given of *Knight's Tale* criticism, challenges to this belief have twice been launched by groups of scholars who have found in the Tale's indebtedness to the *Thebaid* elements more suggestive of epic, chronicle, or tragedy.

The original study of Chaucer's borrowings from Statius by Wise (1911, **642**) has been superseded by the work of Clogan, who has attempted to study Statius as Chaucer knew him, in medieval glossed manuscripts (rather than modern editions of the Roman poet). Clogan identified probable Chaucerian debts to the tradition of Statian glosses (**812**), and analyzed, as Wise had not, some aspects of Chaucer's interweaving of Boccaccian and Statian materials, claiming that for the legend of Thebes, Chaucer took Statius as his 'ultimate source' (**813**). More recently, Anderson **261** has documented the medieval belief in the historicity of the story of Thebes, and the tendency of chroniclers and historians to treat Thebes as a type of the Augustinian earthly city. Influenced by this tradition, Boccaccio developed a 'program of analogies' between his plot and Statius's, centered on the parallelism of Eteocles/Polinices with Palamon/Arcite (**236**). In a third attempt to reconstruct medieval readings of the *Thebaid*, Wetherbee has focused on Dante as a reader of Statius, emphasizing Statius' apparent groping after some power of redemption with which to confront the tragic force in history he so overwhelmingly depicts (**291**, **292**).

Contemporaneously with Clogan's work, Haller (1966, **831**) argued that Chaucer did not abandon epic when he sloughed off the superficial elements of epic in the *Teseida*, but instead borrowed a true epic subject from the *Thebaid*. The conflict over love in the *Knight's Tale* reprises and complements the conflict over lordship in the *Thebaid*, and the proper ordering of the two constitutes the noble life which, for Chaucer, is the only sufficient human emblem of cosmic order. C.D. Benson (1968, **799**) made a similar argument, though emphasizing Chaucer's use of archaizing detail from the *Thebaid* to create a classical setting in which to study an early form of chivalry in the manner of an aristocratic chronicle. In the most recent spate of Statius studies, Anderson (1980, **905**) has presented Chaucer as reading Statius through Boccaccio, strengthening the emphasis he found in Boccaccio on epic strife, Theseus' heroism, and Augustinian typology. Hanning (**962**), like Benson, has emphasized secular rather than cosmic (Haller) or sacred (Anderson) history, suggesting that Chaucer perceived the moral commitment of the *Thebaid* and the moral bankruptcy of the *Teseida*, and drew on the former to study the conflict between violence and order in medieval chivalry.

It has been difficult for Chaucerian students of Statius to establish the importance of the *Thebaid* to the *Knight's Tale*, relative to the importance of the *Teseida* and Boethius' *Consolation*. Whatever the ultimate consensus on that point may prove to be, Statian studies currently promise a harvest of new insights into the *Knight's Tale*.

Relation to *Miller's Tale, Fragment I*, and the *Canterbury Tales*

The relation between the *Knight's Tale* and the *Miller's Tale* was long conceived as a matter of decorum, in the spirit of Dryden's compliment: 'The Matter and Manner of [the pilgrims'] Tales, and of their Telling, are so suited to their different Educations, Humours, and Callings, that each of them would be improper in any other Mouth.' The *Miller's Tale* was thought to offer 'a complete contrast' to the *Knight's Tale* (Tyrwhitt, 'Introductory Discourse,' p 87). Until forty years ago, the two were perhaps not often read together or taught together. In late nineteenth- and early twentieth-century selected editions of the *Canterbury Tales*, the *Knight's Tale* never once appeared with the *Miller's Tale*. One obstacle was the alleged indecency of the fabliaux. Dramatic evidence of changes in taste and critical opinion can be seen in the contrast between the 1908 and the 1958 Everyman editions (**19**, **49**).

The honor of initiating serious discussion of the two tales together seems to belong to Frost (1949, **684**), who found in the *Miller's Tale* an 'aesthetic antithesis' to the *Knight's Tale* on which it cast a critical light. Donaldson (1950, **674**) compared the versions of courtliness in the two tales in his famous study of the idiom of popular poetry. Stokoe (1952, **771**) extended Frost's brief analysis but reversed his thesis, finding in the 'warped and biased' view of the Miller a confirmation of the Knight's wisdom. Stokoe also traced the dramatic fallout of the Miller's polemic through the rest of Fragment I, following in the footsteps of Owen's innovative discussion (1951, **731**) of a thematic unity focused on love and war. Owen's most important contribution, though, was his analysis of the 'aesthetic design' of the Fragment (1954, **732**), emphasizing the balance between idealism and realism and the close association of such predilections with character. In the span of five years, 1949–1954, these pioneering studies introduced new topics – the relations of the first two tales, the artistic unity of Fragment I – which have become a permanent part of our understanding of the *Canterbury Tales*.

Since then resemblances and differences between the two tales in setting, plot, characterization, imagery, and theme have been detailed. The contrast between Emelye and Alisoun has attracted special attention, while discussions of the clash between idealism and realism and of the working out of human and divine justice have dominated discussion. Several critics have emphasized the equality or complementarity of the tales' visions (eg, David **936**), but a slight edge has sometimes been given to the *Miller's Tale*: either by finding in its plot a more perfect justice (Donaldson **675**) or, in its emphasis on nature and carnality, a celebration of the divine bounty (Whittock **897**). It is generally agreed that the fabliau delimits the authority of the romance without wholly undercutting it, and that the ironies in the relationship cut in several directions at once (Howard **842**).

The theme of justice has often been seen as embracing all of Fragment I; other suggestions for unifying themes include McCann's discrimination of various kinds of love and cupidity (**999**), and Joseph's analysis of competing definitions of this world as prison or space for play (**847**). Blodgett **918** has described a fall from spirit to flesh in the Fragment, a movement antithetical to the purposes of pilgrimage. For Kolve, the latter tales exemplify kinds of 'counter-art' which lack the connection between image and hierarchical truth found in the *Knight's Tale*. Siegel (1985, **1125**) has proposed an epistemological theme: the *Knight's Tale* presents a mysterious world that must be encountered by faith; the *Miller's Tale* misleadingly portrays a knowable world that can be manipulated by intelligence. As the dramatic relationship between tale and teller grows stronger in the Fragment, the ability to sustain philosophical inquiry declines. These last three readings interpret what Howard (**974**) has called 'a degenerative movement' in the Fragment: the *Knight's Tale* is sometimes seen as presenting the exemplar from which the other tales of the Fragment fall away, but sometimes as itself participating in a failure of values and vision. This difference of opinion is especially significant for the question of how the Tale functions as the first of the *Canterbury Tales.*

Generally, those studies that present a 'triumphal' reading of the Tale can be assumed to imply that it presents in some form the vision that is the goal of the pilgrimage, while those that present tragic, satiric, or skeptical readings can be assumed to imply that the Tale demonstrates the need for pilgrimage. Relatively few critics have addressed the question directly. Westlund's balanced conclusion **896** stresses the way the Tale reveals the need for pilgrimage and faith in a world where the tragic failure of human order points to some transcendent order. The first Canterbury Tale has also been seen as a programmatic text, with Allen and Moritz **1064** suggesting it introduces the four kinds of change, and Howard, the three kinds of conduct, explored in the rest of the work. Many critics have compared it with one or more of a small group of key texts. Baldwin **649** saw the *Knight's Tale* and *Parson's Tale* as two pillars representing secular and spiritual excellence; Thundy **1042** described a progression from reliance on reason to an acceptance of revelation in the movement from *Knight's Tale* to *Melibee* to *Parson's Tale*; Ruggiers **752** discovered a complementary relationship between the noble philosophy of the opening Tale, the religious guidance provided by the *Man of Law's Tale* and the 'final admonition' of the *Parsons's Tale*. For Gardner **954** the *Knight's Tale* exhibited a 'nominalist-inspired scepticism' that is countered by an affirmation of faith in the *Retraction*, while Herzman **970** distinguished between the affirmation of art in the *Knight's Tale* as an analogue of divine perfection and the qualified rejection of art in the *Retraction* as only a means to a spiritual end. Obviously and inevitably, readings of the *Knight's Tale* have implications for the interpretation of the *Canterbury Tales* as a whole.

Chaucer's *Knight's Tale*

Editions and Translations

The third edition of F.N. Robinson's text **39**, now entitled *The Riverside Chaucer*, has recently appeared under the general editorship of Larry D. Benson (Boston: Houghton Mifflin, 1987). Another separate edition of the *KnT*, as part of the *Variorum Chaucer* **69**, is being prepared by Alan Gaylord. Essential reading is *Editing Chaucer: The Great Tradition*, ed. Paul G. Ruggiers (Norman, Oklahoma: Pilgrim Books, 1984). It contains essays by several hands on early editors not treated in this section — Stow, Speght, Urry, Tyrwhitt, and Wright — as well as essays on Thynne **17** and Caxton **61** and the great modern editors: Furnivall **1**, Skeat **3**, Robinson **39**, and Manly-Rickert **42**.

1 *A Six-Text Print of Chaucer's Canterbury Tales. Part I. The Prologue and the Knight's Tale*. Ed. Frederick J. Furnivall. Chaucer Society Publications, First Series, Number 1. London: N. Trübner, 1868. Pp 25–88.

The text is printed in parallel columns as it appears in these mss: Ellesmere, Hengwrt, Cambridge Gg.4.27, Corpus, Petworth, and Lansdowne. The Cambridge and Lansdowne texts of the *KnT* are accompanied by marginal annotations prepared by Henry Ward which indicate Chaucer's borrowings from the *Tes*. See **2, 3, 4, 7, 13, 16, 20, 345, 541, 619, 636, 642.**

- Frederick J. Furnivall, *A Temporary Preface to the Six-Text Edition*. Chaucer Society Publications, Second Series, Number 3. London: N. Trübner, 1868. Furnival summarizes Ward's analysis as indicating 270 lines translated from the *Tes*, 374 showing a general likeness and 132 showing a slight likeness; he defends the *KnT* as an adaptation, not a mere translation, of Boccaccio's work (pp 104–5).
- Donald C. Baker, 'Frederick James Furnivall,' in *Editing Chaucer* (see Headnote), pp 157–69: In accuracy of presentation, 'the texts are remarkably clean and, to put it bluntly, compare favorably with

similar modern work' (p 165). The 'brilliant idea' of the parallel text was apparently Furnivall's alone (p 166).

2 *The Prologue, the Knightes Tale, the Nonne Preestes Tale from the Canterbury Tales*. Ed. Richard Morris. A New Edition with Collations and Additional Notes by Walter W. Skeat. Oxford: Clarendon, 1888; rpt through 1957. Text: pp 31–105; notes: pp 170–94.
Morris' original edition of 1867 was based on ms Harley 7334. Skeat's revised text is based on Ellesmere, collated with the other mss of the *Six-Text* edition **1**. Variants from Ellesmere appear at the foot of the page. Skeat also revised the Notes, adding half again as much material, and the Glossary. Morris' expurgations, preserved by Skeat, include the allusion to Mars' adultery with Venus in Arcite's prayer (*KnT* 1527–32; I.2385–90). See **3**, **10**, **13**.

3 *The Complete Works of Geoffrey Chaucer*. Ed. W.W. Skeat. London: Oxford University Press, 1894. The Oxford Chaucer, in six volumes with a supplementary volume VII, 1897; rpt 1899, and many times thereafter through 1963. Volume IV: *The Canterbury Tales*: *Text*: pp 26–88.
Presents the first complete printed edition of the *CT* founded on Ellesmere, collated with the other mss of the *Six-Text* edition **1** and with Harley 7334, printed separately by the Society. 'Of all the MSS. E[llesmere] is the best in nearly every respect. It not only gives good lines and good sense, but is also (usually) grammatically accurate and thoroughly well spelt' (xvii). Selective textual notes appear at the foot of the page. The *GP*, *KnT*, *MilT*, *RvT*, and *CkT* comprise Group A of the tales. Ellesmere subdivides the *KnT* into four parts (A 859–1354, 1355–1880, 1881–2482, 2483–3108), and lacks A 2681–2, supplied by Skeat. Volume V: *Notes to the Canterbury Tales*; pp 60–95. The illustrative notes are extensive, an important source for later editors and students. Many of the notes to the *KnT* were written by Morris **2**, though because of their close collaboration, Skeat finds it difficult to say which (xxvi). Volume VI contains a glossary in double columns, with line references, of more than 300 pages. See **6**, **7**, **8**, **10**, **13**, **15**, **19**, **21**, **25**, **31**, **32**, **33**, **35**, **39**, **46**, **55**, **62**. For the Knight and *KnT* see **344** and **625**.

- A.S.G. Edwards, 'Walter W. Skeat,' in *Editing Chaucer* (see Headnote), pp 171–89: Skeat's notes, though an outstanding achievement, have suffered from obsolescence, partly because many of them reflect earlier work of Skeat's, particularly on the Clarendon Press series (pp 187–8).

4 *Chaucer: Canterbury Tales. The Prologue and The Knight's Tale*. Ed. A.J. Wyatt. London: W.B. Clive, 1895. Rpt four times through 1903. University Tutorial Series. Text: pp 59–123; notes: pp 148–58.
The basis of the text is not indicated. There is a substantive introduction and an analytic glossary (pp 165–208). Appendix B gives Ward's analysis (1) of borrowings from the *Tes*. For *KnT* see **644**.

5 *The Student's Chaucer*. Ed. W.W. Skeat. New York and London: Macmillan; Oxford: Clarendon, 1895. Pp 430–57.
This work became the Oxford Standard Authors edition, and was reprinted many times under various imprints through 1967. It presents the 1894 text (**3**) without textual or explanatory notes. An appendix lists doubtful readings and editor's emendations. The double-column glossary of 149 pages is still of value. This text was also published in 3 volumes for the World's Classics Series (London: Oxford University Press, 1903–6) and in 1 volume, with a short introduction by Louis Untermeyer, for the Modern Library (New York: Random House, 1929). These later printings contain a short glossary.

6 *The Works of Geoffrey Chaucer* [The Kelmscott Chaucer]. Hammersmith, Middlesex: The Kelmscott Press, 1896. Pp 9–30.
A distinguished production of William Morris' famed press. F.S. Ellis' edition of the Middle English, based on Skeat **3** (then being published), includes additional corrections approved by Skeat, but no introduction, notes, or glossary. There are no portraits of the pilgrims, but the eighty-seven illustrations by Edward Burne-Jones include six for the *KnT*: 1) Palamon and Arcite, in their prison cell, observe Emelye in the garden; 2) Palamon, hiding in a stand of trees, observes Arcite in the grove; 3) Palamon prays to Venus; 4) Emelye prays to Diana; 5) Arcite prays to Mars; 6) Palamon and Emelye stand before the bier of Arcite. By contrast, there are no illustrations for the *MilT*. For facsimile editions see **51**, **64**.

7 *The Works of Geoffrey Chaucer* [The Globe Chaucer]. Ed. Alfred W. Pollard, H. Frank Heath, Mark H. Liddell, W.S. McCormick. London and New York: Macmillan, 1898/rev 1928. Rpt many times, including Freeport, New York: Books for Libraries Press, 1972. Pp 13–42.
The text of the *CT* is based on Ellesmere, conservatively emended by collation with the other mss in the *Six-Text* edition **1** and with the Chaucer Society's edition of Harley 7334. This conservative emendation, by comparison with Skeat's (**3**), dictated the choice of the Globe Chaucer as the basis of the *Concordance to the Works of Geoffrey Chaucer*, ed. J.S.P. Tatlock and A.G. Kennedy (Washington: Carnegie Institution of Washington, 1927). In 1928 Pollard incorporated

corrected readings from the *Concordance* (xi). Explanatory and textual notes appear at the foot of the page. In the Introduction to the *CT*, Pollard dismisses Brink's theory (**529**) concerning an early version of the *KnT* in seven-line stanzas (xxvi–ii). Pollard had earlier published a separate edition of the *CT*: London: Macmillan, 1894. See also: **14**, **16**.

8 *The Prologue, The Knight's Tale, and The Nun's Priest's Tale from Chaucer's Canterbury Tales*. Ed. Frank Jewett Mather. Boston: Houghton Mifflin, 1899; rpt 1908. Text: pp 35–112; textual notes, pp 140–2.
The text is based on Ellesmere corrected by readings from Corpus, Petworth, and Lansdowne. An 'Appendix of Various Readings' (pp 137–42) lists only the variants from Skeat **3**. The extensive introductory materials include a summary of the *Tes* with commentary, in parallel columns, on Chaucer's uses of his source (lxii–lxix). The explanatory notes, whose value is noted by Robinson **39**, appear at the foot of the page, and there is a glossary. For the Knight see **338**; for *KnT*, **606**.

9 *The Cambridge Ms. Dd.4.24 of Chaucer's Canterbury Tales. Completed by the Egerton Ms. 2726 (the Haistwell Ms.)*. Parts I and II. Ed. Frederick J. Furnivall. 2 volumes. Chaucer Society Publications, First Series, Numbers 95 and 96. London: Kegan Paul, Trench, Trübner & Co, 1901. Volume 1: 26–88.
Lines I.920–1170, 1582–1931, and 2927–3016 of the *KnT* are supplied from the Egerton ms. Volume 2 contains woodcuts of the Ellesmere miniatures of the pilgrims.

10 Chaucer's *Prologue and Knightes Tale*. Ed. Stephen H. Carpenter. Boston: Ginn & Company, 1901. Text: pp 26–90; notes, pp 191–249.
Completed by 1872, this edition is based on Morris **2** but goes even further in bowdlerizing the text, omitting the woman in childbirth (*KnT* 1225–8; I.2083–6), and Emelye's desire to remain a maid (*KnT* 1452–3; I.2310–11) as well as part of Arcite's prayer (*KnT* 1525–32; I.2383–90). The copious notes are largely grammatical and philological.

11 *The Prologue to the Canterbury Tales, The Knightes Tale, The Nonnes Prestes Tale*. Ed. Mark H. Liddell. New York and London: Macmillan, 1901; rpt 1910, 1922, 1926. Text: pp 32–110; notes, pp 160–75.
Presents Chaucer's text in conjunction with a hundred-page historical treatment of Middle English grammar (ix–cviii). The text is based on Ellesmere; textual notes are at the foot of the page. The explanatory notes, whose value is noted by Robinson **39**, treat grammar, phonet-

ics, philology, and metrics, in addition to clarifying allusions and backgrounds.

12 *Geoffrey Chaucer's The Prologue to the Book of the Tales of Canterbury, The Knight's Tale, The Nun's Priest's Tale.* Ed. Andrew Ingraham. New York and London: MacMillan, 1902. Rpt several times through 1938. Text: pp 36–126; notes: pp 259–79.
The basis of the text is not indicated. Glossary with line references.

13 *The Select Chaucer.* Ed. J. Logie Robertson. Edinburgh and London: Blackwood, 1902. Text: pp 71–94; notes: pp 94–7.
Includes the *GP*, seventeen tales (excerpted), and a selection of Minor Poems. For the *KnT* Robertson prints I.1033–1184 ('Palamon and Arcite – rivals in love'), 1491–1880 ('The Fight in the Forest'); and 2485–662, 2671–99 ('The Fight in the Lists'), with the remaining portions summarized in prose. The text is based on Ellesmere and Harley 7334, collated with other mss in the *Six-Text* edition **1** and with the editions of Morris **2** and Skeat **3**. Brief introduction and glossary.

14 *The Knight's Tale.* Ed. Alfred W. Pollard. London: Macmillan, 1903. The text is based on Ellesmere. The extensive notes, to which Robinson **39** is indebted, are printed at the end of the text (pp 77–120). The edition includes 'Illustrations of Chaucer's Grammar from the "Knight's Tale"' (pp 121–5), an appendix that prints passages from the *Anel*, *PF*, and *TC* indebted to Boccaccio's *Tes*, and a glossary.

15 *The Knight's Tale, or Palamon and Arcite, by Geoffrey Chaucer, Done into Modern English.* Trans. W.W. Skeat. London: De la Mare Press, 1904.
Based on **3**, this translation attempts to preserve Chaucer's exact words wherever rhyme, meter, and diction make it possible.

16 *Chaucer's Canterbury Tales: The Prologue, The Knightes Tale, The Man of Lawes Tale, the Prioresses Tale and the Clerkes Tale.* Ed. Alfred W. Pollard. London: Kegan Paul, Trench & Co., 1905. The Dryden Series. Volume 1 of 2. Pp 39–122.
Pollard takes 'the easiest readings' from the mss of the *Six-Text* edition **1** and Harley 7334 to produce a text for general readers, not grammarians (xxv–xxvi). Each volume includes a brief introduction and brief glossary; there are no notes.

17 *The Works of Geoffrey Chaucer and Others, Being a Reproduction in Facsimile of the First Collected Edition 1532* [William Thynne]. Introduction by W.W. Skeat. Oxford: Oxford University Press, 1905. Pp 21–45.

Thynne presents almost the entire canon of Chaucer's work along with nineteen spurious pieces. In his introduction, Skeat reviews the history of the five earlier printed editions of the *CT*: Caxton[1] (1477–8), Caxton[2] (1483: see **61**, **68**), Pynson[1] (1493), Wynkyn de Worde (1498: see **68**), and Pynson[2] (1526). Thynne's edition of the *CT* became the standard edition for another 250 years. 'Unfortunately, this is the least satisfactory portion' of Thynne's volume (xxv), since he based his text on Caxton's inferior first edition. From Caxton's second edition, Thynne drew thirteen woodcuts depicting the pilgrims; they are placed here at the openings of the tales. Only those of the Knight [copied from Pynson[2]] and Squire are new. The Knight, in full armor, rides a richly caparisoned horse and holds the bridle in his left hand, a sword in his right. Large plumes adorn the horse's mane and the Knight's helmet. For later sixteenth- and seventeenth-century versions of Thynne, see **58**, and see James E. Blodgett, 'William Thynne,' in *Editing Chaucer* (see Headnote), pp 35–52.

18 *Selections from Chaucer*. Ed. Edwin A. Greenlaw. Chicago: Scott, Foresman, 1907. Text: pp 98–179; notes: pp 251–65.
Includes the *GP, KnT, MkT* (selections), *NPT*, and *PardT* (condensed), and a glossary. The text is based on Ellesmere.

19 *Chaucer's Canterbury Tales for the Modern Reader*. Ed. Arthur Burrell. Everyman's Library. London: Dent; New York: Dutton, 1908. Rpt many times through 1948.
Prints all of the *CT* except the *CkP* and *Tale*. The *GP, KnT*, and fifteen other tales are presented with modernized spelling, punctuation, and vocabulary. The *MilT* and six others are printed in Middle English because no amount of editing can make their plain-spokenness acceptable to the twentieth century (vii–viii). The basis of the text is not indicated, though reference is made to Skeat **3**. 'There is no pretence that this version is the Chaucer of the scholar, or the Chaucer of any recognised text' (viii). Burrell's text of the *KnT* was also published in *The Canterbury Tales by Geoffrey Chaucer: Part I, Prologue, The Knightes Tale, The Clerkes Tale*. London: Dent, 1913. [Not seen] For the later Everyman edition, see **49**.

20 *The Prologue and the Knight's Tale*. Ed. M. Bentinck-Smith. Cambridge: Cambridge University Press; New York: Putnam, 1909; rpt through 1929. Text: pp 29–100; notes, pp 143–67.
The text is based on Ellesmere, with many of Furnivall's emendations (**1**). Textual notes are printed at the foot of the page; explanatory notes, at the end of the text. The glossary (pp 169–229) is analytic, and the introductory matter, extensive (ix–lxxxvii). For the Knight and *KnT* see **321** and **525**.

21 *The Ellesmere Chaucer, reproduced in facsimile.* Preface by Alix Egerton. 2 volumes. Manchester: Manchester University Press, 1911.
This important text of the *CT*, the most lavishly decorated of Chaucer mss, was made available for reproduction by its then owner, the third Earl of Ellesmere. The famous miniatures of the pilgrims occur at the openings of the tales. The first page of each of the four parts of the *KnT* (see Skeat **3**) is decorated with a demivinet border, and the text of each part begins with a large decorative capital. Smaller decorative capitals appear at lines I 893, where the Knight resumes his narration after alluding to the story-telling contest, and 1347, where the Knight addresses his *demande d'amour* to the audience. This facsimile edition is now rare. For fuller accounts and descriptions of the ms, now owned by the Huntington Library, San Marino, California, see **437a** and **493**. For discussion of the Knight's miniature, see **339, 347, 353, 362, 363, 422, 426, 470, 488, 491, 517**.

22 *Poems of Chaucer: Selections from His Earlier and Later Works.* Ed. Oliver Farrar Emerson. New York: Macmillan, 1911. Text: pp 31–8; notes: 153–6.
The *KnT* is represented by lines 1023–1234 (I.1881–2092) under the title 'The Tourney Field in the Knight's Tale.' Emerson compares Chaucer's tournament to Scott's in *Ivanhoe*, Ch. vii (p 154). The text is based on the mss printed by the Chaucer Society.

23 *The Complete Poetical Works of Geoffrey Chaucer.* Trans. John S.P. Tatlock and Percy MacKaye. The Modern Reader's Chaucer, with 32 Illustrations by Warwick Goble. New York: Macmillan, 1912/rev 1938. Pp 15–51.
This first (prose) translation of the complete works into Modern English bowdlerizes the text to eliminate 'excessive coarseness' in words and phrases, and in a few cases, whole episodes 'incurably gross or voluptuous' (vii). The first sort of excision is silent, the second is announced by asterisks. There are no acknowledged cuts in the *KnT*; the text of the *MilT* eliminates the misplaced kiss. The *KnT* has three of the highly romantic illustrations: 'Theseus returning in Triumph,' 'Emily in the Garden,' and 'The Meeting [of Palamon and Arcite] in the Wood.' Reissued without illustrations in paperback; Toronto: Collier-Macmillan, 1966 [not seen].

24 *Selections from Chaucer, Including His Earlier and His Later Verse and an Example of His Prose.* Ed. Clarence Griffin Child. Boston: D.C. Heath, 1912. Text: pp 28–96; notes: pp 163–72.
Includes the *GP, KnT, Headlink* to *Thop, NPT*, and *PardT*. The source of the text is not indicated. Blake's 'Canterbury Pilgrims' appears as the frontispiece.

25 *The Canterbury Tales. Illustrated after drawings by W. Russell Flint.* 3 volumes. A Riccardi Press book published for the Medici Society. London: Philip Lee Warner, 1913. Volume 1: 26–90.
The Middle English text is Skeat's (3). The colored plates include a frontispiece representing the displacement of the forest gods in the *KnT* and four others illustrating the siege of Ypolita, Palamon's first view of Emelye, the women appealing to Theseus in the grove, and the figure of Meschaunce in Mars' temple. Produced in 500 copies on paper and 12 on vellum. Also published in a one-volume popular edition (London: Jonathan Cape and the Medici Society, 1928).

26 *The College Chaucer.* Ed. Henry Noble MacCracken. New Haven: Yale University Press, 1913; rpt 1915, 1918, 1920. Pp 26–90.
Includes the *GP, KnT*, thirteen other tales, several links, and the *Ret*; omits the *MilT*, *RvT*, and *CkT*. The text is based on Ellesmere, with a few variants printed at the foot of the page. There are no explanatory notes, but the Glossary is extensive (pp 605–713).

27 *Selections from Chaucer.* Ed. S.E. Winbolt. Bell's English Texts. London: G. Bell, 1913.
Includes *GP*, *KnT*, and the Prol to *LGW* [not seen].

28 *Geoffrey Chaucer's 'Canterbury Tales,' nach dem Ellesmere Manuscript mit Lesarten, Anmerkungen und einum Glossar.* Ed. John Koch. Heidelberg: Carl Winter, 1915. Pp 27–66.
The text is based on Ellesmere, with notes on the variants at the foot of the page. The introduction emphasizes mss, editions and sources of the *CT*, and there is an extensive glossary.

29 *Chaucer-Handbuch für Studierende: augsgewählte Texte mit Einleitungen, einem Abriss von Chaucers Versbau und Sprache und einem Wörterverzeichnis.* Ed. Max Kaluza. Leipzig: Tauchnitz, 1915/rev 1927. Pp 135–58.
Presents seven excerpts from the *KnT* based on Ellesmere: the capture of Palamon and Arcite through the end of Part I (I.1001–-1354); the scene in the grove (1663–1880); the preparations for the tournament (2483–2522); the procession to the lists (2565–2699); Arcite's injury and death (2743–2826); the calling of the parliament (2967–86); and Theseus' words to Emelye (3075–3108). The excluded sections are represented by prose summaries. Textual notes appear at the foot of the page; there are no explanatory notes.

30 *The Knightes Tale.* Ed. R.J. Cunliffe. The Plain-text Poets Series. London: Blackie, 1915.
The source of the text is not indicated. There is an analytic glossary but there are no notes.

31 *Selections from Chaucer*. Ed. William Allan Neilson and Howard Rollin Patch. New York: Harcourt, Brace, 1921. Pp 286–336.
Includes the *GP*, *KnT*, *PrT*, *NPT*, *PardT*, *WBT*, and *ClT*. The text is based on Skeat **3**, collated with the mss printed by the Chaucer Society. There are no explanatory notes: glossary, pp 423–505.

32 *Chaucer and Spenser, Contrasted as Narrative Poets*. Ed. Guy Boas. London and Edinburgh: Nelson, 1926. Pp 48–75.
Prints Skeat's text (**3**) of the *GP, ClT, MkT*, and *NPT*, with these selections from the *KnT*: 'Palamon and Arcite fall in love with Emily' (I.1030–1122), 'The Duel' (1623–1880), 'The Tournament' (2483–2699), 'Death of Arcite' (2700–2966), and 'Palamon is married to Emily' (2977–3108).

33 *Canterbury Tales*. Ed. J.M. Manly. New York: Holt; London: Harrap, 1928. Text: pp 171–230; notes: pp 539–58.
An incomplete and bowdlerized edition; eg, it prints excerpts only from the *MilT* and *RvT*. Manly was at work on **42** when he published this edition, which he characterizes as 'in no sense an attempt at a critical text' (vi). He prints the text of Ellesmere corrected from other good mss, and retains the Ellesmere order of the tales, in preference to Skeat's order (**3**), presenting the tales in ten Fragments numbered I (Group A) through X. The introductory matter treats Chaucer's life and historical setting in illuminating detail and includes a section on astronomy and astrology (pp 132–44). The notes influenced later scholarly editions. A black-and-white reproduction of 'A May Party' from the *Très Riches Heures* of Jehan duc de Berri adorns the *KnT*. For the Knight see **337**; for *KnT* **605a**.

34 *The Works of Geoffrey Chaucer*. 8 volumes. Shakespeare Head Press. Oxford: Blackwell, 1928–9. Pp 30–105.
This fine edition prints the Middle English text of the Globe edition **7**. Portraits of the pilgrims by Hugh Chesterman, modelled on the Ellesmere miniatures, stand with the descriptions in the *GP* and again at the heads of the tales. 375 copies and 11 on vellum.

35 *The Canterbury Tales by Geoffrey Chaucer*. With Wood Engravings by Eric Gill. 4 volumes. Waltham Saint Lawrence, Berkshire, England: Golden Cockerel Press, 1929. Volume 1: 31–106.
The Middle English text of this fine art edition is Skeat's (**3**). 15 copies on vellum; 485 on paper.

36 *The Canterbury Tales of Geoffrey Chaucer, together with a version in modern English verse by William Van Wyck, illustrated by Rockwell Kent*. 2 volumes. New York: Covici, Friede, 1930. Volume 1: 23–70.
Van Wyck's translation, in iambic pentameter couplets, and the Middle English text, whose source is not indicated, are printed in

parallel columns. Kent's portraits of the pilgrims, placed at the openings of the tales, attempt to interpret character rather than to illustrate the descriptions in the *GP*. His Knight is an older man with a meditative expression, leaning on a sword and dressed in a robe and cape. 924 copies.

37 *The Canterbury Tales: The Prologue and Four Tales with The Book of the Duchess and Six Lyrics by Geoffrey Chaucer*. Trans. Frank Ernest Hill. Illustrations by Herman Rosse. London: Longmans, 1930; rpt 1940. Pp 35–114.

The first poetic translation to be widely available includes the *GP, KnT, PrT, NPT,* and *PardT*. The romantic black-and-white illustrations for the *KnT* are placed at the beginnings of its four divisions as in Ellesmere (see **3**): Part I, a full-page illustration of the wedding of Theseus and Ypolita and a smaller representation of knights and footsoldiers arrayed for battle; Part II, a full-page illustration of Palamon and Arcite in their cell and of Emelye in the garden, and a small drawing of the duel; Part III, a full-page drawing of Venus, Mars, and Diana, and a small picture of knights gathering outside the lists; and Part IV, a full-page drawing of the tournament, and a small illustration of Arcite's fatal fall. In his introduction, Hill praises the descriptions and actions of the Tale, finding in Mars' temple and the final speeches of Arcite and Theseus, 'bitter protests against human fate ... a strong and even supreme aspect of Chaucer' (xvi–xvii). Hill published a complete translation of the *CT* in 2 volumes: London: Limited Editions Club, 1934/rev 1946 with miniatures by Arthur Szyk.

- See G.K. Chesterton **357**, pp 207–9: Chesterton comments on Hill's translation of I.2779: 'Alone, alone, with none for company.' Hill 'has broken the backbone of the tragic line with a load of repetition ... while the original ... is like a desolate yet living cry, echoing in a vault of stone' (p 209). See **759**.

38 *Tales from Chaucer*. Re-told by Eleanor Farjean. Illustrations by Marjorie Walters. London: Medici Society, 1930. Rpt London: Oxford University Press; Newton, Mass.: Branford, 1959. Pp 16–41.

This prose translation of the *CT*, which contains texts that have been cut and altered for young readers, omits the descriptions of the temples. A colored illustration depicts the meeting of Arcite and Palamon in the woods (opposite p 24). Also published with illustrations by W. Russell Flint (New York: Jonathan Cape and Harrison Smith, 1930), where a colored illustration depicts Palamon and Arcite asking mercy of Theseus (opposite p 26).

39 *The Poetical Works of Chaucer*. Ed. F.N. Robinson. Cambridge, Mass.: Houghton Mifflin; London: Oxford University Press, 1933. Second edition published as *The Works of Geoffrey Chaucer.* Boston: Houghton-Mifflin, 1957. Rpt in paperback, London: Oxford University Press, 1974. Text, pp 29–56/25–47; explanatory notes, pp 770–86/ 669–83; textual notes, p 1006/890.

The standard edition of the Works, superseding Skeat's (**3**). For the *CT*, Ellesmere is the basis of the text, collated 1) with the other seven mss printed by the Chaucer Society (Hengwrt, Cambridge Dd.4.24, Cambridge Gg.4.27, Corpus, Petworth, Lansdowne, and Harley 7334); 2) with Thynne's edition **17**; and 3) with the unpublished Cardigan and Morgan mss. 'In textual method the present editor does not belong to the severest critical school. When the readings of the "critical text" or of a superior archetype appeared unsatisfactory or manifestly inferior, he has accepted help from other authorities more often than the strict constructionists might approve' (xxxvii). The textual notes record selected variants of literary interest. Robinson presents the tales in the Ellesmere order, in ten Fragments labelled I(A)–X. In the second edition, in response to Manly-Rickert **42**, Robinson altered nineteen of his 1933 readings of the *KnT* (pp 883–5). The introductions to the separate works, which are essentially the same in both editions, and the explanatory notes emphasize Chaucer's literary sources, the history of his ideas, and the development of the literary forms in which he worked. Bibliographical references in the notes to the first edition constitute a compendium of scholarship to 1930; in the second edition, the notes were revised chiefly by the addition of more recent references. For the Knight and *KnT* see **388** and **751**; and see **8, 11, 14, 40, 45, 46, 49, 53, 56, 57, 60, 63, 65, 67, 72, 727, 1017.**

- George R. Reinecke, 'F.N. Robinson,' in *Editing Chaucer* (see Headnote), pp 231–51: Reinecke reproduces Robinson's 'Tentative Rule' for emending Ellesmere (pp 230 and 241) and examines its application to several passages, including A(I)3005–108, Theseus' final speech (pp 243–4). Reinecke finds that Robinson does not acknowledge all of his emendations in his textual notes.

40 *The Prologue, The Knight's Tale, and the Nun's Priest's Tale.* Ed. Max J. Herzberg. Boston: Houghton Mifflin, 1936. Pp 39–122.
The text is that of Robinson's first edition **39**, and is accompanied by glosses and brief explanatory notes at the foot of the page.

41 *The Canterbury Tales: The Prologue, the Knightes Tale, the Wife of Bath's Prologue, the Tale of the Wyf of Bathe.* Ed. Sanki Ichikawa. Kenkyusha English Classics. Tokyo: Kenkyushan, 1937.
[Not seen]

42 *The Text of the Canterbury Tales, studied on the basis of all known Manuscripts*. Ed. John M. Manly and Edith Rickert, with the aid of Mabel Dean, Helen McIntosh and Others. With a Chapter on Illuminations by Margaret Rickert. 8 volumes. Chicago: University of Chicago Press; London: Cambridge University Press, 1940.
This study was made possible by the collection, at the University of Chicago, of photostatic copies of all known mss. Volume I: Descriptions of the Manuscripts. Detailed studies of the physical features, dates, dialects and spellings, and provenance of the mss. 'Because of its great freedom from accidental errors and its entire freedom from editorial variants,' Hengwrt is 'a MS of the highest importance' (p 276). The authority usually ascribed to Ellesmere must be qualified because of its total of unique variants, many of them errors, and because of its having been heavily edited (p 159). Volume II: *Classification of the Manuscripts*. The editors, attempting to establish through recension the archetype of the mss, discuss the 'extraordinary shifts and obscurations of relationships' among the mss (p 41). The genetic groupings vary so greatly from part to part of the *CT* that each tale must be treated individually. For the *KnT*, see pp 97–135; and see **717**. Volume III: *Text and Critical Notes, Part I*: *KnT*: text, pp 48–126; notes, pp 426–38 and see **717**. The text is printed without punctuation. The *KnT* appears in the four-part division of Ellesmere. Selected variants recording the most important mss that support the reading given in the text are printed at the foot of the page. The full Corpus of Variants, perhaps the most valuable part of the edition, records all readings that differ from the editors' text and is presented in Volumes V–VIII; *KnT*, Volume V: 80–306. See **39**, **56**, **59**, **60**, **992**. For Critical Notes on the Knight's portrait, see **380**.

- George Kane, 'John M. Manly and Edith Rickert,' in *Editing Chaucer* (see Headnote), pp 207–29: Kane criticizes the editors' understanding and application of the method of recension, and suggests that misunderstandings of the processes of scribal variation and limited command of Middle English undermine their arguments both for deliberate editing of Ellesmere by someone other than Chaucer and for authorial revision. Kane reviews and rejects thirteen alleged instances of editing in the Ellesmere *KnT* (p 221). The editors do not convincingly establish the superiority of Hengwrt to Ellesmere.

43 *The Canterbury Tales of Geoffrey Chaucer*. Ed. Edwin Johnston Howard and Gordon Donley Wilson. 2nd ed. New York: Prentice Hall, 1947. Text, pp 59–123; notes, pp 309–19.

Includes introduction and glossary. The source of the text is not indicated. The *KnT* does not appear in the first edition (1937/rev 1942).

44 *Chaucer's Canterbury Tales (Selected): An Interlinear Translation*. Ed. Vincent F. Hopper. Great Neck, New York: Barron's Educational Series, 1948. Rpt many times through 1962. Pp 55–196.
Includes the *GP, KnT, PrT, NPT, PardT, WBT,* and *FranT*. The source of the Middle English text is not indicated. Beneath each line of Middle English appears a translation into Modern English. Minimal introduction and notes.

45 Morrison, Theodore, trans. and ed. *The Portable Chaucer*. New York: Viking, 1949; rev 1975. Pp 84–133. Rpt Harmondsworth: Penguin, 1977 and through 1987.
Contains the *GP*, most of the links, twelve tales, and the *Ret*, all in verse translation and based on Robinson's first edition **39**. Morrison frequently condenses where Chaucer is 'prolix'; his *KnT* is about half as long as Chaucer's, 'the result of simple squeezing down of expression' (p 52/p 45).

46 *The Canterbury Tales*. Trans. Nevill Coghill. London: Penguin, 1951/rev 1958, 1960. Pp 42–102.
A verse translation in rhymed iambic pentameter, complete except for *Mel* and *ParsT*, which are represented by brief synopses. The translation is based on both Skeat **3** and Robinson **39**. This most widely read translation of the *CT* has been reprinted many times. In a later illustrated edition, the *KnT* is accompanied by ten color plates of medieval artifacts and by a commentary on 'War and the Feudal System' by Bernard Moore (pp 72–3): Penguin, 1977; rpt 1981. See also **62, 519, 1099**.

47 *The Canterbury Tales (Selections), Together with Sections from the Shorter Poems*. Ed. Robert Archibald Jelliffe. The Modern Student's Library. New York: Scribner's, 1952. Pp 76–138.
Includes the *GP, KnT, PrT, NPT, PardT, WBT, ClT, FranT,* and several links. The text is based on Ellesmere. There is a glossary but no notes.

48 *The Knight's Tale*. Ed. J.A.W. Bennett. London: Harrap, 1954/rev 1958. Rpt several times through 1976.
The text is based on Ellesmere, with departures from it and a selection of variants from other mss printed in the footnotes. The introductory matter includes a summary of the *Tes* (pp 27–32) indicating the main differences from the *KnT*. The notes of this respected edition (pp 108–48 and 206–8) contain explanatory,

illustrative, and critical matter. Glossary, pp 165–205. For *KnT* see **657**.

49 *Canterbury Tales*. Ed. A.C. Cawley. Everyman's Library. London: Dent; New York: Dutton, 1958/rev 1975. Pp 26–82.
The text of this widely used work is that of Robinson's second edition **39**. Glosses are printed conveniently in the right margin, and translations of difficult lines, together with a few explanatory notes, appear at the foot of the page. Cawley cites the juxtaposition of *KnT* and *MilT* — 'a dish of caviare beside a platter of blood puddings' (xii) — as an example of the balanced seriousness of the *CT*.

50 *Chaucer's Poetry: An Anthology for the Modern Reader*. Ed. E. Talbot Donaldson. New York: Ronald Press, 1958/rev 1975. Text, pp 34–104 in both editions; notes, pp 901–5/1061–6.
Hengwrt is the base for the text, but the tales are presented in the Ellesmere order, and the *KnT* is divided into four parts as in Ellesmere (see **3**). Lines I.2681–2 and 2779–82 of the *KnT* and lines VII.2771–90 [B^2.3961–80] of the *NPP* (which present an address to the Monk assigned in some mss to the Knight), all missing in Hengwrt, are silently restored. There are no textual notes; glosses and explanatory notes appear at the foot of the page. Spellings have been made consistent throughout the text, and for still current words the forms closest to Modern English are given. The influential 'Commentary' deliberately avoids a historical approach: 'the criticism is in general based firmly on the text' (vii). The commentaries on the Knight and *KnT* are the same in both editions, though the pagination differs; see **365** and **675**.

51 *The Works of Geoffrey Chaucer. A Facsimile of the William Morris Kelmscott Chaucer, with the original 87 illustrations by Edward Burne-Jones*. Introduction by John T. Winterich. Cleveland and New York: World Publishing Company, 1958. Pp 9–30.
The Kelmscott Chaucer **6** was the fortieth of fifty-three books to be produced between 1891 and 1898 by the most important private press in the history of printing (xii). The full-page woodcut title, fourteen large borders, eighteen frames for the Burne-Jones pictures, twenty-six large initial words, and the ornamental initial letters large and small, were designed by Morris. The 'Chaucer' type face, used for the text, and the 'Troy' type face, used for the headings, are also Morris' work. See **64**.

52 *The Knight's Tale*. Ed. F.W. Robinson. London: Brodie, 1960.
The source of this text, intended for use in secondary schools, is not indicated; it is accompanied by brief plot summaries. See **65**.

53 *Chaucer*. Ed. Louis O. Coxe. New York: Dell, 1963. The Laurel Poetry Series. Pp 50–106.
Includes the *GP, KnT, MilT, WBP, MerT, FranT, PardT, NPT,* and *PrT*; the text is based on Skeat **3** and Robinson **39**.

54 *Chaucer's Major Poetry*. Ed. Albert C. Baugh. New York: Appleton Century Crofts; London: Routledge and Kegan Paul, 1963. Pp 256–90.
Includes all of the *CT* except *Mel* and *ParsT*. The text is based on Ellesmere. Explanatory notes and glosses, printed at the foot of the page, are supplemented by a lengthy and valuable glossary with line references.

55 *Chaucer: Canterbury Tales/Tales of Canterbury*. Ed. A. Kent Hieatt and Constance Hieatt. Bantam Dual-Language Series. New York: Bantam Books, 1964. Rpt through 1982.
The text, based on Skeat **3**, is accompanied by a facing-page, line-for-line translation in Modern English; a few brief notes are printed at the end.

56 *Selections from The Tales of Canterbury and Short Poems*. Ed. Robert A. Pratt. Boston: Houghton Mifflin, 1966. Pp 26–78.
Includes the *GP*; eighteen tales with associated prologues; the prologues to the *MkT, SNT, CYT*, and *ParsT*; and the *Ret*. The basis of the *CT* text is Robinson **39**, though Pratt has admitted more readings from Manly-Rickert **42** than does Robinson. Explanatory notes appear at the foot of the page; glosses are in the right margin. For Pratt's complete edition of the *CT*, see **63**.

57 *The Knight's Tale*. Ed. A.C. Spearing. Cambridge: Cambridge University Press, 1966; rpt 1974 and several times through 1982.
The text of this useful teaching edition is based on Robinson **39**. The portrait of the Knight from the *GP* appears in an appendix. The notes, frequently devoted to explaining conventions of medieval literature, are printed at the end of the text (pp 154–90). Glossary, pp 193–219. The introduction (pp 1–79) covers a broad range of background topics and presents Spearing's interpretation of the Tale; see **888**.

58 *Geoffrey Chaucer. The Works, 1532, With supplementary material from the Editions of 1542, 1561, 1598 and 1602.* Facsimile edition. Ed. D.S. Brewer. Menston, Yorkshire: Scolar Press, 1969. Rpt London: Scolar Press, 1974 and 1976.
Thynne's 1532 edition **17** is the basis of this edition, with new material from subsequent sixteenth- and seventeenth-century editions added in order. This facsimile presents Chaucer's work in the form

in which Spenser, Shakespeare, Milton, Dryden, and Pope knew it. See Hieatt **971**.

59 *The Canterbury Tales, A Selection*. Ed. Donald R. Howard, with the assistance of James Dean. The Signet Classic Poetry Series. New York: New American Library, 1969. Pp 95–161.
This well-designed edition includes the *GP*, thirteen tales and associated prologues, *MkP, ParsP*, and *Ret*. The text is 'eclectic' but indebted to Manly-Rickert **42** (xxxix). The spelling has been normalized and modernized. Explanatory notes and glosses appear at the foot of the page. The introduction touches briefly on the Knight as an ideal figure (xiv), on his providential selection as first tale-teller (xv–xvi), and on the presence of an ironic voice in the *KnT* that arouses skepticism about romantic and aristocratic conventions (xxiii–xxiv).

60 *The Canterbury Tales*. Ed. John Halverson. The Library of Literature. New York: Bobbs-Merrill, 1971. Pp 32–100.
Includes the *GP*, twelve tales and associated prologues, summaries (with excerpts) of the remaining tales, and the *Ret*. The text is based on Robinson **39**, compared line for line with the text and variants of Manly-Rickert **42**. Brief explanatory notes and glosses at the foot of the page; glossary.

61 Bennett, J.A.W., ed. *The Canterbury Tales*. A Facsimile Edition of Caxton's Second Edition. Cambridge: Cornmarket Reprints, 1972.
Reproduces Pepys' copy of the *CT*. Caxton^2 (1483), based on a ms of the *a* type, is superior to Caxton^1 (1477–8), based on a manuscript of the *b* type. Twenty-two woodcuts of the pilgrims appear in the *GP* and again at the beginnings of their respective tales. The Knight appears mounted, in armor, with a single plume on his helmet. The *KnT* is printed without divisions; nineteen large red capitals are distributed unevenly throughout the tale. See Beverly Boyd, 'William Caxton,' in *Editing Chaucer* (see Headnote), pp 13–34, and see **68**.

62 *A Choice of Chaucer's Verse*. Selected with an introduction by Nevill Coghill. London: Faber & Faber, 1972.
Presents original texts based on Skeat (**3**) with facing Modern English paraphrases in verse. The *KnT* is represented by four excerpts: 'A Duel for Love' (I.1633–2604 with omissions); 'A Tournament for Love' (2483–2714); 'The Death of Arcite' (2743–2812); and 'First Cause and Last Effect' (2987–3044).

63 *The Tales of Canterbury, Complete*. Ed. Robert A. Pratt. Boston: Houghton Mifflin, 1974. Pp 26–77.
An expanded version of **56** (without the short poems). A new 'Comment on the Text' (pp 561–79) clarifies the relationship of

Pratt's text to Robinson's **39**, and lists all of the altered readings. For the *KnT* there are 82 new readings. The explanatory notes have been expanded, and there are three illustrations for the *KnT*: a photograph of the helm of Sir Richard Pembridge, a ms illustration of 'Diagnosis-Prognosis by Astrology,' and a ms illustration for the *Tes* depicting 'Emilia in the Garden.'

64 *The Kelmscott Chaucer*, a facsimile edition, with *A Companion Volume to the Kelmscott Chaucer* by Duncan Robinson. London: Basilisk Press, 1975.
The *Companion Volume* reproduces finished pencil drawings for the Burne-Jones illustrations (see **6**), including six for the *KnT* (plates 2–7), as well as early drafts, including eight sketches for the temples of Venus (p 30), Diana (pp 38–41), and Mars (pp 43–4). Robinson notes Burne-Jones' 'clear preference for the more chivalric and courtly elements in Chaucer's work' (p 27). His distaste for the *MilT*, *RvT*, and *CkT* apparently prevailed over Morris' wish to have them illustrated. Robinson analyzes the drawing of Emily in the garden as an example of Burne-Jones' 'three-layered composition' (p 48). Robert Catterson-Smith's description of how he converted the pencil drawings into inked drawings is quoted (pp 53–4). The facsimile edition and the Companion were produced in 515 copies on paper.

65 Robinson, F.W. *Brodie's Notes on Chaucer's The Knight's Tale*. London: Brodie, 1976. Rev ed, London and Sydney: Pan Books, 1978.
Prints parallel texts in Middle and Modern English. The Middle English text is based on F.N. Robinson **39**, with revisions to spelling and punctuation by James Winny. F.W. Robinson provides a commentary on sources, setting, plot, and characters. [Not seen]

66 *The Complete Poetry and Prose of Geoffrey Chaucer*. Ed. John H. Fisher. New York: Holt, Rinehart, and Winston, 1977/rev 1982. Pp 25–56.
The text is based on Ellesmere and preserves the Ellesmere order of the tales. All substantive variants in Hengwrt are listed in the textual notes, which, with the explanatory notes, appear at the foot of the page. Plate 1 (p 5) is a black-and-white reproduction of the opening of the *KnT* in Ellesmere. An extensive bibliography (pp 975–1018) is exhaustive for the period 1964–74 and includes important items both earlier and later; the revised bibliography extends through 1979. Includes a glossary.

67 *Geoffroy Chaucer: Les Contes de Cantorbéry, Ière partie*. Trans. Juliette de Caluwé-Dor. Gand, Belgique: Editions Scientifiques E. Story-Scientia, 1977. Pp 25–86.

Contains line-by-line translations into French prose of the *GP, KnT, MilT,* and *NPT*, based on Robinson **39**. Divergences from Robinson are acknowledged in the notes, which also contain explanatory matter and are printed at the end (pp 129–41). The first part of a projected complete edition.

- Review by Roy J. Pearcy, *SAC* 3(1981), 128–34: Pearcy praises the 'creditable degree of accuracy' (p 129) of the translation while noting difficulties with I.1199–1200, 1512, 1540, 1609, 1659, 1699, 2605–6 and 3063.

68 *Wynknyn de Worde and Chaucer's Canterbury Tales: A Transcription and Collation of the 1498 Edition with Caxton² from the General Prologue through the Knight's Tale*. Ed. William F. Hutmacher. Costerus, New Series, Number 10. Amsterdam: Rodopi, 1978.

Hutmacher confirms earlier scholarly opinion that the sole source of Wynkyn de Worde's 1498 edition was Caxton² (**61**). In a discussion of variants from Caxton² (pp 23–33), Hutmacher calls attention to Wynkyn's 'correction' of *fewe* to *ferwe* in 2109 (I.2105); to Wynkyn's introduction of errors into 2134 (I.2130: *namly* for Caxton's *manly*), 2387 (I.2382: *tyre* for Caxton's *fyre*) and 2402 (I.2398: *shente* for Caxton's *she me*); and to Wynkyn's substitution of *Athens* for *Thebes* in 862 (I.861) and of '*And eke thrugh Juno jalous and eke wood*' for Caxton's '*And thourgh hym unhappy and eek wood*' in I.1329. This work is a version of the author's dissertation: see *DAI* 38(1977), 779A. Texas Tech University, 1976.

- Review by N.F. Blake, *N&Q* 224[26](1979), 160–1: More recent scholarship indicates that Wynkyn also used a ms (though not for the *KnT*). There is an average of three transcription errors per page in this collation.

69 *The Canterbury Tales: Geoffrey Chaucer. A Facsimile and Transcription of the Hengwrt Manuscript, with Variants from the Ellesmere Manuscript*. Ed. Paul G. Ruggiers. Introductions by Donald C. Baker and by A.I. Doyle and M.B. Parkes. Volume I of *A Variorum Edition of the Works of Geoffrey Chaucer*. General Editor, Paul G. Ruggiers. Norman: University of Oklahoma Press; Folkstone, Kent: Wm. Dawson & Sons, 1979.

This inaugural volume presents the ms chosen as the base text for the *CT* in the new *Variorum Chaucer*. 'Hengwrt's age (1400–10), its unedited state, and its accuracy ... have now placed it in the forefront of the *Canterbury Tales* manuscripts, ahead even of the magnificent and more nearly complete, but heavily edited, Ellesmere' (xvii). In their paleographical introduction, Doyle and Parkes divide the ms into five structural sections, the first of which, fol. 2–57, contains

Group A (I). Hengwrt lacks the *CYT*, some links, and a few short passages, including *KnT* I[A].2681–2 and 2779–82 and VII.2771–90 [B^2.3961–80] (part of an address to the Monk assigned in Ellesmere to the Knight). In the *KnT* the heading 'Incipit narracio' occurs before line 893, and the rest of the Tale is divided into three parts (rather than four as in Ellesmere): 893–1880; 1881–2742; 2743–3108. Each of these divisions is marked by a decorated letter. The variants from Ellesmere appear in the right margin of the transcription. The opening leaf of the ms is reproduced in color. See **1017, 1069**.

70 Parkes, M. B., and Richard Beadle, eds. *Poetical Works: Geoffrey Chaucer. A Facsimile of Cambridge University Ms Gg.4.27* [With Introductions]. 3 vols. Norman, Oklahoma: Pilgrim Books; Cambridge: D.S. Brewer, 1979.
This ms represents the 'only surviving example of a fifteenth-century attempt to collect Chaucer's major poetical works in one volume' (III:1). Using Henry Bradshaw's corrected foliation, the editors describe the presentation of the *KnT* and adjacent texts: 'Gen. Prol. beginning abruptly (fol. 132) at A, 37; ending abruptly (fol. 141v) at A, 756. (Leaves missing.) Knight's Tale beginning abruptly (fol. 145) at A, 965; lines 3073–88 lost from mutilated leaf (fol. 174). Miller's Prol. without heading (fol. 175)' (III:3). This incomplete text of the *KnT* appears in Volume I. Supply leaves for I.859–964, provided by the antiquarian Joseph Holland in the seventeenth century, appear in Volume III. The *KnT* appears without divisions; sub-headings in the margins, probably by the main scribe, may have been intended as guides to the rubricator (III:43). The ms was mutilated in the late sixteenth century, with pictures, borders, and accompanying texts cut out. The editors print several color plates, including the six surviving pilgrim portraits, which do not include the Knight.

71 *The Canterbury Tales*. Ed. N.F. Blake. York Medieval Texts, second series. London: Edward Arnold, 1980. Pp 66–133.
Blake adopts Hengwrt as the basis of the text and presents the tales in the Hengwrt order (corrected for misbinding). The editing is conservative, aimed at avoiding emendations that have become traditional in favor of presenting 'a "plain" text ... of what is actually in the best manuscript' (p 12). Blake presents those parts of *CT* that appear in Hengwrt with the addition of the *Ret* on the supposition that it was originally in the final lost leaves. He presents in appendices those parts of Ellesmere not found in Hengwrt, including I[A].2779–82, and VII.2771–90 [B^2.3961–80] (an address to the Monk assigned in Ellesmere to the Knight). The *KnT* is presented

with the Hengwrt subdivisions; see **69**. Explanatory notes appear at the foot of the page. See **1069**.

72 *The Canterbury Tales/Die Canterbury-Erzählungen*: *Mittelenglisch/Deutsch*. Trans. and annotated by Heinz Bergner, Waltraud Böttcher, Günter Hagel and Hilmar Sperber. Ed. Heinz Bergner. Stuttgart: Philipp Reclam, 1982. Text: pp 57–185; commentary, notes and bibliography, 451–78.
The Middle English text is based on Robinson **39**. The German prose translation of the *KnT* and the accompanying critical material are by Hagel. For *KnT* see **1097**.

73 *The Canterbury Tales*. Trans. David Wright. Oxford: Oxford University Press, 1985. Rpt in World Classics Series. Oxford, 1986. *KnT*, pp 23–79.
A verse translation that aims to capture the 'immediacy, directness, and plain speech that make up the real poetry of the original' (xx). Wright believes that the difficulty of reading Chaucer in the original has been understated; his translation is not a substitute but 'an introductory prolusion to the real thing' (xxi).

- Derek Pearsall, *SAC* 9(1987), 199–203: The padding necessitated by modern verse translation of the inflected Middle English can produce 'effects of utter banality,' as in Wright's treatment of line I.2779: 'Alone, and with no kind of company' (p 201). See also comments on I.1984 and 2048. The translation is highly accurate, but 'every line read in translation seals off Chaucer and his English more finally' (p 200).

Backgrounds and General Studies

Chaucer and Italy

74 Boitani, Piero, ed. *Chaucer and the Italian Trecento*. Cambridge: Cambridge University Press, 1983.
A collection of twelve essays by various hands, exploring English and Italian cultural relations (see **76** and **78**) and Chaucer's relations with the works of Dante, Petrarch, and Boccaccio, with eight essays on Chaucer and Boccaccio (see **75**, **914**, **1071**). A bibliography (pp 297–304) by Enrico Giaccherini includes selected Italian scholarship before Praz' essay of 1927 (**83**).

75 —. 'What Dante Meant to Chaucer.' In *Chaucer and the Italian Trecento*. See **74**. Pp 115–39.
'Chaucer's relationship to Dante is still mysterious, puzzling and elusive' (p 116). In *HF* Chaucer, reacting to Dante as 'The Poet of Heaven and Hell,' chose instead poetics and philosophy as his own subject matter. The treatment of Arcite's soul (I.2809–14) is evidence of the same decision (p 126). The adaptation of Boccaccio's text on Arcite's soul in *TC* (V.1807–22) is one sign that *TC* is 'Chaucer's most serious effort to create his own equivalent of the *Divine Comedy* (and of the *Teseida*)' (p 127). Dante 'The Wise Poet' influenced Chaucer's concept of *gentilesse* through his *canzone* 'Le dolce rime d'amor' (pp 130–3). Chaucer acknowledged Dante as 'The Great Poet'(pp 133–7), a superior craftsman, in his remarks on Dante's story of Ugolino (*MkT* VII.2458–62).

76 Childs, Wendy. 'Anglo-Italian Contacts in the Fourteenth Century.' In *Chaucer and the Italian Trecento*. See **74**. Pp 65–87.
Childs explores Chaucer's opportunities for contact with Italy through the City of London (pp 67–75), the Court (pp 75–7), and the Church and universities (pp 77–84). She explains the necessary contacts between the Controller of Customs and Italian merchants and financiers, and sketches the background to Chaucer's mission to Genoa in 1373, but finds no evidence that Chaucer accompanied

Lionel to Milan in 1368. Chaucer's Italian contacts probably prepared him well for his journeys but are unlikely to have familiarized him fully with its new literature.

77 Coleman, William E. 'Chaucer, the *Teseida*, and the Visconti Library at Pavia: A Hypothesis.' *MAE* 51(1982), 92–101.

Coleman presents new evidence for Pratt's argument (**81**) that Chaucer might have secured a copy of the *Tes* from the Visconti library during his 1378 trip to Lombardy. A fifteenth-century copy of an inventory made in 1426 includes two copies of the *Tes*. Ms 881, an inexpensive 'private' book, lacks Boccaccio's name, a title, Boccaccio's commentary, and some parts of the text. Ms 935, a costly 'public' or commissioned book, is complete, but appears in the inventory without a title or author's name, and no gloss is mentioned. Of the 53 complete mss extant, all have titles, but the attribution to Boccaccio is missing in 20. It is not known whether mss 881 and 935 were in the Pavia library in 1378. Yet Chaucer makes no use of the parts of the *Tes* missing from ms 881, the wealth of information in the commentary, Boccaccio's title, or his name. 'Chaucer's *Teseida* was a corrupt MS of the work ... it resembled Pavia MS 881 or was a copy of it, and the lacunae in Chaucer's MS produced a corresponding change in Chaucer's understanding of the *Teseida* and his use of Boccaccio's work' (p 99).

78 Larner, John. 'Chaucer's Italy.' In *Chaucer and the Italian Trecento*. See **74**. Pp 7–32.

Larner surveys differences between Italian and Northern European culture (pp 7–16), observing that Chaucer's interest in Italian literature must have been 'the fruit of a very powerful intellectual and literary curiosity' (p 19), since mss were difficult to acquire, he probably did not know Italian, and Latin literature enjoyed greater prestige. Even Dante appeared, to such as Petrarch, to belong to a now remote world, and Boccaccio celebrated Dante partly by misrepresenting him as a Latinist. Chaucer was fortunate to encounter Italian literature in the Florence of 1373 when Dante was being declared a classic. By contrast, in Milan in 1368, Chaucer might have heard Petrarch condemn vernacular literature; and by the 1390's Florence was renowned for Greek scholarship and Tuscan literature seemed part of a past age.

79 Lewis, C.S. 'What Chaucer Really Did to *Il Filostrato*.' *E&S* 17(1932), 56–75.

In this influential study Lewis characterizes Chaucer, who 'had never heard of a renaissance' (p 57), as a poet who submitted Boccaccio's work, specifically *Il Filos*, to a process of '*medievalization*' (p 56).

Chaucer's medieval qualities are discussed under four headings: '"historical" poet,' 'pupil of the rhetoricians,' 'poet of *doctryne*,' and 'poet of courtly love.' See **87, 254, 692.**

80 Parks, George B. *The English Traveler to Italy*. Volume 1, *The Middle Ages (To 1525)*. Stanford: Stanford University Press, 1954.
For the period 1300–1530, Parks treats English kings and diplomats, clerics and pilgrims, soldiers and merchants, and students (pp 277–617). The routes and times of Chaucer's trips in 1372[–73] and 1378 are discussed in detail (pp 511–19), and more briefly, the effects of Italian literature on Chaucer (pp 613–5). Other topics of interest include Prince Lionel's marriage in Milan in 1368 (pp 278–84) and the activities of Sir John Hawkwood and English mercenaries (pp 383–95).

81 Pratt, R[obert] A. 'Chaucer and the Visconti Librairies.' *ELH* 6(1939), 191–99.
On his first authenticated trip to Italy in 1373, Chaucer seems to have become acquainted only with the *Div Com*. Works showing his indebtedness to Dante's *Convivio* and to the writings of Petrarch and Boccaccio seem to have been composed after his second trip in 1378. Very little information survives about Bernabo Visconti's library at Milan, but an inventory prepared in 1426 survives for Galeazzo Visconti's library at Pavia. It lists Dante's *Monarchia* and several works by Petrarch and Boccaccio, though not the *Tes* [but see Coleman **77**]. Many of Petrarch's and Boccaccio's writings were probably added later, but 'nothing definitely militates against' the library's containing such works in 1378. 'Chaucer may not have obtained the bulk of his Italian material until he went to Lombardy, and ... the Visconti may have owned the very manuscripts in question' (p 197).

82 — 'Conjectures Regarding Chaucer's Manuscript of the *Teseida*.' *SP* 42(1945), 745–63.
Pratt reviews the evidence for Chaucer's use of Boccaccio's commentary to his *Tes* (p 746). Pratt cites these four possible parallels between the glosses and Chaucer's works: gloss to *Tes* VII.72.5 and A[I].2283; *Tes* XI.19.1–3 and I.2915–7; *Tes* XI.24.1 and *PF* 179; and *Tes* VII.57.2 and *PF* 231 (pp 751–5). None of the parallels is at all certain, and if Chaucer did have access to the commentary, the paucity of his borrowings is remarkable. Pratt then considers the textual relationship of Chaucer's ms of the *Tes* to the families of extant mss and concludes that 'Chaucer used a corrupt copy of the most widely published type of ms, a type ... which lacked the

commentary' (p 761). Presumably, then, Chaucer did not obtain his copy from Boccaccio himself in Florence in 1373. See **742, 922.**

83 Praz, Mario. 'Chaucer and the Great Italian Writers of the Trecento.' *Monthly Criterion* 6(1927), 18–39, 131–57, and 238–42. Rpt in *The Flaming Heart: Essays on Crashaw, Machiavelli, and Other Studies in the Relations between Italian and English Literature from Chaucer to T.S. Eliot* (New York: Doubleday, 1958; rpt Gloucester, Mass.: Peter Smith, 1966), pp 29–89 [cited here]; in *Machiavelli in Inghilterra ed ultri saggi*, 2nd ed. (Florence, 1960), pp 29–91; and in *Chaucer: The Critical Heritage*. Ed. Derek Brewer (London: Routledge & Kegan Paul, 1978), Volume 2, pp 403–29.

This landmark study characterizes Chaucer's ways of using sources and evaluates his indebtedness to Dante and Boccaccio, with lesser attention to Petrarch. Chaucer frequently disposes different aspects of a single source passage in various parts of his own work, often in response to an association of ideas triggered by a second source. For example, the proem to *PF* suggests that Chaucer traced Boccaccio's description of the flight of Arcita's soul (*Tes* XI.1–3) to its source in Cicero's *Somnium Scipionis*, and then linked both to *Inf* V, itself indebted to Cicero (pp 43–4). But 'the bourgeois Chaucer' was not always in harmony with 'that disdainful aristocrat,' Dante (p 470), and several parallel passages show 'the deep spiritual difference between the two poets' (p 48) [for A[I].2809–14 see **615**]. Still Chaucer's veneration for authority led him to replace Boccaccio's lines with lines from Dante to which they are indebted. Boccaccio's work may have reached Chaucer anonymously or under Petrarch's name. Chaucer borrows more lines from Boccaccio, but the influence of Dante is 'the more deeply interfused and widespread' (p 78). See **914.**

84 Ruggiers, Paul G. 'The Italian Influence on Chaucer.' In *Companion to Chaucer Studies*. Ed. Beryl Rowland. New York: Oxford University Press, 1968/rev 1979. Pp 160–84/139–61.

Emphasizing the cumulative nature of Chaucer's development, in contradistinction to the once common division of his career into French, Italian, and English segments, Ruggiers points out the indebtedness of Italian literature to French and classical traditions. Ruggiers then reviews the limited evidence for and the scholarly speculations on Chaucer's trips to Italy and comments on the impact of Italy on Chaucer: 'Unfortunately Chaucer says almost nothing about Italian landscape, art or the personality of the Italians ... No English poet has been so immune to those aspects of Italian life which are usually fervently praised' (p 164).

85 Schless, Howard. 'Chaucer and Dante.' In *Critical Approaches To Medieval Literature: Selected Papers from the English Institute, 1958-1959*. Ed. Dorothy Bethurum. New York: Columbia University Press, 1960. Pp 134–54.
Schless critiques the 'linked atoms' method of identifying Chaucerian sources advanced by J.L. Lowes ('Chaucer and Dante's *Convivio*,' *MP* 13[1915], 19–33; 'Chaucer and Dante,' *MP* 14[1917], 705–35) by which lines in Chaucer are said to be indebted to Dante through the medium of another poem or poems whose words and phrases are said to remind Chaucer of more or less similar words and phrases in Dante. Schless objects to the assumption that Chaucer had almost total recall of Dante, and to the treatment of a few texts in isolation, without consideration of other specific sources, general knowledge, etc.

86 — 'Transformations: Chaucer's Use of Italian.' In *Writers and Their Background: Geoffrey Chaucer*. Ed. Derek Brewer. Athens, Ohio: Ohio University Press, 1975; rpt 1976. Pp 184–223.
Schless discusses the limitations of some methods of influence study, such as the 'linked atoms' approach (pp 184–6; see **85**). Chaucer probably went to Italy for the first time in 1368 (see Edith Rickert, 'Chaucer Abroad in 1368,' *MP* 25[1928], 511–2; and Margaret Galway, 'Chaucer's Journeys in 1368,' *TLS* 4 April 1958, 183). He might have learned Italian two years earlier as a member of Lionel's household in anticipation of the prince's marriage to Violante of Milan, and he would have encountered Italian bankers and merchants both as a member of Edward III's household and as a Customs officer. These same Italians or the many English persons who traveled to Italy might have introduced the *Div Com* into England before 1372. The examples of influence Schless treats here include the *Tes* and *PF*. Another version of this discussion appears in **1121**, pp 3–27.

87 Spearing, A.C. *Medieval to Renaissance in English Poetry*. Cambridge: Cambridge University Press, 1985.
The Renaissance was characterized by new concepts of the dignity of poetry and the poet, and of history. In Italy the stature achieved by Dante's *Div Com* was an important influence, as was Boccaccio's defense of poetry in *De genealogia* **231** and Petrarch's invention of the historical scheme, antiquity, middle ages, renaissance. Dante's Virgil is a renaissance figure – historically remote, stylistically accessible (pp 1–14). In fourteenth-century England there was no sense of a cultural rebirth, clerk and knight had not yet melded in the courtier, and literature was viewed as merely instrumental. Chaucer shared this

outlook but was strongly affected by his contacts with Italy. Earlier scholars like Mackail **605** and Ker **584** were correct in viewing Chaucer as in some sense a renaissance poet; C.S. Lewis' influential account of Chaucer as a 'medievalizer' of Boccaccio (**79**) fails to explain what attracted Chaucer to the Italian writers. Modern Chaucerians overemphasize Chaucer's medievalism for both scholarly and temperamental reasons (pp 15–22). For KnT see **1130**.

- Review by A.J. Minnis, *SAC* 9(1987), 253–60: Since, as Spearing recognizes, little that was typical of Renaissance culture was entirely new, it proves difficult to isolate the proto-Renaissance aspects of Chaucer. Chaucer's attribution of philosophical questioning to his pagan characters, for example, can be accounted for by appeals to Boethius and late-medieval *moderni.*

Romance and Romances

88 Auerbach, Erich. 'The Knight Sets Forth.' *Mimesis: The Representation of Reality in Western Literature.* Trans. Willard Trask. Princeton: Princeton University Press, 1953. Originally published in German (Berne: A. Francke, 1946). Pp 107–24.

This classic essay defines 'a self-portrayal of feudal knighthood with its mores and ideals' as 'the fundamental purpose of the courtly romance' (p 114). The portrayal includes realistic depiction of external forms of life joined to a fairy-tale treatment of time and space, limitation of the fictional world to the life of one class, and a focus on *avanture* wholly devoid of historical and political purpose. In romance *corteisie* replaces the *vasselage* of the *chanson de geste* (p 117). The emphasis on 'self-realization,' the achievement of 'a personal and absolute ideal' (p 117), requires an unrealistic art, one that may reflect or anticipate the crisis of the feudal class as to its function (p 120). Yet the early courtly romance did not make use of an elevated style (pp 115–6); this occurred only later when the classical doctrine of levels of style was revived (p 121). Restrictions on subject matter were always severe, however; love and war define the knight. Although the relationships between men and women vary, courtly love has the distinctive function of substituting for other kinds of motivation, historical and political, which the romance excludes (p 123). 'Courtly culture was decidedly unfavorable to the development of a literary art which should apprehend reality in its full breadth and depth' (p 124).

89 Beer, Gillian. *The Romance*. The Critical Idiom Series. London: Methuen, 1970.
Beer defines romance as having a 'cluster of properties: the themes of love and adventure, a certain withdrawal from their own societies on the part of both reader and romance hero, profuse sensuous detail, simplified characters (often with a suggestion of allegorical significance), a serene intermingling of the unexpected and the everyday, a complex and prolonged succession of incidents usually without a single climax, a happy ending, amplitude of proportions, a strongly enforced code of conduct' (p 10). In discussing medieval romance (pp 17–31), Beer emphasizes its Jungian treatment of character, its inclusiveness or 'polyphonic form' (p 20), and its mingling of the marvelous and the historical. She reviews such developments as the polarity of ideality and realism in *Don Quixote*, the appeal of the romance to later centuries, and the critiques offered of it.

90 Boitani, Piero. 'The World of Romance.' *English Medieval Narrative in the Thirteenth and Fourteenth Centuries*. Trans. Joan Krakover Hall. Cambridge: Cambridge University Press, 1982. Originally published as *La Narrativa del Medioevo Inglese* (Adriatica: Bari, 1980). Pp 36–70. Chaucer's romances are 'the watershed in the development of the genre' (p 38), creating a new, more sophisticated taste. As in the *KnT*, where he turns romance into 'a platform for discussion of problems of social order and disorder, Fortune, astral influences, nobility and death,' (p 39), Chaucer both uses and transfigures the genre and shows himself, in the *SqT*, conscious of doing so. Chaucer's philosophical and psychological tendencies are eccentric; English romance in general revolves around the poles of chronicle and epic, but its tendency to use a wide variety of kinds of material prepares the way for Chaucer. The romance became a bridge between unofficial folk culture and the official culture of the church and chivalry, and helped develop the art of narrative. For *KnT*, see **1070**.

91 Brownlee, Kevin, and Marina Scordilis Brownlee, ed. *Romance: Generic Transformation from Chretien de Troyes to Cervantes*. Hanover, New Hampshire: University Press of New England, 1985.
A collection of twelve essays devoted mostly to single works or authors. 'Romance — and, more generally, any literary genre — has no meaningful existence as a static category ... the functional literary life of romance involves a series of generic transformations over time resulting in a kind of dynamic continuum' (editors' 'Introduction,' p 1). These interactions typically reflect a dialectical interplay with social and political history. The editors review (pp 2–10) several

kinds of modern genre theory, for which the romance is seen as an especially important case.

92 Frye, Northrop. 'The Mythos of Summer: Romance.' In *Anatomy of Criticism*: *Four Essays*. Princeton: Princeton University Press, 1957; rpt through 1973. Pp 186–206.
Frye discusses romance as one of four 'pregeneric' elements of literature (the others being tragedy, comedy, and satire). Romance has a paradoxical social role since it projects the ideals of a ruling class while also embodying some degree of dissatisfaction; it shows an 'extraordinarily persistent nostalgia' for an imagined golden age (p 186). The central formal element is the quest with its three stages: the initial adventures or conflicts, the central battle or death-struggle, and the recognition and exaltation of the hero (p 187 f). In contrasting the romance with the novel, Frye observes: 'The essential difference ... lies in the conception of characterization. The romancer does not attempt to create "real people" so much as stylized figures which expand into psychological archetypes ... A suggestion of allegory is constantly creeping in' (pp 304).

93 Gist, Margaret Adlum. *Love and War in the Middle English Romances*. Philadelphia: University of Pennsylvania Press; London: Oxford University Press, 1947.
The romances are valuably revealing about their cultural milieu. By depicting woman as man's social inferior, a means to his ends, they faithfully reflect the historical record rather than the doctrines of chivalry. Although they suppress the moralists' ambivalence about war and idealize combat, they also present brutal as well as noble behavior, depicting the interaction between reality and aspiration so typical of the age.

94 Gradon, Pamela. 'The Romance Mode.' In *Form and Style in Early English Literature*. London: Methuen, 1971. Pp 212–72.
While basing itself in social actuality, the romance strives, as in its use of the marvelous, 'to disengage the emotions and to project the tale into an unreal world' (p 237), especially an ideal world of the past. Characters are treated as 'typical figures acting in a typical manner' (p 238). Attempts to differentiate Palamon and Arcite are a prime example of bringing inappropriate mimetic expectations to the romance (pp 246–7). The conventionalized language of courtly love, like the idealized depiction of chivalry, helps both to make the characters remote and to generalize them; they do not develop but represent their social milieu in the service of a theme. It is doubtful that a romance genre can be defined, but as a mode, the romance has close affiliations with the chronicle and chivalric biography (pp 270–

2) and can be contrasted with a more realistic medieval mode represented in part by the fabliau (pp 273–331).

95 Green, D.H. *Irony in the Medieval Romance.* Cambridge: Cambridge University Press, 1979.

Green develops the thesis that medieval romance, a genre dedicated to the legitimization of the chivalric and courtly ideals, is paradoxically welcoming to the ironic mode and to a critical spirit. His last chapter summarizes the reasons (pp 359–93), including conditions of composition, such as the status of the poet as an outsider in the court (here he cites Chaucer, pp. 363–4), and the nature of the genre itself: its very conservatism rhetorically, for example, created a context in which irony could be especially effective. 'Medieval irony, unlike the admittedly often nihilistic corrosiveness of modern irony, still has a positive function in strengthening the ideal' by 'more accurately defining and refining it, reducing it to what is essential by stripping away what is false or questionable or merely superficial' (p 393). Other chapters treat particular romantic themes or ironic devices. Especially relevant for the *KnT* are 'Irony and chivalry' (pp 51–90), 'Irony and love' (pp 91–131) and 'The irony of values' (pp 287–325). Irony often arises from the variety of perspectives within the ideals themselves (eg, competing definitions of love), from conflicts between ideals (eg, between love and chivalry), and from the relativizing of these ideals when a different or larger perspective is invoked (e.g., the way these secular values appear less absolute when a religious perspective is included). The variety of courtly genres also provides a seed-bed for irony, as in the relationship of romance to fabliau (*KnT* and *MilT*, pp 119–3). The *MilT* is 'an external means, complementing the internal ironies of the *Knight's Tale*, of placing that romance ... at a distance ... We can admire [the Knight's world] without living in it so wholeheartedly' (p 122).

95a Jameson, Frederic. 'Magical Narratives: Romance as Genre.' *New Literary History* 7(1975), 135–63. Cf 'Magical Narratives: On the Dialectical Use of Genre Criticism.' In *The Political Unconscious: Narrative as Socially Symbolic Act.* Ithaca: Cornell University Press, 1981. Pp 103–50.

Jameson reviews the approach to romance as a mode, exemplified by Frye's work (**92**), and the approach to it as fixed form, exemplified by Vladimir Propp's *Morphology of the Folktale* (1968). The former reveals the 'contemplative' nature of romance in which acts are states of being (p 139), and the latter shows the hero to be more accurately apprehended as an 'actant' (pp 148–9). The generic categories themselves should not be thought of as archetypes but as aspects of constructed systems always comparativist in nature: eg, Frye's concept of romance is linked to his concept of comedy (p 53). From a Marxist perspective, Jameson emphasizes the necessity of grounding generic criticism in history. The crucial question concerns the origin of medieval romance. It emerged when concepts of good and evil were more magical than ethical, and when a feeling of nostalgia was created for an older social order threatened by nascent capitalism. The transition from *chanson de geste* to romance was made possible by the disappearance of barbarian invaders and the emergence of class solidarity among the feudal nobility; the human antagonist then ceases to be a villain and evil is projected into a magical, non-human realm (pp 158–61).

96 Jauss, Hans-Robert. 'Theory of Genres and Medieval Literature.' *Toward An Aesthetic of Reception*. Trans. Timothy Bahti. Minneapolis: University of Minnesota Press, 1982.
Jauss defends the concept of genre against Croce's attack, which emphasized the unique expressibility of each literary work, but calls for an alternative to the classical conception of genre as an essence having fixed characteristics and subject to an organic process of growth and decay through which it moves by an inevitable teleological process. A genre should be thought of instead as a group or historical family, or as 'an undetermined norm' (p 80) which serves as both example and model; the history of genres would then appear as 'the continual founding and altering of horizons ... the playing out of a limited number of possibilities' (p 94). Jauss surveys the issues – reception, social function, relations among genres – which full appreciation of the historical dimension of genre would require, and the potential or actual contributions made to these issues by various schools of criticism. He provides an exemplary analysis of *chanson de geste*, romance, and novella, compared as to mode of narration (relation of author and text), forms of representation (eg, levels of style), nature of what is represented (action, character, reality), and social function (pp 82–7).

97 Jordan, Robert M. 'Chaucerian Romance?' In *Approaches to Medieval Romance*. Ed. Peter Haidu. *Yale French Studies* 51(1974), 223–34.
Citing the insufficiency of generic classification by subject matter, Jordan turns to structural analysis to test the similarity among Chaucer's supposed romances: *TC*, *KnT*, *SqT*, *FranT*, *WBT*, and *Thop*. Chaucer is a learned poet in the tradition of Chrétien who practices *conjointure*, the interpretative elaboration of a simple narrative; his method of composition is additive and inorganic. 'The essence of the form is variety of allusion and multiplicity of focus, even occasionally

to the point of incongruity and incoherence' (p 232). Yet this method characterizes all of Chaucer's work except the dream visions and short lyrics. 'The term romance would seem to retain little critical value ... our proper study must be narrative structures, not genres' (pp 232–4). See **982**.

98 Ker, W.P. *Epic and Romance: Essays on Medieval Literature*. 1st ed., 1896; 2nd ed., London: Macmillan, 1908; rpt through 1957.
Ker shows a preference for epic and a nineteenth-century conception of the romantic. Epic, which implies 'weight and solidity,' typically involves the defense of a narrow place against odds; romance, which implies 'mystery and fantasy,' involves blind encounters in duels or tournaments (pp 4–6). The social worlds of aristocrat and churl are not sharply distinguished in Epic as they are in Romance. The great strength of Epic lies in its dramatic treatment of character; in Romance, 'there is one voice, the voice of the story-teller, and his theory of the characters is made to do duty for the characters themselves' (p 33). The *KnT* is 'a complete and perfect version of a medieval romance' (p 365). Yet Chaucer compromises between 'the pathetic mood of pure romance and a fuller dramatic method' (p 366); Palamon and Arcite are treated dramatically but Emelye is not. See **611**.

99 Koretsky, Allen C. 'The Heroes of Chaucer's Romances.' *AnM* 17(1976), 22–47.
Chaucer 'de-emphasizes purely military activity and eschews random "aventures" in favor of plots which lead to moments of moral crisis ... Through his pervasive irony, through the imperfections of his characters and the credible confusion suffered by them, and through the universal philosophical significance that he ascribes to their predicaments, Chaucer ... brings the romances into the range of recognizable human experience' (pp 46–7). References to the *KnT passim*.

100 Lenaghan, R.T. 'The Clerk of Venus: Chaucer and Medieval Romance.' In *The Learned and the Lewed: Studies in Chaucer and Medieval Literature*. Ed. Larry Benson. Cambridge, Ma.: Harvard University Press, 1974. Pp 31–43.
Why was Chaucer, 'so clearheaded a realist' (p 31), attracted to the romance? Through romance a poet could discharge the two traditional clerkly roles, that of moralist and that of instructor in the sentiments and ceremonies of love, and qualify himself as the equal of a knight. 'The romance offered Chaucer a literary ... role that corresponded significantly with one he took, or perhaps felt he ought to take, in the real world.' The *KnT* balances Boethian and courtly

values and serves as a kind of humanist instruction for princes (pp 40–1).

101 Muscatine, Charles. 'The Courtly Tradition.' *Chaucer and the French Tradition*. Berkeley: University of California Press, 1957. Pp 11–57.
Conventional traits of courtly style work to express the narrow idealism of the courtly vision. Courtly style is non-representational, tending toward the symbolic, emblematic, or allegorical; it is characterized by 'exotic setting, formal portraiture, undramatic discourse, and semiotic gesture' (p 40). Its implications for Chaucer are especially important in the interpretation of character. The 'type-characters' of the courtly style 'find their meaningfulness through enmeshment in patterns of relationships, in consequential actions, in themes which ... figure forth significant human concerns. For medieval literature, as for modern, "characterization" in the ordinary sense is ... a function of realism' (p 41). Passages or traits of a realistic style often appear in works predominantly courtly but usually not in such a way as to qualify the courtly attitude itself or to pit one attitude against the other (pp 41–57). For *KnT* see **726**.

102 Ryding, William W. *Structure in Medieval Narrative*. The Hague: Mouton, 1971.
Medieval narratives do not lack structure so much as they exemplify non-Aristotelian concepts of structure. Romance shows the tendency of all serious medieval literature toward amplification; only lesser forms such as fabliau aimed at brevity and logical sequence (p 63). The most talented authors of both *chanson de geste* and romance developed, first, bipartite, and later, interlace structures to organize their lengthy works. [See pp 69–71 and 141–5 on simple forms of interlace analogous to those of the *KnT*.] In *Il Filos* Boccaccio began the movement toward modern narrative structures by isolating and developing one plot line, a tendency Chaucer continued in *TC* (pp 155–6). Malory's *Morte D'Arthur* is the major late medieval achievement in the new type of logically unified structure.

103 Stevens, John. *Medieval Romance: Themes and Approaches*. New York: Hillary House; London: Hutchison, 1973; rpt New York: Norton, 1974.
Romance is a plurality of genres whose central concerns, a set of idealisms, are of permanent interest while the means of expressing them are constantly being re-created. The idealized sexual relation was also regarded as the ground of social well-being, as seen in Chaucer's 'social romances,' *WBT*, *FranT*, and *KnT* (see **1035**) (pp 29–71). The idealized concept of integrity generates a plot in which the hero searches for his true self and this romance of honor also has

social dimensions, particularly in Chaucer (pp 72–95). The marvellous in romance is not necessarily religious (pp 96–118), and yet there is a 'general interpenetration of religious with romantic experiences' (p 119), with the religion of love, as enacted by Palamon, being one form of the relationship (pp 119–41). Shifting from themes to modes, Stevens discusses images, characters, rhetoric, and the story-teller. The images of romance assume a metaphysical connection between visible and invisible phenomena (142–67). 'Medieval romances have to be read in a different way from nineteenth-century realist novels because the people who wrote them had different views about the visible world' (p 150). Similarly, characterization is designed to support 'the claim of the ideal' (pp 168–87); the hero's illumination is usually intended to develop a general concept rather than to explore individual psychology. Palamon and Arcite are clear examples, and the *KnT* is 'a safe place to start the study of "characterization" in medieval romance' (p 174). The formal, discursive rhetoric of romance is another way of substantiating the 'claim of the ideal' (pp 188–207). The narrator typically establishes a distance between himself and his tale which he may exploit in a number of ways – eg, to direct the audience's feelings; the most complex case is offered by *TC* (pp 208–26).

- Review by Lillian Herlands Hornstein, *M&H* ns 7(1976), 189–94: Stevens' discussion of idealisms is not new; more important are the later chapters on modes, especially his treatment of 'images' or normative, symbolic scenes. He does not fully relate scenes to whole works, however; thus he misses the ironies in the allegedly happy ending of the *KnT*.

104 Strohm, Paul. 'The Origin and Meaning of Middle English *Romaunce*.' *Genre* 10(1977), 1–28.
From the twelfth century on, the French word *romans* developed from a term signifying 'composed in French' (rather than Latin) to a generic term indicating an entire narrative focused on the deeds of one protagonist from among a group of familiar heroes. *Romaunce* first appears in Middle English in the fourteenth century indicating works having French antecedents, but it gradually acquired the broader generic sense as well as further specifying a work including amatory as well as martial interests and marvelous elements. Chaucer never refers to the *KnT*, *WBT*, *SqT*, *FranT*, or *TC* as romances, probably because he restricted the term to popular Middle English works and to French works (p 17). Various shadings of meaning distinguish *romaunce* from *storie*, *geste*, and *lai* (pp 18–28).

105 Vinaver, Eugene. *The Rise of Romance*. Oxford: Oxford University Press, 1971.
The supplantation of *chanson de geste* by romance was not due so much to a shift in the subject matter of story as to a shift in the way of telling a story. Aiming to move and impress, the *chanson* concentrates on event; aiming to explain and question, the romance concentrates on theme. The interpretative nature of romance and a new stage of biblical exegesis have a common origin in the cathedral schools of twelfth-century France; in the works of Chrétien de Troyes, eg, the interior monologues of the characters are related to events much as the interlinear and marginal glosses of the exegetes are related to the biblical text (pp 1–32). Early attempts to unite event and meaning sometimes produced troubling incongruities (pp 33–52), and the more successful romances use unfamiliar structural forms such as interlace (pp 68–98) and analogy (pp 99–122). Late-nineteenth and twentieth century critics wrongly criticized romance for lacking linear forms of organzation and organic unity; more recently, critics have fled into the study of legend to the neglect of the romances (pp 53–67). Malory exhibits the movement toward the shaping of single, independent narratives, and with it, the modern preference for a tragic vision (pp 123–39).

106 Wittig, Susan. *Stylistic and Narrative Structures in the Middle English Romances*. Austin: University of Texas Press, 1979.
Taking a linguistic and structuralist approach, Wittig examines formulaic elements in the romances, from syntagmemes through motifemes and type-scenes to episodes. Eg, motifemes include the device 'now-we-leave-and-turn-to' (p 61), and type-scenes, the single combat (pp 81–101). The Middle English romance is a conservative genre whose formulas refer to the real-world language of social gesture and ritual; it rejects change and innovation and cannot be used to ask questions (pp 45–6). Defined by the reciprocal relations it establishes between the two episodes 'separation-restoration' and 'love-marriage' (p 182), it emphasizes the individual's relation to the social world as opposed to the spiritual and natural worlds (p 183), and mediates between classes by entertaining the idea of the merits of the lowly-born while ultimately identifying worth with birth (p 186). Such an analysis may serve as a point of departure for studying less formulaic works that violate or question these generic patterns (p 6).

Courtliness and Courtly Love

107 Boase, Roger. *The Origin and Meaning of Courtly Love: A Critical Study of European Scholarship.* Manchester: Manchester University Press, 1977.
Boase provides a chronological survey of scholarship to 1975 with an especially useful reconstruction of early work, 1500–1900. Theories of origin are analyzed under seven headings and theories of meaning under five. Boase himself rejects the view that courtly love is a universally possible experience, emphasizing instead its ties to time, place, and class. 'Courtly Love was ... a comprehensive cultural phenomenon: a literary movement, an ideology, an ethical system, a style of life, and an expression of the play element in culture, which arose in an aristocratic Christian environment exposed to Hispano-Arabic influences' (pp 129–30). Acknowledging that courtly love is 'inherently ambiguous,' Boase nevertheless hopes that his work has vindicated the use of the term (p 129). An appendix devoted to 'amor hereos' (cf I.1373–4) notes Lowes' work (**599**) and adds several medieval citations (pp 132–3).

108 Donaldson, E. Talbot. 'The Myth of Courtly Love.' *Ventures: Magazine of the Yale Graduate School* 5(1965). Rpt in *Speaking of Chaucer.* New York: Norton, 1970. Pp 154–63 [cited here].
'Amour courtois' was effectively invented by Gaston Paris and achieved wide acceptance through Lewis' work **115**. The weakest aspect of Lewis' definition is its insistence on adultery, which appears only occasionally in medieval texts amd rarely in English literature, being confined largely to Chaucer and largely to his fabliau. More central to courtly love is its tendency to sublimation.

109 Economou, George D. 'The Two Venuses and Courtly Love.' In *In Pursuit of Perfection: Courtly Love in Medieval Literature.* Ed. Joan M. Ferrante and George D. Economou. Port Washington, New York: Kennikat, 1975. Pp 17–50.
The common distinction between *caritas* and *amor* did not imply that all earthly love was merely sinful. In the dominant interpretation of Genesis, the duty to love in accordance with Nature's laws continued despite the Fall's corrupting effects. The two dispositions within earthly love – 'the one, legitimate, sacramental, natural, and in harmony with cosmic law; the other, illegitimate, perverted, selfish, and sinful' – were often represented by the double Venus, as in Boccaccio's glosses to the *Tes.* Bernardus Silvestris identified the good Venus with cosmic harmony, and Vatican Mythographer III identified her with the planet. Economou examines the adaptations of this

mythographical tradition by Alanus de Insulis, Jean de Meun, Gower, Chrétien, Wolfram, Gottfried, and Chaucer (in *PF* and *TC*).

110 Ferrante, Joan M. 'The Conflict of Lyric Conventions and Romance Form.' In *In Pursuit of Perfection: Courtly Love in Medieval Literature*. Ed. Joan M. Ferrante and George D. Economou. Port Washington, New York: Kennikat Press, 1975. Pp 135–78.

Courtly love is compatible with lyric genres in ways that it is not with narrative genres. The love lyric describes the emotions of one person engaged in a game never meant to be concluded with a lady who may be partly a projection of his own fantasy; the romance narrative relates actions that pose problems to which the hero must find solutions and that involve real persons to whom the hero has many, potentially conflicting, loyalties. Courtly love supports the lover's personal growth in the lyric but almost always puts him at odds with society in the romance. The French romances of antiquity seem to introduce love only to condemn it. The Arthurian romances, most prominently Chrétien's, explore the ethical and social potentialities of love within an ideal world but typically reject love, finally, as incompatible with other important values. The Tristan stories weave the two traditions together in a way that leads to tragedy in a realistically conceived world. The late prose romances, such as Malory's, reject courtly love as socially destructive, but not without a sense of loss.

111 Green, Richard Firth. 'The Court of Cupid.' *Poets and Prince-pleasers: Literature and the English Court in the Late Middle Ages*. Toronto: University of Toronto Press, 1980. Pp 101–34.

Green assesses the place of love poetry in the fourteenth-century English court and in the careers of newly emergent court poets, successors of the minstrels. Among well-educated courtiers familiar with love conventions who themselves composed love verse, the poet could not pose as an authority but had to adapt self-effacing narrative strategies. Although there is very little evidence in England of the formal courts of love depicted in allegorical poems, courtiers engaged in informal discussions may have regarded themselves as courts of love and may have generated controversies like the attack on *TC* reported in *LGW*. The association of love with courtliness, as in the shared concept of service, may have suggested virtual identification of a royal court with Cupid's court. Lyric verse may have been regarded as an extension of love-talk, and longer narratives may have been adapted to game by such devices as the *demande* of the *KnT* (I.1347–8; pp 126–7). The love-poet participated as an amateur among amateurs; he was more likely to acquire special recognition for chronicles, translations, and various didactic works.

112 Jaeger, C. Stephen. *The Origins of Courtliness: Civilizing Trends and the Formation of Courtly Ideals 939-1210*. Philadephia, University of Pennsylvania Press, 1985.

The origins of courtliness are not to be found in the knightly class and in French literary productions of the twelfth century, but in a long-standing, panEuropean desire, especially associated with the German imperial courts, to emulate ancient Roman values. Key figures were Otto the Great of Germany and his brother, Brun, called to the court in 939 to become an educator and later an archbishop. Generations of courtier-bishops carried out an educational program aimed at civilizing the courts themselves and the warrior class. The qualities at first used to describe the ideal courtier cleric, qualities derived from classical ethical texts, were later extended to kings, in chronicle and biography, and then to knights, in romance. The romance was the chief means by which this civilizing program was carried to the warrior class, and this theory of origin explains the circumstance that so many romancers were clerics. Gottfried von Strassburg's *Tristan*, nearly completed by 1210, is a key text revealing this connection, since Tristan is in part modelled on the courtier cleric. Although the French did not create courtly values, they were among the first to adopt them, partly because of traditions of lay literacy. Romance eventually offered two views of courtliness: in the 'courtier narrative' (pp 236–41) the court is a place of intrigue and corruption where noble natures preserve their integrity in secret, sometimes adulterous love. In the 'chivalric narrative' (pp 242–53), courtliness is an ideal code and the romance offers not a mirror of the court but a model of a knight's process of education. The historical sources do not document the existence of courtly love, but that is not an argument against the probable existence of a new mode of feeling; similarly, women no doubt played a role in this civilizing process, but it is difficult to document. (pp 267–8). See **194R**.

113 Kane, George. 'Chaucer, Love Poetry, and Romantic Love.' In *Acts of Interpretation: The Text in Its Contexts 700-1600: Essays on Medieval and Renaissance Literature in Honor of E. Talbot Donaldson*. Ed. Mary J. Carruthers and Elizabeth D. Kirk. Norman, Oklahoma: Pilgrim Books, 1982. Pp 237–55.

Kane defines 'fyn lovynge' (*LGWP* F 544/G 534) as 'a shifting nexus of forms of thought and expression ... developed to express a fairly narrow class of emotions'; forms 'having the appearance of conventionally established rhetorical and stylistic correlatives; but ...

represented as accepted values in the milieu where the relationship was set' (pp 237–8). Kane surveys Chaucer's acquaintance with *fin amour* in a range of texts from troubadour poetry to Machaut, suggesting that Chaucer was puzzled by the lack of definition of the concept. This lack arose from both a deliberate cultivation of ambiguity in the tradition and from the successive modifications the phenomenon underwent. Chaucer would also have known contrasting traditions of love poetry, such as those that presented the woman's point of view, or defined the sexual relation in moral terms. Chaucer seems to have accepted the confusion as a rich artistic resource and as true to experience; it is unlikely we will ever find him taking an unqualified position toward 'fyn lovynge.'

114 Kelly, Henry Ansgar. *Love and Marriage in the Age of Chaucer*. Ithaca: Cornell University Press, 1975.
Kelly marshalls arguments and evidence against the wide-spread belief (cf Lewis **115**) that love and marriage were viewed as incompatible in the Middle Ages. He finds little evidence for the anti-matrimonial doctrine in the French texts (eg, Chrétien, Andreas; pp 31–48), stresses the medieval indebtedness to Ovid, whom he characterizes as a champion of conjugal love (pp 71–100), and shows that poets often and theologians sometimes viewed sexual delight as a good in marriage (pp 245–332).

115 Lewis, C.S. 'Courtly Love.' In *The Allegory of Love: A Study in Medieval Tradition*. Oxford: Oxford University Press, 1936; rpt New York, 1958.
In this classic – to some, notorious – study, Lewis defines courtly love as a new phenomenon of the late eleventh century that has four characteristics: 'Humility, Courtesy, Adultery, and the Religion of Love' (p 2). He emphasizes the differences between courtly love and the views of love entertained by classical times and the Dark Ages, and the links between courtly love and continuing western beliefs and customs. He attributes the Humility of courtly love to the influence of the feudal bond of vassalage, and the Courtesy to the role of the lord's wife and her circle of ladies in courts populated principally by landless young knights. The feature of Adultery flows from the feudal practice of arranged marriages and from the ecclesiastical theory that all passion was sinful even in marriage. The Religion of Love is partly an inheritance from Ovid and partly an extension of, escape from, and rival to the Christian religion. See **108**, **709**.

116 Mathew, Gervase. 'Marriage and *Amour Courtois* in Late Fourteenth-Century England.' In *Essays Presented to Charles Williams*. [No editor] Oxford: Oxford University Press, 1947. Pp 128–35. Rpt in *Chaucer*

and His Contemporaries: Essays on Medieval Literature and Thought. Ed. Helaine Newstead. Greenwich, Conn.: Fawcett, 1968. Pp 104–11 [cited here].

Mathew surveys what we can know about attitudes toward marriage among the lowest classes; a middle class made up of guildsmen, reeves, millers, and others; and the knightly class, with emphasis on the last. A conventional view among the knightly class was that marriage 'was not only compatible with romantic love but ideally an expression of it' (p 107). The majority of English knightly romances in the late fourteenth century show a union of romantic love and marriage, and the *KnT* offers a perfect example of the expected happy ending.

117 Newman, F.X. *The Meaning of Courtly Love.* Albany: State University of New York Press, 1968.

A set of five papers notable for its challenge to the historicity of courtly love and to the usefulness of the term in literary criticism. Most frequently cited are D.W. Robertson's 'The Concept of Courtly Love as an Impediment to the Understanding of Medieval Texts' (pp 1–18), and John F. Benton's 'Clio and Venus: An Historical View of Medieval Love' (pp 19–42). Robertson argues that the true subject of Chrétien, Andreas, and the *RR* is not courtly love but idolatrous passion, treated satirically. Benton emphasizes the evidence for love in and before marriage and the penalties for adultery in the Middle Ages.

118 Singer, Irving. *Courtly and Romantic.* Volume 2 of *The Nature of Love.* Chicago: University of Chicago Press, 1984.

Since Plato, thinking about love has divided between an idealist tradition that seeks 'ultimate oneness through the magic of merging with another person' (p 10), and a realist tradition, both preceding the idealist position and serving as its critique, that sees love as 'a natural phenomenon distorted by man's propensity to formulate idealistic philosophies' (pp 11, 14). Two problems for the idealists are to reconcile spirituality with sexuality, and love with marriage. Imperfect solutions were worked out under the 'caritas-synthesis' of the Middle Ages (see Volume 1, *Plato to Luther*). Courtly love 'cannot be defined in terms of fixed and invariable attributes, necessary and sufficient conditions'; instead we should seek 'a cluster of ideas that ... often go together in a characteristic manner' during the medieval period: eg, that 'sexual love between men and women is *in itself* ... an ideal'; that 'love ennobles both the lover and the beloved'; that 'love pertains to courtesy and courtship but is not necessarily related to ... marriage' (pp 22–3). Singer goes on to discuss the troubadours, Andreas Capellanus, and medieval romance (pp 37–128). He distinguishes romantic from courtly love by, among other things, its new concepts of feeling as a source of truth and of sympathetic identification with another (pp 283–302).

119 Steadman, John M. '"Courtly Love" as a Problem of Style.' In *Chaucer und Seine Zeit: Symposion für Walter F. Schirmer*. Ed. Arno Esch. Tübingen: Max Niemeyer, 1968. Pp 1–33.

Steadman emphasizes the considerations of genre and style that governed what he calls not 'courtly love' but '*love between persons of courtly rank*' (p 6). After reviewing principles of decorum for presenting courtly, bourgeois, and rural persons, and love as a subject for treatment in the most elevated styles and genres, Steadman explores in several works the various kinds of behavior ascribed to lovers according to their class. In both medicine and poetry consistent traditions from the Middle Ages through the Renaissance characterized 'the loveris maladye / Of hereos' (I.1373–4) as a disease of young and noble persons. Ethically, however, this love was antithetical to the ideal of the noble life understood as based on reason and virtue. Few poets addressed this contradiction, though some dealt with it by distinguishing true nobility from false, Christian values from pagan, and love as an irrational passion from love as a heroic virtue. The poets' primary object was to preserve rhetorical decorum in representing the lover. 'As a system courtly love is a myth ... As a rhetorical concept, however, "courtly love" possesses a definite, though limited, validity' (p 26).

120 Stevens, John. 'Courtly Love and the Courtly Lyric.' *Music & Poetry in the Early Tudor Court*. Lincoln: University of Nebraska Press, 1961. Pp 147–229.

Stevens defines courtly love as occupying a 'middle space' between life and literature in which the social setting, including the presence of ladies, was more important than the musical setting. The relation was not unlike that between religious verse and liturgy, though much of the evidence for courtly life is now lost. In a relatively closed society of leisured aristocrats, the fiction of being a lover functioned as the ground for being a courtier: reading of love, talking of love, and various kinds of enactment, including dances and games, provided both an education in conducting life at court, in a broad sense, and an opportunity to display one's skill at it. Stevens cites a staged event during the marriage celebrations for King James of Scotland and Princess Margaret (1503) as offering an analogy to the sequence of actions in the *KnT*: duel, intervention by king and ladies, tournament (pp 166–7). Works such as the *KnT* and *Anel* were probably read as part of a sentimental education (p 213).

121 Utley, Francis L. 'Must We Abandon the Concept of Courtly Love?' *M&H* n.s. 3(1972), 299–324.
Utley reviews several works, including **108** and **117**. Granting that *amour courtois* is a nineteenth-century coinage, he recommends use of *fin' amors* and other 'sensitized words' from the period (p 317). Admitting the difficulty of defining courtly love, he insists on the characteristic richness of the medieval preoccupation with love. Adultery has been overemphasized, but much of the literature is equivocal. Concerning the realism of courtly representations, it should be remembered that a culture's fictions can be as significant as its charters. The formalized codes of love were an important restraint on behavior even if life did not conform to the ideal. Critics should beware of too frequent recourse to irony as a way of supporting controversial positions. 'There is not one courtly love but twenty or thirty of them, warring with theories of divine love and with popular reductions' (p 322).

122 Zweig, Paul. *The Heresy of Self-love: A Study of Subversive Individualism*. 1968. Rpt New York: Harper & Row, 1970.
In this study of courtly love as part of the West's narcissistic cultivation of self, Zweig connects the troubadour idea of love with permissive attitudes toward feudal and religious authority in the Midi, and contrasts it with the more violent anti-social stances of certain heresies and of the Tristan tradition. Troubadour love undermines the patriarchy of feudal service and at the same time retains its control on excess through the *gilos* or jealous husband, who is in part responsible for the lover's distance from his lady. From another point of view, the lover invents the lady's coldness in order to be alone with his own emotions. Central to troubadour love is the boy Narcissus, a figure of the lover's self.

Chaucer and Women

123 Ames, Ruth M. 'Faith and Feminism.' *God's Plenty: Chaucer's Christian Humanism*. Chicago: Loyola University Press, 1984. Pp 145–78.
Chaucer undoubtedly knew of, and may have met, Christine de Pisan, and his *LGW*, in which he declares his independence of both chauvinists and feminists, may have been inspired in part by French controversies over *RR* (pp 146–53). While using the debate over

women and marriage as a source of humor throughout his career, he had an interest in the relation between feminism and Christianity. He appreciated the male bias in the primary works of Christianity and in the commentaries on them (pp 157–61). He probably intended his use of women characters to represent "feminine" virtues like patience as a compliment to women (p 166); still, his most successful feminist heroine is the aggressive St Cecilia (pp 171–3). Heroines like Prudence in *Mel* and Cecilia cure men of chauvinism as they draw them closer to Christian truth, suggesting that for Chaucer, feminism and faith were compatible (pp 177–8). See **133**, **495**, **1065**.

124 Diamond, Arlyn. 'Chaucer's Women and Women's Chaucer.' In *The Authority of Experience*. Ed. Arlyn Diamond and Lee R. Edwards. Amherst: The University of Massachusetts Press, 1977. Pp 60–83.
Chaucer concentrates on medieval theory about women rather than on daily realities, and the equivocal nature of his statements makes him 'one of the most elusive friends women have ever had' (p 65). His views can be known, if at all, only by studying the relationships depicted in his works, as in the Marriage Group. Among the pilgrims there is no woman who is the 'moral equivalent' of the Knight: 'if admirable, his women are bloodless abstractions; if vivid personalities, they are limited ... or seriously flawed' (p 82). 'He can pity women, he can see some way into them,' but he is 'limited by his fundamental conservatism' (p 82).

125 Ferrante, Joan M. *Woman As Image In Medieval Literature From the Twelfth Century to Dante*. New York: Columbia University Press, 1975.
Ferrante examines symbolic representations of woman in works of biblical exegesis, philosophy, and literature. The most positive treatments of female figures, as allegorical personifications and as the lady of love lyric and romance, arose together in the twelfth century, presenting the female as part of the male and tending to suggest the possibility of harmonious union. The courtly lady is in fact 'a kind of super-personification' (p 66) representing Love itself or the ideal self the lover strives to become. Thirteenth-century works exhibit strong anti-feminism, and see woman as wholly separate from man and often a source of evil to him. Dante's vision of the unity of human and divine love, in which Beatrice is both a mediatrix and a complete human being, is thus both triumphant and slightly anachronistic.

126 Gold, Penny Schine. *The Lady & the Virgin: Image, Attitude, and Experience in Twelfth-Century France*. Chicago: University of Chicago Press, 1985.
We distort history when we identify 'good' and 'bad' images of women and use them to chart declines and advances in that artificial

construct, the 'status' of women. Instead we should study women in particular situations, prepared to admit the ambivalences and contradictions within and between images and experiences. Gold studies the relation of the lady in twelfth-century French literature to the roles of aristocratic women in property transactions, and the relation of visual images of the Virgin Mary to the place of nunneries in religious life. 'Secular Image: Women in *Chanson de Geste* and Romance' (pp 1–42): In the *chanson de geste* women have important but peripheral roles as nurturers and advisors who pursue with men shared goals defined largely by family interests. In the romance the hero experiences a conflict between love and his allegiance to woman, and prowess and his allegiance to men. Woman is both the inspiration of his love and the helpless client of his prowess. As a 'romantic object' (p 38), she is essential to the action of romance, the hero's quest for balanced self-development, and yet she is less powerful than the woman of the *chanson*; her own experience of passion does not matter and she cannot help the hero resolve this conflict. The actual experience of ladies, as seen in property relations – where women play secondary roles in the pursuit of family goals – more nearly reflects the situation in the *chanson*.

• Review by R. Howard Bloch, *MP* 84(1986), 209–10: In 'a sophisticated performance that avoids many of the critical pitfalls' common to studies of women in the Middle Ages, Gold examines 'some of the most spent preconceptions' and produces surprising results, as in her discussion of epic and romance. She 'remains constantly aware of the difference between an object or event and its representation,' but she may too confidently locate ambivalences in individual experience, which is unknowable except through images.

127 Green, Richard Firth. 'Women in Chaucer's Audience.' *ChauR* 18(1983), 146–54.

Chaucer's actual historical audience, as opposed to his fictional implied audience, probably included very few women. Before the end of the fourteenth century at least, royal courts typically contained few women; the queen and her small entourage were not always in residence with the king and when they were, they lived separately. *Demandes* in Chaucer's work, as in I.1347–8, typically concern male characters and elicit a male point of view; the Knight's remark on women (I.2681–2) was probably intended for a male audience. Fabliau like the *MilT* and *RvT* fell out of favor when the presence of women increased.

• Comment by Alan Gaylord, 'Chaucer's Audience: Discussion,' *ChauR* 18(1983), 175–81: The hypothesis that Chaucer read his works at court is unproved; if his works were disseminated by a variety of means, women might have made up a majority of his actual audience (p 175).

128 Haskell, Ann S. 'The Portrayal of Women by Chaucer and His Age.' In *What Manner of Woman: Essays on English and American Life and Literature*. Ed. Marlene Springer. New York: New York University Press, 1977. Pp 1–14.
The romance, a showcase for the aristocratic hero in which ladies like Emily typically do nothing (pp 2, 7–8), was a dying form at the end of the fourteenth century, soon to be succeeded by genres that focused on the bourgeoisie and represented women more fully.

129 Kleinbaum, Abby Wettan. *The War Against the Amazons*. New York: McGraw-Hill, 1983.
A broad survey of the uses of the Amazon, eg, to certify the heroism of man in Greek and Roman history. In the Middle Ages (pp 39–70), Amazons, typically deprived of their sexuality or their prowess or both, played a prominent role in the Troy narratives of Benôit de Sainte-Maure, Joseph of Exeter, and Guido de Colonna and in the works of Christine de Pisan. The *KnT* and Boccaccio's *De Claris Mulieribus* are briefly mentioned, pp 61–2.

130 Schibanoff, Susan. 'The Crooked Rib: Women in Medieval Literature.' In *Approaches to Teaching Chaucer's 'Canterbury Tales'*. Ed. Joseph Gibaldi. New York: Modern Language Association of America, 1980. Pp 121–8.
The undergraduate course described here explores the relationships between women's literary roles and their actual lives by construing genre as a rule-bound game which may mirror society's current or outmoded values, or both, as well as its fantasies. In the *KnT* Emily breaks the courtly rule that says the lady should encourage her lover. Despite his many innovations in the *CT*, Chaucer does not seem to offer a significantly new vision of woman.

131 Weissman, Hope Phyllis. 'Antifeminism and Chaucer's Characterizations of Women.' In *Geoffrey Chaucer: A Collection of Original Articles*. Ed. George D. Economou. New York: McGraw-Hill, 1975. Pp 93–110.
Chaucer understood antifeminism as 'not simply satirical caricatures of women but any presentation of a woman's nature intended to conform her to male expectations of what she is or ought to be, not her own' (p 94). In his works he examines the four primary images of women in his culture, the religious images of Eve and Mary and the corresponding secular images of the bourgeois woman and the courtly lady. The latter also includes the Courtly Damsel, a trophy

men strive for and a figure indebted to Virgil's Lavinia in the *Aen.* For *KnT* see **1052.**

132 Wright, Celeste Turner. 'The Amazons in Elizabethan Literature.' *SP* 37(1940), 433–56.
In both the *KnT* and Shakespeare's *TNK*, Hippolyta is portrayed 'as a tamed and contented bride' (p 437). Most Elizabethans 'appear to have accepted unchanged the views of the Middle Ages: they regarded the Amazons as picturesque ornaments to a pageant or a romance but their social system as a dangerous example of unwomanly conduct,' a violation of that traditional order under which women are subject to man.

Paganism and the Gods

133 Ames, Ruth. 'Pagans and Paganism.' *God's Plenty.* 1984. See **123.** Pp 205–26.
Chaucer subscribed to a Christian humanism that recognized the possibility of salvation outside the Church and admired good pagans for their moral virtue and anticipations of Christian moral truths. The *HF* in particular presents Chaucer as the heir of a pagan and Christian tradition presided over by a universal God (pp 224–6). See **495, 1065.**

134 Coleman, Janet. *Piers Plowman and the 'Moderni.'* Rome: Edizioni di storia e letteratura, 1981.
The theologians known as *moderni* (eg, Holcot, Buckingham, Woodham) were semi-pelagian in their emphasis on man's ability to work out his salvation, and at the same time emphasized God's absolute freedom – among other things, to save whom he would (pp 117–35). Coleman traces the theological debate on who can be saved from Paul through Augustine, Abelard, and Aquinas to the fourteenth-century theologians, with special emphasis on the case of Trajan, the second-century Roman emperor (pp 108–46). Bradwardine denied the possibility of salvation for righteous heathens; Holcot held that God might save those who made right use of natural reason; Buckingham suggested that righteous heathen might be assigned to limbo to await the Second Coming. Langland represents the variety of opinions without committing himself to any one. The shifts in opinion responded to the varying military fortunes of the Christians in the East, to the Lollard interest in conversions, and to the interest of English friars and others in pagan antiquity.

135 Hahn, Thomas George. *God's Friends: Virtuous Heathen in Later Medieval Thought and English Literature.* University of California, Los Angeles Dissertation, 1974. Directors: Henry Ansgar Kelly and William Matthews. See also *DAI* 35(1975), 4428–9A.
From the twelfth century on, changing concepts of nature, and other developments such as new contacts with Moslems and Jews and a new emphasis on conscience in Christian spirituality, combined to suggest that the heathen might achieve salvation. The influence of these ideas can be traced in Mandeville's *Travels*, *Saint Erkenwald*, *Piers*, and *TC* (pp 396–417). In *TC* the 'contrast between the ease of Christian refuge in God and the ambiguity of the heathen's situation' is an important aspect of Chaucer's sense of history (p 415; cf. Bloomfield **207**), a sense especially marked in the tales with pre-Christian settings (p 398). Chaucer is more interested in the pagan's experience in this life than in his fate after death (p 417). The lines on Arcite's soul (I.2809–14) remind us that Chaucer never refers to a pagan who is certainly saved and generally avoids metaphysical speculation (pp 396–8).

136 Klibansky, Raymond, Erwin Panofsky, and Fritz Saxl. *Saturn and Melancholy: Studies in the History of Natural Philosophy, Religion, and Art.* London: Nelson, 1964.
This work surveys ancient and medieval treatments of the doctrine of the four humors, of melancholy, and of Saturn. 'Saturn in Literary Tradition' (pp 127–95) considers Saturn's role in Arabic astrology, Kronos-Saturn as a mythological figure and planet, and Saturn's place in controversies of the Church Fathers and in later medieval theology, mythography, and astrology. 'Saturn in the Pictorial Tradition' (pp 196–214) ranges from ancient to early Renaissance art and includes discussion of 'Saturn and his Children' and of medieval mythograpical illustrations. Includes 146 illustrations. The Saturn of the *KnT* is mentioned briefly (pp 193–4).

137 Kurose, Tamotsu. 'Rhetorical Use of "Jupiter" in Medieval and Elizabethan Literature.' *Anglica* (1964), 1–34.
Examines literary references to Jupiter with respect to his functions as ruler of destiny, ruler of common fortune, ruler of personal fortune, and revenger of the wicked. Theseus' final speech is cited in the discussions of destiny (pp 6–12) and common fortune (p 20).

138 McCall, John P. *Chaucer Among the Gods: The Poetics of Classical Myth.* University Park and London: Pennsylvania State University Press, 1979.
Ch 1, 'The Backgrounds' (pp 1–17): Methods of interpreting myths in the classical period were varied – etymological, physical, and moral

– and in the early Christian period, 'there was no *new* allegorization as such ... [and] pagan mythology, legend, and literature were not Christianized to any significant degree' (p 7). Bernard Silvester's commentary on the *Aen* (twelfth century) is one of the first works to use spiritual interpretation. Only in the fourteenth century were moral and spiritual lessons 'freely and ingeniously developed without any real concern for the obvious meaning of a story or text' as seen in the *Ovide Moralisé* and other works. This untraditional approach was rejected by medieval as well as renaissance humanism. 'Chaucer was not inclined to treat pagan myths or deities as if they held hidden Christian doctrines or as if they were suitable material for pious reflection' (p 16). His strong historical sense and reverence for the integrity of the old stories led him to rework them 'with a purpose which was broadly moral and from a stance of sympathetic irony' toward all human beings (p 17). For *KnT* see **998**.

139 Minnis, A.J. *Chaucer and Pagan Antiquity*. Woodbridge, Suffolk: Boydell & Brewer; Totowa, New Jersey: Rowman & Littlefield, 1982. Ch 1, 'An Historical Approach to Chaucerian Antiquity' (pp 7–30): Chaucer's interest in antiquity was 'literal and historical but rarely, if ever, spiritual or moral' (p 16). Chaucer was 'a sympathetic observer rather than a dogmatic exegete ... a writer of *historia* rather than [moralized] *fabula*' (p 22). Robertson's allegorical interpretation of Arcite (**879**) must be rejected (pp 14–6). Chaucer's realistic treatment of Mars' statue (I.2041–50) contrasts with Bersuire's moralizations of Mars (pp 20–1). *TC* and *KnT* are 'located in historical time and place, not in the timeless land of ethical verities reached by *moralizatio*'; Chaucer is concerned with 'how actual pagans might have lived, loved and philosophized' (pp 29–30). Ch 2, 'The Shadowy Perfection of the Pagans' (pp 31–60), surveys medieval critiques of pagan theology, specifically its idolatry and faith in oracles, and of its philosophy, specifically its emphasis on fate. Bradwardine rejected fatalists, particularly those who believed in astral determinism, but credited Stoics and some other pagans with anticipating Christian notions of divine providence. 'The desire to harmonize Christian and pagan opinion on common intellectual problems is one of the most characteristic features of late-medieval scholastic procedure' (p 47). Bradwardine and others also believed that God revealed truth to the prophets of the Old Testament and to such as Virgil. Certain pagans – eg, Socrates, Seneca, and pre-eminently Trajan – were accepted as secular saints. Holcot argued that God granted the grace of salvation to good Jews and pagans who earned it by following the best light they had. See **1130**. For *KnT* see **1112**.

140 Panofsky, Erwin. *Studies In Iconology: Humanistic Themes in the Art of the Renaissance*. Oxford: Oxford University Press, 1939. Rpt New York: Harper Torchbooks, 1962; rpt 1967.
Panofsky traces the steps by which the Greek Chronos, representing Opportunity or Eternity, became associated with Kronos (the Roman Saturn), the eldest of the gods, and in the Middle Ages, with Saturn, the most malign of the planets. The Renaissance image of Time the Destroyer represents a fusion of the classical Chronos and the medieval Saturn (pp 69–94). Panofsky also comments on the Neoplatonic interpretation of the two Venuses (pp 142–5).

141 Schreiber, Earl G. 'Venus in the Medieval Mythographic Tradition.' *JEGP* 74(1975), 519–35.
Schreiber presents a compendium of interpretations of Venus drawn from Boccaccio's *Genealogie Deorum Gentilium* (**231**), which emphasizes natural and historical interpretations, supplemented by the allegorical interpretations of other writers of the twelfth through fourteenth centuries. 'From the time of the earliest mythographers [Venus] is invested with the dual potential of human love that can be either generous or selfish. The demarcation between these two modes is never sharp or stable' (p 522). Unlike earlier commentators, Boccaccio seems to have been aware of this ambiguity. Aspects of the goddess treated here include her birth from the sea, her nudity, and her relationship with Adonis.

142 Seznec, Jean. *The Survival of the Pagan Gods: The Mythological Tradition and Its Place in Renaissance Humanism and Art*. Trans. Barbara F. Sessions. New York: Pantheon, 1953.
In the Renaissance 'the gods were not *restored* to life, for they had never disappeared from the memory or imagination of man' (p 3). The historical, physical, and moral traditions of interpretation originating in antiquity preserved the significance of the gods in the Middle Ages as, respectively, heroes, planetary deities, and allegorical figures. The volume is richly illustrated.

143 Smalley, Beryl. *English Friars and Antiquity in the Early Fourteenth Century*. Oxford: Basil Blackwell, 1960.
A small group of 'classicizing' friars, including Thomas Waleys, John Ridevall, Robert Holcot, and John Lathbury, introduced extensive studies of pagan antiquity into commentaries on the Bible and the fathers, sermons, and aids to preaching. They were primarily interested in information and wisdom rather than style, and saw no conflict between scholasticism and their literary interests. These features distinguish them from early humanists, who are also differentiated by their perception of the pastness of the past and

sensitivity to anachronism. This short-lived classicizing activity did not help to produce a proto-renaissance in England. Nevertheless, the friars had a share 'in accustoming the public to listen to classical and pseudo-classical sayings and stories. Demand and supply stimulated each other ... when Chaucer mocked at the friars, he was biting the hand that fed him. They educated his audience' (p 307).

144 Wilkins, Ernest H. 'Descriptions of Pagan Divinities from Petrarch to Chaucer.' *Spec* 32(1957), 511–22.
Although four earlier writers – Fulgentius, Isidore of Seville, Hrabanus Maurus, and Mythographus III (Alexander Neckam) – had made brief descriptive comments on the gods, 'Petrarch was the first writer to compose a sequence of pictorial descriptions of pagan divinities freed from interpretative incrustations and designed solely for the purpose of adornment' (p 513). The key text, Petrarch's *Africa* III, 138–264 (composed 1338–42), a description of what appear to be bas-reliefs of gods in a palace hall, became the chief source for Bersuire's treatment of the gods in *Ovidius moralizatus* (Form A completed 1342). Of the many descendants of the *Ovidius*, the *Libellus de deorum imaginibus* (c 1342–1380?) is especially important as a source for Chaucer's *HF* (II.131–39) and *KnT* (see **786**).

Chaucer and Science, especially Astrology

145 Eade, J.C. *The Forgotten Sky: A Guide to Astrology in English Literature*. Oxford: Clarendon, 1984.
Eade provides a detailed but concise hundred-page handbook, explaining technical concepts and terms, and then examines briefly a selection of literary texts. For *KnT* see **1089**.

146 Eisner, Sigmund, ed. *The Kalendarium of Nicholas of Lynn*. Trans. Gary Mac Eoin and Sigmund Eisner. The Chaucer Library. Athens: University of Georgia Press, 1980.
This Latin work is here printed for the first time, with facing English translation, from MS Laud Miscellaneous 662 (Bodleian). Nicholas of Lynn, a Carmelite friar at Oxford, composed his *Kalendarium* in 1386 and dedicated it to John of Gaunt. The work contains a Prologue, a month-by-month calendar, astronomical tables and charts, and canons or rules explaining the foregoing. The latter include canons on the equal and unequal hours of the artificial day and on giving and receiving medicine (pp 208–22). Chaucer acknowledges his familiarity with this work in the Prologue to his *Astr* (line 86).

147 Grimm, Florence. *Astronomical Lore in Chaucer*. Lincoln: University of Nebraska. *Studies in Language, Literature, and Criticism*, No. 2, 1919. Rpt New York: AMS Press, 1970.
A concise overview of the history of astronomy and astrology (pp 3–13) with explanations of many difficult terms and concepts (pp 13–27) and illustration from Chaucer's works (pp 27–51). Grimm traces the shifting influence of the Ptolemaic system, including the competition from a biblical vision of the universe, and the resurgence of theoretical astronomy in the fourteenth century. Astronomy was the most fully developed science in the Middle Ages and Chaucer's view was the educated one (pp 9–13). His interest in it centered on questions about free will and providence and on the usefulness of attitudes toward astrology as a means of characterization (pp 55–67). An appendix offers further technical explanations (pp 79–94). For *KnT* see **565**.

148 Lewis, C.S. *The Discarded Image: An Introduction to Medieval and Renaissance Literature*. Cambridge: Cambridge University Press, 1964; rpt 1967.
A classic work in which Lewis attempts to describe the medieval 'Model of the Universe,' a popular synthesis of theology, science, and history drawn principally from books and of special value to poets. In Ch 5, 'The Heavens' (pp 92–121), Lewis contrasts the modern metaphor of 'law' to describe physical forces with the medieval metaphor of 'desire'; contrasts the finiteness of the medieval universe with the infiniteness of modern 'space'; and reviews the characteristics of the seven planets. Lewis urges the reader to conduct experiments in imagination by taking night walks under the stars.

149 Manzalaoui, Mahmoud. 'Chaucer and Science.' In *Writers and Their Background: Geoffrey Chaucer*. Ed. Derek Brewer. Athens, Ohio: Ohio University Press, 1974. Pp 224–61.
It is probably impossible to determine Chaucer's beliefs about the scientific theories of his day, such as astral influence: 'Chaucer in this matter does not depart from his usual stance, of introducing a questioning even as he asserts an ideal' (p 229). Manzalaoui reviews Chaucer's reading in science; his own scientific works, *Astr* and possibly *Equat* **150**; and his artistic uses of several sciences. A section on astrology and astronomy (pp 235–47) offers criticisms of North **873** and Wood **157**. For *KnT* see **997**.

150 Price, Derek J., ed. *The Equatorie of the Planetis*. Edited from Peterhouse MS.75.I. With a Linguistic Analysis by R.M. Wilson. Cambridge: Cambridge University Press, 1955.

The *Equat* is a Middle English adaptation or translation of a lost Latin version of an Arab treatise describing a common medieval instrument for determining the positions of the planets. The possibility that the *Equat* was composed by Chaucer as a companion piece to his *Astr* bears on the depth of his interest in and knowledge of astrology. Composed about 1392, the *Equat* consists of eight folios of text and 70 folios of astronomical tables. Price presents a transcription of the text with facsimiles, a translation with notes, and full discussion of the manuscript, its contents and their backgrounds, and the ascription to Chaucer. See **149**.

151 Saxl, Fritz, and Hans Meier. *Verzeichnis Astrologischer und Mythologischer illustrierter Handschriften des lateinischen Mittelalters*. 3 vols in 4. Heidelberg: C. Winter, 1915–53.

Wood **156** describes this catalogue of manuscript illuminations as an 'excellent scholarly aid that has not been much used by literary scholars' (p 203). Volume III treats mss in England. For supplementary materials see Patrick McGurk, *Catalogue of Astrological and Mythological Illuminated Manuscripts of the Latin Middle Ages: IV. Astrological Manuscripts in Italian Libraries (Other than Rome)*. London: Warburg Institute, 1966.

152 Smyser, Hamilton M. 'A View of Chaucer's Astronomy.' *Spec* 45(1970), 359–73.

Between 1380 and 1387, when he was composing *Mars*, *KnT*, *TC*, and the *Hypermnestra*, Chaucer felt, perhaps under Boethius' influence, a new interest in astrology and was solving astronomical problems by the use of tables, observation, and the astrolabe (p 366). In the *KnT* the planetary gods, not humans, decide the outcome, and 'give the poem much of its special dignity and grandeur' (p 368). *MLT* 202–3 and 309–15 are evidence of Chaucer's belief in the predictive power of astrology. See **901**.

153 Thorndike, Lynn. *A History of Magic and Experimental Science*. 8 volumes. New York and London: Columbia University Press, 1923–1958.

The volumes are organized by authors and works, with astronomy and astrology receiving repeated and extensive treatment. Volumes 1 and 2 deal with the first through thirteenth centuries; volumes 3 and 4, with the fourteenth and fifteenth centuries. Thorndike discusses, for example, Bernard Silvester's Neo-platonic characterization of the stars as gods (2: 99–123) and Albertus Magnus' Aristotelian treatment of them as instruments of the First Cause (pp 517–92). He presents Aquinas as believing that 'God rules inferior through superior creatures and earthly bodies by the stars ... But ... the human will is free and ... the soul as an intellectual substance cannot be coerced by corporeal substances, however superior' (pp 609–10). There is a detailed chapter on the attitudes toward astrology of Chaucer's contemporary Nicolas Oresme (3: 398–423). See **156, 157.**

154 Wedel, Theodore Otto. *The Mediaeval Attitude Toward Astrology, Particularly in England.* New Haven: Yale University Press; London: Oxford University Press, 1920. Rpt Hamden, Conn.: Anchor, 1968.
In the early Middle Ages astrology was condemned both by Church Fathers and philosophers. As part of the incorporation of Aristotelian and Arabic science in the thirteenth century, astrology became acceptable, subject to such qualifications as preserving freedom of the will (pp 60–89). In literature astrology appeared prominently in romances, where it mingled with Celtic magic (pp 100–12). Gower apparently accepted astrology as a science dealing with celestial influences but rejected it as a fatalistic philosophy (p 132 f). Chaucer sometimes introduces references to astrology where there are none in his sources, as in the blending of the planet Mars with the god of war in the *KnT*. Arcite's speech on the stars (I.1084–91) seems to represent an 'extreme fatalistic philosophy' (p 146). Chaucer's *Astr* (esp 2.4) shows, however, that outside of fiction, Chaucer felt constrained by religious orthodoxy to reject such views. See **157, 955.**

155 Winny, James. 'Chaucer's Science.' In Maurice Hussey, A.C. Spearing, and Winny. *An Introduction to Chaucer.* Cambridge: Cambridge University Press, 1965. Pp 153–84.
Winny presents a detailed account, for students, of the interconnections of the four elements, the four humors, astrological influence, planetary hours (*KnT*, pp 173–4), and bodily spirits (*KnT*, pp 179–80).

156 Wood, Chauncey. 'Chaucer and Astrology.' In *Companion to Chaucer Studies*. Ed. Beryl Rowland. New York: Oxford University Press, 1968/ rev 1979. Pp 176–91/202–20.
Wood notes the scholarly emphasis on the technical aspects of medieval astrology to the neglect of the poetic. Reviewing background works, he finds Thorndike's (**153**) 'partisanship' for astrology and against the church 'intrusive' (p 203), and recommends Grimm's explanations of the terms and phenomena (**147**) and Lewis' appreciation of the imaginative appeal of the old cosmology (**148**). After arguing for the importance of Chaucer's rejection of judicial astrology in the *Astr*, he treats the poetic texts briefly and provides an excellent bibliography (pp 215–20). For *KnT* see **901**.

157 — *Chaucer and the Country of the Stars: Poetic Uses of Astrological Imagery.* Princeton: Princeton University Press, 1970.

Ch 1, 'Chaucer's Attitude toward Astrology' (pp 3–50): It is difficult to distinguish between those who believed in astrology in the Middle Ages and those who did not, as exemplified by Nicole Oresme, Chaucer's French contemporary. Chaucer's statements in the *Astr* (I, 21, 49–62 and II, 4, 1–8 f) show him to 'rank high among the unbelievers' (p 17), however, and should be given more weight than the speeches of his characters (*pace* Wedel **154**). Modern tendencies to emphasize the determinism of fourteenth-century philosophy, to exaggerate the influence granted to stars by Aquinas and Boethius, and to associate astrology honorifically with science (see Thorndike **153** and Wedel) distort the genuine Boethian sense that celestial influence dignifies human beings without abrogating their freedom. Ch 2, 'Conventions and Possibilities of Astrology' (pp 51–102): Chaucer's interest in astrology was more literary than philosophical or scientific, and other medieval artists, as well as the church itself, made artistic use of materials in which they did not repose belief. From ancient times the planets and the gods were identified with each other, so that astrology is often linked to mythology, which is then moralized. Chaucer used astrology only incidentally and wrote only one astrological poem, *CM*. An appendix (pp 298–305) provides a brief sketch of medieval astronomy and astrology for the uninitiate; there are 33 illustrations. See **149**. For *KnT* see **902**.

- Review by J.D. North, *RES* 22(1971), 471–4: Wood makes a strong argument for Chaucer's scepticism, but he dismisses too many poetic astrological passages on the grounds of their alleged humor and he does not consider possible changes in Chaucer's views over time.

Estates and Social Status

158 Brewer, D.S. 'Class Distinction in Chaucer.' *Spec* 43(1968), 290–305. Rpt in *Tradition and Innovation in Chaucer*. London: Macmillan, 1982. Pp 54–72.

Brewer examines three overlapping class systems. The multi-layered system based on rank required money to maintain one's degree, imposed an obligation to act appropriately, especially toward inferiors, and allowed some mobility. Chaucer sometimes exhibits a favorable attitude toward social mobility, but also shows both worldly cynicism and religious scepticism about the degree-structure of society. The second set of distinctions, between 'gentils' and 'churls,' tends to be chiefly moral in Chaucer, though it remains based in class. Even the

Knight's portrait, 'the rightly most famous evocation of a "gentil wight" does not deny a class basis ... [It is] a personal and class portrait whose power endures today, summed up for ever in Chaucer's best-known line: "He was a verray, parfit gentil knyght"' (p 300). This binary system, by attributing virtue to the upper section of society, supports acceptance of the social order, but also contains the revolutionary suggestion that only the good should be considered *gentil.* Finally, Chaucer never explicitly mentions the division of society into knights, clergy, and ploughmen, but it may have influenced the pattern of idealized portraits in the *GP.* This system treats all persons as potentially equal, condemning only those who fail to fulfill one of the three functions. Chaucer was a 'new man' who did not fit into this system, a possible cause of his 'pervasive irony,' and 'notable ambivalence' (p 304).

159 Duby, Georges. *The Three Orders: Feudal Society Imagined.* Trans. Arthur Goldhammer. Chicago: University of Chicago Press, 1980. Originally published as *Les trois ordres ou l'imaginaire du feodalisme.* Paris: Editions Gallimard, 1978.

This is the only book-length study of the social theory that would identify Chaucer's Knight, Parson, and Plowman as representatives of an ideal tripartite society made up of those who fight, those who pray, and those who work. Duby traces the idea from the writings of Gerard of Cambrai and Adalbero of Laon, composed shortly after 1000 with the purpose of strengthening the power of the king, joined with that of the church, especially over men-at-arms. Later the idea was modified to aggrandize the functions of the newly emerging knightly class at the expense of both the monarch and the church; and finally, in the late twelfth century, writers like Benedict of Sainte-Maure redefined it again to place monarchs like Philip Augustus outside and above the structure. In this process, an idea that was originally sacral, viewed as reflecting principles of a divinely ordered universe, became secularized. Throughout its history the idea of the three orders remained a 'category of the imagination' which was never realized in society in any of its forms.

- Review by Elizabeth A.R. Brown, *Viator* 17(1986), 51–64: This 'rich, poetic, and complex book' has already become a classic (p 51). It raises questions it does not fully answer, such as why a thinker chooses a particular model to describe a society, when 'numerous schematic models can be applied to any society' (p 61). Duby's work is notable for setting ideas in their social and intellectual surroundings, yet his focus on France somewhat obscures the history of the trifunctional image in the rest of

Eutorpe, and even that larger history needs to be placed within 'the pervasive medieval concern for establishing and defining rank, precedence, and order within earthly society' (p 63).

160 Girouard, Mark. *The Return to Camelot: Chivalry and the English Gentleman*. New Haven and London: Yale University Press, 1981.
Girouard opens this detailed work of synthesis by considering certain events of 1912 which were shaped by or interpreted in the light of the concept of the gentleman, including the sinking of the Titanic and Robert Scott's expedition to the South Pole. The work ends with a consideration of how World War I largely destroyed the cult of the gentleman which had evolved over almost two centuries partly through nostalgic revivals of chivalric ideals. Girouard's account of the evolution of that cult touches on such matters as the influence of Walter Scott and the modern rediscovery of Froissart **183**. Richly illustrated.

161 Mann, Jill. *Chaucer and Medieval Estates Satire: The Literature of Social Classes and the 'General Prologue' to the 'Canterbury Tales'*. Cambridge: Cambridge University Press, 1973.
Mann redefines the *GP* as an example of the 'neglected medieval genre' (p 1) of the estates satire. Thus Chaucer did not draw his characters directly from 'a world of eternal human types' (p 2) but from contemporary social life, as Manly **335** emphasized, though mediated by the 'social stereotypes' (pp 7–10) upon which the estates satire drew and to which it contributed. Both the comprehensiveness and the order of the *GP* can be better understood by reference to this genre. Eg, clergy usually precede knights in such lists; Chaucer's use of a more irregular order of presentation is one way in which he sets aside the absolute viewpoint associated with the idea of a divinely established social order and introduces a relativist viewpoint. For similar purposes, Chaucer places an unusual emphasis on the skills, duties, and jargon of the individual estates (pp 10–16, 187–202). 'We are in a world of "experts", where the moral views of the layman become irrelevant ... All excellence becomes "tricks of the trade" ... we are in a world of means rather than ends' (p 194). For reviews, see **474**.

162 Mohl, Ruth. *The Three Estates in Medieval and Renaissance Literature*. New York: Columbia University Press, 1933.
The genre of estates literature has four characteristics: the enumerating of the estates; lament over their shortcomings; insistence on the divine ordination of the estates, their importance to the community as a whole, and the duty of contentment with one's station; and an attempt to find remedies for their defects (pp 6–7). Adopted in

England in the fourteenth century, this French form was a vehicle for analyzing the evils of the time, and reached its culmination with Lydgate and Caxton. (Chaucer is mentioned briefly, pp 102–3). In the Renaissance the form was adopted to new circumstances such as the enclosures and protestantism. It died out by the mid-seventeenth century when the term *estate* lost its old meaning (pp 254–5). Medieval authors stressed moral shortcomings as the cause of defects while renaissance writers included economic and social causes; medieval authors urged love as a remedy while renaissance writers turned to the law.

163 Pitt-Rivers, Julian. 'Honour and Social Status.' In *Honour and Shame: The Values of Mediterranean Society*. Ed. J.G. Peristiany. Chicago: University of Chicago Press, 1966. Pp 19–77.
The more general and most often cited part of this essay (pp 21–39) defines honor as the value a person has both in his own eyes and in the eyes of his society. Pitt-Rivers emphasizes the link between right and might and the ambiguous relationship of honor and virtue. 'Respect and precedence are paid to those who claim it and are sufficiently powerful to enforce their claim' (p 24). 'The ultimate vindication of honour lies in physical violence' (p 29). The confusion of honor with virtue 'fulfils the function of social integration by ensuring the legitimation of established power' (p 38). See **168**.

164 Strohm, Paul. 'Chaucer's Audience.' *Literature and History* 5(1977), 26–41.
Chaucer's most important audience was the upwardly mobile class of knights, esquires, and other gentry, many of them, like Chaucer, born in the middle classes or petty gentry. The form of his poetry, characterized by juxtaposition of conflicting elements, and the content, marked by unresolved debate, are exemplified by the way 'the determinism of the *Knight's Tale* is not so much supplanted by the rampant free will and comic justice of the *Miller's Tale* [as] *completed* by it' (p 36). This style would have had particular appeal for a group 'who not only lived with uncertainty and change, but stood to benefit by it' (p 39).

165 —— 'Chaucer's Fifteenth-Century Audience and the Narrowing of the "Chaucer Tradition".' *SAC* 4(1982), 3–32.
Just before and after the year 1400 Chaucer's original audience was dispersed – by deaths, retirements, and political upheaval – and failed to renew itself. One cause was the shift of government functions away from the court under Henry IV and his successors. That early audience was replaced by a more mixed audience of aristocrats and members of the urban middle classes whose tastes

were largely limited to courtly love, advice to princes, and morality; who preferred works that satisfied rather than challenged their horizons of generic expectation; and who welcomed works that supported established social hierarchies. These tastes were another manifestation of the tendency of these groups to protect their privileges and consolidate their social positions in a period of economic decline.

Chivalry, including Tournaments

Essential reading is the recently published *The Study of Chivalry: Resources and Approaches*, ed. Howell Chickering and Thomas H. Seiler (Kalamazoo: Medieval Institute Publications, 1988). For bibliographic guidance, see especially: Jeremy duQuesnay Adams, 'Modern Views of Medieval Chivalry, 1884–1984,' pp 41–90. An important new work falling outside the chronological limits of this volume is Juliet Barker's *The Tournament in England, 1100-1400* (Woodbridge, Suffolk: 1986).

166 Atiya, Aziz Suryal. *The Crusade in the Later Middle Ages*. London: 1938.
The standard work on the subject, this study rejects an earlier view that the crusading movement essentially came to an end with the fall of Acre in 1291 and instead assigns that development to the Christian defeat at Nicopolis in 1396. Atiya treats extensively the propagandistic crusading literature in the West (pp 29–232), especially that produced by pilgrims to the East, but also including work by such figures as Lull **197** and Philippe de Mézières **198**, **199**. His accounts of the expeditions highlight the activities of Pierre de Lusignan (pp 319–78), especially the attack on Alexandria. The study concludes with a treatment of Eastern reactions to the West in the form of counter-propaganda and counter-crusades (pp 463–79).

167 Barber, Richard. *The Knight and Chivalry*. Woodbridge, Suffolk: Boydell, 1970; rpt Totowa, New Jersey: Rowman and Littlefield, 1982.
A readable synthesis that tends to obscure points of controversy. 'The Feudal Warrior' (pp 17–70) gives an account of the origins of knighthood. 'Chivalry and Literature' (pp 71–158) offers a broad survey, with a valuable chapter on chivalric biographies and hand-books. 'Chivalry in Action' (pp 159–212) analyzes tournaments and warfare, and relates both to politics. 'Chivalry and Religion' (pp 213–90) emphasizes the religious military orders, including the Teutonic

Knights. 'Chivalry and the State' (pp 291–336) examines the secular orders and the shifting relationships of chivalry to kings and princes.

168 Barnie, John. 'Aristocracy, Knighthood and Chivalry.' *War in Medieval Society: Social Values and the Hundred Years War 1337-99*. London: Weidenfeld and Nicolson, 1974. Pp 56–96.

Both the religious and the romance ideals of chivalry were relatively weak influences on fighting men. Legists such as Bonet **171**, treating mundane issues from a variety of perspectives, came closest to the views of men-at-arms. By applying chivalric values only within the ranks of a military elite, these men were able to regard war as an ennobling experience while commanding non-noble soldiers who engaged in rapine. Charny **173** described knighthood as a kind of martyrdom to honor, illustrating Pitt-Rivers' observation of the link between honor and violence (**163**). The career of the Black Prince **204** exemplifies the fundamental cultural difference between modern and medieval perceptions. Many contemporary sources described his ferocity as a commander, as at the sack of Limoges (cf Froissart **183**), but none condemned it. Barnie contrasts Sir John Chandos, a representative of traditional chivalric values, with Sir Thomas Gray, a professional soldier concerned with strategy. See also '... The Debate on War' (pp 117–38) where Barnie finds that Gower **185** and Chaucer, although not pacifists, were opposed to the war with France from about 1380 on.

169 Benson, Larry D. 'The tournament in the romances of Chrétien de Troyes & *L'Histoire de Guillaume Le Maréchal*.' In **170**. Pp 1–24.

Until the late twelfth century, the tournament was 'a brutal and informal affair ... [showing] little concern for matters of chivalric honor' (p 10). The biography of William the Marshall **187** offers the first descriptions of actual tournaments. Chrétien was the first of the romancers to describe tournaments, and his imitators made tournaments a characteristic feature of both the romance genre and chivalric virtue. Jean the Minstrel drew on this new tradition in telling William's story, as seen in the importance he gives to William's tournaments as compared with his crusades, in his emphasis on honor and devotion to ladies, and in his use of elements of romance style.

170 —, and John Leyerle, ed. *Chivalric Literature: Essays on relations between literature & life in the later middle ages*. *SMC*, 14. Kalamazoo, Michigan: Medieval Institute Publications, 1980.

A collection of ten essays by various hands. 'The golden age of chivalry came at the end of the Middle Ages and was characterized by complex, traditional interconnections between aristocratic literature and aristocratic life' (p 142). The discrepancy between chivalric ideal and aristocratic practice shows that 'chivalry belongs to the history of ideas and its main record is in literary texts' (p 143). See **169** and **181**.

171 Bonet [Bouvet], Honoré. *The Tree of Battles*. Ed. and trans. C.W. Coopland. Liverpool: Liverpool University Press, 1949.
Bonet (c 1340–1405), a Benedictine prior and scholar, composed his *L'arbre des Batailles* in 1387 and dedicated it to Charles VI. It won him a position as an administrator and ambassador at the French court, proved very popular, and was drawn on by Christine de Pisan (**175**) for her *Livre de Fais d'Armes et de Chevalrie* (c 1410). Its first two parts discuss the origins of war in relation to a historical survey. The third and fourth parts pose and answer questions about the conduct of war: eg, the practice of ransom and its abuses; the legality of a knight's breaking prison when he has been lawfully taken; and the treatment of non-combatants. The French text has been edited by Ernest Nys, Brussels: 1883. See **168, 175, 188, 192, 195, 200, 514, 1105.**

172 Bumke, Joachim. *The Concept of Knighthood in the Middle Ages*. Trans. W.T.H. Jackson and Erika Jackson. New York: AMS Press, 1982. Originally published as *Studien zum Ritterbegriff im 12. und 13. Jahrhundert*. Heidelberg, 1964.
Bumke traces the revaluation of the word *Ritter* from a colorless technical term to '*the* poetic noun of courtly poetry' (p 17), a development parallel to the adoption of knighthood by the higher nobility at the end of the twelfth century. A separate knightly class did not evolve from military knighthood, however; in German culture the distinction between lordship and service was basic, and the lord's retainers could be of various legal and social statuses. 'The aristocratic knighthood of which courtly poetry tells cannot be explained by shifting it into the social hierarchy. It is ... a phenomenon of intellectual history rather than social history' (p 120).

173 Charny, Geoffroi de. *Livre de chevalerie*. In *Oeuvres de Froissart* **183**, Volume 1, part 3, pp 462–533.
Charny's career included a crusade (1347) and service in the Hundred Years War. Probably a member of King John's Order of the Star, he died at the battle of Poitiers (1356) while guarding the Oriflamme. In the text cited here, Kervyn De Lettenhove presents the prose *Livre* without apparatus as an introduction to the times and culture of Froissart. Selections from a briefer version in verse have been edited by Arthur Piaget in 'Le Livre Messire Geoffroi de Charny,' *Romania* 26 (1897), 394–411. In both versions Charny compares knighthood with the priesthood, and both are divided into three parts, on jousts,

tournaments, and warfare. There are no English or Modern French editions. See **168, 192, 194, 200, 934.**

174 Christiansen, Eric. *The Northern Crusades: The Baltic and the Catholic Frontier, 1100-1525.* Minneapolis: University of Minnesota Press, 1980. Christiansen examines the military conflicts in the Baltic as part of the extension of Latin Christendom to that area, and defends the contemporary construction of those conflicts as crusades (eg, pp 250–51). He also comments on the special importance of the Baltic to England (p 3). Of special interest are his history of the Teutonic Knights ('The Armed Monks: Ideology and Efficiency,' pp 70–88), his treatment of 'The Interminable Crusade, 1283–1410' (pp 132–70), which includes discussion of the fourteenth-century crusades in Lithuania and Russia, and his account of the debate over the Teutonic Order at the Council of Constance, 1414–1418 (pp 223–32).

175 Christine de Pisan. *The Book of Faytess of Armes and of Chyvalrye Translated and Printed by William Caxton From the French Original by Christine de Pisan.* Ed. A.T.P. Byles. Early English Text Society, Old Series, Number 189. London: Humphrey Milford, 1932/corrected 1937. Christine (1364–1430?) composed *Le Livre des Fais d'Armes et de Chevalrie* about 1410, possibly at the request of John the Fearless, Duke of Burgundy, as part of his educational program for Louis of Guyenne, the Dauphin. Books 1 and 2 contain discussions of the just war, the ideal commander, and the upbringing of boys, and accounts of the fortification and besieging of castles, and are indebted to Vegetius, other classical sources, and a contemporary anonymous writer on sieges. Books 3 and 4 deal with legal questions about the relations between commanders and their men and between countries at war, and are indebted to Bonet (**171**). Byles collates Christine's discussion with Bonet's in an appendix. Caxton's translation (1489) was undertaken at the request of Henry VII. There is no modern edition of the French text. See **168, 195, 514, 1105.**

176 Cline, Ruth. 'The Influence of Romances on Tournaments of the Middle Ages.' *Spec* 20(1945), 204–11.
The round table, a form of combat better regulated than the ordinary tournament, was well established in England and on the continent in the thirteenth and fourteenth centuries, and reached its peak with Edward III's round table at Windsor in 1344. Participants often appeared as knights of romance; in two tournaments a woman was the victor's prize. The dependence of actual tournaments on romances is a sign that 'the real life and spirit of the tournament was dead' (p 211).

177 Contamine, Philippe. *War in the Middle Ages*. Trans. Michael Jones. Oxford: Blackwell, 1984; rpt 1985, 1986. Originally published as *La Guerre au moyen âge*. Paris: Presses Universitaires de France, 1980.
This work studies war as a cultural phenomenon, as both cause and effect of other aspects of its environment. The first of its three parts traces medieval military history chronologically from the fifth century to the end of the fifteenth century, giving particular attention to the transition from knightly warfare to the first permanent armies. A second part, organized thematically, treats such topics as the 'History of courage' (pp 250–9), including an assessment of the risks of knightly warfare, and the concept of the just war, including a consideration of 'Medieval pacifism and its limits' (pp 292–6). The last part presents a fifty-page bibliography.

178 Denholm-Young, N. 'The Tournament in the Thirteenth-Century.' In *Studies in Medieval History Presented to F.M. Powicke*. Ed. R.W.Hunt, W.A. Pantin, and R.W. Southern. Oxford: Oxford University Press, 1948; rpt 1969. Pp 240–68.
This frequently cited essay describes the nature and reputation of the mêlée, the early form of the tournament replaced in the fourteenth and fifteenth centuries by more picturesque and less dangerous jousting.

179 Duby, Georges. *The Chivalrous Society*. Trans. Cynthia Postan. London: Edward Arnold, 1977; rpt Berkeley: University of California Press, 1980.
This collection of fifteen articles, originally published between 1946 and 1972 and exemplifying the *Annales* school of historiography, explores the evolution of nobility and of knighthood and their relationships to the structure of the aristocratic family. The best known of these studies, translated here as 'Youth in Aristocratic Society' (pp 112–22, originally published 1964), identifies a large group of adult men, frequently younger sons excluded from the patrimony, who lived a turbulent life of adventure while pursuing heiresses to marry. Duby suggests that their experiences in war and tournament were reflected in epic and romance, and that their difficulties of access to aristocratic women inspired the literature of courtly love. See also 'The Origins of Knighthood' (pp 158–70), a study of some terms referring to knights.

180 Ferguson, Arthur B. *The Indian Summer of English Chivalry: Studies in the Decline and Transformation of Chivalric Idealism*. Durham: Duke University Press, 1960.
The transformation of the English medieval knight into the gentleman governor of the Tudor era was eased in part by the English

emphasis on maintaining peace and justice as an extension of the knight's military function. Yet, the undermining of the knight's military function by captains of modern warfare and the sharing of administrative functions with the non-knightly gentry increasingly weakened the relation of chivalry to national interests. Attempts to revive chivalry by such as Malory and Caxton, anachronistically applied traditional values to changed circumstances. See also Ferguson's distinction between medieval anti-war sentiment and humanist pacifism (pp 174–6).

181 Ferris, Sumner. 'Chronicle, Chivalric Biography, Family Tradition in Fourteenth-century England.' In *Chivalric Literature* (**170**), pp 25–38. Noting Cook's suggestion (**326**) that Chaucer's Knight was modelled on Henry of Grosmont or Henry of Derby, Ferris examines the relationships of actual knights to those in literature. Romances, chronicles, and chivalric biographies share the same purposes and techniques, as seen in the biography of the Black Prince (**204**). The Prince's homecoming after his famous victories 'is as formal as the homecoming of Theseus' in *KnT* (p 30). Edward's virtues are presented as innate, needing only to be displayed, not developed; the biography presents him as always on campaign and treats only talents and duties that could enhance a chivalric reputation. It may have been intended to inspire Richard II to emulate his father, but Richard seems to have been uninterested even in celebrating Edward; eg, the Black Prince does not seem to be memorialized in the portrait of the Knight by Chaucer, a court poet (p 38).

182 Fleckenstein, Josef, ed. *Das ritterliche Turnier im Mittelalter: Beitrag zu einer vergleichenden Formen- und Verhaltensgeschichte des Rittertums*. Gottingen, 1985.
A collection of twenty-one essays, most in German or French, by various hands, offering comprehensive, international coverage of the tournament in the High and Late Middle Ages. 'The Medieval English Kings and the Tournament,' by Juliet Barker and Maurice Keen, pp 212–28, examines the tournament ordinances of Richard I and Edward I, and stresses the importance of royal policy in two phases: the earlier period when tournaments were associated with the martial training of magnate retinues and thus with factional struggles among magnates and between magnates and the king, and a later period, especially under Edward III and Richard II, when tournaments were associated with the king's wars in France and Scotland. The volume includes color reproductions of knightly seals and black-and-white pictures of armor and of manuscript and book illustrations.

183 Froissart, Jean. *Chroniques*. In *Oeuvres de Jean Froissart*. Ed. Kervyn de Lettenhove. Volumes 1–25. Brussels: 1867–77. Rpt Osnabrück: Biblio Verlag, 1967.
Froissart (1337?–1410?), born in Hainault, was a clerk in the entourage of Queen Philippa from about 1361 until her death in 1369. He was in Prince Lionel's entourage to Italy in 1368, as was perhaps Chaucer also. The *Chronicles* were commissioned by Froissart's next patron, Robert of Namur, of the family of the Count of Flanders, in 1369 or shortly thereafter. They begin with the deposition of Edward II and end with the deposition of Richard II and the accession of Henry IV. Their four books are divided, with some overlapping, in this fashion: I, 1322–78; II, 1376–85; III, 1386–8; and IV, 1389–1400. Part I, through 1361, is indebted to a chronicle by Jean Le Bel; Chaucer is mentioned as a member of a diplomatic mission in 1376. Although modern historical scholarship has found many factual errors in Froissart's accounts, his work is of inestimable value in revealing the mental world of the great princes, the aristocracy, and the ordinary men-at-arms of the fourteenth century. Froissart juxtaposes without comment the actions and language of chivalric idealism with considerations of commercial interest and scenes of savagery. Although it is difficult to single out passages of greater interest than others, these may be mentioned as examples: the English seige of Calais, with Queen Philippa's appeal for the lives of the burghers, the campaigns of Crécy and Poitiers, the Black Prince's sack of Limoges (Book I); the story of Bascot de Mauleon, member of the Free Companies, a trial-by-combat concerning the rape of a knight's wife by a squire (Book III); and the tournaments of Saint-Inglevert and Smithfield (Book IV). De Lettenhove's edition is being superceded by the authoritative edition of the Société de l'Histoire de France, 15 volumes, 1869–1975, a work in progress that has reached Book IV (1387–9) and is most recently edited by Albert Mirot. A complete English translation is by Thomas Johnes (London: 1805). A convenient selected English translation is Geoffrey Brereton's *Froissart: Chronicles* (Baltimore: Penguin, 1968). See **160, 168, 192, 195, 202-4, 335, 506, 534, 551, 616, 737, 758, 834, 934, 1105.**

184 Gloucester, Thomas, Earl of. 'Letter of Thomas, Duke of Gloucester, Constable of England, to Richard II, concerning how to conduct a Judicial Duel.' Pierpont Morgan Library MS 775. Printed in R. Coltman Clephan, *The Tournament: Its Periods and Phases* (London: Methuen, 1919), Appendix H, pp 184–7; and in Harold Arthur, Viscount Dillon, 'On a Manuscript Collection of Ordinances of

Chivalry of the Fifteenth Century Belonging to Lord Hastings,' *Archaeological Journal*, 62(1900), 20–70.
Probably composed between 1385 and 1395, Gloucester's 'Letter' specifies the duties of the King, Constable, heralds, appellant and defendant. Among other things, it provides that each duelist shall have a long sword, a short sword, and a dagger; that the lists shall be sixty paces long and forty paces wide with gates at the east and west ends; and that oaths shall be sworn on a mass-book. A Latin version with the title 'The Ordenaunce and fourme of fightyng within the listes ...' survives in Landsdowne MS 285 and is printed, with a facing fourteenth-century French text of the 'Letter,' in *The Black Book of the Admiralty*, ed. Sir Travers Twiss (London: 1871), Volume I, 301–29. See **609**, **794**.

185 Gower, John. 'To King Henry the Fourth in Praise of Peace.' In *The Complete Works of John Gower*. Ed. G.C. Macaulay. Oxford: Clarendon, 1901. Volume 3. Text, pp 481–94; notes; pp 550–4.
While acknowledging the right of a king to fight for his 'rightful heritage' (lines 57–60), Gower insists that 'Pes is the beste above alle erthely thinges' (63). He urges war against the Saracens, enemies of Christ, but condemns fighting among Christians for worldly profit (183–252). This work, comprised of 385 lines of English verse and an epistola of 56 lines of Latin verse, was composed in 1399 or 1400. See **168**, **353**, **358**, **454**, **514**, **1111**.

186 Harvey, Ruth. 'The Social and Literary Background of the Tournament.' *Moriz von Craûn and the Chivalric World*. Oxford: Clarendon Press, 1961. Pp 112–217.
The tournament was overwhelmingly popular despite the opposition of church and state and the risks of financial loss and injury or death. Intricately connected to knightly values, serving a variety of needs, and evoking a complex of emotions, the tournament held a meaning for its participants which moderns cannot wholly recover. The aspects of honor at stake were not the highest – such as integrity – but a secondary group – valor, courtesy, liberality – and these were practiced with a mixture of idealism and self-interest. The courtly love associated with tournaments was not of the more intellectualized, aetheticized, or platonic types, but of the feudalistic type, in which the knight expected to receive the lady's favors as a reward for service. Actual tournaments were an important link between literature and life as 'a projection into real life of a romantic vision' (p 199).

187 *Histoire de Guillaume le Maréchal*. Ed. Paul Meyer. Société de l'histoire de France. 3 volumes. Paris: Renouard, 1891–1901.

The *Histoire* is the classical source for the early history of the tournament, being devoted in large part to William's exploits in tournaments from 1166–85. William (1144?–1219) also crusaded in Syria; he became Earl of Pembroke through marriage and later regent of England. This verse-biography was composed about 1226 at the order of the Marshal's son William by Jean the Minstrel with the assistance of the Marshal's squire, Jean d'Erlee. Volumes 1 and 2 present the original text; volume 3 offers an abridged version in Modern French prose with notes and introduction. There is no English translation. A detailed portrait is Sidney Painter's *William Marshall: Knight-Errant, Baron, and Regent of England* (Baltimore: Johns Hopkins, 1933; Medieval Academy Reprints for Teaching, Toronto: University of Toronto Press, 1982). Briefer but highly evocative is Georges Duby's *Guillaume le Maréchal* (Librairie Arthème Fayard, 1984; trans. by Richard Howard as *William Marshall, The Flower of Chivalry* [New York: Pantheon Books, 1985]). See **169**, **194**, **202**, **533**.

188 Huizinga, Johan. *The Waning of the Middle Ages: A Study of the Forms of Life, Thought and Art in France and the Netherlands in the XIVth and XVth Centuries*. London: Edward Arnold, 1924. Rpt many times. Originally published in Dutch, 1919; 2nd ed, 1921.

A classic interpretation of the decay of medieval culture through reliance on secular and religious images increasingly devoid of their original animating ideas. Huizinga characterizes chivalry (pp 59–94) as a fiction through which the aristocracy of a violent era explained its politics and history, reducing both to 'a spectacle ... a noble game' (p 57). In the early Middle Ages chivalry imitated the heroes of romance and the classical past; in the later period, the 'perfect knights' of chivalric biography, such as Boucicaut, Jean de Bueill, and Jacques de Lalaing. The erotic element in chivalry was expressed in tournaments, which borrowed elements from romance literature. The tournament and chivalric culture in general were 'marked by an unstable equilibrium between sentimentality and mockery'; perfect seriousness co-existed with a knowing recognition of the gap between ceremonial and reality (p 69). The early orders, such as the Templars and Teutonic Knights, achieved real economic and political power; the later ones, such as Philippe de Mézières' Order of the Passion (**198**, **199**) and the Burgundian Order of the Golden Fleece, expressed a nostalgic sense of chivalry as an aristocratic club or sacred game. The influence of chivalry on political and military decisions appears in plans to recover Jerusalem and in challenges to settle wars by single combat. Chivalry contributed to the idea of international law, as seen in Bonet **171**, and to the sentiment of patriotism. Huizinga's chapters on courtly love (pp 95–114) also emphasize the gap between the ideal and the actual. The nobility developed elaborate rituals for a love that, given the crudities of sexual mores and the practicalities of marriage contracts, could never be more than a literary amusement or a social game. See **190, 193, 194, 194R, 206, 834, 1111.**

189 — 'The Political and Military Significance of Chivalric Ideas in the Late Middle Ages.' *Men and Ideas: History, the Middle Ages, the Renaissance.* Trans. James S. Holmes and Hans van Marle. New York: Meridian, 1959, pp 196–206. Originally published, *Revue d'histoire diplomatique*, 35 (1921), 126–38.
A version of Ch 7 of **188** in which Huizinga defends the revival of chivalry in the fourteenth and fifteenth centuries against the disparagement of economic and social historians. As an attempt 'to recreate in real life an ideal image of the past,' and as 'a naive and imperfect prelude to the Renaissance,' that revival is an 'historical fact of primary importance' (p 197).

190 Keen, Maurice H. *The Laws of War in the Late Middle Ages.* London: Routledge & Kegan Paul; Toronto: University of Toronto Press, 1965.
Keen examines the links between the legal theory of just war, chivalry and its ideals, and the practice of military profiteering. Part One (pp 7–59) shows how civil and canon law fused with military customs to form an international law. What the lawyer viewed as a matter of contract, however, the soldier was likely to see as a matter of honor (p 20). Part Two (pp 63–133) defines just war, distinguishing public from private wars. For military men, the important point was that public war permitted the taking of spoil, prisoners (for ransom), and payments from civilians. The display of a prince's banner (a pennon was a personal emblem) was the sign of a public war. Although war to the death applied, stricly speaking, only to the crusade, a town taken by assault could be lawfully destroyed since refusal to surrender to a prince was an offense against his majesty. Part Three deals with the spoils of war (pp 137–55) and with ransoms (pp 156–85). The rules governing booty reflect the growing commercialization and legalism of war, both detrimental to chivalry. The relationship of captor and captive was 'a close chivalrous bond' (p 164) in which each party had rights and obligations. 'The man of honour did not mean for a medieval soldier an ideal human being, but a person of a particular social status and calling who kept on the right side of certain technical rules' (p 185). Part Four (pp 239–47) suggests that the laws of war provide the middle term for Huizinga's thesis (**188**)

that the ideal of chivalry prepared the way for modern international law. See **1014**.

191 — 'Chivalrous Culture in Fourteenth-Century England.' *Historical Studies* 10(1976), 1–24.
[Not seen]

192 — 'Chivalry, Nobility, and the Man-at-Arms.' In *War, Literature, and Politics in the Late Middle Ages*. Ed. C.T. Allmand. Liverpool: Liverpool University Press, 1976, pp 32–45.
Citing Sir John Hawkwood as typical of the men-at-arms who devastated much of France and Italy, Keen argues that the medieval idealization of war extended to activities contemporaries recognized as a social bane. Authorities like Bouvet **171**, who focused on the morality of an individual's participation rather than on whether a war was just, tended to confirm the belief that the life of arms was a vocation leading to salvation. This belief is the theme of Charny's *Livre* **173**, where it is combined with an interest in worldly honor, as also in Lull **197**. The association between noble status and arms, as in the Scrope-Grosvenor depositions **201**, led to the belief that service in arms could be a sufficient claim to noble status. The social mystique that saw arms as a way both to salvation and to worldly prosperity was especially important to men of lower rank in the Free Companies, such as Bascot de Mauleon (cf Froissart **183**), but the Free Companies also appealed to men of noble rank who were under economic and social pressure. Crusaders were not different from these; Philippe de Mézières **198**, **199** did not see that the chivalric aspirations he appealed to had created the disorder he wished to remedy.

193 — 'Huizinga, Kilgour and the Decline of Chivalry.' *M&H*, 8(1977), 1–20.
Kilgour's depiction of late medieval chivalry (**195**) shares with Huizinga's (**188**) the mistaken assumption that chivalry of an earlier period was more faithful to an ascetic ideal. Early critics of chivalry made much the same charges as later ones, and chivalry always emphasized *largesse*. The tournament was as powerful an influence as the crusade. Display functioned to create political power, and heraldry shows how ceremony was related to the serious interests of a martial class. The spectacles staged by the dukes of Burgundy reflect not new tastes but greater riches. Crusades became less important and service of the prince, more important, but chivalry was always largely secular.

194 — *Chivalry*. New Haven: Yale University Press, 1984.
Keen's double thesis is that chivalry was always a significant social force and not, as in Huizinga **188**, merely a matter of forms, and that

chivalry was essentially a secular ethic and never an inherently Christian institution. In Ch 1 Keen introduces his emphasis on secularity by interpreting the anonymous *Ordene de Chevalerie* (c 1220), Lull **197** and Charny **173**. Ch 2 traces the evolution of chivalry from roots in Germanic warrior culture to the emergence of a figure like William the Marshall **187**. Crusades (Ch 3) are said to 'thicken the Christian veneer' of the old heroic values but not to replace them (p 57). The secularity of the dubbing ceremony (Ch 4) is argued, against Leon Gautier's characterization of it as an eighth sacrament [cf. *Le Chevalerie* (Paris, 1884)]. The popularity of the tournament (Ch 5) is interpreted in terms of the needs of an aristocratic warrior class, and its persistence in the face of church bans is cited as further evidence of secularity. Tournaments also provided 'a crucial link between the literary expression of chivalrous values and the real world' (p 100). The historical mythology of chivalry (Ch 6), eg, as seen in the scheme of the Nine Worthies, is seen as providing an independent learned culture for this secular ethic. The history of heraldry (Ch 7) is given an original treatment as the priesthood of a secular cult. Ch 8 traces shifts in the definitions of nobility, and Ch 9 explores the practical applications of these ideas, particularly in public recognitions of honor such as the Table of Honor of the Teutonic Knights. Chapters 10 and 11 argue, *pace* Huizinga, for the vital social and political significance of chivalric orders and pageantry in the fourteenth and fifteenth centuries. Concerning war (Ch 12), Keen argues for the reality of the risks knights encountered in battle and for the harmony of chivalric individualism with the military needs of lords. Chivalry's potential for disorder was also real as seen in the difficulty of distinguishing mercenaries like Hawkwood from men like Du Guesclin, Constable of France. Critics prolonged the life of chivalric ideals by invoking them as remedies for chivalry's abuses. Ch 13 reinterprets late developments in chivalry as evidence of adaptive change rather than decline as in Huizinga **188**. Fifty-five illustrations.

- Review by Frederic L. Cheyette, *Journal of Social History* 20(1986), 355–63: Keen, a master of the 'non-literary' literature of chivalry, has made a major contribution through his study of heraldry. He has rehabilitated the ludic, ideological, and intellectual aspects of aristocratic life as constituting a culture worthy of serious study, and in so doing, he has supported rather than opposed Huizinga's efforts (**188**). Keen's attack on Huizinga is more pertinent to the older scholar's reputation than to his work. Keen is also wrong in objecting to Huizinga's recognition of the violence at the heart of chivalry; Keen's own nostalgia blinds him (p 358). The chapters on crusade and dubbing offer a rich elaboration of Keen's thesis that chivalry was a secular culture; yet inattention to the historical relations of nobliity and chivalry is a major weakness of Keen's book, and in particular, he isolates chivalric culture too absolutely from clerical. These chapters will have to be reassessed in the light of Jaeger's work (**112**). Nevertheless, this work deserves 'to join that small pantheon of books on medieval society that every reader interested in the subject should have read' (p 362).

195 Kilgour, Raymond Lincoln. *The Decline of Chivalry as Shown in the French Literature of the Late Middle Ages*. Cambridge, Mass: Harvard University Press, 1936; rpt Gloucester, Mass: Peter Smith, 1966.
Kilgour places the golden age of chivalry in the period of the early crusades, 1100–1250, when warrior and religious values were ideally melded. Thereafter, latent faults such as pride and greed became more pronounced when chivalry was weakened by Eastern luxury and courtly unchastity. Froissart **183** unwittingly revealed chivalry's dark side (pp 58–83). Kilgour presents a valuable compendium of fourteenth- and fifteenth-century criticism by such commentators as Deschamps, Christine de Pisan **175**, Philippe de Mézières **198, 199**, Bonet **171**, Jean Gerson, Alain Chartier, Jean de Bueil, and Philippe de Commines. See **193**.

196 Kyngeston, Richard. *Expeditions to Prussia and the Holy Land Made by Henry Earl of Derby (Afterwards King Henry IV) In the Years 1390-1 and 1392-3. Being the Accounts kept by his Treasurer during two years*. Ed. Lucy Toulmin Smith. Camden Society, new series 52, 1894.
Smith's introduction discusses the relations of the Teutonic Order to England and to crusades into Prussia, and presents itineraries for Henry's expeditions and extracts from chronicles in which they are mentioned. The accounts, in Latin, record such things as the wages of the knights. See also F.R.H. Du Boulay, 'Henry of Derby's Expeditions to Prussia 1390–1 and 1392,' in *The Reign of Richard II*, ed. Du Boulay and Caroline M Barron (London: Athlone Press, 1971), pp 153–72. See **181, 326, 334, 336, 344, 352, 389, 503, 518, 537.**

197 Lull, Ramón. *The Book of the Ordre of Chyvalry. Translated and Printed by William Caxton*. Ed. Alfred T.P. Byles. Early English Text Society, Old Series, 168. London: Humphrey Milford and Oxford University Press, 1926.
Lull (c 1232–1314?) was a poet, a philosopher, and seneschal at the court of James II of Aragon. He later devoted himself to converting the Saracens of North Africa, by whom, tradition has it, he was eventually stoned to death. *Le libre del orde de cauayleria* (c 1276)

treats the origin of chivalry, the office of a knight, the examination of a squire, the ordination of a knight, the significance of a knight's arms, the customs of a knight, and the honor due to a knight. The influential French versions were translated into English by Gilbert of the Haye (1456) and by Caxton (1484). Caxton's version contains his famous exhortation to the knights of England to emulate earlier exemplars of chivalry in history and romance. See **166, 192, 194, 200, 202, 445, 1006.**

198 Mézières, Philippe de. *Letter to King Richard II: A plea made in 1395 for peace between England and France.* Ed. and trans. G.W. Coopland. Liverpool: Liverpool University Press, 1975.
Philippe (1327–1405) was a member of the lesser nobility, chancellor of Cyprus and counsellor to Charles V of France, who, in 1347, conceived the idea of a new crusading order to be called the Order of the Passion. In this letter he urges Richard to make peace with France and to marry Isabel, daughter of Charles VI. Philippe laments the harm done by the Great Schism and the loss of Christian power in the Near East. The new peace and the Order of the Passion are to reunite Western Christians and prepare for a joint French-English crusade to reclaim the Holy Land. This edition contains an introduction, an English translation, and the original text in French. See **166, 188, 192, 195, 417, 504, 514, 1009.**

199 — *Le songe du vieil pelerin.* Ed. G.W. Coopland. 2 volumes. Cambridge: Cambridge University Press, 1969.
This work, completed in 1389 and thus antedating the *Letter* (**198**), is composed of a Prologue and three Books. Philippe urges Western Christians to purify themselves of vices, especially Pride, Avarice, and Luxury, as preparation for the rescue of the Holy Land; he urges Richard II and Charles VI to make peace in order to launch a joint attack on the Saracens and Turks. Coopland provides a 'General Introduction' (pp 1–80) and a lengthy synopsis and commentary for each Book. For references see **198.**

200 Miller, Robert P., ed. 'The Estate of Temporal Rulers: Chivalry.' In *Chaucer: Sources and Backgrounds.* New York: Oxford University Press, 1977. Pp 156–209.
This valuable reference work for teaching prints excerpts in translation from Bonet **171**, Charny **173**, Gower's *Vox clamantis*, Lull **197**, John of Salisbury, and Deschamps, among others. It includes excerpts from a ceremonial for the blessing of a new knight and the blessing of arms from a pontifical of c 1295. The texts are accompanied by highly informative headnotes.

201 Nicolas, Sir N. Harris, ed. *The Scrope and Grosvenor Roll.* 2 volumes. London: 1832.
In 1386 Sir Richard Le Scrope and Sir Robert Grosvenor appeared before the English Court of Chivalry to contest the right to bear a certain coat of arms. The depositions in support of Sir Richard have proved valuable in reconstructing representative careers for fourteenth-century English knights. Chaucer himself testified and several of the deponents were well known to him. Nicolas says of Sir William Scrope that 'he almost realized Chaucer's beau ideal of a Knight,' and cites *KnT* I.3047–56 as a fitting consolation for Sir William's premature death (Volume 2: 105–8). Volume 1 prints the roll in the original French. Depositions in favor of Grosvenor, and the judgment of the court, have been lost. Volume 2 presents the history of the house of Scrope, translations of material parts of the depositions in Sir Richard's favor, and biographical sketches of the deponents. A planned third volume on the house of Grosvenor and on Grosvenor's deponents did not appear. See **192, 210, 218, 335, 336, 353, 360, 411, 470, 504, 510.**

202 Painter, Sidney. *French Chivalry: Chivalric Ideas and Practices in Mediaeval France.* Baltimore: Johns Hopkins, 1940.
This widely-read synthesis offers an analysis of the feudal (pp 28–64), Christian (pp 65–94), and courtly (pp 95–148) aspects of chivalry. The feudal ideals are seen as the most important because of their connection with the warrior's function. William the Marshal **187** and Froissart **183** are cited as examplars, and the popularity of tournaments and of expeditions into Prussia is discussed. The Christian concept of knighthood as a sacred order, though fully described by John of Salisbury for an ecclesiastical audience and by Lull **197** for a more popular audience, found little expression even in crusading. Evidence for the effects of the courtly ideal on the treatment of women is even weaker. These three ideals of chivalry were to a large extent irreconcilable and were so perceived by contemporaries (pp 149–72). Because the Church was sensitive to the economic and social needs of the noble class, its opposition to feudal practices such as tournaments was less absolute than its condemnation of courtly ideas. Poets and biographers produced composite knights with selected, compatible characteristics drawn from the three ideals. See **934.**

203 Palmer, J.J.N., ed. *Froissart: Historian.* Woodbridge, Suffolk: Boydell & Brewer; Totowa, N.J.: Rowman and Littlefield, 1981.
A collection of ten essays on the *Chronicles* **183**. After reviewing Froissart's reputation ('Introduction,' pp 1–5), Palmer advances the

thesis that the several versions of Book I of the *Chronicles* did not reach their final form until the 1390's and that Froissart regarded them all as valid accounts of events: 'Book I (1325–1378) and its Sources,' pp 7–24. In 'Jean Froissart and Edward the Black Prince,' pp 25–35, Richard Barber compares the *Chronicles* with the work of the Chandos Herald **204** and comments on the battle of Limoges. George T. Diller suggests that Froissart shaped his work to satisfy the views and tastes of his audience: 'Froissart: Patrons and Texts,' pp 145–60.

- Review by Sumner Ferris, *SAC* 5(1983), 183–7: This 'first book devoted to the *Chronicles* as a whole ... should be consulted ... by anyone who cites or even reads Froissart' (p 184). Unfortunately, it contains no study of Froissart's treatment of the English and Edward III (p 186).

204 Tyson, Diana B. *La Vie du Prince Noir by Chandos Herald. Beihefte zur Zetschrift Romanische Philologie*, Band 147. Tübingen: Max Niemeyer, 1975.
This narrative and eulogy in verse concerning Edward (1330–76), eldest son of Edward III, was composed about 1385 by the herald of Sir John Chandos, a friend and follower of the Prince. A source for Froissart **183**, it recounts the knighting of the Prince, his role in the battles of Crécy and Poitiers, his rescue of the King at Caen, his Spanish expedition on behalf of Pedro of Castile, and his death. This edition transcribes the University of London Library ms, with textual notes, glossary, and index of names. The Introduction (pp 1–48) explains the relation of this work to the edition of the Oxford ms by Mildred K. Pope and Eleanor C. Lodge (*Life of the Black Prince* [Oxford: Clarendon, 1910]), which includes an English translation, introduction, and historical notes. See **168, 181, 203, 404, 576, 623, 779, 925.**

205 Vale, Juliet. *Edward III and Chivalry: Chivalric Society and Its Context 1270-1350*. Woodbridge, Suffolk: Boydell, 1982.
This revisionist study emphasizes England's participation in European chivalric culture and relates the tournament in particular to a number of other cultural institutions and expressions (pp 4–56). The tournaments of the first half of Edward III's reign show three typical features: a strong relationship to actual warfare, some participation by the bourgeoisie, and the sharing of decorative and dramatic motifs with other kinds of *ludi* (pp 57–75). In founding the Order of the Garter in the middle of his reign, Edward III was imitating the politically successful Arthurianism of his grandfather, Edward I. The two companies of the Order were structured like tournament teams

and reflected the personal and political relationships of the members to Edward and the Black Prince. Participation at Crécy was a common denominator (pp 76–91). Appendices include lists of Edward's tournaments, 1327–55 (pp 172–4) and of the original members of the Order of the Garter (pp 176–7).

206 Vale, Malcolm. *War and Chivalry*: *Warfare and Chivalric Culture in England, France and Burgundy at the End of the Middle Ages*. Athens, Georgia: University of Georgia Press, 1981.
Huizinga's insistence (**188**) on the decline of chivalry into formality and fantasy can be traced in part to themes and influences in his own intellectual development (pp 1–12). In fact, the connection between war and chivalry remained very real. A new 'literature of honour and virtue' among the French and Burgundians, while it did not affect military organization and techniques, did affect personal attitudes and behavior (pp 16–32). The new Orders of Chivalry were a channel by which chivalric ideas were transformed into political reality (pp 33–62). Tournaments and warfare were closely linked (pp 63–99). Such developments as plate armor and the lance rest, and an accepting attitude toward guns, combined to give the cavalryman a new importance rather than to render him obsolete. Another evidence of continuity was the tranformation of the chivalric concept of honor into Renaissance ideas of service to the prince and personal fame.

- Review by Michael Altschul, *M&H* ns 13(1985), 209–10: Vale documents not a decline but a 'fifteenth-century "modernization," as it were, of the chivalric tradition, and its connections, both backwards and forwards in time, with literary *topoi*, with social realities, and above all, with the European code, or set of codes, of masculine honor' (p 210).

Miscellaneous

207 Bloomfield, Morton W. 'Chaucer's Sense of History.' *JEGP* 51(1952), 301–13. Rpt in *Essays and Explorations*: *Studies in Ideas, Language, and Literature*. Cambridge, Mass.: Harvard University Press, 1970. Pp 13–26.
From the twelfth century onward, the historic sense that was fundamental to the Judeo-Christian tradition was more and more applied to matters outside religion. This development, which depended on a conviction that secular matters are important and on scholastic concepts of reason and natural law, manifested itself particularly in concerns for chronology and cultural diversity.

Chaucer's *LGW*, *TC*, and *CT*, despite 'flagrant anachronisms,' display a historic sense relatively unusual in fourteenth-century England as seen, eg, in the Knight's apology for violating chronology (I.2031 f; pp 305–6) and in his uses of the clause 'as was tho the gyse' (I.993, 2279, 2911; p 309). This new awareness helped Chaucer to depict the poignancy of human transience and the humor of clashes of opinion and custom; it also made impossible the kind of Dantean vision based on imagining a point of vantage in eternity (pp 311–2). See **135**, **799**, **1130**.

208 — 'The Problem of the Hero in the Later Medieval Period.' In *Concepts of the Hero in the Middle Ages and the Renaissance*. Ed. Norman T. Burns and Christopher J. Reagan. Albany: State University of New York Press, 1975. Pp 2–48.
The later Middle Ages is like the eighteenth and twentieth centuries in its suppression of the heroic. The English tradition offers no true epic between *Beowulf* and Spenser. Even Chaucer's Knight is disappointing; Moorman's philosophical knight (**430**, **867**) 'is the last type of knight we want as a hero' (p 35). The later Middle Ages tended to displace the traditional hero by making the author the hero or by splitting the hero into several characters. Some causes of this development were doubt about the worth of worldly achievement and an opposition between fame and conscience.

209 Burnley, J.D. *Chaucer's Language and the Philosophers' Tradition*. Woodbridge, Suffolk: D.S. Brewer; Totowa, New Jersey: Rowman & Littlefield, 1979.
Burnley studies collocations of terms in relation to two ethical traditions – rationalist classical philosophy and affective Christian values – explored here through the opposition between the tyrant and the philosopher. In the classical tradition, the tyrant is irrational and arbitrary, and the philosopher is tranquil and self-sufficient. In Middle English the former is associated with terms like *ire*, *wood*, *cruel*, *wraththe*; the latter with terms like *tranquillite*, *pees*, *quiete*, *reste*. Under Christian influence the philosopher became patient, the emphasis shifting from strength and determination to passivity and humility; the tyrant came to be criticized not so much for his irrationality as for his hardheartedness. Distinctions between the tyrant and the just ruler were often made by manipulating such terms, in Latin, as *crudelitas*, *severitas*, *clementia*, *pietas*, and *misericordia*, but these distinctions were imperfectly preserved in their Middle English equivalents. Theseus' forgiveness of Palamon and Arcite identifies him as an ideal philosopher king (eg, pp 26–7 and see Index). Theseus' recommendation of patience in his final speech is undercut by the

Tale's vision of a world ruled by arbitrary Olympians; but Chaucer's target is probably pagan philosophy rather than Theseus himself (p 79). *Gentilesse*, which shows an especially important linkage with *pitee* (pp 151–70), is often verified by tests for the capacity to feel intensely. Unlike Christian charity, these virtues are elitist and have no transcendent goal. Chaucer 'always approaches ... *gentilesse* in a spirit of enquiry rather than participation' (p 163).

210 Crow, Martin M. and Clair C. Olson, eds. *Chaucer Life-Records*. Oxford: Oxford University Press, 1966.
The records are organized topically and appear in their original Latin or French, accompanied by editorial commentary on the documents themselves and on the background of events. They include records of Chaucer's being ransomed by Edward III after his capture by the French in 1359–60 (pp 23–8); his journeys to Genoa and Florence in 1372–3 (pp 32–40) and to Lombardy in 1378 (pp 53–61); his deposition in the Scrope-Grosvenor case in 1386 (**201**) (pp 370–4); and his expenditures, as Clerk of the King's Works, for the tournament at Smithfield in 1390 (pp 472–3).

211 Herbert, Kevin. 'The Theseus Theme: Some Recent Versions.' *CJ* 55(1960), 175–85.
Herbert distinguishes Mary Renault's use of modern psychology and archeology in her historical novel *The King Must Die* (1958); Nikos Kazantzakis' emphasis on the existential need of man for self-knowledge and freedom in his tragedy *Thésée* (1953); Jack Lindsay's treatment of the desertion of Ariadne as representative of human betrayal and isolation in his long poem *Clue of Darkness* (1949); and André Gide's use of the events of Theseus' career to illuminate his own past in his novella *Thésée* (1946).

212 Justman, Stewart. 'Medieval Monism and Abuse of Authority in Chaucer.' *ChauR* 11(1976), 95–111.
Focusing on Paul, Jerome, and Boethius, Justman surveys the problems arising from a plurality of dissenting authorities and from a dilemma internal to authoritative texts, the need to compromise between unitary principle and plurality of cases. He briefly relates Theseus (pp 100, 106, 108) to the theme of abuse of authority in the *CT*.

213 Kane, George. *The Liberating Truth: The Concept of Integrity in Chaucer's Writings*. London: Athlone, 1980.
As he developed from court poet to moralist, Chaucer became concerned with 'the related issues of truth of report and truth of interpretation' (p 9). In the 1360's and 1370's *trouthe* was coming to express a 'moral and philosophical conception ... of integral per-

sonality as we today understand the term' (pp 9–10). After reviewing related terms and concepts in Aquinas and in Biblical texts, and after describing Chaucer's 'techniques of indirect moral representation' (pp 10–7), Kane identifies 'three features of Chaucer's situation': 1) 'the various concepts denoted by the word *trouthe* constitute for him an ideal of morality ... and its extremes of disappointment' (p 18); 2) he 'found it possible to realize the larger ideal of integrity through narrative action only in special settings' such as fairy tale; 3) 'in [his] representations of an actual world the ideal ... is generally realized in specific and limited forms of truth, as keeping the pledged word' (p 19). The Knight is one of the few to whom he attributes 'devotion to integrity, trouthe, in any large, unqualified sense,' and even Theseus has 'a past of *grete untrouthe* in love' (p 19).

214 Lovejoy, Arthur O. *The Great Chain of Being: A Study of the History of an Idea*. Cambridge, Mass.: Harvard University Press, 1936; rpt New York: Harper & Row, 1960.

An aspect of Plato's 'worldliness' was his belief, expressed in the *Timaeus*, in what Lovejoy christens 'the principle of plenitude' (p 52): that all possible kinds of material beings necessarily exist as the perfect expression of the Good. Joined to Aristotle's principles of continuity between kinds and hierarchical arrangement of all kinds in a single series, the principle of plenitude became the concept of 'the Great Chain of Being' (p 59; cf I.2988). In the medieval period (pp 67–98), the assimilation of this philosophy to Christian theology created various conflicts. The concept of the chain seemed to imply that God was constrained to create, and raised the question of whether God could have created better than he did – ie, eliminated evil. The concept also involved contradictory concepts of the Good: as a self-sufficient perfection toward which men ought to ascend and as an over-flowing perfection from which creation flows in a descending order. The first, expressing an attitude of *contemptus mundi*, was the more influential concept in the Middle Ages, but the second, implying a validation of this world, was kept alive by this 'fruitful inconsistency' (p 97).

215 Mathew, Gervase. 'Ideals of Friendship.' In *Patterns of Love and Courtesy*. Ed. John Lawlor. London: Edward Arnold, 1966. Pp 45–53.

A medieval ideal of romantic (but not homosexual) friendship among men united Ciceronian ideas, reshaped by the culture of the Germanic war-band, with scholastic definitions. From the twelfth century on, this same-sex ideal influenced the understanding of heterosexual relations as well, though the two were occasionally contrasted with each other as in the *KnT* (p 52).

215a McFarlane, K.B. *Lancastrian Kings and Lollard Knights*. Oxford: Clarendon, 1972.
The first part of this work approaches the history of Henry IV through his biography. McFarlane notes that Shakespeare's plays and traditional histories have obscured the way Henry 'was worshipped as the conventional hero of chivalry' in the 1390s (p 37). The second set of essays explores the careers (including the military service), wealth, and deaths of seven Lollard knights. McFarlane gives particular attention to John Clanvowe and William Neville (pp 197–206), and reviews Chaucer's acquaintance with this group.

216 Patch, Howard R. *The Goddess Fortuna in Mediaeval Literature*. Cambridge, Mass: Harvard University Press, 1927.
Patch briefly surveys the history of Fortune as a philosophical concept fron the Roman Empire through the Renaissance (pp 8–34). Dante, in *Inf* VII.67–96, reconciled Fortune most satisfactorily with the Christian deity, but Boethius' version had the greater influence. Patch also reviews the literary themes associated with Fortune (pp 35–84), her functions and cults (pp 88–122), and treatments of her dwelling (pp 123–46) and her wheel (pp 147–77). For the *KnT* see his information relevant to destiny (I.1663), p 31; 'aventure' (1465, 1490), p 39; the prison motif (1085 f), p 67; Fortune and astrology (1086–91, 1108–9, 2033–8, 2450–2) p 77; Fortune as playing dice with human beings (1238), p 81; Fortune as trapping humans like birds (1490), p 82; Fortune as giving aid and bestowing victory (915 f), p 113; Fortune as cause of death (925 f), p 119; and Fortune's wheel (925), p 155.

217 Pickering, F.P. 'Fortune.' *Literature and Art in the Middle Ages*. Coral Gables, Florida: University of Miami Press, 1970. Pp 168–222.
Augustine rejected the classical concept of Fortune in evolving a concept of history which could not accommodate purely secular experience. Boethius provided an alternative concept which endowed secular history with Christian significance by making Fortune subject to Divine Providence. The key text is Book II of the *Consol*, and specifically Philosophy's speech impersonating Fortune. Boethius created the hierarchical system – God, Providence, Fate, Fortune, man's Free Will – which became the underpinning for both medieval dynastic history and fictions of various sorts, including romance. Includes several illustrations with commentary.

218 Rickert, Edith, comp. *Chaucer's World*. Ed. Clair C. Olson and Martin M. Crow. Illustrations selected by Margaret Rickert. New York and London: Columbia University Press, 1948.
This collection of documents includes: four depositions (pp 147–50) from the Scrope-Grosvenor trial (**201**) of 1386; an account of the tournament at Smithfield in 1390 (pp 211–4); a description of the expedition against France in which Chaucer participated in 1359–60 (pp 294–7); and two accounts (pp 305–7) of the seige of Calais in 1347, one with Queen Philippa's appeal to Edward III for the lives of the burgesses, linked by some (**576**, **616**, **623**) to the women's appeal to Theseus in the grove.

219 Schlauch, Margaret. 'Chaucer's Doctrine of Kings and Tyrants.' *Spec* 20(1945), 133–56.
Schlauch reviews theories advanced in the twelfth and thirteenth centuries concerning the distinction between legitimate rulers and tyrants (pp 134–40); treats the reshaping of theory during the conflicts between papacy and empire (pp 140–5); and explores the application of theory to the problem of local tyrants by Italian humanists in the fourteenth century, especially in the period of Chaucer's trips to Italy (pp 145–50). Persistent themes in all these periods included: the subjection of the ruler to the law, the importance of the common good, legitimate forms of resistance, and the morality of tyrranicide. The relevant passages in Chaucer's works include I.1773–81 (Theseus' reflection on mercy), a passage that may have been elaborated in *LGW* (G.353–76), and I.941, 961, 1111, 2015 (all concerned with Creon's violence and arbitrariness) (pp 150–6). These passages show Chaucer's knowledge of political theory.

Studies of Sources

An important reference work for scholarship on Chaucer's sources is Lynn King Morris' *Chaucer Source and Analogue Criticism: A Cross-Referenced Guide* (New York: Garland, 1985). Its bibliography of 1477 items (pp 3–89) is indexed by Chaucer's works (*KnT*, pp 127–31), by author of the source or analogue (Boccaccio, pp 220–25; Statius, pp 320–1), by genre or origin of the source, and by title of the source or analogue (*Tes*, pp 560–1; *Theb*, pp 562; *Roman de Thèbes*, pp 543). For the *KnT* Morris includes some nineteenth-century items, and sifts the criticism for references to sources with a fineness that cannot be attempted in this volume.

The *Teseida*

Annual bibliographies of scholarship have appeared in *Studi sul Boccaccio* since 1938. See also the articles by Anna Laura Lepschy, 'Boccaccio Studies in English 1945–69,' *SBoc* 6(1972), 211–29, and 'Boccaccio Studies in English 1974–77,' *SBoc* 13(1979), 473–80; Enzo Esposito and Christopher Kleinhenz, *Boccacciana: Bibliografia delle edizione e degli scritti critici (1939-74)* (Ravenna: Longo, 1975, 1976); and Thomas Bergin, 'Italian Literature,' in *The Present State of Scholarship in Fourteenth-Century Literature*, ed. Thomas D. Cooke (Columbia: University of Missouri Press, 1982), pp 139–94. See also **74**, **227**, **230**. In a work that falls outside the chronological limits of this volume, David Anderson provides guidance through earlier and more recent Italian scholarship: *Before the Knight's Tale* (University of Pennsylvania Press, 1988).

EDITIONS AND TRANSLATIONS

220 *Teseida*. Ed. Salvatore Battaglia. Florence: 1938.
This first critical edition of the *Tes* is based on the autograph ms (**233**), supplemented by a study of twenty-eight other mss and some editions.

Boccaccio's *chiose* or glosses are printed beneath the text, with textual notes at the foot of the page. For discussion of this text, see **742**, pp 82–7.

221 *Giovanni Boccaccio*: *Teseida delle nozze d'Emilia*. Ed. A. Roncaglia. *Opere*. Bari: Scrittori d'Italia, 1941.
The text is based on Battaglia **220** and a new collation of the autograph ms (**233**). Additional glosses are provided and differences from Battaglia's text are noted at the foot of the page. Boccaccio's commentary is printed separately, pp 369–465.

222 *Teseida*. Ed. Alberto Limentani. In *Tutte le opere*. Volume 2. General editor, Vittore Branca. Verona: Mondadori, 1964.
The text of this standard edition (pp 245–664) includes Boccaccio's *chiose*, printed at the bottom of the page. Limentani provides an introduction (pp 231–44), textual notes (pp 873–85) and explanatory notes especially valuable for their comments on literary sources (pp 886–99).

223 *Filostrato*, *Teseida*, *Chiose al Teseida*. Ed. M. Marti. *Opere minori in volgari*. Volume 2. Milan: Rizzoli, 1970. Pp 251–657.
Explanatory notes, predominantly lexical, appear at the foot of the page; the *chiose* are printed separately, pp 663–765.

224 *The Book of Theseus*: *'Teseida delle Nozze d'Emilia' by Giovanni Boccaccio*. Trans. Bernadette Marie McCoy. New York: Medieval Text Association, 1974.
This first complete translation of the *Tes* into English is based on Limentani **222**. The prose is printed in numbered paragraphs corresponding to Boccaccio's stanzas. The text of each Book is followed by the text of Boccaccio's glosses, 'somewhat abridged' (p 47). For the 'Introduction' see **249**.

- Review by Anthony K. Cassell, *MLN* 91(1976), 164–7: The translation is marred by passages that reverse the meaning of the original or fail to convey that meaning in its entirety and by other flaws: 'it can only be employed with the greatest caution and circumspection' (p 167).

225 Havely, N.R., ed. and trans. *Chaucer's Boccaccio*: *Sources of Troilus and the Knight's and Franklin's Tales*. Woodbridge, Suffolk: D.S. Brewer; Totowa, New Jersey: Rowman & Littlefield, 1980.
Depending mainly on Limentani **222**, and diverging frequently from McCoy **224** (p 17), Havely prints English prose translations of passages from all twelve books of the *Tes* (without stanza numbers) and from the *chiose* (pp 103–52). The excerpts present passages that especially influenced Chaucer as well as others that illustrate the differences between the two poets (p 16). The Notes (pp 190–214)

deal with problems of interpretation and with historical and literary contexts; the introduction (pp 1–12) treats the social context of Boccaccio's work and the means by which Chaucer may have gained access to it.

BACKGROUNDS AND GENERAL STUDIES

226 Agostinelli, Edvige [Coleman]. 'A Catalogue of the Manuscripts of *Il Teseida*.' *SBoc* 15(1985–6), 1–83.
Describes sixty-three extant mss, and catalogues twenty-three unrecovered mss. For description of Boccaccio's autograph ms (cf **233**), see pp 17–9. The Appendices list, among other things, illustrations and drawings in the mss. The introduction notes the various titles of the *Tes* in the mss, and outlines further lines of inquiry, on the commentaries and on the owners of *Tes* mss. The catalogue will provide information for the forthcoming Chaucer Library edition. Based on the author's dissertation, 'A Descriptive Catalogue of the Manuscripts of Giovanni Boccaccio's *Il Teseida*.' New York University Dissertation, 1982. *DAI* 43(1983), 460A.

227 Bergin, Thomas. *Boccaccio*. New York: Viking, 1981.
A comprehensive and learned study, intended nevertheless for general as well as specialist readers. Bergin provides a chapter on the fourteenth-century background (pp 1–28) and another on Boccaccio's life (pp 29–65), followed by detailed, chapter-length studies of each of the works. Bibliography, pp 365–79. For *Tes*, see **237**.

228 Branca, Vittore. *Boccaccio: The Man and His Work*. Trans. Richard Monges. Co-trans. and ed. Dennis J. McAuliffe. New York: New York University Press, 1976.
This essential reference work combines material from several of Branca's works, including his revisionist *Boccaccio medievale* (1956; rev 1964, 1970) and *Giovanni Boccaccio: Profilo Biographico* (1964, in *Tutte le opere*; and separately, 1977). 'Boccaccio's Life' (pp 3–193) presents an overview that, among other things, stringently criticizes the romanticized biography derived from Boccaccio's fictions (pp 5–8). The 'Cultural and Artistic Milieu of Naples' (pp 28–40) is described, and the *Tes*, for which Boccaccio may have had a Byzantine source, is briefly discussed as a product of his Neapolitan period (pp 48–9). Book II (pp 197–331) presents Branca's original interpretation of the *Dec* as a medieval rather than proto-Renaissance work, the 'mercantile epic' of a new bourgeois public.

229 —, Paul F. Watson, and V. Kirkham. 'Boccaccio visualizzato.' *SBoc* 15(1985–6), 149–66.

Includes Branca's survey of illustrated mss of Boccaccio's works (pp 121–48), and Watson's survey of subjects from Boccaccio's works in Italian paintings, 1400–1550 (pp 149–66).

230 Hollander, Robert. *Boccaccio's Two Venuses*. New York: Columbia University Press, 1977.

Hollander's provocative thesis is that Boccaccio's minor works in Italian 'make an ironic attack upon the religion of love, an attack ... interspersed with praise of marital love' (p 3). Traditionally, eight early works, including the *Tes*, have been read as praises of fleshly love; the *Corbaccio* has been seen as a kind of retraction. Invoking the mythographical tradition of two Venuses (pp 158–60) and the concept of an ironical narrator, Hollander places Boccaccio on the side of Christian morality from the start; the *Corbaccio* only says explicitly what the others say implicitly. For example, in the *Filocolo*, the Venus associated with carnal love is superceded by the Venus of marital love when the hero insists on marrying Biancifiore before their physical union (pp 37–8). Hollander rejects the 'pseudo-fact' of a 'crisis' in which Boccaccio 'converted' in 1362 from a pagan Renaissance attitude toward love to a medieval Christian attitude, interpreting the famous exchange with Petrarch as being concerned with the value of humanistic literature such as Boccaccio's own Latin works (pp 121–3). Hollander's notes offer a review of Boccaccian scholarship.

231 Osgood, Charles G., ed. and trans. *Boccaccio on Poetry. Being the Preface and the 14th and 15th Books of Boccaccio's Genealogia deorum gentilium*. Princeton: Princeton University Press, 1930. Rpt Indianapolis: Liberal Arts Press; New York: Bobbs-Merrill, 1955.

In this work revised over a thirty-year period, Boccaccio defends poetry as a species of composition containing several kinds of truth protected from the vulgar by a veil of fiction; he defends the study of the great classical texts, the works of men who were moralists, philosophers, and even monotheists, though denied the benefits of Christian revelation. See, eg, his analysis of Vergil's story of Dido and Aeneas (*Aen* IX.13, pp 67–9 here). Osgood's introduction includes a brief discussion of the contents and method of the first thirteen books of the *Genealogia* (xvi–xxix). See **87**, **141**, **252**.

232 Serafini-Sauli, Judith Powers. *Giovanni Boccaccio*. Twayne's World Authors Series. Boston: Twayne, 1982.

This introduction to Boccaccio presents very brief discussions of the historical and social background and treats the works in chronological order. The *Tes* (pp 35–9) 'could be interpreted as an allegory of the movement of the soul from concupiscence and discord to honest love (marriage) and peace' (p 38).

233 Vandelli, G. 'Un autografo della "Teseida".' *Studi di filiologia italiana* 2(1929), 5–76.
Vandelli discovered this manuscript, Biblioteca Laurenziana (Florence), Doni e Acquisti, 325, the basis of all modern editions. Among other things, it gives the title of the work as 'Il Teseida di nozze d'Emilia,' and contains the *chiose*, modelled, Vandelli proposes, on Lactantius' glosses to the *Theb*. According to Hollander **230**, 'the modern history of the *chiose* begins' with this autograph which 'proved conclusively that the laborious allegorizer was none other than Boccaccio himself' (p 184, n 128).

234 Wallace, David. *Chaucer and the Early Writings of Boccaccio*. Woodbridge, Suffolk: D.S. Brewer, 1985.
Emphasizing the importance of studying Chaucer's sources in their own historical contexts, Wallace notes that the Boccaccian works to which Chaucer is most heavily indebted, including the *Tes*, belong to the Italian poet's Neopolitan, rather than Florentine, phase. Wallace provides a comparison of Naples and London with respect to the mixtures of French, Latin, and vernacular elements in their literary traditions, and of mercantile and courtly elements in their wider cultures; he contrasts Chaucer as a courtly insider with Boccaccio as an outsider (pp 23–38). In the *Filocolo* (Book IV), compared here to Chaucer's *TC*, Boccaccio shows an interest in pagans who approach the threshold of Christian truth (pp 61–72). In the *Filos* Boccaccio's narrative has a relation to the popular *cantare* like that of some of Chaucer's narratives to the popular Middle English romances (pp 73–105). Close study of *TC* in relation to source passages in the *Filos* indicates Chaucer's command of Italian (pp 106–40). In brief remarks on the *Tes* (pp 141–3), Wallace contrasts the 'rude vigour' and 'sunny disposition' of the *Tes* with the 'gravity of movement' and 'gloomy inevitability' of the *KnT*.

- Review by B.A. Windeatt, *SAC* 8(1986), 255–7: Wallace's work, the 'long overdue replacement' of Cummings' book (**541**), should settle the question of Chaucer's command of Italian. An examination of the *Tes* combining Wallace's methods of 'large-scale analysis' and 'close-focus study' would be valuable.

235 Wright, Herbert G. *Boccaccio in England from Chaucer to Tennyson*. London: Athlone, 1957.
Wright details England's acquaintance with Boccaccio's works, with frequent comments on the continental situation. Boccaccio was first appreciated as the learned author of Latin works; the Italian verse

narratives were little known. The *Dec* became known slowly and by stages until, by the latter half of the nineteenth century, Boccaccio's reputation rested almost solely on it. For notes on the eighteenth-century English discovery of Boccaccio as the author of the *Tes* and on familiarity with the *Tes* itself, see pp 57–8. For *KnT* see **790**.

CRITICISM

236 Anderson, David. 'The Legendary History of Thebes in Boccaccio's *Teseida* and Chaucer's *Knight's Tale*.' Princeton University Dissertation, 1980. See also *DAI* 40(1980), 4885A.
'... Epic and History in the *Teseida*' (pp 116–95): Boccaccio's borrowings from the *Theb* constitute a 'program of analogies' centering on Eteocles and Polinices, Palamon and Arcite (p 131). *Tes* V.13.7–8, 'signoria / nè amore stan bene con compagnia,' is a reworking of *Theb* I.129–30: 'summo dulcius unum / stare loco, sociisque comes discordia regnis.' Polinices and Eteocles contend for 'signoria,' Palamon and Arcite, for 'amore' (p 151). 'Boccaccio did not "fail" to write a classical epic because he was too "attracted" by medieval romance nor did he parody an epic; he used romance narrative motifs to reinterpret an epic' (p 151). An example of Boccaccio's Christian reinterpretation of Statius is his implication that the real cause of the princes' miseries is not Juno but Fortune, to which they become subject through their own irrational desires. Other departures from Statius, such as giving Teseo a role in controlling violent passion throughout the story, reveal a typological habit of thought: as Thebes is a type of the earthly city, so Athens is a type of the heavenly city and Teseo, of its king, Christ. See **261** and **905**.

237 Bergin, Thomas G. 'The Teseida of the Nuptials of Emilia.' *Boccaccio*. 1981. See **227**. Pp 112–29.
Boccaccio intended to do what Dante, in his *De Vulgari Eloquentia* (Book 2, Ch 2), said had never been done: to write on the theme of arms in Italian. The *Tes* (summarized in pp 112–7) is 'no true epic' (pp 118–9), however, but like all Boccaccio's works, centers on women. It contains classical elements, notably its allegory and mythological glosses (pp 120–2), but even the warlike Theseus has, after Book II, only 'a kind of presidential role' (p 122). The moral and psychological allegory signals Boccaccio's 'topographical-conceptual shift from Neopolitan romance to Tuscan intellectualism' (p 123). The work's chief weakness is 'pallid' characterization. Palemone's puzzling triumph over the nobler Arcita suggests an elevation of sexual passion over all other values (p 124). Emilia's

'finest hour' is her appearance in the garden, for she is 'meant rather to be contemplated than enjoyed' (p 125). Though possibly a sign, with her Tuscan name, of Boccaccio's new intellectualism, she is more convincingly an example of a pictorialism that anticipates the Renaissance (pp 127–8).

238 Boitani, Piero. 'An Essay on Bocaccio's *Teseida*.' *Chaucer and Boccaccio*. Medium Aevum Monographs, New Series, 8. Oxford: Society for the Study of Mediaeval Languages and Literature, 1977. Pp 1–60.

The *Tes* contains two 'knots' of contradictory purposes: the first – Fiammetta-Mars-Venus-Cupid – concerns the tension between love and war as subject matter; the second – Mars-Venus-Fate-Fortune – reflects the inconsistent treatment of causality, with events referred variously to the gods as actors or as allegorical representations of human appetites, and to classical Fate or medieval Fortune (pp 6–32). Boccaccio's layering of the courtly and the epic, of allegory and decoration, of classical erudition and bourgeois wit, constitutes a failed attempt to achieve the polysemous narrative characteristic of the *Div Com* (pp 31–2). Boccaccio borrows from the *Theb*, the *Stilnovisti*, the *Div Com*, Ovid, the *cantari*, and, possibly, the Byzantine romance *Digenis Akritas* (pp 41–5; see pp 61–71, for a table). The *Tes* is flawed by superfluousness, as in the descriptions of the temples; by the violation of suspense in the glosses to VII.91 and IX.5, where the deal between Mars and Venus is explained and its outcome anticipated; and by Boccaccio's failure to emphasize the cruel joke on which the plot turns: that peace-seeking Arcite prays to Mars and takes literally Theseus's words that the winner of the tournament will have Emily (p 47). Arcite is not a 'Mars-hero' nor Palamon a 'Venus-hero,' and the 'tragic irony' of their prayers provides the 'central knot of the characterization' (p 47). Emily is the 'feminine counterpart' of gentle Arcite and 'the most fascinating' of the characters, combining elements of the *Stilnovo* tradition with Boccaccio's psychological study of adolescence on the threshhold of womanhood (pp 49–51). Theseus is a 'synthesis of different elements' (p 51): the great general, the lover, the 'pius Aeneas,' the good bourgeois; he is 'the protagonist behind the curtains: his will becomes event' (p 52). An appendix (pp 198–210) prints the glosses on Mars and Venus. For Chaucer's ms of the *Tes*, and for *KnT*, see **922**.

239 Branca, Daniela. 'La Morte di Tristano e la morte di Arcita.' *SBoc* 4(1967), 255–64.

Tristan's speech to Isolde just before he dies, in the *Roman de Tristan*, is recognizable as Arcita's speech while embracing Emilia;

and Arcita's acceptance of death parallels Tristan's farewell to knighthood. The armed conflict of Arcita and Palemone, as the only path between their estranging loves and their eventual reconciliation, supports the theme that links Arcita and Tristan: that love renders death welcome and beautiful.

240 Branca, Vittore. 'Il Boccaccio del *Filostrato* e del *Teseida* e la tradizione canterina.' *Il cantare trecentesco e il Boccaccio del Filostrato e del Teseida*. Florence: 1938. Pp 51–93.
The standard study of Boccaccio's attempt to wed classical to vernacular tradition by introducing into his epic elements of the *cantari*, popular narratives in *ottava rima*. They give his work a sometimes bourgeois tone and account for such stylistic features as the author's addresses to the audience and formulaic phrases. See **234** and **238**, pp 40–41.

241 Branch, Eren Hostetter. 'Man Alone and Man in Society: Chaucer's *Knight's Tale* and Boccaccio's *Teseida*.' Stanford University PhD Dissertation, 1974. See also *DAI* 35(1974), 7861A.
In the typically proto-Renaissance *Tes*, society, conceived as the sum of human relationships, seems omnicompetent to deal with human problems; no threat of chaos lurks beneath its surface. The characters are psychologically plausible and consistent, and events flow from their intentions as effects from causes. The values are classical: duty, courage, initiative, proud rebellion against fortune, personal fame and glory, friendship. Boccaccio maintains a distance between the Christian and the classical, and develops the ancient setting in a centrifugal fashion: for its own sake and not in relation to his plot. For *KnT* see **923**.

242 — 'Rhetorical Structures and Strategies in Boccaccio's *Teseida*.' In *The Craft of Fiction: Essays in Medieval Poetics*. Ed. Leigh A. Arrathoon. Rochester, Michigan: Solaris, 1984. Pp 143–60.
The two-sided argument, the argument *in utramque partem*, with its variations in the pseudo-legal *controversia*, the poetic debate, and the *quistione d'amore*, is a structural pattern, a motif, and a theme of the *Tes* (p 145). For example, in Book V Palemone and Arcita debate their claims to Emilia; because neither has a chance of attaining her, the dispute is also a *quistione d'amore*. It is succeeded by a *controversia*, as Teseo applies the law to the princes; when he spares both, the contest over Emilia reaches an impasse since both men are equally worthy (pp 146–9). The woodland is a *locus amoenus*, providing a sequestered setting for considering hypothetical questions (pp 149–51). Its peacefulness contrasts with the violence of both Theban history and the princes' dispute (p 151). The murals on Arcita's

monument, which omit his fatal accident, show that rhetoric is both valuable and ineffectual (p 152). Thus Teseo cannot persuade Palemone and Emilia to marry and must order them to do so, and Palemone, the less articulate prince, wins the lady (p 153). Dante evaluates rhetoric within an eschatological perspective; Boccaccio evaluates it within a wordly one. The *Tes* is itself a *locus amoenus* where, free from the Christian perspective, the sufficiency of classical values can be explored (pp 155–6).

243 Ginsberg, Warren. 'Boccaccio's Characters and the Rhetorical "Disputatio in utramque partem".' *The Cast of Character: The Representation of Personality in Ancient and Medieval Literature.* Toronto: University of Toronto Press, 1983. Pp 98–133.
'The arguing of an issue from both sides,' common in ancient rhetoric, became a source for characterization in the Middle Ages. In rhetoric it was directed toward 'the discovery of [the] probable truth' (p 99), and in Boccaccio's works, it supports a world in which 'all phenomena ... have an equal right to be heard' (p 101). Palemone and Arcita are two aspects of Boccaccio's fictional self, the lover and the poet of war. Boccaccio bridges the gap between love and war in several ways: eg, the princes' imprisonment as a consequence of war enforces the idleness that is a necessary preparation for love (pp 110–11); Venus then yields to Mars when the princes become estranged (p 112). The plot gives equal attention to the virtues and divisive potentialities of the two gods. Palemone and Arcita represent the concupiscible and irascible appetites, yet these are not wholly discrete states of being but related powers of the sensitive soul and subject to reason. The *Tes*, *pace* Hollander **244**, presents but does not judge the acts of both appetites, which are also joined in the figure of the narrator. Palemone and Arcite are part of an exposition: they 'provide the reader with the necessary arguments to arrive sufficiently close to the verisimilar, to the probable truth' (p 117).

244 Hollander, Robert. 'The Validity of Boccaccio's Self-Exegesis in His *Teseida*.' *M&H*, ns 8(1977), 163–83.
Of the 1250 or so *chiose*, about 1000 are philological; about 225 concern myth, geography, and custom, for which Boccaccio's source may have been Paolo da Perugia's lost *Liber collectionum*. There are no certain borrowings from Lactantius' glosses to the *Theb* (**269**) (pp 164–8). The *chiose* are keys to the meaning of the *Tes*. 'The exact numerical center of the work' is the thirtieth *ottave* of Book VII, itself the longest book and 'center of significance for the work'; the first of two *chiose* on Mars and Venus depends from that *ottave* (p 169). The 'negative valence' of Mars (p 170) is clear from the first in

text and gloss, while Venus' temple appears at first to be an attractive opposite. But negative details are gradually introduced and Boccaccio's gloss on Mars prepares for the association of Venus with the concupiscible appetite. The gloss on Venus associates corrupt choice with carnal Venus, and rational choice with celestial Venus (pp 171–2). Boccaccio's Christian perspective matches the Aristotelian rejection of carnality in a commentary on Cavalcanti's *Donna mi prega* (pp 172–3). Any expectation that Venus will triumph over Mars is defeated by the opposition of Mars and Venus to Diana, whose temple is 'the *locus* of a better prayer' by Emilia (p 173). The description of Venus' temple in Book XII presents the second, 'good' Venus who presides over the marriage. Arcite 'dies for his lust' and Palamon 'finds a better and matrimonial frame for his' (p 174). See **243, 250.**

245 Kahane, H. and R. 'Akritas and Arcita: A Byzantine Source of Boccaccio's *Teseida*.' *Spec* 20(1945), 415–25.
These parallels are evidence of Boccaccio's probable indebtedness to the medieval Greek epic *Digenis Akritas*: 'the name of the hero; the death of the hero; the Amazon motif; the previous betrothal of the heroine; the encouragement by the heroine during the decisive battle; the scene of the physician; the advice, given by the dying hero to the heroine, to marry again after his death; the tomb' (p 424).

246 Kirkham, V. '"Chiuso parlare" in Boccaccio's *Teseida*.' In *Studies in the Italian Trecento in Honor of Charles S. Singleton*. Ed. Aldo S. Bernardo and Anthony Pellegrini. Binghamton, New York: Center for Medieval & Early Renaissance Studies, State University of New York at Binghamton, 1983. Pp 305–51.
Kirkham uses numerological analysis to reconcile Boccaccio's accurate but incomplete description of the *Tes* as a work about love and arms centering on Palamon and Arcite with the 'more penetrating' perspective which Boccaccio gives to Fiammetta and which is suggested by her title, 'Teseida di nozze d'Emilia.' 'Venus (3) and Mars (5), coupled in the seventh book (VII.30 and VII.50), are emblematic of the marriage celebrated in the poem's numerological plan (5x3=15)' (p 341). The number seven identifies the central and longest book and is associated with the planets and with Teseo and Emilia, sources of moral enlightenment to whom Palemone and Arcita, as representatives of lust and wrath, stand 'in a secondary and antagonistic relationship' (p 341).

247 Librandi, Rita. 'Corte e cavelleria della Napoli angioina nel *Teseida* del Boccaccio.' *Medioevo Romanzo* 4(1977), 53–72.

Boccaccio transforms epic materials in a way that bears the stamp of the Angevin court at Naples and of the romance literature popular in it. Teseo is a medieval monarch and administrator of justice, and Palemon and Arcita, typical medieval barons with the virtues, concerns, and diversions of the Neopolitan aristocracy. The epitome of Boccaccio's approach is the tournament, which, with its elaborately described setting, feminine presence, and sumptuous choreography, reflects both romance literature and the Angevin court (pp 55–63). Robert of Naples staged tournaments as a way of capturing the loyalty of the baronage; he appears to have participated personally and to have tried to mitigate the violence of these events. Thus he is a likely model for Boccaccio's Teseo (pp 64–6). Petrarch, witness to a later period of decline in the Angevin court, condemns tournaments in his *Familiari* (V.3), but speaks approvingly (V.4) of a contemporary 'Amazon,' Maria of Pozzuoli, whose military exploits were probably known to Boccaccio as well. Boccaccio, by contrast, condemns the Amazons of his romance and requires Ippolita to adopt a feminine role centered on beauty and charm (pp 66–72).

248 Limentani, Alberto. 'Boccaccio "traduttore" di Stazio.' *La Rassegna* 8(1960), 231–42.
Limentani briefly surveys the evidence for Statius' influence on Boccaccio's early works, especially the *Filocolo* (pp 231–3). In the *Tes* Boccacio's 'translation' of the *Theb* is marked by greater development of the dramatic potential of scenes and by the underlining and intensifying of emotion. To these ends Boccaccio modified the language and metrics of Statius, and generally attempted to combine classical and *stilnovistic* elements of style (pp 234–7), as seen, for example, in his treatment of the appeal of the Theban women to Theseus (*Theb* XII. 540–6 and *Tes* II.25–8). Boccaccio's most extensive borrowing occurs in *Tes* XI.4–70, indebted to *Theb* VI.26–248, where Boccaccio adapts the mourning over Archemoro to the grief for Arcita (pp 237–40). The *Tes* represents an important stage in Boccaccio's progress from the *Filocolo* to the *Fiammetta* and beyond. The *Tes* is the climactic exercise in the classical study of an extraordinary autodidact. It also represents Boccaccio's effort to revive a passing world of refined feudal aristocracy and unite it with an incipient humanism, but his own ambivalent attitudes prevented his success.

249 McCoy, Bernadette Marie. 'Introduction.' *The Book of Theseus*. 1974. See **224**.
The gods and the human passions they represent are central to the meaning of the *Tes*. The 'good' Venus triumphs in Palamon's success,

but both her triumph and Mars' are shown to be ephermeral. Theseus is 'the perfect hero, the well-ordered knight' (p 10) who pays tribute to Mars but obeys reason (p 14). Arcite, like Theseus, is a client of Mars and 'consistently magnanimous' while Palamon is 'rash and petulant' (p 15). Arcite's funeral is a monument to the knightly ideal and a token of Theseus' affection. Neither prince shows Theseus' pragmatism, as seen in his tactics against Hippolyta and in his urging the marriage of Palamon and Emilia. Palamon seems 'strangely deflated in his new domestic role' and Arcite is quickly forgotten; thus the *Tes* is 'a kind of morality play' in which men are defeated by their own passions and the gods (p 16). As a Boethian work, the *Tes* emphasizes self-mastery more than glorious deeds; still the moralistic elements are subordinated to the story-telling (p 17).

250 McGregor, James H. 'Boccaccio's Athenian Theater: Form and Function of an Ancient Monument in *Teseida*.' *MLN* 99(1984), 1–42.

Boccaccio's treatment of the theater, like his psychology of character as described by Velli **254**, is part of his pioneering classicism (pp 1–13). Theaters did not exist in Boccaccio's Europe, and in a gloss (*Tes* II.20.2), he defines a theater as 'a place to see from' (pp 14–8; cf pp 9–10). His physical models were the Colosseum and the Circus Maximus, but his literary model may have been the rose of Dante's *Par* 20, itself a symbol of the earthly Rome (pp 19–20). Specific features – eg, roundness, circumference, height (*Tes* VII.108, 109) – are also indebted to literary descriptions of Roman monuments (pp 21–6). Its unrealistic number of seats reflects the hyperbolic treatment of Rome as a wonder of the world in the romances (pp 26–9). The classicism of his theater has not been appreciated because he uses it as a setting for a medieval joust, but the conflict between Arcita and Palemone may also be modelled on a gladiatorial combat in Livy's *Ab Urbe Condita* 28, 21 (pp 29–33). While the gods do have allegorical (Hollander **244**) and astrological (Smarr **253**) significances, they also have historical significance in relation to the theater and its games (pp 34–40). Boccaccio follows Christian polemicists in seeing the gods as demons; joined with the appetites of the combatants, they defeat Theseus' justice. 'The theater which begins as an image of Athenian grandeur finally serves as an ironic representation of Theseus' impotence' (p 41). The *Tes* comments on the failure of paganism and corrects the *Theb* by ending in 'not a triumph but a consolation' (p 41).

251 Sells, A. Lytton. 'Boccaccio, Chaucer and Stendhal.' *Rivista di letterature moderne* (1947), 237–48.

The *Tes* is a probable source for Stendhal's *Chartreuse de Parme* [1839]. Stendhal's *Tour Farnèse* as the place of Fabrice's imprisonment, a revision of Boccaccio's palace apartment, parallels Chaucer's introduction of a dungeon into the *KnT*.

252 Smarr, Janet L. 'The Teseida, Boccaccio's Allegorical Epic.' *Northeast Modern Language Association Italian Studies* 1(1977), 29–35.
The *Tes* is a moral allegory in which Books I and II form a chiasmus with Books XI and XII, all four focused on social order, specifically the violation and proper observance of marriage rites. Psychic order is studied through the princes; in his *Genealogia* (**231**, XIII.1), Boccaccio glosses the lion (Arcita) as *ira* and the boar (Palemon) as *concupiscentia*. The fury is a representative of Arcita's own *ira*; the princes in the prison represent the passions within the human body. Teseo, as representative of wisdom, and Fortune, as representative of Providence, restore order. Boccaccio the narrator does not read his poem this way, but Fiammetta supplies a corrective by centering her title for the work on Teseo and marriage.

253 — 'Boccaccio and the Stars: Astrology in the Teseida.' *Traditio* 35(1979), 303–32.
Boccaccio connects the two Venuses – the goddesses of illegitimate love and married love – with the astral influences of Mars and Jupiter, respectively (pp 306–17). The baneful influence of Mars is seen, eg, in the net imagery and in the furies' role in Arcita's death. By contrast, the major astrological stanza of the poem, 3.5, associates Venus with the benign Jupiter, a horoscope realized in the marriage of Palemon and Emilia and echoed in Palemon's prayer (12.34–6). This outcome is effected by Teseo, an astrological child of Jupiter. Boccaccio uses astrological settings to reinforce the thematic meanings of narrative events (pp 317–22). Eg, at the eighth hour after sunrise on the day of the tournament, Libra is ascending, one of the houses of Venus, portending the eventual triumph of Venus' protege, Palemon. The astrological passages do not define a historical year or years in the fourteenth century (pp 322–7), but one can align the twelve Books of the poem with the signs of the zodiac, beginning with Pisces and ending with Aquarius (pp 327–32): eg, the tournament occurs in Book 6 under Leo, the sign of valiant knights. Boccaccio linked astrology to the theme of reason and the passions, and has his Teseo identify the fate dictated by the stars with divine providence. See McGregor **250**.

254 Velli, Giuseppe. 'L'apoteosi di Arcita: ideologia e coscienza storica nel "Teseida".' *Studi e problemi di critica textuale* 5(1972), 33–66.

The first three ottave of Book XI of the *Tes*, describing Arcita's ascent into the heavens, are indebted primarily to Lucan and secondarily to Statius, Valerio Massimo, and Virgil. The borrowings from Lucan are melded with materials from Books I to III of the *Consol* to produce a note of *contemptus mundi*. This melding of classicizing and 'medievalizing' elements (cf Lewis **79**) is suggestive of the ambiguity that typifies the character of Arcita and of the *Tes* as a whole. While Chaucer's *KnT* expresses faith in divine order despite human blindness, Boccaccio seems uncertain of any Providence transcending Fate, and emphasizes instead altruistic human interactions. Boccaccio makes a serious attempt, through his classical literary borrowings, to reconstruct, psychologically and morally, the outlook of the ancient world, yet Arcita's heavenly reward is ultimately justified neither by classical nor Christian values but by courtly-chivalric ones. Paradoxically, the kind of historical consciousness that inspired Boccaccio's classical reconstruction can never wholly escape the limits of the contemporary experience that gives it birth. Chaucer, wholly lacking in historical consciousness, squandered the archaeological quality of the *Tes*. See **250**.

255 Wilson, H.S. '*The Knight's Tale* and the *Teseida* Again.' *UTQ* 18(1948), 131–46.
Although Arcita elicits more sympathy than Palemone, neither knight is clearly superior to the other or more guilty of disloyalty. Rather Boccaccio shows that love is not subject to justice or friendship, and that Fortune rules lovers without regard to merit (p 137). Inspired by Dante, Boccaccio was reaching toward a philosophical approach to love which would embrace Palemone's experience of earthly bliss and Arcita's attainment to heavenly bliss (p 137). The equality of the two knights, Emilia's inability to choose between them, and the nobility of all three are essential to a plot in which the ennoblement of human passion results from its conflict with fate. 'The ironic reversals which all three characters experience bring out the best that is in them. The pathos of the death of Arcita is not more significant than the reconciliation of all three lovers before his death, and the discipline in sorrow and humility of Palemone and Emilia that precedes their final union ... the climax transcends the measure of a simple love story and approaches the plane of philosophical generalization' (p 139). For *KnT* see **787**.

The *Thebaid*

For further bibliographical guidance, readers are referred to the bibliography in Frederick M. Ahl's 'Statius' "Thebaid": A Reconsideration' in *Aufstieg und Niedergang der Römischen Welt*: *Sprache und Literatur*, Band 32.5 (Berlin and New York: Walter de Gruyter, 1986), 2803–2912.

EDITIONS AND TRANSLATIONS

256 *Thebais et Achilleis*. Ed. H.W. Garrod. Oxford: Clarendon Press, 1906; rpt through 1965.
Presents the Latin text with textual notes at the foot of the page; brief preface in Latin. See **266**.

257 *Thebaid*. In *Statius*. Ed. and trans. J.H. Mozley. 2 volumes. Loeb Classical Library. Cambridge, Mass. and London: 1928; rpt through 1967.
The Latin verse and the English prose translation are on facing pages, with brief explanatory notes at the foot of the page. See **282**.

258 *Thebaid*. Trans. J.B. Poyton. 3 volumes. Oxford: Shakespeare Head Press, 1971, 1975.
A highly regarded English verse translation.

259 *Thebais*. Ed. Alfred Klotz. Corrections by Thomas C. Klinnert. Leipzig: B.G. Teubner, 1973.
An edition of the Latin text with explanatory and textual notes at the foot of the page; apparatus in Latin; index of names. An appendix prints Latin arguments for the twelve books. See **270**.

260 *Thebaidos*: *Libri XII*. Ed. D.E. Hill. *Mnemosyne*, Supplement 79. Leyden: E.J. Brill, 1983.
An edition of the Latin text with notes, mostly textual, at the foot of the page; apparatus in Latin; index of names.

BACKGROUNDS AND GENERAL STUDIES

261 Anderson, David. 'The Legendary History of Thebes in Boccaccio's *Teseida* and Chaucer's *Knight's Tale*.' 1980. See **236**.
'The Theban Kingdom in Medieval Historical Writing' (pp 28–115): In universal chronicles Thebes was seen as one of a series of idolatrous empires. Late medieval interpreters of ancient history brought Thebes within Augustine's scheme of sacred history as a type of the earthly city. The city's chief features were a history of misfortune due to divine vengeance, a pattern of fraternal strife, and

a reputation for adultery and incest. Literary treatments were typically read as history, as seen in the incorporations of the *RTh* into historical works and in statements about the *Theb* in medieval commentaries and *accessus*; the gods were seen as fictional, however. For *KnT* see **905**.

262 Clogan, Paul Maurice. 'Chaucer and the Medieval Statius.' PhD dissertation, University of Illinois, 1961. Director: Robert A. Pratt. See also *DAI* 22(1961), 3641.
Section I evaluates Statius' reputation and influence in the Middle Ages through study of the extant mss of the *Theb* and the *Achilleid*, of the evidence provided by medieval library catalogues, and of the *Nachleben* of Statius in medieval literature. For *KnT* see **811**.

263 — 'An Argument of Book I of Statius' *Thebaid*.' *Manuscripta* 7(1963), 30–1.
MS. Ii. III. 13 of Cambridge University Library contains a twelve-line metrical argument, possibly the lost argument referred to by Lactantius in his commentary to I.61. Cf **272**.

264 — 'Chaucer and the *Thebaid* Scholia.' *SP* 61(1964), 599–615.
Chaucer probably knew the *Theb* in a glossed manuscript. Fourteen of eighteen late medieval mss are heavily glossed, and five of these preserve the commentary of Lactantius. Jahnke's edition **269** omits variant and additional glosses from Chaucer's period. Probable borrowings from extant glosses are to be found in *Anel*, *HF*, *TC*, and *KnT* (see **812**).

265 — 'Medieval Glossed Manuscripts of the *Thebaid*.' *Manuscripta* 11(1967), 102–12.
Brief descriptions of mss containing annotations, scholia, and glosses.

266 Deferrari, R.J., and M.C. Eagan. *A Concordance to the Works of Statius*. 1943.
Based on Garrod's edition (**256**). See **270**.

267 Duff, J. Wright, and A.M. Duff. *A Literary History of Rome in the Silver Age*. 3rd ed. London: Benn; New York: Barnes & Noble, 1964.
The authors praise the 'strikingly human note' (p 6) sometimes found in the literature of this period (14–138 AD), and discuss imperial patronage and censorship; the influence of declamation and the study of poetry, especially Virgil; Stoicism; and the interest in encyclopedic learning (pp 3–19). They review Statius' life and provide a book-by-book summary of the *Theb*, commenting on its slow pace and digressiveness, vigor in narrative and speech, and debts to Virgil (pp 373–96).

268 Helm. R. *Fabii Planciadis Fulgentii opera*. Leipzig: Tübner, 1898. Pp 180–6.

Helm presents the Latin text of a brief commentary, *Super Thebaidem*, possibly composed by the sixth-century mythographer (but see **274**). It moralizes Thebes as the soul, Etiocles and Polynices as greed and lust, and Theseus as God. For an English version see Leslie George Whitbread, trans., *Fulgentius the Mythographer* (Ohio State University Press, 1971), pp 235–44. See **273**.

269 Jahnke, Richard, ed. *Lactantii Placidi Commentarios in Statii Thebaida et Commentarium in Achilleida*. Leipzig: Teubner, 1898.
Prints the glosses to the *Theb* supplied by Lactantius Placidus in the fifth or sixth century (pp 1–484). Apparatus in Latin. A definitive modern edition is still awaited; see **264**, **275**.

270 Klecka, Joseph. *Concordantia in Publium Papinium Statium*. Hildesheim, Zürich, New York: Georg Olms, 1983.
Based on Klotz' edition of the *Theb* (**259**).

271 MacKay, L. 'Statius in Purgatory.' *Classical Miscellany* 26(1965), 293–305.
Dante described Statius' conversion to Christianity as a secret partly because it was his own invention. Dante was not inspired by Statius' likeness to Virgil – the *Theb* is more like the *Iliad* than the *Aen* – but by the fact that the *Theb* is 'a poem of love ... often violated, but ... ultimately triumphant' (p 298). Dante's Statius does not mistranslate the Virgilian line *quid non mortalia pectora cogis / auri sacra fames* [*Aen* III.56–7], but interpreted it allegorically, suggesting that Statius represented for Dante poetic intuition which, along with human reason and divine revelation, is a path to truth.

272 Magoun, Francis P., Jr. 'Chaucer's Summary of Statius' Thebaid II–XII.' *Traditio* 11(1955), 409–20.
Magoun prints twelve Latin hexameters outlining the twelve books of the *Theb* and a set of twelve-line Latin arguments to Books II–XII of the *Theb*, all with English translations. [For Book I, see **263**]. Magoun regards these texts as sources for Cassandra's speech in *TC* V.1457–1533, with which he compares them in detail. The twelve Latin hexameters appear between stanzas 214 and 215 in sixteen mss of *TC*.

273 Padoan, Giorgio. 'Teseo "Figura Redemptoris" e il cristianesimo di Stazio.' *Lettere Italiane* 11(1959), 432–57. Rpt in *Il pio Enea, l'empio Ulisse: Tradizione classica e intendimento medievale in Dante*. Ravenna: Longo Editore, 1980. Pp 125–50.
The Christianity attributed to Statius in *Purg* 21–5 may not be Dante's invention but the product of a scholarly tradition in which Dante believed. Commentaries in the *Theb* link Statius' Altar of Clemency with Paul's altar of the Unknown God [in *Acts of the*

Apostles 17.22–34]. Other classical poets, including Ovid, were also believed to be Christians, as seen in the accessus and in a commentary for the *Met*; and Statius specifically was said to be a Christian by Dante's contemporary, Giovanni Colonna. The *Theb* was also sometimes read allegorically, as in Fulgentius' interpretation of Theseus' liberation of Thebes as the freeing of the human soul from sin by the coming of divine goodness (pp 134–6) [cf **268**, **274**]. In the twelfth and thirteenth centuries, figural interpretations identified Theseus, Hercules, and other classical figures with Christ, and an early commentator on the *Div Com* treated Dante's own Theseus (*Inf* IX.54), not inappropriately, as a Christ figure. In his *Convivio* Dante showed his familiarity with allegorical interpretations of other classical works – the *Aen*, the *Met*, and Lucan's *Pharsalia* – and with the kind of figural interpretation so central to the characterization of Beatrice (*Purg* XXX). Far from inventing Statius' conversion, Dante probably had no intention of altering a story that was then generally accepted.

274 Stock, Brian. 'A Note on Thebaid Commentaries: Paris B.N. lat. 3012.' *Traditio* 27(1971), 468–71.
A commentary sometimes attributed to the sixth-century mythographer Fulgentius (**268**) probably dates from c. 1120–80 and shows the influence of the School of Chartres.

275 Sweeney, Robert Dale. *Prolegomena to An Edition of the Scholia to the Works of Statius. Mnemosyne*, Supplement 8. Leyden, 1969.
Sweeney describes the extant mss of Lactantius' commentary on the *Theb*, including a manuscript owned by Boccaccio, with some folios in his hand (p 12–3). The faults of Jahnke's edition (**269**) are identified (pp 5–6), and the history of Lactantius' commentary is summarized (pp 84–5).

CRITICISM

276 Ahl, Frederick M. 'Lucan and Statius.' In *Ancient Writers. Greece and Rome II. Lucretius to Ammianus Marcellinus*. Ed. J. Luce. New York: 1982. Pp 914–41.
The *Theb* (pp 926–39) is a mythic treatment of contemporary political realities in which Statius' choice of Oedipus as a starting point suggests a history of human conflict reaching down to the present of Domitian's rule (pp 926–9). Oedipus rejects reason and allies himself with evil, but Jupiter's plan to punish Thebes is no more just (pp 929–31). Adrastus' naiveté about men and gods only advances the tragedy (pp 931–2), and the episode of Hypsipyle (pp

932–4) illustrates the destruction of innocent bystanders in the mad rivalries of the powerful. Statius does not allow any virtuous character to stand free of the entanglements of evil; this status is reserved for ideals like clemency, which is not equated with any god or political ruler (pp 934–5). Theseus, for example, is both the ally of the Argive women and the enslaver of the Amazons, and his heroism in defeating old Creon is of a very limited kind (pp 935–6). All the characters view human and divine reality from fixed, often irrelevant, perspectives, and the consequent 'dissociation of power from reason' is the central theme (p 937). Statius suggests that while human beings must accept the madness of nature and the gods, there ought to be rational alternatives in human government; yet he is forced to depict a reality is which beauty is routinely destroyed as humanity progresses toward self-annihilation (pp 938–9).

277 Burgess, John F. 'Pietas in Virgil and Statius.' *Proceedings of the Virgil Society* 11(1971–2), 48–61.
In the *Aen* (pp 48–53) *pietas* is not equivalent with 'humanity' but consists in the fulfillment of certain specific obligations. Aeneas' *pietas* aligns him with the gods and fate while it inflicts suffering on him and others and requires acts of inhumane violence. In the *Theb* (pp 53–8) *pietas* does have the broader meaning but is associated only with human beings and is always defeated. *Impietas*, associated with the gods and fate, embraces all violence, including traditional warfare. Virgil asks whether the sacrifices required by *pietas* are too great; Statius asks whether *pietas* can have any effect in the world. The *Aen* expresses 'guarded optimism,' the *Theb*, 'unmitigated despair' (p 59).

278 — 'Statius' Altar of Mercy.' *Classical Quarterly* 22(1972), 339–49.
In *Theb* XII.481 f, Statius redefines the concept of *clementia* in order to offer comfort to human beings in their tragic circumstances. In its traditional usage, as in works by Seneca, Cicero, and others, *clementia* refers to situations in which 'one man ... in a position of superior power over another who has caused him offence ... refrains from exacting the penalty which he has either the legal right or the power to exact' (p 340). As an advertisement of power, *clementia* became a symbol of the despotism of the emperors, and as such was treated with systematic irony by Tacitus (pp 340–1). In the *Theb* Clementia is not a victimizing superior but a responsible and disinterested power that offers pity and assistance rather than pardon (pp 343–4). Statius implicitly recommends this *clementia* to Domitian (pp 354–6, 348–9).

279 Gossage, A.J. 'Virgil and the Flavian Epic.' In *Virgil*. Ed. D.R. Dudley. New York: Basic Books, 1969. Pp 67–93.
The Virgilian humanity of Statius' many scenes of pathos and Statius' Virgilian interpretation of *pietas* (pp 72–3) probably caused Dante to see him as a link between Virgil and Christianity (p 89). Statius' Jupiter has benign qualities reminiscent of Virgil's, but he is also more autocratic, like the Flavian emperors.

280 — 'Statius.' In *Neronians and Flavians: Silver Latin I*. Ed. D.R. Dudley. London: Routledge & Kegan Paul, 1972. Pp 184–235.
Gossage answers criticism of the *Thebaid's* allegedly irrelevant parts (including Book XII), its lack of a central hero, and especially its double motivation: ie, Oedipus' curse on his sons and Jupiter's desire to punish mankind for past evils (pp 189–207). Statius unifies the action by studying the sources of human unhappiness in both human wickedness and divine purpose (pp 196, 198). He explores human psychology principally through the opposition of *furor* and *pietas*, and he exemplifies this opposition several times through conflicts over the proper burial of the dead (pp 199–203). The deaths of Polynices and Eteocles in Book XI are the dramatic end of the story, but Book XII, with its unique altar of Clemency, is necessary to provide the final moral triumph of *pietas* (pp 203–4). Gossage reviews briefly Statius' influence on later authors, including Chaucer, Lydgate, and Dante (pp 217–23).

281 Greene, Thomas M. *The Descent from Heaven: A Study in Epic Continuity*. New Haven: Yale University Press, 1963.
Mercury's descent to Tartarus (I.303–11) has as its purpose to foment discord between Eteocles and Polyneices. The episode is typical of a work whose world is without justice and whose only theme is violence. The spirit of the poem is best represented by the Furies and by Mars, who makes two descents (III.227 f and 7.1 ff) and who is 'a fearful incarnation of destructiveness' (pp 100–102).

282 Hakanson, Lennart. *Statius' Thebaid: Critical and Exegetical Remarks*. Lund: Gleerup, 1973.
'Notes on the Thebaid' (pp 7–73) focus on textual readings and problems of translation. A survey of 'the major errors' in Mozley's translation (**257**) (pp 79–85) supports the view that 'a thorough revision of this presumably widely distributed and frequently used translation is a desideratum.'

283 Juhnke, Herbert. *Homerisches in römischer Epik flavischer Zeit: Untersuchungen zu Szenennachbildungen und Strukturentsprechungen in Statius' Thebais und Achilleis und in Silius' Punica*. Munich: Beck, 1972.

Includes a book-by-book commentary on the *Theb* (pp 51–161).

284 Lewis, C.S. *The Allegory of Love: A Study in Medieval Tradition*. Oxford: Oxford University Press, 1936; rpt through 1960. Pp 49–56.
The *Theb* illustrates the 'drift towards allegory, in its early stages' (p 49). Mars represents 'the martial or pugnacious spirit' and needs no specific motive for his acts (pp 50–2). Although Clementia represents only a state of mind, she is treated with 'something like real religious emotion' (p 53). The gods of the poem 'are only abstractions, and its abstractions, though confessedly belonging to the inner world, are almost gods' (p 56).

285 — 'Dante's Statius.' *MAE* 25(1957), 133–9. Rpt in *Studies in Medieval and Renaissance Literature*. Cambridge: Cambridge University Press, 1966. Pp 94–102 [cited here].
An important early study which argues that Dante found in the *Theb* itself convincing grouds for believing or pretending that Statius was a Christian. Statius' Nature seems close to the neo-Platonic *Natura* of the Middle Ages, especially when she supports 'what is almost the Pagan equivalent of a Crusade,' Theseus' attack on Thebes (p 96). The *Theb* also presents a Stoic doctrine of human brotherhood; a seeming endorsement of the doctrine of the Fall, in its emphasis on human evil; a portrayal of the Olympians as, in effect, devils; something like 'Christian feeling' in its celebration of *Virtus*, *Pietas*, and *Clementia* (p 99); a special treatment of Jupiter that brings him close to the Creator of Christian tradition; an approximation of the doctrine of grace in its explanation of Menoeceus' heroism (X.629–30); and an attitude toward sexual life reminiscent of the more rigorous medieval moralists. Dante saw that Virgil was the greater poet but that Statius had the truer vision. See **290R**.

286 Snijder, H. *Thebaid: A Commentary on Book III, with Text and Introduction*. Amsterdam: Hakkert, 1968.
The text is followed by a line-by-line commentary. In his introduction (pp 11–21), Snijder characterizes the *Theb* as 'a poem of horror, cruelty and destruction' in which the characters exhibit extremes of piety and impiety. Theseus effects a moral restoration by prosecuting 'a *holy* war' in defense of humane principles (p 17).

287 Tillyard, E.M. 'Statius.' *The English Epic and Its Background*. New York: Oxford University Press, 1954. Pp 99–104.
Statius imposes 'a semblance of unity' on the disparate materials of the *Theb* principally through Book XII, 'a gallant, if hopeless, effort to give meaning to the welter of horror and carnage that has gone before' (p 100). The statement that the Altar of Mercy is unknown

to the fortunate (XII.496) gives the famous passage psychological depth.

288 Venini, Paola. '*Furor* e psicologia nella Tebaide di Stazio.' *Athenaeum* ns 42(1964), 201–13.
Venini expands upon earlier scholarship on *furor* in the *Theb* by emphasizing the psychological dimension. Typically, a demon or god acts from without, producing a sudden, irresistible change in the human agent. Yet the external action always coincides with a pre-existing psychological cause. The fury simply makes Polinices and Eteocles aware of their criminal inclinations, for example, and Venus' instigation of the massacre of Lemnos parallels the women's own pain as a motivation. Similarly, Oedipus' grief over his sons signals not only the departure of the fury from him, but the abating of his own hatred now that his desire for revenge has been accomplished. The *Aen* provided models for the intervention of a fury, but Statius introduced cases in a greater variety of circumstances and insisted on the psychological aspect. *Furor* is both the most important cause of action in the *Theb* and one of its chief themes.

289 Verrall, A.W. 'The Altar of Mercy.' In *Collected Literary Essays: Classical and Modern*. Ed. M.A. Bayfield and John Duff. Cambridge: Cambridge University Press, 1913. Pp 219–35.
Statius intended the *Theb* to share in the sacred quality he attributed to the *Aen*. The passage on the Altar of Mercy shares an important sentiment with Christianity, emphasizing the power 'to console the miserable and the guilty, to heal the wounds of the world and the sense of sin' (p 230). By contrast the gods have lost their connections to reality.

290 Vessey, David. *Statius and the Thebaid*. Cambridge: Cambridge University Press, 1973.
In this first book-length study of Statius in English, the *Theb* is presented as 'above all an epic of emotion' (p 58), reflecting the emphasis on pathos in the schools of rhetoric, and unified by psychological and philosophical themes rather than by the career of a single hero. 'If the Aeneid is the epic of *pietas*, then the *Thebaid* is the epic of *ira*. Whereas Virgil envisages providence as benevolent and creative, Statius ... appears to see fate as maleficent and destructive' (p 59). Statius' human characters are 'monochromatic' (p 65), 'virtually allegorical' representatives of varieties of *pietas* and *ira* (p 67). The causes of war lie in human character, specifically in Oedipus and his sons (pp 71–81), but Fate concurs and provides the means. In Statius' Stoic universe (pp 82–91), Jupiter is the 'executive agent' of an implacable fate; his speech expounding the meaning of

fate and the relations of mercy and justice, in the last scene of Book VII, presents 'a succinct and comprehensive exposition of the philosophy' of the *Theb* (p 91). Theseus' role in Book XII is prepared for by the famous description of the altar of Clementia, which suggests that 'man's only hope of salvation lies within himself' (p 310). Theseus is 'a man of steel, an instrument of divine justice and human clemency through whom the world is purified and improved' (p 316). Book XII saves the *Theb* from being 'a statement of despairing nihilism' and makes it 'an epic ... of redemption, a chronicle ... of triumphant good' (p 316).

• Review by Frederick M. Ahl, *PQ* 53(1974), 141–4: Lewis' article (**284**) laid the groundwork for a full study of Statius, a need that is only partially met by Vessey's book. His introduction is excellent and his book contains much useful analysis of and insight into Silver Latin epic. But in discussing Statius' politics and philosophy, he relies too much on assertion without evidence or argumentation. It is difficult to reconcile Statius' traditional epic treatment of Jupiter with what Vessey alleges to be the poet's stoicism (p 144).

291 Wetherbee, Winthrop. '"*Per Te Poeta Fui, Per Te Cristiano*": Dante, Statius, and the Narrator of Chaucer's *Troilus*.' In *Vernacular Poetics in the Middle Ages*. Ed. Lois Ebin. Kalamazoo: Medieval Institute, 1984. Pp 153–76.

In the dark vision of the *Theb*, even Theseus can effect peace only through violence, and Clementia is 'emphatically a last resort' (p 161). In reaction against this harsh world, Statius prefers the innocence of the Arcadian warrior Parthenopaeus to the heroic virtue of Creon's son, Menoeceus (pp 161–4). Statius' indecisiveness, his moral and spiritual doubt, commended him to Dante and Chaucer. His 'conversion,' as portrayed by Dante (*Purg* 21–25), is occasioned by reinterpreting Vergil's *Fourth Eclogue* (lines 5–7) and can be understood as a new appreciation of the 'spiritual challenge' represented by Menoeceus (p 164). Dante's account of the divine *virtu* coming to the human embryo is modelled on Menoeceus' infusion with *virtu* (*Theb* X); Dante seems to point to an 'embryonic' quality in the spirituality of the *Theb*. Statius' experience is 'a symbolic prefiguration of Dante's own growth to spiritual maturity through poetry' (p 165).

292 — 'Thebes and Troy: Statius and Dante's Statius.' *Chaucer and the Poets: An Essay on 'Troilus and Criseyde'*. Ithaca: Cornell University Press, 1984. Pp 111–44.

Incorporates portions of **291**. Looking at the *Theb* as a medieval Christian poet might have, Wetherbee sees it as opposing the tragic force of history, located in fate and the indifferent gods, to virtue and piety, associated nostalgically with youth; a happier afterlife is hinted at for some characters, but Statius withholds judgment on the action of his story (pp 113–5). Statius' religious values are associated particularly with Parthenopaeus and Menoeceus: the former associated with a traditional religion of cult and pagan practice; the latter, with 'something genuinely transformative, which [Statius] can express only tentatively' (p 138), an anticipation of Christian vision which affirms the value of human virtue and suffering. The Virtus who inspires Menoeceus is a kind of grace. See also the 'Introduction,' on parallels between the spiritual growth of Statius and that of the *Troilus* narrator; and see pp 228–31, on Dante's view of Statius.

- Review by John V. Fleming, *SAC* 7(1985), 262–7: The discussions of Virgil, Ovid, and Statius 'are clearly among the most informed studies yet published on "Chaucer and the classics"' (p 263).

293 Williams, R.D, ed. *Thebaidos: Liber Decimus. Mnemosyne*, Supplement 22. Leyden: Brill, 1972.
The text is followed by a line-by-line commentary. In the introduction (xi–xxiv) the *Theb* is said to exhibit a 'tremendous tension between the scenes of violence and horror ... and the sad and bewildered sympathy for those who suffer' (xix). Its sense of futility arises from the politics of the era; in the commitment to humane values represented by the personifications — Virtus, Pietas, Clementia — and by Theseus, 'no remedy is found, but a refuge is offered' (xxi).

The *Roman de Thèbes*

EDITIONS AND TRANSLATIONS

294 Constans, Léopold, ed. *Le Roman de Thèbes, Publié d'après tous les Manuscrits*. Société des Anciens Textes Français. 2 volumes. Paris: Firmin Didot, 1890. Rpt New York: Johnson Reprint Corporation (Harcourt Brace), 1968.
The text is based on the 'S' ms (British Library Manuscript Additional 34114), a poem of 11,546 lines copied in the latter half of the fourteenth century. In an effort to reconstruct the original version, now lost, Constans adds, deletes, changes, and re-orders lines and passages, with the aid of the other extant mss.

295 Ripley, Dana Phelps, ed. *A Critical Edition of the "Roman de Thèbes" (lines 1-5394), with an Introduction, Notes, and Glossary*. Ann Arbor, Michigan: University Microfilms, 1960.

A partial edition of the 'C' text (Bibliothèque Nationale Manuscript French 784). A poem of 10,562 lines, it is the shortest of the *RTh* texts, and was copied in the thirteenth century.

296 Raynaud de Lage, Guy, ed. *Le Roman de Thèbes*. Les classiques Français du moyen âge. Volumes 94 and 96. Paris: Honoré Champion, 1967 and 1968.
This is a complete edition of the 'C' text (see **295**).

297 Coley, John Smartt, trans. *Le Roman de Thèbes (The Story of Thebes)*. Garland Library of Medieval Literature, Volume 44, Series B. New York and London: Garland, 1986.
Coley provides a complete, line-for-line English translation of the *RTh* as found in Constans' version (**294**).

- Review by Caroline D. Eckhardt, *SAC* 9(1987), 203–6: Because of Coley's use of Constans' nineteenth-century 'editorial creation' (p 204), 'it would be dangerous ... to use this translation for any close inquiry into Chaucer's relationship to the *Roman*' (p 205); the translation of Constans is generally excellent, however. An English translation based on a specific manuscript is needed.

BACKGROUNDS

298 Blumenfeld-Kosinski, Renate. 'Old French Narrative Genres: Towards the Definition of the *Roman Antique*.' *RPh* 34(1980), 143–59.
The *roman antique* can be defined by its three-fold relation to the *translatio* topos. As *translatio studii* it treats subject matter drawn from the text of a school *auctor*; as *translatio imperii* it deals with political issues (in the *RTh*, the evils of civil war) important to the new Norman-Angevin kingdom; and it translates Latin into the vernacular. The *RTh* stands midway between the *Roman d'Énéas* and the *Roman de Troie* in the explicitness with which it acknowledges its source. Its Statius is not the ancient poet but 'a Statius FIGURE, poeticized and utilized for specific ends' (p 154), principally as a guarantor of truth.

299 Cormier, R. 'The Problems of Anachronism: Recent Scholarship on the French Medieval Romances of Antiquity.' *PQ* 53(1974), 145–57.
Some aspects of antique life are presented authentically in these texts, challenging the belief that medieval people had no consciousness of a past distinct from the present. The audience for the *romans antiques* were probably literate or pre-literate, and may have had an interest in conserving the past. Anachronism can serve functions of communication, rationalization, and renewal of the past.

300 Hanning, R.W. 'The Social Significance of Twelfth-Century Romance.' *M&H* 3(1972), 3–29.
The *topos* of chivalry ('love inspires prowess, prowess inspires love') antedates the chivalric romance (p 3). The *topos* first appears in Geoffrey of Monmouth's *Historia*, then in Wace's *Brut* and in the *RTh*. In the last the chivarlic *topos* motivates heroism in war for the first time and becomes an ironic subplot in love relationships that are frustrated by the fates of war (pp 5–6). The possibilities of love as an inward experience of self-discovery, explored in the Ovidian *contes*, influenced the *Roman d'Aneas*, but the plots of the *romans antiques* inhibited development of the *topos*; it reached its full development only in the chivalric romance, where there is no context larger than the life of the hero. See also Hanning's *The Individual in Twelfth-Century Romance* (New Haven: Yale University Press, 1977).

301 — 'The Audience as Co-Creator of the First Chivalric Romances.' *YES* 11(1981). 1–28.
The audience for chivalric romance included 'clerics, educated women, and cadet members of the aggressive feudal aristocracy' (p 7). Characterized by a humanistic interest in classical antiquity and by a flexible ability to enjoy a variety of genres, they were constituted *ad hoc* as an audience for chivalric romance by cues within the works, as can be illustrated from the opening lines of the *RTh* (pp 10–12). Those lines emphasize the role of the 'poet-performer-creator' and the story's claim to provide wisdom; they define the audience as they invite it to confer unity on the work by interpreting and evaluating it.

302 Köhler, Erich. 'Quelques observations d'ordre historico-sociologique sur les rapports entre la chanson de geste et le roman courtois.' In *Chanson de Geste und Höfischer Roman*. Ed. Kurt Baldinger, et al. Heidelberg Colloquium, 1961. Heidelberg: Carl Winter, 1963. *Studia Romanica* 4. Pp 21–30.
The opening of the *RTh* (pp 22–5) is evidence for the emergence of a socially stratified audience and of a sense of contestable truths, both associated with the *roman*, as contrasted with the homogeneous audience and universal truths assumed by the *chanson*. The *romans antiques* mark a transition between the two genres.

303 Petit, Aimé. 'Le traitement courtois du thème des Amazones d'après trois romans antiques: *Enéas*, *Troie* et *Alexandre*.' *MA* 89(1983), 63–84.
The myth of the Amazons is 'humanized' and the women themselves are 'feminized'; their self-mutilization and their practice of killing male offspring are suppressed, and they are shown as capable of

loving men. Their prowess in battle is linked to a new emphasis on their virginity: the romancers create a new feminine type characterized by *fortitude-pulchritudo-pudicitia* and intended to be the equal of the male warrior.

304 Raynaud de Lage, Guy. 'L'Antiquité dans les Romans Antiques.' *MA* 67(1961), 247–91.
The anachronism with which the romancers treat ancient times was not the result of ignorance. In a spirit of play the poets created in their works a world of ideal feudality which corresponds exactly with neither their own nor the ancient world. They were restrained, however, in assimilating ancient religion to their own, lest they be guilty of blasphemy.

CRITICISM

305 Adler, A. 'The *Roman de Thèbes*, A "Consolatio Philosophia".' *Romanische Forschungen* 72(1960), 257–76.
The subject matter of the *RTh* is a *desolatio*; the treatment, inspired by the humanism of the mid-twelfth century, provides a *consolatio*. The poet uses elegant language, describes beautiful objects and ceremonies, introduces courtly love and Ciceronian friendship, and appreciates war as strategy. The mixed epic-courtly inspiration of many scenes distracts the audience's attention from the *desolatio* to questions of aesthetics. The poet's success in creating beauty suggests a tentative hope for the world of the *RTh*.

306 Blumenfeld-Kosinski, Renate Elisabeth. 'The Traditions of the Old French *Roman de Thèbes*: A Poetico-Historical Analysis.' *DAI* 41(1980), 1582A. PhD dissertation, Princeton University. Director: Karl D. Uitti.
The earlier, shorter version of the *RTh* (see **317**) shows the influence of learned Latin narrative in its historico-political purpose, to comment on the danger of civil war between Henry II and his sons. The longer version shows the influence of later romance literature in its concentration on apolitical *aventure*. The *RTh* was reconstituted as a historical text when it was absorbed into the prose *Histoire ancienne jusqu'à César* in 1213.

307 — 'The Earliest Development of the French Novel: the *Roman de Thèbes* in Verse and Prose.' *French Literary Series* 11(1984), 1–10. [Not seen]

308 — 'The Gods as Metaphor in the *Roman de Thèbes*.' *MP* 83(1985), 1–11.

As 'one of the first texts that made pagan mythology available to a vernacular audience,' the *RTh* is 'a crucial text for the further development of the mythological tradition in vernacular literature' (p 3). Under the influence of Chartrian uses of myth, the *RTh* strips the gods of their divinity and revalorizes them as representatives of legitimate social authority, artistic excellence, and ancient learning. Jupiter speaks for the poet when he condemns Capaneus, blasphemer against civilized values.

309 Donovan, Lewis-Gary. *Recherches sur le "Roman de Thèbes."* Paris: Société d'Edition d'Enseignement Supérieur, 1975.
Emphasizing the originality of the *RTh* as the first French romance, Donovan studies its author's adaptations of the epic, represented by the *Theb*, and of the *chanson de geste*, represented by the *Chanson de Roland*, in the process of creating the romance genre. Donovan demonstrates the poet's direct indebtedness to the *Theb* itself, rather than a Latin intermediary, and his learned mastery of that classical text as well as of medieval rhetoric. The structure of the *RTh*, Donovan argues, suggests as much a '*Chanson d'Atys*' as a story of Etioles and Polynices, representing the poet's chief departure from Statius. The *RTh* is a didactic work, incorporating in the epic manner much scientific and scholarly matter. Stylistically, the influence of the *chanson de geste* is rather slight. Donovan gives extended attention to the portraits and to Parthenope. See **310**.

310 Dufournet, Jean. 'La *Thébaide* de Stace et le *Roman de Thèbes* (A propos du livre de G. Donovan).' *Revue des Langues Romanes* 82(1976), 139–60.
After commenting favorably on **309** (pp 139–47), Dufournet balances Donovan's account of the French poet's uses of the *Theb* with an analysis of what he rejected (pp 147–55). The French poet eliminates scenes of horror and introduces scenes of pathos, often with the intent of developing the chivalric grandeur and humanism of the narrative; he also suppresses Homeric similes and matter concerned with the gods. Finally, Dufournet comments on the portraits (pp 156–60), emphasizing the pairing of antithetical portraits.

311 Grout, Patricia B. 'Religion and Mythology in the *Roman de Thèbes*.' In *The Classical Tradition in French Literature: Essays Presented to R.C. Knight*. Ed. H.T. Barnwell. London: Grant and Cutler, 1977. Pp 23–30.
The poet has reduced references to the gods to the minimum necessary to the plot, and adapted religious ceremonies to Christian forms. He presents a concept of sin which brings the views of Statius and Virgil still closer to those of his audience.

312 Jones, Rosemarie. *'Le Roman de Thèbes.' The Theme of Love in the 'Romans d'Antiquité.'* London: Modern Humanities Research Association, 1972. Pp 19–29.
The author introduces love relationships not found in Statius, incidental references to courtly love, and a general atmosphere of courtliness; he focuses on pre-marital rather than married love, and emphasizes the woman's point of view. Yet the influence of Ovid is notably absent: the love interest is peripheral, not central.

313 Micha, A. 'Coleur épique dans le *Roman de Thébes.*' *Romania* 91(1970), 145–60.
Despite the introduction of an elementary sentiment of love, the *RTh* remains epical in matter and to a large extent in manner, as in the use of traditional clichés.

314 Payen, Jean-Charles. 'Structure et sens du *Roman de Thèbes.*' *MA* 76(1970), 493–514.
The *RTh* belongs more to the epic than to the romance. Its verse form, sharply visualized presentation of male warriors, and handling of soliloquy and dialogue are reminiscent of the *chanson de geste* and of quasi-historical works. Its ideology superimposes an ancient legend on events of the Middle Ages: Eteocles and the Thebans represent the pagan enemies of the Christian crusaders, here represented by Polinices and Theseus. This superimposition is accomplished partly by deliberate anachronism, inspired by what medieval readers understood as anticipations of Christian thought in Statius' *Theb.*

315 — 'La mise en roman de la matière antique: Le cas du *Roman de Thèbes.*' In *Etudes de philologie romane et d'histoire littéraire offerts à Jules Horent à l'occasion de son soixantième anniversaire*. Ed. Jean Marie D'Heur and Nicoletta Cherubini. Tournai: Gedit, 1980. Pp 325–32.
An examination of selected passages in mss C (see **295**), S (see **294**), and P suggests that the 'mise en roman' was not fully realized in C, the earliest ms, but evolved in stages. As the epic vigor of the work was weakened, objective descriptions of scenes and characters' displays of affectivity were expanded, and depictions of paganism were reconciled with Christian ideology.

316 Raynaud de Lage, Guy. 'Le premier roman.' In *Orbis Mediaevalis: Mélanges de langue et de littérature médiévales offerts á Reto Raduolf Bezzola à l'occasion de son quatre-vingtième anniversaire*. Ed. George Güntert, et al. Berne: Editions Francke, 1978. Pp 323–7.
The author of the *RTh* adapted his work to the new courtly audience of the second feudal age. He desacralized the world of the *chanson de geste* and fictionalized the world of Statius; he introduced

courtoisie, but not *fin amors*, under the influence of women in the audience. As narrator he interprets and moralizes, in line with the didactic thrust of the *roman*.

317 Ripley, Dana Phelps. 'The Genesis of the *Roman de Thèbes*.' In *Mediaeval Studies in Honor of Urban T. Holmes, Jr.* Ed. John Mahoney and John Esten Keller. Chapel Hill: University of North Carolina Press, 1965. Pp 157–67.

The *RTh* survives in five mss dating from the thirteenth and fourteenth centuries, with Mss. C, B, and S representing earlier, shorter versions of the poem, and Mss P and A representing later, longer versions. The primitive *RTh*, composed near the beginning of the second half of the twelfth century, is lost, and the two versions in the mss date from the last part of the century. The poem we have, a product of individual and collective authorship, passed through a process of evolution: its style changed, it was corrected with reference to the *Theb*, and it acquired new episodes, an expanded love interest, and allusions to contemporary events.

The Knight in the General Prologue (and the Links)

Fine Edition of the General Prologue

318 *The Prologue to the Canterbury Tales, with original screen images designed by Ronald King.* Introduction by Kevin Power. London: Editions Alecto, 1966; rpt Surrey: Circle Press, 1967/2nd ed, 1978.
Presents fourteen drawings inspired in part by the traditions of the African mask and accompanied by a Middle English text whose source is not indicated. The Knight's is predominantly black, gold, and violet; its general shape is suggestive of a helmet, and on it sword-like and cross-like designs intersect with each other. Twenty additional drawings [not seen] are distributed one-to-a-set; they include a lithograph of the Knight in two colors and a screen-print of his horse in four colors.

Musical Treatments of the General Prologue

319 Dyson, George. *The Canterbury Pilgrims: Portraits Chosen from the Prologue to Chaucer's Canterbury Tales and set to music for Chorus, Orchestra & Three Soloists (Soprano, Tenor & Baritone).* London: Oxford University Press, 1930. Pp 16–25.
The portrait of the Knight is sung by the chorus. Lines I.43–50 are to be performed 'broadly'; beginning with line 51 and the mention of the first battle, the expression is to be 'Poco a poco piu mosso,' with a return to the original tempo at line 64. Lines 68–71 are marked 'Slow' and line 72 – 'He was a verray, parfit gentil knyght' – is marked 'molto sostenuto.' The musical portrait closes with this famous line and omits lines 73–8. A 'L' Envoi' treats lines 747–858 and the first four lines of the *KnT*. The part of the Knight is assigned to the tenor; the part of the Host, to the baritone.

320 Trimble, Lester. *Four Fragments from the Canterbury Tales*. New York: C.F. Peters, [n d].
A composition for soprano, flute, clarinet, and harpsichord or piano which treats excerpts from the opening lines of the *GP*, the Knight's portrait, Squire's portrait, and *WBP*. The section on the Knight omits the list of battles (the Squire's battles are also omitted), and begins 'allegro quasi pesante'; line 71 is marked 'rallentando poco' and line 72, 'meno mosso,' with a return to the initial tempo thereafter. The clarinet suggests the Knight's maturity; the flute, the Squire's youth.

Criticism

1900–1930

This section contains some pre–1900 items.

321 Bentinck-Smith, M. *The Prologue and the Knight's Tale*. 1909. See **20**.
Even more than Sir Roger de Coverley [of Addison and Steele's *Spectator*], Chaucer's knight is the 'image of a gentleman or worthy person fashioned in vertuous and gentle discipline.' The Squire will excel his father, his manly virtues refined by knowledge and love of the arts. The yeoman is 'the faithful follower and servant of expiring feudalism' (lxxv). For *KnT* see **525**.

322 Berkelman, Robert G. 'Chaucer and Masefield.' *EJ* 16(1927), 698–705.
Masefield's Sir Peter Bynd in *Reynard* was inspired by Chaucer's Knight. 'An old, grave soldier, sweet and kind, / A courtier with a knightly mind' (p 701). For *KnT* see **526**.

323 Bond, Richard P. 'Some Eighteenth Century Chaucer Allusions.' *SP* 25(1928), 316–39.
The anonymous *A Poem on the Civil Wars of the Old-Baily* (1713) cites 'knights renown'd of old, / For warlike deeds, as great as e're were told; / *By Chaucer*' (p 321). See **528**.

324 Bryant, Frank E. 'Did Boccaccio Suggest the Character of Chaucer's Knight?' *MLN* 17(1902), 235–6.
Certain features of the Knight, that he shows the stains of his armor, that he is not 'gay' (I.74) but 'worthy' and 'wise' (68), that he is 'meek as a maid' and speaks courteously to all (69–71), are anticipated in Boccaccio's description of King Evander (*Tes* VI.40). Chaucer may have hoped to harmonize the Knight's portrait with his tale by taking both from the same source.

325 Cook, Albert S. 'Beginning the Board in Prussia.' *JEGP* 14(1915), 375–88.
To explain the distinction implied in beginning the board at the table of honor of the Teutonic Order, Cook analyzes two texts: an article of accusation by a Polish procurator of 1415, charging that the Order used the custom to extort money from knights, and a poem by Peter Suchenwirt, herald and minstrel, describing the experiences of Duke Albert III of Austria in Prussia in 1377. Cook concludes that the table was reserved for a small number – ten to fourteen knights; that the right to hold the table was conferred or confirmed by the Pope and Emperor; that seats were assigned by heralds who were well informed about the Knights' careers; and that the table of honor, announced in advance, 'proved a powerful magnet to attract the bravest knights from foreign lands to the service of the order' (p 387). See **353**.

326 — 'The Historical Background of Chaucer's Knight.' *TCAAS* 20(1916), 165–240. Rpt New York: Haskell House, 1966.
1, 'Chaucer and Henry, Earl of Derby' (pp 165–215): Cook argues that the participation of Henry, son of John of Gaunt, in the siege of Vilna in 1390 (**196**) stands behind Chaucer's Knight's activities in Lithuania; that Henry was the probable source of Chaucer's information about the table of honor of the Teutonic Order; and that therefore the portrait of the Knight is unlikely to have been composed before the summer of 1393. 2, 'Chaucer's Knight and his Exploits in the South' (pp 216–38): Cook surveys the battles of Palatia, Satalia, Lyeys, Alexandria, Tlemcen, and Algeciras, and those in Morocco, giving particular attention to the participation of Englishmen. He concludes that although Chaucer's Knight is 'a typical, in some sense a composite, figure ... no one contributed more noble traits' to his portrait (p 237) than the elder Earl of Derby, grandfather to Henry IV, who participated in the siege of Algeciras. See **336**, **388**, **448**. For *KnT* see **537**.

327 — 'Two Notes on Chaucer.' *MLN* 31(1916), 441–2.
The fact that 'Lyeys' (I.58) was in Lesser Armenia supports the interpretation of 'Ermony' in *Anel* (72) as Armenia.

328 Coulton, G.G. *Chaucer and his England*. London: Methuen, 1908; rpt in several editions through 1968 and with a new bibliography by T.W. Craik in 1963.
'In days when the distinctions of rank were so marked and so unforgettable, even to the smallest details of costume, the Knight's dignity risked nothing by unbending to familiar jest with the Host' (p 126). Yet the Knight makes no display of his rank, which can be

guessed only from the excellence of his behavior. No one could dispute his right to tell the first tale (pp 133–4). Ironically, the Monk is interrupted by the Knight, who never spoke villainy to anyone (p 140).

329 Flügel, Ewald. 'Gower's Mirour de L'Omme und Chaucer's Prolog.' *Anglia* 24(1901), 437–508.
Flügel briefly compares Chaucer's treatment of knighthood with Gower's more highly critical treatment in his three major works. He cites other literary references to crusading in Prussia and documentary evidence of English knights' activities there. He suggests that 'reyse' was a term especially associated with excursions into Eastern Europe and that contemporary opinion was often critical of such trips.

330 Hammond, Eleanor P. *Chaucer: A Bibliographical Manual.* Boston: Macmillan, 1908; rpt. New York: P. Smith, 1933.
The Long and Short forms of the *NPP* represent a rare clear instance of Chaucerian revision (pp 241–3). Mss and early printed editions having the short form differ in attributing the interruption, some to the Host, some to the Knight; 'Knight' may have been written in the archetype above or beside the original 'Host' in preparation for Chaucer's elimination of the 'inartistic repetition' (p 243) of having the Host interrupt both *Thop* and the *MkT*. Hammond summarizes editorial treatments of *ariue* and *armee* in I.60 (p 273). For *KnT* see **568**.

331 Hinckley, Henry Barrett. 'The Prolog.' *Notes on Chaucer: A Commentary on the Prolog and Six Canterbury Tales.* Northhampton, Mass.: Nonotuck Press, 1907. Rpt New York: Haskell House, 1964. Pp 1–49.
For the Knight's portrait (pp 5–7) Hinckley includes notes on the Teutonic knights, Lettow, *armee* ('muster'?), *worthy* ('of social position'), *vileynye*, and *gypoun* ('often emblazoned with the arms of the wearer'). For *KnT* see **576**.

332 Kittredge, George Lyman. *Chaucer and His Poetry.* Cambridge, Mass.: Harvard University Press, 1915. Rpt many times; with an Introduction by B.J. Whiting, 1970.
Although Harry Bailly is the 'master of ceremonies' of the pilgrimage, 'the ruler of the company is actually the Knight. It is he that asserts himself whenever the case requires an appeal to the controlling forces of the social world' (pp 163–4), as in the matter of the Monk's tragedies (p 165). See **379**; for *KnT* see **587**.

333 Legouis, Émile. *Geoffrey Chaucer.* Trans. L. Lailavoix. New York: Dutton, 1913. Rpt New York: Russell & Russell, 1961. Originally published in French: *Geoffroy Chaucer.* Paris: Bloud, 1910.

The didactic side of Chaucer's art is most apparent in his ideal figures. 'The Knight with his purity of morals, his piety, his modesty, his courtesy to all, might very well be a pattern of primitive chivalry, set as a model for imitation by a degenerate age, where the order had drifted towards ambition, luxury, and sensuality' (pp 155–6). For *KnT* see **591**.

334 Lounsbury, Thomas R. *Studies in Chaucer: His Life and Writings*. 3 volumes. New York: 1892. Rpt New York: Russell & Russell, 1962. Chaucer may have modelled the Knight on the son of John of Gaunt, later Henry IV (**196**), who participated in two crusades, in Barbary and in Lithuania (1:93). *Worthy* means 'of high rank,' and lines I.68–9 mean that there was in the Knight's deportment 'nothing of the arrogance often seen in men of noble birth or exalted position' (p 93, n 1). Chaucer shared the attitudes of his class, in favor of the military order and against the ecclesiastical order. The Knight is 'the ideal soldier and gentleman. Even his Christianity is, in its way, of a higher type [than that of the clergy] ... His crowning merit ... is his consideration for the feelings of others, no matter what their station in life' as indicated by lines 70–1 (2: 480). For *KnT* see **594**.

335 Manly, John Matthews. 'A Knight Ther Was.' *Transactions and Proceedings of the American Philological Association* 38(1907), 89–107. Rpt in *Chaucer: Modern Essays in Criticism*. Ed. Edward Wagenknecht. London: Oxford University Press, 1959. Pp 46–59. Believing that the Knight's portrait has faded with time, Manly sets out 'to apply to it a "reviver" made of extracts from certain old documents' (p 89). Although knighthood was already doomed by cannon and commerce, 'the flame of devotion flared wider and higher and burned for a moment with unwonted intensity and purity. Knighthood was no longer a mere feudal obligation, it had become an ever-alluring ideal' (p 90). The Knight's campaigns fall into three groups (pp 92–103). His activities at Algezir, in Belmarye and in Tramissene were part of the attempt to push the Moors out of Spain and to punish their piracy. Letters preserved in Rymer's *Foedera* document English participation in these efforts. Manly prints a long extract from Froissart **183** on the single combat in battle. A second group of campaigns, at Alexandria, Lyeys, and Satalye, and in Turkey, were all associated with Peter of Cyprus. The ambivalent attitudes of European leaders toward Peter's exploits are illustrated by Froissart's account of Edward III's response. The Knight's battles in Pruce, Lettow, and Ruce, possibly his most recent, make up a third group, all associated with the Teutonic Order. If the siege of Algezir in 1344 was the Knight's first battle, he is probably sixty to sixty-five years old. Testimony in the Scrope-Grosvenor case indicates that among knights and esquires Chaucer knew there existed more than one 'approximate model' (p 104) for such a career. While the opinion of Sir Harris Nicholas, editor of *The Scrope-Grosvenor Roll* **201** , that Sir William Scrope provided the model for the Knight is 'perhaps an exaggeration,' we can be certain 'that Chaucer was painting no picture of fancy, but giving us a figure at once realistic and typical' (p 107). See **161, 336, 353, 369, 372, 388, 504.**

336 — *Some New Light on Chaucer.* New York: Holt, 1926; rpt 1951. Rpt Gloucester, Mass.: Peter Smith, 1959.
Characterizing his earlier discussion **335**, Manly says that the evidence did not identify a single individual as a model but showed the Knight's career to be a 'possible and natural' one 'illustrated even in minute detail' by knights of a well–known family [the Scropes **201**] (p 254). Concerning Cook's arguments (**326**) for Henry Earl of Derby and Henry IV (**196**) as models, Manly observes that 'Chaucer's Knight belonged rather to the social rank of the Scropes than to the more exalted rank of the Derbys' (p 256).

337 — *The Canterbury Tales.* 1928. See **33**.
In his notes to the Knight's portrait, pp 498–501, Manly summarizes material from his earlier article **335** and takes issue with Skeat (**344**, V: 5). 'Chaucer's Knight was not ... a mercenary soldier who sought employment under foreign lords when there was no fighting going on at home. The campaigns to which he devoted his life ... had a twofold interest; first, they were all crusades against the infidel; secondly, they were all fought on the very borders of European civilization' (p 499).

338 Mather, Frank Jewett. *The Prologue, The Knight's Tale, and The Nun's Priest's Tale.* 1899. See **8**.
The order of the portraits is deliberately haphazard. 'First a Knight well-mounted, but bearing the stains of battle for our faith; sage in council and brave in fight, the very prototype of the sturdy, unassuming English gentleman. His son follows ... a dandy who has given and taken hard knocks in the Low Countries. You may find his like on our warships and in colonial posts. Their single attendant is ... a stupid, faithful, crop-headed yeoman' (lvi–lvii). For *KnT* see **606**.

339 Piper, Edwin Ford. 'The Miniatures of the Ellesmere Chaucer.' *PQ* 3(1924), 241–56.
For the Knight (p 242), Piper notes the gilt and red ornaments on his gown, the 'bagsleeves' with close-fitting cuffs, the fingerless gloves, the 'roundlet' head-covering, and the gilt on all his accouterments. The spirited horse suggests the good horsemanship of the Knight.

The brand on the horse's flank — M(?) for *Miles* — is in ink and may be a later addition (n 5).

340 Quiller-Couch, Sir Arthur T. *The Age of Chaucer*. London: Dent, 1926; rpt 1931.
In I.70–1 'vileynye' means not 'coarse speech' but 'the true gentleman's delicacy which forbade hurting the feelings of others, especially of his social inferiors; by "no manner wight," ... we should understand "not even the humblest person"' (p. 105). The Knight has 'that particular gentleness of speech and manner which so often belongs to the English officer who has seen hard service' (p 106). Quiller-Couch cites Thackeray's Colonel Newcome and General Charles Gordon. The Knight is probably a younger son of a county family; 'he is obviously not well off' (p 107).

341 Root, Chaucer. *The Poetry of Chaucer*. Boston: Houghton-Mifflin, 1906/rev 1922; rpt 1934. Rpt Gloucester, Mass.: Peter Smith, 1950, 1957.
When the cuts are drawn to determine the first teller, 'either by fortune or over-ruling providence, or perhaps by the manipulation of the Host, the lot falls to the Knight, whom every one feels should be the first to tell his story' (p 163). Although the Knight has traveled widely, 'he has lived ... in the fair dream of chivalry ... he is as unworldly as his squire-son' (pp 168–9). For *KnT* see **619**.

342 Schofield, William Henry. *Chivalry in English Literature: Chaucer, Malory, Spenser and Shakespeare*. Cambridge, Mass.: Harvard University Press, 1912. Rpt Port Washington, New York: Kennikat Press, 1964.
Schofield examines the resemblance of the Knight's portrait to Watriquet de Couvin's description of Gauchier de Chatillon, Constable of France (pp 31–3). Next he contrasts the Knight with the luxury-loving Monk, and compares the Knight both with the Parson, 'a Knight of peace' (p 35), and with Saint Louis' ideal of the *preud'omme*. 'Chaucer has fixed forever our conception of knighthood, beautiful, almost holy. Historians without number may tell us: "knights were not all like that;" and we reply (with some unreason): "No doubt, but here was at least one"'(p 36). See **474**. For *KnT* see **623**.

343 Sedwick, W.B. 'Satalye (Chaucer, *C. T. Prol.* 58).' *RES* 2(1926), 346.
The 'S' of Satalye is a survival of the Greek preposition, and the city referred to is Attalia, the modern Adalia.

344 Skeat, W.W. 'The Knight.' *The Complete Works*. 1894. See **3**.
Volume V: 5–9: Knights commonly sought employment in foreign wars. In I.47 and 50, *worthy* means 'distinguished, honourable,' and *in*

his lordes werre refers to 'the king's service.' Line 52 means 'he had been placed at the head of the dais, or *table* of state' on the evidence of passages from Gower's *CA* and from *Sir Beves of Hamptoun.* Tyrwhitt **640** is cited on the frequency with which English knights fought in Prussia, and the service there of Thomas Duke of Gloucester and of Henry earl of Derby **196** is noted. In I.60 Skeat prefers *aryve* to *armee*, which 'gives no good sense.' In I.74 *hors* is plural. The relation of the habergeoun (I.76) to the hauberk is explained. The Knight had vowed a pilgrimage for his safe return (I.77–8). See **337**, **368**, **450**; for *KnT* see **625**.

345 — *The Eight-Text Edition of the Canterbury Tales, with Remarks upon the Classification of the Manuscripts and upon the Harleian Manuscript 7334.* London: Kegan Paul, Trench Trübner and Co., and Oxford University Press, 1909. Chaucer Society Publications, 2nd Series 43 (1909 for the issue of 1905).
'On the Word *Arivee* in the General Prologue [I. 601]' (pp 55–7): The *NED* lists *armee*, following Tyrwhitt **640**, rather than *aryve*, following Skeat **344**. But *aryve* fits the preposition *at* and is attested in fourteenth-century French.

346 Spurgeon, Caroline F.E. *Five Hundred Years of Chaucer Criticism and Allusion 1357-1900.* Cambridge: Cambridge University Press, 1925. 3 volumes and a Supplement. Rpt New York: Russell and Russell, 1961.
The Index contains only one reference for the Knight, to Richard Hakluyt's *Principal Navigations*, 1598. Other hard-to-find items include: in Part I, John Shirley (p 53); in Part II, Scott (p 18), W. Carey (p 36), Blake (p 43), Crabbe (p 57), Digby (p 137); in Part III, Tennyson (p 75). For *KnT* see **629**.

347 Stevens, William O. 'The "Gipoun" of Chaucer's Knight.' *MLN* 18(1903), 140–1.
The *gipoun* seems to have been a short surcoat worn *over* the armor, as seen on fourteenth-century effigies. How then did the Knight's *gipoun* become 'bismotered with his habergeoun' (I.76)? Stevens suggests that stains showed through from the underside of the *gipoun*. The long surcoat of the Ellesmere miniature is a civil garment of the fifteenth century.

348 Tupper, Frederick. *Types of Society in Medieval Literature*. New York: Holt, 1926. Rpt New York: Biblo and Tannen, 1968.
Concerning I.68 Tupper appeals to the *Chess Book* of Jacobus de Cessolis for interpretations of the Knight's worthiness as 'prowess' and of his wisdom as the 'prudence' born of experience in battle (p 34). Other uses of the worthy-and-wise formula appear in Hoccleve's

Regement of Princes, Beowulf, the *Song of Roland*, and various medieval romances. A knight's 'freedom' (I.46) or liberality is important so that the heralds will make known his deeds (p 38).

1931-1960

349 Baldwin, Ralph. *The Unity of the Canterbury Tales. Anglistica*, Vol. 5. Copenhagen: Rosenkilde and Bagger, 1955. Excerpts rpt in *Chaucer Criticism: The Canterbury Tales.* Ed. Richard Schoeck and Jerome Taylor. Notre Dame: University of Notre Dame Press, 1960. Pp 14–51.
Baldwin discusses the Knight in relation to various medieval methods of characterization and to the tradition of estates. 'In such a summary tag as "He was a verray, parfit gentil knight," there is the "incorporation" of many virtues' Christian and chivalric. 'We have a kind of metonymic exchange between the particular knight and his class: the one verifies and makes real the other' (pp 40–1). The Knight is given no physical traits. 'We do not know *the* knight directly, but only *a* knight through the composite of the battlestained campaigner and the Christian military-apologist. He is idealized to the point of complete depersonalization' by the list of virtues, the repetition of the word 'worthy,' the catalogue of battles, and his unpretentious horse and attire (pp 44–5). The Knight, Parson, and Plowman are 'classically typical, but are *substantiated* as anti-types of the current, rather degenerate exemplar' (p 46). The Knight's 'radix trait' is worthiness (p 49). See **465** and for *KnT* see **649**.

350 Birney, Earle. 'The Squire's Yeoman.' *REL* 1(1960), 9–18.
Birney identifies the Yeoman as the Squire's attendant, not the Knight's. The lavishness of the Yeoman's equipment continues the emphasis on chivalric externals seen in the Squire's portrait, and contrasts with the Knight's humble appearance. This evidence outweighs the grammatical possibility that lines I.101–2 refer back to the Knight.

351 Bond, Richard P., John W. Boyer, C.B. Millican and G. Hubert Smith. 'A Collection of Chaucer Allusions.' *SP* 28(1931), 481–512.
Robert Lowth cited I.69–72 as an illustration of the double negative in his *A Short Introduction to English Grammar, with critical notes* (Philadelphia, 1775), pp 499–500.

352 Borowy, Waclaw. 'English Visitors to Prussia, Lithuania and Poland in the Fourteenth Century.' Trans. from the Polish by A. Truszkowski. *Baltic Countries*, 2(1936), 247–52.

The forays of the Teutonic Knights into largely Christian Lithuania and Poland were ruthless, as reported by the German poet Peter Suchenwirt. Viewed as 'crusades' in the West, they were sometimes more popular than expeditions to the Holy Land and became 'almost a fashion and a kind of sport' [citing Chaucer's Knight] (p 248). English participation was especially notable, extending from 1331–94 with the most famous expedition that of Henry Bolingbroke in 1390–92 (**196**). Difficulties over trade, greater awareness of the Christian identity of the Order's enemies, and defeat by Lithuanian and Polish forces in 1410 led to a cooling of relations with England.

353 Bowden, Muriel. 'The Perfect Knight.' *A Commentary on the General Prologue to the Canterbury Tales*. New York: Macmillan, 1948; 2nd ed, 1967. Pp 44–73.

Relating the Knight to the history of chivalry as a set of ideals seldom realized in practice, Bowden says: 'he is the personification of those ideals, yet ... like the other pilgrims ... he is flesh and blood. He is one of those exceptional heroes who strive to live according to a great ideal yet who are at the same time understandably and understandingly human' (p 44). Bowden summarizes Schofield's analysis (**342**) of the likenesses between this knight and Gauchier de Chatillon as described by Watriquet de Couvin, and reviews some medieval meanings of *chivalrie, trouthe, honour, freedom,* and *curteisie* (pp 46–9). In line 68 she defines *worthy* as 'brave' and *wys* as 'prudent' and indicates the commonplace nature of the formula (p 49). She notes that the Knight has avoided the costly array often complained of in sermons, and that his horses reflect the knightly duty to be properly mounted. She defines *gypon* and *habergeon*, and observes that the Ellesmere illustration presents the Knight without armor (pp 49–51). She suggests that for Chaucer's audience the list of battles (pp 51–66) 'was no mere catalogue of expeditions ... but a chapter of romance' (p 51). She follows Manly **335** in treating the battles in three groups associated with the Moors, Peter of Cyprus, and the Teutonic knights, and prints contemporary accounts of Peter of Cyprus and an excerpt from Cook's translation (**325**) of Suchenwirt's poem on the Prussian campaign of 1377. She reviews Manly's discussion of three members of the Scrope family as offering 'an approximate model' for the Knight (p 67; and see **201**), and closes with a discussion of medieval attitudes toward war (pp 67–9). *Pace* Gower (cf **185**) and Wyclif, 'Christian opinion was almost undivided in approving holy wars ... This may in large part explain why Chaucer lays stress only on those expeditions of the Knight which were against the infidel' (p 67). The phrase 'his lordes werre'

(I.47) may refer to a nonreligious war, but this battle receives little emphasis (p 68). Bowden balances the anti-war emphasis of *Mel* against the observations that 'Chaucer was a man of the court, and in no sense a reformer' and that in many of his works, 'the poet frequently saw only the excitement, the adventure, and the pageantry of war' (p 69). Against Malone's claim (**379**) that Chaucer is not concerned to make the pilgrims true-to-life, Bowden argues that though the Knight and the Parson are exceptionally good, they are none the less realistic for that (p 318). She compares the Knight's 'gypon' with that of the Black Prince, on display in Canterbury Cathedral (p 319). See **401, 429, 474.**

- Review by Margaret Galway, *RES* 1(1950), 357–8: Bowden mentions Manly's theory of the Knight as a composite figure (**335**), but not Cook's (**326**), and thus obscures the probability that Chaucer 'was thinking of several, if not all, of the Englishmen who took part in the crusades from about 1340 onwards' (p 358).
- Review by Howard R. Patch, *MLN* 65(1950), 64–6: 'A judiciously assembled digest of important material' (p 64), the *Commentary* overemphasizes the limitations of feudalism and medieval religion to the neglect of the positive achievements of the age, and fails to treat the literary history of the portraits and Chaucer's Italian journeys. The narrow interpretation of *worthy* (I.68) as 'brave' excludes the ironical overtones of the word in the *GP*.
- See Hoffman **841**, pp 46–7: 'One of the most widely read books on Chaucer ever produced' (p 46). 'No teacher-critic, college student, or armchair reader of the *Tales* can quite afford to be without it, for ... these observations on the General Prologue form an essential introduction to all of *The Canterbury Tales*' (p 47).

354 Brett-James, Norman G. *Introducing Chaucer*. London: Harrap, 1949.
The Knight 'earns almost the warmest of all Chaucer's encomiums — he never abused anyone, and was a very perfect and gentle knight' (p 103).

355 Brown, Carleton. 'Chaucer's Squire and the Number of the Canterbury Pilgrims.' *MLN* 49(1934), 216–22.
The number twenty-nine (I.24) represents an original plan that Chaucer modified by inserting the portrait of the Squire as the thirtieth pilgrim. The Squire's military campaigns do not overlap with the Knight's, a possible evidence of composition at different times. Lines I.101–2 originally concluded the Knight's portrait, the 'he' of this couplet being the Knight; his preference for a small retinue echoes his modest dress, and 'that tyme' refers to his just having come 'from his viage' (I.77). See **452.**

356 Camden, Carroll, Jr. 'Chauceriana.' *MLN* 47(1932), 360–2.
Camden defines *worthy* (A[I].43) as 'able,' 'fit,' 'suitable,' 'having such qualities as to be deserving of or adapted to some specified thing' (p 360). To apply the definition, 'one would have to know what the medieval Englishman thought the characteristics of a "worthy" or typical person (of any status) were' (p 360).

357 Chesterton, G.K. *Chaucer*. London: Faber and Faber, 1932; rpt 1948, 1960, 1965. New York: Pellegrini & Cudahy, 1948.
In the Knight's portrait 'the poet seems actually to take a detour in order to avoid the fields of Crecy and Poictiers ... Chaucer goes out of his way to say that his hero fought for the Cross and not the Crown ... The Knight comes from ... those ultimate enmities in which Christianity is in collision with the things really outside itself. He is the ghost of a grander Europe ... The Knight is of a larger make or framework than the rest; and throws a giant shadow ... [that] lies on us and on our children. It is a problem of the present and even more of the future, whether we can make even so large a commonwealth of nations as combined in the Crusade' (pp 63–4).

358 Chute, Marchette. *Geoffrey Chaucer of England*. New York: Dutton, 1946.
The Knight is 'everything that a knight should be and usually was not – honorable, courteous to all classes, gallant in war and very conscientious about the religious significance of a pilgrimage. He may have been Chaucer's answer to the rising tide of criticism from men like Gower [cf **185**] and Deschamps as to the worthlessness of the current crop of knights' (p 249). Chaucer individualizes the Knight by listing his battles and describing his horse and stained tunic. For *KnT* see **668**.

359 Coghill, Nevill. *The Poet Chaucer*. London: Oxford University Press, 1949/2nd ed, 1967.
The Knight (pp 95–8) is a 'pattern of authority, humility, candour, and kindness' (p 93). He fits the Medieval Latin term for a gentleman, *generosus*. Dante, Chaucer, and Langland all believed that this 'largesse or freedom of nature' was due not to an individual's heredity but to his imitation of Christ (p 95). In literature the Knight can be compared to Sir Roger de Coverley [of *The Spectator*]. For *KnT* see **670**.

360 — *Geoffrey Chaucer*. Writers and Their Work, No. 79. London: Longmans, 1956.
The Knight is 'the finest figure of courtesy' in the *CT* (p 26) and just as realistically drawn as Chaucer's rogues. Both his military career, echoing those of participants in the Scropes-Grosvenor trial of 1386

(**201**), and his character would have seemed authentic to Chaucer's audience.

361 Davies, R.T. *Chaucer: The Prologue to the Canterbury Tales*. London, Harrap, 1953; rpt many times through 1973.
The Knight is 'a model of the perfect military man described in the didactic literature of the later Middle Ages'; his career as a crusader is emphasized (p 68). The ideal of being 'fierce in the field' and 'gentle in the hall' goes back to *Beowulf* (p 68). Davies analyzes 'chivalrie,' 'trouthe,' 'fredom,' 'curteseiye,' 'honour,' 'gentleness,' and 'vileinye,' showing the general dependence of aristocratic virtue on great wealth and the special Christian coloring of these virtues in the Knight's case (pp 69–70). Chaucer's characterization of the Knight as a gentleman and as an ascetic older man preparing for judgment is conveyed partly by the orderly structure of his portrait: 'built in three blocks with a tail-piece about outward appearance' (p 73).

362 Dent, A.A. 'Chaucer and the Horse.' *Proceedings of the Leeds Philosophical and Literary Society* 9 (1959–62), 1–2.
Dent comments on the Ellesmere miniature, describing the Knight as 'a recently retired cavalry officer' who is 'frankly mercenary' (p 9). The branding of his horse ('M' for Munster or Mecklenburg?) is characteristic of German horse-breeding establishments. The war-horses given to the Knight and the Squire would not be suitable for pilgrimage but identify them as belonging to 'the *stede*-owning class' (p 9). For *KnT* see **673**.

363 — 'Pictures from Chaucer.' *History Today* 10(August, 1960), 542–53.
Dent contrasts the Ellesmere miniatures with the woodcuts of Pynson's 1491 edition. The miniature presents the Knight (p 544) in civilian dress; the woodcut presents him in armor of the heavy, complex type typical of the late fifteenth-century.

364 Donaldson, E. Talbot. 'Chaucer the Pilgrim.' *PMLA* 69(1954), 928–36. Rpt in *Chaucer Criticism: The Canterbury Tales*, ed. Richard J. Schoeck and Jerome Taylor (Notre Dame: Notre Dame University Press, 1960), pp 1–13; in *Discussions of the 'Canterbury Tales,'* ed. Charles A. Owen, Jr. (Lexington, Mass.: D.C. Heath, 1961), pp 18–24; and in Donaldson's *Speaking of Chaucer* (New York: Norton, 1970), pp 1–12.
Donaldson defines the narrator of the *GP* as a fictional reporter who is 'usually, acutely unaware of the significance of what he sees, no matter how sharply he sees it' (p 929). 'One might reasonably ask how the narrator's uncertain sense of values may be reconciled with the enthusiasm he shows for [the] rigorous integrity [of the Knight,

Parson, and Plowman] ... It is the nature of the pilgrim to admire all kinds of superlatives ... He is ... merely an average man, or mankind; ... showing himself, too frequently, able to recognize the good only when it is spectacularly so .... The pilgrim's ready appreciation for the virtuous characters is perhaps the greatest tribute that could be paid to their virtue, and their spiritual simplicity is, I think, enhanced by the intellectual simplicity of the reporter' (pp 933–4).

365 — *Chaucer's Poetry*. 1958/rev 1975. See **50**. Pp 881–3/1044–3.
The Knight is both 'a pattern of perfection against which all the other pilgrims may be measured' (p 881/1041) and 'the dominant figure' of the age (p 881/1042). Chaucer shows his participation only in holy wars, and the lord he serves (I.47) 'almost seems' to be God, not an earthly lord. He is 'less ... an experienced veteran than ... a perfect knight,' both a valiant warrior and a sage counselor, and with the Parson, one of the pilgrims who seems 'most aware of the real purpose of the pilgrimage' (p 882/1043). Balancing the Knight's 'august attributes,' are the Squire's 'more human and perhaps more endearing ones' (p 882/1043). 'What the Squire is, the Knight once was, and what the Knight is, the Squire may yet be' (883/1043). 'The portrait of the Yeoman carries into the lower-class milieu the sense of purposeful order that we associate with the Knight he serves' (p 883/1044). For *KnT* see **675**.

366 Duncan, Edgar Hill. 'Narrator's Points of View in the Portrait-Sketches, Prologue to the *Canterbury Tales.*' In *Essays in Honor of Walter Clyde Curry*. [No editor.] *Vanderbilt Studies in the Humanities*, Volume Two. Nashville: Vanderbilt University Press, 1954. Pp 77–102.
Duncan divides the Knight's portrait into three sections. Lines I.43–67 are dominated by the omniscient point of view and include summary statements 'particularized, omnisciently, by precise references' and ended by 'omniscient generalization' (p 78). Lines 68–72 'form a bridge of transition from the omniscient to the completely limited' point of view, and include personal observation (69) and the Narrator's conclusion about the Knight's character (72). Lines 73–8 'are strictly limited to the Narrator's point of view in the dramatic situation ... Their effect is to give the knight a local situation in the immediate dramatic context, ... to make him dramatically real' (p 78).

367 Elliott, R.W.V. *Chaucer's Prologue to the Canterbury Tales*. Notes on English Literature Series. Oxford: Blackwell, 1960; New York, Barnes & Noble, 1963.
Comparable in rank to the Prioress, the Knight is closest morally to the idealized Parson, though rendered more life-like by the references

to his appearance. The Knight's virtue is emphasized by the four negatives in lines I.70–1. He is meant to remind the audience of a neglected ideal and of the true nature of worthiness, founded on character rather than wealth (pp 27–9).

368 Ethel, Garland. 'Horse or Horses: A Chaucerian Textual Problem.' *MLN* 75(1960), 97–101.
Ethel contests Skeat's translation (**344** V: 8) of line A [I].74, which is meant to reveal that the Knight avoids the elaborate equestrian equipage condemned by Church moralists. The key is *were*, here, as in line 68, a subjunctive third person singular preterit. Line 74 is 'a conditional sentence consisting of an hypothetical and a completing principal clause' (p 99) with omission of an initial *though*. See **413**.

369 Fink, Z.S. 'Another Knight There Was.' *PQ* 17(1938), 321–30.
Fink explores the parallels between Chaucer's Knight and Jörg von Ehingen, a German knight born in 1428 who left an autobiographical account of his campaigns. 'Both ... were associated with military orders in fighting on the borders of Christendom, and von Ehingen fought at both ends of the Mediterranean as Chaucer's knight had done, and in part at the same places. Both knights fought in combats against heathen champions, ... and were honored "aboven alle naciouns," the one in Prussia, the other in North Africa' (p 328). Manly **335** was justified in characterizing the Knight's career as 'possible and natural' rather than excessively idealized; and since many knights may have had similar careers, arguments for particular persons as models cannot be convincing (pp 329–330).

370 Héraucourt, W. *Die Wertwelt Chaucers, die Wertwelt einer Zeitwende*. Heidelberg: Carl Winter, 1939.
In this study of key words in their cultural contexts, of special interest for the Knight's portrait are the discussions of *gentillese* (pp 51–8), *honour* (pp 64–71), *curteisye* (pp 71–5), *trouthe* (pp 184–91), *knight* (pp 240–5), and *worthinesse* (pp 245–8). See pp 30–1 for Chaucer's views on knighthood, and see p 377 for an index to lines in the *GP*. For *KnT* see **695**.

371 Hoffman, Arthur W. 'Chaucer's Prologue to Pilgrimage: The Two Voices.' *ELH* 21(1954), 1–16. Rpt in *Chaucer: Modern Essays in Criticism*, ed. Edward Wagenknecht (London: Oxford University Press, 1959), pp 30–45; in *Discussions of the 'Canterbury Tales'*, ed. Charles A. Owen, Jr. (Lexington, Mass.: D. C. Heath, 1961), pp 9–17; and in *Chaucer: The Canterbury Tales, A Casebook*, ed. J.J. Anderson (London: Macmillan, 1974), pp 105–20.
The 'double view of pilgrimage' represented by nature and supernature, by the 'voices' of the bird and the saint (I.1–18), appears in

the portraits as a 'range of motivation ... from the sacred to the secular and on to the profane' (p 4). 'In the Knight, the acquired, tutored, disciplined, elevated, enlarged love, the piety; and in the Squire, the love channelled into an elaborate social ritual, a parody piety, but still emphatically fresh and full of natural impulse' (p 6). The Squire's pilgrimage is allied to the voice of the bird; the Knight's, to the voice of the saint (p 6). The concluding couplet of the Squire's portrait (I.99–100) suggests the son's submitting to his father, to the values of the past he represents and to the supernatural goal he seeks (p 6). 'A host of relative judgments' are set up by the sequencing of portraits, and the ideal portraits of the Knight, Parson, and Plowman provide 'a kind of penultimate judgment' (p 11). See **408**, **429**.

372 Hulbert, J.R. 'Chaucer's Pilgrims.' *PMLA* 64(1949), 823–8. Rpt in *Chaucer: Modern Essays in Criticism*. Ed. Edward Wagenknecht. London: Oxford University Press, 1959, pp 23–9.
There is only one Knight in the *GP* because he is meant to represent his class and, possibly, an actual individual. Noting the disagreement between Manly **335** and Robinson **388** as to the nature of the Knight's career, Hulbert argues against its being merely typical, since it does not include Crécy and Poitiers, and since it has 'a perfect consistency not likely to be found in a composite' (p 826).

373 Kaske, R.E. 'The Knight's Interruption of the *Monk's Tale*.' *ELH* 24(1957), 249–68.
'Why has Chaucer used the ... interruption of the *Monk's Tale* to make [a] belated, fairly extended, and to all appearances thematically isolated observation on the Knight?' (p 251). The interruption is not an instance of 'vileynye' nor of literary naiveté as Malone **379** suggests (p 251); rather the link provides the climax to Chaucer's pairing of Knight and Monk, who are 'virtually antitypes' (p 252). The Monk has had a soft life, the Knight, a harsh one; the Monk has accomplished little, the Knight is renowned for his achievements; the Monk speaks brusquely, the Knight, with reserve. Monasticism and chivalry are the two great depositories of Christian idealism, and Chaucer seems to see the hunting monk as 'a kind of comic imitation of knighthood' (p 254). Knight and Monk are paired again when the Host invites the Monk to 'quite' the *KnT* (I.3118–9). The Knight's interruption 'completes a sort of double chiasmus ... in which the *Monk's Tale*, seemingly at odds with his individual character, is broadly in keeping with the ideal of which he himself is an inadequate representative; while the Knight's opinions, which appear suspiciously shallow for his own ideally conceived character, accord

well enough with what might be expected of some nearly actual or more conventionally romantic representatives of knighthood' (p 260). The pattern may also be psychologically significant: the comfortable Monk can enjoy tragedy, the weary Knight prefers to contemplate life's lighter side. See **1082**. For *KnT* see **703**.

374 Loomis, Roger S. 'Was Chaucer a Laodicean?' *Essays and Studies in Honor of Carleton Brown*. [No editor] New York: New York University Press, 1940. Pp 129–48. Rpt in *Chaucer Criticism: The Canterbury Tales*. Ed. Richard Schoeck and Jerome Taylor. Notre Dame: Notre Dame University Press, 1960. Pp 291–310 [cited here].
Was Chaucer 'wholly lukewarm, wholly neutral' on the controversies of his time? Loomis answers in the negative, seeing in the *GP* a protest against the Hundred Years' War. The 'doctrine' of the Knight's portrait accords with that of Wyclif, defining as just wars only those 'in the cause of the Church or for the honour of Christ' (p 298). 'The mature Chaucer of 1387 must have been convinced of the futility of war, except for some high cause far transcending the territorial pretensions of monarchs' (p 299). Knights as a group were sympathetic to Lollardy, and four of the most prominent Lollard Knights – Clifford, Stury, Neville, and Clanvowe – were friends of Chaucer's. The Knight's making a pilgrimage 'does disqualify him as a good Wycliffite,' but Chaucer's idealized portrait may yet be 'an expression of sympathy with a suspect class' (p 301). See **398**, **440**.

375 Lumiansky, R.M. 'Chaucer's Philosophical Knight.' *Tulane Studies in English* 3(1952), 47–68.
Presents the same analysis as **376** below, with these additions. Each of the nouns in lines I.45–6 suggests two meanings: one 'limited to strictly military excellence,' the other having 'a general moral application' (p 51). The teachings of Boethius interest the Knight, yet he is not 'overly sober'; he plays the role of 'assistant manager' of the group with tact and good humor (p 52). See **713**.

376 — *Of Sondry Folk: The Dramatic Principle in the Canterbury Tales*. Austin: Texas University Press, 1955.
The reader accepts the pilgrims as 'realistic persons' (p 20) because of the 'combination of typical and individual traits,' or better, the 'combination of the expected and the unexpected' (p 22). Lines I.43–67 of the Knight's portrait present the expected: 'brave and honorable qualities and campaigns representative of the age of chivalry' (p 23); lines 68–78 present the unexpected, 'a professional military man' who is 'prudent, humble, circumspect in speech, modest in dress, and serious in religious devotion' (p 23). Lines I.68–9 and especially the word *though* indicate the Knight's moral superiority to many in his

profession (pp 33–4). The assignment to tell the first tale falls to the Knight either by chance or because of the Host's respect for rank (p 27). Because of this scene, we see the *KnT* as 'a recital by the Knight,' not just as a tale by Chauncer (p 27). See **474**, **713**.

377 — 'Benoit's Portraits and Chaucer's General Prologue.' *JEGP* 55(1956), 431–8. Esp. pp 437–8.
The portraits of Hector and Troilus in the *Roman de Troie* (5093–582) show similarities to the Knight-Squire pair. 'Both the Knight and Hector are mature and experienced individuals, worthy and wise, bold in war and courteous in speech; while both the Squire and Troilus are young, gay, attractive, interested in love, and brave in battle' (p 437).

378 Malone, Kemp. 'Style and Structure in the Prologue to the Canterbury Tales.' *ELH* 13(1946). Rpt with minor additions as Ch 8 in **379**.

379 — *Chapters on Chaucer*. Baltimore: Johns Hopkins, 1951; rpt 1961. Ch 8: The portraits are organized by rank, as indicated by the Knight's primacy of place, and by special groupings such as the 'household group' (p 149) formed by Knight, Squire, and Yeoman. Ch 9: Chaucer does not dwell on the Knight's campaigns in Christendom because he wants to make him 'a great champion of Christianity against the heathen' (p 168). A perfect knight who has never spoken 'vileynye,' he 'breaks the habits of a lifetime to stint the monk of his tale' (p 169). In this 'new characterization of the knight,' 'we discover that our military hero has the taste of a child, or at any rate of a thoroughly unsophisticated person ... Tragedy he cannot abide. A story must end happily' (p 170). Perhaps Chaucer wanted to make the knight 'more human by making him less perfect' (p 170). Kittredge **332** treats the pilgrims as actual persons and undervalues their dramatic aspects. The Knight is 'a perfect knight, not a perfect man' (p 173). Ch 10: The realistic passages in the portraits are intended to give the illusion of actuality and do not constitute evidence that Chaucer drew his pilgrims from actual models. Some statements in the Knight's portrait present him as an ideal [eg, lines I.68–72]; some give him individuality [eg, 73–80]; and some serve both purposes at once [eg, 68–9] (pp 198–9). See **353**, **373**, **440**.

380 Manly, John Matthews, and Rickert, Edith. *The Text of the Canterbury Tales*. 1940. See **42**.
The 'Critical Notes' (III, 421–8) include only two for the Knight's portrait: a note on the phrase 'as in' in I.49 and another on *armee* in I.60. For comment on the editors' view that *armee* is the correct

term, misread by some fifteenth-century scribes as *aryue*, see Donaldson **450** and Görlach **463**. For *KnT* see **717**.

381 McCormick, Sir William. *The Manuscripts of Chaucer's Canterbury Tales: A Critical Description of Their Contents*. With the assistance of Janet E. Heseltine. Oxford: Clarendon, 1933.
The Knight-Miller link (A[I].3109–86) is found in place in all but two (McCormick and Phillips 8137) of 57 complete or practically complete mss (xv). The Monk-Nun's Priest's link (B^2.3957–4010 [VII.2767–2820]) was originally lacking or is missing or misplaced or breaks off at some point in thirteen mss (xix). The Long and Short forms of this link are probably the result of 'an uncertainty in Chaucer's own mind,' and the scribes' confusion was increased by the problem of placing the Modern Instances in the *MkT* (xxix–xxx).

382 Owen, Charles A., Jr. 'The Development of the *Canterbury Tales*.' *JEGP* 57(1958), 449–76.
Early in his work on the *CT*, Chaucer composed the Knight's portrait without any thought of linking it to *P&A*, already in existence on the evidence of *LGW* (F.420–1). The references to the Teutonic knights in the Knight's portrait and to the Despenser 'crusade' in the Squire's indicate a date in 1387 or after for their composition (p 455). The Knight's replacement of the Host as the interrupter of the *MkT* was intended to introduce variety (since the Host had already interrupted *Thop*), and may have been suggested by the Knight's role at the end of the *PardT*, already composed (p 472). For *KnT* see **733**.

383 Parr, Johnstone. 'Chaucer and *Partonope of Blois*.' *MLN* 60(1945), 486–7.
I.60–3 (on the Knight's mortal battles and fights in lists) parallels *Partonope* 11858–60. For *KnT* see **736**.

384 Patch, Howard Rollin. *On Rereading Chaucer*. Cambridge, Mass.: Harvard University Press, 1939.
The Knight's dignity is enhanced by meekness, valor, and simplicity of dress and manner (p 155), but somewhat qualified by the implication that his 'worthinesse,' like the Franklin's, is only respectability (p 156). For *KnT* see **611**.

385 Piper, Edwin Ford. *Canterbury Pilgrims*. Iowa City, Iowa: Clio Press, 1935.
In this set of poems inspired by the *CT*, one (p 18) celebrates the Knight's chivalry and courtly qualities; another (p 19), his battles.

386 Preston, Raymond. *Chaucer*. New York and London: Sheed & Ward, 1952. Rpt New York: Greenwood Press, 1969.
Preston points out grounds for criticism of the Knight in I.68–71: eg, the Knight may love but not practice chivalric virtues, and avoiding

villainous speech is a 'safely negative virtue.' But Preston rejects this reading. 'The Knight is five times called *worthy* – not, I believe, because we are to consider him the reverse, but because the worth of knights in his day could hardly be taken for granted' (p 155). The best Knights achieved only a qualified perfection. For *KnT* see **746**.

387 Rickert, Edith, and John M. Manly. *The Text of the Canterbury Tales*. 1940. See **42**.
See Manly **380**.

388 Robinson, F.N. *The Works of Chaucer*. 1933/1957. See **39**. P 652.
Robinson reviews the Knight's battles in chronological order, following Manly's reconstruction (**335**). He rejects Cook's linkage of the portrait with the siege of Vilna in 1390–1 (**326**) since the date is too late for the probable time of composition of the *GP* [c 1387]. Robinson is skeptical of attempts to find specific literary and historical models for the Knight. The character, and probably the career, is typical. 'Chaucer presents in the Knight a completely ideal figure. Although chivalry in the fourteenth century was in its decline and had a very sordid side, Chaucer has wholly refrained from satirizing the institution. It has been suggested, indeed, that in this very ideal presentation the keenest satire was concealed. But it may be doubted if such was Chaucer's intention' (p 652). See **372**, **510**; for *KnT* see **751**.

389 Schlauch, Margaret. 'King Arthur in the Baltic Towns.' *Bulletin Bibliographique de la Société Internationale Arthurienne* 11(1959), 75–80.
Schlauch describes the formation in Danzig during the fourteenth century of 'Brotherhoods of King Arthur' (p 75) by 'members of families of noble origin who had turned to trade' (p 76). Both these societies and the Teutonic Order may have been inspired by Edward III's Order of the Garter. The many English visitors to Prussia – eg, Henry Hotspur, John Beaufort, Henry Bolingbroke (**196**) – may have reported on the Danzig societies, providing 'one reason for [Chaucer's] envisaging the Baltic area as an appropriate scene for his Knight's adventurings' (p 80).

390 Sedgwick, Henry Dwight. *Dan Chaucer*. Indianapolis: Bobbs-Merrill, 1934.
The Knight is 'the portrait of an English gentleman. He brings with him an atmosphere of quiet, courtly dignity, and his modesty, in spite of all his adventures in foreign lands, bears, as it were, ... the stamp of Eton and Cambridge' (p 20). Referring to I.72, Sedgwick says: 'what a felicitous verse by which to sum up his character, no wonder it is proverbial. And, how well the poet, even after that verse, adds

to the effect of the description, by telling how careless the Knight is of his appearance' (p 20). For *KnT* see **757**.

391 — *In Praise of Gentlemen*. Boston: Little, Brown, 1935.
In this defense of 'the Guild of Gentlemen' against democracy and other 'forces of destruction,' Sedgwick sees Christianity as both detracting from and enhancing the gentlemanly ideal. Asserting that 'no one has delineated the Christian gentleman better than Chaucer,' Sedgwick cites the Knight's meekness and his casualness about his appearance as unfortunate results of Christian influence, contrary to the pride and elegance of a gentleman (pp 85–6).

392 Smith, Roland M. 'Chaucer Allusions in the Letters of Sir Walter Scott.' *MLN* 65(1950), 448–55.
Letter to Richard Heber, 29 Oct. 1823 (Vol. VIII, p 109 in the Grierson edition): Scott describes his son Walter as 'just the stuff out of which would have been made in former days "A verie parfite gentle knight"'(p 454). For *KnT* see **762**.

393 Speirs, John. 'The Prologue.' *Chaucer the Maker*. London: Faber and Faber, 1951. Rpt 1964, 1967, 1972. Pp 99–121.
The Prologue gives us 'an impression of a people, the English people' (p 102). 'The rather faded, crusading Knight is felt as already passing into the past, rememberable for an inner beauty of life beneath his battered exterior expressed in the tenderly nostalgic line "He was a verray parfit gentil knight"'(p 103). The 'fadedness' of the Knight contrasts with 'the gay extravagance of the young Squire and with the spectacular Robin Hood-like apparition of the Yeoman who is, underneath, simply a solid English countryman' (p 103). For *KnT* see **767**.

394 Stillwell, Gardiner. 'Chaucer's Knight.' 1944.
See Webb **398**.

395 Swart, J. 'The Construction of Chaucer's *General Prologue*.' *Neophil* 38(1954), 127–36.
The portraits can be divided into two groups representing social order and disorder. In the first, the Knight, Squire, and Yeoman represent the nobility and are followed by the clergy and by various sub-groups of commoners. The Parson and the Plowman close the group representing order and replicate the pattern of nobleman, priest, and commoner because they are linked to the Knight by their 'perfect Christian virtues' (p 130). Chaucer's choice of the Knight to tell the first tale, with the implication that the Host uses sleight of hand to arrange it, is a device to make the scene realistic (p 135).

396 Thompson, W.H. 'The Men of Arms.' *Chaucer and His Times*. London: A. Brown & Sons, 1936. Rpt Folcroft, Pennsylvania: Folcroft Library Editions, 1975. Pp 84–7.
The Knight is 'the gentle Don Quixote in his sound mind ... in deportment there is nothing of the coarse mercenary about him, even though he has been on fifteen deadly battlefields.' 'An indefinable old-world air' clings to him; his 'simple, unadorned courtesy' needs 'no outside finery or trappings to bespeak the true gentleman.' The type is seen again in Thackeray's Colonel Newcome and in General Charles Gordon. Everyone is drawn to such a man, including the Host and the churls. For *KnT* see **774**.

397 Waggoner, George R. 'Allusions to Chaucer.' *TLS* 21 Nov. 1952, 761.
In *The Duello or Single Combat* (1610), John Selden relates 'trouthe,' 'honour,' 'fredom' and 'curteisie' to the offenses which lead to duels: 'the *Lie* given, *Fame* impeached, *Body* wronged, or *Curtesie* taxed.'

398 Webb, Henry J. and Gardiner Stillwell. 'Chaucer's Knight and the Hundred Years' War.' *MLN* 59(1944), 45–7.
Stillwell and Webb contest Loomis' argument (**374**) that the Knight fought mainly against heathens and that this circumstance indicates Chaucer's opposition to the Hundred Years' War and all secular wars. They respond that the Squire must have been the Knight's attendant in battle, and that his campaigns (I.86) are to be understood as the Knight's too.

399 Whiting, B.J. 'Some Chaucer Allusions, 1923–1942.' *N&Q* 187(1944), 288–91.
In *His Majesty of Corsica* (London, 1939), Valerie Pirie attributes the Knight's loves (I.45–6) to Francis II. Rakoczi, Prince of Transylvania (p 290). For KnT see **783**.

400 Woolf, Rosemary. 'Chaucer as Satirist in the General Prologue to the Canterbury Tales.' *Critical Quarterly* 1(1959), 150–7.
Chaucer speaks in his own voice in the portraits of the Knight, Parson, Plowman, and Clerk, establishing the 'true moral standard' by which the rest of the pilgrimage may be judged. Chaucer's satire is not so angry as Langland's and is perhaps less hopeful. 'The virtuous characters, however, by their very presence, imply a censure of the rest, which dispels any impression of over-sophisticated aloofness' (p 155).

1961-1970

401 Badendyck, J. Lawrence. 'Chaucer's Portrait Technique and the Dream Vision Tradition.' *EngR* 21(1970), 113–25.

Chaucer makes the Knight seem a creature of 'flesh and blood,' Bowden's term (**353**), not by the use of visual or psychological detail, but by locating him in time and space through the list of battles. 'They are the ground of whatever substantiality the Knight has. In modern terms they would have the effect of reciting World War II battles' (p 119). Deliberately placed before the description of the Knight's traits, 'the history does more than balance the abstract qualities. It lashes the whole construct to reality' (p 119).

402 Beidler, Peter G. 'Chaucer's "Knight's Tale" and Its Teller.' *EngR* 18(1968), 54–60.
In his three appearances in the frame, at the ends of the *GP, MkT,* and *PardT*, the Knight shows the same cheerful disposition and interest in preserving light-hearted play seen in his tale. For *KnT* see **798**.

402a Birch, P.M. *Four Essays*. 1967.
See Bright **405**.

403 Bowden, Muriel. 'The Influence of Chaucer's Chivalric World.' *A Reader's Guide to Geoffrey Chaucer*. New York: Farrar, Strauss, and Giroux, 1964; rpt 1966. Pp 17–45.
Bowden sketches the influence of the crusades and courtly love on the concept of chivalry. The decline of courtly love by the fourteenth century accounts for the absence of references to love in the Knight's portrait. The Knight's initial position reflects his excellence in virtue and not just his social standing. The Knight's battles – all against the heathen as Pope Urban commanded – and his appearance support the statements about his character. The claims that he has been honored by the Teutonic Knights 'ful ofte tyme' (I. 52) and that he has slain his foes in 'lystes thries' (I.63) are poetic exaggerations that point to truths about the Knight. His stained clothes signal his pious eagerness to start his pilgrimage. His horses and attendants are appropriate according to the rules of the chivalric orders. For *KnT* see **804**.

404 Brewer, Derek. *Chaucer in His Time*. London: Nelson, 1963; Longman, 1973; rpt through 1977.
Brewer describes the ideal of chivalry, particularly the qualities of loyalty, bravery, pity, generosity, and courtesy (pp 157–63): the 'chivalric and courtly view of life is entirely accepted by Chaucer,' who 'deepens and ennobles the ideal' in the *GP* where the Squire represents 'the more obviously youthful parts of the idea,' and the Knight, 'the deeper moral qualities' (p 163). Brewer comments briefly on the Knight's virtues, modesty in dress, and prudence in battle, comparing him with several of Chaucer's acquaintances who were

companions of the Black Prince **204**. They were not feudal retainers but served for pay, as the Knight did with the lord of Palatye. 'Chaucer's portrait is not only of greater moral beauty than the average contemporary description, it is also more realistic' (p 164). For *KnT* see **805**.

405 Bright, J.C., and P.M. Birch. *Four Essays on Chaucer*. Australian High School English. Sydney: William Brooks, 1967.
Contains brief references to the Knight in four wide-ranging essays on medieval society, thought, and literary traditions. Bright characterizes the Knight's portrait as 'slightly ironical' (p 7); Birch says the Knight is an ideal representative of 'an order of society which Chaucer wholly endorses' (pp 27, 32–4). For *KnT* see **806**.

406 Brooks, Harold F. *Chaucer's Pilgrims: The Artistic Order of the Portraits in the Prologue*. New York: Barnes & Noble; London: Methuen, 1962; rpt 1968.
The Knight properly comes first in the *GP* and tells the first tale. He is 'a lofty, serious, ideal figure,' individualized by his parenthood and his military career. His family group is arranged in descending order of individualization, rank, relationship, and ideals. 'The Squire's good qualities ... are more secular ... than his father's. Yet some of them are moral as well as social, while the Yeoman's are all matters of practical skill and of workmanlike pride' (pp 13–4). 'The Knight and Squire are strongly contrasted, on a basis of affinities.' They represent the same military class but different stages of life. 'The youth, fashion, grace, exuberance, and promise of the Squire contrast with the Knight's maturity and experience, his long record of achievement, his concentration on essentials, like good horses and prompt thanksgiving, at the expense if necessary of his appearance' (p 14).

407 Corsa, Helen Storm. *Chaucer: Poet of Mirth and Morality*. Notre Dame: University of Notre Dame Press, 1964.
The description of the Knight is unironic but suggestive of comedy. 'The Knight is truly and unromantically "worthy" in all the ways it is possible for him to be ... But as the reiteration [of the word] suggests, he is limited, uncomplex, single in vision.' The Squire is 'fresshe,' the Yeoman, efficient. Like the royal eagles of the *PF*, these three fighters are not themselves comic, but their limitations show up when they are compared with the other pilgrims (p 81). When the Host and Pardoner quarrel, the Knight re-establishes the perspective necessary for mirth (p 193). His action recalls his primacy of place in the *GP* and the fact that his own tale emphasized such values as order, justice, and pity. He becomes 'almost a symbol of Order, restoring into harmonious coexistence the elements that threaten

disorder,' a function he also performs at the end of the *MkT* (p 194). The Knight releases the audience's sense of comic surprise at the hedonistic Monk's telling tragic stories. The Knight's concept of comedy is Chaucer's despite the 'apparent unsophisticated simplicity' of the definition (p 210). For *KnT* see **815**.

408 Courtney, Neil. 'Chaucer's Poetic Vision.' *CR* 8(1965), 129–40.
Courtney questions Hoffman's separating out of natural and supernatural characteristics and motives in the pilgrims (**371**), preferring to emphasize the wholeness of individual pilgrims. The Knight's portrait begins with unequivocal praise which is given 'a slight, comic qualification' by the list of battles, in which the Knight's 'boastful tone' can be heard, and by the insistence on his worthiness. Line 68, distinguishing between his worthiness and his wisdom, is 'overtly comic'; the reference to his stained garment is the 'one sharp personal touch,' serving to emphasize the Knight's formality and remoteness. The Knight is not an ideal type nor are chilvaric ideals debunked, but 'they are not established in the Knight without some cost' (pp 134–5).

409 Delasanta, Rodney. 'The Horsemen of the *Canterbury Tales*.' *ChauR* 3(1968), 29–36.
The Knight, Clerk, Nun's Priest, Plowman, and Parson dress simply and ride poor, or at least un-caparisoned, horses. Cf the *ParsT* (I [X].412 and 430 f) for a condemnation of the 'synne of adornement or of apparaille' (p 33–4).

410 Dunleavy, Gareth W. 'Natural Law as Chaucer's Ethical Absolute.' *Transactions of the Wisconsin Academy of Sciences, Arts and Letters* 52(1963), 177–87. Rpt in *Geoffrey Chaucer*. Ed. Willi Erzgräber. *Wege der Forschumg*, Volume 253. Darmstadt: Wissenschaftliche Buchgesellschaft, 1983. Pp 196–209.
The Knight, Parson, and Plowman are the 'most complete Christians' in the *GP*. 'In a day when man-made laws of chivalry are close to becoming superannuated, the Knight independently adheres to the natural law concept of "trouthe and honour" translated to mean "sense of honor, honourable dealing"' (pp 208–9).

411 Engel, Claire-Elaine. 'Les Croisades du Chevalier.' *Revue des Sciences Humaines*, No. 120(1965), 577–85.
The Knight's battles 'n'ont rien de fantaisiste' although the Knight is 'un personnage fictif' and 'le symbole du plus haut idëal chevaleresque' (p 577). His campaigns in Grenada, Algezir, Belmarye, and Prussia parallel the career of Henry of Derby (pp 578–81); his battles in Asia Minor echo the experiences of Sir Richard Scrope (pp 582–3; see **201**). Tramyssene, usually identified as Tlemcen, may actually

be Termessos, an ancient site near Sattalia (pp 583–4). The siege of Alexandria in 1365 is the latest campaign mentioned, although the *GP* was probably not composed until 1387 (pp 584–5). The portrait presents the familiar chivalric ideal and a new idea: the thirst for exotic adventure and knowledge of new places (p 585).

412 Farrell, William J. 'Chaucer's Use of the Catalogue.' *TSLL* 5(1963), 64–78.
Farrell compares *BD* 1020–6 with I.51–66 of the *GP*. Listing the places to which Fair White will not send a man – Pruyse, Tartarye, Alysaundre, Turkye – is merely an exercise in amplification, while in the Knight's portrait, each place-name is 'a testimony to his "worthiness," a proof of the essential virtue that is synonymous with the Knight himself' (p 73). We are meant to contrast the Knight's 'far-flung experience' with the Squire's 'provincial adventures' (p 73). The Knight's motives are more serious.

413 French, W.H. 'General Prologue 74: Horse or Horses?' *MLN* 76(1961), 293–5.
French rejects Ethel's reading (**368**) of I.74. *Goode* 'determines the number of the entire construction' (p 294); *goode* and *hors* are plural and *he* refers to the Knight, who is 'nat gay.'

414 Greaves, Margaret. *The Blazon of Honour: A Study in Renaissance Magnanimity*. New York: Barnes & Noble, 1964. Pp 37–8.
Although Chaucer nowhere portrays the magnanimous man 'in his wholeness,' the portrait of the Knight 'comes nearest to a complete statement of the idea' (p 37). Pagan courage, truth, and honour are joined to medieval gentleness, freedom, and courtesy. For *KnT* see **827**.

415 Grennen, Joseph E. 'Chaucer in A Chapel Perilous: *The Waste Land*, 1–18 and 230–242.' *EngR* 13(1962), 42–4.
Eliot's line, 'Bin gar keine Russin, stamm' aus Litauen, echt deutsch' (12) recalls I.53–4. Compare also 'And makes a welcome of indifference' (242) with I.3042.

416 Griffith, Richard R. 'The Knight.' *A Critical Study Guide to Chaucer's The Canterbury Tales*. Totowa, New Jersey: Littlefield, Adams, 1968. Pp 25–8.
This summary of the Knight's portrait is accompanied by comments on the decline of chivalry, on the war-horse, and on historical models for the knight. For *KnT* see **828**.

417 Hatton, Thomas J. 'Chaucer's Crusading Knight, A Slanted Ideal.' *ChauR* 3 (1968), 77–87.
The portrait of the Knight is an idealization slanted to reflect the ideas of the French propagandist of crusading, Philippe de Mézières

(**198**, **199**). References to the Knight's worthiness — understood as embracing both bravery and battle-field skill and experience — frame the list of his battles, which is an *exemplum* of his worthiness (p 78). Similarly, reference to the Knight's wisdom — understood as embracing both prudence and the philosophic and social ideals of chivalry — introduces the account of his behavior off the battlefield (pp 79–80). The list of battles, the portrait's most original element (p 80), includes many of fourteenth-century Europe's campaigns against the heathen, but conspicuously omits England's victories in the Hundred Years' War (pp 80–1). 'The message of the Knight's portrait,' that 'true worthiness and true wisdom are best demonstrated in crusading' (p 82), accords with Philippe's program to end the Hundred Years' War and the Schism so that a reunited Europe might launch a crusade, spearheaded by Philippe's Order of the Passion of Jesus Christ, to recover the Holy Land. This program enjoyed significant support in England in the last decade of the century. See **934**.

418 Hira, Toshinori. 'Chaucer's Gentry in the Historical Background.' In *Nakayama Kyoju Kanreki Kinen Ei Bei Bungaku Ronso Kankokai (Essays in English and American Literature in Commemoration of Professor Takejiro Nakayama's Sixty-first Birthday)*. [No editor] Tokyo: Shohokuska, 1961. Pp 31–44.
The Knight belongs to a gentry group that was losing its traditional functions and its influence while new men of squire's rank, such as the Merchant, were growing in power. Chaucer presents his Knight in a traditional way and avoids political controversy, probably out of deference to his patrons.

419 Hodgson, Phyllis. *General Prologue: The Canterbury Tales*. London: Athlone, 1969.
The Knight is either a knight banneret or a knight bachelor. The repetition of *worthy* 'in a eulogy free from reservation' (p 74) connotes 'high social standing,' 'praiseworthiness,' 'bravery,' 'goodness,' and 'efficiency.' The Knight has the qualities (I.44–6) of a romance hero and the proven manhood of an actual fighter. The list of battles may seem hyperbolic, and yet may reflect a living model. Individualizing touches are the Knight's gentleness and piety and his memorably stained tunic (p 75). The Knight is a 'convincing exception' to self-seeking crusaders and knights given to luxurious living (p 75). The contrast between Knight and Squire opposes 'passionate youth and wise maturity' and crusades and courtly love (p 77).

420 Howard, Edwin J. *Geoffrey Chaucer*. New York: Twayne, 1964.
Chaucer uses understatement to treat abuses of the time. His Knight, a 'paragon of virtue,' contrasts with the imperfect knights of Chaucer's time (p 123). For *KnT* see **843**.

421 Huppé, Bernard F. *A Reading of the 'Canterbury Tales'*. Albany: State University of New York, 1964.
The key word of the Knight's portrait is 'worthy.' At first it associates him with the ideals of knight-errantry. Then the list of his battles, all crusades against the infidel, identifies the 'lord' the Knight serves (I.47) as God Himself. His worthiness is now associated with wisdom and Christian humility (pp 31–2). The Knight's portrait provides a foil for the Squire's (pp 32–3). See **487**; for *KnT* see **844**.

422 Hussey, Maurice. *Chaucer's World: A Pictorial Companion*. Cambridge: Cambridge University Press, 1967.
The Knight is 'an epitome of chivalric virtues' (p 37). Hussey identifies the Knight's hat in the Ellesmere miniature as of a 'fashionable long-tailed type known as the *liripipe*' (p 37), and discusses armor (pp 38–9), siege warfare, jousts and tournaments (pp 39–41), and castles (pp 41–7). The Knight, a noble of 'relatively modest social standing,' might have owned a manor such as Stokesay Castle in Shropshire (pp 41–2).

423 King, Francis, and Bruce Steele. *Selections from Geoffrey Chaucer's The Canterbury Tales*. Melbourne: F.W. Cheshire, 1969.
'Does Chaucer ... view the Knight with the same unsmiling idealism that he gives the Parson and his brother? There is at least room for doubt' (p 340). The incongruity between the ideal figure and the context of contemporary politics in which he appears makes the Knight 'something of a melancholy anachronism, even perhaps slightly comic' (p 340).

424 Kiralis, Karl. 'William Blake as an Intellectual and Spiritual Guide to Chaucer's *Canterbury Pilgrims*.' *BlakeS* 1(1969), 139–90.
In his engraving, Blake uses the figure of the Host to divide the pilgrims into two groups, the foremost group constituting the upper levels of society and headed by the Knight and the Squire. The Knight is contrasted with the Poet at the rear of the procession: the one noted for physical prowess and concerned with temporal affairs, the other, an observer of men concerned with eternal matters. The Knight tutors the Squire; the Poet, the Clerk.

425 Lenaghan, R.T. 'Chaucer's *General Prologue* as History and Literature.' *Comparative Studies in Society and History* 12(1970), 73–82.
The pilgrims can be divided into three groups according to the sources of their livelihood: land, the Church, and trade, with the

Knight belonging to the first. Landed wealth supported activities such as the Knight's crusading. 'The agents [peasants] work and the principals amuse themselves and render public service' (p 76). The *GP* shows a 'stress on hustle and competition' transcended by the 'exemplars of the three estates, the Knight, the Parson, and the Plowman,' who do so 'by a moral force unique to them' (p 79). The wealthy, including the Knight, appear to be exempt from sexual and economic competition (p 80), but historical evidence suggests that this was not really so. This appearance may reflect Chaucer's point of view as an insecure, upwardly mobile civil servant.

426 Loomis, Roger S. *A Mirror of Chaucer's World*. Princeton: Princeton University Press, 1965.
'The Knight' (Fig 80): Chaucer describes the Knight as wearing his *gypon*, for an example of which Loomis refers the reader to the effigy of the Black Prince in Canterbury Cathedral (Fig 19); but the Ellesmere artist has presented the Knight in 'an apparently padded, knee-length gown with wide sleeves and close-fitting cuffs.' His horse is sturdy and has an 'M' brand on its flank. For *KnT* see **854**.

427 Maclaine, Allan H. 'The General Prologue.' *The Student's Comprehensive Guide to the Canterbury Tales*. Woodbury, New York: Barron's Educational Series, 1964. Pp 11–42.
Maclaine provides a summary of the text, selective glosses, and a digest of interpretations; for the Knight, pp 15–7. For *KnT* see **855**.

428 Magoun, Francis P., Jr. *A Chaucer Gazeteer*. Chicago: University of Chicago Press, 1961.
This alphabetical listing and discussion of all geographical names, and terms of geographical origin or with geographical connections, used by Chaucer brings together the materials of Magoun's articles in *MS* 15(1953); 16(1954); and 17(1955). See entries for Algezir, Alisaundre, Belmarye, Gernade, Lettow, Lyeys, Mediterranean Sea, Palatye, Pruce, Ruce, and Satalye. For *KnT* see **856**.

429 Mitchell, Charles. 'The Worthiness of Chaucer's Knight.' *MLQ* 25(1964), 66–75.
Mitchell rejects Hoffman's association of the Knight with the Parson (**371**), positioning the Knight midway between the evil of the Pardoner and the Summoner and the good of the Parson and the Plowman (p 66). The Knight's perfection lies only in martial activity and courtly manners, and the ostensibly religious motives of his fighting may conceal a quest for glory. Mitchell cites Bowden **353** on the political and economic value of Satalye and Lyeys; notes that the Knight has fought for and against heathens and Christians; and contrasts the gentleness of his speech with the savagery of the victory

at Alexandria as reported by Bowden (pp 68–9). The Knight's chivalric values (I.44–6) are unlikely to bear the 'lofty moral significance' Hoffman ascribes to them (p 71). The Yeoman 'externalizes' the Knight's efficiency in killing the enemy (p 72). The word *curteys* links Knight, Squire, Prioress, and Friar, degenerating in meaning with each use. The Knight's interest in 'prys' and honor (I.50, 67) suggests an interest in courtly, not spiritual, perfection (p 74). The ambiguity of the Knight is summed up in the word *worthy*, whose meanings vary from 'estimable' (I.43) to merely 'brave' (I.68) (p 74). The Knight shares with the other pilgrims the spiritual sickness symbolized by the Cook's sore (p 75). See **485**.

430 Moorman, Charles. 'The Philosophical Knights of *The Canterbury Tales*.' *SAQ* 64(1965), 87–99. Rpt in *A Knyght There was: The Evolution of the Knight in Literature*. Lexington: University of Kentucky Press, 1967. Pp 76–95.
The Knight is an 'idealized reality – an actual bismotered fighter ... tempered by a set of values presumably extinct in the chivalric class; and he is a realized ideal, a ... piece of literary perfection, in stained clothing' (p 92). He is 'a living paradox' (I.72) since 'knights were ordinarily not both "true" and "perfect"'(p 92). Chaucer 'has defined a new concept of chivalry for a new age, a chivalry stripped of its immorality and criminal violence and ready to stand in the midst of the new mercantilism as a symbol of the conservative, middle-class values that Chaucer everywhere praises' (p 99). For *KnT* see **869**. See **208**.

431 Neuse, Richard. 'The Knight: The First Mover in Chaucer's Human Comedy.' *UTQ* 31(1962), 299–315. Rpt in *Geoffrey Chaucer: A Critical Anthology*. Ed. J.A. Burrow. Baltimore: Penguin, 1969. Pp 242–63.
Commenting on the seeming inconsistency between the 'playful narrator' of the *KnT* and the 'imposing' yet meek figure of the *GP*, Neuse says that in the *GP* 'it is mainly external "identity" that counts. The pilgrims appear as self-sufficient "concrete universals" while their potentialities ... remain largely hidden until they enter upon the stage of action' (p 301). Neuse links this relation between portrait and tale to the 'movement toward transcendence' (p 311) of the *CT*. The *KnT* also reflects the Knight's relation to the Squire, and the problem of being both 'worthy' and 'wys' (I.68); see **871**.

432 Nevo, Ruth. 'Chaucer: Motive and Mask in the "General Prologue".' *MLR* 58(1963), 1–9.
'The pilgrim's characteristic behavior is defined in every case in terms of the acquisition and use of wealth' (p 2). The order of appearance of the pilgrims constitutes a design whose *leitmotif* is money: Knight,

Squire, and Yeoman are members of the landowning feudal aristocracy; next come the members of the great propertied religious houses and orders; at the end appear all those of peasant origin and the parasites whose income is derived from graft. The Knight, as a knight banneret, the Plowman, and the Parson are 'each placed on the humblest, the most productive and serviceable rung of the respective functional orders – the warriors, the workers, and the worshippers' (p 6).

433 Pearsall, Derek A. '*The Canterbury Tales.*' *History of Literature in the English Language.* Volume 1, *The Middle Ages.* London: Barrie & Jenkins, 1970. Pp 163–93.
In interrupting the Monk, the Knight exhibits his unique 'moral authority' (shown also in his tale) and his 'authority of rank' (exercised again in reconciling the Host and the Pardoner) (p 168). In the *GP*, the ideal portraits of Knight, Parson and Plowman provide 'touchstones' for the three estates (p 175). Within an overall pattern that proceeds from the landed gentry to the peasantry (with a final group of parasites), 'particular sequences are morally significant: Knight-Squire-Yeoman, for instance, sifting through the reality of chivalric idealism until only a handful of peacock-feathers is left' (p 175). For *KnT* see **875**.

434 Reidy, John. 'Grouping of Pilgrims in the General Prologue to *The Canterbury Tales.*' *Publications of the Michigan Academy of Science, Arts, and Letters* 47(1962), 595–603.
The literary function of the first group of pilgrims is to gain 'the initial goodwill of the audience towards a new kind of poem' (p 596). The perfect Knight, likeable Squire, and model soldier (Yeoman) reflect the predispositions of the aristocratic audience and lead them gently toward the satire to come.

435 Robertson, D.W., Jr. *A Preface to Chaucer: Studies in Medieval Perspectives.* Princeton: Princeton University Press, 1962.
The details of the Knight's portrait are iconographic, not realistic, and emphasize, in climactic order, the ideas of worthiness, wisdom, and humility. The portrait represents 'an ideal that was still very much alive' rather than social reality (p 248). For *KnT* see **879**.

436 Salter, Elizabeth. *Chaucer: The Knight's Tale and the Clerk's Tale.* Studies in English Literature, No. 5. London: Edward Arnold; Great Neck, New York: Barron's Educational Series, 1962.
The portraits of the Knight and Clerk are 'pure' portraits in which Chaucer makes no use of 'the innuendo, the deliberately incongruous detail, the disclaimer of damaging intent' (p 7–8). By skillful use of circumstantial evidence – 'the carefully charted career of the Knight,

his travel-stained clothes' — Chaucer establishes their 'living connection with fourteenth-century society'; at the same time, 'they are beings dedicated to higher service — each in his own way, to God' (p 8). For *KnT* see **833**.

437 Schaar, Claes. *The Golden Mirror: Studies in Chaucer's Descriptive Technique and Its Literary Background*. Lund: C.W.K. Gleerup, 1967. In 'The Portraits' (pp 167–252) Schaar distinguishes nine types of descriptions of human beings, three of which appear in the portrait of the Knight. 'The idealization of his character enframes the description of habits, and is, then, followed by the concrete view of the Knight's appearance ... That [Chaucer] had no intention at all to satirize the figure can be taken for granted' (p 202). In 'The Problem of the Portraits' (pp 301–32), Schaar discusses various reasons for the more abstract representation of persons of high social status and the more concrete representation of persons of low status. For *KnT* see **885**.

437a Schulz, Herbert C. *The Ellesmere Manuscript of Chaucer's 'Canterbury Tales'*. San Marino: Huntington Library, 1966.
Describes the illumination, text, history, and physical makeup of the manuscript, and includes color reproductions of all the pilgrim portraits, which are said to be 'a unique graphic heritage from medieval times' (p 18).

438 Spencer, William. 'Are Chaucer's Pilgrims Keyed to the Zodiac?' *ChauR* 4(1970), 147–70.
'The hidden ground plan' of the *GP* (p 149) is a pattern based on the planets' rulership of the signs of the zodiac. The Knight (pp 149–50) occupies the first position, Aries ruled by Mars. His love of war, fierceness, fame, qualities of leadership, and wide travels associate him with Mars; his involvement with beginnings associates him with Aries, the sign under which the sun begins its yearly course and under which God was believed to have created the world.

438a Steele, Bruce. *Selections from ... 'The Canterbury Tales'*. 1969.
See King **423**.

439 Strange, W.C. 'The *Monk's Tale*: A Generous View.' *ChauR* 1(1967), 167–80.
In interrupting the *MkT*, the Knight asks for 'a narcotic art limited to pleasantness' (p 177). By his treatment of Fortune, the Monk 'raises a dark spirit never far from the Knight's own consciousness .... With Peter of Cyprus, the Monk thrusts this doubt ... into the proud stuff of the Knight's own life ... [and] questions forcefully that order and justice in the world's events which the Knight had asserted in his own tale. This painfully efficient and close questioning, not the

Monk's lack of narrative ability, prompts the Knight to break in upon him' (p 177).

440 Wagenknecht, Edward. *The Personality of Chaucer*. Norman: University of Oklahoma Press, 1968.
Chaucer may have portrayed a Knight who devotes himself to religious wars because, as Loomis **374** suggests, he sympathized with the Wycliffite position that only religious wars are justifiable. Against this possibility are the reference to 'his lordes werre' (I.47), the Squire's expeditions, and Chaucer's participation in the Hundred Years' War. Yet Chaucer did not become a knight, nor celebrate war in his verse (p 57), and he did write the pacifist *Mel*. There is no contradiction between pacifist sympathies and the idealization of a figure like the Knight. The Knight's interruption of the *MkT* does not show, as Malone **379** asserts, the taste of a child. Matthew Arnold, too, objected to a type of tragedy that offers no catharsis (p 55).

441 Whittock, Trevor. *A Reading of the Canterbury Tales*. Cambridge: Cambridge University Press, 1968.
Chaucer emphasizes the spiritual condition of the Knight (pp 50–2). The glance at the Knight's youth (I.44–5) shows his years of dedication and his large experience, as do his travels and battles. His meekness suggests a paradoxical tenderness in a warrior (p 50). His rusty surcoat suggests 'how his arduous life is beginning to leave its marks upon him' (p 50). His decision to ride with only one servant 'hints at a person who knows when to cut out of his life the redundant and the luxurious' (p 50). The Knight's pilgrimage is a 'chivalric duty' and penitential exercise after war (p 52). The Knight has two motives for interrupting the Monk: boredom and the Monk's references to Alexander and Julius Caesar as 'knights.' 'The Knight's protest is almost as simple-minded as the Monk's definition of tragedy, for it also puts the whole emphasis on the events and none on their presentation ... the Knight's remarks here suggest he never fully appreciated the darker undertones of his own tale (though, of course, Chaucer did)' (p 222). For *KnT* see **897**.

442 Winny, James. *The General Prologue to the Canterbury Tales*. Cambridge: Cambridge University Press, 1965.
The Knight is 'an outstanding example of human goodness, by which the moral worth of the other pilgrims can be measured' (p 80). His crusading constitutes a 'form of active Christian life,' and 'his politeness, modesty and piety build up an impression of virtuous character which is confirmed by his "bismotered habergeon"'(p 81). His pilgrimage is 'a brief interval between campaigns,' which may have been occasioned by a vow. It is appropriate that the habergeon

should be the only detail of physical appearance in the portrait of a subject who 'shapes his life by an exalted standard which separates him from the materialistic temper of his age' (p 82).

1971-1980

443 Allen, Orphia Jane. 'Blake's Archetypal Criticism: *The Canterbury Pilgrims*.' *Genre* 11(1978), 173–89.
Blake associates the Knight with Urizen, at once a representative of reason and a Satanic figure. Blake can call the Knight a hero and a good man, in the *Descriptive Catalogue* for the 1809 Exhibition, because the Knight has made the Urizenic principle his servant rather than his master (p 176).

444 Bowden, Betsy. 'The Artistic and Interpretive Context of Blake's "Canterbury Pilgrims".' *Blake* 13(1980), 164–90.
The 'spiritual ambivalence' surrounding the Knight in Blake's 1810 engraving is at odds with the praise of the Knight in Blake's *Descriptive Catalogue* for the 1809 exhibition (p 180). Plate armor, a deviation from the *GP* common in sixteenth-century representations, makes the Knight seem sinister (p 180). His layers of clothing contradict Blake's description of him as being 'without ostentation' (p 181). Blake's characterization of the Knight as the 'guardian of man against the oppressor' might be reinterpreted in the light of the engraving: 'the Knight, as an eternal type, takes it upon himself to define man's oppressor. And with the rules and trappings of chivalry, he guards against forces that man – if left to his own inspiration – might embrace rather than fear' (p 181).

445 Coghill, Nevill. *Chaucer's Idea of What Is Noble*. Oxford: Oxford University Press, 1971. Rpt in *The Collected Papers of Nevill Coghill, Shakespearian and Medievalist*. Ed. Douglas Gray. Sussex: Harvester Press; New York: St. Martin's Press, 1988. Pp 54–73.
The topic of this eighteen-page presidential address to the English Association was suggested to Coghill by a three-fold coincidence: his reading of Auden's remark in *A Certain World* – 'Today gentlemen are no longer in demand'; his own experience that 'to recommend a man as a Christian gentleman is virtually to lose him the job'; and his encounter with a hitch-hiking ex-convict who had read *Lady Chatterley's Lover*: 'that gamekeeper having that Ladyship! It properly cut her and her class down to size!' (p 1). Coghill recalls that the idea of the gentleman was both minted in and immediately challenged by the fourteenth century: 'Whan Adam dalf and Eva span, / Who was then the gentil man?' To this question, Chaucer, who 'created the

images by which we know the idea, especially in its secular context' (p 6), offered the best answer, and his Knight and Squire are the pre-eminent representatives of *gentilesse*, a concept that has its origins in the Sermon on the Mount and in the Passion of Christ (pp 6–7). Dante re-defined *nobleness* as a moral concept, and Lull **197** re-defined chivalry as a sacred order (pp 8–9). Although the 'sneering critic' dismisses the Knight's portrait as mere nostalgia for an institution 'already being blown up by gunpowder,' the factual accuracy of the portrait's historical references provides 'a kind of guarantee that we can trust Chaucer in spiritual matters, too' (p 9). The Knight's pursuit of an unattainable ideal mirrors the Christian's pursuit of moral perfection. The concept of the gentleman is central to our civilization, and it ought to be our goal to 'keep green the meaning of our more ancient texts, lest some precious part of our inheritance be negligently thrown away' (p 17).

446 David, Alfred. *The Strumpet Muse: Art and Morals in Chaucer's Poetry*. Bloomington: Indiana University Press, 1976.
The 'most comprehensive standard of judgement' for the pilgrims is the worthiness that the Knight, along with the Parson and Plowman, represents (p 58). The Knight 'embodies the values that should ideally accompany noble rank' (p 59). If the phrase 'his lordes werre' (I.47) refers to the French wars, the brevity of the reference implies Chaucer's disapproval of wars among Christians. As a crusader and a penitent, the Knight is a *miles Christi* (p 59). He is 'a figure of the romantic past' (p 61) who must seek adventure on crusade because gunpowder and the longbow have made him obsolete at home. Nevertheless the ideal he represents is still powerful (p 62). His reconciliation of the Pardoner with the Host is 'more truly chivalrous than anything in the Knight's Tale' and may anticipate Christ's forgiveness (p 203). The Monk's conception of tragedy may have been the younger Chaucer's and the Knight's objection to it may voice the sentiment of the mature poet (p 222). For *KnT* see **936**.

447 DiMarco, Vincent Joseph. 'Literary and Historical Researches Respecting Chaucer's Knight and Squire.' University of Pennsylvania Dissertation, 1972. Director: Robert A. Pratt. See also *DAI* 33(1972), 1677A.
An uncritical reliance on a romantic image of the Crusades has obscured the irony of Chaucer's portrait. The Knight's campaigns in Algezir, Belmarye and Tramyssene reflect a fourteenth-century strategy that implied the probability that the Holy land was irrevocably lost. His campaigns with Peter of Cyprus suggest the impracticality and inherent contradictions of the crusading ideal. His

association with the Teutonic Order involves him with an organization that had abandoned the ideal in favor of territorial expansion. The Squire represents romantic values capable of enriching and correcting the Knight's warrior values. For *KnT* see **938**.

448 — 'Chaucer, Walter Sibile, and the Composition of the General Prologue.' *Revue belge de philologie et d'histoire* 46(1978), 650–62.
Giving partial support to Cook **326**, DiMarco argues that the *GP* was probably composed later than the traditional date of 1387. Strained relations between England and the Hanseatic League, of which the Teutonic Order was a member, culminated in a government ban on travel to the Baltic lands in 1385. Relations were restored in 1388 by a treaty negotiated in part by Walter Sibile, one of Chaucer's former subordinates in the Customs office. Since it is unlikely Chaucer would have represented the Knight as traveling to the Baltic during this troubled period, 1388 is at least a *terminus a quo* for the Knight's portrait.

449 Donaldson, E. Talbot. 'The Manuscripts of Chaucer's Works and Their Use.' In *Writers and Their Background: Geoffrey Chaucer*. Ed. Derek Brewer. Athens: Ohio University Press, 1975. Pp 85–108.
In a discussion of how scribal error arises from confusion of minims, Donaldson briefly argues for the reading *arivee* rather than *armee* in I.60. 'But it is probable that we shall never be certain which Chaucer intended' (pp 90–1). See **450**, **505**.

450 — 'Some Readings in the *Canterbury Tales.*' In *Medieval Studies in Honor of Lillian Herlands Hornstein*. Ed. Jess B. Bessinger, Jr. and Robert R. Raymo. New York: New York University Press, 1976. Pp 99–110.
The reading *aryue* is to be preferred to Manly and Rickert's *armee* in I.60 (**380**). While both the *OED* and the *MED* list *aryue* as a probable error for *armee*, they also list I.60 as the first known use of *armee* in English; thus the two words would have presented equally difficult readings for the scribes. The evidence of the mss does not clearly favor either term. Skeat's view (**344**, V: 8) that *arme* is a misreading of *ariue* is supported by scribal habits in dealing with minims.

451 Ebner, Dean. 'Chaucer's Precarious Knight.' In *Imagination and the Spirit: Essays in Literature and the Christian Faith presented to Clide S. Kilby*. Ed. Charles A. Huttar. Grand Rapids, Michigan: William B. Eerdmans, 1971. Pp 87–100.
Like the protagonists of the Monk's tragedies, the Knight is precariously perched at the top of Fortune's wheel, and his fear of falling causes him to interrupt the *MkT*. The Knight's portrait provides

evidence of pursuit of fame, high social position, and attachment to worldly goods. For *KnT* see **941**.

452 Eckhardt, Caroline D. 'The Number of Chaucer's Pilgrims: A Review and Reappraisal.' *YES* 5(1975), 1–18. Rpt in *Essays in the Numerical Criticism of Medieval Literature*. Ed. Caroline D. Eckhardt. Lewisburg: Bucknell University Press; London: Associated University Presses, 1980. Pp 156–84.
Eckhardt rejects Brown's suggestion (**355**) that the Squire's portrait is a later addition. The belated reference to the Knight in A[I].101–2 is typical of the narrator's 'apparently inconsequential process' (p 2), and is prepared for by the reference to 'fader' in 100. The Squire's campaigns do not overlap with the Knight's because the Squire belongs to a different generation and probably did not serve under his father. The contrast between the Knight's 'distant and holy war' and the Squire's 'more local and profane' war contributes to their characterizations (p 3).

453 Eliason, Norman E. 'Personal Names in the Canterbury Tales.' *Names* 21(1973), 137–52.
Chaucer's avoidance of names for most of the pilgrims allowed him to emphasize professions in setting up dramatic relations. The *KnT* 'is the kind of tale any proper knight might tell and he is the kind of knight who might tell so proper a tale' (p 152).

454 Engelhardt, George J. 'The Lay Pilgrims of the *Canterbury Tales*: A Study in Ethology.' *MS* 36(1974), 278–330.
The Knight's perfection caused him to be placed first even though Chaucer accepted the primacy of the spiritual estate over the military (p 284). A 'ternary formula' governs the presentation of the Knight: 'verray, parfit gentil' (pp 289–90). He is a (modified) *miles Christi* of the type described by Bernard of Clairvaux: he wages war against Christ's enemies, lives a continent life as a presumptive widower, and exhibits humility (p 291). The Knight has progressed to crusading from the political wars in which the Squire still fights; Chaucer does not, like Gower [cf **185**], ask questions about the worldly motives of the men under whom father and son serve and the motives of Knight and Squire are 'beyond question' (pp 291–2). For *KnT* see **946**.

455 Evans, Gillian. *Chaucer*. Glasgow and London: Blackie, 1977.
The Knight is a mercenary who fought only in worthy causes, a pious and courteous man who represents a literary ideal rather than the actuality of knighthood (p 68).

456 Fichte, Joerg O. 'Man's Free Will and the Poet's Choice: The Creation of Artistic Order in Chaucer's *Knight's Tale*.' *Anglia* 93(1975), 335–60.

Fichte discusses the Knight's portrait in Section 1 (pp 334–9) of his essay, as part of his argument that 'the aristocratic teller of the *KnT* is used by Chaucer as mouth-piece for his own views' (p 335). The Knight is a 'personification' of worthiness, which comprises the traditional virtues of fortitude and wisdom. His fortitude has been demonstrated by his military career, and his wisdom is to be demonstrated by his tale. Chaucer idealizes the Knight, distinguishing him from the actual knights criticized by Geoffroy de la Tour-Landry and Deschamps, in order to strengthen his qualifications as the poet's spokesman. For *KnT* see **947**, **948**.

457 Finlayson, John. 'The Satiric Mode and the *Parson's Tale*.' *ChauR* 6(1971), 94–116.
In an introductory commentary on the *GP* (pp 94–105), Knight, Plowman, and Parson are said to 'provide not only the ideal social framework of feudal theory ... but ... also a reminder of the moral norms of that social structure' (p 99). Yet the ideal portraits 'lack identifiable humanity and the artistic dynamism that is attendant upon the "immoral" characters' (p 104). The Knight's portrait 'states an ideal of life which is gradually eroded as we move throughout the sequence of portraits' (p 105). Chaucer's more or less random placement of the ideal portraits suggests that the world is 'a curious *melange* of folly, vice, and virtue' (p 105).

458 Fisher, John H. 'Chaucer's Last Revision of the "Canterbury Tales".' *MLR* 67(1972), 241–51.
Fragments I to V 'represent wholesale revision' in response to a principle of dramatic interplay that had emerged in Fragment VII (p 243). The *NPP* evolved from a version limited to expressing the Host's views to a more fully dramatic one in which the Knight and the Host discuss prosperity, fortune, and tragedy. Applying his new dramatic principle to the opening, where the Man of Law may have been assigned to the first tale (Brown, **667**), and after deciding to add the fabliaux and the churls, Chaucer chose to put the Knight and his chivalric tale first, thus emphasizing a secular ideal and providing a 'yardstick of genteel behaviour against which the rest of the collection can be measured' (p 248).

459 Fry, Donald K. 'The Ending of *The Monk's Tale*.' *JEGP* 71(1972), pp 355–68.
Part I (pp 355–68) traces the historical connections between the Knight and Pedro of Cyprus and Pedro of Spain, two subjects of the Modern Instances in the *MkT*. In Part II (pp 357–64) Fry classifies the mss according to the ways they combine three variables: whether the interrupter is the Host or the Knight, whether the interruption

appears in the Long Form (B2.3957–95 [VII.2767–2805]) or the Short Form (without B2.3961–80 [VII.2771–907]), and whether the Modern Instances appear in a medial or a final position. He then offers a reconstruction of how the text evolved, suggesting that the Knight's replacement of the Host as interrupter inspired the addition of the two Pedros to the Modern Instances, and that Chaucer moved the Modern Instances from the medial to the final position to make it clear that the Knight was interrupting a tale still in progress and perhaps to diminish the distance between the Pedros and the interruption (p 363). The Knight's interruption has a 'personal and emotional' motive (p 365) as shown by references to his distress added to the Long Form: 'I seye for me ... allas ... as it thynketh me.' As an aristocrat and an older man at the peak of his career, the Knight is like the Monk's modern tragic figures (p 366). Fry suggests various reasons for the Knight's delay in interrupting the Monk, and concludes: 'What the Knight calls for is ... a balance of happiness and sorrow. It is the...Monk's reiteration of his tragic theme which wears down the listeners, especially one for whom the tragedies strike home' (p 368).

460 Fyler, John M. *Chaucer and Ovid.* New Haven: Yale University Press, 1979.
The Knight's reaction to the *MkT* does not show him to be a pollyanna. Rather his commitment to the chivalric ideal transcends the Monk's bleak view, which the Knight nevertheless shares, much as Theseus' First Mover speech incorporates and goes beyond Egeus' simpler stoicism (pp 146–7). For *KnT* see **952.**

461 Gardner, John. *The Poetry of Chaucer.* Carbondale: Southern Illinois University Press, 1977.
The Knight is a figure of the rational soul, a true leader shown heading up his household; the phrase 'his lordes werre' contains a pun referring to the god of the crusading, worthy knight (p 233). The Squire represents the concupiscent and irascible soul, but may yet rise to his father's status (p 233); the Yeoman represents healthy concupiscence (p, 234). It is appropriate that the Host and Pardoner should be reconciled by the Knight, 'Chaucer's symbol of natural balance and proportion,' the man who 'upholds not Christian doctrine (directly, anyway) but social order and the order of nature' (p 303). For *KnT* see **954.**

462 Gilbert, A.J. *Literary Language from Chaucer to Johnson.* London: Macmillan, 1979.
The Knight, Parson, and Ploughman are described in 'a sacred version of the low style which combined a degree of conventional realism

with a strong sense of the moral imperative' (p 61). 'Gentle' (I.72) 'has the sacred plain-style sense of "noble", not the middle-style sense "well-bred"'(p 62). 'Meeke as is a mayde' (69) is a traditional formula in the sacred low style: 'we are meant to see the moral idea, and not the person.' 'Vileynye' (70) implies 'both "moral reproach" (sacred plain style) and "discourtesy" (middle style).' For *KnT* see **956.**

463 Görlach, Manfred. '"Canterbury Tales" Prologue, 60: The Knight's Army.' *N&Q* 20[218](1973), 363–5.
The *MED* lists only two (later) uses of *armee* with the relevant meaning and no occurrences of *aryve.* But mss of the legend of *Alban* in the *Gilte Legende* (c 1438) provide evidence for *arive* as an English word in the early fifteenth century (p 365). In 1400, *armee* was a new word in French, adopted from Italian. While Manly **380** thought a few scribes misunderstood *armee* and substituted *aryve*, the scribes may have substituted the newly popular *armee* for the difficult *aryve.* See **505.**

464 Green, Eugene. 'The Voices of the Pilgrims in the *General Prologue* to the *Canterbury Tales.*' *Style* 9(1975), 55–81.
Green attempts to show by stylistic analysis how the voices of the narrator and the pilgrims blend in the portraits. We hear the narrator's enthusiasm (pp 57–8) and the Knight's dignity and reserve (p 71). A paratactic arrangement of clauses of certain types has the effect of stating simply, 'as if the Knight were speaking, what his accomplishments had been in a life of service' (p 72).

465 Hatton, Thomas J. 'Thematic Relationships between Chaucer's Squire's Portrait and Tale and the Knight's Portrait and Tale.' *SMC* 4(1974), 452–8.
Youth is not the Squire's 'radix trait,' as Baldwin suggests (**349**), but rather his condition as lover, as indicated by the grammatical parallelism between I.43 and 79–80. Nor is subservience to love an inevitable trait in youth, as shown by the Knight's youthful devotion to other values (I.44–6). It is unlikely that the Squire's dedication to love would have been viewed as 'the more human side of the perfect knight' (p 454); rather contemporary works on chivalry indicate that it might have been tolerated with amusement. For *KnT* and *SqT* see **966.**

466 Helterman, Jeffrey. 'The Dehumanizing Metamorphoses of The Knight's Tale.' *ELH* 38(1971), 493–511.
The Knight is a paradoxical figure, a man of mild, Christ-like aspect who must slay his foe (p 504). The battles in which he engaged typically produced bloodshed and martial victory, but few converts

and no permanent tenure for Christian forces (pp 505–7). The Knight's haste in going on pilgrimage suggests that he is seeking 'something not to be found on the field of battle' (p 505) and the stain on his *gypon* suggests that knighthood has been tarnished in the crusades (p 506). For *KnT* see **969.**

467 Higdon, David Leon. 'Diverse Melodies in Chaucer's "General Prologue".' *Criticism* 14(1972), 97–108. Esp pp 106–7.
The references to music in the *GP* have metaphorical significance, and the pilgrims can be classified according to their relations to the theme of concord and discord. The Knight, Clerk, Parson, and Plowman 'have neither songs nor instruments. They are openly hostile to music and share a distrust of "high style" in rhetoric' (p 106). Their song is 'the New Song of the New Man who participates in and reflects the music governing the harmony of the spheres' (p 107).

468 Howard, Donald R. *The Idea of the Canterbury Tales*. Berkeley: University of California Press, 1976.
The Knight is an 'obsolescent hero' (p 94), as indicated by his forty years of battles, his participation in lists during wartime, his service in crusades instead of in the war with France, and his old-fashioned values, and by the contrasting portrait of the Squire, which shows knighthood in decline. The Knight's motives were not the worst – conquest and booty – and perhaps not the best – 'to do good, to do justice, to punish the wicked' – but rather a desire for glory (p 97). The idealized figures divide the portraits into three symmetrical groups (the Knight heads the group Squire-Yeoman-Prioress-Monk-Friar-Merchant) and their 'emblematic' quality (p 151) links them to the 'images' of medieval artificial memory systems. The Knight's peace-making between the Host and the Pardoner is 'a courtly gesture which reflects the aristocrat's preference for smooth surfaces' and a charitable act, reflecting the Knight's compassion for the Pardoner, but it is probably not symbolical of Christian charity (p 368). See **502**. For *KnT* see **974**.

- Review by D.W. Robertson, Jr., *M&H* 8(1977), 252–5: Robertson objects to the characterization of chivalry as obsolescent. 'From the perspective of history it is true that chivalric ideals would soon weaken and almost disappear, but Chaucer would not have known this ... Men like Clanvowe and Stury, not to mention Chaucer himself, would have thought the function of chivalry to be something like that of a modern defense establishment, and although they may well have thought that it had declined in England, they could observe ... that it had begun to flourish in France' (p 253).

469 Johnson, Judith A. '*Ye* and *Thou* among the Canterbury Pilgrims.' *MichA* 10(1977), 71–6.
A long-standing exception to the rule that one addresses an inferior as 'thou' allowed 'a member of the top rung of the social ladder' to address everyone as 'ye' (p 71). The Knight exemplifies this behavior in his addresses to the Host (VI.964–5) and the Monk (VII.2768 [B2.3958]), but he addresses the Pardoner as 'thee' (VI.966). The Knight may be attempting to conciliate the Pardoner, or he may feel that on this occasion he must invoke his social superiority to restore order (p 72).

470 Jones, Terry. *Chaucer's Knight: The Portrait of a Medieval Mercenary.* London: Weidenfeld and Nicolson; Baton Rouge: Louisiana State University Press, 1980. Rev ed, London: Methuen, 1985.
Ch 1 (pp 1–3) announces Jones' thesis: 'The Knight's career, instead of conforming to a pattern of Christian chivalry, has more in common with the mercenaries ... who brought the concept of chivalry into disrepute and eventual disuse' (p 2). Ch 2 (pp 4–30) distinguishes between the indentured knight and the mercenary (pp 4–13); traces the development of the Free Companies (pp 13–8); and cites contemporary fears of mercenaries (pp 18–25) and suspicion of 'poor knights' as being mercenaries (pp 25–7). The 'M' brand on the Knight's horse in the Ellesmere miniature may associate him with the Teutonic Order or with Sir John Hawkwood's White Company (pp 27–30). Ch 3 (pp 31–140) divides the portrait into twenty parts. In lines I.43–6 (pp 31–4) Chaucer introduces the Knight 'with apparent praise before proceeding to reveal his true nature' (p 31). The possibility that these lines contain hints of criticism is pursued in an appendix (pp 223–30) where, for example, the Knight's 'trouthe' is said to mean only that he fulfilled his contracts. Contemporary accounts and modern historical studies suggest satiric intent in the account of the Knight's career (I.47–67). For example: I.51 (pp 42–9): the looting and abandonment of Alexandria, carried out largely by mercenaries, was widely regarded as a cause of shame; I.52–4 (pp 49–55): the Teutonic Order was commonly regarded as a merely secular power, noted for its savagery and welcoming attitude toward mercenaries; I.54–5 (pp 55–9): the Knight's activities in Russia, a Christian country, consisted in banditry or in service to the Tartars. Chaucer's use of the Italian-French term *armee* (I.59–60; pp 73–6) identifies the Knight as that English 'export,' the mercenary soldier. The Knight is an 'efficient killer' who has slain at least eighteen men, some of them in tournaments, a practice regarded as shameful (I.61–3; pp 76–86). The Knight seems not to have participated in

England's own wars (pp 94–100); a chart contrasts his career with those of several knights who did: Henry of Lancaster, Sir John Chandos, and three members of the Scrope family. Six final sections (pp 100–39) discuss the virtues ascribed to the Knight in I.68–78, suggesting, for example, that the Knight's plain dress and lack of coat-of-arms are a sign of chivalry's decline. Contemporary readers 'would not have seen a militant Christian idealist but a shabby mercenary without morals or scruples – the typical product of an age which saw war turned into a business' (p 140). Jones compares Chaucer's Knight to the knight depicted in Bruegel's *Massacre of the Innocents* (pp 85–6, 110, 125), and defines the Knight, Squire, and Yeoman as constituting a 'lance,' the distinctive fighting unit of Hawkwood's White Company (p 211). Ch 5, 'Why does the Knight interrupt the Monk?' (pp 217–22) links the interruption to the Host's earlier invitation to the Monk to 'quit' the *KnT*, and argues that Chaucer always intended the *MkT* as a reply to the *KnT* (p 218). The Monk's tales are directed against those who trust worldly glory. The modern instances concern tyrants and contain references to the treachery of mercenaries and to an event from the Knight's own career, the battle of Alexandria. The Knight's interruption is a response to 'this onslaught – almost a personal attack' (p 221). The Knight's portrait, the *KnT*, the *MkT*, and the Knight's interruption constitute a 'whole cycle ... vibrant with the political realities that Chaucer saw around him – the established tyrannies abroad and the nascent tyranny at home' (p 222). See **499**, **504**, **507**, **508**, **510**, **514**, **515**, **518**. For *KnT* see **981**.

- Review by J.A. Burrow, *TLS* 15 February 1980, 163: While praising the line-by-line analysis of the portrait as the best part of Jones' book, Burrow rejects criticism of the Knight for supposedly not participating in the war against the French. Lines 47–9 must refer to the French wars, unless the Knight's lord is God, a reading that Jones also rejects. In spite of other 'manifest absurdities' and tendentious arguments, Jones is 'absolutely right ... to reject as too bland and insipid the conventional account of the Knight.' The Knight's service in Palatye and Russia suggests that he is neither a simple nor a completely ideal figure.
- Review by Jill Mann, *Listener* 103(1980), 157: 'Its historical orientation is the limitation of this book as well as its strength. What it lacks is literary analysis worthy a writer as subtle and profound as Chaucer ... Discussion of the portrait is hamstrung by its very simple conceptions of irony and satire ... It is assumed that the only alternatives we have ... are blind admiration or a knowing

sneer. That is, we are only supposed to be thinking about the Knight, never about the way he is described ... nor about the connection of his portrait with the rest of the General Prologue' (p 157).

- Review by G.C. Britton, *N&Q* (1982), 431: Jones' argument concerning the list of battles is 'undeniable,' but its ironic function in the portrait does not require a demotion of such terms as 'gentil' nor an identification of the Knight with mercenaries.
- Review by Phillipa Hardman, *RES* 23(1982), 311–3: 'What we need to know is how [the Knight's campaigns] were regarded by Chaucer and his contemporaries, and here Mr Jones relies on documentation from hostile sources ... hardly accessible to English readers, sometimes on selective quotations ... and on a bit of bullying' (p 312). Jones' ironic reading depends on believing that Chaucer and his readers were 'liberally pacifist ... regarding wars against infidels, and ... belligerently patriotic regarding European wars; but we have no consistent evidence for this' (p 312).
- Review by G.A. Lester, *MAE* 52(1983), 122–5: Jones makes his best case in attacking the battle for Alexandria, but he is unable to show that the documents he cites were known to Chaucer or their ideas widely familiar. While his analysis of the battles has 'a nagging element of remote possibility,' his discussions of tournaments are wrong-headed.

471 Kahrl, Stanley J. 'Chaucer's "Squire's Tale" and the Decline of Chivalry.' *ChauR* 7(1973), 194–209.
'If the *Knight's Tale* is a celebration of classical order in the chivalric world, the *Squire's Tale* presents the growing impulse toward exoticism and disorder at work in the courts of late medieval Europe' (p 195). The qualities of the two tales reflect the careers of the two men. The Knight's crusades 'were among the last to be fought ... under the original ideals of chivalry' (p 207); the Squire's participation in the Bishop of Norwich's crusade and in the Hundred Years' War reveal him to be one of the 'new men' of Richard II's court (p 208).

472 Keenan, Hugh T. 'Curious Correspondence: Canterbury Tales A 24–25, Mirk's Festival and Becket's Martyrdom.' *AN&Q* 16(1978), 66–7.
Twenty-nine, the number of pilgrims (A[I].24–5), may be an allusion to Thomas Becket's feast day, December 29; the portrait of a meek Christian Knight in service to a secular lord may recall the characterization of Becket in Mirk's sermon for the feast day.

473 Knight, Stephen. *The Poetry of the Canterbury Tales*. Sydney: Angus and Robertson, 1973.

The Knight's appearance is not stressed: 'it is the inner man who is striking.' His nobility is conveyed by 'measured and formal' poetry, as in the 'almost liturgical list' of battles, the confidence of line 72, and the three balanced couplets that conclude the portrait (pp 8–9). For *KnT* see **988**.

474 Mann, Jill. 'The Knight.' *Chaucer and Medieval Estates Satire*. 1973. See **161**. Pp 106–15.

Mann studies the portraits in relation to the traditions of medieval satire on social classes in texts from 1100–1400. The Knight's worthiness, devotion to chivalric virtues, wisdom, and meekness suggest that he is an ideal knight. The virtues listed in I.45–7 may be indebted to Watriquet de Couvin, as Schofield **342** suggests, but it is unlikely that this grouping had a specific meaning for either poet, since slightly different lists can be found in Watriquet's work and in other works on chivalry. The Knight's 'array' associates him with St. Bernard's monk-like ideal of crusading knighthood, and aligns him against the plundering and self-indulgence criticized by satirists. The armor-stained 'gypon' gives an impression of realism, particularly by creating a time-dimension. The earlier reference to the Knight's youth (I.44–5) gives him 'an "estates" past' (p 109). Little emphasis is placed on the Knight's service to his secular lord (I.47), a relationship stressed by chivalric and estates writers. The listing of places in the description of the Knight's career is a convention borrowed from the *chansons de geste*. 'Despite the undoubted topicality of the campaigns in Chaucer's list, its *framework* is a literary one, whose function is to place the Knight in a line of heroes of chivalry' (p 113). The 'tenor' of the list is religious (p 114), stressing the traditional duty of knights to fight the heathen. But estates satire in general, and Langland in particular, places greater stress on the knight's duty to protect the church and the poor and to punish wrong-doers. 'The immediate ends [of the Knight's] professional activities are undefined. Is their aim conversion of the heathen? or their extermination, to make way for the permanent occupation of the Holy Land by Christians? The Knight's role ... is merely to fight, win, and move on ... His campaigns have a religious *character*, but not a religious *aim* ... Like the other pilgrims, he is a professional specialist' (p 115). Chaucer gives his Squire a different chivalric motive from the Knight's — the desire to win his lady's favor — but 'betrays no *system* of ethics which would lead us to prefer one to the other' (p 117). See also pp 10–11, where the list of the Knight's battles is said to create a 'professional mystique' rather than Bowden's 'chapter of romance' (**353**); and see pp 188–9, where the traits Lumiansky **376** classifies as 'unexpected' are said to belong to the stereotyped ideal of the Knight's estate. See **501**.

- Review by A.G. Rigg, *RES* 25(1974), 456–7. In 'the best critical study of Chaucer for many years,' Mann explains how Chaucer uses the estates material not to elicit praise or blame, but to create a 'moral neutrality' that 'produces, and is produced by, the semantic vagueness of terms such as *worthy, courtesie, conscience*, which shift meaning throughout the General Prologue' (pp 456–7).
- Review by S.S. Hussey, *MLR* 70(1975), 387–8: Mann's account of how Chaucer causes us to view each pilgrim according to his own values is convincing and explains the hyperbole in many of the portraits (p 387). She shows how the estates tradition conditioned readers' expectations, concerning the virtues to be expected of a knight, for example. 'The strongest evidence from estates literature is, in fact, for the Monk, Friar, and Knight, the weakest for the Franklin and Miller' (p 387).

475 Mannuci, Loretta Valtz. *Fourteenth-Century England and the Canterbury Tales*. Milan: Coopli, 1975.
The Knight is not the 'mundane and modest figure' he might be as a member of the lowest rank of the nobility ; he is 'the epitome of the knightly concept,' as indicated by the repetition of 'worthy' (p 102). Yet the lack of physical description and of reference to his duties in England make the Knight somewhat dream-like (p 103). There is 'something less than an outright criticism, something less, as well, than full praise, almost respectful elegy' (p 104).

476 Martin, Loy D. 'History and Form in the General Prologue to the Canterbury Tales.' *ELH* 45(1978), 1–17.
The portraits present a contrast between pilgrimage and daily life (p 4). The Knight's portrait describes 'a life of danger and strife, toil and death' – in effect, 'what the Knight has *left behind* in joining the travelers' (p 5). The variety of pilgrims reflects the 'new possibilities of intimacy and interpersonal exchange among persons of different professions or trades and ... ranks' in the fourteenth century (p 12).

477 McAlpine, Monica E. *The Genre of 'Troilus and Criseyde.'* Ithaca: Cornell University Press, 1978.
The Knight's comment on the *MkT* echoes the conventional medieval definition of comedy and reminds us that human beings are sometimes able to overcome obstacles and achieve their objectives. Still 'it is probably the grimness of his actuality that motivates his determined optimism' (p 111); he may be seeking mere escape. Moreover, his definition of comedy replicates the defect in the Monk's definition of

tragedy by emphasizing external change while de-emphasizing freedom and responsibility (p 113).

478 Mehl, Dieter. *Geoffrey Chaucer: Eine Einführung in seine erzählenden Dichtungen*. Berlin: Erich Schmidt, 1973. Trans. as *Geoffrey Chaucer: An Introduction to His Narrative Poetry*. Cambridge: Cambridge University Press, 1986 [cited here].
The typical and the individual reinforce each other in the portraits. The Knight gives us 'a vivid idea of all that is most admirable in courtly chivalry within a single biography, credible and idealized at the same time' (pp 133–4). The idealized figures like the Knight are as much 'unmatchable and lonely experts' as the other pilgrims, leaving the relevance of their ideals in doubt (p 140). For *KnT* see **1001**.

479 Miskimin, Alice. 'The Illustrated Eighteenth-Century Chaucer.' *MP* 77(1979), 26–55.
In George Vertue's engravings of the pilgrims for Urry's edition (1721), 'horses, gestures, and symbolic attributes (the Wife's whip, the Knight's sword) are clearly outlined' (p 33). Stothard's realistic approach to the *GP* was derived from eighteenth-century criticism. William Carey, in an 'Appreciation' of Stothard, described Chaucer's Knight as combining 'the minute accuracy' of Durer with 'the fine colouring and dignity' of Holbein, and suggested that Chaucer modelled him on courtiers at the court of Edward III (p 53). For *KnT* see **1004**.

480 Morgan, Gerald. 'The Universality of the Portraits in the *General Prologue* to the *Canterbury Tales*.' *ES* 58(1977), 481–93.
The portraits are organized by 'a general concept of social class' (pp 482–3). Morgan discusses the Knight's virtues – *chivalrie*, *trouthe*, *honour*, *fredom*, *curteisie* – in relation to the concept of knighthood; they serve religion as well since the 'lord' of A[I].47 is God (pp 483–4). Details in the portraits are also determined by the general conception (or concrete universal in Aristotelian terms) and do not signify the individuality of the pilgrims. Thus the Knight's battles (pp 486–7) exhibit prowess. The Knight is 'ideal' in the sense of being archetypal as well as in the sense of being morally excellent (p 490).

481 —— 'The Design of the *General Prologue* to the *Canterbury Tales*.' *ES* 59(1978), 481–98.
The *GP* presents a 'coherent sequence of portraits, ordered in accord with the gradations of fourteenth-century society' (p 486). The perspective is essentially secular, as indicated by the Knight's being given first position (p 487). The series starting with the Knight and ending with the Franklin represents the 'gentils'; the rest, the

commonalty (p 490). The ancestor of the modern gentleman is not the Knight, but the Franklin, one of the new squirearchy that was taking over the administrative duties of knights (p 491).

482 Owen, Charles A., Jr. *Pilgrimage and Storytelling in the Canterbury Tales: The Dialectic of 'Ernest' and 'Game'*. Norman: University of Oklahoma Press, 1977.
Ch 2: In an early version (1387?–88), the portraits started with the Knight and ended with the Parson, and emphasized 'selfless dedication' on the borders of Christendom and within it (p 45). In a second version (c 1396), Chaucer added the Monk, Friar, and churls, creating a community threatened not by the Knight's enemies but by church corruption. Ch 3: The Knight's retinue suggests in various ways his gentleness, effectiveness, and sincerity (p 51). His portrait 'emphasizes the devotion of a lifetime to the ideals of chivalry' (p 51). The list of battles distinguishes the Knight from romance heroes, and his 'curteisie' has nothing to do with courtly love, but 'represents a purity of manner that has resisted the crudities of camp life' (p 52). The impressionistic order of the battles grounds the Knight's idealism in the contemporary world (p 52). Although in I.68 'worthy' suggests mere rank or wealth, the knight fulfills a higher standard; the concessive 'though' suggests that others do not (p 53). Line I.72 is grammatically distinct and gains further emphasis from the rhyme and its summary quality (p 53). The stains on the Knight's 'gypon' authenticate his virtues as soldier, pilgrim, and man (p 53). The poet exhibits 'unequivocal admiration' for the Knight (p 55). The Friar is the Knight's moral opposite (p 65). Ch 4: The choice of the Knight to tell the first tale is providential, emerging 'from an order not man made, not even rationally testable' (p 88). Ch 5: The Knight interrupts the Monk because he is a 'defender of the status quo ... Stories featuring repeated falls from high estate make him uneasy for the stability of the society he has spent his life defending' (p 133). Ch 6: In reconciling the Host and the Pardoner, the Knight shows a 'sense of responsibility and delicacy of feeling' (pp 181–2). For *KnT* see **1010**.

483 Palmer, David Andrew. 'Chaucer and the Nature of Chivalric Ideas.' *DAI* 37(1977), 6507–8A. McMaster University Dissertation, 1976.
Chivalric ideas cannot be fully appreciated by reference only to the activities of knights since they had the symbolic potential to represent theories about secular life in general. The Knight of the *GP* is 'mainly an emblem of right spiritual orientation rather than an endorsement of specifically knightly duties or contemporary crusade projects.' As the study of several romances shows, the pursuit of love

was viewed as 'inversion of the knight's responsibilities to God and society,' and a 'polarity between love-service and Christian knighthood' structures the portraits of Knight and Squire. For *KnT* see **1011**.

484 Parr, Roger P. 'Chaucer's Art of Portraiture.' *SMC* 4(1974), 428–36.
The first thirty lines of the Knight's portrait constitute *notatio*, moral description; only the last six, *effictio*, physical description. Chaucer unifies the portrait around the concept of worthiness by using *traductio* (the five-fold repetition of 'worthy' in I.43, 47, 50, 64, 68), *distributio* (the list of battles), *conclusio* (the summary statement in 72), and *superlatio* (hyperbole in 48, 52, 67, 70, 72).

485 Pichaske, David R. 'Knight's Tale.' *The Movement of the 'Canterbury Tales': Chaucer's Literary Pilgrimage*. [Place?]: Norwood Editions, 1977. Pp 27–36.
Citing Mitchell **429** approvingly, Pichaske suggests that both the notion of virtue and the word 'worthy' are tainted in the *GP*; the Knight's virtue concerns mainly prowess and courtesy. He has fought for heathens, killed often, and participated in partially commercial enterprises at Satalye and Lyeys. He has served *a* lord but not *the* Lord, and his stained clothing suggests Pauline armor mainly by contrast (pp 27–9). 'His reverence is for truth *as he sees it* ... it may be his easy submission to a-Christian, secular rule ... that necessitates [his] pilgrimage' (p 29). See **1012** for *KnT*.

486 Pison, Thomas. 'Liminality in *The Canterbury Tales*.' *Genre* 10(1977), 157–71.
As part of the pilgrims' 'withdrawal from profane society,' distinctions are modified or eliminated (p 160). The Knight's preeminent status is reflected in his being described first and in his telling the first tale, yet the obligation to offer the first story is 'a liability,' and one that comes about by caprice. The Knight's good-humored submission shows that as a man as well as a knight, he deserves Chaucer's approbation as 'verray, parfit, gentil' (p 161).

487 Raffel, Burton. 'Chaucer's Knight as Don Quijote.' *Notre Dame English Journal* 10(1976), 1–11.
In an age of decayed chivalry, the Knight is neither an exemplar nor a Platonic Ideal but 'an actionable reality ... a Good capable of being realized and ... profoundly to be desired' (p 3). He is contrasted with the Monk, who exhibits some of the excesses that disabled both ecclesiastics and degenerate knights as leaders (pp 4–5). The Knight is 'more Christian, less chivalric, and ... more of a Lollard' than conventional knights were (pp 5–6). Raffel extends Huppé's comment

on I.67–8 (**421**), emphasizing the atypicality of the Knight's Christian humility. For *KnT* see **1013**.

488 Rowland, Beryl. *Blind Beasts: Chaucer's Animal World*. Kent, Ohio: Kent State University Press, 1971.
'The Horse' (pp 112–40): In the Ellesmere illustrations the Knight and the Squire appear to be riding destrers, or warhorses, although away from the battlefield a knight would ordinarily use a palfrey and a squire, a cob or rouncy (p 121). For *KnT* see **1022**.

489 Schmidt, A.V.C. *The General Prologue to the Canterbury Tales and the Canon's Yeoman's Prologue and Tale*. Medieval and Renaissance Texts. London: University of London Press, 1974; New York: Holmes & Meier, 1976.
Schmidt suggests placing a colon at the end of I.45. 'The various abstract qualities [in line 46] then become not *further* objects of the knight's "love" but rather *component elements* of an all-embracing ideal' (p 127). 'Chaucer has isolated one aspect of the many-sided reality of the fourteenth-century knight (part sportsman, part landlord, part justice, part mercenary-soldier) in order to make him the personification of the ideal of chivalry' (p 127). The Knight's campaigns from c 1345–85 place him in his late fifties. His soiled clothes suggest his awareness of the need for penitence (p 128).

490 Sklute, Larry. 'Catalogue Form and Catalogue Style in the General Prologue of the *Canterbury Tales*.' *Studia Neophilologica* 52(1980), 35–46.
The Knight is an ideal figure whose list of battles convinces us of his heroic qualities; subsequent lines on his other virtues soften our sense of him as a soldier but sustain our sense of him as a *Miles Christianum* (pp 36–7).

491 Stemmler, Theo, ed. *The Ellesmere Miniatures of the Canterbury Pilgrims*. Mannheim: University of Mannheim, 1976; 2nd ed, 1977; 3rd ed, 1979.
Presents unretouched color photographs of high quality. The Knight appears as a 'strong, determined fighter (his black eye is due to discolouration, though) riding on a sturdy battle-horse' (xiv). Gold, in the decorations on his gown, his dagger, spurs, and harness, dominates the miniature and indicates his high rank. The brands on the horse's neck may be M's and may stand for *Miles*.

492 Stevenson, Warren. 'Interpreting Blake's Canterbury Pilgrims.' *Colby Library Quarterly* 13(1977), 115–26.
What appears to be Blake's wholly favorable view of the Knight in the *Descriptive Catalogue* is qualified in the engraving. The full armor connects the Knight with the figure of Satan covered with scales in

Blake's Job engravings. The red draperies, the cross on his breast, and the direction of his gaze connect the Knight with the Prioress, the embodiment of corrupt religious institutions. The Knight is counter-balanced by the Poet, recalling the Blakean antithesis between the 'war of swords' and 'intellectual war.' Blake could speak of the Knight as a good man while disapproving of his knighthood; he invites us to forgive the Knight his knightliness (p 120).

493 Thorpe, James. *A Noble Heritage: The Ellesmere Manuscript of Chaucer's Canterbury Tales*. San Marino: The Huntington Library, 1974.
The miniatures are remarkably faithful to Chaucer's descriptions. The horses may have been drawn first, and then mounted figures added. The scale of the Knight's portrait is 'appropriately large' in relation to his rank; his horse is 'massive and aggressive' (p 10). A foldout reproduces all the portraits in color.

494 Zacher, Christian K. *Curiosity and Pilgrimage: The Literature of Discovery in Fourteenth-Century England.* Baltimore: Johns Hopkins, 1976.
The Knight's initial position in the *GP* 'symbolizes the receding ideal of pilgrimage'; his travels, motivated by 'dutiful love for church and country,' contrast with those of the ecclesiastical pilgrims, motivated by restlessness and a desire to exploit others (pp 93–4). He is distinguished by his poverty of dress, service to others, and orderly household group (pp 95–7). The Pardoner, placed last in the series, challenges the order represented by the knight (p 97), and the Knight is more effective than the Host in preserving harmony (p 99). For *KnT* see **1062**.

1981-1985

495 Ames, Ruth M. *God's Plenty*. 1984. See **123**.
Chaucer may have hated war but admired the good soldier, or, influenced by the Lollards, may have condemned war unless motivated by a spiritual revelation. He does not comment on the Knight's battles, but presents the man as admirable (pp 87–8). For *KnT* see **1065**.

496 Beidler, Peter G. 'Chaucer and the Trots: What to Do about Those Modern English Translations.' *ChauR* 19(1985), 290–31.
Includes a brief review of translators' treatments of 'sovereyn prys' (I.67) (p 293).

497 Burchfield, Robert. 'Realms and Approximations: Sources of Chaucer's Power.' *E&S* 35(1982), 1–13.

The Middle Eastern part of what we now call the Third World was for Chaucer 'a poetical rather than a geographical entity' (p 8). The Knight's portrait presents 'a generalized heathendom or "Barbarie"' whose battlefields were meant to seem 'romantically distant and remote' (pp 8–9).

498 Burnley, David. *A Guide to Chaucer's Language*. Norman: University of Oklahoma Press, 1983.
The three time spheres – the narrative present, the time of the pilgrimage, the Knight's past – are not consistently distinguished by tense; both the preterit and the pluperfect are used to refer to the Knight's past (pp 47–8). For *KnT* see **1075**.

499 Cooper, Helen. *The Structure of the Canterbury Tales*. London: Duckworth, 1983.
The *GP* sets up relations between pilgrims comparable to those between tales. The Knight (pp 77–9), in whom Chaucer, *pace* Jones **470**, recalls 'the solid tradition of Christian chivalry' (p 78), is contrasted with the Monk. We might have expected the Knight to be a 'well-to-do secular country gentlemen,' but he is 'an ascetic who has devoted his life to the service of Christianity' (p 78). Chaucer describes the exploits of the reticent Knight while the Monk's own voice and self-estimate are heard in his portrait. The Knight's portrait is dominated by abstract moral adjectives and the 'Miltonic roll-call' of his battles; the Monk's, by concrete references to such things as food, clothing, and animals (p 79). For *KnT* see **1083**.

500 Edsall, Donna Marie. 'Chaucer and the Chivalric Tradition.' Ohio University Dissertation, 1981. Director: R. Vance Ramsey. See also *DAI* 42(1981), 2663A.
Chaucer's audience approved of war and chivalry and Chaucer wrote to please an audience with whom he probably agreed. The Knight (pp 74–80) is an admirable figure. For *KnT* see **1090**.

501 Fisher, John H. 'Chaucer's Prescience: The Presidential Address [to the New Chaucer Society], 1982.' *SAC* 5(1983), 3–15.
Fisher notes the link between the Knight's eastern European campaigns and the contemporary American 'winter of ... discontent with Poland and Russia' (p 8). Chaucer's placing of the Knight at the beginning anticipates modern secularism; in most medieval estates satires (Mann **474**), ecclesiastical figures appear first (pp 8–9).

502 Higgs, Elton D. 'The Old Order and the "Newe World" in the General Prologue to the *Canterbury Tales*,' *Huntington Library Quarterly* 45(1982), 155–73.
Higgs expands upon Howard's tripartite division of the pilgrims (**468**) into groups headed by the ideal Knight, Clerk, and Parson and

Plowman. Each ideal figure represents a virtue and the other members of the group, contrasting vices. The Knight represents feudal fealty and faithful service for the good of society while the vain Squire and Yeoman, socially ambitious Prioress, Monk, and Friar, and mercenary Merchant represent 'new mobility' and mere appearances (pp 158–9, 161–3).

503 Kane, George. *Chaucer.* Past Masters Series. Oxford: Oxford University Press, 1984.
The list of the Knight's battles sketches a tradition of knight errantry reaching from Henry Duke of Lancaster to Henry Bolingbroke (**196**) (pp 103–4). These men were not mercenaries and the Knight's virtues are not treated ironically (p 104). Chaucer's Knight is 'an enlightened creation, not as a deeply ironic advocacy of non-violence but because he embodies the best compromise possible in his time between the ideals of a religion founded on charity and natural human aggressiveness' (p 105).

504 Keen, Maurice. 'Chaucer's Knight, the English Aristocracy and the Crusade.' In *English Court Culture in the Later Middle Ages.* Ed. V.J. Scattergood and J.W. Sherborne. New York: St. Martin's Press, 1983. Pp 45–61.
Rejecting a view of the Knight as an 'anomaly' embodying antique values and Jones' view of him as a mercenary (**470**), Keen suggests that the Knight represents a 'pattern of virtuous living' followed by only a few, and that the crusading ideal and experience were somewhat more powerful in the period than is usually thought (p 47). Keen examines the records of three armorial disputes before the English Court of Chivalry: Scrope v Grosvenor (**201**), Lovell v Morley, and Grey v Hastings. Four of these families had crusading experience, and the extensive activity of the Scropes justifies Manly's suggestion (**335**) that collectively they provided a model for Chaucer (pp 50–2). The witnesses with crusading experience included men from different parts of the country and different degrees of wealth as well as professional and semi-professional warriors (pp 52–3). In some comital families there was a crusading tradition (pp 54–5). Several men in the royal circle of Edward III went on crusade; an Anglo-French expedition against the Turks was planned; and several men in Richard's court enrolled in Philippe de Mézières' Order of the Passion (**198**, **199**) (pp 56–7). Chaucer's Knight is 'the best kind of knight of his time ... a figure idealised somewhat, perhaps, but by no means antiquated in his outlook or remote, in his described life-style and ideals, from the English aristocrats and knights whom Chaucer knew personally' (pp 57–8). Jones' skepticism about the

motives for crusading is justified, but greed was probably not a powerful one since no money was to be made in Prussia, the principal crusading area for western knights; Alexandria was an exception (pp 58–9). The mystique that the Teutonic Knights created to attract men suggests other motives: 'conformist acceptance of established ideals, together with the prospect of winning repute and the lure of adventure' (p 60).

505 Kuhn, Sherman M. 'Chaucer's ARMEE: Its French Ancestors and Its English Posterity.' In *Medieval Studies Conference Aachen 1983: Language and Literature*. Bamberger Beiträge zur Englischen Sprachwissenschaft 15. Ed. Wolf-Dietrich Bald and Horst Weinstock. Frankfurt: Peter Lang, 1984. Pp 85–102.
In I.60 *armee* is favored by the best and the earliest manuscripts, and by a majority of all manuscripts (p 91). Donaldson **449** exaggerates manuscript authority for *aryve*, and Görlach **463** underrepresents the currency of *armee* in French and Anglo-French sources (pp 92–6). *Aryve* does not occur in English outside the manuscripts of the *GP* and is not securely attested in French. Fifteenth-century English uses of *armee* are listed, p 97.

506 Leland, Virginia E. 'Chaucer As Commissioner of Dikes and Ditches, 1390.' *MichA* 14(1981), 71–9.
Chaucer's fellow-commissioners have counterparts in the *GP*. The Knight is very like Sir Richard Stury, a supporter of Richard II, accused by some of being a Lollard but praised by Froissart **183** for his bravery and courtesy (pp 75, 77).

507 Lester, G.A. 'Chaucer's Knight and the Earl of Warwick.' *N&Q* 28[226](1981), 200–2.
Lester argues against Jones' characterization of the Knight as a mercenary and merciless killer (**470**), citing the fifteenth-century *Warwick Pageant*, a biography of Richard Beauchamp, Earl of Warwick (1381–1439). Lester notes many similarities between the Knight's career and the Earl's: Warwick's participation in wars against other Christians, his being invited to 'begin the board' at noble feasts, his service in Russia and Prussia, and his participation in tournaments and jousts, in one of which he killed his opponent. The biography presents the Earl as a paragon of knighthood and as having a reputation as such with both the English and the French.

508 — 'Chaucer's Knight and the Medieval Tournament.' *Neophil* 66(1982), 460–8.
Replying to Jones' criticism (**470**) of the Knight's behavior in tournaments, Lester distinguishes among jousts, foot combats, and mêlées, all 'theoretically friendly, sporting affairs' (p 461), and the

duel, a judicial combat that ordinarily ended in death (pp 460–1). At the end of the fourteenth century, the word 'tournament' probably referred only to the mêlée (p 461). The phrase 'In lystes thries' (I.63) refers not to a tournament but to a duel; the Church condemned mêlées, but not duels (until the Council of Trent in 1561) (p 462). Thus the Knight was 'fighting Muslims, under conditions akin to those regulated in the ordinances' (p 462). 'It is wildly wrong to deduce "the Knight's homicidal character"'(quoting Jones, p 85) (p 463). For *KnT* see **1108**.

509 Lindahl, Carl. 'The Festive Form of the *Canterbury Tales*.' *ELH* 52(1985), 531–74. Rpt in part in Ch 4 of *Folkloric Patterns in the Canterbury Tales*. Indiana University Press, 1987. Pp 44–61.
The *CT* shares features with medieval oral forms of entertainment. There is a strong competitive element, with nobles like the Knight focusing on individual competition and exhibiting humility, while churls like the Miller and Reeve focus on class and occupational rivalry and exhibit contentiousness. Festivals mirror society in having a hierarchical structure but allow for sanctioned inversions, such as the Miller's 'quitting' the Knight (pp 548–57).

510 McColly, William. 'Why Chaucer's Knight Has No Coat of Arms.' *ELN* 21(1984), 1–6.
Jones **470** says that the lack of a coat of arms identifies the Knight as a poor knight and a mercenary. Yet Bertilak in *SGGK*, Youth in *The Parlement of the Three Ages*, and many of the knights in the alliterative *Morte Arthure* and in Malory appear without coats of arms (p 2). Heraldic devices advance characterization or theme in specific ways: eg, Sir Gawain's pentangle, Theseus' banner and pennon (I.975–80). But the Knight is an ideal figure, as described by Robinson **388**, whose typicality requires a degree of depersonalization (p 4). The Scrope-Grosvenor case (**210**) would have made Chaucer aware of the embarrassment that could arise from assigning to a fictional character arms that might already be in use by an actual person (pp 5–6).

511 —— 'Chaucer's Yeoman and the Rank of His Knight.' *ChauR* 20(1985), 14–27.
The Yeoman was not of lowly status, a hunter or gamekeeper, but a law enforcement official of considerable authority. The Knight's ownership of a forest and his retention of a forester suggest his degree among the kinds of knights: he is 'an idealized image of the baronial class' (p 23).

512 Morgan, Gerald. 'Rhetorical Perspectives in the *General Prologue* to the *Canterbury Tales*.' *ES* 62(1981), 411–22.

Because the *GP* is not satire but moral comedy conducted within a tradition of rhetorical description, it represents virtue as well as vice. The Knight is one of the virtuous figures meant to be appreciated 'in and for themselves' (p 416), not because they provide standards by which other pilgrims are to be judged. 'There is no suggestion here of a distinction between poet and pilgrim, no sense in which our admiration for the Knight is qualified' (p 417).

513 Owen, Charles A., Jr. 'Development of the Art of Portraiture in Chaucer's *General Prologue.*' *LeedsSE* ns 14(1983), 116–33.
The Knight's portrait exhibits one of the governing principles of the portraits – that they should 'build toward an identity rather than assert it' (p 117). The list of battles, 'neither entirely random nor entirely systematic,' conveys convincingly 'the religious motivation, [and] the lifetime commitment' (p 119). Lines 67–9 contain the portrait's only logical subordination and only overt comparison, and clearly imply the Knight's superiority in wisdom to men loosely called 'worthy.' Lines 70–2 juxtapose two striking statements, the negatives in 70–1 constituting a kind of superlative. The last lines constitute an *effictio* that implies a *notatio*: the lesser importance of the physical presence (p 120).

514 Porter, Elizabeth. 'Chaucer's Knight, the Alliterative *Morte Arthure*, and Medieval Laws of War: A Reconsideration.' *Nottingham Medieval Studies* 27(1983), 56–78.
Porter links Jones' re-interpretation of the Knight as a mercenary (**470**) with William Matthews' re-assessment of Arthur as a war-monger (*The Tragedy of Arthur*, 1960), and replies that both characters are celebrated by poets who accept the crusading ideal. Reviewing medieval treatises on the causes and conduct of just wars, particularly the works of Honoré Bouvet **171** and Christine de Pisan **175** (pp 58–73), Porter concludes that both the crusades to regain the Holy Land and Arthur's wars to secure the throne of the Roman Empire were justified by the right to defend a patrimony (pp 60–1), and that other laws concerning non-Christians 'left enough latitude' to justify the Knight's campaigns in Lithuania, Armenia and Grenada (p 61). As to the brutality of the attack on Alexandria, 'the devastation and suffering ... was both usual and legitimate according to the contemporary *ius in bello*' (p 64). Siege warfare was directed in large part at civilians (pp 64–6), and the type of war known as *guerre mortelle* justified the sacking of Alexandria, which was 'hailed with delight in Christendom' (p 67). Texts like Gower's *In Praise of Peace* **185** do not support pacifism but urge an end to the war between England and France because of the need for a crusade (p 75). The

Knight's apparent poverty is part of his idealization as a crusader, while the Squire may represent those knights whom Gower blamed for profiting from war (p 77). The *Mel* may express war-weariness but not pacifism, and, with the Knight's portrait, may express Chaucer's support for the crusading program of Philippe de Mézières (**198, 199**) (pp 77–8).

515 Siberry, Elizabeth. 'Criticism of Crusading in Fourteenth-Century England.' In *Crusade and Settlement: Papers read at the First Conference of the Society for the Study of the Crusades and the Latin East and presented to R.C. Small.* Ed. Peter W. Edbury. Cardiff: University College of Cardiff Press, 1985. Pp 127–34.
Jones' claim of a rising tide of anti-crusade sentiment (**470**) is not convincing because he ignores the numbers of English knights, including members of Richard's court and even Lollard knights, who took the cross, and because he treats comments by Wyclif and Gower in isolation from their works as a whole. Wyclif attacked the Flanders Crusade of Bishop Dispenser (1383) as an abuse of papal power, and Gower [cf **185**] complained of strife among Christians, but there is no evidence that either rejected the use of force against the Muslims. Similarly, Langland seems to have accepted the use of force even as he advocated missions of conversion.

516 Spearing, A.C. 'Chaucerian Authority and Inheritance.' In *Literature in Fourteenth-Century England.* Ed. Piero Boitani and Anna Torti. Tübinger Beiträge zur Anglistik, 5. Gunter Narr, 1983. Pp 185–202.
Surveying Chaucer's absent or cruel fathers, Spearing notes that we learn nothing in the *GP* of the Knight's paternal relation to the Squire; I.100 refers only to a squire's appropriate behavior toward his lord (p 187). For *KnT* see **1127**.

517 Stevens, Martin. 'The Ellesmere Miniatures as Illustrations of Chaucer's Canterbury Tales.' *Studies in Iconography*, 7–8(1981–2), 113–34.
The Ellesmere illustrators produced individual portraits rather than types, 'mnemonic aids' (p 122) that link the pilgrims to the tales they tell and before which their portraits appear. Chaucer presents the Knight (pp 123–4) as both a chivalric figure and a gentleman; though the physical description (I.74–6) focuses on the soldier alone, the illustrator presents the gentleman. The Knight's stately horse is equipped for riding not jousting; gold adorns horse and rider; the Knight's gown, boots, gloves, and hat identify him as a modish member of the upper class. This treatment would appeal to a noble audience, and links the Knight to his tale, in which Theseus appears first as warrior and then as nobleman.

518 Urban, William. 'When Was Chaucer's Knight in "Ruce"?' *ChauR* 18(1984), 347–53.
No English knights have been identified as crusaders in Russia (pp 347–8), yet Jones **470** cites the Knight's raids into Christian Russia as evidence of his being a mercenary (p 349). England had no contacts with Russia, and 'Ruce' is probably Rossenia, a district of Samogithia, between Livonia and Prussia (p 349). The most well known of several English crusaders to visit Samogithia was Henry, Earl of Derby **196**, who went to Prussia in 1390, and made a pilgrimage to Bridlington on his return in 1391. The portrait may be 'a flattering reference' to Henry, making 1390–1 the earliest date for its composition (p 350). There was no significant English participation in the Prussian crusades after 1390; the reputation of the Teutonic Knights declined; the Hundred Years' War resumed. 'For Englishmen of the next generation the Knight was almost as remote a figure as he is to us' (p 351).

The Knight's Tale

Illustration

519 *Etchings illustrating Chaucer's 'Canterbury Tales' by Elizabeth Frink.* Introduction and translation by Nevill Coghill. London: Leslie Waddington Prints Ltd., 1972.

One of the 19 plates depicts a nude, 'classical' Theseus on a white horse, greeting ten Theban ladies dressed in black robes and veils. The accompanying text is Coghill's translation of I.893–904 as in **46**. Two bound editions of 50 copies each; one unbound edition of 175 copies.

Dramatization

520 *Canterbury Tales: Chaucer Made Modern.* By Phil Woods with Michael Bogdanov. North Shields: Iron Press, 1980; rpt through 1985. Pp 2–6.

This stage version, first performed in 1974, presents a 'Canterbury Tales-telling competition' set in the present. The *KnT* is reduced to a set of brief scenes and narrative summaries: omitted, eg, are the descriptions of the temples, Arcite's funeral, and Theseus' final speech. The *MilT*, it is hinted, will be the audience's choice for best tale.

521 *The Two Knights.* Adapted from the Canterbury Tales by Geoffrey Chaucer. Dramatised as a Pageant Play for Costume Representation by Sivori Levey. The Pilgrimage Plays, Number 2. Roehampton: Fountain Publishing Company, 1919.

The story is presented in tableau form in Levey's Modern English translation. It is divided into two parts, of seven and six scenes each, with the major break coming at the end of the scene in the grove. A curtained recess at the back of the stage serves as the prison cell, the temples, and the 'royal box' at the tournament.

Criticism

1900-1930

This section contains some pre–1900 items.

522 Anders, H.R.D. *Shakespeare's Books: A Dissertation on Shakespeare's Reading and the Immediate Sources of His Works.* Berlin: George Reimer, 1904. Rpt New York: AMS Press, 1965.
The name 'Philostrate,' Theseus' title of 'Duke,' the Athenian wood, and the romantic costume of the classical characters in *MND* are drawn from the *KnT*. 'Philostrate' and Theseus' title were apparently also part of Richard Edwardes' play 'Palamon and Arcite' (1566). It is likely that Theseus' hunt, with the music of the hounds, in *MND* IV.i derives from a stage tradition originating with Edwardes. See Coghill **671**.

523 Baker, Courtland D. 'A Note on Chaucer's *Knight's Tale*.' *MLN* 45(1930), 460–2.
Baker objects to Hulbert's emphasis (**578**) on the equal merits of Palamon and Arcite. Palamon's 'affeccioun of holinesse' is worthier than Arcite's 'love, as to a creature' (I.1158–9) as is shown by Palamon's 'martirdom' (1460) in love; by Arcite's violation of the covenant of blood brotherhood; by Palamon's prayer for love; by Arcite's dying recantation and recommendation of Palamon; and by Saturn's intervention on Palamon's behalf. See **650**.

524 Ballmann, O. 'Chaucers Einfluss auf das englische Drama.' *Anglia* 25(1902), 1–85.
Elizabethan and Jacobean plays indebted to the *KnT* include: *Palamon and Arcite*, 1566 (now lost); another play of the same name, 1594; Shakespeare's *Love's Labor's Lost*, and *The Passionate Pilgrim*, both of which allude to I.1155–9; *MND* (the marriage of Theseus and Hippolyta); and *TNK* (many allusions: see Leuschner **592**).

525 Bentinck-Smith, M. *The Prologue and the Knight's Tale*. 1909. See **20**.
Bentinck-Smith rejects Brink's theory of a *P&A* in seven-line stanzas (**529**). The *KnT* and the work referred to in *LGW* (Prol F.420–1) 'are to all intents the same poem'; *KnT* and *TC* were composed at about the same time; and *Anel* is 'a first experiment' in the treatment of the *Tes* (lxxxiii). Tyrwhitt's account (**640**) of the superiority of the *KnT* to the *Tes* does not convince. Palamon's seeing Emelye first cannot support justice in a poem 'based upon the conception of human beings as toys in the hands of the gods' (lxxxv). The love and jealousy of Chaucer's princes are merely conventional (lxxxv). Emelye may be

unaware of the princes' initial interest, but she does know that she is a 'fers' in a game of chess (lxxxv). Chaucer's characters behave less chivalrously than Boccaccio's, as when Palamon rushes on Arcite in the grove 'with words which must forever exclude him from the ranks of those who "nevere yet no vileynye ne sayde"' (lxxxv).

526 Berkelman, Robert G. 'Chaucer and Masefield.' 1927. See **322**.
Arcite's death-bed questions (I.2777–9) are echoed in Masefield's *The Passing Strange*: 'Fasten to lover or to friend, / Until the heart break at the end, / ... then to lie useless, held-less, still, / Down in the earth.'

527 Bethel, John Perceval. 'The Influence of Dante on Chaucer's Thought and Expression.' Harvard University Dissertation, 1927.
The *KnT* exhibits three facets of Dante's influence on Chaucer: verbal borrowings, elevated tone, and philosophy. The last is treated in a discussion of I.1663–9 in relation to *Inf* VII.67–96 (pp 249 f). An appendix lists fifteen passages showing Dante's influence, for which see Schless **1121**.

528 Bond, Richard P. 'Some Eighteenth Century Chaucer Allusions.' 1928. See **323**.
In *An Essay on Criticism; As It Regards Design, Thought, and Expression, in Prose and Verse* (1728), pp 38–9, John Oldmixon compared the *KnT* and Dryden's *Pal*.

529 Brink, Bernhard ten. *Chaucer: Studien zu Geschichte Seiner Entwicklung und zur Chronologie Seiner Schriften*. Münster, 1870.
The original *P&A* was a close translation of the *Tes* in seven-line stanzas, its relationship to its Italian original being much like that of *TC* to the *Filos*. *Anel* is a later, lightly modified fragment of *P&A*, and the *KnT* is a still later work in which Chaucer re-cast *P&A* into heroic couplets, greatly condensed the work, and adopted a lighter, more comical tone (pp 39–70). The original *P&A* no doubt contained Arcite's ascension; in eliminating it from the *KnT*, Chaucer was poking fun at both Boccaccio and himself (p 61). See **7**, **525**, **573**, **589**, **590**, **605a**, **607**, **613**, **620**, **625**, **632**, **644**, **751**.

530 —— *History of English Literature*. Volume 2. Trans. William Clarke Robinson. London: George Bell, 1901.
Boccaccio miscalculated both the suitability of his story for epic treatment and his own talent for treating heroic themes (pp 63–7). Chaucer's early stanzaic version (see **529**) must have been condensed, modified in conception and infused with humor in becoming the *KnT*, which, shorn of Boccaccio's epic pretensions, 'breathes the atmosphere of a romance tale' (p 68). While Boccaccio prefers Arcite, Chaucer attempts to treat the two knights equally and is the first to

work out fully the implications of their two different prayers. Theseus fights only in the interests of humanity as befits his double role as an 'earthly Providence' and a 'privileged exponent of Chaucer's humor and worldly wisdom' (p 70). The descriptions of the temples exemplify both the medieval art of amplification and the renaissance taste for 'plastic beauty' (p 71). Lycurgus reflects Palamon's character, and Emetrius, Arcite's (p 72).

531 Browne, Matthew [pseudonym of William Brightly Rands]. *Chaucer's England*. 1869. 2 volumes. Excerpted in *Chaucer: The Critical Heritage*. Ed. Derek Brewer (London: Routledge & Kegan Paul, 1978), Volume 2, 128–31 [cited here].

As evidence for his claim that 'Nature, in the Wordsworthian sense, plays no part in Chaucer' (p 129), Brown cites the description of dawn (I. 1491–6). 'This is beautiful ... but it is all homely; it is all the *face* of nature; ... there is no undercurrent ... Thought of an inner secret or soul in nature there is none, — even if there is of a heart' (p 130).

532 Browne, William Hand. 'Notes on Chaucer's Astrology.' *MLN* 23(1908), 53–4.

Arcite is fatally wounded during one of the three hours on a Tuesday when Saturn could act, the thirteenth hour or sunset. See **550**, **901**.

533 Cook, Albert S. 'The Arming of the Combatants in the Knight's Tale.' *JEGP* 4(1902), 50–4.

Cook compares Chaucer's description of the preparations for the tournament (*KnT* 1625–64; I.2483–2522) with the account of an actual tournament of about 1180 in *L'Histoire de Guillaume le Marchal* **187**.

534 — 'Miscellaneous Notes: Chaucer, *Knight's Tale* 810–811.' *MLN* 22(1907), 207.

Cook supports the designation of these lines — 'yet somtyme it shal fallen on a day / That falleth not eft withinne a thousand yere' (I.1668–9) — as proverbial by citing their attribution to John of Gaunt in Froissart's *Chronicle* **183** and their use by Nicholas, alias 'Proverbs,' in Henry Porter's *Two Angry Women of Abington* (1599).

535 — 'Chaucer's Alaunts' in 'The Last Months of Chaucer's Earliest Patron.' *TCAAS* 21(1916). New Haven: Tuttle, Morehouse & Taylor, 1916; rpt New York: AMS Press, 1973. Pp 128–40.

Contemporary documents suggest that the 'alaunt' (*KnT* 1290–4; I.2148–52) looked something like a Great Dane and was noted for its large size, whiteness, and fierceness. There is no evidence of alaunts in England; Chaucer may have seen such dogs in Paris or Milan.

536 — 'Chaucer's *fraknes*.' *MLN* 31(1916), 315.
Entries for *pock-frecken* and *pock-freckled* under '*Pock*' in the *NED* suggest that *fraknes* in *KnT* 1311 (I.2169) might be a euphemism for pock-marks.

537 — 'The Historical Background of Chaucer's Knight.' 1916. See **326**.
Henry, Earl of Derby, later Henry IV, provided a model, particularly on the occasion of his progress from Dartford to London on July 5, 1393 (**196**), for Chaucer's portrait of Emetrius (*KnT* 1297–1328; I.2155–86) (pp 165–215). See **751**, **898**.

538 — 'Chaucer: *Knight's Tale* 2012–8.' *RomR* 9(1918), 317.
These lines describing the adornment of Arcite's bier and corpse (I.2870–6) are indebted to *Tes* XI.15. Boccaccio may have drawn on his own observations of Petrarch's funeral.

539 — 'Chauceriana.' *TCAAS* 23(1919), 1–63.
The dogs depicted in a fifteenth-century fresco by Andrea Montegna may be alaunts, as in *KnT* 1290 (I.2148) (p 30).

540 Cowling, George H. *Chaucer*. London: Methuen, 1927; rpt Freeport, New York: Books for Libraries Press, 1971.
The theme of the *KnT* is 'honour amongst friends,' and its climax is Arcite's renunciation of Emily, a noble action 'too lofty for real life' (p 153). Characterization is generally weak, but Theseus is a 'dominating personality' whose 'genial cynicism and ... openness are evidently Chaucer's own' (p 154). The Tale's success lies in its magnificent descriptions.

541 Cummings, Hubertis M. 'Chaucer's Use of the *Teseide*.' *The Indebtedness of Chaucer's Works to the Italian Works of Boccaccio (A Review and Summary)*. University of Cincinnati Studies, No 10, pt 2. Cincinnati: University of Cincinnati, 1916. Rpt New York: Haskell House, 1965; Phaeton Press, 1967. Pp 123–46.
The necessity of fitting the *KnT* to the *CT* motivated Chaucer's compression of the *Tes*, not any deficiencies in the *Tes* itself. Some of Chaucer's changes were not for the better, such as his substitution of Boethian philosophy for romantic sentiment (p 127). Cummings presents (pp 128–31) attempts to quantify Chaucer's indebtedness to the *Tes* by Ward **1**, Skeat **625**, and Tatlock **632**, and adds his own (pp 131–4). A second table (pp 134–5) lists ten 'New Elements' added by Chaucer. Cummings then lists (pp 135–7) nineteen 'beauties' of the *Tes* discarded by Chaucer. Cummings objects, eg, to Chaucer's 'almost crude' treatment (p 137) of the knights' first sight of Emelye as compared with Boccaccio's, and to his less detailed characterization of Emelye. Chaucer improved upon the *Tes* by strengthening the justice of the outcome by having Palamon see

Emelye first; rearranging the meeting of the two knights in the grove to emphasize fierce passion and knightly generosity; adding Theseus' pardoning of the lovers at the ladies' request; locating the gods' altars in the theater; and putting Palamon's prayer first, thus emphasizing his meritorious loyalty to Venus. Chaucer also retains the device by which 'through the wording of prayer the Gordian knot of Boccaccio's [love problem] was solved' (p 142). After reviewing the pseudo-classical elements Chaucer excised, Cummings lists the realistic medieval elements he introduced, according to S. Robertson **616**, and adds several: eg, the 'proper English' observance of May; the 'mediaeval phenomena' depicted on the walls of Mars' temple; the details about armor, the spectators, and the herald at the tournament (p 145). 'Chaucer's greatest contribution to the story of Palamon and Arcite is this new atmosphere' of English feudalism, appropriate to a knight (p 146). See **234R**.

542 Curry, Walter Clyde. 'Two Notes on Chaucer.' *MLN* 36(1921), 272–76.
The 'tempest' of I.884 is not a storm but the tumult occasioned by the triumphant return of Theseus to Athens with his bride (pp 272–4). See **595, 778**.

543 — 'Astrologizing the Gods.' *Anglia* 47(1923), 213–43. Rpt in *Chaucer and the Mediaeval Sciences*. New York: Barnes & Noble, 1926/rev 1960; rpt 1962, 1968, pp 119–63.
For the pagan gods, whom his audience regarded as poetic fancies, Chaucer substituted the planets, in whose astrological influence the audience believed, as seen in the description of Mars' temple (I.2016–29), for example, and in the assignment of the prayers to the hours of astrological influence of their respective gods. Lycurgus, with his black hair, olive complexion, and heavy brows is a Saturnian figure and Emetrius, with his yellowish hair, red complexion, and freckles, is a Martian figure. Saturn sends the fury during one of the hours of his influence and causes Arcite's final illness by strengthening the retentive virtue, which falls under his planetary sway. 'The final scene of conflict between the planets is in the body of Arcite' (p 147). Chaucer fits the otherwise mechanical processes presided over by the planets into a consoling Boethian scheme of cosmic governance, as seen most explicitly in the narrator's comment on destiny (I.1663 f) and in Theseus' 'First Mover' speech (pp 161–3). See **559, 799, 807, 853, 885, 901, 947, 955**.

544 — 'Arcite's Intellect.' *JEGP* 29(1930), 83–99. Rpt in *Chaucer and the Mediaeval Sciences*. 2nd ed. New York: Barnes & Noble, 1960; rpt 1962, 1968. Pp 299–315.

In the account of Arcite's death (I.2765–2812) 'intellect' is the supreme essence of the rational soul, synonymous with spirit. Chaucer chooses sides on controversial points when he locates the intellect in the heart and suggests that the spirit 'houses' itself in another body of some sort after death (pp 83–93). Chaucer chose not to be specific about the fate of Arcite's soul (pp 193–7) because the story is concerned not with his merits but with his destiny. Chaucer's flippant tone may be directed against 'the smugness and futility of scholastic dialectic' on the subject of the pagan's salvation (p 97).

545 [Cyples, William]. 'Chaucer's Love Poetry.' *Cornhill Magazine*, 35 (1877), 280–97; excerpted in *Chaucer: The Critical Heritage*. Ed. Derek Brewer (London: Routledge & Kegan Paul, 1978), Volume 2, 188–207 [cited here].

In this anonymously published article, Cyples seeks to demonstrate the 'incredible sentimentality' (p 195) of Chaucer's treatment of love, his chief subject. In explaining the medieval style of love, Cyples cites the *KnT* to exemplify the irresistible power of love, the suddenness of falling in love, and the terrible sufferings of men in love (pp 196–9). The 'silly presentation' of men is one cause of readers' neglect of Chaucer's works, but the historical value of these poems should increase 'since there is no doubt that, in modern Christianised civilisation, the influence of sex is waning' (p 207).

546 Day, Mabel. 'A Note on "The Knightes Tale".' *MLR* 23(1928), 208.

Day rejects Dustoor's interpretation of *tweye* in I.2625 as 'twice' (**551**) in favor of the gloss 'two.' Chaucer's two heroes, like Boccaccio's in *Tes* VIII.12, engage in a single combat.

547 Derocquigny, J. 'Notes sur Chaucer.' *Revue Germanique* 6(1910), 203–6.

Offers glosses for *desirynge* (I.1922), *devisynge* (2496), *Nailynge the speres* (2503), and *Giggynge of sheeldes* (2504).

548 Dodd, William George. 'The Knight's Tale.' *Courtly Love in Chaucer and Gower*. Milford, Mass.: Ginn, 1913. Rpt Gloucester, Mass.: Peter Smith, 1959. Pp 234–46.

In the *KnT* Chaucer uses 'the stock ideas of love literature' (p 234): a god of love of absolute power; Venus and Cupid as love deities; the lady as the indifferent superior to her lovers and the recipient of their services; the lovers' customary symptoms and sufferings; and the wounding of the heart by beauty entering through the eyes. Arcite's sensitivity to music (I.1367–8) is probably original with Chaucer. Chaucer changed Boccaccio's story by greatly abridging the material, building up Palamon to make a more effective contrast with Arcite, and making Emilia 'almost characterless' (p 239). Dodd surveys in detail (pp 239–45) Emilia's greater role in the *Tes*, finding her character particularly impressive in five scenes: her prayer to Diana, her reflections on her responsibility for the lovers' conflict, her response to Arcite's injury, her interview with Palamon, and the death scene of Arcite. Chaucer has 'sacrificed much in his original that is beautiful and attractive' yet we can be certain that he appreciated the beauty of Emilia's character. His motive was to focus attention on the love-passion of the two men, making what had been artificial in the *Tes* 'not only earnest but absolutely genuine' (p 245).

549 Durand, W.Y. '*Palaemon and Arcyte, Progne, Marcus Geminus*, and the Theatre in Which They Were Acted as Described by John Bereblock (1566).' *PMLA* 20(1905), 502–28.
Durand translates into English the Latin *Commentarii* in which John Bereblock recounts the performance of Richard Edwards' *Palaemon and Arcyte*, now lost, in the Common Hall at Christ's Church in Oxford before Queen Elizabeth in 1566. The play was performed in two parts, on two evenings, the division being made at the end of the scene in the grove when Theseus decrees the tournament. Bereblock's synopsis indicates one clear change from Chaucer's version: Venus appeals to Saturn only after Arcite has won the tournament. The audience reacted to the fighting with 'a great shudder' (p 511) and greeted the marriage of Palamon and Emelye 'with a tremendous shout and clapping of hands' (p 512). Durand prints two briefer accounts, by Nicholas Robinson and Richard Stephens, but rejects Robinson's statement that Edwards' play was a translation of an unknown Latin version of the *KnT*.

550 Dustoor, P.E. 'Chaucer's Astrology in "The Knightes Tale".' *TLS* May 5, 1927, 318.
Extending Browne's analysis (**532**), Dustoor suggests that Palamon escapes from prison in one of Mercury's hours. Mercury rescues Palamon as he earlier acted to return Arcite from exile. See **901**.

551 — 'Notes on "The Knightes Tale".' *MLR* 22(1927), 438–41.
Dustoor cites three parallels between the *KnT* and Froissart's *Chronicles* (**183**) as evidence of Chaucer's realism: Palamon and Arcite's helping to arm each other (I.1612–14) and the account of the tilting match between John Bouchmel and Nicholas Clifford (*Chronicles*, I); the construction of the lists (I.1882–4) and the match between John de Carogne and James le Gris (*Chronicles*, II); and Arcite's funeral (I.2887 f) and the funeral of the Earl of Flanders (*Chronicles*, II). Glosses: In I.2153 and 2179 Palamon and Arcite are each accompanied by 99 knights for a total of 100 on each side. In I.2450 *drede* may mean 'anger,' 'fury,' 'violence,' 'rage.' I.2625 should

be read 'Each had unhorsed the other twice.' In I.2815 *Ther* means 'thereupon.' See **546**.

552 Edmunds, E.W. *Chaucer and His Poetry*. London: Harrap, 1914. Rpt New York: AMS, 1971. Pp 144–51.
The *KnT* is the *'pièce de résistance'* of the *CT* and an improvement upon the *Tes* (p 144). 'The characterization is ... quite modern in its psychological subtlety. The rather melancholy Palamon ... is an effective contrast with Arcite ... headstrong, passionate, but generous'; Emilia is 'not the usual pretty doll of chivalry, but has a beautiful personality in keeping with her external charms; and Theseus is royal, every inch of him' (pp 145–6).

553 Egg, Walter. 'Chaucers Knight's Tale: Eine literarische Skizze.' *Jahresbericht der Stattsrealschule in Marburg* 42(1911–2), 3–26.
Egg comments on the humorous aspects of the *KnT* (pp 7–13), eg, the princes' quarrel over an unattainable lady. He comments briefly on classical, medieval, and renaissance elements (pp 13–5), and discusses the work's division into parts, combination of epic and dramatic elements, and combination of objective reporting with direct addresses to the reader (pp 15–21).

554 Emerson, Oliver Farrar. 'Chaucer's "Opie of Thebes Fyn".' *MP* 17(1919), 287–91. Rpt in *Chaucer: Essays and Studies*. Western Reserve University Press, 1929. Pp 312–19.
Chaucer's references to opium in *LGW* 2668–70 and *KnT* 612–6 (I.1470–74), references not found in his sources, illustrate his medical knowledge. Thebes, a city in Egypt, was a source of especially fine opium according to the testimony of fourteenth- and sixteenth-century botanists. Narcotics, and especially opium, were recognized as remedies for love-melancholy such as Palamon suffers.

555 — 'Chaucer and Medieval Hunting.' *RomR* 13(1922), 115–50. Rpt in *Chaucer Essays and Studies*. 1929. See **554**. Pp 320–77.
Esp pp 139–43. Although the *KnT* is based on an Italian work, it depicts hunting as it was known in England: eg, the mention of a bear, native to northern latitudes (I.1637–48) (p 139). The *grete hert* is a technical term indicating a hart appropriate for hunting, and Theseus hunts him in the proper time (May) and place (in the plains). The green costumes of Theseus' party reflect the hunting dress of the period. The 'whyte alaunts' (2148–52) are English hunting dogs, which required a 'mozel' or muzzle because of their fierceness. They wear 'tourettes,' that is, 'swivels to allow free play of the leash' (p 142).

556 — 'Some Notes on Chaucer and Some Conjectures.' *PQ* 2(1923), 81–96. Rpt in *Chaucer Essays and Studies*. 1929. See **554**. Pp 378–404.
In *KnT* A[I].979–80 Theseus' pennon is 'Of gold ful riche, in which ther was y-bete / The Minotaur.' In his notes Skeat **625** implies that gold hammered into thin sheets was used as a decoration. But three passages in *SGGK* (77–8, 2027–8, 1832–3) and a passage in *RR* (824–6) translated in the *Rom* (836–8) show that *gold beten* refers to 'gold (or metallic) thread used in textile fabrics.' Thus the figure of the Minotaur is woven or embroidered in gold thread (pp 88–9).

557 Fairchild, Hoxie Neale. 'Active Arcite, Contemplative Palamon.' *JEGP* 26(1927), 285–93.
In differentiating Palamon and Arcite Chaucer may have drawn on the distinction between the active and contemplative lives. The Knight's *demande d'amour* (A[I].1347–54) may ask which life was the superior one. On first seeing Emily, Palamon reacts as a visionary, Arcite as a lover, and Arcite's distinction between 'affeccioun of holinesse' and love 'as to a creature' (1158–9) 'is precisely the distinction between Contemplative Life and Active Life' (p 287). After years of futile activity, Arcite turns toward contemplation, in the grove, while Palamon, escaping from prison, turns to action. But in their prayers the princes revert to type: Palamon focusing on the end he seeks, Arcite, on means (p 291). Arcite's excessive emphasis on activity is the tragic error which leads to his death. Palamon corrects his excessive devotion to contemplation by escaping from prison, and becomes the ideally balanced 'working dreamer' (p 292). See **718**, **751**.

558 Fansler, Dean Spruill. *Chaucer and the Roman de la Rose*. New York: Columbia University Press, 1914. Rpt Gloucester, Mass.: Peter Smith, 1965.
Chaucer refers inconsistently to Venus as both Jove's daughter (A[I].2222) and Saturn's (I.2453, and see Brooks **666**); the latter identification comes from *RR* 6270–5 and 11592–5. The specification of Cithaeron as her dwelling (1936–7) is indebted to *RR* 16596–604; the reference to her net (1951–2), to *RR* 11664–5; her role as enemy of chastity (2233–7), to *RR* 22087–94; her involvement with Mars (2388–90), to *RR* 14785–815, 15100–129, and 18996–19204. Chaucer probably took his conception of Venus as a representative of voluptuous love from the classical poets rather than from Jean de Meun (pp 56–60). *Pace* Skeat **625**, who sees a debt to *RR* in I.2921–3, Chaucer chose his own woods for his tree list (p 114). Three proverbs in the *KnT* can be traced to the *RR* (pp 194–5): those on

love and lordship (I.1625–6, *RR* 9198–9202), on age and wisdom (I.2447–8, *RR* 13759–61), and on making a virtue of necessity (I.3041–2, *RR* 14960–1). And see index.

559 French, Robert Dudley. 'The Knightes Tale.' *A Chaucer Handbook.* New York: F.S. Crofts, 1927/rev 1947. Pp 210–5.
French reports a consensus that the *KnT* is essentially the same work as the *P&A* mentioned in the *LGW* (p 210). He reproduces Tyrwhitt's summary (**640**) of the *Tes* (pp 211–4), and he notes Chaucer's familiarity with the *Theb* and the deep influence of Boethius particularly 'as the romance darkens into tragedy towards its close' (p 214). Finally he cites Curry's interpretation (**543**) of the significance of the astrological elements.

560 Getty, Agnes K. 'Chaucer's Changing Conceptions of the Humble Lover.' *PMLA* 44(1929), 202–16.
Palamon and Arcite are 'the most ideal pair of Chaucer's romantic lovers,' yet the Tale as a whole shows 'strong revolt' against the courtly code (p 210) as suggested by the narrator's impatience with Arcite's love-sickness (I.1380–2), the ladies' defense of the princes on the ground that 'nothyng but for love was this debaat' (1754), and Theseus' scoffing at love (1796–1817). 'Chaucer slyly suggests ... that allegiance to the code was merely a popular pose' (p 211); yet his return to the pattern in Arcite's death-bed speech seems sincere. Chaucer 'has drawn himself more clearly than either the knight or Theseus ... the odd combination of satire, human sympathy, ridicule and wistful regret is intrinsically Chaucer's own' (p 212).

561 Gibbs, Lincoln R. 'The Meaning of *Feeldes* in Chaucer's *Knight's Tale*, vv. 975–977.' *MLN* 24 (1909), 197–8.
Gibbs argues for the literal interpretation, 'plains,' against the alternative possibility, 'heraldic fields or grounds,' suggested by Skeat (**625**), and cites as an analogue a passage in Chrétien de Troyes' *Perceval* (1832–40). See **562**, **586**.

562 Gildersleeve, Virginia C. 'Chaucer and Sir Aldingar.' *MLN* 25(1910), 30.
The *Ballad of Sir Aldingar* (Child, no. 59, A, stanza 43) is an additional analogue supporting Gibbs' interpretation (**561**) of *feeldes* (I.975–7) as 'plains.'

563 Graves, Thornton S. 'Some Chaucer Allusions (1561–1700).' *SP* 20(1923), 469–78.
Thomas Campion alludes to the *KnT* in his *Poemata* (1595) where he says of Chaucer: '*Ille Palaemonios varie depinxit amores*' (*Works*, ed. Vivian, p 336). See **663**.

564 Greg, W.W. 'Early Printed Editions of the *Canterbury Tales.*' *PMLA* 39 (1924), 737–61.
Gregg examines the editions by Caxton (1478, 1484), Pynson (1490, 1526), Wynkyn de Worde (1498), and Thynne (1532) to determine their status as independent authorities for the text. A table (pp 744–9) presents a collation of the first 116 lines of the *KnT* as they appear in these six editions and in two mss: Trinity College R.3.15 and Corpus 198. Greg concludes that only Caxton's first edition was set up from manuscript and thus ranks with the manuscripts as a textual authority.

565 Grimm, Florence M. *Astronomical Lore in Chaucer.* 1919. See **147**.
The kind of fatalism typically displayed by Chaucer's characters consists of a general belief in destiny, modified by the hope that destiny can somehow be altered in particular ways (pp 67–8). The speeches of Arcite (I.1084–91, 1163–9) and Palamon (1303–8) state a doctrine of necessity but show the princes' attitude of resistance to fate (pp 71–2). In the *KnT* humans cannot escape the determinations of destiny and the gods, but Chaucer emphasizes the humorous side of this dilemma here and the tragic side in *TC* (p 75).

566 Hadow, Grace E. *Chaucer and His Times.* New York: Henry Holt and Co.; London: Williams and Norgate, 1914.
Hadow commends Chaucer's condensation of the *Tes*, but thinks some elements need more elaboration (pp 74–5). Characterization is undeveloped, and only rarely, as in the description of the tournament crowd or in the comment on Arcite's death, does Chaucer's 'shrewd observation and dry humour' show in this apprentice tale (p 76). Chaucer portrays woman's 'fierce shrinking from the thought of matrimony' (p 128) in Emily, whom Hadow compares with Blanche in the *BD* and with the Emily of *TNK.* Chaucer does not fully describe the duel; his uncharacteristically full description of the tournament may reflect his own military and administrative experiences. As compared with human emotion, 'chivalry has ... little glamour in Chaucer's eye' (p 182).

567 Hall, James Norman. *Flying with Chaucer.* Boston: Houghton Mifflin, 1930.
A memoir by an American airman, co-author of *Mutiny on the Bounty*, who read the *CT* while imprisoned in Germany in 1918. In a final flight over the deserted front lines after the armistice, Hall remembers his dead friends and finds 'cold comfort' in the consolation offered by Theseus, 'that good soldier' (citing I.3047–53) (pp 52–3).

568 Hammond, Eleanor P. *A Bibliographical Manual*. 1908. See **330**.
Hammond lists editions, modernizations and translations, discussions of source and date, other versions of the story of Palamon and Arcite, and notes on the Tale, including a review of scholarship on 'shippes hoppesteres' (*KnT* 1159; I.2017) (pp 270–4). She cites the relationship between *Anel* and the *KnT* as 'an enduring Chaucer-crux' (p 358).

569 — 'Chaucer and Lydgate Notes.' *MLN* 27(1912), 91–2.
'*Shippes hoppesteres*' (I .1159) should be compared with Lydgate's reference to ships chained together (*Fall of Princes*, iv, cap.1).

570 — *English Verse between Chaucer and Surrey*. Durham: Duke University Press; London: Cambridge University Press, 1927.
Annotating an anonymous fifteenth-century English translation of a ballad by Charles D'Orleans (p 226), Hammond cites parallels for the line 'has ie suy seul sans compagnie' ('Allas alone am y without compane'; cf. I.2779), including works by Machaut, Christine de Pisan, Dante, Petrarch, Gower, and others.

571 Hart, William Morris. 'The Lady in the Garden.' *MLN* 22(1907), 241–2.
Henri d'Andeli's *Lai d'Aristote* provides an analogue to Chaucer's description of Emelye in the garden (I.1033 f).

572 Hazlitt, William. 'On Chaucer and Spenser.' *Lectures on the English Poets*. 1818. Excerpted in *Geoffrey Chaucer: A Critical Anthology*, ed. J. A. Burrow (Baltimore: Penguin, 1969), pp 85–8; and in *Chaucer: The Critical Heritage*, ed. Derek Brewer (London: Routledge & Kegan Paul, 1978), Volume 1, 276–84 [here cited].
The two poets are opposites. 'As Spenser was the most romantic and visionary, Chaucer was the most practical of all the great poets' (p 278). Hazlitt cites the descriptions of Emelye (I. 1033–9), of the hunter (1639–42), and of Palamon in prison (1277–80) as examples of Chaucer's fidelity to fact. 'He exhibits for the most part the naked object, with little drapery thrown over it' (p 279). There are 'no borrowed roseate tints' (p 280). Hazlitt cites the 'terrible beauty' of the descriptions of Lygurge and Emetrius (I.2128–86) (p 281); the deep pathos of the accounts of Arcite's love-sickness (1355–71) and of his death-bed (2771–9) (p 282); the beauty and grandeur of the paintings in Mars' temple (1967–80); and the 'terrific images' of Mars himself and of the wolf eating the man (2041–8) (p 282).

573 Hempl, G.F., J. Mather, and J.S.P. Tatlock. 'Palamon and Arcite.' *MLN* 23(1908), 127–8.
Consists of three letters to the editor. Hempl reports that in a paper delivered to the MLA in 1895, he questioned Brink's theory of an

early stanzaic version of the *KnT* (**529**). Yet Mather **607** and Tatlock **632** credit Pollard **7** with being the first to question the hypothesis. Tatlock and Mather express their regrets for the oversight.

574 Hibbard, Laura A. 'Chaucer's "Shapen was my sherte".' *PQ* 1(1923), 222–5.
Hibbard cites three passages in which Chaucer links the making of a shirt or cloth with the beginning of life (I.1566; *Hypermnestra*, 68; *TC* III.733), and relates them to similar passages in other medieval works. The shirt seems to be 'a transcendental garment, symbolic of human life and destiny' (p 22).

575 Hinckley, Henry Barrett. 'Chaucer and *Ywaine and Gawin*.' *Academy* 71(1906), 640–1.
Hinckley cites three parallels: *Ywaine and Gawin* 421–2 and I.2645–6, Emetrius' experience in the tournament; 633–4 and I.1649, the duel in the grove; and 3531–59 and I.2603–16, the alliterative description of the tournament. *Ywaine and Gawin* was composed in the first half of the fourteenth century and Chaucer knew the work.

576 — 'The Knight's Tale.' *Notes on Chaucer*. 1907. Pp 50–120. See **331**.
The *KnT* is 'a poem of burning youth. Critics who insist on the canons of realism rarely enjoy it as a whole ... Charged with fierce and turbulent emotion, the poem is likewise tempered with exquisite satire and with admirable philosophy ... The speeches lack the flexibility of Chaucer's later work, but possess an anti-strophic character that is an artistic compensation ... The madcap Palamon and the equally ardent but more rational Arcite are skillfully contrasted at every turn ... If it is Palamon who wins his lady, it is Arcite who wins our sympathy' (p 53). Theseus is a 'hot-blooded Plantagenet' who nevertheless dominates by shrewd wisdom, and Emily, 'a poetic vision of the eternal feminine' (p 53). More than any other of Chaucer's works, the *KnT* reflects historical events of the period (p 52): Theseus' entry into Athens recalls King John of France's arrival in London; Theseus' forgiveness of Palamon and Arcite in the grove after the appeals of Hippolyta, Edward III's revocation of the death sentence for six citizens of Calais after the entreaty of Queen Philippa; Theseus' entertainment of Palamon and Arcite before the tournament, the captivity of King John in London; and Arcite's death, the early death of the Black Prince **204** (see Hinckley's notes to I.1027, 1748, 1881, 3047–54). See **836**.

577 — 'Chauceriana.' *MP* 14(1916/17), 317–8.
Hinckley cites sources and analogues for several lines. I.1422: see *Joshua* 9: 21, 23: 'hewers of wood and drawers of water.' I.1660: for fighting in blood up to the ankles, see *Roman de Troie*, 24372–3.

I.1697: for a phrase similar to 'Under the sonne,' see the Flemish *Reinart de Vos*, 759–60. I.1910: for coral used as a building material, see *Sir Ferumbras*, 1324–7; for alabaster, *Roman de Troie*, 14631. I.2160: 'clothe of Tars' comes from Tarsus; see *Sir Ferumbras*, 4463–4 and 5077. I.2698: 'in memorie' means 'conscious,' 'in his senses'; see Milton's *Comus*, 205–6, and Webster's *Duchess of Malfi*, I.1 and *Devil's Law Case*, 2.1. I. 2803–5: correcting an earlier gloss (**576**), Hinckley suggests that the idea of the heart as the seat of the intellect comes not from Aristotle but from 1*Kings* 3:9.

578 Hulbert, J.R. 'What Was Chaucer's Aim in the *Knight's Tale*?' *SP* 26(1929), 375–85.
Chaucer's changes to the *Tes* cannot be explained simply as improvements since the *Tes* is the superior work, especially in characterization (p 377). Chaucer re-shaped the story as a problem of courtly love: 'which of two young men, of equal worth and with almost equal claims, shall (or should) win the lady' (p 380). Chaucer's conclusion, 'that Palamon should get the lady because he had the sense to petition Venus rather than Mars for success must have seemed both a satisfactory and an ingenious solution' (p 381). Chaucer equalized Palamon and Arcite 'to keep the problem entirely in the field of intellect' (p 381). He eliminated Emilia's awareness of Arcite's interest so that no attraction on Emelye's part should seem an argument for Arcite's winning her. He introduced the term 'loveres maladye of Hereos' (*KnT* 516–7; I.1373–4) as a marker of his interest in courtly love, and focused Theseus' speech in the grove on courtly love (pp 382–3). He strengthened Palamon's claim by letting him see Emelye first. This change allowed him to introduce two minor 'questions of love': 'whether the lover who sees a lady first has a better right to her than one who sees her later and what the duties of a sworn brother are in such a case' (p 384). See **523**, **650**, **672**, **833**.

579 Hunt, Leigh. 'Preface' to *Stories in Verse*. 1855. P 20. Rpt in *Geoffrey Chaucer: A Critical Anthology*, ed. J. A. Burrow (Baltimore: Penguin, 1969), pp 90–4 [cited here]; and in *Chaucer: The Critical Heritage*, ed. Derek Brewer (London: Routledge & Kegan Paul, 1978), Volume 2, 75–88.
Hunt defends I.2273 – 'Uprose the sun, and uprose Emily' – against charges of artificiality. 'It is pure morning freshness, enthusiasm, and music' (p 91). Chaucer attempts to do equal justice to 'the brightest of material creatures, and the beautifulest of human creatures' partly by 'repeating the accent on a repeated syllable, and dividing the *rhythm* into two equal parts' (p 91). Although the line contains simile

and analogy by implication, 'the poet lets nature speak for herself. He points to the two beautiful objects before us, and is content with simply hailing them in their combination' (p 91). See **933**.

580 Hustvedt, S.B. '"Under the Soune He Looketh".' *MLN* 44(1929), 182. Hustvedt interprets Chaucer's phrase in I.1697 by reference to a similar phrase in the ballad 'Johnie of Cocklesmuir,' which means to look at a low point between dark ground and the faint light from the sky at twilight.

581 Jack, Adolphus Alfred. *A Commentary on the Poetry of Chaucer & Spenser*. Cambridge: Maclehose, Jackson & Co.; London: Macmillan, 1920; rpt Folcroft, Pa.: Folcroft Press, 1969.
The 'vein of romance' is present everywhere in Chaucer's work, but is often qualified by 'droppings into realism' or by 'longuers that speak plainly of a task' (p 102). 'A tale of love in which there is no lovemaking, and in which, in fact, the heroine only speaks when praying for escape from her lovers, can have no great sympathetic interest' (p 103).

582 Jefferson, Bernard L. *Chaucer and the Consolation of Philosophy of Boethius*. Princeton: Princeton University Press, 1917. Rpt New York: Gordian Press, 1968.
Jefferson supports Tatlock's identification (**631**) of Dantean influence in I.1663–6, citing 'ministre general' as an echo of Dante's *general ministra* (*Inf* 7.78). But in Dante this term and his *destino* are always equivalent to Fortune. Chaucer follows Boethius, especially IV. pr 6, in making destiny God's minister (pp 61–2). Such references as 'aventure or cas' (I.1074) and 'aventure or destinee' (1465–6), which Tatlock traces to *Inf* 15. 46–7 and 32.76–8, are more profoundly indebted to the *Consol*, V. pr 1 and IV. pr 6, where the idea of multiple, distinct agents of divine providence is fully developed (pp 62–5). Another means of providential intervention is the 'bond of love,' celebrated by Boethius in three meters: II. met 8, III. met 9, and IV. met 6 (pp 65–8). Chaucer's treatment of God's justice in permitting evil, in Palamon's speech (I.1303–33), follows a pattern indebted to I.met 5 and perhaps to IV. pr 1: The omnipotence of God is recognized, the question is asked why God permits evil, the matter is left to clerks (p 69). Nowhere in his poetry does Chaucer present the answer of Philosophy (pp 70–1). Skeat (**625**, V, 93–4) is mistaken in tracing Theseus' lines on the bond of love (I.2987–3015, 3035–40) to II. met 8; rather IV. met 6 is the source (p 118). Boethian influence in the *KnT* (pp 130–32) is concentrated in three long speeches (p 131). Arcite (I.1251–72) blames himself for pursuing false happiness blindly, echoing III. pr 2; Palamon (1303–33) blames

the gods for permitting the innocent to suffer, echoing I. met 5; Theseus (2987–3040) explains the divine plan as Philosophy does in IV. pr 6 and met 6. 'More pity is aroused for Arcite, that he who acknowledges that God's ways are always just meets in the moment of his greatest triumph a sudden and tragic death, whereas Palamon who complains against heaven receives the high reward. The speech of Theseus ... points back to the speeches of the two younger and less wise men and is made to appear more noble and dignified by contrast with theirs' (p 131). In a list of passages from Chaucer's works showing Boethian influence, there are 17 for the *KnT* (pp 142–3). A chart (p 150) indicates that 18 lines of the *KnT* show a general Boethian influence, and 48 lines, verbal influence. Boethius' influence on Chaucer falls into three periods; the *KnT* belongs to the second, most intense period (1381–6) (pp 150–1). See **672**, **775**.

583 Ker, W.P. 'Chaucer.' *Essays in Medieval Literature*. London: Macmillan, 1905. Pp 76–100.

Ker compares the *KnT* with the *Tes*, *TC*, and *TNK*. The *Tes* is 'overburdened in its heroic accoutrements'; the *KnT*, brought down to the romance form, possibly the form of Boccaccio's lost source, is 'well designed, and nothing in it is superfluous' (p 88). But Chaucer 'saw that the story would not bear a strong dramatic treatment' (p 89), and deliberately avoided the development of character typical of *TC* in favor of a 'sequence of pictures' (p 89). In Fletcher's 'rash experiment ... the story is refuted as soon as it is made to bear the weight of tragic passion or thought' (p 89). There is pathos in the *KnT* but 'no true tragedy' (p 90). The art of the *KnT* is 'perfect in its own kind, but that kind not the greatest' (p 91).

584 — 'Chaucer and the Renaissance.' *Form and Style in Poetry: Lectures and Notes by W.P. Ker.* Ed. R.W. Chambers. London: Macmillan, 1928. Pp 64–79. Excerpted in *Geoffrey Chaucer: A Critical Anthology*, ed. J. A. Burrow (Baltimore: Penguin, 1969), pp 104–11.

In *Anel*, Chaucer attempts to copy the Renaissance epic poetry of Boccaccio's *Tes*, but lapses into the late medieval French manner of the 'abstract sentimental case' (p 66). The *KnT* 'could bear the most exacting tests with regard to its composition ... it is a classical poem ... there is nothing weak or inharmonious or out of place. If such virtues as these are the ideal of the Renaissance, then Chaucer's poem belongs to the Renaissance. But ... they are due to Chaucer's mind working critically on a Renaissance formula — the artificial epic poem — and rejecting many of the things on which the Renaissance poets and critics were disposed to set most value' (p 75–6). See **87**.

585 Kittredge, G.L. 'Chaucer and Some of His Friends.' *MP* 1(1903), 1–18.
Kittredge argues for Sir Thomas Clanvowe as the author of the *Book of Cupid*, whose first two lines reproduce *KnT* 927–8 (I.1785–6) (p 13). The probability that the *Book of Cupid* was composed before 1392 and perhaps before 1391 helps to date the *KnT* (p 18).

586 — 'On "Feeldes" in the *Knight's Tale*.' *MLN* 25(1910), 28.
Kittredge adds three analogues to those cited by Gibbs **561** in support of the meaning 'plains' for *feeldes* (I.977): *Partonope*, 6374 f; *Perceval li Gallois*, 13512; and *Roman de Troie*, 13000 f.

587 — *Chaucer and His Poetry*. 1915. See **332**.
Chaucer's condensation of the *Tes* is 'a truly marvelous performance' (p 19), but all of Dryden's versions of Chaucer's texts are longer than their originals – his *Pal* about ten percent so. 'The artistic economy of Chaucer ... goes quite beyond all Dryden's power of self-control' (p 19). Kittredge cites for comparison the temple of Mars in *KnT* I.1990–4 and in *Pal* 1164–9.

588 Klaeber, Fr. '"Looking under the Sun".' *MLN* 37(1922), 376–7.
Klaeber supports C. Alphonso Smith's interpretation (**627**) of *KnT* 839 (I.1697) by citing similar phrasing in the Old English *Phoenix* (101), in *Heliand* (655 f), in *Elene* (87 f), and in the *Metres of Boethius* (14.7). See **618**.

589 Koch, John. 'Alte Chaucerprobleme und neue Lösungsversuche.' *Englische Studien* 55(1921), 161–225.
Koch defends Brink's theory (**529**) of an early *P&A* distinct from the *KnT*, particularly against the recent attacks of Langhans **590**. It is unlikely that Chaucer produced the *KnT* by a relatively simple process of direct translation from the *Tes* involving only decisions about inclusion and exclusion. For example, while Chaucer translated the description of Mars' temple and the prayers fairly closely, he apparently constructed the narrative portions by borrowing only from the beginnings and ends of Boccaccio's stanzas (p 206). Just as the *P&A* must have represented a substantial re-working of the *Tes*, so the *KnT* seems to represent a substantial revision of the earlier *P&A*, since the Tale shows so many characteristics of Chaucer's late period (pp 208–9).

590 Langhans, Viktor. 'Chaucers Anelida and Arcite.' *Anglia* 44(1920), 226–44.
Langhans rejects Brink's theory (**529**) of a lost version of the *KnT*, a *P&A* in seven-line stanzas, to which *Anel* is indebted. Supporting Tatlock **632**, Langhans argues that the reference in the *Prol* to the *LGW* names the storial matter of Palamon and Arcite rather than the

title of a work substantially different from the *KnT*, and that the poet who had written the *KnT* would not then have gone on to write *Anel.* Palamon's reference in I.1145 to 'false Arcite' is probably a reminiscence of the earlier, unfinished *Anel. Anel* was probably composed in 1373–4 and the *KnT* in 1382.

591 Legouis, Émile. *Geoffrey Chaucer.* 1913. See **333.**
Legouis recognizes Chaucer's 'never failing realism and familiarity' (p 120), as in the humor he assigns to Theseus and in his attention to the crowd at the tournament. But Chaucer's changes are few in comparison to his debt to the *Tes*, as seen in his depictions of Emelye in the garden, the knights gathering for the tournament, the theater, the temples, the combats. 'These pages far excel the rest of the poem: ... Chaucer's principle merit, therefore, is to have taken poetry where he found it' (p 121).

592 Leuschner, Bruno. 'Uber das Verhältnis von "The Two Noble Kinsmen" zu Chaucer's "Knight's Tale".' Halle: Heinrich John, 1903.
Shakespeare introduces scenes (I.ii and II.i) that emphasize the friendship of Palamon and Arcite before they fall in love with Emily, and scenes (III.iii and vi) that show their later noble behavior toward each other. Shakespeare's Emily has a larger role than Chaucer's, beseeching Theseus to oppose Creon (I.i) and soliloquizing about her anguish at causing the kinsmen's dispute (IV.ii). Theseus is saved from any association with the looting of dead bodies, and his noble friendship with Pirithous is more fully developed. The net effect is a greater idealization of the characters in Shakespeare's version. See **524.**

593 Liebermann, Felix. 'Theseus' Herzogstitel bei Chaucer.' *Archiv* 145(1923), 101–2.
Theseus was first given the title 'duke' (as in I.860) by Walter von Brienne, who died at Poitiers in 1356. See H.E. Madden, *The Collected Works of Sir Francis Palgrave*, Volume 10 (1922).

594 Lounsbury, Thomas R. *Studies in Chaucer.* 1892. See **334.**
As evidence of Chaucer's later, skeptical attitude toward religion, after *TC*, Lounsbury cites the account of Arcite's soul (*KnT* 1951–56; I.2809–14). It reveals that Chaucer had no faith in a future life and felt contempt for those who presumed to talk about it (2: 513–4). But Palamon's speech on the cruel gods (445–63; I.1303–21) is an example of Chaucer's interest in the 'mysterious things of faith' (pp 531–2). Contrasting Dryden's tendency toward expansion with the compression of style typical of the *KnT* (3: 162–75), Lounsbury cites, always to Chaucer's advantage, the description of the May morning (*KnT* 633–38; I.1491–6); Felony (1137–8; I.1995–6) and the assassin

or 'smiler' (1141; I.1999); Arcite's song (651–4; I.1509–12); Palamon's prayer to Venus (1363–5; I.2221–3); and Arcite's death-bed speech (1913–24; I.2771–82), among others. Lounsbury criticizes Chaucer's 'passion for dialectics' (p 373), which led him to introduce irrelevant passages from Boethius, such as Theseus' final speech. And see index. See **773**, **1039**.

595 Lowes, John Livingston. '"The Tempest at Hir Hoom-cominge".' *MLN* 19(1904), 240–3.
The tempest on Hippolyta's arrival in Athens (I.884), of which there is no mention in Statius or Boccaccio, may allude to the famous storm on 18 December 1381 when Anne of Bohemia arrived at Dover for her marriage to Richard II. See **542**, **751**, **778**.

596 — 'The Prologue to the *Legend of Good Women* Considered in Its Chronological Relations.' *PMLA* 20(1905), 749–864.
Although *P&A* antedates the Prologue, the *Ariadne* and *Phyllis* antedate *P&A*. Chaucer's 'exquisite rendering' of the garden scene in the *KnT* must postdate a similar scene involving a privy in the *Ariadne*; his 'finished' treatment of Theseus in the *KnT* must have followed his 'crude' sketches of him in the *Ariadne* and *Phyllis* (p 809–10). *P&A* antedates *TC*: May 3 is part of an elaborate scheme of days and astrological hours in the *KnT* whereas it has only an accidental relationship to the story in *TC* in its second, derivative use (p 843). Mather's account (**607**) of how Chaucer used the *Tes* in *P&A* and in the composition and revision of *TC* must be rejected. Chaucer's treatment of Arcite's soul (A[I].2809–15) is consonant with 'the profoundly human and frankly naturalistic' treatment of Arcite's dying (p 847); Chaucer is not filling a gap left by his prior use of the stanza from the *Tes* in *TC*. As to meter, Chaucer had not yet demonstrated the full possibilities of the couplet in the *KnT*, and thus returned to the more familiar stanza in *TC* (p 849). His six-fold use of the *Tes* (in *Ariadne*, *Anel*, *PF*, *TC*, *P&A*, and *KnT*) suggests it was his introduction to Italian literature (pp 850–1). As compared with *TC*, the *KnT* exhibits the simple characterization and mechanical treatment of fate suggestive of an early work (pp 852–3). See **632**, **720**.

597 — 'Hereos.' *Nation* 97(1913), 233.
In A[I]1372–6 this term does not refer to Eros but is a technical medical term referring to a specific malady. See **599**.

598 — 'Chaucer's Friday.' *MLR* 9(1914), 94.
Alexander Neckam's *De Naturis Rerum*, Book I. cap. VII is the source of the characterization of Friday as Venus' day (I.1534–9). Line 1535 does not mean that it alternately shines and rains on each Friday, but

that it rains on the Friday of a sunny week and shines on the Friday of a rainy week. See **712**, **972**.

599 — 'The Loveres Maladye of Hereos.' *MP* 11(1914), 491–546.
Lowes reviews the treatment of this crux by editors (pp 491–5). In his 1598 edition Speght printed the term *hereos* in his text but said in his notes, 'Read *Eros*, i. Cupide'. In his *Animadversions*, Francis Thynne argued for the interpretation 'heroes.' Speght then changed his 1602 text to read *Eros*, and retained the gloss 'Cupide' in his notes but admitted the possibility of Thynne's interpretation. With the exception of Morell (1737), who followed Thynne, all editors have accepted Speght's treatment of the crux. Lowes then presents extensive evidence from Greek, Arabic, and medieval European medical texts (pp 495–520) to show that *eros* was a technical term for a species of 'mental alienation' (p 495), a malady. The connections Chaucer draws between this malady and mania, the melancholy humor, and the cells in the front of the head suggest that he was intimately acquainted with the medical views of his day (pp 525–8). The term retained its technical meaning in Richard of Bury's *Philobiblon*, Chapter 11, and in Burton's *Anatomy of Melancholy*, IX.1538–42, but this connection had been lost when Pope spoke of 'heroic love' in his *Moral Essays* (p 542). See **107**, **636**.

600 — '*Hereos* Again.' *MLN* 31(1916), 185–7.
Loews adds Lydgate's *Fabula duorum mercatorum*, stanzas 46 and 48–50, to the list of occurrences of the phrase *amor hereos* (*ereos*) cited in **599**.

601 — 'Chaucer and Dante.' *MP* 14 (1917), 705–35.
The allusion to Juno's anger against Thebes (I.1329–31), for which there is no corresponding passage in the *Tes*, is indebted to the *Inf* XXX.1–2.22–3 (p 715).

602 — 'The *Franklin's Tale*, the *Teseide* and the *Filocolo*.' *MP*, 15(1917/8), 689–728.
Behind the 'murmuringe / Full lowe and dim' of Mars' statue (I.2431–3) stands not the phrase '*Con dolce romore*' of *Tes* VII.40.5–6, but the phrase '*un touto mormorio*' of *Filocolo* I.207–8.

603 Macaulay, G.C. 'Notes on Chaucer.' *MLR* 4(1908), 14–9.
To love 'par amour,' *KnT* 297 (I.1155): 'to be in love with' as distinct from 'to worship, in a religious sense.' 'Positif lawe,' 309 (I.1167): law dependent solely upon man's decrees as opposed to law derived from nature. 'In ech degree,' 310 (I.1168): 'in every degree of kinship' or 'in every case' (pp 16–8).

604 MacCracken, H.N. '"The Laborer and the bouchour and the smyth".' *MLN* 28(1913), 230.

The substitution of 'laborer' for 'barbour' in I.2025 by the scribes of the Ellesmere and Cambridge Gg mss may have been inspired by Vegetius' statement that butchers, smiths, and those '*in labore nutritur*' make good soldiers while barbers do not.

605 Mackail, John William. *The Springs of Helicon*. London: Longmans Green & Co., 1909. Excerpted in *Chaucer: The Critical Heritage*. Ed. Derek Brewer (London: Routledge & Kegan Paul, 1978), Volume 2, 285–99 [cited here].
Mackail distinguishes among Chaucer's narrative, dramatic, and poetic gifts, preferring *TC* to all Chaucer's other works. The *KnT* 'with its stately movement and lavish richness of ornament, does not bring us into the heart of things' even though it is 'one of the chief splendours of our literature' (p 289). Poetically, it is 'the single poem which represents Chaucer most fully ... It has more range than any other single poem of his; it supplies more memorable phrases and lovely lines. It ranges from the sweet garrulous manner of the romance-writer, to a loftiness and incisiveness that are almost Homeric, almost Virgilian' (pp 289–90). As evidence of Chaucer's classicism, Mackail cites a number of lines concerned with fate (eg, I.1251–4 and 3041–2), and the comparison of Palamon and Arcite with the lion hunter as an epic simile (pp 290–1). By contrast both the 'flicker of a smile' in the reference to Arcite's soul (2809–10) and the 'strange sob' of his death-bed speech (2777–9) belong to the world of romance (pp 291–2). See **87**.

605a Manly, John Mathews. *Canterbury Tales*. 1928. See **33**.
In his Notes (pp 539–58), Manly rejects Brink's theory (**529**) of a stanzaic *P&A*, and sees Chaucer as turning Boccaccio's courtly epic into a dramatic work centered on the conflict between love and friendship. Manly questions Skeat's linkage (**625**) of the Tale's internal dates to actual calendars, and regards May 3 as a traditionally unlucky day (pp 549–51). He explains geomancy (cf I.2045) and reproduces a manuscript page showing geomantic figures (pp 553–4). For comment on Manly's notes, see **686, 751, 755, 760-1, 1079**.

606 Mather, Frank Jewett. *The Prologue, The Knight's Tale, and the Nun's Priest's Tale*. 1899. See **8**.
Mather cites several passages to illustrate Chaucer's artistry: the wind in the forest surrounding Mars' temple (*KnT* 1117–22; I.1975–80); line 1921 (I.2779) of Arcite's death-bed speech; the preparations for the tournament (*KnT* 1644–51; I.2502–9); and Arcite's being removed from his armor (*KnT* 1858; I.2716) (xxxv–xlvii). The *KnT* is superior to the *Tes* in several respects: the immediate rivalry of Palamon and Arcite on seeing Emily; the strengthening of Palamon's claim to

Emily by having him see her first; the role of chance in the meeting in the wood; the portrayal of Palamon's jealousy in the same scene; the description of a general mêlée in the tournament rather than of a series of single combats; the omission of Arcite's triumphal procession and wedding to Emily; and Arcite's gentle suggestion to Emily that she consider Palamon as a husband (lxiii–lxviii). Theseus, a vaguely kingly figure in the *Tes*, is 'the smiling providence of the romance,' an ironical, genial man who 'plays nobly [the] role of chorus to the drama' (lxxi). Asserting that the 'strife ... between brotherhood and love is the real subject of the poem' (lxxi), Mather cites Pater's comments in *The Renaissance*: 'Chaucer [expresses] the sentiment of [comradeship] so strongly ... that one knows not whether the love of both Palamon and Arcite for Emelya, or of these two for each other, is the chiefer subject' (lxxii). Also admirable are the descriptions: Emily in the garden, Lygurge, the theater, the tournament. The characters are developed only enough to sustain the necessary illusion.

607 — 'On the Date of the "Knight's Tale".' In *An English Miscellany Presented to Dr. Furnivall in Honour of His Seventy-fifth Birthday.* [No editor] Oxford: Clarendon, 1901; rpt New York: Benjamin Blom, 1969. Pp 301–13.

Mather expands Pollard's attack (**7**, **613**) on the hypothesis originated by Brink **529** that *P&A* was a work in seven-line stanzas, now lost, parts of which Chaucer later assigned to *TC*, *Anel*, and *PF*. Chaucer was not capable of 'self-criticism so heroic' (p 306) as to dismember a major completed work; a work of such high quality could not have been suppressed once circulated; the existence of scraps in stanza form does not establish the existence of a whole poem; *Anel* would not stop at the description of Mars' temple if a completed *P&A* already existed. Mather presents a new hypothesis: 'After writing *Troilus*, Chaucer began *Anelida* as a pendant, or rather offset, to the greater poem. Relinquishing this plan in favour of the poem later known as the *Knight's Tale*, much of the descriptive matter of the *Teseide* was left free for other uses' [for insertion into *TC* V.1807–27 and *PF* 183–294] (pp 312–3). Using Skeat's analysis of internal dates (**625**), Mather assigns Chaucer's work on the *Tes* and *KnT* to 1381–2 (pp 309–10). The reference to meter in the *LGW* (Prol 562) may mean that decasyllabic couplets were an unfamiliar meter but does not exclude the possibility of their use in *P&A*. See **573**, **596**, **632**, **751**.

608 Meyer, Emil. *Die Charakterzeichnung bei Chaucer. Studien zur englischen Philologie* 48. Halle: Niemeyer, 1913.

Esp. pp 37–41 and 46–9. The passion of Palamon and Arcite for Emily fits the pattern of love-yearning and service to women in youth typical of all Chaucer's knightly characters. Their attempt to resolve their rivalry by a duel is related to their primary identity as knights. Palamon is the more naive and idealistic; Arcite, the more sophisticated and pragmatic.

609 Neilson, George. *Trial by Combat.* New York: Macmillan, 1891.
Chaucer's tournament conforms in several details with Gloucester's ordinance governing judicial combat (**184**): eg, the order in which the combatants enter the lists, their taking refreshment only with Theseus' permission, the conclusion of the fighting at sunset (pp 182–8).

610 Patch, Howard R. 'Under the Sonne.' *MLN* 38(1923), 60.
Parallel to Chaucer's phrase in I.1697 is 'under sunnan' in the Old English *Andreas* (1013).

611 — 'Chaucer and Mediaeval Romance.' In *Essays in Memory of Barrett Wendell.* [No editor] Cambridge: Harvard University Press, 1926. Pp 93–108. Rpt in *On Rereading Chaucer* (Cambridge: Harvard University Press, 1939). Pp 195–212.
Patch objects to Ker's characterization of the *KnT* as the 'perfect version of a medieval romance' (**98**), citing these Chaucerian modifications of the *Tes*: less emphasis on chivalry and love and more on character; less emphasis on chance and more on providence; the introduction of irony and humor. 'Arcite is the more manly figure, a true knight; Palamon is steadfastly the lover, who is willing to turn state's evidence to win his game' (p 104). The appeal to providence as causing Theseus' appearance in the grove 'strengthens the plot at the moment of its greatest weakness' (p 102). Imitating the Knight's use of *occupatio*, Patch lists the ironies that don't need listing: the lament of the Athenian women, the platitudes of 'delicious Egeus,' the speech of his son, who has inherited his father's tediousness, and the interminable account of the funeral. 'It is the tone of something rather like levity which is most surprising in this tale. The Knight seems to have cared less for the mysterious and the uncanny than for some other things, and above all, he has a sense of humor. With a sympathy the more wholesome for this grace, he gives us the tragedy of youth, by means of a characterization which is not over-individualized but sure' (p 106).

612 — 'Chaucer and Lady Fortune.' *MLR* 22(1927), 377–88.
Boccaccio appeals to pure chance to account for Teseo's arrival in the grove. But Chaucer had already devised a more realistic plot, and so in I.1663–9, he attributes Theseus' arrival to Destiny, borrowing

phrases from Dante's description of Fortune in *Inf* VII.78 and perhaps from *Tes* VI.1 f. The change of Fortune to Destiny may have been suggested by the *Consol*, Book IV. pr. 6.35 f.

613 Pollard, Alfred W. *Chaucer*. London: Macmillan, 1893; 2nd ed, 1931. *Pace* Brink **529**, *P&A* was not a literal translation of the *Tes*, now lost, but probably contained 'reminiscences' of the *Tes* and survives in the *KnT* (p 42), which may be the comedy referred to in *TC* V.1786–8 (p 44). The *KnT* cannot be dated on the basis of its calendrical references (Skeat **625**), since Chaucer sought only 'astrological appropriateness' (p 47); *P&A*, 'nearly as in the *KnT*,' probably belongs to 1385. The *KnT* is the 'most splendid and ornate' of the tales; the descriptions of the temples are 'the most famous of all the "purple patches" in Chaucer'; and Theseus' entry into Athens, the princes' view of Emily from the prison, their meeting in the woods and its interruption, the preparations for the tournament, and the death of Arcite constitute 'a succession of pictures of singular vividness and colour' (p 111). Palamon and Arcite are 'slightly sketched'; Theseus is the 'much more finished portrait' (p 112). See **573**, **607**.

614 Potts, Abbie Findlay. 'A Letter from Wordsworth to Thomas Powell.' *MLN* 45(1930), 215–8.
In this undated letter from 1839 or 1840 Wordsworth gives Dryden credit for the 'spirit & harmony' of his translation of the *KnT* but complains that he 'suffered ... much of the simplicity, & with that of the beauty, & occasional pathos of the original to escape.'

615 Praz, Mario. 'Chaucer and the Great Italian Writers.' 1927. See **83**.
Dante's conception of his pilgrimage as 'no fiction, but a reality greater than any mundane reality' did not appeal to 'the bourgeois Chaucer' as seen in *KnT* A[I].2809–14 and *LGW* 1–9 where the term 'divinistre' may refer to Dante (p 53). 'Any speculation on the other world must have seemed unrealistic to Chaucer' (p 53). In I.1761, 'For pitee renneth sone in gentil herte,' Chaucer substituted pity for the love in Dante's famous line, 'Amor, che a cor gentil ratto s'apprende.' Chaucer responded to the 'human and touching' in the *Div Com* but not to 'the sublimer side of Dante's genius' (p 56). See **914**.

616 Robertson, Stuart. 'Elements of Realism in the "Knight's Tale".' *JEGP* 14(1915), 226–55.
Drawing parallels between Froissart's *Chronicles* **183** and the *KnT*, Robertson argues that the Tale is 'replete with realism' (p 226). 1) Several details of Theseus' attack on Thebes reflect contemporary realities as seen in the English attack on the Flemish town of

Cadsant, in the Black Prince's razing of Limoges, and in Edward III's general practice (pp 227–8). 2) The taking of ransom for knightly prisoners was a well established practice, and the hint in I.1022–4 and 1204–6 that Theseus is unusual in not accepting them, indicates that the Knight has accommodated himself to the mercenary aspects of contemporary chivalry (pp 228–30). 3) The life-long banishment of Arcite on pain of death recalls Richard II's sentence on Mowbray (pp 230–1). 4) The duel is unusual in having no judges or spectators and in the chivalrous behavior of Palamon and Arcite toward each other; but the use of spears and swords reflects contemporary practice (pp 231–3). 5) The intercession of Ypolita and her ladies recalls the intercession of Philippa with Edward III on behalf of the citizens of Calais (pp 233–4). 6) Authentic elements of the tournament include the great enthusiasm it inspires, the feasting and processions, the concern with rank and with having an audience. The numbers involved are unusually large. A judicial tournament was not impossible in Chaucer's day, but had been more common earlier. Theseus' rules are realistic in that common practice excluded such weapons as missiles, pole-axes, and short knives; called for one course with spears and defense on foot with the sword; and provided for the defeated to be taken prisoner at a stake. In the most realistic passages, Chaucer owes few debts to Boccaccio; in the least realistic, the descriptions of the temples and the speeches of the suppliants and the gods, Chaucer is most heavily indebted to the *Tes* (pp 242–55). See **218**, **541**, **779**, **799**, **934**.

617 — 'Old English Verse in Chaucer.' *MLN* 43(1928), 234–6.
Chaucer's description of the tournament in I.2600–2619 imitates Old English verse in its use of alliteration and of four stresses per line.

618 Roosbroeck, Gustave L. van. '"Under the Sonne he loketh".' *MLN* 38(1923), 59.
A phrase similar to Chaucer's in I.1697 occurs in a Flemish ballad, *Mi Adel en Hir Alewijn*, confirming Klaeber's belief (**588**) that the phrase is based on an old Germanic idiom, and supporting Tatlock's translation (**635**) as against C.A. Smith's (**627**).

619 Root, Robert K. *The Poetry of Chaucer*. 1906/rev 1922. See **341**.
Root commends Chaucer's condensation of the *Tes*, citing Henry Ward's statistics (**1**) in support of Chaucer's originality (pp 163–6). Noting the unworldliness and idealism of the Knight, Root says of the Tale: 'we must give ourselves up to the spirit of romance; we must not look for subtle characterization, nor for strict probability of action; we must delight in the fair shows of things, and not ask too many questions' (p 169). 'Palamon is the dreamer, Arcite the man of

action ... it is Arcite who determines the destiny of the two; while Palamon merely drifts with the current of circumstance' (p 170.) Arcite prays for victory, 'the definite practical means to the attainment of his desires,' while Palamon prays for success in love, 'leaving the means of its attainment to the providence of the heavenly synod' (p 170). Emily is 'a fair vision of womanly beauty and grace, and little more ... she *does* nothing' (p 171). Theseus is 'the most actual personage in the tale ... the motive power of the plot' (p 171). The greatness of the *KnT* lies in its descriptions: Theseus' home-coming, Emily in the garden, the meeting of the princes in the wood, the theatre, Emetrius and Lygurge, the tournament. 'The *Knight's Tale* is preeminently a web of splendidly pictured tapestry, in which the eye may take delight, and on which the memory may fondly linger. In the dying words of Arcite ... the terrible reality of the mystery of life, its tragedy and its pathos, are vividly suggested; but it is only suggested, as a great painting may touch on what is most sacred and most deep' (pp 171–2). Fletcher's *TNK* fails because it cannot exploit the 'essentially pictorial character' of Chaucer's poem and because it exposes the 'slenderness of the plot, and the inconsistency of the characters' (p 172). See **684**, **726**.

620 Schirmer, W.F. 'Boccaccios Werke als Quelle Geoffrey Chaucers.' *Germanisch-Romanische Monatsschrift* 12(1924), 288–305.
Schirmer accepts Brink's theory (**529**) concerning an early *P&A* in seven-line stanzas. Chaucer not only re-cast it in heroic couplets, but also shortened it, modified its pathetic tone, and individualized its characterizations in order to make it suit the Knight. A comparison of *PF* 183–294 with *KnT* A (I).1918–35 gives some idea of what that process of re-casting was like. Yet the *Tes* and the *KnT* remain alike in several ways – eg, in the artificiality of the monologues, lack of psychological insight, etc (pp 298–300). Chaucer's work is more highly unified work than Boccaccio's, not because he perceived the incongruity between a romance plot and classical form, but because he failed to comprehend Boccaccio's classical aspirations (pp 300–305).

621 Schöffler, Herbert. 'Chauceriana.' *Beiblatt Zur Anglia* 29(1918), 42–8.
That 'save' (A[I].2713) is 'a medicinal potion, to be drunk' is evident from its use in medicinal texts and from verb forms referring to drinking (p 42–6)

622 Schofield, William Henry. *English Literature from the Norman Conquest to Chaucer*. 1906. Rpt New York: Haskell House, 1968; Phaeton Press, 1969.

Chaucer does more than condense the *Tes*; he unifies the work and makes it more realistic. The opening lines 'transfer us at once into the medieval atmosphere of formal chivalry' (p 296).

623 — *Chivalry in English Literature*. 1912. See **342**.
The *KnT* provides 'one of the best pictures we have of English courtly life in the fourteenth century' (p 40), especially in its references to armor, costumes, and manners. Hippolyta's pleas for Palamon and Arcite in the grove recall Queen Philippa's intervention on behalf of the burgesses of Calais. Arcite's generous behavior toward the unarmed Palamon is one of the earliest representations in English literature of the knightly ideal of fair play. The tournament reflects Edward III's interest in such spectacles. In I.2125, 'Ther is no newe gyse ...,' Chaucer comments slyly on his provision of fourteenth-century armor to ancient Greeks. The theme of Theseus' final speech – that kings and pages both must die – echoes the French poem composed by the Black Prince **204** for his tomb; the consolation for Arcite's death – that he died at the height of his fame – is the only solace the English people had for the death of the Black Prince. See **218**.

624 Shannon, Edgar Finley. *Chaucer and the Roman Poets*. Cambridge, Mass.: Harvard University Press, 1929; rpt 1957. Rpt New York: Russell & Russell, 1964.
'Chaucer, Ovid, and Virgil' (pp 302–7): The description of Mercury's appearance before Argus (I.1385–90) is taken from Ovid's *Met* I.671–2 and 720–1, not from Claudian's *De Raptu Proserpinae* I.76 (cf Skeat **625**, V: 70). I.1761, 'For pitee renneth sone in gentil herte,' echoes *Tristia* III.v.31–2. The idea for the paintings on the temple walls came from the description of Juno's temple in *Aen* I.446–93 (see also pp 103–5). Only Diana's temple shows classical influence, all of the following being presented with details found in Ovid's works but not in the *Tes*: Callisto (I.2056–61), Daphne (2062–4), Actaeon (2065–8), and Atalanta and Meleager (2069–71). The depiction of Lucina (2083–6) and the story of Venus, Mars, and Vulcan (2388–90) are also indebted to various Ovidian works. The wood nymphs (2925–8) are indebted to *Met* I.192–3, 680–1, and 688–91, and the term 'vale of Galgopheye' (2626) comes from *Met* III.155–6. See **1039**.

625 Skeat, W.W. *Oxford Chaucer*. 1894/1899. See **3**.
See I:529–30 for the relationship of *Anel* and *KnT*. In III:389–95, Skeat supports Brink's theory (**529**) of an earlier stanzaic *P&A*, prints Tyrwhitt's summary (**640**) of the *Tes*, and suggests that the Knight was meant to win the story-telling prize. In his Notes to the *KnT* (V:60–95), Skeat presents a table showing the indebtedness of the

KnT to the *Tes*. He shows that the internal dates in the Tale fit the calendars for 1386 and 1387, probable years of the Tale's composition. For I.2045, he explains how geomantic figures are formed. For comment on Skeat's notes, see: **541, 556, 558, 561, 582, 605a, 607, 613, 624, 632, 642, 741-2, 751, 811, 836, 964, 1039.**

626 — *The Evolution of the Canterbury Tales*. London: Kegan Paul, Trench, Trübner & Co., 1907. Chaucer Society Publications, 2nd Series, 38 (1907 for the issue of 1903).
The Hengwrt scribe introduced the 'ghost-word' *sertres* in A[I]2037 where the proper reading is *sterres*. Ellesmere and several other mss seem to follow Hengwrt, while Harley 7334, often independent, has the correct reading (p 37).

627 Smith, C. Alphonso. '"Under the sonne he loketh".' *MLN* 37(1922), 120–1.
The phrase in *KnT* 839 (I.1697) means that Theseus looked all around, from one point of the compass to another; the idiom survives in popular ballads, eg, *Fair Annie* (Child 62) and *Bewick and Graham* (Child 211). See **618, 635, 761.**

628 Snell, F.J. *The Age of Chaucer*. London: George Bell and Sons, 1901.
The conclusion to the *KnT* (pp 201–5) is 'unsatisfying' since Palamon, who is less chivalrous than Arcite, wins the lady; still this 'rude' justice is appropriate to our 'imperfect state' (p 205). Palamon and Arcite are 'human and vitally alike' as Boccaccio's 'marionettes' are not (p 205); Chaucer sacrifices consistency in fashioning the Amazon Emelye 'after the best models of contemporary maidenhood' (p 205).

629 Spurgeon, Caroline F.E. *Five Hundred Years of Chaucer Criticism*. 1925. See **346.**
Only a small portion of the references to the *KnT* are listed under that heading in the index. Other hard-to-find items include: in Part I, Pope (p 319), T. Gray (p 420), T. Warton (p 439), Unknown (p 480), J. H. Mortimer (p 447); in Part II, D. Wordsworth (p 14), R. Wharton (p 22), Hazlitt (p 70), G. F. Nott (pp 78–90), 'C.B.' (p 94), W. Gifford (p 96), Hazlitt (pp 115–6), L. Hunt (pp 124–5), E. B. Browning (p 160), Landor (p 162), Unknown (p 164), Hippisley (p 215), E. B. Browning (p 243), J. Saunders (pp 264–6), Ruskin (p 286); in Part III, Emerson (p 1), L. Hunt (p 21), Longfellow (p 90), Lanier (p 124); in Part IV, Douglas (p 9), Unknown (p 44), Isaac D'Israeli (p 99), W. Beloe (p 103), Mrs Markham (p 105); in Part 5, Yart (p 30), Gomont (p 60). See Alderson **793.**

630 Stewart, George R., Jr. 'The Moral Chaucer.' In *Essays in Criticism, by Members of the Department of English, University of California.*

University of California Publications in English, No. 1, 1929. Pp 91–109.
Seeing Chaucer as a 'serious teacher' as well as a 'genial man of the world' (p 93), Stewart cites the *KnT* as a work dealing with 'the ethical problem of love *versus* friendship,' although because of the Church's opposition to courtly love, it must also be counted as one of the tales that 'sounen in-to sinne' (pp 94–5). Along with *Bo* and *TC*, the *KnT* belongs to a middle period when Chaucer 'became greatly interested in the deeper problems of life to which he was able to see no solution except through religion' (p 106).

631 Tatlock, John S.P. 'Chaucer and Dante.' *MP* 3(1906), 367–72.
Esp. pp 370–2. Chaucer's interest in fate and chance, divine foreknowledge and human free-will, are reflected in *KnT* I.2987 f, which has a source in the *Tes*, and in I.1086–91, 1108–9, and 1303–6, which do not. Although Boethius' *Consol* was Chaucer's chief source of ideas in this area, Dante was also an influence, especially his discussion of Fortune in *Inf* VII.68–88, to which I.1663–9 is chiefly indebted. Chaucer's stylistic trait of listing several possible destinal causes of an event, as in I.1074 and 1465–6, may echo *Inf* XV.46, 47 and XXXII.76–8. See Jefferson **582**.

632 — *The Development and Chronology of Chaucer's Works*. Chaucer Society, Series 2, Number 37. London: Kegan, Paul, Trench, Trübner & Co., 1907.
Tatlock attacks the stanza-theory originated by Brink **529**, citing the theory's improbability, evidence that the passages from the *Tes* in the extant stanzaic poems (*TC*, *PF*, and *Anel*), show no signs of having been imported from another work, and lack of evidence in the *KnT* of indebtedness to an earlier English version in stanzaic form (pp 45–66). On the question of whether *P&A* was substantially revised for inclusion in the *CT*, Tatlock acknowledges only two clear additions, I.889–92 (or perhaps 875–92) and 3107–8, and argues against much alteration on the grounds of probability and Chaucer's usual practice. Tatlock attacks Lowe's arguments for dating the *KnT* before *TC* (**596**). The *KnT* was composed after *TC* (1377) and before the *LGW* (1386), works with which it shares a large number of similar or identical phrases and lines, and after *PF* (1381) in which Chaucer used Boccaccio's version of Venus' temple. Historical allusions suggest a date of 1382 at the earliest. Tatlock comments skeptically on Skeat's 'calendar method' of dating the work (**625**), suggests that Chaucer's interest in the *Tes* extended over at least six years (cf Mather **607**), and concludes that the *KnT* was composed shortly before, and revised soon after, 1385, and put into its present position

in the *CT* about 1388–90 (pp 70–83). Appendices present a table of parallels between the *Tes* and the *KnT* (pp 226–30) and a discussion of positive features of the *Tes* (pp 231–3) Chaucer has omitted: eg, the more vivid portrait of Emily. Chaucer's Palamon is inferior to his 'honourable and generous' Arcite, who 'shows the last magnanimity in commending Palamon to Emily' (p 232). The basing of Palamon's claim to Emily on his loving her first shows the 'half-deliberate satire' characteristic of the *KnT* (p 232) and seen in other instances of levity – eg, Emily's bathing, and Egeus' simple-minded consolation. See **541, 573, 590, 667, 737, 744, 778.**

633 — 'Notes on Chaucer: The Canterbury Tales.' *MLN* 29(1914), 140–4. The saying that Friday is seldom like the rest of the week (I.1539) is explained by Alexander Neckam in his *De Naturis Rerum*. Friday is Venus' day and the planet Venus nourishes earthly beings by ensuring periods of hot and wet weather (p 142).

634 — 'The Source of the *Legend*, and Other Chauceriana.' *SP* 18(1921), 419–28.
The Prologue to the *LGW* is reminiscent of the scene in which Theseus comes upon the dueling princes: a sovereign discovers offenders against his authority; he does not recognize one of them at first, but then rebukes and threatens him; a queen dressed in green and her ladies plead for the offenders; the sovereign reminds himself of the need for mercy, pardons the offenders, and assigns them a task whose performance provides the substance of the rest of the poem (p 419). Chaucer wrote the story of Palamon and Arcite shortly before the *LGW*, he has Alceste refer to that work, and he uses in the *LGW* (F. 503) a line he first composed for the *KnT*: 'pitee renneth soone in gentil herte' (I. 1761) (p 420). Alceste's 'other holynesse' (F.424) means not '*sanctitas*' but merely 'piety' or 'religion.' Palamon's 'affeccioun of holinesse" (I.1158) is 'a feeling of devoutness' (p 423).

635 — 'Under the Sonne'. *MLN* 37(1922), 377.
Tatlock rejects C.A. Smith's interpretation (**627**) of *KnT* 839 (I.1697) and suggests that Chaucer describes Theseus as looking in the direction of the sun. See **618, 761.**

636 Thynne, Francis. *Animadversions* [upon Speght's edition of 1598]. [Originally published 1599] Ed. F.J. Furnivall. Chaucer Society Publications, Second Series, No. 13. London: N. Trübner, 1875.
Thynne objects to seven of Speght's readings in the *KnT* (pp 43–52), preferring 'Campaneus' to Speght's 'Capaneus' in A[I].932; 'Heroes' to 'Eros' in 1374, a famous crux; 'unserial' to 'cerriall' in 2290; 'everye' to 'eyther' in 2570; 'save onlye the intellecte' to 'and also the intellecte' in 2803; 'straughte' to 'haughte' in 2916; and 'vassallage' to

'visage' in 3054. Furnivall's footnotes review the status of each reading in Speght's 1598 and 1602 editions and in the mss of the *Six-text* edition **1**. On I.1374, see **599**, **791**; and see Derek Pearsall, 'Thomas Speght,' in *Editing Chaucer* (see Headnote to 'Editions'), pp 83–5.

637 Tobler, Alfred. *Geoffrey Chaucer's Influence on English Literature*. University of Zurich Dissertation. Berne: Haller, 1905.
Tobler inventories authors who imitate, finish, enlarge, use, modernize, or adapt for children, Chaucer's works. For the *KnT* see Gavin Douglas (pp 1–2), Lydgate (pp 20–1, 45), James I of Scotland (pp 46–8), Shakespeare (pp 50–1), Fletcher (p 53), Dryden (pp 66–70), George Ogle (pp 92–100), Edward Hovel Thurlow (pp 104–5), George Cowden Clarke (pp 105, 115–6), John Saunders (p 111), Frederick Clarke (p 112), Frank Pitt Taylor (p 112), Mrs. H.R. Haweis (pp 113–5), Francis Storr and Hawes Turner (p 114), and Mary Seymour (p 114).

638 Torraca, F. 'The Knightes Tale e la Teseide.' *Societate Reale di Napoli: atti della reale Accademia di Archeologia, Lettere e Belle Arti* ns 10(1928), 201–217. Rpt in *Scritti Vari*. Milan: 1928. Pp 91–107.
Torraca emphasizes Chaucer's debt to the *Tes*, against early commentators who minimized it. Chaucer's condensation was achieved simply by cutting out large tracts of the work, and his deviations from Boccaccio often complicate what had been simple, or lack credibility, or eliminate a charming scene. For example, Chaucer omits Emilia's glimpse of the princely prisoners, and inserts the improbable construction of the theater in a mere fifty weeks. He introduces a contradiction between the completed movements of the altar fires and Diana's forecasts about them (I.2331–6 and 2355–7). The philosophical speeches of Arcite, Palamon, and Theseus are irrelevant and merely indulge Chaucer's moralizing tendencies. Many of the best parts of the *KnT* are taken directly from the *Tes* or from Dante (the description of the dawn: I.1493–4) or Statius (the minotaur on Theseus' pennon). Chaucer's work displays a novice's touch.

639 Tuckwell, Reverend W. *Chaucer*. Bell's Miniature Series of Great Writers. London: Bell, 1904.
Arcite's maying (I.1491–1512) is an example of Chaucer's 'finest style' and the account of the tournament (2599–2613) is the product of Chaucer's eye-witness experience. The *KnT* is a 'splendid original poem' but we may wish that the *MilT* and *RvT* had never been written (pp 57–60).

640 Tyrwhitt, Thomas. *An Introductory Discourse to the Canterbury Tales.* [Originally published 1775] Folcroft, Pa.: Folcroft Library Editions, 1973.
In this preface to his edition of the *CT*, Tyrwhitt praises the choice of the Knight by lot to tell the first tale since this device provides for a splendid opening while not impairing the 'apparent equality' necessary to the social occasion (p 13). Chaucer may first have prepared a translation of the *Tes*, which he revised when he incorporated it into the *CT* (p 13). Tyrwhitt provides a brief summary of the *Tes* (pp 15–21), and approves of three Chaucerian changes: that Palamon sees Emilia first, 'which makes the catastrophe more consonant to poetical justice'; that the princes exhibit jealousy, the lack of which in the *Tes* 'if not absolutely unnatural, is certainly very insipid and unpoetical'; and that Emilia is unaware of her suitors, since no consequences follow from her knowledge of them in the *Tes* (p 16). Chaucer's placement of the temples in the lists is a 'more natural fiction' than Boccaccio's flight of personified prayers to distant shrines (p 18). The combat is anachronistically medieval in both works (p 18). See **344-5, 525, 559, 625, 644, 707, 964.**

641 Williams, W.H. '"Palamon and Arcite" and "The Knightes Tale".' *MLR* 9(1914), 161–72 and 309–23.
Dryden's modernization of the *KnT* faithfully reflects the method of paraphrase he defined in the Preface to the *Fables*. Dryden attempts 'to make the language more pointed, epigrammatic, and antithetical; to render the vague more definite, and the allusive more explicit; to fill in outlines and to complete pictures; to make the narrative logical and consistent; to supply missing links in the chain of thought; to dignify, polish, and adorn; in short, to array what he considered to be the primitive and crude simplicity of Chaucer's language in the elegant and ornate court-dress of Restoration rhetoric' (p 161). Citing Dryden's 'Omissions,' 'Additions,' and 'General Changes,' Williams concludes that Dryden's most impressive achievement is his version of Theseus' final speech, 'where he has rendered his fine original with an added vigour and eloquence which fully justify the expansions he has admitted' (p 323).

642 Wise, Boyd Ashby. *The Influence of Statius upon Chaucer.* Baltimore: J.H. Furst, 1911; rpt New York: Phaeton Press, 1967.
Ch 1, 'Direct Influence of the Thebaid ... ' (pp 46–54): Chaucer probably had the *Theb* open before him as he composed and could not have confused the 'tempest' (A[I].884) at Theseus' homecoming with a figurative storm mentioned later in Statius' narrative, as suggested by Skeat (**625**). Line 884 should be emended to read *feste*

(based on *Tes* II.19), or 'tempest' should be interpreted figuratively. Chaucer's direct debts to the *Theb* include: the night march (970), the Minotaur (980), the mention of Fortune (915), the 'waste walles wyde' (1331), the simile of the wild boars (1699, 1658), the hill on which Mars' temple stands (1981), the 'vese' (1983), the northern light (1987), 'adamante' (1990), the description of Felonye (1995–6), the tower of Conquest (2527–8), the peaceful habitation of the gods (2925–8), and the cloth of gold and jewels (2933–4). Ch 2 A, 'Indirect Influence of the Thebaid ... ' (pp 78–115): Wise offers two corrections to Ward's comparison (1) of the *KnT* and the Tes: A[I].893–900 is indebted to *Tes* II.25, and 989–90 has no source in the *Tes* (p 78). Wise details Chaucer's indebtedness to parts of the *Tes* which themselves are indebted to the *Theb*, giving particular attention to three long passages: Theseus' Amazonian triumph and attack on Thebes (I.859–996; pp 78–87), the temple of Mars (1967–2050; pp 92–6), and Arcite's funeral (2863–2962; pp 107–15). Ch 2 B, 'Did Chaucer Know the *Roman de Thèbes*?' (pp 127–37): Wise answers in the affirmative, citing particularly A[I].893–1004. The description of the Theban women as 'caitifs' (924), and the epithet 'olde' for Creon (938) may be indebted to the *Roman*, for example; but more important are the specifications that Theseus rode on horseback, won the city by assault and destroyed it. In the *Theb* and *Tes*, Theseus is a classical conqueror; in the *Roman* and the *KnT*, a medieval knight of chivalry. See **811**.

643 Woolf, Virginia. 'The Pastons and Chaucer.' *The Common Reader*. New York: Harcourt, Brace, 1925. Pp 13–38. Excerpted in *Geoffrey Chaucer*, ed. J. A. Burrow (Baltimore: Penguin, 1969), pp 125–6; in *Critics on Chaucer: Readings in Literary Criticism*, ed. Sheila Sullivan (London: Allen and Unwin, 1970), pp 17–22; and in *Chaucer: The Critical Heritage*, ed. Derek Brewer (London: Routledge & Kegan Paul, 1978), Volume 2, 377–84.

In this famous essay on the elder Paston's 'passion to acquire' (p 17) and on the younger Sir John Paston's passion for books, among them Chaucer's poems, Woolf says of Chaucer: 'he never flinched from the life that was being lived at the moment before his eyes ... If he withdraws to the time of the Greeks or the Romans, it is only that his story leads him there. He has no desire to wrap himself round in antiquity, to take refuge in age, or to shirk the associations of common grocer's English' (pp 29–30). She notes Palamon's address to the cruel gods (I.1303–8), his remark on the world's 'greet pyne' (1323–4), and Arcite's death-bed questions (2777–9), saying: '[Chaucer] was little given to abstract contemplation. He deprecated, with peculiar archness, any competition with the scholars and divines ... [Chaucer] asks questions, but he is too true a poet to answer them; he leaves them unsolved, uncramped by the solution of the moment, thus fresh for the generations that come after him' (p 31).

644 Wyatt, A.J. *The Prologue and the Knight's Tale*. 1895. See **4**.
Wyatt rejects Skeat's argument for a lost stanzaic *P&A* (**625**), suggesting that Chaucer would have lacked the patience to revise such a long work. If such a *P&A* existed, it was probably a nearly complete version of the *Tes*, since its supposed fragments in *Anel*, *TC*, and *PF* are drawn from Books I through XI of the *Tes* (pp 17–8). Wyatt gives Tyrwhitt's summary (**640**) of the *Tes* (pp 19–21), and lists eighteen contrasts between the *Tes* and the *KnT* (pp 21–4). For example, Boccaccio prefers Arcite while Chaucer is impartial and interested in the question of justice; the *Tes* is slow moving while the *KnT* is a 'rapid succession of brilliant pictures' (p 23). Partly on the evidence of the 'purple patches' describing the temples, Wyatt surmises that Chaucer intended the Knight to win the prize supper (p 24).

1931-1960

645 Ackerman, Robert W. 'Tester: *Knight's Tale*, 2499.' *MLN* 49(1934), 397–400.
Ackerman questions the usual gloss, 'helmets,' for *testeres* (I.2499) since 'helmes' are mentioned in the next line. Latin and Old French sources suggest the meaning 'a headpiece for a horse or an ass,' especially head-armor for the destrier or war-horse.

646 Aiken, Pauline. 'Arcite's Illness and Vincent of Beauvais.' *PMLA* 51(1936), 361–9.
The medical theory, practice and terminology of Chaucer's description of Arcite's illness (I.2743–60), an addition to Boccaccio's story, can be found in Vincent of Beauvais' *Speculum Majus*. Arcite's 'sore' is an abscess, its underlying cause an excess of a humor which then putrefies: Chaucer's 'clothered blood' that 'corrupteth.' 'Veyne-blood' and 'ventusinge' are two kinds of bloodletting. The natural virtue, of which the expulsive is a subdivision, works through the veins, now congested with excess blood; thus Chaucer is correct in saying that the natural virtue must be purged. The animal virtue functions through the nerves, and since Arcite's have been injured, his brain can no longer direct his breathing. The inability to breathe spreads infection to Arcite's 'pypes' and 'lacertes' since air was believed to purify the blood. The administration of laxatives and emetics was a

traditional means of supporting the body's *virtus expulsiva*. Finally Arcite arrives at the 'hora status,' the last struggle between nature and disease when the physician is essentially helpless.

647 Atkinson, Dorothy. 'Some Notes on Heraldry and Chaucer.' *MLN* 51(1936), 328–31.
John Guillim's *A Display of Heraldrie* (1611), Sect. vi, Ch 5 quotes I.2159–64 and explains Emetrius' mantle as a garment intended to indicate a commander's rank and to protect his armor.

648 — 'Some Further Chaucer Allusions.' *MLN* 55(1940), 361–2.
Randle Holme, in *The Academy of Armory* (completed 1649; published by the Roxburghe Club 1905) speculates on the drapery or, in heraldic terms, 'doubling' of Emetrius' mantle in I.2159–64 (p 320).

649 Baldwin, Ralph. *The Unity of the Canterbury Tales*. 1955. See **349**.
The *ParT* represents spiritual excellence and the *KnT*, a similar but subordinate secular excellence. The *GP* and the *KnT*, on the one hand, and the *ParT* and the *Ret*, on the other, are the 'supports' of Chaucer's pilgrimage structure (p 106).

650 Baum, Paull F. 'Characterization in the "Knight's Tale".' *MLN* 46(1931), 302–4.
Baum supports Hulbert's contention (**578**) that Chaucer weakened Boccaccio's characterizations, and contests Baker's insistence (**523**) that Chaucer clearly differentiates Arcite's and Palamon's attitudes toward love. 'The simple distinction of Arcite's as earthly and Palamon's as heavenly love (1155 ff.) is a neat tentative, but Chaucer lays no stress upon it' (p 303). Chaucer is chiefly interested in courtly love and destiny, topics he treats 'with a certain air of jocosity' (p 304).

651 — 'Chaucer's Puns.' *PMLA* 71(1956), 225–46.
To Kökeritz' citations (**706**), Baum adds several instances of play on sound, including A[I].1076, 1013, 1026, and 2725 (p 227 n8). Baum emphasizes play on sense. See entries for *array* (A[I].934), *cart* (2022), *charity* (1623), *degrees* (1889), *disjoint* (2962), *divinistre* (2809), *noise* (2674), *rebelling* (2459), *space* (1895), and *streams* (1495).

652 — 'Chaucer's Puns: A Supplementary List.' *PMLA* 73(1958), 167–70.
See entry for *May* (A[I].1037).

653 — 'The Knight's Tale.' *Chaucer: A Critical Appreciation*. Durham: Duke University Press, 1958. Pp 84–104.
Chaucer was an '*amateur of genius*' (x) whose kindly and worldly-wise art is without spiritual and philosophical depths. The *KnT* has unrealistic scenes, an inappropriate mixture of high and low styles, humor that is sometimes misapplied (eg, the comments on Arcite's

soul), and a number of inconsistencies (eg, the overlap between the roles of Saturn and Mars) (pp 85–94). The parliament is an artistic blunder (pp 94–5), and although the Tale's symmetrical structure is praiseworthy (pp 96–7), the characters are only '*dramatis personae*' in a 'purely literary' treatment of the story (p 98). *Pace* Frost **684** and Muscatine **726**, 'the moral is simply that somehow things come right in the end ... Arcite, who put his trust in Mars, is rewarded by victory in battle and a fine funeral, but the astuteness of Palamon, who put his trust in Venus, is ultimately justified. This is perhaps not very edifying, but it has a Chaucerian flavor' (p 99). Chaucer was chiefly interested in the *demande d'amour*; the Tale 'exists for its ambiguity and its ingenious solution' (p 101). Its appeal lies in the beauty of particular passages; 'the setting, the figures, the situations are all *romantic* to the last degree' (p 102). The *KnT* is 'an imperfect poem,' probably an early work that Chaucer did not significantly revise (p 104).

654 Bayley, John. *The Characters of Love: A Study in the Literature of Personality.* London: Constable, 1960.
In excising Arcite's ascent to the ninth sphere, as in the *Tes*, Chaucer replaces the 'orthodox comforts of mediaeval philosophy' with a 'heroic spirit of his own discerning [citing I.2778–9] (pp 74–5). Chaucer's re-use of line 2779 in the *MilT* (I.3204) shows Chaucer's 'sophisticated assembly of different worlds [epic, chivalric, fabliau-esque] in one phrase made appropriate to Arcite, the Knight, and the Miller' (p 76). Chaucer's patriarchal ancient world gives an important place to Egeus and his counsels. The 'tragic resignation' of the *KnT* 'depends on this quality of platitude as well as truth, a "twice-told" tale as well as a moving reality' (p 77).

655 Bennett, H.S. *Chaucer and the Fifteenth Century.* Volume 2, Part 1 of the Oxford History of English Literature. Oxford: Clarendon Press, 1947; rpt with corrections, 1965.
The effect of I.2779 depends on its position, at a point where Arcite's cries have built up an 'emotional pitch' (p 83), and on the way Chaucer manages the diction, pauses, and phrasing. The 'deliberate artistry' of this passage can be seen by consulting *MilT* I.3204 where 'the whole weight given to the phrase in the *Knight's Tale* is lacking' (p 84).

656 Bennett, J.A.W. 'Chaucer, Dante, and Boccaccio.' *MAE* 22(1953), 114–5.
KnT 635–6 (I.1493–4) conflate Dante's description of the hour before sunrise in *Purg* I.19–21 (where the planet is Venus, not Phoebus) and *Tes* III.5–8, where Boccaccio describes the hours after sunrise on the

morning when Palamon and Arcite first see Emelye. The later passage may itself be a reminiscence of the *Purg*. For another example of conflation, see Bennett **914**.

657 — 'The Knight's Tale.' *The Knight's Tale*. 1954/rev 1958. See **48**. Pp 16–27.
Bennett reviews Chaucer's uses of the *Tes* in the *KnT* and the relations of the *KnT* to an earlier *P&A* (pp 16–8). As part of the 'medievalization' of the classical story (pp 18–9), Chaucer astrologizes the gods and uses the Tale to express his view of divine providence. Chaucer's debt to Boethius 'unobtrusively alters the tale's total effect' (p 20). The Knight's presence as narrator is signalled by many details associated with Theseus, the duel, and the tournament (pp 20–3). Theseus' 'blend of humorous wisdom and sane realism certainly makes him the most "Chaucerian" of the characters' (p 23). He is 'more god-like' than Teseo and 'closer to what the Knight's own concept of an ideal prince would be' (p 24). Palamon and Arcite are more alike than their counterparts in Boccaccio, bringing out the conflict between love and brotherhood (pp 25–6). Boccaccio's Emilia is artful, coy, and vain; Chaucer's Emilye is 'the English prototype of the passive heroine,' an ancestor of Edith in Scott's *Old Mortality* (p 27).

658 — *The Parliament of Foules: An Interpretation*. Oxford: Clarendon, 1957.
Ch 2 (pp 62–106) contains detailed comparisons of the Venus of *PF* and the Venus of *KnT*. The latter is very like 'a deputy of Nature,' and the former is more 'distasteful to Nature' (pp 95–8). A 'neo-Aristotelian emphasis on generation and corruption' (p 110) can be seen in *PF* and in Theseus' final speech (pp 110–1; cf 179–80). Bennett compares the royal tercel with Arcite (pp 162–4), and the formel with Emily (pp 176–7). And see his summary (pp 186–93).

659 Bethurum, Dorothy [Loomis]. 'Shakespeare's Comment on Medieval Romance in *Midsummer-Night's Dream*.' *MLN* 60(1945), 85–94.
'The whole conception' of Shakespeare's Theseus is Chaucer's (p 86): a benevolent, responsible ruler sympathetic to the follies of love for which he provides a common sense norm. The plot of the four lovers is developed in ways that heighten Chaucer's ironies into a satire against romance (pp 87–9). See **671, 852**.

660 Bivar, A.D.H. 'The Death of Eucratides in Medieval Tradition.' *Journal of the Royal Asiatic Society*, Parts 1–2 (1950–1), 7–13.
Emetrius is probably Demetrius of Bactria, a figure rarely mentioned in classical literature whose importance as a successor of Alexander and conqueror of India was revealed by modern numismatics. How

did Chaucer hear of him? References in Justin (XLI.6), in Boccaccio's *De Casibus Virorum Illustrium* (VI.6), and in Laurence de Premierfait's French translation of the *De Casibus* suggest that Boccaccio, Chaucer, and Laurence may have had access to a version of Trogus [ie, the *Historiae Philippicae*, a lost work by the fourth-century Roman historian] or to a text derived from Trogus.

661 Bowers, R.H. 'Impingham's Borrowings from Chaucer.' *MLN* 73(1958), 327–9.
One of the thirteen proverbs composed, compiled, or at least copied by one Impingham and preserved in Brit Mus MS Harley 7333, fol 121v–122r (c 1460) is adapted from I.1523–4: 'Gode it is a man to bere him even / For al day men mete at vnset steven.' See **1103**.

662 Boys, Richard C. 'Some Chaucer Allusions 1705–1799.' *PQ* 17(1938), 263–70.
The anonymous author of 'Parallel between the French and English Writers,' *The Universal Museum and Complete Magazine* (August, 1765) says *P&A* is 'a poem of more merit than could be expected from the rude age in which its author lived' (p 267). The anonymous author of 'The Design of Poetry,' *The Microcosm*, 9(January 29, 1787), cites I.989–90 and 2019–20 as evoking in the reader an unpleasant state 'between horror and laughter' (p 268).

663 Bradner, Leicester. 'References to Chaucer in Campion's "Poemata",' *RES* 12(1936), 322–3.
Bradner quotes more of the context in Campion's poem for the allusion to the *KnT* reported by Graves **563**.

664 Brewer, Derek S. *Chaucer*. London: Longmans, 1953/2nd ed, 1960/ 3rd ed, 1973.
The *KnT* shares with Chaucer's dream visions an emphasis on theme, and with *PF* details of its central situation, at the same time that it shows a new interest in narrative (pp 67–8). Its strengths lie in 'splendour and vividness of description' and 'nobility of sentiment' (p 70). The characters are generalized, but Arcite is more arrogant than the humble Palamon. Theseus' attitudes toward love enrich the work but are not in any simple sense Chaucer's. Love and death are interrelated throughout and in Theseus' final speech, whose 'exalted conception of life' produces the effect of 'true metaphysical poetry' (pp 75–6). 'Serene acceptance crowns the nobility of *The Knight's Tale*' (p 76).

665 — 'The Ideal of Feminine Beauty in Medieval Literature,' *MLR* 50(1955), 257–69. Esp pp 265–7. Rpt in Brewer. *Tradition and Innovation in Chaucer*. London: Macmillan, 1982. Pp 30–45.

Brewer describes the type of the beautiful woman set forth by Dares Phrygius, Maximian, Matthew of Vendome, Geoffrey of Vinsauf and others, and examines its use in the Harley lyrics and in Chaucer's Blanche, Criseyde, Emily, and Alisoun. While Boccaccio supplies many of the traditional physical details for his Emilia, Chaucer 'almost entirely omits the description of the heroine' (p 265) and appeals instead to the reader's imagination (p 266). His Emily does not sing love-songs. 'Her remoteness, her purity, her passiveness ... are therefore enhanced. She is indeed like a goddess; her ideal supramundane beauty removes all worldly stain from her' (p 266). Yet Chaucer's success depends on the tradition: only a few details – her long hair, the red and white flowers – are needed to evoke the stock response. 'Such girls, in medieval literature at least, represent not realistic individuals ... but universals in concrete form ... The idealized beautiful girl corresponds to a basic element in man's experience' (p 267).

666 Brooks, Cleanth. 'Chaucer: Saturn's Daughter.' *MLN* 49(1934), 459–61.
Brooks corrects Robinson's note to I.2453 (**751**) by showing that *doghter* here and in I.2668 means 'female member of a family' and identifies Venus as Saturn's granddaughter, consistent with the references in I.2222 and I.2477. See **558**.

667 Brown, Carleton. 'The Man of Law's Head-Link and the Prologue of the Canterbury Tales.' *SP* 34(1937), 8–35.
Mel, assigned to the Man of Law, was originally intended to be the first of the *CT* (pp 8–33). The phrase 'allone withouten any companye' in *Mel* B^{2}2749–50 (VII.1559–60) does not echo A[I].2778–9 of an earlier *P&A* (Tatlock **632**) but was a familiar formula always available to Chaucer (Robinson **751**) (pp 19–20). The present Group A is made up of the *GP* and *KnT*, which are early work, and the fabliaux and links, which are late work (p 26). The *KnT* was incorporated after 1394 when it is still referred to as *P&A* in the revised Prologue to *LGW* (pp 27–8). The present arrangement of Group A is Chaucer's work as indicated by the 'almost unanimous' agreement among the mss (pp 29–30). The *GP* originally ended at A[I].825–6. The next 32 lines, which contain verbal echoes of the ML Head-link and repeat the penalty for opposing the Host's judgment (cf 805–6 and 833–4), were inserted at the same time as lines 875–92 (Wager **778**) in order to adapt the *KnT* to its position as the first tale. See **458, 734**.

668 Chute, Marchette. *Geoffrey Chaucer of England*. 1946. See **358**.
Chaucer's problem was to preserve the courtliness of the *Tes* while

cutting away the extraneous epic detail (p 260). His use of *occupatio* in describing Arcite's funeral reflects his own 'anxiety to condense' (p 261); the tournament, his experience as Clerk of the Works; his medievalizing of his Greek story, his belief that 'ther is no newe gise that is nat old' (p 261). He adapts the story to his medieval audience by transforming the gods into planets. Chaucer's love story is not undermined but is made more entertaining by the humorous passages, the elements of realism, and the veins of medical and astrological lore (p 263).

669 Cloyd, Marie G. 'Chaucer's Romance Element.' *PQ* 11(1932), 80–91. Summarizes the results of a statistical study of Chaucer's use of words of Romance origin in the *GP*, *KnT*, *MLT*, and *SNT*. 'Chaucer used the same percentage of words of Romance origin [11 % for *KnT*] when writing independently as when taking the material from a Romance source' (p 91). See **720**.

670 Coghill, Nevill. *The Poet Chaucer*. 1949. See **359**. In adapting the *Tes*, Chaucer emphasized 'the rigours of courtly love' (p 96), inventing 'the deliciously absurd debate' on which Arcite's tragedy depends, as to which prince has priority as Emilia's lover (p 97). Chaucer depicts noble chivalry in the scene in which the two knights arm each other for the duel; he shows his 'genius for wise digression' by adding philosophical depths to Arcite's speech on fortune (1259–64), and his powers of description in his treatment of the lists and the tournament. Emilia's lack of interest in the lovers indicates 'a temperament fully feminine and fully virginal' (p 98). The gods defeat Arcite because he is a 'recreant from the Code,' but he shows magnanimity in his final speech, 'among the finest things in Chaucer' (p 98). Its emotional appeal is balanced by Chaucer's account of Arcite's soul, in which the 'imperturbable balance of the High and Colloquial styles matches the mystery and agnosticism of this moment of poetry' (p 98).

671 — 'Shakespeare's Reading in Chaucer.' In *Elizabethan and Jacobean Studies Presented to Frank Percy Wilson in honour of his seventieth birthday*. [No Editor] Oxford: Clarendon, 1959. Pp 86–99. Reviewing the scholarship on the influence of the *KnT* on *MND* (pp 87–91), Coghill points out how H.R.D. Anders **522** weakened J.W. Hales' characterization of Shakespeare's debts to Chaucer ['Chaucer and Shakespeare,' *Quarterly Review* 134(1873), 225–55]. Coghill finds Bethurum's suggestions of Chaucerian influence on *MND* (**659**) 'highly speculative' (p 91), but goes on to suggest other borrowings from the *KnT*: the image of the bucket in the well (I.1550–3 and *Richard II*, IV.i.184–7) and the contrast between earthly and heavenly loves (I.1158–9 and *Love's Labour's Lost*, IV.iii.62). An important influence on Shakespeare in his early thirties, Chaucer lacked a vision of evil, later Shakespeare's main interest.

672 Dempster, Germaine. 'The "Knight's Tale".' *Dramatic Irony in Chaucer*. Stanford: Stanford University Press, 1932. Rpt New York: Humanities Press, 1959. Pp 87–91.
Dempster approves Hulbert's theory (**578**) that Chaucer reshaped Boccaccio's story as an unanswerable problem of love, which requires indistinguishable lovers and a lady without preferences. Without strong characters, there is little opportunity for typical Chaucerian ironies. Dempster lists only three instances: that it is Arcite, about to be freed, who is resigned to imprisonment; that once released, Arcite reflects on Palamon's good luck and Palamon, on his; and, following Jefferson **582**, that it is Arcite, who thinks the gods just, who suffers a tragic death whereas Palamon, who charges the gods with cruelty, receives a reward (p 89).

673 Dent, A.A. 'Chaucer and the Horse.' 1959. See **362**.
In I.2506–7 *brydel* refers to the bit alone; in I.2887–91 *foundre* means to stumble; in I.2613–4 a fallen rider uses a traditional means of avoiding injury by rolling like a ball (p 8).

674 Donaldson, E. Talbot. 'Idiom of Popular Poetry in the Miller's Tale.' In *English Institute Essays 1950*. Ed. Alan S. Downer. New York: Columbia University Press, 1951. Pp 116–40. Rpt in *Explication as Criticism: Selected Papers from the English Institute 1941-1952*, ed. W.K. Wimsatt, Jr. (New York: Columbia University Press, 1963), pp 27–51; in *Chaucer and His Contemporaries: Essays on Medieval Literature and Thought*, ed. Helaine Newstead (Greenwich, Conn.: Fawcett, 1968), pp 174–89; in E. Talbot Donaldson, *Speaking of Chaucer* (New York: Norton, 1972), pp 13–29; in *Chaucer: The Canterbury Tales, A Casebook*, ed. J.J. Anderson (London: Macmillan, 1974), pp 143–60.
Exploring the implications of the Miller's description of Alison, Donaldson concludes: 'Beneath the Miller's remorseless criticism the Blanchefleurs and even the Emilys of Middle English romance degenerate into the complacent targets of a lewd whistle' (p 134). The phrase *love-longinge*, used in connection with Absolon, seems to imply 'a desire of the flesh irreconcilable with courtly idealism' (p 135) and is never used in reference to Arcite and other aristocratic lovers. Chaucer's use of the popular idiom in the *MilT* strengthens its link with the *KnT* 'for it emphasizes the parallelism between the two ... love-rivalries ... [and] tends to turn the [Miller's] tale into a parody

of all courtly romance, the ideals of which are subjected to the harshly naturalistic criticism of the fabliau' (p 139).

675 — *Chaucer's Poetry*. 1958/rev 1975. See **50**. Pp 901–5/1061–6. The philosophic problem of the *KnT* is 'why of two young men equally worthy (or unworthy) one should live to attain happiness with the woman he loves and the other should end, through the most capricious of accidents, in his grave' (p 902/1063). The answer is that there is no reason humans can understand, but they must believe in a beneficent deity while making a virtue of necessity and trying to live life fully. The equality of the two heroes is essential to this theme. The ultimate victory of Palamon, who saw Emelye first and offered the proper prayer, may distantly reflect the divine plan, but Palamon is not morally superior to Arcite, nor is Venus morally superior to Mars. The Tale's most memorable character is Theseus, whose attempts to bring order out of chaos sometimes involve cruelty, a 'practical compromise that, moral or not, medieval chivalry believed in' (p 904/1065). As narrator, the Knight shows 'firm self-control' (p 905/1065), responding to the excesses of the plot with restraint and humor; he does not expect justice but shows an attitude like Shakespeare's 'readiness is all.' The *MilT* both comments sardonically on the courtly love of the *KnT* and shows a world of more obvious and more even-handed justice (p 908/1069).

676 Doran, Madelein. '*A Midsummer Night's Dream*: A Metamorphosis.' *Rice Institute Pamphlet* 46(1960), 113–35. Shakespeare constructed his Theseus out of borrowings from Ovid, Plutarch, and Chaucer and yet created 'a new and whole character: a quite satisfactory Renaissance prince' (p 124). To Chaucer's *KnT*, Shakespeare's Theseus seems to owe 'his keeping "state" in the wedding of Hippolyta, the conquered bride; his riding to hounds and his change of service from Mars to Diana; his role as an arbiter in a romantic love story; perhaps something of his amused and tolerant attitude towards the lovers' (p 120).

677 Empson, William. *The Structure of Complex Words*. London: Chatto & Windus, 1951. Rpt Ann Arbor: University of Michigan Press, 1967. Excerpted in *Geoffrey Chaucer: A Critical Anthology*. Ed. J. A. Burrow. Baltimore: Penguin, 1969. Pp 159–60. 'Honest Man' (pp 185–201): In exploring this phrase, Empson discusses A.[I].1440–3 in which we are told that Arcite 'honestly and slyly' spent his income while living in disguise in Theseus' court. *Slyly* means 'cleverly' and *honestly* means 'not in the riotous pleasures that attract attention,' 'in a respectable way,' 'steadily and carefully, like a good tradesman' (p 186).

678 Ericson, Eston Everett. '"Reaving the Dead" in the Age of Chivalry.' *MLN* 52(1937), 353–5.
Germane to I.1005–8. Citing the *FQ*, the *Iliad*, Malory's *Morte D'Arthur*, *Beowulf*, the Bayeux Tapestry, the Perceval stories, Gilbert the Haye's *Buke of the Law of Armys*, and Holinshed, Ericson concludes that a knight might honorably divest a fallen enemy of his weapons and his armor, and that 'wholesale pillaging by the soldiery was a practice approved by army leaders' (p 355).

679 Everett, Dorothy. 'Chaucer's "Good Ear".' *RES* 23(1947), 201–8. Rpt in *Essays on Middle English Literature*. Ed. Patricia Kean. Oxford: Clarendon, 1955. Pp 139–48.
Chaucer's use of alliteration in the account of the tournament (I.2602 f) does more than suggest the effect of the meter, as Robinson **751** claims. Rather 'there are lines in it (eg, 2605, 2610, 2611) which could have come straight from a poem in that metre' (p 202). Everett cites R. Smith **761** on the possible relations of the *KnT* to *Ipomadon A* and *Partonope*, but prefers Parr's view (**736**), saying that the similarities do not account for 'the most striking thing in Chaucer's description, the "feel" of alliterative verse' (p 203). Chaucer seems to have deliberately adopted the 'tune' appropriate to the subject of battle as established by the Old English tradition (p 203).

680 — 'Some Reflections on Chaucer's "Art Poetical".' *Proceedings of the British Academy* 36(1952), 131–54. Rpt in *Essays on Middle English Literature*, ed. Patricia Kean (Oxford: Clarendon, 1955), pp 149–74; and in *Chaucer's Mind and Art*, ed. A.C. Cawley (London: Oliver and Boyd, 1969; New York: Barnes & Noble, 1970), pp 99–124.
The organization of the *KnT* depends on parallelism. Palamon and Arcite are alike in everything but their manner of loving Emily, and from this difference flows the entire plot (p 168). The parallel relationships of gods and humans embody Chaucer's theme: the power of destiny, ultimately subordinate to the divine plan evoked by Theseus' final speech. Everett cites approvingly Frost's discussion of the Tale's 'formal regularity of design' (**684**), but takes issue with him on four points: the central motif is not the conflict between love and friendship but rivalry in love; while the poem is philosophical, it is not theological; the Tale is in no sense tragic; the Tale does not reveal the Knight's character because it was composed before Chaucer began the *CT* (p 166, n 1).

681 Ford, Ford Madox. *The March of Literature: From Confucius' Day to Our Own*. New York: Dial Press, 1938.
The *KnT* is 'one of the type problem stories of all time ... it is as breathless as Stockton's *Lady or the Tiger*' (p 421).

682 Francis, W. Nelson. 'Chaucer Shortens a Tale.' *PMLA* 68(1953), 1126–41.
Five of Chaucer's nine uses of *occupatio* occur in the *KnT*, including the sentence of forty-four lines (I.2919–62) describing Arcite's funeral (p 1127). Chaucer's use of abbreviation in the descriptions of the temples may be a reaction against his own tendency toward prolixity. In works where he is most dependent on a source, it may reflect his sense of the necessity of re-shaping the material to his own artistic ends; thus the 'faintly regretful' *occupatio* (I.875–92) as he re-focuses Boccaccio's story of Theseus on the fates of Palamon and Arcite (p 1132).

683 French, Robert Dudley. 'The Lovers in the *Knight's Tale*.' *JEGP* 48(1949), 320–8.
Boccaccio intended Arcite, his representative, to be the more truly chivalric, magnanimous lover, thus suggesting to Fiammetta the unwisdom of her rejection of the poet. Chaucer intended Palamon and Arcite to be equally noble, in the tradition of the courtly literature to which his *demande d'amour* alludes. He introduces one, qualitatively neutral, distinction between the lovers: preference for the battlefield (Arcite) and preference for the bower (Palamon).

684 Frost, William. 'An Interpretation of Chaucer's Knight's Tale.' *RES* 25(1949), 290–304. Rpt in *Chaucer Criticism: The Canterbury Tales*, ed. Richard Schoeck and Jerome Taylor (Notre Dame: University of Notre Dame Press, 1960), pp 98–116; and in *Chaucer: The Canterbury Tales, A Casebook*, ed. J.J. Anderson (London: Macmillan, 1974), pp 121–42.
Frost dissents from Webb's view (**779**) that Theseus is ignoble and cruel. A proper understanding of Theseus requires a review of the entire poem and an alternative to Root's conception (**619**) of the *KnT* as 'a splendidly pictured tapestry.' The plot consists of 'three widening concentric circles of interest: the merely human interest of the rivalry between two young heroes ... for the hand of a heroine ... the ethical interest of a conflict of obligations between romantic love and military comradeship; and finally the theological interest attaching to the method by which a just providence fully stabilizes a disintegrating human situation' (p 292). The similarities between Palamon and Arcite, echoed in the Tale's rhetorical parallelism and 'formal regularity of design' (p 293), make all the more violent the rupture of their comradeship. Their differences validate the justice of their fates. Palamon is 'the spokesman of the greater idealism' (p 295), who 'includes his passion in a wider conception of Venus-worship; and ... puts his love for Emelye above life itself' (p 296).

Arcite, though not base, experiences desire rather than devotion, and treats the situation as merely 'a practical problem of satisfying a desire by pursuit of the local means to attain it' (p 296). Theseus is 'the executant of destiny' (p 297), as established by lines 1662 ff. 'As a personality he is appropriately impressive: terrifying in action, philosophical in outlook; richly experienced yet detached in point of view; warmly sympathetic to misfortune yet mockingly ironical at the expense of youthful enthusiasm' (p 297–8). Destiny is represented by Mars, Venus, Diana, and Saturn, and is subject to Providence, represented by Jupiter (p 298). The tragedy, which lies in the disasters that befall the central characters and Thebes, in those depicted on the temple walls, and in those reviewed by Saturn (I.2453–69), is summed up by Egeus' concept of pilgrimage and by the pervasive fact and image of imprisonment. Yet 'the very vicissitudes of life fall into an ultimate pattern decipherable by wisdom and philosophy; even the destructive divinities are still divine' and beyond them is the First Mover. Theseus' speech is the climax of the poem. 'Man's proper wisdom is ... nobly to accept his destiny ... Hence the importance of Arcite: his nobility, his education, his tragedy. His death was not meaningless to him since it empowered him to reassert his proper relation to Palamon' (p 302). The *KnT* is a 'dramatic utterance' mirroring the Knight's Christian faith, chivalry and heroic disposition (p 302). The *MilT*, an 'artistic antithesis' to the *KnT* in its depiction of love, its setting, plot, manners and use of religion, is the 'principal external means by which the Knight's Tale is made dramatic'; the chief internal means is the 'ingenuousness of the Knight as a commentator on his own story' (p 304). See **653, 680, 690, 691, 710, 771, 821, 885, 887, 896, 916, 982, 1013, 1014.**

685 — *Dryden and the Art of Translation. Yale Studies in English*, Vol. 128. New Haven: Yale University Press, 1955. Rpt Hamden, Conn.: Archon Books, 1969.

Frost comments on Dryden's versions of I.2919–24, the list of trees (pp 36–8); 1260–7, Arcite's description of the drunken man (pp 39–40); 1995–8, description of Mars' temple (pp 45–6); 1940–2, description of Venus' temple (pp 46–7); and 975–80, Theseus' banner and pennon (p 61). Dryden's version is 'ambitious' and 'brilliant' — but 'only a partial success' (pp 72–3). The nineteenth-century critic John Wilson ('Christopher North') faulted Dryden for introducing Arcite's 'remorse of conscience' at having 'wrongfully won' Emily (p 73), and for having expanded the death-bed speech: in Chaucer 'the weight of death seems actually to lie upon the tongue that speaks in few interrupted accents. Dryden's Moribund runs on, quite at his ease, in eloquent disquisition' (p 73). In the Preface to the *Fables*, Dryden says that 'Chaucer makes Arcite violent in his love, and unjust in the pursuit of it' (p 74), and Frost cites evidence of Dryden's shaping the tale to fit this judgment: eg, making Arcite a representative of William III, of 'military success vitiated by personal disloyalty' (p 76). Still Dryden preserves Theseus' significance as 'an embodiment of destiny' (p 78), and Emelye's, as an embodiment of May. His version of Arcite's death-bed questions may be 'a sophistication' of the famous lines, but it is true to 'Chaucer's sense of the precariousness of the human situation – a perception essential to the existence of a heroic view of life' (p 79). Theseus' final speech, 'one of the great philosophical passages of Chaucerian poetry,' 'became in Dryden one of the finest of the seventeenth century, its Boethian vigor and loftiness undiminished' (p 79). Because Dryden treats the tale as a free-standing work, his version lacks the 'sly' irony which presupposes the Knight-narrator, who is sometimes the object of this irony (p 80).

686 Garvin, Kathleen. 'Note on the Tournament in the *Knightes Tale*.' *MLN* 46(1931), 453–4.
Chaucer's tournament takes place on a Tuesday (I.2486–93) not only because as Mars' day, Tuesday was especially propitious for Arcite (Manly **605a**), but also because the 'etiquette of romantic war' (p 454), as in the fifteenth-century *Partonope* (3067–72) and the twelfth-century *Partenopeu* (2349 f), identified Tuesday as the day for tournaments.

687 Gesner, Carl. 'A Note on Henry Vaughan.' *MLR* 50(1955), 172–3.
Vaughan [1621–95] alludes to the *KnT* in his references to Venus, Mars, and Saturn in '*The importunate Fortune, written to Doctor* Powel *of* Cantre,' lines 63–4, 67–8, and 71–4. He associates 'dark Imaginations' with Saturn rather than Mars (cf I.1995).

688 Getty, Agnes K. 'The Medieval-Modern Conflict in Chaucer's Poetry.' *PMLA* 47(1932), 385–402.
The medieval narrative conventions of enumeration and detailed description were in conflict with Chaucer's modern admiration of economy. Chaucer's treatment of the temples constitutes 'a veritable orgy of description' (p 393); in the account of Arcite's funeral, Chaucer compromises by enumerating what he will not enumerate.

689 Graves, Robert. 'Official and Unofficial Literature.' *The Common Asphodel: Collected Essays on Poetry 1922-1949*. London: Hamish Hamilton, 1949. Pp 258–61.
The *KnT* is 'typical official literature'; the *MilT* is 'a purely criminal piece;' and the *RvT* is 'in the same style but somewhat more obscene'

(p 258). Chaucer awards the prize for the best story to the Knight [*sic*]; but, by devoting his art equally to the *MilT* and *RvT*, 'he reveals how strong his criminal sympathies are' (p 258).

690 Green, Richard Hamilton. 'Classical Fable and English Poetry in the Fourteenth Century.' In *Critical Approaches to Medieval Literature. Selected Papers from the English Institute, 1958-1959.* Ed. Dorothy Bethurum. New York: Columbia University Press, 1960. Pp 110–33.
Green illustrates the uses of medieval traditions of commentary on classical texts and aims to extend and correct the 'articles of major importance' (p 129) by Frost **684** and Muscatine **726** in which Theseus emerges for the first time as the Tale's central figure. Theseus is the link to the classical 'fables of the poets' (p 129), Palamon and Arcite and Emily all having been invented by Boccaccio. Three episodes in particular depend on traditions of mythological commentary. In his conquest of the Amazons, Theseus appears not just as an historical hero but also as a 'figure of the rational soul' (p 131). His marriage to Hippolyta suggests the 'natural perfection of the human person in whom action is governed by reason' (p 131). The war between Theseus and Creon, Athens and Thebes, suggests the opposition of order and discord, rational virtue and shameful vice. The memory of Eteocles and Polynices provides 'a figurative context from which the new fiction of Theban "brothers," changed by concupiscence from friends to mortal enemies, will draw extended meaning' (p 131). The Minotaur in Theseus' pennon recalls his 'personal conquest of the monstrous product of Pasiphae's lust' (p 132), and implies a negative view of Palamon and Arcite. 'A passion which leads to broken friendship, treachery, madness, and bloodshed would seem at least youthful folly rather than chivalrous devotion; Theseus' speech on the behavior of the lovers is an adverse criticism of disorderly conduct, rather than "a mature appraisal ... of courtly love" [Muscatine **726**, p 185]' (p 132). These traditional interpretations cannot provide a key to the tone of the poem, however, as represented by Theseus' 'urbane humor' (p 133). The tone seems to 'mitigate the seriousness of [the young knights'] folly, to qualify the dreadful implications of the conventional details in the descriptions of the temples of Mars and Venus' (p 133).

691 Halverson, John. 'Aspects of Order in the "Knight's Tale".' *SP* 57(1960), 606–21.
Halverson elaborates the theme of order identified by Frost **684** and Muscatine **726** by distinguishing three aspects. For his treatment of 'natural order,' Chaucer draws on folk rituals. In the rivalry of Palamon and Arcite and in Palamon's marriage to Emily, the May

Queen, appear the sacred combat, the seeming death of a god, the mourning for him, and the sacred marriage typical of mid-winter and spring festivals (pp 606–12). 'Social order' is represented by the noble life, of which Theseus is the exemplar; he has known adventure and love; he restores piety in Thebes; he transforms the unlawful duel into a lawful tournament; he subdues the wilderness by building the theater (pp 612–6). Both the natural and the social order reflect a third, 'cosmic order' introduced principally through the Boethian additions. While Palamon and Arcite are versions of the Boethian persona, failing to see that they can free themselves from chance by submitting to divine providence, Theseus is a version of Philosophy, possessed of theoretical and practical wisdom. The characters do not change, but the poem progresses toward a marriage which is an aspect and a symbol of cosmic order (pp 616–20). The theme of order is supported by the narrative movement from the crisis of the duel to the serenity of the marriage; by the characterization, which uses exemplary or symbolic figures; and by the three-fold setting: gardens and woods, palace and lists, heavens and temples (pp 620–1). See **808, 887, 916, 1105R.**

692 Ham, Edward B. 'Knight's Tale 38.' *ELH* 17(1950), 252–61.
Citing sixteen interpretations of the *KnT*, Ham argues for 'some simplification of perspective' (p 253). Through his emphasis on *courtoisie*, Chaucer 'medievalizes' the *Tes* much as C.S. Lewis has shown he 'medievalized' *Filos* in his *TC* (**79**). The Tales's humor and attention to astrology do not detract from its courtliness, and the characterizations of Palamon and Arcite are consistent with it, since 'everything they do, except Arcite's choice of Mars, follows the rules' (p 259).

693 Harris, Brice. 'Some Seventeenth-Century Chaucer Allusions.' *PQ* 18(1939), 395–405.
Samuel Purchase, in his *A Theatre of Political Flying-Insects* (1657), pp 144–5, quotes I.2907–8, on the ancients' custom of casting riches onto the funeral pyre. William Seymor [Ramesay?], in his *Conjugium Conjurgium: Or, Some Serious Considerations on Marriage* (1675), pp 75 and 77, quotes I.1077–9, Palamon's first sight of Emelye; 1361–6, Arcite's love-sickness; and 2805–10, Arcite's last words to Emelye, to illustrate the susceptibility of men young and old to love.

694 Heather, P.J. 'The Seven Planets.' *Folk-lore* 54(1943), 338–61.
Examining the treatment of the planets in the *Early South English Legendary* and in works of Middle English verse, particularly those by Gower and Chaucer, Heather cites the emphasis on the astrological aspects of Mars (I.1967–74, 2033–8), and the descriptions of Saturn's

powers (1087–91, 2453–69). Gower summarizes conventional thought on astrology; Chaucer seems to be skeptically weighing these beliefs (p 351).

695 Héraucourt, W. *Die Wertwelt Chaucers*. 1939. See **370**.
Includes a discussion of *pitee* and related terms (pp 208–19). See indices to words (pp 372–6) and to lines in the *KnT* (pp 377–8).

696 Herben, Stephen J., Jr. 'Arms and Armor in Chaucer.' *Spec* 12(1937), 475–87.
Many details concerning arms and armor found on English monumental brasses are illustrated in Chaucer's works, especially in the *KnT*, *Thop*, *Rom* and *TC*. They include: the helm, body armor, coat-armor, the spear, axe and mace, knife and dagger, targe and shield, horse-trappings, and the bow.

697 — '*Knight's Tale*, A.1881 ff.' *MLN* 53(1938), 595.
Chaucer reduced the number of tiers in the stadium from the 500 mentioned in the *Tes* (VII.108, 110) to 60, which still would have provided room for 180,000 spectators, four-and-a-half times the population of fourteenth-century London. Chaucer replaced one absurdity with another.

698 Hinckley, Henry Barrett. 'The Grete Emetreus the King of Inde.' *MLN* 48(1933), 148–9.
Emetreus is Demetrius, son of Euthydemus, a Greco-Bactrian prince who ruled a large part of India. Chaucer's description of his appearance coincides with Polybius' description of Euthydemus and with Emetreus' image as preserved on coins.

699 Housman, A.E. *The Name and Nature of Poetry*. New York: Macmillan; Cambridge: Cambridge University Press, 1933. Excerpted in *Geoffrey Chaucer: A Critical Anthology*, ed. J. A. Burrow (Baltimore: Penguin, 1969), pp 136–7; and in *Chaucer: The Critical Heritage*, ed. Derek Brewer (London: Routledge & Kegan Paul, 1978), Volume 2, pp 491–3.
Housman cites Dryden's treatment of certain lines from the *KnT* as illustrative of the vices of eighteenth-century poetic diction, 'a thick, stiff, unaccommodating medium' (p 20). He commends Dryden for leaving unchanged such lines as I.2273, 'Up rose the sun and up rose Emily,' and 2005, 'The slayer of himself yet saw I there.' But he condemns the expansion of 1999, 'The smiler with the knife under the cloke,' into a three-line passage centering on a personified 'Hypocrisy'; a similar expansion of 1542; and a seven-line expansion of 1748–50, a description of the weeping of Hippolyta, Emelye, and their ladies.

700 Hulbert, J. R. '*The Canterbury Tales* and Their Narrators.' *SP* 45(1948), 565–77.
Chaucer did not rewrite the *KnT* to fit its narrator (p 569), and while the Tale has a general appropriateness to any knight, as a story of young love, it would be more appropriate to the Squire (p 575).

701 Immaculate, Sister Mary. '"Sixty" as a Conventional Number and Other Chauceriana.' *MLQ* 2(1941), 59–66.
The number sixty, as in I.1890, often meant 'a large but indefinite number' (p 61).

702 Kane, George. *Middle English Literature: A Critical Study of the Romances, the Religious Lyrics, Piers Plowman*. London: Methuen, 1951; rpt Folcroft, Pa.: Folcroft Press, 1969.
'The whole strength of The Knight's Tale is crustaceous, external and superficial ... [Chaucer] evidently saw that this material would best be presented by concentration upon the perfection of its outward form, and by this means he made ... a romance externally so near perfection that only the closest scrutiny reveals its internal defects' (p 88). 'To the eye it offers a feast of images splendidly chivalric, to the ear some of the noblest verse that Chaucer wrote, and to the mind an exceptionally smooth mixture of ancient matter and mediaeval conception. It is genuinely of no consequence that the characters are shallow, the plot wanting in verisimilitude or the emotions light' (p 89).

703 Kaske, R.E. 'The Knight's Interruption of the *Monk's Tale*.' 1957. See **373**.
The *KnT* is 'a philosophically true representation of good fortune apparently evil' (p 261). It analyzes the most difficult possibility arising from the Boethian critique of Fortune: 'apparently evil fortune, sent for the "exercise" of good men' (p 264). Theseus' great speech contrasts with the merely 'popular recognition of Fortune as the leveller of the proud' (p 265) in the *MkT* and with the Monk's glance at the Stoic injunction to know oneself (VII.2139). The *KnT* is complemented by the kind of story the Knight recommends in interrupting the Monk, stories in which good men enjoy obvious good fortune. The interruption is also a semi-tacit criticism of the philosophical inadequacy of the Monk's presentation of the fortunes of evil men (p 267). The *KnT* borrows heavily from the treatment of Fortune in Book IV of the *Consol*; the *MkT* borrows almost exclusively from Books II and III. See **887**.

704 Kirby, Thomas A. 'J.Q. Adams and Chaucer.' *MLN* 61(1946), 185–6.

An autograph ms preserves this poem composed by John Quincy Adams in 1834. 'To Miss Emily Ward': "Up rose the Sun — and up rose Emily" / Five Hundred years have pass'd away / Since Chaucer, in that single line, / Pourtray'd a damsel of *his* day, / Whose Soul was pure and fair as Thine. / And *Thou* art rising like the Sun / And, be thy destiny the same — / With him a cloudless race to run, / And close in still serener flame.'

705 Kleinstück, Johannes Walter. *Chaucers Stellung in der Mittelalterlichen Literatur.* Hamburg: Cram, de Gruyter & Co., 1956.
Chaucer goes beyond Boccaccio by treating sympathy as something based on conviction as well as emotion, as seen in the grove, where the representation of Theseus' thought processes is Chaucer's invention (pp 55–60). Following Boethius, Chaucer greatly expanded the role of chance in the plot, and the role of fate as represented by the gods. Theseus is an instrument of Providence, and alone among the characters is able to act with significant freedom. Chaucer departs from Boethius in putting Theseus' wisdom in the service of love (pp 78–94). The marriage is compatible with courtly love because Palamon will continue to serve his lady. Chaucer uses the description of Arcite's love-sickness (I.1355 f) to invite both laughter and judgment, for love itself is both comical and earnest (pp 109–16).

706 Kökeritz, Helge. 'Rhetorical Word-Play in Chaucer.' *PMLA* 69(1954), 937–52.
Kökeritz notes the consensus — as in Skeat (**625**, V, 374) and Robinson (**751**, p 760) — that Chaucer seldom puns. After examining the rhetorical background of Chaucer's punning, Kökeritz cites nine instances in the *KnT*: 2247–8, *armes: armes*; 1837–8, *lief: leef*; 2171–2, *caste: caste*; 1239–40, *absence: presence*; 2333–37, *queynte: queynte, queynte, queynte*; 953, *herte: herde*; 2328–9, *mayde-kepere: maydenhede-kepe*; 2338–9, *brondes-brennynge-brondes*; 2430–4, *fyr-brente: fyr-brenneth* (pp 945–50). See Baum **651**.

707 Kovetz, Gene H. 'Canterbury Tales, A.2349–52.' *N&Q* 5[203](1958), 236–7.
In the *Tes* the scene in which the gods decide how to satisfy both Palamon and Arcite precedes Emilia's prayer. In the *KnT* it follows all the prayers. Thus Diana's announcement to her devotee that a decision has already been reached makes sense in *Tes* VII.67 but not in *KnT* A[I].2349–52. Tyhrwhitt **640** pointed out a similar inconsistency in A[I].2356–7, where Diana refers to an omen yet to be revealed, as in the *Tes*, whereas in Chaucer, the omen has been presented.

708 Kuhl, Ernest P. 'Chaucer and the Red Rose,' *PQ* 24(1945),33–8. Rpt in *Studies in Chaucer and Shakespeare by Ernest P. Kuhl*. Ed. Elizabeth K. Belting. Beloit, Wisconsin: Belting Publications, 1971. Pp 161–8. Emily's red and white flowers (I.1035–9, 1053–4) express a hope for the union of the Lancaster and Mortimer factions (p 37).

709 Lewis, C. S. *The Allegory of Love*. 1936. See **115**.
Lewis compares Palamon's first view of Emelye with the passage in which the lady is seen from the window in the *KQ* [c 1424]: 'Chaucer for the moment is not looking beyond the lachrymose and dejecting aspects of love which the tradition has made so familiar; the Scottish poet ... recalls us to the essential geniality, the rejuvenating and health-giving virtues of awakened passion' (p 237).

710 Lloyd, Michael. 'A Defence of Arcite.' *EM* 10(1959), 10–25.
Lloyd contests Frost's characterization of Palamon as 'the spokesman of the greater idealism in love' and the worthier lover of Emelye (**684**). It is Arcite who proclaims that love is the greatest law and who conceives of it as a service continuing into eternity (pp 14–5). Palamon seeks possession of Emelye rather than chaste service of her, and he is driven mad by jealousy while Arcite only suffers a lover's melancholy (pp 16–7). Arcite's death-bed recommendation of Palamon does not balance any disloyalty of his to Palamon, but rather balances Palamon's wish that Arcite should die rather than come into possession of Emelye (p 18). Arcite's right to Emelye is never challenged since Palamon's marriage to her is a political union with no relation to the tournament (pp 18–9). Arcite exemplifies the patient acceptance of Fortune; Palamon continually rebels against the cruel gods. The marriage is an appropriate reward for Palamon, who prayed to Venus for mortal possession; Arcite goes back to God, love's source. 'Arcite's concept of love is larger than Palamon's worship of Venus: it approximates a worldly love to the whole "cheyne", so that worldly love is not ultimately to be rejected, but translated to a super-mortal sphere' (p 25).

711 Looten, Camille. *Chaucer, ses modèles, ses sources, sa religion*. Lille: Memoires et travaux des Facultés catholiques, 1931.
Chaucer surpasses his sources in his depiction of the preparations for the tournament and in his descriptions of Emetreus and Lygurge (pp 57–9, 61–5), but the immaturity of the *KnT* shows in the weakness of the characterizations (pp 69–72). For example, while Chaucer's restrained treatment of Emelye produces 'une surprise pathétique' (p 68) when she intercedes for the princes in the grove, her inability to love is never satisfactorally explained. Chaucer excels in describing murals (pp 148–53). His interest in scholastic dialectic appears in

Theseus' opposition of mutable and immutable creation in his final speech (pp 170–2).

712 Lowes, John Livingston. *Geoffrey Chaucer and the Development of His Genius.* Boston: Houghton Mifflin, 1934 [cited here]. Rpt (with different pagination) Bloomington: Indiana University Press, 1958; rpt through 1962.

Lowes explains the relationships of the days of the week, and of the 'artificial day' with its 'unequal' hours, to the planets, and reviews the hours specially devoted to the gods' observances (pp 13–8). He then comments on the 'strange, twisted mythology' which the association of planets with gods produced, as in the 'bizarre occurrences' and the 'amazing company' associated with Mars (pp 18–9). In the description of Arcite's moods as lover (I.1528–39), 'the lore of the planets, and the traits of the days of the week, and the idiosyncracies of lovers, have all rolled their sweetness up into one ball with complexions' (p 36). Lowes repeats his explanation **598** of the reference to Friday. He remarks on Chaucer's expansion of the *Filos* in *TC* and his abbreviation of the *Tes* in *KnT*. Emelye, 'in startling contrast with Criseyde, speaks but twice' (p 215). *TC* and the *KnT* 'stand to each other almost as *Hamlet* stands to *Henry V*' (p 215).

713 Lumiansky, R.M. 'Chaucer's Philosophical Knight.' 1952. See **375**. Rpt with revisions as 'The Knight' in *Of Sondry Folk*. 1955. See **376**. Pp 29–49.

The *KnT* is appropriate to the Knight both as a chivalric romance, and because it develops a philosophical theme suitable to the wise and courteous Knight of the *GP*. 'The relation of Providence to man's happiness' (p 34) is considered in three major Boethian speeches introduced by Chaucer: Arcite's (1251–74), Palamon's (1303–33), and Theseus' (2987–3040). Of fourteen major actions in the plot, nine are explicitly explained as caused by an agent in the Boethian hierarchy — Providence, Destiny, Fortune, Nature, 'cas,' or 'aventure' — and three others may be so interpreted. Palamon, like Boethius at the beginning of the *Consol*, can find no benevolent order in the universe, and he maintains this point of view until after Arcite's death, when he accepts the Boethian chain of love propounded by Theseus, and thereby earns Emily's hand (pp 40–1). From the first, Arcite, like the enlightened Boethius, acknowledges an established order that must be patiently accepted. After seeing Emelye, he feels his life is controlled by Fortune and Love, and he struggles with these larger powers to achieve happiness. Mercury is not a deceitful oracle (see Worcester **788**); rather Arcite 'conjured up Mercury to instruct him as he wants to be instructed' (p 44). Arcite prays to Mars because he hopes to escape the double evil of death from love-sickness and the sentence of exile on pain of death. On his death-bed, he 'states his final bewilderment at the workings of a universe which, though ordained by "purveiaunce of God," has defeated him at every turn' (p 45). Although Chaucer leaves Arcite's questions unanswered and omits the vision Arcite enjoys in the *Tes*, the Tale is saved from being wholly tragic by Theseus' explanation of God's plan (p 49) and by the marriage of Palamon and Emelye. See **877**.

714 MacCallum, Sir Mungo. *Chaucer's Debt to Italy*. Sydney: Angus & Robertson, 1934.
Chaucer's abridgement of the *Tes* is an improvement since the plot is slight (p 15), but Chaucer learned from it how to construct a story (p 15–6).

715 Madden, William. 'Some Philosophical Aspects of the Knight's Tale: A Reply.' *CE* 20(1959), 193–4.
Madden objects to Ruggiers' assignment of the philosophy of the *KnT* to Chaucer rather than to the Knight, and to his characterization of the Tale as 'carrying the principal philosophical burden' of the *CT* (**753**). The Tale reveals an honorable and courteous knight whose faith has been dampened by experience and partly replaced by Stoic detachment.

716 Makarewicz, Sister Mary Raynelda. *The Patristic Influence on Chaucer*. Washington, D.C.: The Catholic University of America Press, 1953.
Chaucer deviates from the traditional treatment of courtly love. The narrator treats Arcite's sufferings in love ironically; Theseus rejects the practice of a woman's having a husband and a lover by saying that Palamon and Arcite cannot both have Emelye, and he interprets the cosmic chain of love to be the marriage bond (pp 103–6).

717 Manly, John M., and Edith Rickert. *The Text of the Canterbury Tales*. 1940. See **42**.
Volume 2, *Classification of the Manuscripts*. 'The Knight's Tale' (pp 97–135): The *KnT* appears in 57 mss, including all the relatively complete mss (except McCormick) and Harley 1239 and Longleat 257. Lines lacking by scribal omission include A[I].2681–2, in Ellesmere, and these and 2779–82 in Hengwrt; in some mss such omissions are numerous. Substantial passages are missing in 23 mss, mainly because of loss of leaves. The classification of the mss is complicated 'by many shifts of exemplar, and by more [contamination] and independent editing than in [the *GP*], as well as by the possibility that some of the extant mss have been affected by the pre-CT version of the Tale [*P&A*]' (p 97). The editors divide the mss into a larger group

descended from a common ancestor designated O^1 (discussed on pp 98–122), and a smaller group, including Hengwrt and Ellesmere, descended from 'a somewhat later and slightly modified copy of the original,' O^2 (p 97; O^2 discussed on pp 122–33). The editors divide the *KnT* into three sections 'in which the MSS show different connections and characteristics': A[I].859–1740; 1741–2798; 2799–3108 (p 133). The last section 'is markedly different from all that precedes' (p 134), showing an increase in variants in both Ellesmere and Hengwrt, an increase in uncorrected scribal errors in almost all mss, extensive independent emendation, numerous changes of affiliation and much contamination. The *KnT* 'represents unfinished work ... [and] such revision as Chaucer made stopped short about 300 lines from the end' (p 135). 'Early and Revised Versions' (pp 495–518): Manly suggests that 'superior' readings in some mss may be Chaucerian revisions, and 'inferior' readings, early unrevised work by the poet. He cites 22 'inferior' lines and 13 'improved' lines after A[I].1740 in the mss of Group d (pp 496–8). Volume 3: *Text and Critical Notes*. The 'Critical Notes' contain brief discussions of ms authority for various readings; speculations on how errors, emendations, and omissions may have come about; and comments on spelling, grammar, and meter (pp 426–38). The *KnT* is divided in several different ways (p 533): four mss divide the tale into two parts at I.1880; three mss, including Hengwrt, into three parts (at 1880 and 2742); Ellesmere, into four parts (at 1354, 1880, and 2482); and Hatton, into five parts (at 1880, 2094, 2482, and 2742). In a discussion of glosses, those for the *KnT* are given in full (pp 484–90).

718 Marckwardt, Albert H. 'Characterization in Chaucer's Knight's Tale.' *University of Michigan Contributions in Modern Philology* 5(1947), 1–23.

In a study of thirteen scenes Marckwardt reverses Fairchild's characterization of Palamon as the passive man and Arcite as the active man (**557**). For example, in the prison scene, Palamon is restive, while Arcite counsels patience (pp 7–8). On first seeing Emelye, Palamon prays to Venus for release from prison, but Arcite asks only to be able to see Emelye. The phrase 'affecioun of holinesse' (I.1158) may not be an accurate qualifier of Palamon's love since it is spoken by Arcite, 'probably in a lightly satirical vein' (p 9). With respect to the prayers, it is inaccurate to say that Arcite forgets his true goal and thinks only of means. The phrase 'I aske thee namoore' (I.2420) should be interpreted 'I shall ask no further,' not 'I ask for nothing else' (p 19). Palamon's focus on ends is not 'based on a consistent, thought-out scheme of life' as Fairchild suggests, but is an instance of his 'jumping over means, disregarding them because of his impetuosity and impatience' (p 19). Palamon is 'impulsive, not profound intellectually, and certainly less gracious and courtly than he appeared in the *Teseide*' (p 23). Arcite ... is 'a more profound thinker ... he is the contemplative and the introvert. Yet ... his keen intellect makes him a realist and not an extravagant idealist unconcerned with reality' (p 23).

719 McKenzie, James J. 'A Chaucer Emendation.' *N&Q* 1[199](1954), 463.
The phrase 'double soor and hevynesse' (I.1454) should be printed 'double so(o)r[we] and hevynesse'; similar phrasings occur in *TC* I.1; *Bo* III met. 12.29; and *WBT* III.1079.

720 Mersand, Joseph. *Chaucer's Romance Vocabulary.* New York: Comet Press, 1937/2nd ed, 1939. Rpt Port Washington, New York: Kennikat, 1968.
Mersand rejects Cloyd's conclusion (**669**) that the percentage of Romance words Chaucer uses does not vary with his source, pointing out that she does not compare the *KnT* with the *MilT* (pp 35–6). The *KnT* contains the largest number of Romance words of any of the *CT*, a fact which Mersand attributes to its dependence on the *Tes* (p 80). All the statistical categories, but especially the use of Romance words in rhyming positions, indicate that the *KnT* was composed after the *HF* and before *TC*. The same tests confirm Lowes' argument (**596**) that the *Ariadne* was composed before the *KnT*. The influence of Boccaccio can be seen in such passages as I.1981–90, where Chaucer draws six Romance words from *Tes* VII.32: *entree*; *burned*; *streit*; *adamant*; and two new words, *armipotente* and *etern* (p 113). 'Chaucer was enlarging his Romance vocabulary in a crescendo arrangement which had as the successive stages the *Knight's Tale*, *Troilus*, and *Prologue G* of the *Legend*. Then came Chaucer's separation from Court circles [when he lost his Customs post in 1386] and Court linguistic influences and a return to a language characterized by a smaller Romance element' (p 115).

721 Mitchell, Edward R. 'The Two Mayings in Chaucer's "Knight's Tale".' *MLN* 71(1956), 560–4.
The two passages in which Emelye and Arcite 'do observance to May' (I.1034–55 and 1499–1512, respectively) are not found in the *Tes* and may reflect Chaucer's familiarity with the folk custom of gathering hawthorn boughs in May and with French works such as Froissart's *Un Trettié Amourous à la Loenge dou Joli Mois de May*. The *Guillaume de Dôle* includes a six-line May song comparable to Arcite's three-line song.

722 Moore, Arthur K. 'Chaucer's Use of Lyric as an Ornament of Style.' *CL* 3(1951), 32–46.
Arcite's 'fragment of a roundel' (I.1510–2) may have evoked audience response especially if the song were familiar. But lyric intercalations are few and brief in the *CT*, by contrast with *TC*, perhaps reflecting Chaucer's rejection of French conventions (pp 44–5).

723 Mroczkowski, Przemyslaw. *Opowiesci Kanterberyjskie: Na TleEpoki.* Lublin: Katolickiega Uniwersytetu Lubelskiego, 1956.
Contains chapters on the backgrounds, on the framework of *CT*, and on individual tales, with a summary in English (pp 435–41). In the discussion of the *KnT*, 'emphasis is laid on the typically feudal setting and on Chaucer's shaping of this material, as well as on comparison with the "Teseide" and with contemporary art' (p 438).

724 — 'Medieval Art and Aesthetics in *The Canterbury Tales.*' *Spec* 33(1958), 204–21.
The descriptions of the temples reflect the popularity of the fresco, of which Chaucer could see magnificent examples in Florence (p 209). Chaucer's Venus could be described as a painted high-relief (p 209). Although the awareness of female beauty it reflects used to be thought an anticipation of renaissance art, the same quality appears in such medieval works as the North Italian tray showing 'Tristram, Lancelot, and other Devotees of Venus' (p 219, and n 42). The description of Mars' temple illustrates the 'evocation of the reader's pleasure as a result of a proper presentation of the ugly' (p 219). The use of astrology reflects the Chartrian tendency to present the entire world as a work of art. 'The arrangement of the cosmic motors,' like the order praised in Theseus' final speech, has an element of beauty but may not constitute divine providence (p 221).

725 Muscatine, Charles. 'Form, Texture, and Meaning in Chaucer's "Knight's Tale".' *PMLA* 65(1950), 911–29. Rpt in *Chaucer: Modern Essays in Criticism*. Ed. Edward Wagenknecht. London: Oxford University Press, 1959. Pp 60–82. Excerpted in *Critics on Chaucer: Readings in Literary Criticism*. Ed. Sheila Sullivan. London: Allen and Unwin, 1970. Pp 123–8.
See **726** for this essay in substantially the same form. See **776, 1014**.

726 — 'The *Knight's Tale.*' *Chaucer and the French Tradition*. 1957. See **101**. Pp 175–90.
The conventional style of the *KnT*, derived from French courtly tradition, has been ignored by those who pay attention 'to its poor dramatics rather than its rich symbolism, to its surface rather than its structure' (p 175). Root **619**, recognizing weaknesses in plot and characterization, urged readers to admire the Tale as a splendid but

possibly meaningless tapestry. This approach misses the way in which 'form and style ... point directly to the meaning' (p 177). 'The symmetry of scene, action, and character grouping, the slow pace of the narrative and the large proportion of static description, the predominantly rhetorical kind of discourse ... point to a nonrepresentational, symbolic method ... The *Knight's Tale* is essentially neither a story nor a static picture, but rather a sort of poetic pageant. Its design expresses the nature of the noble life ... Order, which characterizes the structure of the poem, is also the heart of its meaning. The society depicted is one ... in which life's pattern is itself a reflection ... of the order of the universe. And what gives this conception of life its perspective, its depth and seriousness, is its constant awareness of a formidably antagonistic element – chaos, disorder ... clearly exemplified in the erratic reversals of the poem's plot, and deeply embedded in the poem's texture' (pp 180–1). As examples of how the poetry enacts the noble life, Muscatine cites the portraits of Emetrius and Lygurge, the description of Theseus' banners, and the poem's opening lines, which depict Theseus 'as variously the ruler, the conqueror, the judge and, not least, the man of pity' (p 183). Like the descriptions, the speeches have 'metaphoric value.' Theseus' speeches show him to be the central figure and the 'representative of the highest chivalric conception of nobility ... His final oration is a masterpiece of dignity ... [It shows] perfect agreement in organization and content, with the principle of order which Theseus both invokes and represents throughout the tale. In a sense the representative of Fate on earth, the earthly sovereign interprets the will of the divine one' (p 183–4). Theseus' actions and speeches are normative: those of Palamon and Arcite provide the questions that Theseus resolves (p 184). Theseus' speech on love (I.1785–1820) is a 'mature appraisal, not an adverse criticism, of courtly love' (p 185). Its balance of common sense and recognition of the power of love (p 185) rules out satire but not irony. Irony is not used moralistically, however, to suggest that one knight is superior to the other; Palamon represents the worship of Venus and Arcite, the worship of Mars, equally important parts of the noble life. Chaucer is particularly careful to avoid intimations of moral judgment or tragical attitudes in his treatment of Arcite's death. He focuses on 'physical data' and the Knight's colloquial comment (I.2759–80) is 'a deftly administered antidote for tragedy' not 'an actively satiric strain' (p 187). 'The real moral issue of the poem' concerns Palamon and Arcite's 'common position in relation to the universe' (p 187). This issue is presented partly through 'an ever-swelling undertheme of disaster' (p 189), detected in Arcite's deathbed speech, in his and Palamon's early laments, in the descriptions of the temples, and climactically, in the monologue of Saturn, with a final echo in Theseus' insistence on the universality of death in his oration. 'This subsurface insistence on disorder is the poem's crowning complexity, its most compelling claim to maturity ... The impressive, patterned edifice of the noble life, its dignity and richness, its regard for law and decorum, are all bulwarks against the ever-threatening forces of chaos, and in constant collision with them. And the crowning nobility ... goes beyond a grasp of the forms of social and civil order, beyond magnificence in any earthly sense, to a perception of the order beyond chaos. When the earthly designs suddenly crumble, true nobility is faith in the ultimate order of things. Saturn, disorder, nothing more nor less, is the agent of Arcite's death, and Theseus, noble in the highest sense, interprets it in the deepest perspective ... The history of Thebes had perpetual interest for Chaucer as an example of the struggle between noble designs and chaos' (p 190). Virtually every paragraph of this highly influential study has been cited or commented on by later critics. See **653, 690, 691, 846, 883, 887, 896, 897, 904, 915, 916, 918, 936, 943, 955, 962, 982, 1008, 1018, 1025, 1035, 1092, 1097, 1110, 1117.**

727 Nathan, Norman. 'Pronouns of Address in the "Canterbury Tales".' *MS* 21(1959), 193–201.
According to Skeat, '*Thou* is the language of a lord to a servant, of an equal to an equal, and expresses also companionship, love, permission, defiance, scorn, threatening; whilst *ye* is the language of a servant to a lord, and of compliment, and further expresses honour, submission or entreaty' (*3*, V: 175). Of the 2281 uses in Robinson's first edition (**39**), 98% are correct. Twenty-three 'incorrect' addresses to the Christian deity and the pagan gods in the *KnT* and *FranT* are not counted as errors here since they suggest that there was 'no firmly established usage in addressing a deity' (p 194). The *KnT* contains more errors (18) than any other tale, probably because it is early work, unsystematically revised (p 201, n 21).

728 Neville, Marie. 'The Function of the *Squire's Tale* in the Canterbury Scheme.' *JEGP* 50(1951), 167–79.
Wishing 'to compliment and to surpass his father' (p 169), the Squire loads his tale with romantic elements. His opening description of Cambuskyan plagiarizes and extends the Knight's opening description of Theseus; he reproduces certain of the Knight's narrative tricks, promises to describe several battles where the Knight had described only one, multiplies sub-plots, gives Cambalo two champions to

oppose, where Palamon and Arcite had engaged in a simple duel, and assigns to Canacee Theseus' 'pitee' (A[I].1761; F[V].479). The *SqT* lacks the humor of the *KnT*, especially about love (pp 168–74).

729 Oliver, Anna M. 'Chaucer Allusions in XVII-Century Minor Poetry.' *N&Q* 174(1938), 97–8.
In the Preface to *The Thebaid of Statius*, 2nd ed (London, 1773), an English verse translation, William Lillington Lewis says that 'nothing is a greater Argument of Statius' Merit, than the verbal Imitations of Chaucer.' In notes to *Theb* VI.279 and XII.709, 795, 803, and 869, he cites Chaucerian borrowings in the *KnT*.

730 Olson, Paul A. 'A Midsummer Night's Dream and the Meaning of Court Marriage.' *ELH* 24(1957), 95–119.
Shakespeare was trying to breathe new life into ideas that had been made familiar through texts like the *KnT*. Theseus' final speech was one source for the traditional idea that marriage is part of the love that orders the universe. Chaucer's Duke shows that Theseus was already regarded as a representative of the reasonable man and ideal ruler. Hyppolita and her Amazons represented a violation of order in both the Middle Ages and the Renaissance. Chaucer's Diana, whose Proserpina aspects are emphasized in Emelye's prayer, may have inspired Shakespeare's paradoxical treatment of Titania as a 'licentious goddess of chastity' (p 109).

731 Owen, Charles A., Jr. 'The Plan of the Canterbury Pilgrimage.' *PMLA* 66(1951), 820–6.
Owen argues for a five-day, two-way pilgrimage. The first day 'opens with a strong presentation of the chivalric ideal in love and war. Then the theme is inverted as the disorderly Miller presents his version of how men really love and the choleric Reeve shows in his tale and in his conduct two versions of how they fight' (p 825). The pairing of the Pardoner and the Parson on the fifth day balances the conjunction of Knight and Miller on the first day (p 825).

732 —— 'Chaucer's Canterbury Tales: Aesthetic Design in Stories of the First Day.' *ES* 35(1954), 49–56.
The tales of Fragment A emphasize character as do the portraits of the *GP*. 'As a story of chivalry, of combat, of delight in convention and pageantry [the *KnT*] befits that ideal paladin of expanding feudal Christianity. Even its weaknesses in the portrayal of women suggest ... the man more at home in the field than the bower' (p 49). Parallelism and paradox mark the plot, structure, and characterization. 'Equal in grief at the end of Part I, the two knights are equally happy at the end of Part II and equally hopeful at the end of Part III' (p 51). Their fates are equivalent: 'Arcite's death at the

height of his glory and Palamon's attainment of love and happiness are equally desireable' (p 51). It is the paradoxical theme that links the Tale in a profound way to the Knight: 'Courage and devotion to an ideal are valuable not for the results they bring about but precisely because they make the results irrelevant ... For a man whose life had been spent ... in combat ... life and death were constant alternatives, but there was no alternative to honor. In each of his many combats he had faced the fates of Palamon and Arcite and had regarded them as equally desirable' (p 51). The Miller responds to the *KnT* with 'a crude realism' that indicates his impatience with the 'exalted conduct' of knights and their ladies (p 53). The *CkT* indicates that the last three tales of Fragment A were intended to balance the *KnT* by emphasizing themes of betrayal and deception (p 55).

733 — 'The Development of the *Canterbury Tales*.' 1958. See **382**.
References to the *KnT* in the *MilP* indicate that the *KnT* was not inserted into an already developed Frag A. Instead 'a series of fresh intuitions, *Palamon and Arcite* as the *Knight's Tale*, the displacement of the Man of Law as the first storyteller ... the startling contrast between the Knight and the "cherles" ... resulted in the creation of Fragment A,' which may have been 'Chaucer's last work as a poet' (p 457). The *ParsT* belongs to a period of 'overt religious feeling' in 1390–4, and Fragment A to a later one of 'subtle indirection, where morality is experienced rather than expressed' (p 464).

734 — 'The Earliest Plan of the "Canterbury Tales".' *MS* 21(1959), 202–10.
To strengthen Brown's argument (**667**) that *P&A* did not become the *KnT* until after the 1394 revision of the Prologue to *LGW*, Owen points out that the reference to *P&A* occurs in a single couplet [G. 408–9] which could have been omitted without any changes to the context. 'For at least eight years then after Chaucer started to work on the *Canterbury Tales*, the *Knight's Tale* in all probability did not stand as the first of the series' (pp 204–5). The probable original sequence, the *Mel* told by the Man of Law followed by the *ShT* told by the Wife, anticipated the present *KnT-MilT* sequence (p 210).

735 Panofsky, Erwin. *Renaissance and Renascences in Western Art*. Stockholm: Almquist & Wiksells, 1960. Rpt New York: Harper Torchbooks, 1969; rpt 1972.
Panofsky rejects Wilkins' argument (**786**) that Chaucer must have borrowed the details of Venus' holding an object in her *right* hand and of having roses *both* white and red from the *Libellus de imaginibus deorum* since these details do not appear in Bersuire's *Ovidius Moralizatus*. Panofsky points out that Chaucer follows neither of these

texts in replacing Venus' *conca* with a citole, and suggests that Chaucer may have had other textual and visual sources (pp 79–80, n 2). This lengthy note succinctly summarizes the relations among the *Ovide Moralisé*, Bersuire, and the *Libellus*.

736 Parr, Johnstone. 'Chaucer and Partonope of Blois.' 1945. See **383**.
Parr cites two additional parallels between the *KnT* and *Partonope*: I.2630–3 (on Palamon's desire to kill Arcite) and *Partonope* 10577–80; and I.2645–7 (on Emetreus being lifted out of his saddle) and *Partonope* 9930–1, 10853–4 and 10972–3. Parr rejects R. Smith's argument (**761**) for the influence of *Partonope* on Chaucer, noting that no ms of *Partonope* antedates the fifteenth century, and that Chaucer's references to a 'Partonope' (*Anel* 58 and *TC* V.1503) are to one of the Seven against Thebes. The parallels are due to Chaucerian influence on the fifteenth-century English translator of the French romance. See **679, 1000.**

737 — 'The Date and Revision of Chaucer's *Knight's Tale*.' *PMLA* 60(1945), 307–24.
Parr argues, against Tatlock **632**, that *P&A* was significantly revised, not earlier than the middle of 1390. The reference to Saturn's 'vengeance and pleyn correccioun' (I.2461) has no counterpart in the astrological textbooks and may refer to Gloucester's purges and Richard's recovery of power in 1387–8 (pp 307–14). The tempest (884) may refer to the entrance of Isabella of Bavaria into Paris in 1389; the alliances with certain countries (2973), to the truce of 1389 with France, Scotland, and Castile; and Hyppolita's intercession for the princes, to Queen Anne's appeal to Gloucester for Sir Simon Burley in 1388 (pp 314–17). Details concerning the tournament which are not found in the *Tes* are paralleled in Froissart's accounts of the Smithfield tournament of 1390 (**183**) for which Chaucer as Clerk of the King's Works supervised the construction of the lists (pp 317–24). See **744, 781, 901.**

738 — 'Was Chaucer's *Knight's Tale* Extensively Revised after the Middle of 1390?' *PMLA* 63(1948), 736–9.
In this rejoinder to Pratt **744**, Parr doubts that the phrase 'vengeance and pleyn correccioun' (I.2461) could have been understood as a warning of future events since it has no astrological tradition behind it. Concerning the competing suggestions for historical allusions, Parr observes that interpretations offered first do not thereby gain any additional plausibility. Parr lists new details of Chaucer's tournament that do not appear in the *Tes*, and observes that the astrological scheme of the poem, to which Pratt appeals, requires only that

Emetrius and Lygurge arrive before Monday, not specifically on Sunday.

739 — '"Life is a Pilgrimage" in Chaucer's *Knight's Tale.*' *MLN* 67(1952), 340–1.
The fourteenth-century lyric 'Child, thou ert a pilgrim in wikidnes ibor' (Harleian MS 913) is an analogue for Egeus's use of the proverb.

740 — 'Chaucer's "Cherles Rebellyng".' *MLN* 69(1954), 393–4.
'Cherles rebellyng' (I.2459) is not a reference to the Peasants' Revolt of 1381; similar descriptions of Saturn's effects appear in the works of Albohazen Haly and Guido Bonatus. See Wood **901**.

741 Patch, Howard R. 'Chauceriana.' *ES* 65(1931), 351–9.
For being wounded by love through the eye (I.1096–7), Patch cites the Provencal tradition represented by Dante's *Vita Nuova*, cap 19. canz 1.64–7, and the tradition of debate represented by the *Disputatio inter Cor et Oculum* attributed to Walter Mapes. In I.1533 the 'now – now' formula is one often used in descriptions of Fortune; for the allusion to buckets in a well, Patch refers to Burton's *Anatomy of Melancholy* as discussed in Skeat's note (**625**, V: 72).

742 Pratt, Robert A. 'The Knight's Tale.' *Sources and Analogues of Chaucer's Canterbury Tales*. Ed. W.F. Bryan and Germaine Dempster. Chicago: University of Chicago Press, 1941. Rpt New York: Humanities Press, 1958. Pp 82–105.
Pratt summarizes the discussion by Salvatore Battaglia **220**, in his 1938 edition of the *Tes*, of the relationships between the autograph ms and two distinct families of other mss (pp 82–5). Evidence for the classification of Chaucer's ms of the *Tes* is 'extremely slight' (p 87; but see **82**). Other sources of the *KnT* are briefly listed (p 88), and several scholarly studies of Chaucer's treatment of the *Tes* are reviewed (pp 88–90). Skeat's table of correspondences between the *KnT* and the *Tes* (**625**), as modified by Robinson **751**, is reprinted (p 91), and Pratt provides a new table of verbal correspondences (p 92). There follows a summary of the *Tes* in English (pp 93–105).

743 — 'Chaucer's Use of the "Teseida".' *PMLA* 62(1947), 598–621.
The kinds of uses Chaucer made of the *Tes* changed over time and promoted his own growth as a poet. Especially revealing are the ways Chaucer dealt with three problems he faced in composing the *KnT* (pp 613–20). First, while Boccaccio had scattered the temples of the gods around Athens and sent personified prayers off to distant shrines, Chaucer concentrated scene and action in the amphitheater. He had moved beyond translating and elaborating Boccaccio's descriptions, as in *PF*, and was now adapting and imitating them.

Secondly, in I.1491–6, the description of dawn, he created his own 'heightened time passage' (p 618), whereas he had adapted several of Boccaccio's in *TC*. Thirdly, in reducing Boccaccio's lengthy epic catalogue of warriors to the highly individualized portraits of Lygurge and Emetrius, he advanced toward the sophisticated art of the *GP*. Blessed with psychological insight and great descriptive powers, Boccaccio was a 'poet's poet,' who 'had written effective poetry if no great poem' (p 621). Chaucer gradually surpassed his model.

744 — 'Was Chaucer's *Knight's Tale* Extensively Revised after the Middle of 1390?' *PMLA* 63(1948), 726–36.
Pratt answers in the negative, supporting Tatlock **632** and rejecting Parr's evidence (**737**). The astrological reference to Saturn's 'vengeance and pleyn correccioun' (I.2461) may have been intended as a warning to Richard of future dangers rather than as an allusion to past events (p 727). In suggesting several novel historical allusions, Parr offers no evidence against previous interpretations of these passages (pp 727–8). Some details concerning the tournament can in fact be found in the *Tes*, and others may have been drawn from Chaucer's general knowledge rather than from the Smithfield tournament of 1390 (pp 728–36). The arrival of Emetrius and Lygurge on a Sunday is required by the astrological scheme and must belong to an early version of the Tale (pp 730–1). See Parr's rejoinder (**738**).

745 — '"Joye after Wo" in the "Knight's Tale".' *JEGP* 57(1958), 416–23.
The unifying idea of the *KnT* is '"joye after wo" brought about both by the plot and by Boethian Destiny ... for this tale of Palamon and Arcite begins in sorrow and ends in gladness' (p 416). The chief sorrows of the princes are their imprisonment and their sufferings in love (pp 417–9). Theseus is the *deus ex machina*. The comment on destiny (I.1663–72), besides being an 'apology' for Theseus' role and for the coincidence of the characters' meeting in the wood, answers Arcite's earlier philosophical query (1251–9; 1266–7) by giving assurance that human appetites are ruled by divine providence (pp 419–20). Saturn's intervention is also presented as the work of providence; he acts as a peacemaker and as 'the solver of a kind of destinal problem or puzzle': how to insure that both Venus and Mars have their will and that both Palamon and Arcite have joy (pp 420–1). Egeus' speech (I.2842–9) provides an answer to Palamon's philosophical complaint (I.1303–24) (p 421). Theseus' speech shows that Arcite's joy consists in being freed from the prison of this life and in dying with honor. On his death bed, Arcite prepared this

ending by commending his soul to Jupiter and Palamon to Emily. Chaucer opens the *CT* by showing that life is both a prison and a pilgrimage (pp 422–3). See **887**.

746 Preston, Raymond. *Chaucer*. 1952. See **386**.
The *KnT* has been overpraised partly because critics have taken too seriously Dryden's characterization of it as an epic (p 183). Dryden's translations of I.1799–814 and 2787–8 show that he did not always understand Chaucer's intention. Theseus' speech on love shows 'the humour of an experienced Officer in Command indulging a sudden access of hearty sympathy and worldly wisdom as he condones a serious breach of discipline'; Dryden reduces it to 'full Epic vacancy' (pp 184–5). The *KnT* is too often read apart from the *MilT* and *RvT* 'so that its exaggerations are not seen in comic relation to the contrary exaggerations' of those tales (p 186). 'What is distinctive about the tale is a bold combination of mockery and pathos, of mock-epic and genuine rhetorical dignity, of lovers and buckets and gods and butchers' (p 187). Perhaps Chaucer meant to criticize Renaissance epics such as the *Tes* for their lack of substance. Though not a great narrative poem, the *KnT* contains a number of entertaining passages, including the Theban women's lament (2835–6) which Pope adapted as a parodic couplet on the death of Lord Orrery's dog (p 189). The *KnT* also extends the characterization of the Knight: 'It is possible to see in Theseus ... an aggressive side of the narrator's character, an impulse to cruelty which the *parfit knight*, perhaps with difficulty, controlled' (p 190). See **887**.

747 Priestley, F.E.L. 'Keats and Chaucer.' *MLQ* 5(1944), 439–47.
Keats admired Hazlitt's lectures on Chaucer and Spenser, in one of which Hazlitt commented on Arcite's lovesickness: I.1355–66. Keats uses phrases from the passage in several works, most importantly in *Isabella* (pp 440–2).

748 Raith, J. *Boccaccio in der englischen Literatur von Chaucer bis Painters Palace of Pleasure*. Leipzig: R. Noske, 1936. Pp 57–60.
Chaucer made more important and extensive changes in transforming the *Tes* into the *KnT* than he did in transforming the *Filos* into *TC*. He substituted feudal realism for Boccaccio's attempts at constructing a classical setting; he transferred the powers Boccaccio ascribed to the pagan gods to the planets of the same names; and he dropped Boccaccio's contrast between a choleric Palamon and a melancholic Arcite in favor of an opposition between two early medieval attitudes toward love: Palamon's 'affeccioun of hoolynesse' (I.1158) and Arcite's 'love as to a creature' (1159).

749 Renoir, Alain. 'A Note on Chaucer's Women.' *N&Q* 203(1958), 283–4.
The image of a woman 'whose hair, either braided or loosely tied, is allowed to fall casually down her back' occurs in the *KnT* (Emelye, I.1048–50), *PF* (Venus, 267–8), and *TC* (Criseyde, V.808–12). In *Metamorphoses*, Apuleius provides a similar image (Book II.x) and an explanation for its effectiveness (viii). The common source for both Apuleius and Chaucer may have been Virgil's description of Venus in *Aen* I.318–20.

750 Rickert, Edith, and John M. Manly. *The Text of the Canterbury Tales*. 1940. See **717**.

751 Robinson, F.N. *The Works of Chaucer*. 1933/1957. See **39**.
Chaucer claims the ancient authority of Statius but actually follows the *Tes* (p 4). Still, some of the Tale's 'most memorable features' – the temples, the tournament, the philosophical reflection – are largely independent of Boccaccio (p 4). Chaucer made the Tale more realistic and more humorous but he does not satirize chivalry or courtly love (p 4). In the 'Explanatory Notes' Robinson declares the hypothesis of a stanzaic *P&A* (Brink **529**) 'unnecessary' and, citing I.1201, suggests that *P&A* was lightly revised on becoming the *KnT* 'not earlier than 1382' (p 669). He accepts the possible allusion to Anne of Bohemia in I.884; see Lowes **595**. The *KnT* probably preceded *TC*, though there is no definite evidence. Robinson dismisses Skeat's **625** and Mather's **607** attempts to relate the poem's internal dates to the actual calendar in the 1380's and cites Manly (**605a**) on the subject. He rejects Cook's suggestion (**537**) of a date in the 1390's (note to I.2155). He reviews opinion on the sources of the *Tes*, and provides a table, based on Skeat's **625**, of correspondences between the *KnT* and the *Tes* (pp 669–70). Of Fairchild's invocation of the active and the contemplative lives (**557**), he says that the 'allegory is somewhat forced' (p 670). He grants Hulbert **578** that a 'question of love' is important in the Tale, but rejoins that the *KnT* 'would never have engaged, as it does, the sympathy of the reader if it had been written primarily as a discussion of such an academic problem' (p 670). For comment on Robinson's notes, see **666, 667, 679, 706, 742, 760, 761, 763, 811, 836, 964, 976, 1099.**

752 Ruggiers, Paul G. 'The Form of the *Canterbury Tales*: *Respice Fines*.' *CE* 17(1956), 439–44.
As his opening tale Chaucer presents 'a Boethian test case,' applying the noblest philosophy he knew to man's problems and finding 'a partial explanation and resolution in the Great Chain of Love and its provisions for the immortality of species' (p 441). The Tale's anti-

courtly emphasis provides appropriate instruction for such as the Squire. Metaphorically, it assures us of order in the universe and provides a rationale of this world without resort to faith or revelation (p 442). The Miller misses the philosophical implications and makes his own point, that the Arcites of the world are much more likely to win the lady than the Palamons. To the philosophical guidance of the *KnT*, Chaucer later adds the religious guidance of the *MLT* and the 'final admonition' of the *ParsT* that 'penitence and ... virtue are the keys to the kingdom' (p 444). See **887, 1012.**

753 — 'Some Philosophical Aspects of *The Knight's Tale.*' *CE* 19(1959), 296–302.
The first 170 lines predict what is to come: a conflict is resolved by a wedding, the power of Fortune is articulated by the Theban women, the superiority of divine to human law is implied in the controversy over burial rites, and Theseus acts as the defender of divine law (p 296). This pattern helps us deal with two problems: why Chaucer excised the flight of Arcite's soul, and what the relation is of the many gods to the one God (pp 296–7). The god each prince prays to 'objectifies and clarifies the personality of the agent' (p 298). Venus is associated with the First Mover and the Christian God; thus Palamon 'is praying with a wisdom that transcends his present knowledge of the Providence of God' (p 298). The Tale does not emphasize human freedom and responsibility, however, but justifies the divine will and shows the accommodation of human wills to it (p 299). What seem to men so many gods are, along with Fortune, Fate, and the fury, manifestations of the First Mover (p 299). The laments of Palamon and Arcite in Part I and the narrator's comment on Destiny (I.1663–72) all posit a divine will which Theseus, 'spokesman of the Divine,' interprets in his final speech (pp 300–1). Arcite's death, including his reconciliation with Palamon and achievement of a hero's name, is dictated by the universal principle of love, which also provides that Palamon and Emily shall love and ensure progeny through marriage. The consolation reconciles Palamon to the inevitability of death and the necessity of living, and 'sympathy for the living' (p 302) caused Chaucer to eliminate Arcite's laughter from the spheres. See **715, 881.**

754 Savage, Henry. '"Under the sonne": Knight's Tale, 1697–8.' *TLS*, 14 June 1934, 424.
Savage translates the phrase 'against the sun,' citing the parallel phrase 'undir the wynde' (ie, 'against the wind') in the Middle English *The Master of Game.*

755 — 'Arcite's Maying.' *MLN* 55(1940), 207–9.
The illustration for May in the *Heures de Turin* prepared for Jean, Duc de Berry, depicts a group of aristocrats picking blossoms and cutting branches from trees. The Calendar of Months includes persons of all classes, however (p 208, n2), suggesting that anyone might go a-maying (p 208). This evidence weighs against Manly's suggestion (**605a**) that Arcite's maying (I.1506–14) alludes to the controversy over the Flower and the Leaf.

756 Schaar, Claes. *Some Types of Narrative in Chaucer's Poetry.* Lund Studies in English, 25. Lund: C.W.K. Gleerup; Copenhagen: Ejnar Munksgaard, 1954.
Ch 2, 'Summary Narrative' (pp 17–105): The *KnT* contains two examples: the accounts of Theseus' campaign against the Amazons and of his attack on Thebes. There are no summary narratives in the *MilT* or *RvT*. Ch 3, 'Close Chronological Narrative' (pp 106–93): Schaar cites the accounts of Arcite's accident and of the construction of the pyre. In the former, the reader's attention is 'continually riveted' on Arcite, while in the *Tes*, the focus shifts frequently to the fury, the crowd, or the horse. Ch 4, 'Loose Chronological Narrative' (pp 194–227): Schaar cites the accounts of Theseus' encounter with the Theban women, Arcite's decision to return to Athens, Theseus' hunting party and the duel, and Diana's response to Emelye's prayer. The first three lead up to climactic events; the last is itself a climax, which lays greater stress than does the *Tes* on Emelye's fear. All three types of narrative are rare in the *Tes* and *Theb*.

757 Sedgwick, Henry Dwight. *Dan Chaucer.* 1934. See **390**.
The characters are somewhat unrealistic, 'like figures in early Flemish tapestry' (p 277–8). The Tale is characteristic of Chaucer's Italianate period, but shows signs, as in the description of the crowd at the tournament, of the new artistic direction Chaucer later took in the *CT* (p 278).

758 Sells, A. Lytton. *The Italian Influence in English Poetry from Chaucer to Southwell.* Bloomington, Ind.: Indiana University Press, 1955.
The *KnT*, despite its derivation from the *Tes*, is a 'new poem' (p 28), principally because of a difference in spirit (p 37). Sells' comparison of the two works touches on the knights' first view of Emily, the duel, Theseus' appearance in the grove, the descriptions of the oratories, the tournament, the comments on Arcite's soul, and the funeral. For example, Palamon's seeing Emily first gives him a 'better moral claim' to her; the cousins' jealously is 'more true to human nature'; and Emily's lack of awareness 'creates a more delicate ... more interesting situation' (p 31). The duel and the tournament are

more violent than in the *Tes* and probably reflect Froissart's accounts (**183**) and contemporary practices. Theseus, in Boccaccio 'a grand, knightly person,' is in Chaucer 'a bluff English baron' (p 33).

759 Shelly, Percy Van Dyke. *The Living Chaucer*. University of Pennsylvania Press, 1940. Rpt New York: Russell & Russell, 1968.
Shelly rejects both Chesterton's modernization (**357**) of Arcite's dying words (I.2777–9) and Hill's translation (**37**), noting that both neglect or distort Chaucer's true rhyme, feminine endings, and patterns of assonance and caesurae (p 8). The effect of the last line is due to its 'climactic relationship' to the preceding two, a relationship lacking in the *MilT* 3203–4 (pp 8–9). In a discussion of Arnold's estimate of Chaucer (pp 26–38), Shelly cites Theseus' oration, 'obviously and directly a criticism of life,' and Arcite's death, 'a very moving and tragic bit of life portrayed with perfect truth and art,' as having the quality of high seriousness (p 35). '*The Knight's Tale*' (pp 228–41): In its treatment of chivalry, feasting, dress, tournament and customs of love, the *KnT* 'is entirely romantic only to us. To Chaucer and his contemporaries it was largely realistic' (p 232). The story celebrates Theseus' greatness; he is 'proud, autocratic ... and ruthless' (p 234), but possessed of a heart 'almost womanly in its capacity for pity' (p 235). Palamon is 'the gentler, more honorable and straightforward of the two [knights]' (p 236) while Arcite is 'the hotter-headed, harder, and more aggressive' (p 237). He rises to a new level when he is reconciled with Palamon. Though indifferent to love, Emelye is made appealing through the description of the effects of her beauty upon the princes (p 239).

760 Smith, Roland M. 'Two Chaucer Notes.' *MLN* 51(1936), 314–7.
Pace Robinson **751** and Manly **605a** (notes to I.1462f), there is no tradition establishing May 3 as an unlucky day. According to *Partonope* 3067–72, Tuesday, Mars' day, was a traditional day for tournaments (pp 316–7).

761 — 'Three Notes on the Knight's Tale.' *MLN* 51(1936), 318–22.
Citing the fifteenth-century ballad *Robin and Gandeleyn* (Child 115), Roland Smith supports C.A. Smith's interpretation (**627**) of the phrase 'Under the sonne' (I.1697) as 'in every direction' against Tatlock (**635**) and Robinson (**751**) (p 318). Citing *The King of Tars*, Smith argues that the use of May 3 (I.1462f) as a day of misfortune was a romance convention, making it unlikely that Chaucer used the date for personal reasons (Robinson **751**) or borrowed it from a list of unlucky days or really meant the night of May 2 (Manly **605a**) (pp 319–20). Chaucer's account of the tournament may contain borrowings from English romances. Smith cites verbal similarities between

I.2605–10 and *Ipomodon A* 7989–95, and between I.2600–37 and *Partonope* 11128–42 (pp 320–2). See **679, 736, 1000.**

762 — 'Chaucer Allusions in the Letters of Sir Walter Scott.' 1950. See **392.**
Scott's use of the phrase 'to make a virtue of necessity' may be an allusion to I.3042 (Journal, 16 December 1825), and a reminiscence of 2777–9 appears in another passage beginning 'What is this world?' (Journal, 13 May 1827) (p 455).

763 — 'Three Obscure English Proverbs.' *MLN* 65(1950), 441–7.
Egeus' reference to the world as a 'thurghfare ful of wo' (I.2847) was a stock expression, perhaps indebted to such visions as that of Tundale. The characterization of life as a pilgrimage (2848) may be indebted to *Hebrews* xi.13 f as Robinson **751** suggests, but a closer resemblance is provided by *Ecclesiastes* vii.1. The idea was already proverbial when it was cited in Plato's *Axiochus*.

764 — 'Five Notes on Chaucer and Froissart.' *MLN* 66(1951), 27–32.
The 'complainte de l'amant' in Froissart's *L'Espinette Amoureuse* (1556–1794) is the source for Chaucer's identification of Dane as Daphne and for the poet's remarks on being correctly understood (I.2062–4). Actaeon's story (I.2065–8) also appears in *L'Espinette* (1317, 2799f), but Chaucer's details may be taken from Froissart's *Buisson de Jeunesse* (2256–88) (pp 27–8).

765 Spector, R.D. 'Dryden's Translation of Chaucer: A Problem in Neo-Classical Diction.' *N&Q* 3[201](1956), 23–6.
Why did Dryden choose to translate the *KnT* and not the fabliaux? To ward off charges of ribaldry, he would have had to alter much of the diction of the fabliaux. But he believed in a 'propriety of thoughts and words.' The *KnT* was one of the few Chaucerian works in a high style that appealed to neo-classical taste, and even there Dryden often dropped colloquial elements such as Arcite's reference to the mouse (I.1261–4).

766 Speirs, John. 'Chaucer (III): The Canterbury Tales (II),' *Scrutiny* 12(1943), 35–57.
The general assumption that the *KnT* is the best of the *CT* is probably due to its fitting the Romantic notion of a medieval romance; yet its 'mature tone of amused observation' does not fit the Romantic idea (p 39, n 10). The rhetoric of the Mars passage (I.1967–2050) consists of 'a series of *exempla* of violence, treachery and death – each distinct image, shocking in effect by itself, contributing to the ultimate effect of the whole series, the gathered vision of universal violence which leaves the mind shaken and appalled' (p 56). The domestic images of the child eaten by the sow

and the cook scalded by his ladle show a Shakespearean freedom from pomposity (p 57). In the Saturn passage (2453–69), the reference to 'the mynour or the carpenter' gives original force to lines reminiscent of mediaeval Mutability poetry (p 57).

767 — *Chaucer the Maker*. 1951. See **393**.
The line 'For pitee renneth sone in gentil herte' (I.1761) 'distils the essential spirit' of the *KnT* (p 121). 'The sense that passion, death, forces of disorder undermine continually the splendid chivalric order gives the *Knight's Tale* its depth' (p 122). Emily is not a personification but 'a young English girl' clearly visualized (p 122). The naturalness of Palamon's 'a!' (1078) on seeing Emily reminds us of Criseyde's 'Who yaf me drinke' (*TC* II.651). 'The *Knight's Tale* is continually on the point of moving beyond itself (as *par excellence* a courtly romance) into a further actuality that would be comedy or tragedy' (p 123). The source of this 'inner tendency towards a completer reality' lies in Chaucer's English (p 123). Comedy is present 'when the colloquial element ... asserts itself' (p 123), as in the references to the man drunk as a mouse (1261), Arcite's up-and-down mood (1533), and the women's reaction to Arcite's death (2835–6). The tragic perceptions, too, depend on Chaucer's English, as in the image of a cold sword gliding through Palamon's heart (1574–5) and Arcite's death-bed questions. There follows an abbreviated version of **766**. See **1018**.

768 Steadman, John M. 'Venus' Citole in Chaucer's Knight's Tale and Berchorius.' *Spec* 34(1959), 620–4.
Chaucer's depiction of Venus holding a citole in her right hand (I.1959) indicates that he was not indebted only to the *Libellus de deorum imaginibus*, as Wilkins **786** claims, but was also indebted to the *Ovidius moralizatus* of Berchorius, where the more traditional sea shell is interpreted as a symbol of music. Chaucer probably preferred the citole to the shell because it was less hackneyed, more clearly suggestive of the voluptuous life associated with Venus, and appropriate to the courtliness of the Knight's romance. See **878**, **1048**.

769 Stewart, George R. 'The Meaning of *Bacheler* in Middle English.' *PQ* 13(1934), 40–7.
Cf. I.3085. For the period before 1500, Stewart rejects the meaning 'aspirant to knighthood' and accepts three: 1) 'a knight-bacheler,' sometimes implying a youthful knight, sometimes implying a distinction from the knight-banneret; 2) 'an unmarried man,' rarely; and 3) 'a young man.'

770 Stillwell, Gardiner. 'Chaucer's *Complaint of Mars.*' *PQ* 35(1956), 69–89.
Stillwell compares *Mars* and *KnT* with respect to the changeableness of lovers' moods (p 73), the treatment of the gods, especially Mars (pp 81–2), and the questioning of undeserved suffering by Mars and Palamon, respectively (pp 86–7). Chaucer expresses similar attitudes toward young lovers in *Mars*, *KnT*, and *TC*, emphasizing the fascination of their 'busynesse' and the pathos and the humor of their 'basing their lives on so unstable a foundation' (p 88).

771 Stokoe, William C., Jr. 'Structure and Intention in the First Fragment of *The Canterbury Tales.*' *UTQ* 21(1952), 120–7.
Extending Frost's remarks (**684**) on the relations of the *KnT* and the *MilT*, Stokoe stresses the Miller's 'warped and biased' (p 121) interpretation of the *KnT*. Responding 'polemically' (p 122) to the Knight, the Miller uses his portrait of Alisoun to show 'his contempt for the Knight's idealization of Emelye' (p 122). He turns Arcite into Nicholas, the kind of man who has a collection of etchings, and Palamon into Absolon, the 'bashful admirer of women from a distance' who has a collection of pin-ups (p 123). John the Carpenter shows 'how little [the Miller] believes in the reality of a man as wise as Theseus' (p 124). Where the Knight sees divine providence, as executed by such wise agents as Theseus, leading to general happiness, the Miller sees the gods callously resolving their conflicts by the 'costly expedient of causing Arcite's death' and Theseus 'straighten[ing] out the mess the gods have made' (p 124). The Miller takes a 'statistical' approach, demonstrating that 'for every tournament winner killed by a fall from a horse frightened by a fury sent from hell to answer conflicting prayers, there are numbers of old fools taken in by astrologers, soothsayers, false prophets of doom, and fortune tellers' (p 125). The 'unedifying' aftermath as seen in the behavior of Reeve, Cook, and Host, is Chaucer's way of dramatizing the evil of the Miller's view of life and love and the wisdom of the Knight's (p 127).

772 Tatlock, J.S.P. '*The Knight's Tale.*' *The Mind and Art of Chaucer.* Syracuse: Syracuse University Press, 1950. Rpt New York: Gordian Press, 1966. Pp 94–7.
The most 'thoroughly Chaucerian' of the poet's work, the *KnT* shows his typical 'amusing touches' and 'delicate ridicule' (p 95): the Knight's roguishness in describing Emily's ritual bathing; Venus' crying tears into the lists; Theseus' comments on love in the grove; Egeus' simplistic consolation; the displacement of the forest gods; the use of *occupatio*. The Tale is also 'highly decorative and full of

chivalry ... full of ideal romantic love, not of artificial "courtly love"' (p 96). Palamon is 'sentimental, less magnanimous and masculine, Arcite a fully attractive young male preferring disappointment to dishonor. Yet the account of his death, though touching, is detached ... A keen reading shows a trace of ironic reality in the reward going to the less worthy lover' (p 96). Theseus is 'the true hero from beginning to end ... virile, humane and above all adult' (p 96–7).

773 Thomas, Mary Edith. *Medieval Skepticism and Chaucer*. New York: The William-Frederick Press, 1950. Rpt New York: Cooper Square Publishers, 1971.
Thomas rejects Lounsbury's interpretation (**594**) of the lines on Arcite's soul (I.2809–14) as evidence of Chaucer's agnosticism in later life, pointing out that *TC*, which Lounsbury assigns to the poet's religious phase, was probably composed after the *KnT* (pp 104–5). Chaucer was not challenging the doctrine of immortality but reflecting the uncertainty of contemporary theologians concerning the salvation of righteous heathens (pp 105–6; cf pp 64–71). Palamon's speech on the 'cruel goddes' (1303–27) is one of several discussions of the problem of evil which Chaucer interpolated into his poems where there were not corresponding passages in his sources (pp 126–8). Chaucer 'stands out ... [for] his understanding and sympathy ... [with] the frailty of human nature in regard to faith ... Perhaps ... he was not certain of the fundamental doctrines of the faith he stoutly embraced' (p 130).

774 Thompson, W.H. *Chaucer and His Times*. 1936. See **396**.
The *KnT* (pp 57–8) strikes a 'keynote of tragedy' and exhibits the romantic treatment of classical fable in the Middle Ages. Thompson commends the account of the tournament.

775 Ueno, Naozo. *The Religious View of Chaucer in His Italian Period*. Tokyo: Narr'un-do, 1956.
Like Boethius' Philosophy, Jean de Meun's Reason, and Chaucer's Pandarus, Arcite is a 'mouthpiece' for Fortune speaking in her own defense (citing I.1084–6 and 1251–6) (p 64). His death-bed speech could become a Boethian realization of the vanity of worldly joys, but remains 'a pathetic cry of doubt about the intention of God' (p 65). Lines 1251–2 and 1663–5 indicate the close association Chaucer came to make between Fortune and Providence in his Italian period (pp 67, 71). Like Troilus and Dorigen, Palamon asks the meaning of human suffering (lines 1303 f) (pp 115–8). Egeus gives one answer, that suffering is a phase of human life; the Boethian answer is that suffering arises from seeking false felicity (p 118). The bodily pleasure Boethius rejects is not sinful, but only ephemeral, and Chaucer

departs from Boethius more than Jefferson **582** allows by emphasizing the beauty of human love (pp 119–23). The divine love that binds the universe, as described in Theseus' final speech, in Troilus' lyric (*TC* III.1744–71), and in *Consol* II. m 8 is not different in kind from human love (p 130).

776 Underwood, Dale. 'The First of *The Canterbury Tales*.' *ELH* 26(1959), 455–69.
The *KnT* is more critical of the world it depicts than Muscatine **725** allows (p 455), revealing 'mutability, transmutation, and incessant fluctuation between radically juxtaposed extremes' (p 456). Theseus' conquest of the Amazons is followed by his wedding with their queen; his marriage feast, by the destructive tempest; his triumphant homecoming, by the grief of the Theban widows – a pattern that depicts the mechanical order of Fortune's turning wheel (pp 456–8). Opposed to Fortune is the principle of purposive human order which seeks to insure both stability and development (p 458). Human order is represented by the lists, where disorder is converted into order, simultaneously shown to contain disorder (p 459). These ambivalences center on Theseus whose attack on Thebes extends a pattern in which Laius and Oedipus damn the city while trying to save it. The 'progressive line' of these actions 'becomes at the same time an increasing line of disorder' (p 460). In decreeing a tournament, eg, Theseus contradicts his own analysis of the love situation in the grove, and extends the folly of the princes (p 462). As shown by his final speech, Theseus reflects both the order of the First Mover and the disorder of Saturn (p 463). The laments of Arcite and Palamon in Part 1, Egeus' consolation, and Theseus' final speech roughly recapitulate the argument of the *Consol* (pp 463–5), but Theseus' speech omits the questioning of divine order at the beginning of the *Consol*, and the acceptance of human freedom and responsibility at its close (p 466). Like Oedipus, Theseus cannot fully understand the relation of divine will to human will. 'He fails to see the essential crux of the human situation. And the crux is not only that, though partially blind, man is responsible for his destiny; it is also that this apparent disorder and injustice in terms of human logic is part of the logic, justice, and order of the divine' (p 466). Theseus does not see that he has contributed to Arcite's death and turned his world into a prison (p 466). Yet the Tale also reveals a principle of divine order that is super-human but not mechanical, cyclical but still progressive (p 467). Arcite restores the bond of man with man by recommending Palamon; Theseus, the bond of man with god through his speech; Palamon and Emelye, the bond between Thebes and Athens, and the

bond between man and woman (pp 467–8). See **846**, **887**, **916**, **947**, **955**.

777 Van Doren, Mark. *John Dryden: A Study of His Poetry*. 3rd ed. Bloomington: Indiana University Press, 1946; rpt 1960, 1963. 1st ed published as *The Poetry of John Dryden*, 1920.
In translating the *KnT*, 'Dryden has drawn the sting of Chaucer's colloquial charm and injected with a blunt needle the false dignity of Almanzor and Aureng-Zebe ... Epithets, circumlocutions, latinisms, grave conceits, and standard allusions are run profusely in to thicken but not ennoble the original texture' (pp 223–4). The 'gross' psychology (p 224) of Dryden's version is illustrated by his treatments of the women's weeping in the grove (I.1748–50) — 'Through the bright choir the infectious virtue ran' — and of the duel (1658–60). Redeeming features are the 'regal' Lycurgus and Emetrius, the prayers, the settings, and the way Dryden occasionally 'slashed with a shining malice through the tissue of knightly palaver' (p 224), as in his 'caustic' treatment (p 225) of the crowd's speculations about the next-day's tournament (I.2512–22).

778 Wager, Willis J. 'The So-Called Prologue to the *Knight's Tale*.' *MLN* 50(1935), 296–307.
Wager supports Tatlock's suggestion (**632**) that A[I].875–92 is a late insertion meant to adapt *P&A* to its place in the *CT* as the *KnT*. Thirteen mss designate the first thirty-four lines as a prologue to the Tale. Shifts of tense and repeated material and rhymes suggest that Chaucer was inserting a 'post script' (p 299). As a late insertion, these lines cannot be used to date the Tale, but Lowes' evidence (**595**) for the 'tempest' (884) as an allusion to an actual storm in 1391 is unsound in any case: see Curry **542** and the references to disturbances in Boccaccio and Statius (*Tes* II.25; *Theb* XII.472–80 and 512 f) (p 304). See **667**.

779 Webb, Henry J. 'A Reinterpretation of Chaucer's Theseus.' *RES* 23(1947), 289–96.
Chaucer intended to show that 'Theseus, even at the time he was performing his most knightly deeds, was possessed of those frailties which, in later life, caused him to be damned' — and to be criticized by Chaucer in *LGW* 2171 f, and in *HF* 408 (p 289). His four most objectionable acts are: the razing of Thebes, the general pillage, the imprisoning of the princes without ransom, and the freeing of Arcite alone at Perotheus' request. The destruction of Thebes does not occur at all in the *Tes*, and appears as an act of war preceding Creon's death in *RTh*. Pillage and imprisonment without ransom were practices frequently condemned by critics of medieval warfare.

Theseus' refusal of ransom is not unmercenary as S. Robertson **616** suggests but cruel. Unlike Teseo, Theseus does not send out men to look after the wounded, nor does he maintain Palamon and Arcite in conditions befitting their rank as the Black Prince **204** did King John in 1356. His freeing of Arcite makes Palamon's situation all the more painful, and the Duke's failure to mete out equal justice on this occasion directly foreshadows his mistreatment of Ariadne. Even in Theseus' deeds of pity there are 'hints of selfish motives' (p 295): eg, he thinks of the fame an attack on Creon would bring him. Chaucer's repeated references to Theseus as 'noble' are probably ironic (p 296). See **684, 1014, 1031.**

780 Webster, C.M. 'Chaucer's Turkish Bows.' *MLN* 47(1932), 260.
The Turkish bow of the *KnT* (I.2895) and the *Rom* (A. 923–30) was a strong, reflexed bow, fashioned of layers of horn, wood, and sinew. The Turkish bow surpassed the English long-bow in the distance it could achieve.

781 Weese, Walter E. '"Vengeance and Pleyn Correccioun," *KnT* 2461.' *MLN* 63(1948), 331–3.
Parr **737**, in citing I.2461 in support of a late date for the revision of the *KnT*, did not offer a translation of the line. If 'vengeance' is translated as 'retributive or vindictive punishment,' and 'correccioun' as 'corporal punishment' (p 333), then I.2461 sums up the traditional activities ascribed to Saturn in 2457–60 — hangings, imprisonments, etc — but does not fit the historical events to which Parr claimed it alluded. Chaucer, who lost friends and his controllership during the period of Gloucester's ascendancy, would have been unlikely to refer to Gloucester's activities as 'vengeance,' and Richard's later self-assertion was characterized by a calm that does not fit 'correccioun.' See **901, 902.**

782 Whiting, Bartlett Jere. *Chaucer's Use of Proverbs. Harvard Studies in Comparative Literature*, Volume 11. Cambridge, Mass.: Harvard University Press, 1934. Rpt New York: AMS Press, 1973.
The *KnT* (pp 78–83) contains twelve proverbs, three spoken by Arcite (I.1163–6, 1181–2, 1606), two spoken by Theseus (3026, 3041–2), and seven spoken by the narrator (2636, 1521–2, 1523–4, 1539, 1623–6, 1668–9, 2449). There are eighteen sententious remarks, the largest numbers being used by Theseus, Arcite, and the narrator. In the *KnT*, as in *TC*, the stronger characters use proverbs (p 82). A chart (pp 7–9) indicates that there are 32 proverbial comparisons for the *KnT* and six other proverbial phrases.

783 — 'Some Chaucer Allusions, 1923–1942.' 1944. See **399**.
Chaucer's 'smylere with the knyf' (I.1999) is referred to by both I.H. Irwin, in *A Body Rolled Downstairs* (1938), p 191, and Leslie Ford (Mrs. Zenith Brown), in *Murder in the O.P.M.* (1942), pp 100–1. In Gwyn Jones' *Garland of Bays* (1938), p 487, a character is said to be 'fresher than Chaucer's Emily'; cf I.1037.

784 — 'A Fifteenth-Century English Chaucerian: the Translator of *Partonope of Blois*.' *MS* 7(1945), 40–54.
The English translator of the French romance of Partonope borrowed extensively from Chaucer's works. There are eight probable borrowings from the *KnT* and twelve passages showing similarities of a typical Chaucerian kind. Although he usually worked from memory, the translator seems to have had the text of Chaucer's tournament scene open before him.

785 Whittock, Trevor. 'Chaucer's *Knight's Tale*.' *Theoria* 13(1953), 27–38.
The descriptions of Theseus' conquests of the Amazons and Thebans introduce an ideal world of chivalry threatened by disruptive Fortune (p 28). The audience's sympathies are invited equally for Palamon and Arcite, and Emelye is the 'archetype of feminine grace and beauty' (p 29). Then the princes' quarrel shows that 'man is the torn victim of conflicting passions and duties' (p 30). This universal relevance is particularly clear in Arcite's lament (I.1251–64) with its figure of the drunk man, 'a distinctively Chaucerian image in its compassionate humour and humanity' (p 31). The prayers are comic, since none of the three characters knows what the other two are doing, but the comedy 'shows the terrible irreconcilabilities inherent in life' (p 32). The 'secret justice of Saturn' is that he gives each man what he deserves (p 33). The tournament is 'emblematic of all human strife' (p 33), and Arcite's end 'is the common lot all men must share' (p 34). His death-bed speech makes us feel both the fragility and the value of love (p 34). The grimness of his death is elaborated by the women's obtuseness (I.2833–6) – which nevertheless articulates a fundamental question – and by Egeus' despairing counsel (p 35). But the description of the funeral pyre, a rhetorical *tour de force*, expresses a balanced attitude (p 35). Both the grandeur of the description and the richness of the things thrown into the fire convey the value of human life (p 36). Theseus' final speech helps us to 'see life whole again. What is necessary must be accepted, and the goodness of the universe rejoiced in' (p 37). The marriage of Palamon and Emily shows 'how joy can exist despite, and perhaps because of, anguish and suffering' (p 38). See **825**, **897**.

786 Wilkins, Ernest H. 'Descriptions of Pagan Divinities from Petrarch to Chaucer.' 1957. See **144**.
The source of Chaucer's description of Venus (I.1955–66) is the *Libellus de deorum imaginibus* (1342–1380?). Of the two other possible sources, Petrarch's *Africa* did not circulate after 1343, and Bersuire's *Ovidius moralizatus* does not specify in which hand Venus holds her shell while Chaucer agrees with the *Libellus* in placing an object in her *right* hand (p 520). Chaucer's descriptions of Mercury and Mars (I.1387–8, 2041–8) may derive from the same source, and Venus' 'wawes grene,' from a manuscript illustration like that in the Reginensis ms of the *Libellus*. See **735, 768, 878, 1038, 1048.**

787 Wilson, H.S. '*The Knight's Tale* and the *Teseida* Again.' 1949. See **255.**
Esp pp 139–46. Chaucer, like Boccaccio, intended Palamon and Arcite to be seen as equally worthy, but Chaucer agrees with Arcite that natural law takes precedence of positive law. In the meeting in the grove, Palamon's bitterness dramatizes his sufferings, but Arcite's behavior clears him of Palamon's accusations. The plot functions as 'an *exemplum* of the power of love which overrules all fellowship' and both antagonists illustrate this theme (p 143). The tournament emphasizes their equality, and their reconciliation at Arcite's death bed shows the power of love. Where Boccaccio referred only to fate, Chaucer supplies references to Christian providence. He shows 'how the Divine Love providentially works through imperfect love to a higher end' (p 145); the development of this theme, implicit in the *Tes*, is Chaucer's most significant improvement. The humor in the *KnT* is justified, for Chaucer 'sees the comic ironies of life even in its moments of tragedy,' as in the Athenian women's laments (p 146). See **887, 896.**

788 Worcester, David. *The Art of Satire*. Cambridge, Mass.: Harvard University Press, 1940. Rpt New York: Russell & Russell, 1960.
The *KnT* presents a double instance of the deceitful oracle in Mercury's promise of an end to Arcite's woe (I.1391–2) and in the seeming signal of victory from Mars' statue (2431–33). 'Both prophecies are fulfilled to the letter: Arcite loses his life in the hour of victory, and so his woe is at an end' (p 116). The second prophecy is also an instance of 'the granted wish that boomerangs back on the petitioner' (p 116), and it is prepared for in Arcite's 'ironical meditation' (1251–61) in which Chaucer relates oracles to the problem of predestination and free will (p 117). See Lumiansky **713.**

789 Wordsworth, Jonathan. 'A Link between the Knight's Tale and the Miller's.' *MAE* 27(1958), 21.

The Miller's single rhetorical question, 'Who rubbeth now, who froteth now his lippes' (I.3747–9) – marking Absolom's mishap in love – is a deliberate verbal echo of the Knight's series of rhetorical questions marking changes of fortune for Palamon and Arcite (1454–6, 1870–1, 2652–3). Its second line, 'With dust, with sond, with straw, with clooth, with chippes' is 'a parody of the high-style devices of catalogue and repetition.'

790 Wright, Herbert G. 'The *Teseida.*' *Boccaccio in England from Chaucer to Tennyson*. 1957. See **235**. Pp 44–58.
Wright reviews Chaucer's condensation of the *Tes* (pp 45–6), and then considers his treatment of the characters. Teseo is a great warrior but a humane victor, one whose love for Hippolyta makes plausible his later sympathy with the lovers. Theseus is a stern ruler, ruthless towards Thebes and severe towards Palamon and Arcite. Emilia's gradual maturation in love is carefully drawn, but Emelye is 'an angel hovering in the background, a colorless abstraction' (p 49). In the *Tes*, the emotional states of the princes are detailed, and the antagonism between them is juxtaposed with evidence of their abiding friendship. The friendship of Chaucer's princes seems 'formal and superficial rather than deep and intimate' (p 51). While Boccaccio favors Arcite, Chaucer attempts to win sympathy for Palamon – perhaps to justify his eventual victory – by extending his imprisonment, allowing him the first sight of Emelye, and making his defeat in the tournament more dignified. Chaucer makes the tournament more realistic and contemporary, and incorporates his own experience, perhaps, in Arcite's role as Theseus' servant. In the philosophical additions, Egeus' metaphor of life as a pilgrimage (2847–9) and Theseus' final speech adequately answer the earlier questionings of Arcite and Palamon. Although Arcite's death constitutes the kind of reversal of fortune that fascinated the Middle Ages, the Tale is not tragic. Chaucer does not seem deeply moved by it, as evidenced by his light remarks on love (1531–3 and 1806–12), Arcite's illness (2758–60), and Arcite's soul (2809–12) (p 57). Chaucer's version of Boccaccio's story is 'more a tale of action than a psychological study,' a story well suited to the Knight (p 57).

791 — 'Thomas Speght as a Lexicographer and Annotator of Chaucer's Works.' *ES* 40(1959), 194–208.
Wright compares the annotations of Speght's 1602 edition with those of the 1598 edition, noting particularly the influence of Francis Thynne's *Animadversions* **636**. In his note to A[I].1374, Speght defends his reading *Eros* and his interpretation, 'Cupid,' but adds this reference to Thynne's reading: 'Wheras some will haue vs read

Heroes, *i.* noble men; I cannot dislike their opinion, for it may fitly stand with the sense of the place' (pp 197–8). By the end of the sixteenth century, 'the code of courtly love was no longer appreciated, and in its place an ideal of loftiness and self-control had begun to emerge' (p 204). Its influence is seen in Speght's note on Arcite: 'Arcyte, in this furye of his love, did not shewe those courses of gover[n]mente, whiche the Heroes, or valiante persons, in tymes paste vsed ... for the Heroes sholde so love, as that they sholde not forgett, what they were in place, valor, or magnanymytye, whiche Arcite, in this passione, did not observe' (p 204).

1961–1970

792 Adams, George R., and Bernard S. Levy. 'Good and Bad Fridays and May 3 in Chaucer.' *ELN* 3(1966), 243–8.
'Gereful' Friday and its goddess, 'geery' Venus (I.1534–9), remind readers that Adam was believed to have sinned on a Friday, and that Christ died on a Friday. May 3 was also the feast of the Invention of the True Cross. This Venus-Christ conflict supports the larger theme of the *KnT*: that devotion to Venus must be rejected in favor of a love that supports the friendships of men and nations and the marriage bonds of man and woman.

793 Alderson, William L. and Arnold C. Henderson. *Chaucer and Augustan Scholarship*. Berkeley: University of California Press, 1970.
The discussion of the *Fables* (pp 53–68) treats four passages from the *KnT*. In I.2062–4 Dryden correctly interpreted *Dane* as 'Daphne' and established the reading *Peneus* in place of Speght's *Venus*. In I.2922 he helped to establish the reading *lynde*. Dryden's treatment of I.1372–6, the description of Arcite's love sickness, 'a passage which remained a Chaucerian crux until early in the twentieth century' (p 63), 'would not be accepted today ... but constitutes an intelligent approach to a formidable passage' (p 64). Dryden's version of the preparations for the tournament 'shows great care in re-creating an atmosphere of feudal chivalry' and illustrates his principles concerning the restoration of old words (p 65). 'A Collection of Chaucer Allusions' supplements Spurgeon **629** and includes five references to the *KnT*: 1722 John Dart (p 209), 1745 Sneyd Davies (p 217), 1783–4 Thomas Davies (p 230), 1826 Richard Ryan (p 239), and 1905 W.B. Yeats (p 240).

794 Arnott, Peter D. 'The Origins of Medieval Theatre in the Round.' *Theatre Notebook* 15(1961), 84–7.

Chaucer's description of the 'noble theatre' (I.1881–8) follows contemporary English practice, on the evidence of the Duke of Gloucester's rules for lists **184** and other sources. Such lists provided the model for medieval theatre-in-the-round.

795 Bartholomew, Barbara. 'The Knight's Tale.' *Fortuna and Natura: A Reading of Three Chaucerian Narratives*. The Hague: Mouton, 1966. Pp 73–107.

Chaucer heightens the role of Fortuna, who had been only an epic agent in the *Tes*, and introduces the role of Natura (pp 74–8). Theseus' character (pp 78–85) 'follows a definite line of development as he rises above the tyranny of Fortuna to an acceptance of the ordered love of Natura' (p 79), but his progress is uneven. He submits the princes' fate to Fortuna in the tournament and despoils the grove of Nature to prepare Arcite's over-elaborate funeral. Emily 'shows obedience to Natura in agreeing to marry if Destiny commands' (p 88) but then confuses Fortuna with Destiny when Arcite triumphs in the tournament. Palamon (pp 88–94) allies himself initially with the 'good' Venus, an aspect of Natura, but falls prey to the 'bad' Venus, an aspect of Fortuna, through his jealousy. He prays to the 'good' Venus, however, and is eventually cured of his unnatural grief by Theseus' final speech. What initially seems like patient resignation in Arcite (I.1086–91) is actually a life-denying pessimism, and in his speech lamenting his freedom (I.1244–74), he misuses Boethian philosophy to justify the pursuit of false felicity (pp 96–8). His allegiance to Mars brings him to the point where 'Nature hath now no dominacioun' (I.2758) (p 101). Fortuna seems triumphant at the point where Theseus' final speech gives the victory to Natura (p 103). Its germinal idea is contained in the counsels of Egeus, which Theseus transcends by a deeper understanding of love (p 104). Chaucer implies that 'ability to cope with God's ordered universe comes with age and understanding' (p 105).

796 Baum, Paul M. *Chaucer's Verse*. Durham, North Carolina: Duke University Press, 1961.

Baum faults the Tale's use of *-ye* rhymes in some twenty pairs, often with *Emelye*. The use of alliteration in the tournament scene imitates the Anglo-Saxon long line (p 56). The several 'irregular lines' in the *KnT* (p 65) may be evidence of an early date of composition (p 66). Arcite's song (I.1510–2), an instance of Chaucer's 'verbal music' (p 91), is characterized by its repetition of *may/May*, the *f* and *g* alliteration, and the ironic phrase 'som grene,' with its suggestion of transience (p 93).

797 Bawcutt, Priscilla. 'Gavin Douglas and Chaucer.' *RES* 21(1970), 401–21.
In Douglas' *Eneados* (completed 1513), Bawcutt finds four echoes of the *KnT* in the Prologues to the twelve Virgilian books: I. Prol. 45–7 and I.1236–7; IV. Prol. 36 f and I.1785 f, I.2988 f; IV. Prol. 21 and I.2235; IV. Prol. 52 and I.1198–200. There are two echoes in the translation of Virgil: X.vi.50 and I.2511–2, and possibly IV.iv.57 and I.1502. In Douglas' thirteenth book, a version of a fifteenth-century work by the Italian humanist Maphaeus Veguis, there are two: Prol. 167–8 and I.1491–2, and XIII.x.111–2 and I.2809–10. Among Chaucer's works, Douglas alludes most frequently to *TC, LGW* and *KnT*.

798 Beidler, Peter G. 'Chaucer's "Knight's Tale" and Its Teller.' 1968. See **402**.
The 'aging Knight' is an appropriate narrator for the *KnT*, a light-hearted romance (p 54). The Knight's sense of humor has fun as its object, not the philosophical purposes suggested by Neuse **871** and Huppé **844** (p 57). The veteran fighter is amused by the tournament, and the husband and father, by courtly love.

799 Benson, C. David. 'The *Knight's Tale* as History.' *ChauR* 3(1968), 107–23.
Chaucer uses characteristics of the aristocratic chronicle – an emphasis on human will in political action, and a formal, even shallow, presentation of character (pp 107–11) – to establish a classical setting rather than a medieval one (cf S. Robertson **616**). This interest is signalled by Chaucer's repetition of the phrase 'as was tho the gyse,' (cf Bloomfield **207**) and by his adding archaizing details from the *Theb* (pp 113–20). The description of the tournament resembles Statius' account of the fight between Polyneices and Eteocles before Thebes; the duel in the grove, the fight between Polyneices and Tydeus; Arcite's love for Emelye and his death, Artys' love and death in the *Theb*. Other archaizing touches include the treatment of Arcite's soul, the portrayal of the gods as classical deities (astrologized, as Curry **543** argues, but only faintly), and the mêlée of the tournament. Chaucer examines by reason alone 'the practice and ideals of the chivalry he believed antedated Christianity' (p 120). The limits of pagan wisdom are seen in Theseus' final speech whose 'central flaw' is its claim that corruptibility proves the existence of an incorruptible First Mover (p 121). The speech prefigures the Christian vision through its 'universal projection of Theseus' own role' in ending the crimes of Thebes and establishing love in the place of hatred (pp 122–3). See **934**.

799a Birch, P.M. *Four Essays*. 1967.
See Bright **806**.

800 Bishop, Ian. *Pearl in Its Setting: A Critical Study of the Structure and Meaning of the Middle English Poem*. Oxford: Basil Blackwell, 1968.
Chaucer's introduction of a consolatory topic not found in his sources – 'The grete tounes se we wane and wende' (A[I].3025) – and his reference to comforting the grief-stricken (2850–2) indicate his familiarity with the genre of consolation. Egeus' speech contains three topics: death is the common human lot, life is a pilgrimage, and death is an end of suffering. Theseus adds two: the futility of opposing God's will (3035–46) and the timeliness of a death (3047–56)(pp 21–2).

801 Blake, N.F. 'Chaucer and the Alliterative Romances.' *ChauR* 3(1968/9), 163–9.
An analysis of the alliterative patterns and vocabulary of I.2605–16 (and *LGW* 635–48) shows that Chaucer either was not familiar with the alliterative romances or was not trying to copy them.

802 Bloomfield, Morton. 'The Miller's Tale – An UnBoethian Interpretation.' In *Medieval Literature and Folklore Studies: Essays in Honor of Francis Lee Utley*. Ed. Jerome Mandel and Bruce A. Rosenberg. New Brunswick, New Jersey: Rutgers University Press, 1970. Pp 205–11.
In the *KnT*, the irrationalities are only seeming, and the providence of Theseus on earth, and of God in heaven, ultimately produces good. In the *RvT*, the universe is committed to justice and fair play. In the *MilT*, the world 'seems rational but is not really so' (p 207) as seen in Alisoun's escape from deserved punishment and John's experience of undeserved punishment.

803 Bolton, W.F. 'The Topic of the *Knight's Tale*.' *ChauR* 1(1967), 217–27.
In Part I of the *KnT*, Theseus opposes Fortune with wisdom and chivalry while Palamon and Arcite submit to it (pp 217–8), and Theseus shows himself capable of a charitable love in his friendship with Pirotheus while the princes are capable only of carnal loves for Emelye (pp 219–21). The duel in Part II shows the princes to be animal-like (pp 221–2). Part III shows that 'the world is indeed what men ask to have, that is, it becomes the thing they desire it to be' (p 222). The temples show Mars and Venus to be aspects of 'the degrading promptings of carnal love and their disastrous effects' (p 224). In Part IV Theseus' god-like role as an embodiment of reason is emphasized (pp 224–5). Arcite's death-bed speech merely restates the illusions that caused him fruitlessly to love Emelye in disloyalty to Palamon (p 255). In his final speech Theseus replaces the lovers'

selfish schemes with 'high statecraft' (p 226), and explains the cosmic chain of love against which they had complained. The *KnT* is about love and death; its major love scene is also its major death scene, and 'Arcite dies because he has seen love only in the mortal dimension' (p 227). See **1067**.

804 Bowden, Muriel. *A Reader's Guide to Geoffrey Chaucer*. 1964. See **403**. 'Chaucer's Chivalric World' (pp 17–45) considers Chaucer's enthusiastic 'eyewitness' account (p 27) of the tournament in relation to ecclesiastical attitudes; the cousins' pledge as sworn brothers; and the chivalry of the first meeting in the woods as well as Arcite's deathbed recommendation of Palamon. 'Chaucer's Religious and Philosophic World' (pp 46–93) examines evidence from the Tale for Chaucer's interest in the stars and Fortune. 'Chaucer's Scientific World' (pp 94–105) explains the 'unequal' hours of the 'artificial day'; presents a chart showing the hours of the various days of the week dedicated to each planet; and reviews the medical detail of Arcite's love sickness and his fatal injury. 'Chaucer's Everyday World' (pp 106–34) contrasts Alisoun with Emelye, a symbol of 'the maidenly ideal' (p 117). 'Chaucer's World of Literature' (pp 135–40) examines the use of the long complaint, the elaborate description, *occupatio*, and the list in the *KnT*.

805 Brewer, Derek S. *Chaucer in His Time*. 1963. See **404**.
Brewer describes the tournament: its various functions as practice for war, substitute for war, and sport; the distinction between the older mêlée, represented in the *KnT*, and the late fourteenth-century joust; and the tournament in Smithfield in 1390 for which Chaucer had responsibility as Clerk of the King's Works (pp 170–6). He comments on feasting and music (pp 176–84), citing I.2197–206, and explains the customs of Maying reflected in 1507–12 (pp 186–7).

806 Bright, J.C., and P.M. Birch. *Four Essays*. 1967. See **405**.
In 'Chaucerian and Medieval Thought' (pp 15–21), the *KnT* is Bright's chief example of Chaucer's intellectual interests: Boethian philosophy, astrology, controversies over the soul, medicine.

807 Brooks, Douglas, and Alastair Fowler. 'The Meaning of Chaucer's *Knight's Tale*.' *MAE* 39(1970), 123–46.
The balance a character achieves in his relationships to the gods is the measure of his psychological maturity. Theseus' past links him to Mars, Venus, and Diana, and in the present he is allied to Jupiter as judge and ruler; he needs to be instructed in the ways of Saturn, god of time (p 126). Emily must progress from Diana's patronage to Venus'. Her experience in Diana's temple is a psychological allegory, revealing the next stages of her maturity (pp 126–8). The close

relationships of gods and humans are expressed in the construction of the theater as a zodiac, with the siting of the temples reflecting the actual state of the heavens on May 7 in the late fourteenth century (pp 128–30). The import of the planetary influences is revealed through the descriptions of the two kings. As Curry **543** argues, Lygurge is Saturnian, but Emetrius is not simply a Martian figure but a Martian-Solar composite (pp 130–3). The kings represent the heroes' 'deepest psychological resources' (p 134), and indicate Palamon's moral and psychological superiority to Arcite (pp 134–7). Arcite represents the Martian, choleric prime of the typical knight, superseding the early sanguinic, Venerean phase represented by Palamon; thus Arcite's brief victory in the tournament. The Martian phase is superseded by a Saturnian Middle Age, when Arcite acknowledges, on his death bed, the superiority of Palamon's values. What survives is the 'more mature stage of the supercharacter Palamon-Arcite-Emetrius-Lygurge' (p 138). Theseus does not achieve the highest level of Saturnian maturity (pp 140–1). He occasionally shows Martian rigor, he engages in Jovinian busyness to the end, and in his final speech he shows incomplete detachment from the world and imperfect submission to Saturn. The ambivalence surrounding Theseus issues from the Knight-narrator, who shares the Duke's faults, some of his virtues and his stage of development (pp 141–2). At every level the *KnT* treats of 'growth to wise maturity through a succession of ages and attitudes' and 'the soul's formation and ascent through a series of planetary stages' (p 142). See **955**, **1008**, **1076**, **1122**.

808 Cameron, Allen Barry. 'The Heroine in *The Knight's Tale.*' *Studies in Short Fiction* 5(1968), 119–27.
Emily represents man's idea of perfecting himself, his quest for harmony. She has a three-fold significance, matching the three realms of order identified by Halverson **691**. In the natural order, she is the May Queen, a figure of physical regeneration; in the social order, she represents the aristocratic ideal, as the vehicle of its preservation; and in the cosmic order, she is a representative of Fortune.

809 Champion, L.S. '*A Midsummer Night's Dream*: The Problem of Source.' *PLL* 4(1968), 13–9.
In *MND* Shakespeare adapted the *KnT* as a romantic comedy. Both works have three layers of action: the Theseus-Hyppolita relationship, framing the main action; the lovers' sufferings, at the center; and the intervention of gods or fairy gods, complicating and resolving the action. Shakespeare's most important modifications are the introduction of the rustics with their parody of the lovers, and the substitu-

tion of the relatively harmless and benign fairies for Chaucer's powerful Olympians.

810 Cherniss, Michael D. 'Chaucer's *Anelida and Arcite*: Some Conjectures.' *ChauR* 5(1970), 9–21.
Chaucer may have intended *Anel* to be a dream-vision presenting a version of the story of Arcite as in the *Tes* and the *KnT*. Arcite's betrayal of Anelida would justify his death, and his punishment would show that a just Providence rules. Anelida was apparently to pray to Mars, who would lead Arcite to his death. Chaucer may have left *Anel* unfinished because of the difficulty of keeping both the Anelida-Arcite story and the Palamon-Arcite story before the audience simultaneously and because it would have been out of character for Anelida to be consoled by retribution against Arcite (pp 17–21).

811 Clogan, Paul M. 'Chaucer and the Medieval Statius.' 1961. See **262**.
Clogan reviews (pp 60–8) Chaucer's debts to the *Theb* as listed by Skeat **625**, Wise **642**, and Robinson **751**, and confirms most of them. He identifies two new borrowings: the description of Conquest as 'in a tour' (I.2027–9), from *Theb* VII. 55–6, and the straw thrown on the funeral pyre (I.2933), from VI.56. The spellings of place names in the Statian apigraph to the *KnT* and details in I.868 and 2027 indicate a medieval (rather than a classical) Latin source, much like Magdalen College Ms 18. Clogan supports Skeat's suggestion that the 'tempest' of I.883–4 may come from *Theb* XII.650–5, but rejects his definition of 'feelds' (I.977) as a heraldic term. He also questions, on grounds of manuscript evidence, Skeat's and Robinson's view that a confusion about *bellatrices* (*Theb* VII.57, *Tes* VII.37) produced 'shippes hoppesteres' (I.2017). Chaucer's knowledge of the *Theb* goes well beyond what he could have derived from arguments to the separate books or from the kind of argument that appears in mss of *TC* (see **272**); he borrows most heavily from Book XII, often for details not found in the *Tes* or *RTh*. Clogan reviews Chaucer's debts to the *Roman* (pp 91–6) as identified by Wise and Robinson and lists one new one: 'with herte pitous' (I.953), from *Roman* 9996. Chaucer must have known the *Roman* itself or one of its prose redactions.

812 — 'Chaucer and the *Thebaid* Scholia.' 1964. See **264**.
Chaucer's probable borrowings from medieval glosses to the *Theb* include: his description of Theseus' setting out for Thebes (I.969–70); the confusion of Mount Cithaeron with the island of Cythera (1936–7); the 'Compleint' and 'Outhees' (2012) and the 'tour' (2027) of his temple of Mars; his identification of Lygurge as king of Thrace (2129); and his idea of the tree nymphs as living spirits (2925–8).

813 — 'Chaucer's Use of the "Thebaid."' *EM* 18(1967), 9–32.
Clogan traces the development of Chaucer's interest in the story of Thebes and in Statius as a narrative poet through the early short poems, *Anel*, *TC*, and *KnT*. While imitating the *Tes*, Chaucer regarded the *Theb* as the ultimate source of his *KnT*, and drew from it many details not present in Boccaccio's story: the tempest (I.883–4), the role of the eldest Argive widow, Theseus' night march to Thebes, the Minotaur on his pennon, the Duke's replacement of Emily as the one to discover the dueling lovers in the grove, and the 'veze' or blast (I.1985) associated with Mars' temple (pp 25–8).

814 Coghill, Nevill. 'Chaucer's Narrative Art in *The Canterbury Tales*.' In *Chaucer and Chaucerians: Critical Studies in Middle English Literature*. Ed. D.S. Brewer. London: Nelson; University, Alabama: University of Alabama Press, 1966. Pp 114–39.
Coghill discusses the different effects of Arcite's 'melancholy line,' as it appears in the *KnT* (I.2779) and the *MilT* (I.3204) (pp 115–6). Theme dominates in the *KnT* where each climax is followed by a great debate or speech: eg, the lovers' first sight of Emelye is followed by their argument; Arcite's release from prison, by their Boethian soliloquies. The indistinguishability of Palamon and Arcite is realistic 'since any two young men, brought up in the same strict code, cannot but wear the moral uniform of their class' (p 123). At the same time, Arcite represents chivalry, and Palamon, romantic love. Emelye represents virginity, and Chaucer may hint at a connection between Diana and Mary (p 124). Theseus, representing Boethian philosophy, asserts the reality of divine providence and the dignity of human free will (pp 124–5).

815 Corsa, Helen Storm. 'Modes of Comedy in the First Fragment.' *Chaucer: Poet of Mirth and Morality*. 1964. See **407**. Pp 73–120.
The *KnT* proclaims the existence of order through its division into four parts and through the patterning of two's in both plot and narrative details, as in the complaints of the two prisoners and the question about which suffers most. 'The answer is ... that neither has "the worse" since both have equal woe'; a second question is implied: 'which of the two will eventually have "the best"' (p 102). At the end of Part II the Knight 'rejoices in the re-establishment of rule' through the planned tournament (p 104), but the multiplicity of gods and prayers in Part III indicates that the right to Emelye's hand is not to be settled by might. In a love story the devotee of Venus should win, but more basic is 'the principle of Distributive Justice: as each prays so each receives' (p 104). This principle is born out in Part IV; and yet Arcite shares equally in bliss with Palamon because

he is released from the prison of this life. The Knight's story 'indicates his limitations, revealing simplifications about Human Nature and Reality that Chaucer, even in his earliest poems, never conceded to' (p 107). The *KnT* 'skeletalizes' Boethian philosophy, presenting in a simple way the essential vision of the *CT* (p 107). With the exception of Emelye, the characters speak alike, as 'projections' of the Knight himself: 'worthy, wise, and prudent' (p 108). The *MilT* makes the *KnT* seem 'less incredibly idealized' (p 108). The views of reality in the two tales complement each other much as do the views of the royal and common birds in *PF*. The word *quite* is the key to the First Fragment, 'unifying [the tales] dramatically, qualifying the nature of "the game" they are a part of, and joining them together as explorations of a common subject: justice, distributive and retributive' (p 109).

816 Cozart, William R. 'Chaucer's Knight's Tale: A Philosophical Re-Appraisal of a Medieval Romance.' In *Medieval Epic to the 'Epic Theater' of Brecht*. Eds. Rosario P. Armato and John M. Spalek. *University of Southern California Studies in Comparative Literature*, No. 1. Los Angeles: University of Southern California Press, 1968. Pp 25–34.

Theseus' 'First Moevere' speech, 'a conclusion in which nothing is concluded' (p 31), may reflect Chaucer's preoccupation with Nominalism. 'Although there may be an essential connection between the justice of God and the arbitrariness of human destiny, one cannot demonstrate it rationally; it is a matter of faith' (p 32).

817 Craik, T.W. *The Comic Tales of Chaucer*. London: Methuen, 1964; rpt 1967.

The *KnT* illustrates the typical mixture of comedy and tragedy in Chaucer's work. In spite of its happy ending 'what we most strongly recall ... is the force of destiny, expressing itself in the tragedy of Arcite's death' (x). Yet the poem is permeated with humour and good sense, as seen in Theseus' speech on love in the grove, which Craik compares to Pandarus' speeches to Troilus (xi).

818 David, Alfred. 'The Man of Law vs. Chaucer: A Case in Poetics.' *PMLA* 82(1967), 217–25.

The *KnT* and *MLT* address the same problem: 'reconciling destiny and divine justice' (p 222). In the *KnT* providence is presented in Boethian terms appropriate to the pagan setting and Theseus exhibits 'a stoic equivalent of the ideal of constancy' (p 222). The Christian god directly dispenses justice and grace in the *MLT* and Constance's 'feminine and passive virtue' replaces Theseus' 'masculine and chivalric virtue' (p 222). There is a 'current of pessimism' in the *KnT* but the *MLT* is gloomier still, partly because it lacks romantic coloring and partly because it draws on the *De contemptu mundi* (of Pope Inocent III, late twelfth century) instead of the *Consol* (pp 222–3).

819 Dean, Christopher. 'The "Place" in "The Knight's Tale".' *N&Q* 13[211](1966), 90–2.
In its five appearances in the *KnT* (I.2399, 2584, 2678, 2690, 2694), *place* is a technical term borrowed from medieval theatrical usage and indicating 'the grassy ground of the arena within the lists.'

820 — 'Imagery in the *Knight's Tale* and the *Miller's Tale.*' *MS* 31(1969), 149–63.
In the *KnT* imagery is concentrated in five passages: the descriptions of Emily in the garden and of Lygurge and Emetrius, Arcite's complaint in the woods, the duel, and the tournament (p 154). The largest groups of images in the *KnT* deal with emotions and abstract ideas, but in the *MilT* the largest groups deal with appearance and physical objects (pp 154–5). The animals of the *KnT* are fierce, wild, and noble; those of the *MilT* belong to the barnyard. In the *KnT* love is a serious emotion associated with images of wounding and death, paradise and hell, and fire (pp 158–9); in the *MilT*, it is a physical necessity associated with images of food and eating (p 161). A variety of images in the *KnT* – the drunken man, the fair chain of love – concern human beings' efforts to control their fates (p 160); in the *MilT*, animal imagery characterizes the expressions of their lustful natures as entirely normal (p 162).

821 Delasanta, Rodney. 'Uncommon Commonplaces in "The Knight's Tale".' *NM* 70(1969), 683–90.
Delasanta supports Frost's characterization of Palamon as the 'spokesman of the greater idealism' (**684**) by contrasting Palamon's world view with Arcite's. Arcite's speech on Fortune (I.1086–91) projects a world from which God has been banished while Palamon's address to Venus (I.1104–1111) relates human will to a divine will (pp 685–6). Arcite's 'almost anarchic disdain' for governance is seen in another way in his idea of every-man-for-himself (I.1186). In their two lamentations (I.1223 f), Arcite focuses on Fortune; Palamon, on the gods (pp 687–8). In their prayers Palamon subjects his will to Venus and Arcite emphasizes Mars' power and his own (pp 688–9). Arcite is converted to Palamon's values on his death bed. Modern readers may be attracted to Arcite's position, but 'for the medieval mind the discernible order of a hierarchical universe was preferable to [his] implicit nihilism' (pp 689–90).

822 Donaldson, E. Talbot. 'The Ending of Chaucer's *Troilus*.' In *Early English and Norse Studies Presented to Hugh Smith*. Ed. Arthur Brown and Peter Foote. London: Methuen, 1963. Pp 26–45. Rpt in *Speaking of Chaucer*. New York: Norton, 1972. Pp 84–101.
The disagreement among critics as to which of the knights suffers most and most deserves to win Emily constitutes 'a kind of protracted response to the Knight's rhetorical question' (I.1347–8) (p 31). The disagreement and the poem itself indicate that the question is wrong. 'On temperamental grounds you may prefer a man who mistakes his lady for Venus to a man who knows a woman when he sees one, or you may not; but such preference has no moral validity' (p 32). The knights are of equal worth, and the poem suggests that we must do our best in a world governed by a Providence we cannot understand. But 'this is an unpalatable moral ... unless it is as hard-won as the Knight's own battles. The experience by which the individual attains the Knight's tempered view of life is an important part of that view ... This experience must include our questioning of relative values, our desire to discover that even-handed justice does prevail in the universe, and our resistance to the conclusion that justice, so far as we can see, operates at best with only one hand' (p 32).

823 Edwards, Philip. 'On the Design of "The Two Noble Kinsmen".' *REL* 5 (no. 4) (1964), 89–105.
The *KnT* is 'a magnificent study of human helplessness' whose central image is that of the drunken man (I.1259–67) (p 93–4). Inspired by its dark vision, Shakespeare put Palamon's address to Venus (V.i.77–136) at the center of the play. Here, and through various disruptions and conflicts in relationships, Shakespeare suggests that the passage from innocence to experience, in submission to chance and one's own nature, often involves the exchange of a greater good for a lesser good. Emilia's role is central to both Tale and play (pp 102–3): Chaucer suggests the absurdity of her fate through her silence; in *TNK*, when events cause her to marry Palamon instead of Arcite, her fate mirrors that of the jailer's daughter (who accepts a pseudo-Palamon as her lover) and clinches Shakespeare's case against Venus. See **1088**.

824 Fifield, Merle. 'The "Knight's Tale": Incident, Idea, Incorporation.' *ChauR* 3(1968), 95–106.
A pattern unites the incidents in Palamon and Arcite's history, the stages in the development of Theseus' character, the subdivisions of Theseus' final speech, and the governing idea of the romance. Initially, Palamon and Arcite are victims of an irresistible Fortune, and Theseus is an irresistible conqueror. Then Palamon and Arcite

attempt individual action in their duel while Theseus becomes the fallible monarch. The tournament represents Theseus' attempt, in his new character as judge and interpreter of human customs, to impose order through corporate law. The description of the theater looks backward to the duel and forward to the tournament as it predicts the defeat of human attempts at order. This defeat is reflected in the exempla concerning mortality in Theseus' speech, while Theseus' character as monarch and judge is echoed in the fair chain of love. Taught by Palamon and Arcite's experience and his own, Theseus becomes a priest-king who defines the reign of mutability and preaches the wisdom of acceptance. See Fichte **947**.

825 Fletcher, P.C.B. 'The Role of Destiny in "The Knight's Tale".' *Theoria* 26(1966), 43–50.
Arcite's death-bed speech (I.2771–80) contains an element of personal feeling lacking in a work like the Old English 'Wanderer's Lament' (pp 43–4). The emotions of Palamon and Arcite, though stylized, help to characterize two sharply distinct individuals, making the tragedy 'at once more human and more acceptable' than it appears in Salter's interpretation emphasizing destiny (**883**), or Whittock's, emphasizing Fortune (**785**) (p 45). In their reactions to Emily, Palamon is the more impetuous lover, and Arcite, the more reasonable lover (pp 45–8). Arcite does not deserve his death, but both men are shown to be moved by destructive passions represented by the gods (p 48). Chaucer undercuts his characters' speeches on destiny, as when he introduces Palamon's speech on the cruel gods with a description of his jealousy (I.1299–1308) (p 49). Fate's rule is complete only in the realm of death; thus Arcite's fall from his horse is the only true intervention of fate (p 50).

826 Foster, Edward E. 'Humor in the "Knight's Tale".' *ChauR* 3(1968), 88–94.
The humor of the *KnT* is unconscious on the Knight's part, but is intended by Chaucer as a way of qualifying the Knight's idealism. Instances of humor include certain puns (on *queynte*, *harneys*), incongruous situations (the princes' debate, the manner of Arcite's death), and the bathetic effects of the Knight's abrupt narrative transitions and lapses from high style. The Tale combines 'the Knight's perception that the ideals are necessary, and Chaucer's that they are artificial and precarious' (p 91). Chaucer's attitude toward the Knight is one of 'admiring sympathy' (p 91), and the ultimate effect of the Tale is to strengthen our belief in the necessity of forms despite their fragility.

826a Fowler, Alastair. 'The Meaning of Chaucer's *Knight's Tale*.' 1970. See Brooks **807**.

827 Greaves, Margaret. *The Blazon of Honour*. 1964. See **414**. Pp 38–9.
Magnanimity is the ideal in the *KnT*, breached by Theseus' refusal of ransom for his prisoners. 'Tacitly he is tried and found wanting' (p 38). Palamon and Arcite's magnanimity is shown in their friendship, an experience available to noble males and unattainable by women.

828 Griffith, Richard R. 'The Knight's Tale.' *A Critical Study Guide*. 1968. See **416**. Pp 67–8.
As a story of young love, the *KnT* does not fit the Knight; as an aristocratic entertainment, it does.

829 Grose, Michael W. 'Astrology and the "Knight's Tale".' *Chaucer*. London: Evans Bros., 1967. Pp 52–7.
Events are determined, not by the gods as in Chaucer's sources, but by planetary influences. In four instances Chaucer specifies times of day associated with the influence of planets: Palamon's and Arcite's births (I.1086–90; Saturn), Palamon's escape from prison (1534–39; Mercury), the visits of Palamon, Arcite, and Emelye to the temples (2271–74 and 2367–74; Venus, Mars and Diana), and the appearance of the fury (2684–7; Saturn).

830 Haller, Robert S. 'Chaucer's *Squire's Tale* and the Uses of Rhetoric.' *MP* 62(1965), 285–95.
Haller contrasts the Squire's uses of rhetoric with the Knight's to show that Chaucer satirizes the Squire. For example, the Squire's description of Cambuskyan has no organic function, but the Knight's opening description of Theseus highlights traits of wisdom and chivalry which Theseus later exhibits (pp 286–7). The Squire's use of *occupatio*, as in the description of the feast (V.63–75), is a meaningless set piece; the Knight's is necessary to the management of a complex narrative (p 288). For the Squire, 'pitee' (V.479) is an ability to identify compassionately with a character; in the *KnT* (I.1761) pity explains the tempering of justice with mercy (p 291). The romance genre indicates that the Squire misunderstands *gentillesse*; the epic shows the Knight to be an exponent of the noble life. 'The *Knight's Tale* is the only one in which the high style is married to a truly noble subject' (p 295).

831 — 'The *Knight's Tale* and the Epic Tradition.' *ChauR* 1(1966), 67–84.
For Chaucer the classical epic was the only genre that could adequately define the noble life in relation to principles of order in society and the cosmos. Chaucer eliminates superficially epic elements from the *Tes*, but borrows an epic subject from the *Theb* (p 68). The

rivalry of Palamon and Arcite over Emily parallels the struggle of Polynices and Eteocles over the throne of Thebes (p 68). The connection is suggested in early speeches of Palamon (I.1104–11) and Arcite (1181–2), but in their laments (1328–33 and 1543–62), they blame Juno for the Theban disasters and fail to see their own responsibility (pp 71–3). The narrator's observation that love and lordship are alike in tolerating no fellowship (I.1623–7) sums up the Tale's central concern. 'What Arcite and Palamon discover about love Polynices and Eteocles had discovered about lordship' (p 74). Principally through Theseus, who becomes less tyrannical (p 82) as the Tale progresses, Chaucer suggests new definitions of love and lordship which incorporate fellowship and show the essential unity of values in the private and public spheres of the noble life. See **934**.

832 Hargest-Gorzelak, Anna. 'A Brief Comparison of the *Knight's Tale* and *Sir Gawain and the Green Knight*.' *Roczniki Humanistyczne* 15(1967), 91–102.
The *KnT* is rhetorically brilliant but confused and confusing in its signification (pp 92–5). The difficulty is not inherent in romance, since *SGGK* displays subtle characterization, greater plausibility of action, equal rhetorical skill, and a more organic use of parallelism. A comparison of the descriptions of the theater (I.1880–1913) and of Bercelak's castle (764–802) shows that in the *KnT*, Chaucer is dominated by his form, and that in *SGGK*, the poet dominates the form (p 101).

833 Harrington, David. 'Rhetoric and Meaning in Chaucer's *Knight's Tale*.' *PLL* 3(1967), 71–9.
Harrington revives Hulbert's thesis (**578**) that the *KnT* is essentially a *demande d'amour*, though one Chaucer has enriched by giving love a cosmic, Boethian sense. Rhetorical questions, balanced elements, and formal transitions keep Palamon and Arcite and their merits before the audience. The use of *occupatio*, as in the treatment of the war against Thebes, keeps Theseus in the background. The elaborate use of *effictio*, and of devices of alliteration, *anaphora*, and figurative language, in the treatment of the tournament keeps the princes, the *demande*, and the theme of Boethian order at the center of the Tale. Theseus' final speech balances Arcite's merits against Palamon's merits, and leads the audience to accept the solution to the *demande* on both practical and philosophical levels.

833a Henderson, Arnold C. *Chaucer and Augustan Scholarship*. 1970.
See Alderson **793**.

834 Herz, Judith Scherer. 'Chaucer's Elegiac Knight.' *Criticism* 6(1964), 212–24.

The 'insistent' realism that the Knight introduces from his own experience conflicts with the 'lyrical and artificial structure of romance' (p 213). The same duality characterizes Froissart's *Chronicles* **183**, which celebrate the pride, gestures, and heroic deeds of chivalry while simultaneously reporting the cruelty and business-like calculation (pp 215–8). Froissart's silence about this duality is not hypocritical: rather he is guided by what Huizinga **188** calls an 'historical ideal of life,' an exalted image that controls what he sees and how he sees it (p 218). In the *KnT* Arcite presents the fullest portrait of the ideal knight (p 220): he wins a martial victory, is devoted to serving his lady even beyond death, senses the instability of the world and preaches fortitude, and makes his final renunciation in terms of the moral implications of chivalry. Yet the Tale shows that events are determined by the gods. The Knight is an elegiac figure like Froissart, who sees selectively, who emphasizes the pageantry of chivalry, and whose philosophic limitations are represented by Egeus' platitudes, which probably seem as valid to him as Theseus' conclusions (pp 221–2). Chaucer sees more than the Knight (p 223), yet he too is unable to achieve a unified vision, for much of the action of the poem is at odds with its Boethian philosophy.

835 Hill, Boyd H., Jr. 'The Grain and the Spirit in Mediaeval Anatomy.' *Spec* 40(1965), 63–73.
Ancient and medieval traditions placed in the human heart the *spiritus*, a term having a range of meanings from 'breath' to 'soul.' Arcite's reference to the 'woful spirit in myn herte' (I.2765) probably ought to be taken literally. The 'hous' that Arcite's spirit has left (I. 2809) may be the heart (p 73).

836 Hoffman, Richard L. 'The *Felaweshipe* of Chaucer's *Love* and *Lordshipe*.' *Classica et Mediaevalia* 25(1964), 263–73. Rpt in *Ovid and the Canterbury Tales* (**839**). Pp 63–7.
The proverb of I.1625–6 is probably drawn from *Tes* V.13.7–8, but *Ars Amatoria* III.564 may also be a source. Hoffman distinguishes two traditions confused by Skeat **625** and diagrammed here in a chart (pp 263–7 and p 273). One, traced to *Met* II.846–7, contrasts love and *maiestas*; the other, traced to *Ars Amatoria* III.564, compares love and rule as both rejecting competition. Hinckley **576** and Robinson **751** mistranslate I.1625–6 as meaning that Love itself, rather than a lover, will tolerate no rival (pp 270–1).

837 — 'Mercury, Argus, and Chaucer's Arcite: "Canterbury Tales" I(A)1384–90.' *N&Q* 12[210](1965), 128–9. Rpt in *Ovid and the Canterbury Tales* (**839**). Pp 61–3.

Chaucer's statement that Mercury appears to Arcite 'As he was when that Argus took his sleep' indicates both Chaucer's direct indebtedness to Ovid's *Met*, I.671–2 and the meaning of the passage. Like Argus, Arcite is persuaded by the deceitful words of the god of eloquence and is consequently led to his death. See **908**, **1039**.

838 — 'Ovid and Chaucer's Myth of Theseus and Pirithous.' *ELN* 2(1965), 252–7. Rpt in *Ovid and the Canterbury Tales* (**839**). Pp 52–6.

Chaucer's reference to the friendship of Theseus and Pirithous (I.1196–1201) may be indebted to three passages in Ovid's *Tristia* (I.v.19–20 and ix.31–2) and *Ex Ponto* (II.iii.43), and possibly to Alanus' *Anticlaudianus* (II.188–90). Chaucer apparently misinterpreted them to mean that Theseus went to Hades to rescue Pirithous, as in *RR* (8148–54). In the *Ovide moralisé* and in Berchorius' commentary on *Met* VIII, Pirithous originated a plan to rescue Proserpina from hell and convinced Theseus to help him.

839 — 'Knight's Tale.' *Ovid and the Canterbury Tales*. Philadelphia: University of Pennsylvania Press, 1967. Pp 39–113.

The *KnT* shows more debts to Ovid than any other tale (p 39). Hoffman comments on twenty-two separate passages, finding clear evidence of indebtedness in fifteen. 1) I.865–66 (pp 41–8): Theseus' conquest of 'Femenye' is related to a literary convention traceable to Ovid and his commentators: 'the regular identification of manliness with moral virtue ... with fidelity ... wisdom, and authority; and the concomitant association of effeminacy with vice ... unfaithfulness, foolishness, and weakness' (p 45). For fuller treatment, see **841**. 2) I.978–80 (pp 49–50): The Minotaur reflects Chaucer's reading of *Met* XII.665–74. 3) I.1191–1201 (pp 52–6): For sources of the allusion to Pirithous, see **838**. 4) I.1299–1302 (p 56): The comparison of Palamon's complexion to the boxtree is indebted to *Met* IV.134–5 and XI.417–8. 5) I.1384–90 (pp 61–3): For Chaucer's treatment of Mercury, see **837**. 6) I.1625–6 (pp 63–7): For the proverb on love and lordship, see **836**. 7) I.1761 (pp 68–71): Chaucer's often repeated line on 'pitee' is traced to *Tristia* III.v.31–2. 8) I.1940–1 (pp 71–82): The figure of Idleness in Venus' temple can be traced through Boccaccio's '*Ozio*' and Guillaume de Lorris' '*Oiseuse*' to Ovid's '*otia*' in *Remedia Amoris* 139; the story of Narcissus, from both Guillaume's *RR* 1439–1506 and from *Met* III.339–510. 9–12) Four of the myths that adorn Diana's temple are drawn from Ovid: Callisto, I.2056–61 (pp 82–5); Daphne, I.2062–4 (pp 85–7); Actaeon, I.2065–8 (pp 87–8); and Atalanta, I.2069–72 (pp 88–89). 13) I.2233–7 (pp 90–3): Palamon's war with chastity recalls the *miles amoris*, developed in

Ovid's *Amores* and *Ars Amatoria.* 14) I.2383–92 (pp 96–9): Arcite's reference to the love of Venus and Mars is probably indebted to *Ars Amatoria* II.561–92 and *Met* IV.171–89, among other texts. 15) I.2626–9 (pp 98–9): The image of the tigress and her whelp is drawn from *Met* III.155–6. Hoffman's text and notes are full of valuable information on sources and meanings even where no indebtedness to Ovid can be established. See **937**.

840 — 'Two Notes on Chaucer's Arcite.' *ELN* 4(1967), 172–5.
Arcite's duties as Emelye's page recall *Joshua* ix: 21, 23, and 27. Theseus parallels Joshua; the Thebans, the Gibeonites; and the Athenians, the Israelites. Arcite's promise (I.2407–18) to sacrifice his beard and hair to Mars suggests that Arcite will lose his life for Emelye as Samson lost his through Delilah, and explains Saturn's reference (I.2466) to Samson.

841 — '*The Canterbury Tales.*' In *Critical Approaches to Six Major English Works: Beowulf through Paradise Lost.* Ed. R.M. Lumiansky and Herschel Baker. Philadelphia: University of Pennsylvania Press, 1968; London: Oxford University Press, 1969. Pp 41–80.
In a tradition derived from Ovid's invocation to Venus in *Fasti* IV.1, celestial Venus is associated with honorable love, *mundana musica*, and divine love, as in Theseus' speech on the 'faire cheyne of love,' and infernal Venus is associated with fornication, sensual music, and original sin, as in the paintings in her temple (pp 56–7). Theseus' role stems from a tradition established by Ovid's treatment of Hercules in *Met* IX: 'the regular identification of manliness with moral virtue ... and ... of effeminacy with vice' (p 64). This dichotomy is reflected in 'several pairs of coordinates' (p 65) in the Tale: wisdom vs. the 'regne of Femenye'; Theseus vs. Hyppolita; Athenians vs. Amazons; Athens vs. Thebes; Theseus vs. Palamon-Arcite. Theseus' conquest of Hyppolita and their marriage represents the rational subordination of woman to man, of flesh to spirit, of concupiscent appetite to reason (pp 65–6). Palamon and Arcite, 'already subject to the "regne of Femenye" within themselves ... surrender easily to a woman' (p 68). The marriage of Palamon and Emelye is the 'proper remedy' to the problem, and Theseus presides over it 'almost as a priest would' (p 68).

842 Howard, Donald R. 'Chaucer the Man.' *PMLA* 80 (1965), 337–43. Rpt. in *Chaucer's Mind and Art.* Ed. A. C. Cawley. London: Oliver and Boyd, 1969; New York: Barnes & Noble, 1970. Pp 31–45.
To exemplify the difficulty of determining Chaucer's own perspective (pp 42–3), Howard cites I.1457–64, on Palamon's martyrdom: is the

Tale or the Knight or Chaucer himself the butt of the joke? A similar mystery is presented by the echoes of the *KnT* in the *MilT*.

843 Howard, Edwin J. *Geoffrey Chaucer*. 1964. See **420**.
Howard reviews the possibilities of the Tale's having been previously published and revised for the *CT*, and provides a plot summary. As a 'dignified story of courtly love,' the *KnT* makes an appropriate opening for the *CT* (p 126). In presenting 'completely unindividualized characters' (p 128), Chaucer's purpose was to show that 'the forces which shape human destiny are outside the individual' (p 130).

844 Huppé, Bernard F. '*The Knight's Tale.*' *A Reading of the 'Canterbury Tales.'* 1964. See **421**. Pp 49–74.
After reviewing problems in interpreting the *KnT*, particularly its combination of Boethian philosophy and rhetorical 'sinking' (pp 49–54), Huppé characterizes the Tale as 'high comedy,' in which laughter is 'a tool by which to reveal human folly and thus to show how it may be avoided' (p 54). The Knight intends to instruct the Squire: 'to lead him from courtly folly back to an ideal of Christian chivalry' (p 54). Theseus is a stand-in for the Knight, an exemplar of chivalric responsibility and a minister of God's Providence; Palamon and Arcite are stand-ins for the Squire and represent all those who become victims of Fate by seeking the false gifts of changeable Fortune (pp 58–67). Theseus' apostrophe to Cupid (I.1785–1814) sums up the older man's 'kindly humor' toward the younger men (pp 66–8). The tournament and its aftermath 'reveal the working out of Theseus' design for peace in a world of confusion ... Arcite's death is beyond his human control; it is a *fatal* event, made comprehensible only in the Great Design, which no mere man can grasp, and of which Theseus' plan is but an emblem' (p 67). Huppé emphasizes comic elements in the prayers (pp 68–71) and in Arcite's dying speech (pp 71–3). 'Comic comprehension' allows us to see 'the rhetoric of romantic grief as illusory, wrong, incongruous' (p 72); Egeus' speech answers Arcite's dying questions. The end is comic because peace has been established, Arcite has achieved what he sought, and Palamon has acquired a wife and the insight that chivalric virtue should be exercised in the service of duty, not a woman – of charity, not *amor* (p 74). See pp 85–8: The Miller does not understand the philosophical import of the *KnT* and finds it unrealistic, particularly in the passive role it assigns to women; Alison chooses her lover. See **798, 887, 1013, 1014.**

845 James, Max. 'Submission to Faithful Providence: *The Knight's Tale.*' 'Pre-Chaucerian and Chaucerian Concern with Providence: The Question of Providence Examined in Representative Theologians and

Poets before Chaucer and as a Major Preoccupation in Chaucer's Poetry.' Claremont Graduate School Dissertation, 1966. Pp 238–62. See also *DAI* 29(1968), 604A.

Chaucer uses astrology to define a kind of 'subpredestination' for his characters: that is, Nature endows each person with a disposition which, in each act of choice, he may affirm or deny, and the temples of the god-planets reveal, not the nature of the divine as Salter **883** takes it, but the characters of the gods' devotees. The sinister aspects of the gods and the stars derive from the common medieval identification of both as demonic powers. Only a divine providence is able to overcome the effects of both human passion and demonic activity to bring good out of evil. Theseus' advice, to submit to providence without rebellion, is also Chaucer's.

846 Jordan, Robert M. 'The Knight's Tale: Nobility in Theseus' World and Chaucer's Art.' *Chaucer and the Shape of Creation: The Aesthetic Possibilities of Inorganic Structure*. Cambridge, Mass.: Harvard University Press, 1967. Pp 152–84.

The formality and symmetry of the *KnT* imply a celebration of rationality as a force in human affairs and in the cosmic order as seen in the first encounter of Palamon and Arcite in the grove (pp 154–6). The two princes set out their charges against each other in balanced speeches (I.1580–1660), and combine chivalry and passion in a 'tense equilibrium' (p 155). Theseus' transformation of the duel into a tournament publicly affirms the ideals enacted by Palamon and Arcite. The accident of Arcite's death occasions the exploration of the idea of order in Theseus' final speech, which advocates 'submission to the perfect harmony of the universe' (p 157). Underwood's assertion (**776**) that the poem itself is Chaucer's image of divine order cannot be demonstrated by analysis of the fictional world but only by analysis of the narrative structure, and such analysis elucidates Muscatine's observation (**726**) of a tension between structure and surface narrative (pp 158–60). Parts I and II are characterized by movement among spatially separated protagonists whose narrative paths converge at especially significant moments. The moment when Palamon first sees Emily, created by the convergence of the independent scenes of Emily in the garden and of the princes in the tower, is both 'an emotional occasion within the fiction, which we experience vicariously' and 'an aesthetic occasion entailing a structural impact, which we experience directly' (p 163). The narrative of Theseus' arrival in the grove supports his role as 'the center of all forces in the world of the tale' (p 165). First, two separate lines of narration bring Palamon and Arcite together, dramatizing the power of chance.

Then the lines on destiny (I.1663–72) emphasize the climactic importance of Theseus' arrival. In line 1673, 'This' may refer backwards or forwards, but links Theseus with destiny 'if only by collocation of the two passages' (p 170). The account of the royal hunt, carried on in ignorance of the bloody duel, prepares for the 'startling yet satisfying convergence' of the two lines of narration (p 171). Description of the emblematic tournament then replaces the narrative of action. The two halves of the poem are not integrated, no reasons being established in Parts I and II for the alignment of the characters with their respective divinities; but the two halves are congruent, both serving 'to exalt man's capacity for noble action' (p 172–3). The treatment of the theater (pp 173–8) draws on Gothic principles of structure, presenting a general view followed by a scholastic analysis of parts. The *KnT* is unique in being about the human capacity to construct as well as being itself exemplary of it (p 178). Chaucer's changes of tone do not serve to characterize the principals or the Knight-teller, but signal Chaucer's reservations about human nobility and call attention to the limits of fiction (pp 180–3). See **916, 970.**

- Stephen T. Knight, 'Some Aspects of Structure in Medieval Literature,' *Parergon* 16(1976), 3–17: Jordan's analysis of the Gothic structure of the *KnT* is 'the only convincing critical account' of the Tale's varied tonalities.

847 Joseph, Gerhard. 'Chaucerian "Game" – "Ernest" and the "Argument of Herbergage" in *The Canterbury Tales.*' *ChauR* 5(1970), 83–96.
The *KnT* and other tales inspired by 'ernest' involve a conception of space, the 'herbergage' (I.4329) or 'lodging of this world,' as a prison from which to escape, while the *MilT*, *RvT*, *CkT*, and other tales told in 'game' advance a conception of space as a joyful enclosure designed for unrestrained play (p 83). In the *KnT* there is a progression from smaller enclosures to larger ones and from shorter to longer intervals of time between events. This expansion is due in part to Theseus' deliberate attempts to order experience by ritualizing it. Theseus' ultimate conception of enclosure as an ordered cosmos does not wholly triumph over the Knight-narrator's apparent conception of the whole world as a prison (pp 84–8).

848 Keen, Maurice. 'Brotherhood in Arms.' *History* 47(1962), 1–17.
'As his cousin, Arcite ... might have been Palamon's rival in love without disparagement; as his brother-in-arms he could not be' (p 2). Keen defines the rites and obligations of brotherhood-in-arms, comparing it to other chivalric, feudal, and kinship ties. When Palamon speaks of a sworn bond (I.1131–4), he may be referring to

the solemn oath and exchange of sealed letters which normally established the relationship (p 5). Obligations of the bond included contributing to each other's ransoms, prosecuting each other's just quarrels, and giving counsel and sharing confidences. These obligations were limited by the requirements of one's honor and by duties to blood kin and to one's lord. Arcite may be referring to these limitations (p 11) when he defies the bond Palamon has cited (I.1604–5).

849 Kreisler, Nicolai von. 'A Recurrent Expression of Devotion in Chaucer's *Book of the Duchess, Parliament of Fowls,* and *Knight's Tale.*' *MP* 68(1970), 62–4.
Theseus' characterization of Palamon's service to Emily, 'with wille[,] herte, and myght' (I.3078) echoes phrases in *BD* 116 and 768 and in *PF* 417, and may be indebted to *Matthew* 22:37 and *Mark* 12:30. The term 'myght' occurs only in the *KnT*, where the lover fights for the lady, and the biblical allusion may suggest the 'spiritual intensity' of Palamon's love (p 64).

850 Lanham, Richard A. 'Game, Play, and High Seriousness in Chaucer's Poetry.' *ES* 48(1967), 1–24. Rpt in *The Motives of Eloquence*. New Haven: Yale University Press, 1976. Pp 65–81.
Chaucer studies character with the ambivalence appropriate to watching or playing a game, not with Arnoldian 'high seriousness.' He does not, like Theseus (I.1789–1810), dismiss Palamon and Arcite's contest over possession of Emily as inherently ridiculous. Nor does he ask whether it is right or wrong, or which is the more worthy of Emily. Rather he shows that as a zero-sum game – one in which one party's gain is the other's loss – the contest must lead to bitterness and frustration (pp 11–3).

851 Loomis, Dorothy Bethurum. 'Saturn in Chaucer's "Knight's Tale".' In *Chaucer und Seine Zeit: Symposion für Walter F. Schirmer*. Ed. Arno Esch. Tübingen: Max Niemeyer, 1968. Pp 149–61.
Chaucer's Saturn may be based on Bernardus Sylvestris' Saturn in his *De Universitate Mundi*, I.v.45–75. There the planet presides over a frigid sphere in which he devours his children and mows down all living things with his scythe. But he is also revered as the father of time and his cruelties are absorbed into a vision of a perfectly ordered cosmos (pp 150–5). Chaucer was acquainted with astrological works that treated Saturn's negative influences, and with the moralizing tradition of Fulgentius and Mythographus III which treated Saturn as a god of heavenly wisdom (pp 155–8). The narrator's introduction of Saturn (I.2443–52) refers to this latter tradition, and Saturn's own description of his powers (2454–69)

accords with the former. The Chaucerian gods are majestic but not benign, and Egeus' and Theseus' speeches cannot drown out Arcite's 'bitter cry' [citing I.2777–9] (p 161). Chaucer's acceptance of destiny's decrees 'is of a Providence which awards more sorrow than joy, and it remains mere submission without even Boethius' consolation' (p 161). See **955**.

852 — 'Chaucer and Shakespeare.' In *The Mind and Art of Chaucer*. Ed. A.C. Cawley. London: Oliver and Boyd, 1969; New York: Barnes & Noble, 1970. Pp 166–90.
The excellence of the *KnT* depends on its long descriptions and cannot be reproduced in drama. The *TNK* is less concerned with aristocratic life and more concerned with love: eg, Theseus enters in his wedding procession, not on his return from Scythia. The weakness of its plot is that Fortune and the planets have lost their power; Arcite dies simply because he rides a poorly trained horse. Shakespeare's characters are more realistic than Chaucer's: Emilia is more responsive to the lovers than Emelye; Palamon and Arcite become Jacobean courtiers who express un-Chaucerian attitudes toward love and war. A simplified Theseus shows little of the pity, honor, magnanimity, or ironic awareness of Chaucer's Duke.

853 — 'The Venus of Alanus de Insulis and the Venus of Chaucer.' In *Philological Essays: Studies in Old and Middle English Language and Literature in Honour of Herbert Dean Meritt*. Ed. James L. Rosier. The Hague: Mouton, 1970. Pp 182–95.
Loomis traces the influence on Chaucer of Alanus' characterization of Venus as Nature's deputy in carrying out the divine work of creation. Drawing on this inspiration, on the morally neutral description of Venus in the *De deorum imaginibus libellus*, and on the late medieval habit of astrologizing the classical gods (Curry **543**), Chaucer made the Venus of the *KnT* a much more powerful figure than the goddess of the *Tes*.

854 Loomis, Roger Sherman. 'The Knight's Tale.' *A Mirror of Chaucer's World*. 1965. See **426**.
Figures 119–27 present nine miniatures and drawings with these titles and line references: 'The Same Death to Man and Beast' (A.[I].1309); 'Venus, Cupid, and the Three Graces' (1955–8, 1962–6); 'Puella and Rubeus,' two figures (2043–5); 'Alaunts' (2148–52); 'Diana' (2346 f); 'Knight's Jousting' (2602 f); 'A Tournament' (2604–13); and 'The Four Elements' (2987–94).

855 Maclaine, Allan H. '*The Knight's Tale*.' *Student's Comprehensive Guide*. 1964. See **427**. Pp 43–62.

The tale is divided into twenty narrative units represented by brief plot summaries with selective glosses and notes.

856 Magoun, Francis P., Jr. *A Chaucer Gazeteer*. 1961. See **428**.
See entries for Arcadye, Amazones, Athens, Cithero, Crete, Femenye, Galgopheye, Greece, Helle, Scithia, Theban, Thebes, and Trace.

857 Mahoney, John F. 'Chaucerian Tragedy and the Christian Tradition.' *AnM* 3(1962), 81–99.
Theseus, like the Man of Law, is an interpreter of Fortune. Both counsel resignation, the one in his final speech, the other in his didactic digressions (pp 86–8). The *KnT* has the structure of a Greek tragedy. Fortune, justice, and Providence are ultimately the same thing, and the merits of Palamon and Arcite are irrelevant (p 91). Theseus functions like the Greek Chorus, at once an agent in the action and a commentator on it whose final speech is addressed to Palamon, to the Knight's fellow-pilgrims, and to Chaucer's audience (pp 92–3). But Theseus' attitude toward Fortune also amounts to an acceptance of the post-lapsarian state, and Chaucer's Christian audience would have automatically completed the analysis by adverting to the redemptive action of the Second Adam (pp 93–4).

858 Markland, Murray F. 'The Order of the *Knight's Tale* and *The Tempest*.' *Research Studies* 33(1965), 1–10.
Chaucer's and Shakespeare's different conceptions of man's responsibility under God can be seen in the careers of Theseus and Prospero, the characters 'most responsible for the initial disorder and the final order' (p 2) in the *KnT* and *The Tempest*, respectively. Theseus begins with a blind confidence in his ability to govern, as seen particularly in his destruction of Thebes; he ends 'in humility [accepting] things as they are, as they have been ordained,' with sadness and resignation (p 6). Prospero begins by neglecting rule, by attempting to lead a life of pure intellect and spirit; he ends by reestablishing the proper balance, choosing to exercise responsibility in the actual world with confidence and determination. In Chaucer's medieval view, 'man must find and accept God's order'; in Shakespeare's renaissance view, 'within God's order man must create his own order' (p 9).

859 Masui, Michio. *The Structure of Chaucer's Rime Words: An Exploration into the Poetical Language of Chaucer*. Tokyo: Kenkyusha, 1964.
Chaucer uses rime-breaking, often accompanied by a distinct change of subject or tone, thirty-two times in the 2250 lines of the *KnT*, apparently to avoid monotony in a long narrative (pp 220–2). The expression 'dwellen in prisoun/ Perpetuelly' is used three times in Parts I and II (I.1022–4, 1175–6, and 1457–8) and once with a

variation (1341–2). The enjambment, the p-p alliteration, and the positioning of 'perpetuelly' at the beginning of a line combine to express effectively the doomed situation of Palamon and Arcite (p 282).

859a Matthews, William. 'The Spiritual Purpose of the Canterbury Tales.' 1970.
See Woo **900**.

860 McCall, John P. 'Chaucer's May 3.' *MLN* 76(1961), 201–5.
The common denominator in Chaucer's uses of the date May 3 in the *KnT* (I.1462 f), the *NPT* (VII.3187 f) and *TC* (II.55–63) is that the promptings of carnal love are felt keenly on this day. Chaucer took the idea from Ovid's *Fasti*, IV.943–8 and V.183–378, where the day is identified as the feast of the goddess Flora, in whose festivities prostitutes played a prominent part.

861 McKenzie, James J. 'Chaucer's *The Knight's Tale*, 1053.' *Expl* 20(1962), No. 69.
The line has been understood in two ways by translators: either to mean that Emily first gathers white flowers and then red ones, or that she gathers flowers which are both white and red. *LGW* F 42–3 supports the latter translation and identifies the flowers as daisies.

862 Meier, T.K. 'Chaucer's Knight as "Persona": Narration as Control.' *EM* 20(1969), 11–21.
In using *occupatio*, the Knight describes only briefly actions that he anticipates at great length: the battle with Creon (5 lines), the duel (14), the tournament (57), the wedding (5) (pp 14–5). This behavior reveals a 'profound pessimism, a sense of the inconsequence of all action' (p 15). At one level the narrative progresses from disorder to order: the battle against Thebes and the unburied dead are replaced by the tournament and Arcite's funeral; Palamon and Arcite break their vows of brotherhood but are reconciled. At a deeper level, the narrative supplies reasons for the progressive dejection of the Knight: Palamon and Arcite are sometimes ignoble, Theseus is ineffectual, the heavens and their gods are disorderly (p 18). The Knight's humor, as in the *demande d'amour* and the description of Arcite's death, deals continually with suffering (pp 16–8). The Tale is not tragic but only pathetic, since the characters' sufferings are not disproportionate to their circumstances, and basic social and religious duties are reasserted. 'While the Knight's view is pessimistic, his stance is stoic; he accepts the natural order of things, but he expects very little from it' (p 20).

863 Middleton, Anne. 'The Modern Art of Fortifying: *Palamon and Arcite* as Epicurean Epic.' *ChauR* 3(1968), 124–43.

In turning the *KnT* into an epic, Dryden eliminated the narrator and the mix of high and low styles, and 'fortified' Chaucer's treatment of 'Love' and 'Arms' through the art of dramatic pictorialism. For example, Dryden's Emily is a conscious, purposive figure who acts in a defined time and space; Chaucer's Emelye is the generic lady of romance and a symbol of man's desires (pp 127–9). Chaucer's Palamon and Arcite are 'puppets of the narrator,' himself perhaps 'the most sensitively drawn character' in the *KnT* (pp 129–30). Dryden's hero is Palamon, loyal servant of love and pious Royalist like the Duke of Ormond; his Arcite is warlike, possibly rebellious, and reminiscent of the demagogue Monmouth (pp 130–1). Chaucer's gods and figures on the temple walls are allegorically significant; Dryden's become human beings acting in time and space, as seen in his treatment of Chaucer's 'smylere' (I.1999; pp 131–3). Chaucer's Saturn represents mortality itself but Dryden's is 'a classical deity with a grudge' (p 133). The tournament, a 'refined game' in the *KnT* (p 134), becomes a war of epic proportions in Dryden (p 135). When Arcite is injured, Dryden's epic begins to fail and the wisdom of Chaucer's method is revealed. Chaucer's narrator refuses to treat the subjects of romance with high seriousness and passes the work of interpreting them to the audience (p 138). Having fortified the romance elements, Dryden extricates himself by means that are 'surprisingly anti-Christian and anti-heroic' (p 139). Arcite's death-bed speech becomes an 'Epicurean lament over the tragic annihilation of the senses' (p 141), and Theseus' speech, an Epicurean celebration of eternal matter and an injunction to enjoy life while we may (pp 141–2).

864 Miller, Robert P. 'The *Miller's Tale* as Complaint.' *ChauR* 5 (1970), 147–60.

The *MilT* is a complaint against the four estates of knights, clergy, workers, and woman, presented from the Miller's 'anti-authoritarian point of view' (p 147). The Miller may be an anti-chivalric 'grotesque,' as indicated by his wrestling (I. 547–8), poor horse-manship (I.3120–3), and bad manners (pp 149–50). Prevented by ignorance from addressing the legitimate functions of the aristocracy, he attacks its superficial mannerisms in courtship (pp 150–3). His comment on Alisoun's suitability as lover for both lord and yeoman (3269–70) exposes his resentment of upper class privilege, and the misplaced kiss is meant to show that manners are a disguise for the physical urge that reveals the equality of all men.

865 Miner, Earl. 'Chaucer in Dryden's Fables.' In *Studies in Criticism and Aesthetics, 1660-1800: Essays in Honor of Samuel Holt Monk*. Ed.

Howard Anderson and John S. Shea. Minneapolis: University of Minnesota Press, 1967. Pp 58–72.
Dryden divides the *KnT* into three parts, the first ending with Arcite's term of service to Theseus and the second, with Palamon and Arcite's return to Thebes to recruit followers for the tournament. 'The refashioning gives a much clearer narrative line' (p 68). Dryden's epic conception led him to express an even greater concern for Fortune than Chaucer, and to depict the gods as more active and less allegorical. Dryden's Theseus is both more cruel and more philosophical. 'Arcite is a cunning, valiant Achilles ... Palamon is a more sensitive, moral Hector' (p 69). Dryden's treatment of Arcite's dying speech is less moving than Chaucer's, but his version of Theseus' final speech affirms 'a continuous beneficence of divine purpose' while Chaucer strikes a *contemptus mundi* theme. In Dryden the Stoicism of Theseus' speech has the tone of Renaissance Christian humanism and a 'Vergilian sense of the epic life' (pp 70–1).

866 Mogan, Joseph., Jr. '*The Knight's Tale.*' *Chaucer and the Theme of Mutability*. The Hague: Mouton, 1969. Pp 145–60.
Palamon and Arcite's Boethian speeches (I.1251–74 and 1303–33) highlight the mutability theme, emphasizing man's mortality and inability to control his own destiny (pp 149–50). The up's and down's of the love story provide a cautionary example of life's vicissitudes, and the concept of a destinal force is repeatedly but unsatisfactorily invoked to explain them (pp 151–5). The threat that mutability poses to human happiness receives climactic expression in Arcite's deathbed speech (p 155). Egeus replies to Arcite's questions in the spirit of the *contemptus mundi* motif (pp 155–7); Theseus asserts that there is a purposeful divine plan, and not just a blind destiny. His speech makes convincing both the hope he expresses for a perfect joy and the Knight's claim that Palamon and Emily enjoyed wedded bliss (pp 158–60).

867 Moorman, Charles. 'The Philosophical Knights of *The Canterbury Tales.*' 1965. See **430**.
The Knight is interested in the Boethian issues of free will and predestination, chance and providence, as they relate specifically to courtly love. Palamon and Arcite 'may be propelled on their way to self-knowledge by a Boethian *fortuna*, but their actions are primarily guided by the dictates of *fin amor*, which clearly run opposed to those of reason' (p 96). Theseus' speech in the grove shows that 'cas' is an agent of the God of Love, and his final speech presents both love and fortune as 'unaccountable, unknowable, unpredictable' (p 97). His advice, to make a virtue of necessity, is 'a thoroughly Boethian

conclusion to the whole problem' (p 97). The *KnT* presents 'a new kind of hero, the questioning, searching, philosophical knight' (p 97). See **208**.

868 Mulvey, Mina. *The Canterbury Tales: Analytic Notes and Review*. New York: American R.D.M. Corp., 1965.
The *KnT* (pp 24–30) 'focuses on the question of how man can live in an unstable world governed by chance' (p 25). Theseus provides a 'stock answer' and Chaucer, 'insight into the problem of human beings subjected to the inexorable decrees of fate' (p 25).

869 Muscatine, Charles. '*The Canterbury Tales*: Style of the Man and Style of the Work.' In *Chaucer and Chaucerians: Critical Studies in Middle English Literature*. Ed. D.S. Brewer. London: Nelson; University of Alabama Press, 1966. Pp 88–113.
Muscatine defines 'the style of the man' by surveying Chaucer's favorite stylistic devices, with frequent reference to the *KnT*: eg, inconsistency of perspective (I.2671–5, confusion of the tournament spectators with the pilgrim audience); use of portraits (Lygurge and Emetrius); extended use of description in support of theme and plot (eg, 1491–6, the coming of dawn; 1987–2000, the door of Mars' temple); exploration of sound and rhythm (2607–13, the alliterative description of the tournament); formal rhetoric, especially in apostrophes or invocations (2771–9, Arcite's death-bed speech). The 'style of the work' is the conventional, non-representational style common to the *KnT*, *SqT*, *FranT*, and *MLT* (pp 104–5).

870 Nakatani, Kiichiro. 'A Perpetual Prison: The Design of Chaucer's *The Knight's Tale*.' *Hiroshima Studies in English Language and Literature* 9(1962), 75–89.
Both Chaucer's detachment in referring to Arcite's dying (I.2758–61) and the fate of his soul (2809–12), and the poet's mixing of high and low styles reflect an 'attitude half-transcendental to the human world' (p 78), a vantage-point from which Chaucer looks down on the earth and up to the heavens. Chaucer places 'the love tragedy in [a] comic frame' (p 81) by introducing the gods and by using Emelye as a link to the gods, one who in a passive but positive way accepts their decrees (pp 79–84). The Tale's repeated characterization of life as a prison reflects Chaucer's macrocosmic perspective (pp 84–8). Human life is painful, but also sometimes joyful, and not tragic. Chaucer's detachment is not cold; he 'never deserts Arcite, but watches warm-heartedly over him' (p 89).

871 Neuse, Richard. 'The Knight: The First Mover in Chaucer's Human Comedy.' 1962. See **431**.

The Knight's vision is different from and superior to Theseus'. 'The Knight's approach is basically comic and ironic. We see him in an unbuttoned, holiday mood' (p 300). He places chivalry and courtly love in an epic context whose paganism is a source of comedy. The quarrels of the gods, who represent both things-as-they-are and human appetites, are as absurd as the conflicts of the humans. Theseus is the 'brilliant political opportunist' (p 306), only briefly baffled by Arcite's death, who quickly returns to 'politics as usual' (p 305). In his oration, the chain of love, 'divorced from its relevance to human beings, ... assumes the scientific neutrality of gravitational force' (p 305). The image of Jupiter (I.3037) leads not to spiritual vision but to the tyrant's plea (3042) (p 305). Thus 'the geometric design of the Knight's Tale functions more as a comic "mechanism" than as a means for expressing a concept of order' (p 306). Theseus' taking pity on the lovers arises from 'a judicious blend of motives' including reasons of state and comical appreciation of love's irrationality (p 306). His actions are governed by a will to power summed up in his god-like pose at the window. All the characters are driven by appetite, and a major irony is that each gets precisely what he wants (p 307). The *MilT* parodies the *KnT* as it 'bluntly manifests desire or will as the source of action, which in the other tale seems to be concealed under the drift of events or happenstance'; but the Knight, 'though no reductionist like the Miller, has a perspective very similar to the Miller's' (p 308). By bringing out the absurdities, the Knight 'consistently presents his story in such a way as to make genuine tragedy impossible' (p 309). Although Theseus sees love as folly (I.1785–90), only the Knight sees that lordship, too, can be destructive (I.1623–6). The *CT* creates a 'comic society' (p 311) in which all love is capable of conversion to a transcendent level, but it is not clear that the Knight fully appreciates this possibility (p 312). Still his explication of Fortuna (I.1663–72) as both comic and subject to destiny, which is in turn subject to God, offers a resolution to the problem of injustice, while Theseus' description of a First Mover presiding over death (I.2995–9) does not (p 312). The Knight's comic vision shows him to be both worthy and wise (I.68) (p 313). See **798, 887, 904, 1076**.

872 Nist, John. 'Chaucer's Apostrophic Mode in *The Canterbury Tales*.' *Tennessee Studies in Literature* 15(1970), 85–98.
Palamon's address to Emily (I.1104–1111) becomes an apostrophe to Venus, a transformation that shows Palamon's idealism and innocence and foreshadows his romantic triumph over Arcite (p 86). Palamon's

superior merit is demonstrated again by his prayer to Venus, 'a reverential form of apostrophe' (p 87).

873 North, J.D. 'Kalenderes Enlumyned Ben They: Some Astronomical Themes in Chaucer.' *RES* 20(1969), 129–54, 257–83, 418–44.
'Chaucer adopted the habit of referring the action in his tales ... to planetary, solar, and lunar configurations subsisting ... within a few years, at the very most, of the time of composition' (p 129). In the *KnT* (pp 149–54) the tournament seems to take place in 1388, one of only two years between 1365 and 1400 when Saturn was in the sign of Leo (I.2462) and the only such year preceded by a year in which either 3 May or 4 May fell on a Friday (I.1462–3 and 1534–5). On the day of the tournament Saturn was in 'the devastating position Chaucer demanded' while Mars was 'in a sorry plight' and Venus 'in an ambiguous situation' (p 154). All of Chaucer's dates, with the exception of those in the *Astr*, belong to the first half of the year, the period covered by Ovid's *Fasti*, his probable source (pp 437–42). Two periods of 49 days, from 15 March to 3 May and from 6 May to 24 June, were regarded as unlucky. Palamon escaped from prison on the first day following an unfortunate period, and Arcite's death may have occurred on 6 May, the first day of a new cycle of misfortune. Chaucer may have believed 'that human affairs were not only paralleled by the movements of stars and planets, but actually determined by them' (p 442). The *KnT* may have been begun in 1387 and finished at about the same time as *TC* (p 443). See **149, 901, 1122.**

874 Owen, Charles A., Jr. 'The Problem of Free Will in Chaucer's Narratives,' *PQ* 46(1967), 433–56.
Chaucer's interest in astrology, with its emphasis on fate, waned as his interest in character, free even of the poet's control, grew. After *Mars*, his 'most deterministic poem' (p 435), Chaucer assembled many of the same elements in *P&A*. At first the characters 'choose ineffectually and judge blindly' (p 437) and their wills are continually thwarted by unforeseen contingencies. The poem is full of complaints against injustice and suffering. Yet human will is not passive; the characters believe in the effectiveness of human will and this belief is justified by Theseus' achievement (p 438). Still 'the characters are differentiated more by what happens to them than by what they are' (p 438), and, supported by the Tale's emphasis on form and pattern, 'the sense of destiny is stronger than the freedom of the characters to choose' (p 439).

875 Pearsall, D[erek] A. 'The Canterbury Tales.' 1970. See **433**.
Chaucer may have intended the *KnT* to be read as 'a fully Boethian poem, a story of men giving up their reason to passion and thus falling under the arbitrary sway of Fortune. Theseus ... plays the part of the man above Fortune, the arbiter of order' (p 183). But Chaucer realizes this purpose only imperfectly as seen in the poem's 'moments of levity' such as the 'flippancy of tone after Arcite's moving death-speech' (p 183); in the 'compelling art' of Palamon and Arcite's complaints against Fortune (p 184); in the way the description of Mars and Saturn 'seems wantonly to extend the scale of suffering in the Tale' (p 184); and in the hollowness of Theseus' consolations for Arcite's death as measured against Arcite's own death-bed complaint. In this 'early work (about 1382) ... the images of disruption which the narrative contains, and must contain if the philosophical explanation is to be at all convincing, break out of their context and disturb us as realities' (p 184.) Still 'the grandeur of its set-piece writing, in descriptions and invocations particularly, was never to be equalled again by Chaucer' (p 184).

876 Penninger, F. Elaine. 'Chaucer's *Knight's Tale* and the Theme of Appearance and Reality in *The Canterbury Tales*.' *SAQ* 63(1964), 398–405.
Chaucer deliberately made Palamon, Arcite, and Emily and much else in the *KnT* unrealistic in order to dramatize the Knight as a believer in a world of appearances, and specifically, in chivalry. Chaucer's attitudes toward chivalry are revealed in *Thop*, where knightly combat is made absurd, and in *Mel*, where it is rejected as unchristian (pp 401–3). The 'unearthly idealism' of the *KnT* stands in need of correction by the 'earthly realism' of the *MilT* and the 'ultimate realism' of the *ParsT* (pp 403–5) See **887**.

877 Presson, Robert K. 'The Aesthetic of Chaucer's Art of Contrast.' *EM* 15(1964), 9–23.
Chaucer's use of contrasts is exemplified at length: eg, the juxtaposition of the courtly *KnT* with the uncourtly *MilT*, the re-use of I.2779 in I.3204 (pp 9–11), the opposing views of Monk and Knight (pp 15–16), and the parallelling of doubt and assertion in the speeches of Palamon (1303–33) and Theseus (2987–3069) (pp 18–9).

878 Quinn, Betty Nye. 'Venus, Chaucer, and Peter Bersuire.' *Spec* 38(1963), 479–80.
Both Steadman **768** and Wilkins **786** used the early sixteenth-century Badian edition of Bersuire's *Ovidius moralizatus*. The earlier Paris edition (1342) supplies new evidence for Steadman's view that

Chaucer's description of Venus (I.1955–66) may be indebted to Bersuire rather than to the anonymous *Libellus de deorum imaginibus*. The Paris edition specifies that Venus carried her shell in her *right* hand, and one ms contains a reading associating the shell with both singing (cf 'citole,' I.1959) and hair (cf 'comb,' *HF* 136). See **1048**.

879 Robertson, D.W., Jr. *A Preface to Chaucer*. 1962. See **435**.
The development of Arcite's lover's malady makes him vulnerable to a destructive 'miracle' of Cupid or Venus: 'as a devotee of Mars (Wrath), he meets his death through the action of an infernal fury (a wrathful passion) sent up by Pluto (Satan) at the instigation of Saturn (Time, who consumes his "children"), who was, in turn, prompted by Venus (Concupiscence). That is, concupiscence frustrated leads to wrath which in time causes self-destruction' (p 110). Robertson discusses the tradition of the 'two Venuses,' one representing virtuous love and cosmic order, the other, unlawful passion (p 126). Palamon prays to the first, and Theseus implicitly invokes her in his final speech; thus Palamon's marriage is part of the harmonious order represented by the celestial Venus (p 127). Theseus is an iconographic figure, representing the wisdom of the New Law which tempers justice with mercy, as when he pardons Palamon and Arcite. The hart-hunt is an iconographic action designed to reinforce Theseus' association with wisdom and virtue (p 264). His conquest of the Amazons, figures of lust, sensuality and effeminacy, and his marriage to Ypolita represent the proper union of reason and sensuality (p 265). The parallel submission of Thebes, the city of Venus and Bacchus, to Athens, the city of Minerva, is established through the marriage of Palamon and Emelye. Theseus' actions are always symbolic. 'They have nothing to do with "psychology" or with "character" in the modern sense' (pp 265–6). Similarly, the long speeches of the characters are intended to present ideas to the audience rather than to other characters (p 270). Chaucer might have drawn the signification of his temple of Venus from Boccaccio's notes to the *Tes*, where Venus represents the concupiscible appetite (p 370), but the interpretation was a well established convention, as in the works of Fulgentius and Vatican Mythographer III. The *KnT* introduces the theme of marriage in the *CT*, presenting it as a solution to the problems raised by the concupiscent and irascible passions (p 375). The scene in which Palamon and Arcite first see Emelye is 'mocking and humorous' (p 466), and Chaucer deprives Arcite of dignity and sympathy through the 'elaborate restraint from Dantean speculation' in the account of his soul (I.2089–15), through the unconvincing 'noise' of the mourners, and through the 'ridiculous

practicality' of the questions of the Athenian women (2835–6) (p 467). Theseus exhibits a form of courteous love in his responses to women, but the two lovers never show 'disinterested benevolence' (p 468). See **139, 1012, 1048, 1099, 1117.**

- Review by Francis Lee Utley, 'Robertsonianism Redivivus,' *RPh* 19(1965), 250–60. Rpt as 'Chaucer and Patristic Exegesis' in *Chaucer's Mind and Art*. Ed. A.C. Cawley. London: Oliver and Boyd, 1969; New York: Barnes & Noble, 1970. Pp 69–85: As an example of Robertson's tendency to allegorize some details of a work and not others, Utley notes his explanation of Arcite's death and then remarks: 'One wonders why Palamon, the real idolater, who identified Emily with Venus, managed to save his life and get the girl' (p 72).

880 Rowland, Beryl. 'Chaucer's *The Knight's Tale*, A.1810.' *Expl* 21(1963), 73.
The mss offer two readings: 'a cokkow or an hare' and 'a cokkow of an hare.' If Chaucer is emphasizing the qualities the cuckoo and hare have in common, ignorance of love and lack of affection, the reading should be 'a cokkow *or* an hare.' If Chaucer is punning on *hare* and on *cokkow*, the phrase is presumably proverbial and means that Emily knows as little of love as a cuckold *of* a whore, ie, of his wife.

881 Ruggiers, Paul G. 'The Knight's Tale.' *The Art of the Canterbury Tales*. Madison: University of Wisconsin Press, 1965. Pp 151–66.
In an expanded version of **753**, Ruggiers treats the *KnT* as a 'didactic romance' falling 'within a range of Christian comedy' opposed to the fabliau vision of irrational humanity (p 152). As an attempt 'to conflate romance with realism and to accommodate philosophical commentary to human suffering,' the *KnT* is 'an experiment of sorts,' like the more successful *TC* (p 154). While it supports the idea of providential order, the Tale remains perplexing, probably because of the 'persistent strain of irony ... which prevents in [Chaucer] any facile affirmation' (p 157); and its lack of attention to characterization and to the problem of free will produces 'a kind of quizzical and thought-provoking literary type' somewhere between the tragedy of fate and serious comedy (p 158). Palamon's praying to Venus may be intended to enlist our sympathies for him (p 160), but Arcite is not guilty of an error in judgment in praying to Mars (p 161). Theseus provides 'a sane vantage point' from which to view the princes, and serves as a bridge between the pagan and Boethian systems through his 'intimately human involvement' and 'faintly godlike detachment' (p 162).

882 Rumble, T.C. 'Chaucer's *Knight's Tale*, 2680–83.' *PQ* 43(1964), 130–3.
Rumble objects to the usual editorial procedures in dealing with this passage: either dropping 2681–2, or retaining them while expressing reservations about their authenticity and emending 2683. The latter – 'And was al his chiere, as in his herte' – should be translated: '[Emily] was now completely of his [Arcite's] state of mind and heart.' It signals a reversal of Emily's earlier indifference; the two preceding lines constitute the Knight's self-conscious attempt to reconcile her contradictory attitudes.

883 Salter, Elizabeth. 'The Knight's Tale.' *Chaucer: The Knight's Tale and the Clerk's Tale*. 1962. See **436**. Pp 9–36.
In reshaping the *Tes* (a process commented on in detail, *passim*), Chaucer 'shows himself far more interested in predicaments than personalities' (p 10). The *KnT* is an atypical romance in its 'varied and powerful use of language' and in the 'philosophic and ... enigmatic ... final impression it leaves' (p 12). In 'the language of power and ritual,' Chaucer emphasizes 'the theme of worldly magnificence'; formulaic speech and theatrical gesture reveal 'the almost ritualistic nature of the life led by man in an elevated and aristocratic society' (p 13). Salter cites, eg, Chaucer's use of fire, wound, and death metaphors for the lovers' passion; and the description of the door of Mars' temple, 'remind[ing] us of the strain of "iren tough" (I.1992) in Chaucer's imagination' (p 17). The 'language of concept, criticism, and realism' (p 18), through its use of philosophical analysis, humorous deflation, and pungent commentary, 'looks intently at the darker implications of divine and human affairs' (p 19). For example, the paintings in Mars' temple undermine the 'protective and glamorous language' used earlier to describe Theseus' banner (p 19). The laments of Arcite (I.1223–74) and Palamon (1303–33) may seem benighted, measured by Boethian philosophy, but they accurately predict the divine indifference and callousness. The Knight's jovial comment on their sufferings, in the *demande*, focuses the problem of Chaucer's use of 'two voices.' 'One reveals for us the pain latent in the narrative, the other, less sensitive, speaks with imperfect comprehension of that pain' (p 23). Thus the narrator introduces the description of the theater in an optimistic mood that ill prepares us for its horrors, and leaves the temples in good spirits, unaffected by spectacles of suffering (pp 25–8). His attitudes are 'pathetically inadequate' to the pitiable state of humans subject to vengeful gods, as summed up in Saturn's speech on his influence (p 28). Arcite's death undermines the happy ending

by showing the unhappiness and waste on which it builds. His death-bed recommendation of Palamon indicts the gods by suggesting that the capacity for charity is 'an entirely human prerogative' (p 29). Chaucer's 'imaginative sympathy was called out most strongly by the spectacle of human life subject to cruel and disproportionate strokes of destiny,' but the story 'is an inadequate vehicle for the emotions so powerfully expressed by the poetry' (p 32). The *KnT* does exhibit the rhetorical order discussed by Muscatine **726**, but 'we ought not to confuse rhetorical ordering with imaginative' (p 33). The *KnT* 'confronts us with active malice and passive suffering to an almost unbearable degree' (p 34). Theseus' speech is 'the crux of the problem' (p 35). Though its opening lines are eloquent, the wisdom of referring to the Firste Moevere the activities of Mars, Venus, and Saturn is questionable (p 35). In the references to Arcite's honorable death and escape from the prison of this life, 'only the confident flow of the poetry disguises the basic illogicality of the appeals' (p 35). A 'great gulf' lies 'between the questions asked by the poet's imagination, and the replies he feels able, in *this* instance, to give' (p 36). See **825, 845, 891R, 897, 904, 936, 947, 1014, 1018, 1025, 1092.**

884 Scaglione, Aldo D. *Nature and Love in the Late Middle Ages*. Berkeley and Los Angeles: University of California Press, 1963.
Arcite professes a 'naturalistic' love for women and a faith in natural law as opposed to social convention (pp 79–80).

885 Schaar, Claes. *The Golden Mirror*. 1967. See **437**.
In the *KnT* (pp 56–62) emotions often lose the nuances they have in the *Tes* and become 'more expressive, pointed, and emphatic' (p 62). The *KnT* is the earliest work to show 'behavioristic description' (p 92; see p 20 for definition), possibly under Statius' influence (p 165). See also the sections on the *Tes* and the *Theb* (pp 147–9). Emelye's portrait combines 'idealizing characterization' with some 'objective characterization' (p 213; see pp 169–70 for definitions). Although her long hair is a striking Chaucerian addition, Boccaccio's description of Emilia is fuller and less conventional (p 214). The 'objective descriptions' in the temple of Mars 'are of a great, almost shocking expressiveness' (p 215). The portraits of Lycurge and Emetrius are 'pieces of particular idealization,' 'gigantic and gorgeous' (p 217). The idealization characteristic of Chaucer's description of Emelye can be found in other portraits in the *Tes* and in the French *romans*. In descriptions of heroes, such as Emetrius and Lycurge, Boccaccio and Statius concentrate on armor and horses while Chaucer focuses on countenance. If Chaucer used physiognomical lore, as Curry **543** argues, he 'created a descriptive novelty' (p 291–3). Chaucer's

treatment of the May morning (I.1488 f) consists of 'factual and impressionistic description' (p 414; see pp 368–71 for definitions). Lines 1495–6 are original and line 1494 is indebted to *Purg* I.19 f. See also the discussions of the *Tes* (pp 448–50) and the *Theb* (pp 470–2).

886 Schmidt, A.V.C. 'The Tragedy of Arcite: A Reconsideration of the *Knight's Tale.*' *EIC* 19(1969), 107–17.
Schmidt challenges Frost's conclusion (**684**) that Palamon is worthier of Emelye, asserting that Arcite is the tragic hero of the poem (p 107). Palamon's identification of Emelye with Venus does not establish his moral superiority since he is objectively mistaken about the lady and subjectively mistaken about his own feelings (pp 108–10). The oath the princes have taken not to hinder each other in love does not apply to their circumstances, in which neither has a relationship with the lady (pp 110–1). Arcite's prayer to Mars cannot be faulted since he sees victory only as the means to winning Emelye (pp 111–2). While Palamon's moral superiority can at most be inferred, Arcite's can be demonstrated (p 112), principally by the resignation and magnanimity of his death-bed speech. He is, like Troilus, the hero of a Boethian tragedy who enjoys the favor of Fortune all too briefly. Theseus' description of Arcite's escape from the 'foule prisoun of this lyf' (I.3061), like Troilus' laughter from the eighth sphere, expresses Boethian contempt for the world, which mixes uneasily with the optimism of Theseus' speech and his anticipation of marital happiness for Palamon and Emelye (p 114). The poem offers no explicit theological interpretation; instead Arcite's defeat shows a 'ghastly parody of true justice' (p 115). Saturn's literal interpretation of Arcite's request for victory parallels Arcite's 'tactical' interpretation of Palamon's identification of Emelye with Venus (p 115). Like *TC*, the *KnT* offers a 'sombre assessment' of chivalry and love while celebrating their inspiring aspects (p 117).

887 Severs, J. Burke. 'The Tales of Romance.' In *Companion to Chaucer Studies*. Ed. Beryl Rowland. Toronto: Oxford University Press, 1968/rev 1979. Pp 229–46/271–95.
Critics have asked too many questions about the *KnT*, especially since concern shifted, about mid-century, from characterization to philosophy. Frost's (**684**) was 'the best general study of the tale' at mid-century (p 231/273). Important studies of the philosophy include those by Muscatine **726**, Lumiansky **713**, Kaske **703**, Ruggiers **752**, Halverson **691**, Pratt **745**. and Westlund **896**. Objections and qualifications have been offered by Underwood **776**, Preston **746**, Neuse **871**, and Penninger **876** among others. Chaucer's humor does

not undermine the seriousness of the work, as Wilson **787** and Huppé **844** have explained. In the revised edition, Severs observes (pp 282–3) that the *KnT* has received more attention than any of the other Chaucerian romances, and that special attention has recently been paid to the theme of order vs disorder (eg, see Blake **916**, Fichte **947**, Van **1050**) and to the relationship of the Tale's humor to its idealism (eg, see Thurston **891**).

888 Spearing, A.C. 'Introduction.' *The Knight's Tale*. 1966. See **57**. Pp 1–79.
The *KnT* is a philosophical poem that depicts the world as governed both by Fortune, without regard to individual merits (51–4), and by the gods, with destructive effects (pp 54–65). Venus, Mars, and Diana represent dangerous human impulses, and Saturn, the external conditions of life that tend toward disaster. Arcite's death shows the callousness of the gods, and his death-bed magnanimity, their pettiness. This pessimistic view is carried out in the Tale's animal imagery (pp 66–70) and prison imagery (p 71). Theseus' relationship to the animal imagery exposes his ambivalent status: eg, the Minotaur suggests that he becomes 'an exponent of the very force he is proud of having destroyed' (p 68). The theater and tournament are permeated by animal imagery, especially in the figures of Emetrius and Lygurge. Theseus' final speech appears to answer Palamon's questioning of the gods (*KnT* 449–50; I.1307–8), but succeeds mainly in showing 'the *difficulty* philosophy has in ordering the universe' (p 76). Theseus is mistaken in identifying Jupiter rather than Saturn as ruler of the world (2716–80; I.3034–8), and Jupiter's grace (2209–11; I.3067–9) is not obvious. But Theseus' practical advice shows 'how to go on living in a world ruled by Saturn' (p 78). See **1018**.

889 Stevens, Michael. 'The Knight's Tale.' *Chaucer's Major Tales*. Michael Hoy and Michael Stevens. London: Norton Bailey, 1969. Pp 23–38.
The *KnT* draws on Boethian philosophy to present the problem of man's subjection to irrational Fortune. Theseus, the only character whose individuality is developed, maintains the ideals of chivalry against the forces of disorder.

890 Taylor, Eric F. '*The Knight's Tale*: A New Source for Spenser's *Muipotmos*.' *Renaissance Papers 1965*. Durham: The Southeastern Renaissance Conference, 1966. Pp 57–63.
Several correspondences establish the *KnT* as a source for Spenser's poem: the circumstances of Arcite's entering the grove (I.1489–1541) and of Clarion's entering the garden (379–435); Chaucer's catalogue of trees and Spenser's list of flowers; the armor of Lygurge (I.2140–7) and of Clarion (65–75); the clash between Mars and Venus in the

KnT and the debate between Venus and Minerva in *Muipotmos*; the characterizations of the world as a 'thurghfare ful of wo' (I.2847) and as a 'spectacle of care' (440). Spenser's poem lacks the kind of consolation offered by Theseus.

891 Thurston, Paul T. *Artistic Ambivalence in Chaucer's Knight's Tale.* Gainesville: University of Florida Press, 1968.
The artistic ambivalence of the *KnT* consists in the possibility of its being read both as 'a glowing tale of chivalry' and as 'a satire of cherished chivalric traditions as well as the literary forms in which they are celebrated' (x). Ch 1, 'The Traditional Point of View' (pp 1–19), reviews critical interpretations that approach the *KnT* as a serious work of romance to the neglect of its humorous and satiric elements. Ch 2, 'Chaucerian Humor and Satire' (pp 20–62), analyzes passages considered humorous or satirical by critics: eg, Theseus' discovery of the dueling princes and the Knight's remarks on Arcite's soul. In the former case, Theseus uses humor to resolve an unmanageable situation; in the latter, Chaucer uses humor to evade a topic unsuitable for his chivalric Knight. Eight characteristics of Chaucer's humor and five qualities of his satire are listed (pp 57–8), and these are referred to by number in later portions of the book. Ch 3, 'Book One' (pp 63–111), identifies, again for later reference, three stylistic characteristics of the Knight's narration: objective reportage; reportage making freer use of figurative language but still without interpretation by the Knight; and actual interpretation of events (pp 66–7). Readers need not accept all of the Knight's assertions and interpretations (p 69). There are contradictions between Theseus' pragmatic politics and the Knight's praise of his chivalry, and comic incongruities in the arguments and complaints of the princes over the inaccessible and indifferent Emelye. These aspects, and Chaucer's omission of the war against the Amazons, make the *KnT* a 'radically different work' from the *Tes* (p 106). Ch 4, 'The Love Complex' (pp 112–49), presents detailed analyses of the *KnT* in relation to the love code of courtly allegory and to the plots and characterizations of metrical romance, concluding that the *KnT* differs fundamentally from these genres. For example, Emelye has neither the desire nor the power of the courtly lady to grant her grace freely to the man of her choice, and the princes, rather than seeking to right injustice or to acquire material gain like the heroes of romance, seek only the lady. Ch 5, 'Book Two' (pp 150–71), examines Arcite's love-sickness, his return to Athens, and the meeting of the princes in the grove. Detailed comparisons are made to Books IV and V of the *Tes*. Boccaccio's Arcita is 'much more like a conventional courtly lover,

while ... Chaucer's Arcite is a delightfully exaggerated misrepresentation of this literary phenomenon' (p 166). Ch 6, 'Book Three' (pp 172–95), finds this part of the *KnT* more like the *Tes* than any other part, both in the extent of Chaucer's direct borrowings and in Chaucer's use of 'extravagant epic paraphernalia' (p 173). The opening lines (1881–1901) are evidence of the Knight's 'exaggerated preoccupation' with the chivalric (pp 176–7), while Chaucer probably intended the extravagance of building lists for the tournament to indicate 'the lengths man will go to in order to reap the harvest of his folly' (p 178). The Knight's treatment of the temples and prayers reveals his emphasis on things military and his unease with things feminine. Ch 7, 'Book Four' (pp 196–223), summarizes Books VIII–XII of the *Tes*, and argues for the very different humorous and satiric effects of the closing events of the *KnT*. For example, Theseus' limitation on the weapons to be used makes anti-climactic what was to have been a fight to the death; the 'freendlich ye' (I.2680) Emelye casts on the apparently victorious Arcite emphasizes her ambivalence as the princes' love object; Arcite's parting speech to Emelye is full of contradictions; the expressions of grief are inappropriately 'plebian' (p 219); and the account of the funeral is satirically excessive. In Ch 8, '"the sentence of this matere"' (pp 224–31), Thurston concludes that 'it is not the ideals of love that are so treated as to convey effective satire and humor but man's interpretation of them through the social edifices of courtly love and the chivalric code' (p 229). The 'external characteristics' (p 230) of courtly allegory and metrical romance in the Tale are there precisely to provide the material for satiric treatment.

- Review by Alfred David, *Spec* 45(1970), 498–500: Commenting on Thurston's perception of a contradiction between Arcite's inability to sleep (I.1361–2) and Mercury's appearing to him in sleep (1384–6), David says that 'Arcite's conventional insomnia is not to be taken so literally as to make his conventional prophetic dream a comic matter ... This kind of literalism – the failure to appreciate convention as such – is characteristic of the book as a whole' (p 499). David prefers studies of the Tale's humor such as Salter's (**883**), which deals with 'true ambivalence, not a false division of the poem into two levels' (p 499). 'Far from increasing the beauty and interest of the Knight's Tale, the kind of humor attributed to it here would cheapen and vulgarize it' (p 500).
- Review by Alan T. Gaylord, *JEGP* 69(1970), 167–9: Gaylord cites Thurston's interpretation of Theseus' failure to accept ransom as typical of his errors of understanding. 'As [Theseus'] attitude, vow,

and banner show, he is going against Thebes to exercise retributive justice ... He was fighting a *guerre mortelle*, as against an infidel ... Ransom, then, would be no more expected than survivors. Thurston must pay more attention to the context' (pp 168–9).

- Review by R.M. Wilson, *YES* 1(1971), 216–7: 'No doubt there is more humour and satire in the *Knight's Tale* than the undiscerning reader might suppose, though not all the illustrations of it will command general agreement — for example it is difficult to believe that lines 2778–9 could ever have been intended as "humorous or satiric or both" ... But whether one agrees with the argument or not, there is much in the book that any reader will find of interest and value: the detailed comparison of the *Teseida* with the *Knight's Tale* ... the comparative study of some of the metrical romances, and the consideration of courtly love as essentially a literary phenomenon' (p 217).

892 Van, Thomas A. 'Second Meanings in Chaucer's "Knight's Tale".' *ChauR* 3(1968), 69–76.
Van examines six words, pairs of words, and phrases whose ambiguities contribute to the serious tone and artistic completeness of Chaucer's tale: *array* ('dress,' 'predicament'); *hart/heart* (with the latter suggesting both 'erotic fantasy' and 'compassion'); *wele/wheel; turning/turneiynge* (I.2557); *boone/bone*; and *righte way* (a phrase having emotional, geographical, and philosophical significances).

893 Vann, J. Dow. 'A Character Reversal in Chaucer's "Knight's Tale".' *AN&Q* 3(1965), 131–2.
Palamon is the warrior and Arcite, the lover in the first two parts of the Tale, but these characterizations are reversed when they pray to the gods in Part Three: Palamon to Venus, and Arcite to Mars.

894 Waldron, R. A. 'Knight's Tale A1037: "fressher than the May".' *ES* 46(1965), 402–6.
Emily is compared not to the month of May but to a blossoming tree of May, probably the hawthorn. The Old French '*mai*' commonly refers to the green branches used in May rituals like those alluded to in Chaucer's description of Arcite's 'maying' (I.1500–12). This interpretation establishes a coherent sequence 'the lylie ... the May ... the rose' (1035–9) (p 406). The play on words here ('May,' 1034; 'may,' 1036) is similar to the one in Arcite's scene ('May,' 1511; 'may,' 1512).

895 Warren, Roger. 'Three Notes on "A Midsummer Night's Dream".' *N&Q* 16[214](1969), 13–4.
Chaucer uses the term 'transfigure' evocatively in *KnT* 246–9 (I.1104–7). Since Shakespeare knew the *KnT* well, drawing even

Theseus' humorous attitude toward the lovers (IV.i.136–7) from Chaucer (*KnT* 927–43; I.1785–1801), it is probable that Hippolyta's use of 'transfigur'd' (V.i.24) suggests not simply change but 'revelation of the true nature of the lovers' minds, and affections' (p 134).

896 Westlund, Joseph. 'The *Knight's Tale* as an Impetus for Pilgrimage.' *PQ* 43(1964), 526–37.
By presenting 'the continual subversion of noble efforts to bring order out of disorder' in a pagan setting (p 526), the *KnT* establishes the need for Christian pilgrimage. The first episode constitutes 'the rehearsal of a pattern' (p 527) as the solemnity of Theseus' triumphal homecoming is disrupted by the war against Thebes with its 'hint ... of ignoble elements' (p 527). The pattern is repeated several times: eg, when the sworn brotherhood of Palamon and Arcite is undone by love, and when the perpetual imprisonment of Arcite is nullified by Perotheus' appeal (pp 528–9). The Tale presents more than what Muscatine **726** calls 'a constant awareness ... of chaos'; rather 'ordered situations are continually prepared only to be reversed' (p 529). The tournament, Theseus' supreme effort, is thwarted by the gods. The quarrel in heaven precedes and qualifies the scene in which Theseus, at the height of his glory, modifies his rules (pp 529–30). The gods are not impartial instruments of fate, but personal, willful actors, and Frost **684** is mistaken in arguing that they grant victory to the worthier lover; rather, as Muscatine shows, it is impossible to distinguish between the two princes (pp 530–1). Frost overemphasizes the significance of 'guidance from above,' for 'whatever we consider the nature of the divinities to be, their presence does not give much meaning to the lives of mortals' (p 532). Theseus' First Mover speech is the poem's strongest assertion of order, but we should not, with Wilson **787**, read Christian doctrine into the speech; instead we should ask why Chaucer did not use Christian materials available in his sources: the fullness of Boethius' arguments, and the flight of Arcite's soul in the *Tes* (p 533–5). The exclusion of Christian elements creates a world view appropriate to the first of the Canterbury tales. 'The poem creates both a sense that men's state is tragic, and that there is some kind of order in the universe. We are convinced that there is a very real need for spiritual quest, and that we must begin with faith and acceptance of our earthly lot' (p 537). See **1125**.

897 Whittock, Trevor. *A Reading of the Canterbury Tales*. 1968. See **441**.
'The Knight's Tale' (pp 57–76) reprints **785** with the addition (pp 64–9) of a reply to Salter **883**. The combination of horror and chivalric splendor forces us to ask, 'What is the significance of this,

and how does Chaucer reconcile his range of tones within the [tale]?' (p 64). Salter's 'radical answer' rests on misunderstandings (p 64). The gods are not sinister powers playing with human puppets but manifestations of human passions or experiences (p 66). The two voices are simply the Knight's voice, telling a tale of chivalry whose issues are resolved within the Tale, and Chaucer's voice, laying out the 'grander design' of issues yet to be explored in the *CT* (p 67). Horror and joy are everywhere balanced, even in Saturn's description of his powers. 'The poetry does not shirk reality nor (what would be the same thing) attack the god' (p 60). The chaos in the poem not only gives depth to the order it celebrates, as Muscatine **726** suggests, 'but the pattern of the poem assimilates even this disorder to itself, capturing it by irony' (p 69). In the *KnT* disasters reflect the helplessness of human beings; in the *MilT* slighter sufferings constitute deserved and laughable retribution (p 81). The *MilT* attempts to answer Arcite's death-bed questions by celebrating God's bounty (p 88). The *MLT* attempts, through a Christian exemplum, to answer Palamon's question concerning the suffering of the innocent (I.1313–4). Chaucer knows that on such issues no one answer can be wholly sufficient.

898 Williams, George. *A New View of Chaucer*. Durham: Duke University Press, 1965.

Williams subjects Chaucer's relationship to John of Gaunt to intricate speculation. In the *KnT* Chaucer may have made Theseus a duke rather than a king 'as a means of subtly associating Theseus' wisdom and courage with ... [the] Duke of Lancaster' (p 154). Theseus' return from Scythia with Hippolyta and Emelye 'irresistibly suggests the return of Gaunt to England, in 1371, with his new-wedded Queen of Spain, and her sister Isabella' (p 154). Palamon's escape from prison on May 3 may have reminded contemporaries of 3 May 1389 when Richard II re-assumed power from the Duke of Gloucester and 'set the wheels in motion for Gaunt's return to England' (pp 154–5). The white eagle, probably a badge of the Lancaster family, (I.2178) supports Cook's argument (**537**) that Emetrius represents Henry Bolingbroke, Gaunt's son (p 155).

899 Wilson, William S. 'Days and Months in Chaucer's Poems.' *AN&Q* 4(1966), 83–4.

Chaucer often cites dates that constitute 'symmetrical numbers.' Taking March as the first month of the year, May 3 in the *KnT* and *TC* is the third day of the third month. The symmetrical numbers do not contribute to meaning but are 'a piece of pure design (p 83).

900 Woo, Constance, and William Matthews. 'The Spiritual Purpose of the Canterbury Tales.' *Comitatus* 1(1970), 85–109.
The Knight was chosen to tell the first tale not because of his rank but because he is a 'model Christian narrator' (p 99). The story of the princes' pursuit of false goods and the final speech of Theseus – like the Knight, Chaucer's alter ego – make the *KnT* a 'sermon toward goodness' (p 100).

901 Wood, Chauncey. 'Chaucer and Astrology.' In *Companion to Chaucer Studies*. 1968/rev 1978. See **156**. Pp 176–91/202–20.
'The artistic function of the astrological images is ... difficult to grasp, because the *tone* of the tale as a whole is slippery' (p 181–207). The difficulty is illustrated by evaluative comments on Browne **532**, Curry **543**, Dustoor **550**, Parr **737**, **740** and Weese **781**. In the revised edition, Wood cites North **873** and Smyser **152** and some reactions to his own work (**157**, **902**).

902 — *Chaucer and the Country of the Stars*. 1970. See **157**.
Palamon and Arcite's determinism (I.1328, 1086–91) is not shared by the Knight-narrator whose observations on destiny (1663–72) emphasize the roles of divine providence and human appetite (pp 45–7). Theseus' advice to make a virtue of necessity refers to mortality, not to fortune; and the lack of stoic attitudes attributed to him suggests that his position is closer to the Knight's than to the lovers' (p 47). There may be an historical allegory in Saturn's speech, I.2461–2, although in reviewing the arguments of Parr **737** and **740**, and Weese **781**, Wood notes (pp 71–2, n 38) that Parr inconsistently favors an historical interpretation of 'vengeance and pleyn correccioun' and an astrological interpretation of 'cherles rebellyng' (I.2459). The poetic meaning of the astrological materials has to do with character, however. Palamon and Arcite's subjection to lust and Emily's self-indulgent refusal to bear children lead to their associations with the destructive aspects of Venus, Mars, and Diana, and with the wholly destructive Saturn. The wise and mature Theseus has no connection with Saturn and allies himself in productive ways with the other gods as the references to his banner (Mars), his hunting (Diana), and his early loves (Venus) indicate (pp 72–5). In the *KnT* Chaucer 'abandon[s] any idea of astral determinism for self-determination on the basis of character' (p 75).

903 Zesmer, David M. 'The Knight's Tale.' *Guide to English Literature from Beowulf through Chaucer and Medieval Drama*. College Outline Series, No. 53. New York: Barnes and Noble, 1961; rpt 1964. Pp 221–3.

Zessmer notes the Tale's balanced rhetoric; lack of characterization; negative attitudes toward love, war, and chastity; parodies of courtly love in the 'fantastic quibble' over ways of loving Emelye and in the 'equally ludicrous' question about which knight suffers most (p 222); and the Knight's detachment, as seen in his handling of Arcite's death. Theseus' final speech is the key to the romance; it recommends acceptance on faith of the justice of Providence as the way to triumph over the vicissitudes of fortune (p 233).

1971-1980

904 Aers, David. 'Imagination, Order and Ideology: *The Knight's Tale.*' *Chaucer, Langland and the Creative Imagination.* London: Routledge & Kegan Paul, 1980. Pp 174–95.
Chaucer's reflexive imagination viewed ideologies as human constructs, not eternal verities. The *KnT* does not, as Muscatine **726** argues, assert an aesthetic, cosmic, and metaphysical order represented by Theseus, but rather, as Neuse **871** and Salter **883** have suggested, scrutinizes 'the versions of order, styles of thought and life embodied in Theseus, rulers like him and their culture' (pp 174–5). The heraldic representation of Mars on Theseus' banner glamorizes violence, but Chaucer chooses to 'de-sublimate this emblem' (p 176) by showing Theseus' cruelties. The imagery in the temple of Mars 'negates the aestheticization of legalized and organized violence' (p 177) by associating it with condemned and purposeless violence (p 178). As appropriate to Theseus' kind of order, Saturn, 'the old pragmatist' (p 178) whose violent influence (I.2456–70) 'thoroughly undermines any claims about benign harmonies' (p 180), provides the solution in the conflict between Mars and Venus. Theseus' modification of the rules for the tournament shows how such gestures of compassion are 'embedded in a form of life which undermines and inverts them' (p 181). His ideas of love, symbolically represented on his pennon, offer no positive alternative to his Martian values. He sanctions Arcite's 'anarchic egotism' (p 182) by accepting the idea that every man works only to advance himself, and he makes love serve violence when he offers Emily as a prize. Arcite's death definitively exposes the limitations of Theseus' order. The clinical focus on the body 'resists the absorption of individual identity and the particulars of misery into ... grandly abstract patterns of consolation' (p 183). Arcite's questions expose the culture's failure to give an adequate account of human existence. He turns away from 'the comforts of theodicy,' preferring 'incarnate human love and friend-

ship' (p 185). As he embraces Emily and recommends Palamon, he offers 'a glimmer of the human potential distorted and perverted by the culture over which Theseus presides' (p 185). Chaucer's refusal to follow Boccaccio in granting Arcite a vision of cosmic order argues against our imposing religious consolations on the text. Egeus' complacent consolation evades the issues; Theseus' speech exemplifies the manipulation of metaphysics to serve the ends of secular power. His appeal to 'immediate and unstructured experience' rather than to a 'real but hidden structure to the phenomenal world' (p 189), his application of the term 'love' to what is only 'the idealization of sheer power over others' (p 190), and his 'sacralization' (p 191) of the existing social order as an absolute add up to a travesty of Boethian philosophy. Far from exalting Theseus, Chaucer's tale makes the 'idea and function of theodicy a topic for reflection' (p 183) while directing special attention to the 'transformations of metaphysics into an ideology of unreflexive secular domination' (p 195). See **1092**.

- Review by Paul Strohm, *Criticism* 22(1980), 376–7: In this invigorating study, Aers does not fully explain the likenesses he sees between the political world of the *KnT* and Chaucer's own world. As a result the 'reflexivity' Aers attributes to Chaucer resembles the ironic Chaucerian consciousness of formalist critics.

905 Anderson, David. 'The Legendary History of Thebes.' 1980. See **236**. Part 3, 'Boccaccio's English Heirs' (pp 196–275): 'Chaucer preserved and in many cases accentuated the analogies Boccaccio had drawn between his two noble kinsmen and the brothers of the *Thebaid*' (p 197). For example, he preserved the key lines on 'signoria' and 'amore' (*Tes* V.13.7–8) in I.1625–6, and moved them to 'the climax of the recognition scene in the grove.' The grove itself has Theban associations: eg, the ankle-deep blood (I.1660) is reminiscent of the bloody lake in *Theb* IV.553. The two flames on Diana's altar recall those on the pyre of Eteocles and Polinices (*Theb* XI) and Chaucer refers here to Statius (I.2292–4). Chaucer invents a new genealogy: Palamon is the son of Polinices by his incestuous union with his sister Antigone, and Arcite is the son of another sister, Ismene. Chaucer departs from Boccaccio to equalize the attention paid to Palamon and Arcite so as to emphasize their strife with each other rather than their relation to Emilye. Although Chaucer uses humor, the *KnT* is not a mock-epic, as evidenced by the way Theseus' admirable role is preserved. Here, as in Gower's *CA*, the motif of Thebes' 'olde walles wyde' (I.1331, 1880) connects Thebes with Babylon and Augustinian typology.

906 [Anonymous]. *Notes on Chaucer's The Knight's Tale*. London: Methuen Educational, 1976.
Offers a literal translation of the *KnT* into Modern English. A two-page 'critical appraisal' asserts that in this 'high-falutin' story, the poet is 'not interested in the persons' (save, momentarily, Theseus), but that nevertheless the Tale 'provides much food for thought' (p 36).

907 Bachman, William Bryant, Jr. 'Materialistic Opposition as an Informing Principle in Chaucer's Philosophical Narratives.' *DAI* 36(1976), 6696A. Syracuse University Dissertation, 1975.
An an inheritor of the 'general progression of medieval epistemology ... towards a rehabilitation of sense experience and the experiential world,' Chaucer probably reacted critically to the idealism of the *Consol*. Chaucer's use of Boethian ideas of destiny and felicity in combination with an emphasis on experiential knowledge turned the *KnT* into 'a deterministic tragedy' (Chapter III).

908 —. 'Mercury, Virgil, and Arcite: *Canterbury Tales*, A 1384–1397.' *ELN* 13(1976), 168–73.
Bachman rejects Hoffman's suggestion (**837**) that this passage is based on Ovid's *Met* and implies that Arcite dies through Mercury's action. Bachman traces the passage to *Aen* IV.556–9; the episode emphasizes the conflict between human desires and human destinies.

909 Bateson, F.W. 'Could Chaucer Spell?' *EIC* 25(1975), 2–24.
As evidence that the sounding of *e*'s was not an archaism intended to impart an epic flavor, Bateson cites the comparable number of such *e*'s in A[I]2340–3108 of the *KnT* and the *MilT* entire (pp 8–9). The spellings of *Emelye/Emelia* and of *Arcite/Arcita* (pp 11–5) are determined in every case by metrical considerations. *Emelye* and *Arcite* are frequently used in rhyming positions; *Emelia*, once; and *Arcita*, never. Bateson cites A[I]2938 (actually 2928) as illustrating the movement of some plurals in *-es* toward a murmur vowel. He cites Cambridge Gg and Ellesmere as reading *Nymphus*, and Gg and Corpus as reading *amadrius* (pp 20–1).
- A.V.C. Schmidt, responding in the same volume, pp 391–2, points out that Gg and Corpus actually read *amadries*.

910 Bawcutt, Priscilla. 'The Lark in Chaucer and Some Later Poets.' *YES* 2(1972), 5–12.
The lark was frequently interpreted as either praising God or greeting the dawn. The second tradition is reflected in I.1491–2. Arcite, and later Palamon (I.2209–16), are characterized as zealous lovers through association with the early-rising lark, 'a type of zeal and industry' (pp 10–1).

911 Beidler, Peter G. 'Art and Scatology in the *Miller's Tale.*' *ChauR* 12(1977), 90–102.
The *MilT* differs from its analogues in having the woman present her buttocks at the window rather than the lover, his. The Miller demonstrates through Alisoun his rejection of the ladylike values represented by Emily (p 93).

912 Bennett, J.A.W. *Chaucer at Oxford and at Cambridge.* Oxford: Oxford University Press; Toronto: University of Toronto Press, 1974.
In the accounts of a Merton College bursar, Bennett finds an expenditure for illumination and cites I.2087–8 (p 4). The College Library contained a *geomancia* (cf I.2045), and medical texts in which Chaucer might have read about the symptoms he ascribed to Arcite's love-sickness and fatal illness (pp 16–7).

913 — *The Knight's Tale: A Commentary.* 4 parts. Cambridge: privately printed, 1976.
[Not seen] Listed in *Medieval Studies for J. A. W. Bennett: Aetatis Suae LXX*, ed P.L. Heyworth (Oxford: Clarendon, 1981), p 410. The press of the Cambridge University Library printed the *Commentary* but the Library reports that it holds no copy.

914 — 'Chaucer, Dante and Boccaccio.' *Quaderno* 234 (1977), 3–22. Rpt slightly altered in *Chaucer and the Italian Trecento.* 1983. See **74**. Pp 89–113.
Bennett examines five passages in which Chaucer enriches his borrowings from the *Tes* by returning to passages in the *Div Com* from which Boccaccio had borrowed. In an expansion of **656**, Bennett shows how Chaucer conflates three incidents in the *Tes* (IV.73–5 and 79, IV.80, V.29 and 37) to produce a 'kinetic' scene in which the lark soars, Phoebus rises, and Arcite mounts his horse (pp 94–7). Line 1501, 'Remembringe on the point of his desir,' echoes *Purg* XII.19–21 and *Par* XXII.25–6 (p 98). The treatment of Fortune in I.1663–72 fuses *Tes* V.77 and VI.1 with *Inf* VII.78–86, itself alluded to in *Tes* IV.80. Chaucer rejects Boccaccio's fatalistic version of Fortune for Dante's providential interpretation (pp 98–101). The account of Emily in Diana's temple (I.2333–40) is indebted to *Tes* VII.92, itself a reminiscence of *Inf* XIII.40–5. From the latter Chaucer reintroduces the 'wete brondes' (2334) and Emily's horror at the sight (pp 102–4). In describing the meeting of Palamon and Arcite in the grove (I.1638–42), Chaucer reintroduces details from *Inf* XIII.112–4, a source for *Tes* VII.106, where the rivals meet in the theater (p 104). Finally, Bennett discusses the relation of I.1761, 'For pitee renneth soone in gentil herte,' to *Inf* V.100. Chaucer does not give the Dantean allusion to Palamon, as Boccaccio does (*Tes* III.27), but

reserves it for Theseus, associating the prince's mercy with 'gentilesse' (cf *Tes* II.43) (pp 104–6). This association challenges Praz' interpretation of Chaucer as bourgeois (**83**, **615**) (p 106).

915 Benson, Robert G. *Medieval Body Language: A Study of the Use of Gesture in Chaucer's Poetry. Anglistica*, No. 21. Copenhagen: Rosenkilde and Bagger, 1980.
In both romances and saints' lives, tranquility is a sign of virtue, and excessive gesturing, a sign of evil (pp 44–5). Chaucer uses gesture to establish Theseus as the central figure in what Muscatine **726** calls the Tale's exposition of 'the nature of the noble life.' The philosophic Theseus has fewer gestures than any other major character; 'he is never passion's slave' (p 51).

916 Blake, Kathleen A. 'Order and the Noble Life in Chaucer's *Knight's Tale?*' *MLQ* 34(1973), 3–19.
Blake questions Muscatine's characterization (**726**) of Theseus as the 'representative of Fate on earth,' given Saturn's 'decisive role' (p 3). The Tale is full of 'futile debates, which are not really open to rational solution but which must be resolved arbitrarily' (p 6), and the rhetoric of symmetry and balance 'has the effect of proposing everything in terms of alternatives ... but grounds for reasoned choosing are remarkably scant' (p 7). Blake cites Palamon's remark to Arcite: 'outher thow shalt dye, / Or thow ne shalt nat loven Emelye. / Chees which thou wolt, for thou shalt nat asterte!' (I.1593–5). The princes' choice among the gods is equally meaningless, as is the choice the reader is invited to make between the two princes. Only Theseus seems qualified to impose a meaningful ending, and the theater and the tournament demonstrate the power and nobility of his will. Yet Arcite dies an ignominious death after Theseus has declared him the tournament's winner. Saturn is the decisive agent, although Theseus, ignorant of this, celebrates Jupiter in his final speech. Nor is it clear, as Underwood **776** claims, that Saturn acts on Jupiter's behalf. Halverson's interpretation (**691**) exaggerates the success of Theseus' attempts at order, and Frost **684** and Jordan **846** misread I.1663–74, which do not identify Theseus as the executor of God's will, but as a human whose actions are determined by Fortune (p 15). Theseus produces only appearances of order, as in the funeral ritual (p 16). The grounds for Muscatine's 'faith in the ultimate order of all things' are shaky (p 18). The Tale reveals that 'the "noble life" is like any made, artificial human order: it offers aesthetic satisfaction, but it is not the earthly embodiment of God's scheme, nor a purposeful, effective agent in the working out of any "ultimate order"' (p 19).

917 Blamires, Alcuin. 'Chaucer's Revaluation of Chivalric Honor.' *Mediaevalia* 5(1979), 245–69.
Blamires surveys Chaucer's works, including *BD, Mars* and *TC*, and especially *Thop, Mel* and *KnT*, to show that Chaucer was opposed to a concept of chivalric honor based on belligerent prowess. 'Chaucer was really straining against his distaste for prowess' throughout the *KnT* (p 261). He turns the duel of Palamon and Arcite into 'a desperate affair of frothing savagery' (p 262) while exalting the peace-making role of Theseus; the anonymity of the action in the tournament undercuts claims of anyone's winning honor while exposing the shame of being dragged to the stake (pp 262–3); and a sense of futility is communicated by Mars' temple, especially by the depiction of Conquest (p 263).

918 Blodgett, E.D. 'Chaucerian *Pryvetee* and the Opposition to Time.' *Spec* 51(1976), 477–93.
Pryvetee is the Chaucerian equivalent of the classical *otium*, withdrawal from the world; it represents an attempt to control and thus to deny time, and its 'negative effects are thoroughly displayed' in Fragment I (p 481). In the *KnT* Theseus' final speech presents a downward view: nature descends into corruption, death is a relief (p 485). The knights do not adventure forth but seek a perilous stasis. 'Hence, Muscatine's analysis **[726]** of the structure of the tale and its symbolic order is attractive without being persuasive,' for order takes the form of prison and exile, which are here 'negative states of liberation' (p 486). The world of the Tale is dominated by Saturn, 'the possessor of death' (p 487). All Theseus can do as a Jovean figure is to establish a 'static order within chaos by providing prisons, temples, and elaborate tournaments. Each is a spatial and geometric response to events, and each issues ... in strife and death' (p 487). The season of May appears to be Jovean, and to offer a new life based on love. But 'every time May comes back, it carries mortality in its wake, ultimately bringing death to Arcite and loss to Palemon and Emily. 'The speech on the First Moevere and the marriage seem natural but anti-climactic arrangements' (p 488). All of the tales of the First Fragment represent a fall from spirit to flesh. 'If it is possible to suggest an anagogic level to the *Knight's Tale*, it is malevolent; if it is possible to suggest a moral level to the *Miller's Tale*, it is an instrument for erotic ends. Allegory is only multiple innuendo in the *Reeve's Tale*, and the literal is the only level that emerges in the *Cook's Tale*' (p 492). 'The descent of the First Fragment ... is a long dramatization of the loss of prefiguration as a character of thought, and without such a sense pilgrimage ... is

impossible. Hence, the aesthetically attractive symmetries of the *Knight's Tale* serve mainly to foreshadow the sinister kinds of retribution which characterize the following tales' (p 493).

919 Boheemen, Christel van. 'Chaucer's *Knight's Tale* and the Structure of Myth.' *DQR* 9(1979), 176–90.
Characterization in the *KnT* illustrates 'decomposition,' the structural principal of myth whereby 'various attributes of a given person are disunited and several individuals are invented, each endowed with one group of the original attributes' (p 185). Together Palamon and Arcite represent Thebes, Dionysian chaos, mutability, death. They are opposed by Theseus and Emily, who represent Athens, Apollonian order, immutability, eternal life. The decomposition allows Athens to triumph over Thebes, in the person of Arcite, and to unite Thebes to itself, after a period of purification, in the person of Palamon. The marriage is the 'grete effect' of the Tale, and Arcite's death is 'the indispensable preliminary' to it (p 188). This pattern is analogous to the Christian schema by which the individual must experience the death of the body in order for his soul to live eternally. See Perryman **1118**.

920 Boitani, Piero. 'Chaucer's Temples of Venus.' *Studi Inglesi* 2(1975), 9–31.
Boitani compares Chaucer's three descriptions of Venus in *HF* (I.119–467), *PF* (172–294), and *KnT* (I.1918–66) to their classical antecedents and to Boccaccio's treatment in the *Tes*. For the Anadyomene of the mythographers, Boccaccio substitutes a bivalent goddess of courtly love and of sensuality. Chaucer restores the idol of the mythographers and places her in a complex with other forces: Fame and Rumor, or Nature, or Mars and Diana. In the *KnT* (pp 27–31) Chaucer revised the *Tes* by replacing the personified prayer with a direct observer, establishing the symmetry of the three temples, and introducing the system of Chinese boxes: murals on walls of oratories within lists. Chaucer depicts Venus as a significant force, both as a goddess and a planet.

921 —— 'Chaucer and Lists of Trees.' *Reading Medieval Studies* 2(1976), 28–44.
Boitani examines Chaucer's use of the *RR* (1351–8), the *Tes* (XI.22–4), *Met* (X.90–108), and *Theb* (VI.98–106) as sources for his tree-lists in the *Rom* (1379–86), *PF* (176–82), and *KnT* (2063–5; I.2921–3). In the *KnT*, Chaucer drops the functional attributes ascribed to the trees in *PF*, probably in the interest of fitting the list to the Knight's use of *occupatio* (pp 35–6).

922 — *Chaucer and Boccaccio*. 1977. See **238**.
Ch 4 (pp 76–102) provides a line-by-line analysis of Chaucer's uses of *Tes* VII in Parts Three and Four of the *KnT*. A table (pp 76–8) shows how Chaucer restructured the material into three groups of four episodes each, with an interpolation from *Tes* VI. In *Tes* VII Chaucer found 'the core of the story, the point at which all Boccaccio's themes converge, and the most interesting iconography' (p 102). Ch 5 (pp 103–12) presents an overview of Chaucer's borrowings. Of the 9,541 lines of the *Tes*, Chaucer omits 8,000, summarizes 1,080 in 139 lines of his own, and uses 461 lines more closely. Ch 6 (pp 113–6) argues that Chaucer's ms of the *Tes* did contain Boccaccio's glosses. To the four parallels Pratt **82** thought possible but unconvincing, Boitani adds twenty-two, of which he regards one as certain, Chaucer's 'bowe Turkeys' (I.2895). Ch 7 (pp 117–26) examines the ways the *Tes* prompted Chaucer to borrow from the *RR, Theb, Met, Div Com,* and *Consol.* Ch 8, on plot and structure (pp 127–34), emphasizes Chaucer's interest in symmetry. Ch 9 concerns characterization (pp 135–47). Chaucer intended each of his characters to be not an individual but an Everyman; the exception is Theseus, whose human individuality is combined with his roles as ideal figure interpreting providence and as typical feudal lord. Ch 10 discusses iconography and decoration. The Knight-narrator's comment on the tournament (*KnT* 1243–67; I.2101–25), analyzed in detail (pp 155–9), represents Chaucer's realistic interest in a medieval present, without historical perspective, as opposed to Boccaccio's archaeological idealizing interest in a classical past. The *Tes* is 'a cultural element that Chaucer absorbs. Some of the cultural strata which form Boccaccio's poem are kept, others adapted and modified, others replaced by elements which, though culturally different, stand for similar meanings: and, finally, new elements are added. This is what we may call *the Chaucerian compromise*' (p 164). Ch 11 concerns style (pp 165–89), and treats the pace and tone of the two works as well as the imagery; the latter includes Chaucer's description of the dawn (*KnT* 633–46; I.1491–1504) and the physical details of Arcite's dying (*KnT* 1885–90; I.2743–8). The *Tes* is an *avant garde* work by a young intellectual; the *KnT* is a bold reshaping of traditional cultural materials by a mature poet (pp 188–9). See **1071**.

923 Branch, Eren Hostetter. 'Man Alone and Man in Society: Chaucer's *Knight's Tale* and Boccaccio's *Teseida*.' 1974. See **241**.
In this typically late medieval work, Chaucer transforms classical epic into philosophical allegory. He presents isolated human beings trying to achieve the proper perspective on suprahuman forces operating in

an irrational world. Treated as abstractions that define a pre-Christian order, ceremonies and customs become protagonists, as do the passions that cause the characters to become manifestations of fortune to each other. Chaucer uses the classical setting in a centripetal manner: to support his delineation of the philosophical perspective available to those denied Christian revelation. The philosophical framework is Chaucer's main thematic addition to Boccaccio's story, and the Knight-narrator is his main narrative addition. Concentrating on chivalry and his hero-worship of Theseus, the Knight is unaware of the way his Tale implies continual threats to human efforts at creating order. Approaching experience principally through the concept of fortune, he does not appreciate the inadequacies of Theseus' vision, and thus his own perspective becomes part of the philosophical structure of the work.

924 Brewer, Derek. 'Honour in Chaucer.' *E&S* 26(1973), 1–19. Rpt in Brewer. *Tradition and Innovation in Chaucer*. London: Macmillan, 1982. Pp 89–109.

Honour is 'Janus-faced,' embracing both inner virtue and external reputation, with a 'continuum of meaning' between the two (p 3). As an example of how 'honour derives from the public recognition of virtue,' Brewer cites Arcite's achievement of honour, as Philostrate, at Theseus' court (p 5).

925 — *Chaucer and His World*. London: Eyre Methuen, 1978.

The *KnT* 'gives us the feeling ... [of Edward III's court] better than any other record': eg, the conception of war in terms of personal honour; the ruthlessness reflected in Arcite's comment on 'Ech man for hymself' (I.1182); his funeral, suggestive of rites for Edward and for the Black Prince **204**; the marriage of Palamon and Emily, reminiscent of Gaunt's marriage to Blanche of Lancaster; Arcite's advancement at court, suggestive of Chaucer's own (pp 108–9). 'Chaucer is the supreme example of the poet as "insider" ... [the *KnT*] can afford to express the court's feeling about itself. It is neither flattering nor self-satirical' (p 109).

926 — 'The Arming of the Warrior in European Literature and Chaucer.' In *Chaucerian Problems and Perspectives: Essays Presented to Paul E. Beichner, C.S.C.* Ed. Edward Vasta and Zacharias P. Thundy. Notre Dame: University of Notre Dame Press, 1979. Pp 221–43. Rpt in Brewer. *Tradition and Innovation in Chaucer*. London: Macmillan, 1982. Pp 142–60.

Brewer traces the *topos* from its use in the *Iliad* to its deployment in the metrical romances. The *Gawain*-poet 'finally naturalizes it, while Chaucer, naturalistic, or realistic in a quite opposite way, effectively kills it' in *Thop* (p 235). Brewer notes that there are opportunities for its use in the *KnT*, particularly in the duel scene, 'but there is nowhere the least hint of the traditional formulae ... What Chaucer finds moving is suffering, not aggression' (p 238).

927 Brody, Saul N. 'The Comic Rejection of Courtly Love.' In *Pursuit of Perfection: Courtly Love in Medieval Literature*. Ed. Joan M. Ferrante and George Economou. Port Washington, New York: Kennikat, 1975. Pp 221–61.
Theseus rightly ridicules Palamon and Arcite, 'first cousins to the Parlement's three tercels' (p 249), for sacrificing themselves for a girl who does not return their love. The marriage of Palamon and Emelye 'legitimizes the courtly love ideal by transforming it into an ideal which serves something outside itself; the Knight gives it a transcendent aim, a metaphysical cause which brings it to serve the world and God' (p 250). The Miller, cousin to the ducks of *PF*, seems to agree that courtly lovers make fools of themselves, but rejects the idea of substituting divine principles for courtly ones. 'Chaucer seems to imply not that divine or courtly principles are themselves foolish, but that being elevated they cannot be followed by men, who are essentially carnal' (p 252).

928 Burlin, Robert B. 'Palamon and Arcite.' *Chaucerian Fiction*. Princeton: Princeton University Press, 1977. Pp 95–111.
The *KnT* is a philosophical work in which the epistemological aspects of fiction are explored. It re-works the *PF* in a more densely human narrative borrowed from the *Tes*, whose pagan setting Chaucer interprets with the aid of Boethius (pp 95–100). Palamon and Arcite are 'counters in a philosophical inquiry' (p 101), representing forces that direct human life; their equality is essential to the issue of justice. Theseus, too, is 'a paradigmatic figure,' his vitality arising more from the plot than from character. All inhabit 'a philosophic parable within which an individualized personality would constitute a serious breach of decorum' (p 101). The action carries a correspondingly greater burden of significance, with the symmetrical relationships of Parts I and II providing an exposition of Fortune's reversals (pp 101–2). In Part III the planetary deities represent human passions, and the forces earlier represented as Fortune reside now in the stars and the human psyche (pp 102–3). In Part IV Theseus attempts to assert human dignity in spite of Fortune. He replaces Saturn with Jupiter, and 'as Jupiter's theologian, presides, like Nature in the *Parliament*, over the union of the surviving lovers' (p 105). The symbolical structure of the Tale, particularly its beginning and ending with marriages, confirms the philosophical

insight that Theseus, as a pagan, cannot fully articulate. 'The limitations of Theseus' speech are serious' (p 105). It places death in the perspective of successions in nature, but cannot explain the individual death; it shows that there is order in the universe, but not necessarily justice; its identification of order with love is unconvincing because it fails to distinguish sufficiently between human and non-human existence. Theseus sees beyond Fortune, but does not grasp the concept of Providence, as seen in the differences between his speech and the *Consol* (pp 106–7). These limitations are consistent with Theseus' role as representative of an intermediary Destiny (I.1663–5), but his actions in that role make his speech 'more profoundly resonant than a literal analysis allows' (p 108). He brings an ethical dimension to his pagan world 'by his gestures if not by his philosophizing' (p 111).

929 Burrow, J.A. *Ricardian Poetry: Chaucer, Gower, Langland and the 'Gawain' Poet.* London: Routledge & Kegan Paul; New Haven: Yale University Press, 1971. Esp pp 53–6, 94–99, 112–4, 116–7, 125–9. By choosing the Knight as narrator rather than the Squire, Chaucer moves away from the lyrical, sentimental character of the *Tes* to produce 'a more objective, more purely "historical" kind of poem' (p 54). Chaucer, lacking a sense of war as a 'great subject,' gives minimal attention to fighting; and his use of alliterative verse in the description of the tournament identifies it as an 'alien matter' (p 56). Chaucer shares with other Ricardian poets 'an unheroic image of man' (p 94). We see Theseus as a civilian; Chaucer does not remind us that Emily is an Amazon. Theseus' speech on love is an example of the humorous manner of Ricardian poetry. It distances us from the princes' view of their situation without entirely undermining our sympathies with them (pp 112–3). An aspect of such humor is 'some acceptance of "things as they are"' (p 116), an acceptance based on the doctrine of the Ages of Man. This doctrine is 'important but implicit' in the *KnT*: Palamon and Arcite, like the Squire, are given to passionate love; Theseus, like the Knight, has known marriage, conquest and rule; and Egeus, like the parson, possesses 'saturnine wisdom' (p 117). The dominance of Theseus makes the *KnT* 'middle-aged' (p 125). 'The Knight is, of course, a fictional person; but I believe that nowhere else in his work does Chaucer decisively transcend the limitations of the Knight's vision; nor, perhaps, do his contemporaries' (p 127). Chaucer maintains a certain distance from intensities of both youth and old age, disappointing the reader's need for 'grandeur of thought, unguarded intensity of feeling, and sublimity of expression' (p 128). But the poetry in which Theseus, Harry Bailey,

Pandarus, Sir Bertilak (*SGGK*), Piers and Will (*Piers Plowman*) play the dominant roles offers a characteristic 'jovial' wisdom. 'Here is the "largeness, freedom, shrewdness, benignity" which Matthew Arnold allowed Chaucer; but also what he denied him, a kind of "high seriousness"' (p 129). See **993**.

930 Cherchi, Paolo. '"The Knight's Tale": Lines 1774–81.' *MP* 76(1978/9), 46–8.
Cherchi traces Theseus' reflection on the proper ways for a lord to treat the proud and the repentant to a proverbial formula ultimately derived from *Aen* VI.853: 'parcere subiectis et debellare superbos.'

931 Ciavolella, M. 'Mediaeval Medicine and Arcite's Love Sickness.' *Florilegium* 1(1979), 222–41.
Chaucer's description of Arcite's love-sickness (I.1358–79) was inspired by Boccaccio's in *Tes* IV, but the two poets use different sources and Chaucer's treatment is the more 'scientific' (pp 223–4). Ciavolella provides a lengthy summary (pp 225–33) of the medical tradition on which Chaucer drew, emphasizing the way in which obsessive concentration on the 'phantasma' of the beloved (p 231) was believed to produce the 'anorexic' lover (p 232). Boccaccio drew on literary sources, including Cavalcanti's 'Donna mi prega' (pp 233–5). Boccaccio works to heighten the dramatic effects (p 236); Chaucer 'considers himself the interpreter of *amour courtois* in England' (p 237).

932 Clogan, Paul M. 'Literary Criticism in William Godwin's *Life of Chaucer.*' *M&H* ns 6(1975), 189–98.
While finding Dryden's estimate of the *KnT* too high, Godwin (1804) praises the Tale as 'full of novelty and surprise' and visual appeal; it presents the most 'powerful portrait of chivalry that was perhaps ever delineated' (p 193).

933 — 'Chaucer and Leigh Hunt.' *M&H* ns 9(1979), 163–74.
Clogan quotes Hunt's discussion of I.2273 – 'Uprose the sun, and uprose Emily' (**579**) and says: 'Hunt's habit of close reading is nowhere so well demonstrated' (p 171).

934 Cowgill, Bruce Kent. 'The *Knight's Tale* and the Hundred Years' War.' *PQ* 54(1975), 670–9.
Chaucer describes an archaic tournament (p 671) in order to associate the Knight with an older concept of chivalry and to dissociate him from contemporary standards and the Hundred Years' War, as Hatton **417** has shown his portrait also does. Cowgill compares Chaucer's tournament with Richard II's pageant at Smithfield in 1390 and with tournaments described by Froissart **183** and Painter **202**, and by the chronicler Holinshed (pp 671–3).

Fourteenth-century tournaments featured jousts and blunted weapons; twelfth- and thirteenth-century tournaments were violent mêlées, practices for actual battle. Thus Chaucer's mêlée is authentically medieval, as S. Robertson **616** and Parr **737** argue, but not contemporary in style. Chaucer's attitude can be seen in the association of jousting with dancing in the Squire's portrait (I.94–6) and in the activities preceding the tournament (I.2486–7). C.D. Benson's and Haller's studies (**799**, **831**) of the genre of the *KnT* and of the Theban allusions show its relevance to the internecine conflict of England and France (p 675–6). Similarities between Chaucer's tournament and proposals by Edward III and Geoffrey de Charny **173** for judicial tourneys to settle the issues of the War indicate that the *KnT* is 'a quiet plea for peace' (p 677).

934a Cox, Robert C. 'Chaucer's May 3.' 1972.
See Kellogg **985**.

935 Crampton, Georgia Ronan. *The Condition of Creatures: Suffering and Action in Chaucer and Spenser*. New Haven and London: Yale University Press, 1974.
Crampton examines the use of the topos 'agere et pati' in the *KnT* and in Books I–IV of the *FQ*. Ch 2, 'Theseus' Scene: Action in the Knight's Tale' (pp 45–75): The other characters are sufferers, Theseus is an actor. His decisiveness is supported by narrative compression, syntactic strategies, and the deployment of epithets, but ambiguities about life as action are implicit throughout. In the grove, Theseus' action consists of making up his mind between vengeance and mercy. In the year that elapses before the tournament, Theseus moves from his early illusion, 'that he is an invincible dealer of death,' to a second illusion, 'that he presides over life' (p 64). In the interval between Arcite's death and the parliament, Theseus finds, in a cosmic commitment to love, the ground for continuing to act without illusions. The lapse of time makes the wisdom in his final speech 'the product of the precise, personal experiences of this duke' (p 66). Yet the audience knows that capricious Saturn, not providential Jupiter, has determined events. Still the subject of an irrational universe is denied tragic treatment: no hero challenges the divine order; the narrator's tone dispels any sense of urgency; and Theseus' speech implies the futility of dwelling upon such subjects. The speech is not evasive but tentative in its affirmations. Ch 3, 'Feasts Perturbed and Prisons: Image in the Knight's Tale' (pp 76–112), explores Palamon's question: 'are human beings no more than sheep to the gods?' (p 76). Theseus' rehearsal of the cycles of life and death in his final speech is a vision toward which the images of the whole poem lead. Chaucer

critiques the feasting mentality by showing how Theseus and his guests delude themselves into believing that all the mishaps in the tournament have been minor. Chaucer's critique of the mourning mentality shows that the tragic perspective on Arcite's death is only one of several, as illustrated by the different view of the wood gods. Unlike the turning of Fortune's wheel, the alternation of festival and mourning applies to all ranks in society, and does not make humans so strictly sufferers of destiny (pp 77–92). More severe restrictions on human freedom are suggested by the imagery of prisons and traps (pp 92–104). The narrator repeatedly refers to his characters as captives. Palamon and Arcite articulate a growing perception of life itself as confining, and the shrines of the gods provide mythic extensions of the princes' prison. Animal imagery (pp 104–12) suggests that human beings are sufferers because of a fundamental appropriateness of that condition to the nature they share with animals. Ch 6, 'Conclusion' (pp 178–202), supports and qualifies the truism that 'Spenser the Renaissance poet celebrates action; Chaucer, a medieval poet, sufferance' (p 178).

936 David, Alfred. 'The Order of Chivalry.' *The Strumpet Muse: Art and Morals in Chaucer's Poetry*. 1976. See **446**. Pp 77–89.
Chaucer's assigning the *P&A* to the Knight and juxtaposing it with the *MilT* 'is a more creative act than any revision could have been' (p 78). The *KnT* is similar to *TC* in subject and theme but different in style. In *TC* 'the ideal of cosmic order ... is overwhelmed by the confusing human reality' (p 80); in the *KnT* Chaucer attempts 'to hold the troubling sense of humanity in abeyance' (p 81) by using characters who are types and a plot that is mathematically ordered. The difference can be seen by comparing the description of Troilus passing before Criseyde's window (II.624–48) with the description of Emetrius entering the lists (I.2155–86). The courtly aspects of the first, noted by Muscatine (**726**, pp 157–8), are qualified by naturalistic and dramatic perspectives; the latter is the 'pure example' (p 82) of the courtly, non-naturalistic style. Arcite's death is moving rather as the death of youth, beauty, and passion than as the death of an individual, and his death-bed questions are answered by Chaucer's vision of a hierarchically ordered universe embodied, as Muscatine demonstrated, in the Tale's symmetrical structure. But this idea of order is disturbed by 'a sense of the ridiculous and ... a sense of evil' (p 86). The 'flippant' voice identified by Salter **883** exposes pain as effectively as the high style (pp 87–8). These 'reflexes of Chaucer's native skepticism' weaken his argument for order, a limitation Chaucer recognized. In the *CT* the *KnT* expresses 'not the prevailing

order but the nostalgic wish for an order that might have been once upon a time' (p 88). See also p 105: the *KnT* stands for 'fidelity to higher principle'; the *MilT*, for 'fidelity to the vital principle of life.'

937 Dillon, Bert. *A Chaucer Dictionary: Proper Names and Allusions Excluding Place Names*. Boston: G. K. Hall, 1974.
Entries are arranged alphabetically, and give variant spellings, identification, references to other literary works and to scholarly studies, and a list of occurrences in Chaucer's works. Eg, the entry for 'Boccaccio' lists passages in the *Tes* to which Chaucer's poems are indebted (pp 44–7) along with additional sources for each passage: for the *KnT*, Statius, Dante, Ovid, Virgil. The entry for 'Pirithous' identifies him, lists sources in the *Met, Tes* and *RR*, and cites Hoffman **839**.

938 DiMarco, Vincent Joseph. 'Literary and Historical Researches Respecting Chaucer's Knight and Squire.' 1972. See **447**.
There exists a potential conflict between Theseus' role as conqueror, with its emphasis on individual deeds of valor, and his role as governor, with its emphasis on the communal welfare. His several accessions to the pleas of others distances him from the churlishness of Creon, but only the conflict between Palamon and Arcite shows him the compatibility of knighthood and love. Love embraces a leader's benevolence to his subjects, respect for women and marriage, recognition of universal mortality, and faith in a providential order. In a variation of the romance motif of sworn brotherhood, Palamon, who believes in the compatibility of love and brotherhood, initially enacts Theseus' identity as governor, while Arcite, who denies this compatibility, enacts the role of conqueror. Later Palamon betrays brotherhood by exposing Arcite to Theseus, and Arcite reestablishes brotherhood by surrendering Emeleye to Palamon. The concept of sworn brotherhood becomes the instrument of Theseus' illumination by showing that Palamon and Arcite overvalued romantic love and that Theseus himself undervalued love in general (pp 113–88).

939 Dolan, Michael. 'Chaucer and the Continental Tradition: A Study in Neoplatonic Influences.' Cornell University PhD dissertation, 1974. *DAI* 35(1975), 4511A–12A.
The *KnT* presents a drama of men suffering from *letargye* – a condition of ethical confusion; the neoplatonic allusions are 'foils to the narrator's Christian point of view within which the difficulties and contradictions of man's post-lapsarian condition are viewed as resolved.'

940 Donaldson, E. Talbot. 'The Masculine Narrator and Four Women of Style.' *Speaking of Chaucer*. New York: Norton, 1972. Pp 46–64.

The plain sense of I.1034–55 is that 'Emily is a pretty, long-haired blonde with a good complexion and an excellent singing voice' (p 49). The complex meaning is that she is youth, beauty, and Spring. The world of the *KnT* 'seems devoid of purpose or significance. Emily is one of the ideas that make this world tolerable, and if she were given a personality, she would lose her symbolic significance' (p 49). Arcite may have been as much deceived in thinking her a woman as Palamon was in thinking her a goddess: 'for she was only an idea, though one of more importance to the ideal of chivalry than a real woman could have been' (p 50). See **1107**.

941 Ebner, Dean. 'Chaucer's Precarious Knight.' 1971. See **451**.
The moral of the *MkT* is an ascetic one: urgent withdrawal from the active life in an unstable world in favor of preparing for a heavenly life. The *KnT* celebrates worldly splendor, often in details Chaucer added to his source, and consistently avoids or neutralizes the tragic implications of the plot, most effectively in Theseus' final speech. The Knight, anxious about his own prosperity and unwilling to grant the absolute existence of evil, must object to the *MkT* for personal and philosophical reasons.

942 Elbow, Peter. 'How Chaucer Transcends Oppositions in the *Knight's Tale*.' *ChauR* 7(1973), 97–112; rpt with minor changes as '*The Knight's Tale*' in *Oppositions in Chaucer*. Middletown, Conn.: Wesleyan University Press, 1975. Pp 73–94.
The *demande d'amour* (I.1347–52) provides the framework for the *KnT*, being complicated and enlarged until many of the elements of the work have been brought into opposition (pp 97–8). Palamon is the more open, impulsive, and naive cousin; Arcite, the more tough-minded, distanced, and pragmatic (pp 98–100). Yet Chaucer refuses to answer the *demande* as to which is worthier, as seen in three paradoxes: Arcite wins Emelye, but Palamon gets her; the wedding is overshadowed by the funeral; and Arcite wins by conduct characteristic of Palamon – following the rules – while Palamon gets Emelye through an extra-legal intervention characteristic of Arcite (pp 100–101). The *demande* itself is shown to be problematic by Chaucer's treatments of Theseus, Saturn, and the First-Mover speech. Theseus exposes the absurdity of the contest over Emelye, is sensitive to the reality of pain and death, and provides a model of thoughtfulness (pp 101–4). In the grove (pp 104–6), he moves through 'a rich sequence of mental processes' showing that he combines Arcite's 'gift for detachment' with Palamon's 'gift for involvement' (p 106). Animal imagery also shows the superiority of Theseus' virtues to the princes' (pp 107–8). Saturn expresses the central theme by making peace

between Mars and Venus without destroying their opposition. His violent means throw into sharper relief Theseus' association with order and mercy (pp 108–9). The First-Mover speech (pp 109–11) shows that neither lover is worthier than the other by incorporating and transcending values associated with each. 'The poem is about the transition from a static, symmetrical opposition to a state of complex, paradoxical process' (p 111). See **1092**.

943 Eliason, Norman. *The Language of Chaucer's Poetry: An Appraisal of the Verse, Style, and Structure. Anglistica*, Vol. 17. Copenhagen: Rosenkilde and Bagger, 1972.
The *KnT* is 'greatly overrated' and its structure is 'decidedly inferior to that of Chaucer's work at its best' (p 13). By imposing order on the episodic structure of the *Tes*, Chaucer sacrificed 'the charm which the haphazard course of events often has in a romance ... [while] he gained only a structural tidiness so conspicuous that it can hardly fail to distract the reader and so rigid that it clearly constrained his treatment of the tale' (pp 159–60). Theseus is not the representative of a principle of order, as Muscatine **726** claims, but a ruler who acts whimsically and arbitrarily (p 159), and the soap-opera plot mitigates against seeing the Tale as a serious philosophical poem (p 160). Nevertheless the *KnT* provides 'a stately if somewhat stuffy prelude' to the other tales (p 160).

944 — 'Chaucer the Love Poet.' In *Chaucer the Love Poet*. Ed. Jerome Mitchell and William Provost. Athens: University of Georgia Press, 1973. Pp 9–26.
Chaucer is most successful in treating 'ordinary love' (p 10), the 'tender and passionate affection for one of the opposite sex' (p 9). The idealization of love in the *KnT* destroys its worth and interest as a love story. 'The rival claims of Palamon and Arcite, two equally hare-brained young men, for the hand of Emelye, possibly the most mindless heroine in all literature, [and] the preposterous series of events which culminate in the winning of the girl ... constitutes a story too fatuous for any serious consideration' (pp 14–5).

945 Elliott, Ralph W.V. *Chaucer's English*. London: André Deutsch, 1974.
Elliott comments on the alliteration, diction, inverted word order, and use of pronouns in the description of the tournament battle scene (I.2605–16); on alliteration and diction in the description of the site of Mars' temple (I.1975–80) (pp 102–7); and on the appropriateness of colloquialisms and *occupatio* to the Knight-narrator (pp 414–6).

946 Engelhardt, George J. 'The Lay Pilgrims of the *Canterbury Tales*.' 1974. See **454**.

The Knight, functioning as a critic of the *Tes*, minimizes the roles of Juno and Fortune; the important role is given to Saturn (pp 293–8), an apotheosis of 'the retributive principle that inheres in the inordinate passions of man.' In Boccaccio's glosses, Palemone is identified with the concupiscible appetite; Arcita, with the irascible. Chaucer refines this differentiation by making Palamon the 'proprietary' lover, and Arcite the 'admirer,' or 'opthalmic' lover (pp 298–9). While the ostensible topic is consolation for the death of a young hero, the real topic is submission to God's will (p 300). Boccaccio's Arcita sees the vanity of earthly goods from the eighth sphere, but his Palemone is unconverted. Ignoring Arcite, the Knight focuses on 'rescuing Palamon from the slough in which Boccaccio left him' through a marriage that participates in Boethian and Pauline definitions of love (pp 300–1). Boccaccio treats the marriage night in the manner of fabliau in both text and gloss, but the Knight blesses the marriage and makes fun of the princes' earlier follies in love (pp 301–2). Boccaccio celebrates the tournament in his text and admits its immorality in his gloss. The Knight characterizes it as an attempt 'to manipulate Providence and to tempt God' partly by his use of the rude alliterative style (p 304). Boccaccio allegorizes his classical gods in his glosses; the Knight subordinates them to Saturn and satirizes them, as in his association of unheroic activities with Mars (pp 304–5).

947 Fichte, Joerg O. 'Man's Free Will and the Poet's Choice: The Creation of Artistic Order in Chaucer's *Knight's Tale*.' 1975. See **456**. Part One of the *KnT* explores 'the themes of mutability, of man's insufficient knowledge, and of what appears to be divine injustice ... Sufferings in love are just a by-product of the general disorder characteristic of this sublunary sphere' (p 342). The Knight's *demande* (A[I].1347–52) is an inadequate comment on this portion of the poem (pp 340–1), even as Theseus' final speech is a 'philosophical appendage' to the plot (p 342). After reviewing criticisms of the speech offered by Curry **543**, Westlund **896**, Salter **883**, Underwood **776**, and Fifield **824**, Fichte adds that the speech 'places an undue emphasis on God's power' (p 344). Chaucer deliberately designed the 'thematic irresolution' of the *KnT* because he believed that 'an *ex cathedra* statement cannot resolve the real issues' (p 345). Fichte then reviews (pp 345–50) the development in fourteenth-century philosophy, preeminently in Ockham, of the thesis that God has both 'ordained power' — expressed through his instituted laws — and 'absolute power' — the power to do everything that is not contradictory. To the question whether such power allows significant human freedom, Ockham answered in the affirmative, defining freedom more radically than did Boethius, as a matter of will rather than intellect. In his attempts to impose order, Theseus underestimates the freedom of others – eg, to ignorantly follow their passions – while in his final speech, he underestimates his own freedom and bows to necessity. Chaucer solves the problem Theseus cannot solve by composing 'a structurally perfect work of art' (pp 352–3). 'By an exercise of free will, the artist has created structural order and superimposed it on Theseus' world, where chaos is caused by the characters' imperfect understanding of God's absolute power in its relation to their freedom of choice' (p 356). The *KnT* provides 'a paradigm of Chaucer's *ars poetica*' (p 359). The structure of the *CT* mirrors the structure of the *KnT*: eg, the *ParsT* (p 360), provides a thematically inadequate ending just as Theseus' speech does in the *KnT*. See **887**, **948**.

948 —— 'The Paradigm of Artistic Order.' *Chaucer's 'Art Poetical': A Study in Chaucerian Poetics*. Tübingen: Gunter Narr, 1980. Pp 81–97.
A reprinting of **947** with a new section on love, one of the major themes of the *CT* (pp 81–4). In the *KnT* love is an irrational, lawless, and arbitrary force, one of the destinal forces that frustrates the characters' attempts at self-assertion. Neither the tournament nor the marriage can resolve the love problem since the one depends on mere chance and the other is dictated by political necessity.

949 Fisher, John H. 'The Three Styles of Fragment I of the Canterbury Tales.' *ChauR* 8(1973), 119–227.
Although we cannot be certain Chaucer knew John of Garland's *Poetria*, the first three Canterbury Tales almost seem designed to illustrate Garland's linkage of the three rhetorical styles – high, middle and low – to a social classification: courtiers, urban citizens and rural folk. The *KnT* involves the Athenian court, an elaborate love service, and no explicit sexual references; the *MilT*, civic Oxford, a seduction plot, and scatological humor; and the *RvT*, the rustic fens of Trumpington, mere sexual adventure, and explicit sexual humor.

950 Friman, Anne. 'Of Bretherhede: The Friendship Motif in Chaucer.' *Innisfree* 3(1976), 24–36.
The bond between Theseus and Perotheus foreshadows the ennobling restoration of friendship between Palamon and Arcite (pp 24–5).

951 Frye, Northrop. *The Secular Scripture: A Study of the Structure of Romance*. Cambridge, Massachusetts: Harvard University Press, 1976.
'The disasters and tragedies wrought by the conjunctions of the stars [in *KnT* and *TC*] make it clear that the heavens are for [Chaucer}, as for most science fiction writers today, much more a symbol of

alienation than of divine presence' (p 98). The goddess Diana symbolizes nature as 'a closed cycle that man is trapped in'; Arcite must be sacrificed to make the marriage of Palamon and Emily possible (p 154).

952 Fyler, John. 'The Narrator and His Double.' *Chaucer and Ovid*. 1979. See **460**. Pp 124–47.
Chaucer substitutes for a Boccaccian surrogate who suffers with the narrator, an Ovidian surrogate who is a detached observer and shaper of order (pp 127–9). Theseus is the surrogate of the Knight, and the development of their characters represents Chaucer's principal departure from the *Tes*. They are alike in their military enthusiasms, indifference to death, detachment from the youthful folly of love, condescension toward woman, and benevolent attempts to maintain order (pp 138–42). Although Theseus initially seems cruel, he becomes more sympathetic as he releases Arcite, forgives the princes in the grove, organizes the tournament, and tries to prevent loss of life (pp 142–4). He shares with the Knight a resilient determination to establish order (p 144). The Knight's intrusions as narrator are as prominent as Theseus' attempts to control events (p 146).

953 Garbáty, Thomas J. 'And Gladly Teche the Tales of Caunterbury.' In *Approaches to Teaching Chaucer's 'Canterbury Tales.'* Ed. Joseph Gibaldi. Consultant editor, Florence H. Ridley. New York: The Modern Language Association of America, 1980, pp 46–56.
The Temple of Mars may shock students. The image of the sow eating the child (A[I].2019) may reflect Chaucer's war-time experience in France. 'Chaucer's geniality, humor, and wise humanity may have been dearly bought' (p 52).

954 Gardner, John. 'Fragment I, from the *General Prologue* to the *Cook's Tale*.' *The Poetry of Chaucer*. 1977. See **461**. Pp 227–62.
'By any standard, the best poem Chaucer ever wrote' (p 241), the *KnT* is a philosophical allegory in which Theseus represents ideal human justice and reason (p 242); Palamon, 'a perversion of the concupiscent or desiring soul;' and Arcite, 'a perversion of the irascible soul, or will' (p 245). Emelye's prayer shows her rejecting both the concupiscent and irascible elements, instead of seeking a right ordering of them (p 249). Theseus' hunting of the hart is an allegory for the subduing of the heart that does not know how to use the things of this world (p 248). In his final speech, Theseus explains why human beings should accept the cosmic plan. Saturn, 'the death principle on which orderly succession depends' (p 253), plays a similar role in heaven by reconciling the wills of individual gods with the common good (p 250). The *KnT* shows men working in co-

operation with the Prime Mover; the *MilT* shows them ruled by concupiscence, and the *RvT* shows them ruled by irascibility. Each tale is 'grounded on the character of its proponent' (p 262). All the characters in the tales receive a kind of justice, but 'in ways which leave human beings fairly helpless' (p 262). The authority for the Knight's world view is uncertain, and this is part of 'the nominalist-inspired skepticism' of the *CT* (p 337), which is replaced by an affirmation of faith in the *Ret.*

955 Gaylord, Alan T. 'The Role of Saturn in the *Knight's Tale*.' *ChauR* 8(1974), 171–90.
Gaylord sets out to reconcile Saturn with the Tale's happy ending, rejecting or qualifying the interpretations of Curry **543**, Muscatine **726**, Underwood **776**, Wedel **154**, and Loomis **851**, all of whom make Saturn responsible for Arcite's death, and of Brooks and Fowler **807**, who criticize Theseus' failure to be more like Saturn (pp 171–4). Chaucer presents Saturn as a planet; 'questions of philosophy, then, must be set within astrology,' whose teaching was that 'the wise man rules the stars' (pp 176–7). Palamon and Arcite are men in whom passion prevails over reason (pp 177–80). The scenes in the temples of Venus and Mars represent both 'an illustration of the mental states of the knights who go there to pray and a prediction of their futures' (p 182). Theseus, who designed the temples to reflect the knights' condition, 'represents the summing up of all that is good' in Venus, Mars, and Diana, and like Jupiter mitigates the severity of Saturn's influence (pp 182–3). Saturn is not the fateful cause of Arcite's death but 'a kind of baleful summary of the implications in the infatuate desires of the lovers' (p 183). He acts 'not because Jupiter is helpless, but because the lovers are not prepared for a reconciliation (p 183). Saturn's role is relatively unimportant; the battle itself, the disruption of brotherhood, is the disaster (p 184). Although Theseus intends the tournament to be an occasion for redemption through 'pitee,' he cannot force men to choose the good (p 185). The necessity Theseus speaks of is only death; although he does not make a full Boethian statement on freedom, he exemplifies it by effecting a reconciliation (pp 185–6). He is not the representative of fate, as Muscatine claims, but one who 'stands in the free service of Providence' (p 186).

956 Gilbert, A.J. *Literary Language*. 1979. See **462**.
Gilbert analyzes the passages on the princes' being found on the battlefield (I.1005–19), Theseus' decision to imprison them (1020–32), Emily's walking in the garden (1033–44), Emetreus (2155–71), Venus' temple (1918–33), and Mars' temple (1995–2008) with

reference to the high, middle, and low styles (pp 33–9). The variety of styles throws a number of lights on courtly love, an archaic ideal treated 'as a secular attempt to give meaning to the human condition, and ... shown to fail in the light of Boethian philosophy' (p 39). Chaucer's 'forensic version' of the low style (1153–64) shows Arcite's view of love to be 'debased and limited' (pp 40–1).

957 Gillmeister, Heiner. *Discrecioun*: *Chaucer und die Via Regia*. Bonn: Grundmann, 1972.
In Chaucer *discrecioun*, 'restraint,' or 'prudence,' is a virtue especially associated with the nobility, as in I.1779, 'That lord hath litel of discrecioun.' Theseus exhibits this virtue in the scene in the grove and in his management of the tournament (cf I.2538). There may be an allusion to Richard II and the political crisis of 1397 (pp 79–84).

958 Gray, Douglas. 'Chaucer and "Pite".' In *J.R.R. Tolkien, Scholar and Storyteller*. Ed. Mary Salu and Robert T. Farrell. Ithaca and London: Cornell University Press, 1979. Pp 173–203; esp pp 177–85.
As an instance of Chaucer's flexibility in using the term, Gray cites I.3075–89, where 'the rational tone of [Theseus' appeal to Emelye to accept Palamon], the hint of theological undertones in the association of *pite* with grace, the application of the adjective *womanly* to *pite*, suggest ... a wider concept of pite' than the merely courtly (p 178). After reviewing the derivation of the word from *pietas* (pp 178–9), Gray cites three aspects of Chaucer's uses of the term: the close connection of *pite* with *gentilesse* and, where rulers are concerned, with humility; the close connection with women; and the importance of those instances where *pite* suggests intense compassion (pp 179–83). The first of these points is illustrated by Theseus' encounters with the Theban women (I.919–21 and 952–4) and with Palamon and Arcite (1756–61 and 1773–80). The latter scene also illustrates the connection of *pite* with women (1748–50 and 1770–1). 'Pite' as intense compassion is illustrated by the Athenian women's grieving over Arcite (2835–6).

959 Green, John Martin. 'World Views and Human Power: The Four Phases of Chaucer's *Knight's Tale*.' University of California at Santa Cruz Dissertation, 1974. See also *DAI* 35(1975), 5403A.
The *KnT* presents four world views. The first, symbolized by Fortune's wheel, suggests that all human power is illusory. Theseus appears to be a god-like conqueror but he cannot wholly resolve the problems he addresses. Human powerlessness is treated ironically in the second view, whose emblem is the prison. The imprisonment of Palamon and Arcite is shown to involve a frame of mind in which they enjoy the impossibility of acting effectively. The tournament and the interven-

tion of the gods then define a third world view in which human control is seen to be possible and significant but limited. Finally, Arcite's death and Theseus' First Mover speech suggest the importance of human beings' reactions to things themselves uncontrollable. The funeral rites recognize Arcite's worth, and Theseus' speech affirms the possibility of belief in universal order. Theseus' struggle to believe is shared by the Knight who in his holy wars has experienced brutal disorder joined to high purpose.

960 Gruber, Loren C. 'The Wanderer and Arcite: Isolation and the Continuity of the English Elegiac Mode.' *Publications of the Society for New Language Study* 1(1972), 1–10.
In the Old English poem, the Wanderer's isolation arises from concrete physical circumstances, and could be remedied by his reincorporation into a comitatus. In the *KnT* Arcite's isolation becomes irremediable psychological alienation as he realizes the insufficiency of language to communicate the perplexities of his tragedy.

961 Hanning, Robert W. 'The Theme of Art and Life in Chaucer's Poetry.' In *Geoffrey Chaucer: A Collection of Original Articles.* Ed. George D. Economou. New York: McGraw-Hill, 1975. Pp 15–36.
The descriptions of the temples show how 'the artist can reduce areas of pain and chaos in actual experience ... to beautiful self-contained artifacts' (p 33). In Mars' temple 'a triple *ecphrasis*' is used: within the temple a wall made to resemble the temple in Thrace has another temple painted on it within whose walls are the paintings the Knight describes. When Arcite's death defeats Theseus' attempt at ordering experience, 'the artist's power in creating images of order seems somehow irrelevant — perhaps even a cruel hoax' (p 34).

962 — '"The Struggle between Noble Designs and Chaos": The Literary Tradition of Chaucer's *Knight's Tale.*' *Literary Review* 23(1980), 519–41.
Hanning offers a double response to Muscatine's claim (**726**) that 'the history of Thebes had perpetual interest for Chaucer as an example of the struggle between noble designs and chaos.' First Hanning confirms that the *Theb* and the *Tes* are concerned with the possibilities for and threats to order. In the *Theb* Theseus represents 'the belated, partial, but real triumph of civilization over passion' (pp 521–22), but Statius' most powerful vision of the noble life remains the funeral pyre on which the spirits of Polyneices and Eteocles rage at each other beyond death. Boccaccio's vision of the noble life is merely aesthetic. Through Teseo Boccaccio celebrates his own virtuosity in combining epic with romance. The other characters invite

us to be both cynically amused and sentimentally involved. This lack of a moral center moves the *Tes* toward an 'interpretive impasse' (p 527). In his 'more revisionist response' (p 520) to Muscatine, Hanning argues that Chaucer's originality lies in equating Theseus' attempts to establish order in the political realm with the Knight's attempts in the artistic realm. The golden bridle (I.2506–7) is the emblem of Theseus' 'precariousness of control,' and *occupatio* is Chaucer's main way of dramatizing the Knight's uncertain control. The construction and description of the lists 'fuse the high point of the Knight's art of language and Theseus' art of government' (p 532). The lists foreshadow the cosmic order later invoked in Theseus' speech, and emblemize the 'socially useful poetry that reflects and promotes cosmic order' (p 532). The Knight's experiences as a warrior, extensively mirrored in the Tale, have produced a 'fatalistic sense of life, amoral in its recognition of the uncontrollable element in human affairs' (p 537). Seeing his characters as playthings of larger forces, the Knight responds with apparent coldness and retreats from the abyss opened up by death and fortune by establishing Theseus as the 'mouthpiece of a philosophical optimism' (p 539). He arranges for Theseus to experience success in the plan for the marriage, but since it is impossible to say whether Theseus' earlier attempts to create order succeeded or led to more misery, his final success is also doubtful. In his speech we hear, 'someone's desperation — whether Theseus' or the Knight's is not clear — ' to escape despair (p 539). Chaucer shows a 'vivid and profound comprehension of the tensions that might well exist within the *Weltanschauung* of a late medieval mercenary warrior' (p 539), in which the attempt to 'moralize and dignify aggression' produces that 'synthetic phenomenon, the idealistic killer' (p 540).

963 Harbert, Bruce. 'Chaucer and the Latin Classics.' In *Writers and Their Background: Geoffrey Chaucer*. Ed. Derek Brewer. Ohio University Press, 1975. Pp 137–53.

Harbert explains the difficulty of determining whether an apparent borrowing comes directly from a classical author or from *florilegia*, and how much of a classical text a medieval poet had read. He estimates Chaucer's knowledge of Statius conservatively, citing for the *KnT* only 'some touches' in Mars' temple drawn from *Theb* VII.34–73 (pp 143–4).

964 Hart, James P., Jr. 'Thomas Tyrwhitt (1730–86) as Annotator and Glossarist of Fragment A of *The Canterbury Tales*, and His Editorial Relations.' University of Pennsylvania PhD dissertation, 1971. Director: Robert A. Pratt. *DAI* 32(1971), 2056A.

Hart compares Tyrwhitt's notes and glosses (**640**) with those of Speght, Urry, Morell, Skeat **625**, and Robinson **751**, confirming both Tyrwhitt's originality and his lasting influence. Ninety-two of his notes to A served as prototypes for both Skeat and Robinson.

965 Hatton, Thomas J. 'Medieval Anticipations of Dryden's Stylistic Revolution: *The Knight's Tale*.' *Language & Style* (1974), 261–9.
The *KnT* is, like Dryden's heroic dramas, a metaphor. Chaucer begins with an abstract concept, the Knight's wisdom (cf I.68), which concerns the way in which Providence works through Fortune, and invents a concrete situation to embody it (pp 263–4). Theseus, like the Knight, understands the transient nature of Fortune's gifts and uses them wisely to advance the common good. Palamon, as shown by his confusion of Emelye and Venus, does not recognize the limitations of earthly goods; Arcite, who sees Emelye as the woman she is, does recognize those limitations but nevertheless commits himself to the world as his ultimate good (p 265). The two princes act out the two ways Fortune can deceive people, according to Boethius (Book II. pr. 4). From one point of view, Arcite enjoys a mixture of good and bad fortune, while Palamon has consistently bad fortune (p 266). From another point of view both princes enjoy good fortune; they survive the war against Thebes and their lives are spared twice by Theseus. These inconsistencies suggest that 'good' or 'bad' fortune is a matter of interpretation, and that Fortune, as in Theseus' final speech, is an agent of Providence (pp 266–7). Providence prepares better fates for the princes than anyone anticipated; Arcite achieves a death with honor and Palamon achieves a desired and socially useful marriage he has done nothing to merit (pp 267–8).

966 — 'Thematic Relationships between Chaucer's Squire's Portrait and Tale and the Knight's Portrait and Tale.' 1974. See **465**.
The *KnT* illustrates its teller's wisdom, and the *SqT*, its teller's immaturity and concupiscence. Palamon and Arcite are lovers like the Squire, who put love of a lady before chivalric virtue, while Theseus is a worthy conqueror and a wise ruler devoted to the common good. In the *SqT*, Cambyuskan presides over an undisciplined court; the hawk has false notions of the good and the tercelet is unfaithful. Chaucer's audience would probably connect these defects with the extravagance and military failures of Richard II's court. 'Chaucer may be gently hinting ... that it is time to return to the values represented by his perfect knight' (p 458).

967 Hawkins, Harriet. *Poetic Freedom and Poetic Truth: Chaucer, Shakespeare, Marlowe, Milton*. Oxford: Clarendon Press, 1976.

Chaucer has altered the *Tes* to make Palamon and Arcite 'as much alike as two gold ingots' (p 15) in order to reveal the cosmic mystery of random injustice. All happens by fortune, chance, unpredictable gods. Chaucer's final emphasis on the consolation of philosophy cannot help Arcite but is 'mildly comforting' to the audience and allows us to celebrate with Palamon (p 17).

968 Haymes, Edward R. 'Chaucer and the Romance Tradition.' *South Atlantic Bulletin* 37(1972), 35–43.
Chaucer's diction is derived in part from the English romances as seen in his use of such phrases as 'makynge his mone' (I.1366), 'looth or lief' (I.1837), 'springing of the day' (822, 2209, etc.), 'great joy and bliss' (1684) and others.

969 Helterman, Jeffrey. 'The Dehumanizing Metamorphoses of The Knight's Tale.' 1971. See **466**.
Chaucer turned what was a random collection of decorative animal images in the *Tes* into a formal pattern of metaphor describing the inner metamorphoses of Palamon and Arcite. Initiated by Venus, these changes show the 'dehumanizing force' of the courtly ideal which, contrary to nature, elevates earthly love to the highest good (p 494). The duel in the grove presents an emblem of 'unchecked cruelty'; Lycurgus and Emetrius are emblems of 'tamed ferocity'; and the tournament is an emblem of 'untamed savagery' (pp 497–9). Arcite's illness and the destruction of the woodland present climactic images of unnaturalness. The Knight's use of *occupatio* signals his reluctance to acknowledge the failure of Theseus' scheme and of his own 'dream of order' (p 504). The opposition of chivalric ceremony and bestial savagery parallels the opposition of idealistic motivation and cruel results in the Knight's career (**466**). The Knight puts too much trust in the ideals of chivalry, and does not grasp the necessity of seeking a supra-terrestrial perfection.

970 Herzman, Ronald B. 'The Paradox of Form: *The Knight's Tale* and Chaucerian Aesthetics.' *PLL* 10(1974), 339–52.
The *KnT* simultaneously celebrates and criticizes both chivalry and art as means of bringing order out of chaos (pp 339–40). The value of the rules of chivalry is expressed in typical medieval fashion by their continual elaboration (p 311). The rules become ends, not means; they become more important than Palamon, Arcite, or Emily (pp 342–3). Their absurdity can be seen in the refusal of the princes to take any advantage in the contest for Emily, and in the length of time that elapses, estimated to be fifteen to twenty years (pp 343–4 and n 6). Similarly, the analysis of structure embedded in the narration, as in its formalized pairings, both celebrates the ordering

powers of art and tends to undermine the telling of the story: 'excess of form defeats the purpose of narrative itself' (p 346). Cf Jordan **846**. Theseus' 'Prime Mover' speech glosses Chaucer's 'dual vision' of chivalry and art by explaining that the effects of fate are an imperfect image of divine harmony (p 346). 'However imperfect [chivalry and composition] may be, they are the earthly analogue of divine perfection of form' (p 347). Theseus' satisfied contemplation of the lists (I.2092), a structure that sums up the aims of chivalry and art, is justified, but the Knight's 'stylistic lapse' in using sustained *occupatio* to describe Arcite's funeral reminds us of the limitations of human forms (pp 347–9). In the *KnT*, as is appropriate to a beginning, Chaucer emphasizes the value of art as an analogue of divine perfection. In the *Ret*, as is appropriate to an ending, he emphasizes the transcendent end to which art is a means (pp 350–1).

971 Hieatt, A. Kent. 'The Knight's Tale, the *Teseida*, and Platonizing Influences.' *Chaucer, Spenser, Milton: Mythopoeic Continuities and Transformations*. Montreal: McGill Queen's University Press, 1975. Pp 29–45.

Hieatt compares the intercession of Hippolyta and her ladies on behalf of Palamon and Arcite (I.1748–59) with Alceste's intercession on behalf of the poet in the *LGW* (G.317 f) and with the appeal of the Theban women at the beginning of the *KnT* (I.912–51). Theseus is not a tyrant like the God of Love in *LGW*, but a practitioner of *pitee* and *gentilesse* like Alceste (p 32). Accepting the former enemy princes into his friendship, Theseus contradicts what is said about lordship while confirming what is said about love in I.1625–6. Chaucer's addition of sworn brotherhood between Palamon and Arcite clarifies the destructive effects of love (pp 35–6). The other destructive force is the pagan gods, 'gracious to man' in Boccaccio but 'uniformly indifferent or malign' in Chaucer where they are contrasted with the Christian God (p 36) to whom Theseus is 'merely vicar in Athens' (p 39). Hieatt comments briefly on the Platonic and Boethian nature of the 'First Moevere' speech (pp 40–41) and suggests two ways of reading the last two lines of the poem (I.3099–100). The marriage of Emelye and Palamon clarifies the forms of love which, according to the *Consol* (II.met.8.22–30), 'mirror in the human heart the harmony of the rest of the universe ... fully committed sexual love, friendship, nation' (pp 44–5). Hieatt summarizes the pattern Spenser took from the *KnT* for repeated use in the *FQ*, especially in Book IV, his version of the *SqT*: 'a stage of anarchic love, another stage of friendship and love among four persons in accord with nature and courtesy, a Theseus figure, and a fixed combat to put an end to sexual competition' (p 45; cf pp 75–94). In the versions of the *CT* available to Spenser, derived from Thynne **58**, the *SqT* followed Fragment A and the *MLT*, perhaps making Spenser more sensitive to likenesses between the *SqT* and *KnT*.

972 Hoeber, Daniel R. 'Chaucer's Friday Knight.' *Chaucer Newsletter* 2.i(1980), 8–10.
Hoeber challenges Lowes' interpretation (**598**) of I.1534–9 as meaning only that Friday differs from the rest of the week, the sense of 1539. Rather Friday's changeable nature is also displayed within the compass of its own twenty-four hours, as indicated by 1534–8 and by Arcite's actual experience in the grove as well as other considerations.

973 Holtz, Nancy Ann. 'The Triumph of Saturn in the *Knight's Tale*: A Clue to Chaucer's Stance Against the Stars.' In *Literature and the Occult: Essays in Comparative Literature*. Ed. Luanne Frank. Arlington: University of Texas at Arlington, 1977. Pp 159–73.
Chaucer repudiates astrological determinism by presenting Saturn as a neutral rather than a malignant force, one whose effect is defined in part by the responses of human beings to events. 'In Palamon, a man who has conquered time through his patient submission to earthly tribulation, we have Chaucer's development of the Saturn-ruled man of destiny' (p 173).

974 Howard, Donald R. *The Idea of the Canterbury Tales*. 1976. See **468**.
The *KnT* establishes the 'narrative now' as a stylistic feature of the *CT* as a whole. For example, in the descriptions of the temples, the claims of the 'I' to have been an eye-witness are a deliberate anachronism intended to achieve immediacy, and as we approach the tournament, the historical present tense is more and more used (pp 86–8). Fragment I is concerned with Civil Conduct (p 215), but the *KnT* introduces all three thematic strands of the *CT* — chivalry (civil conduct), love and marriage (domestic conduct), and philosophic and ethical issues (private conduct) — as well as the tradition of 'knight-lore' (p 228) — questions of religion, honor, courtesy, valor, service to a lady, and 'an epic and fatalistic way of looking at things' (p 229). Chaucer's refusal to describe the journey of Arcite's soul (p 229) indicates that in the *KnT* as in the *CT* our vision is to be limited to this world. The humorous element, as seen in the mock-epic treatment of destiny (I.1663–82) is 'the most controversial aspect of the tale' (p 230) and is part of the 'unimpersonated artistry' (p 231) by which Chaucer's own ironic attitudes are expressed. The 'I' of the tale is Chaucer, not the Knight (p 232); its expressions of boredom

and anti-climactic endings to moving incidents and speeches satirize the 'knightly mentality' (p 234), with its emphasis on pageantry, bravery, idealism, maleness, fame, and a favorable marriage. The gods are 'a super-race of nobles – a ruling class which rules the ruling class' (p 235). The civility of the *KnT* is treated both as a source of dignity and as an artificial code (p 237). In the *MilT* folklore replaces knightlore (p 238) as part of the 'degenerative movement' of Fragment I (p 245). The concatenation of *KnT-MilT* and *MilT-RvT* is part of the interlace structure of the *CT* (pp 224–5, 247). The *CT* also contains two 'metastructures' (p 308; cf pp 215–6): 'a group of ideal narratives leading up to the *ParsT* and a group of romances led off by the *KnT* and leading to the *Mel.* The high-minded sentiments of the *KnT* may have seemed 'a bit Edwardian' to the court of Richard II (p 310). The *Mel* is addressed to 'a new public-spiritedness devoted to the good of a nation' (p 315) as distinct from the older feudal and family ties reflected in the *KnT*. See **1101**.

975 — 'The Idea of a Chaucer Course.' In *Approaches to Teaching Chaucer's Canterbury Tales.* Ed. Joseph Gibaldi. Consultant editor, Florence H. Ridley. New York: The Modern Language Association of America, 1980, pp 57–62.
The *MilT* and *RvT*, and the *CT* as a whole, lose their intended effects if the *KnT* is displaced or omitted. 'It is a high-minded, ceremonious romance that bespeaks the grand old ideas of the medieval knighthood ... What a falling-off is to come after it! And what an irony is established *in* it by that curious voice that can tell us "I nam no divinistre" (I.2811). But that falling-off and that ironic voice are lost on any reader who skips to the Miller's offering' (p 58).

976 Huntsman, Jeffrey F. 'Caveat Editor: Chaucer and Medieval English Dictionaries.' *MP* 73(1976), 276–9.
In mss of the fourteenth-century Latin-English lexicon the *Medulla grammatice*, Huntsman finds circumstantial evidence for the interpretation of *nakers* (I.2511) as 'horns' rather than as 'drums' as in Robinson **751**.

977 Hussey, S.S. 'The Knight's Tale.' *Chaucer: An Introduction*. London: Methuen; New York: Barnes & Noble, 1971/rev 1981. Pp 129–35/125–32.
The *KnT* is like other romances in its unrealistic characterizations, exotic setting, use of an ending that includes a marriage and shows poetic justice, and its leisurely narrative (p 129/125). Its original element is its philosophical questioning. The slight differences between Palamon and Arcite 'should not be elevated into a complete contrast in character' (p 131/127). Chaucer's interest 'to display the

whole chivalric panorama' (p 132/128) may be reflected in the four-part division of the tale, as in Ellesmere. Theseus' speech may be designed to show the philosophical limitations of a pagan (pp 134–5/131). In the revised edition, Hussey dismisses the view of Theseus as a tyrant and a hypocrite as 'far too modern and cynical a reading' (p 128).

978 Jambeck, Thomas J. 'Characterization and Syntax in the *Miller's Tale*.' *Journal of Narrative Technique* 5(1975), 73–85.
Lines I.1653–72 juxtapose the description of the princes' fight in the grove, presented in a paratactic style, with the Knight's comment on 'destinee,' presented in a hypotactic style (p 74). The Knight views human events as occurring on two planes, and the hypotactic style is needed to reflect 'the enigmatic network of causal links which connect the real and the supernal' (p 75). The style of the *MilT*, by contrast, is heavily paratactic, reflecting its teller's 'mindlessly linear perspective' (p 75).

979 Jameson, Hunter Thomas. 'The *Knight's Tale*.' 'Moral Seriousness in the Canterbury Tales: Human Conduct and Providential Order in the Knight's Tale, Franklin's Tale, and Parson's Tale.' Indiana University Dissertation, 1975. Pp 12–66. See also *DAI* 36(1975), 7437A.
Arcite's moral miscalculation in breaking the terms of his friendship with Palamon leads to his later strategic miscalculation in praying to Mars rather than Venus. Saturn's intervention is a part of a Jovian plan existing from all eternity. The reader is offered a privileged view of Arcite's miscalculations and of the gods' providential roles, but Theseus is ignorant of both and thus his final speech is incomplete. He asserts the providence of Jupiter but does not discuss its relationship to a righteous life. In arranging the marriage of Palamon and Emilye, as in his actions throughout the tale, Theseus unknowingly furthers the designs of Providence.

980 Johnson, W.C. 'Chaucer's Language of Inevitability.' In *New Views on Chaucer: Essays in Generative Criticism*. Ed. William C. Johnson. Denver, Colorado: The Society for New Language Study, 1973. Pp 17–26.
Arcite is an 'isolated, sensitive tragic hero' (p 21). Of all the characters, Arcite 'suffers most passionately because most inwardly' (p 22). He believes that both his love and his death are fated (p 24). Theseus' speech increases our sense of pathos by its dependence on an old-fashioned, external concept of necessity. Chaucer moves toward a Renaissance view through his emphasis on the 'internal fires of personality' and on the consolations of art rather than doctrine (p 26).

981 Jones, Terry. '*The Knight's Tale.*' *Chaucer's Knight.* 1980. See **470.** Pp 141–216.
The *KnT* is 'a courtly, philosophical romance ... told by an uncourtly, unphilosophical and totally unromantic professional soldier' (p 145). The intentions of Chaucer, who tells a pacifist tale (*Mel*) and may have sympathized with Richard II's peace policy, can be seen in changes from the *Tes*. For example, Venus' temple is transformed from a garden of delights to a kind of battlefield; Palamon and Arcite, whose love is never wholly broken in the *Tes*, fight like participants in a barrack-room brawl (pp 146–56). The Knight exhibits a variety of faults, including his self-advertising and authoritarian use of *occupatio*, and lapses into a low, colloquial style that betrays the brusque man-of-action unused to courtly usage (pp 164–71). Conspicuously absent from the Tale are *pitee* and romantic feeling (pp 175–8). The general mêlée of the tournament is very different from the stylized combats of contemporary chivalry; Palamon's capture is unchivalric; and Theseus' judgment in favor of Arcite, questionable (pp 178–85). The *KnT* contains several allusions to mercenaries and the tyrants they served: eg, the depiction of many kinds of bloodshed in Mars' temple corresponds to the destruction of non-combatants by the Free Companies. Mars' cart and the emblem of the man-devouring wolf may be allusions to the Italian city-states (pp 185–92). Theseus is a 'typical Italian tyrant' (pp 197–202) whose object is self-aggrandizement, not the common good, as his 'machiavellian' (p 195) motives for the marriage demonstrate. His susceptibility to supplication shows him indulging in those moods that contemporary commentators deplored as a sign of despotism. His 'First Mover' speech is 'the ultimate expression of Theseus' tyranny and of the Knight's own political creed' (p 202). In this travesty of the *Consol*, Theseus urges men to submit passively to a stronger power; uses imagery from nature to explain death rather than cosmic harmony; celebrates the fame Boethius deemed worthless; and makes arrogant claims for the truth of his assertions (pp 202–11). The *KnT* is a 'hymn to tyranny' (pp 212–6) told by a narrator who may resemble Sir John Hawkwood. In his treatment of Arcite's death, the Knight shows the soldier's 'cheerful contempt' for religious speculation and the 'clinical detachment' of one who has seen destruction on a vast scale (p 215). By assigning the *KnT* to 'a new style mercenary captain, Chaucer has created a cold, dark world of fear, oppression and death ... [and has shown] how chivalry and knighthood, divorced from their underlying ideals, had become the tools of tyranny and destruction' (p 216). See **1092, 1108.**

- Review by Jill Mann, *The Listener* 103(1980), 157: In Jones' reading, the *KnT* 'has nothing to say (or even ask) about chance, change, time and death; it becomes just an unremitting *exposé* of the nastiness of its major figures, and of course of its teller ... The constant variations in style are not, in fact, revelations of the Knight's insensitivity. They are utterly characteristic of Chaucer's style as a whole, and, more importantly, of his concern to ask ... whether there is not a constantly-shifting kaleidoscope of experiences and possible attitudes to them, and, if so, what stable centre to living we can find' (p 157).
- Review by V.J. Scattergood, *British Book News*, July, 1980, pp 435–6: 'The tough-minded, harshly practical, at times rather cynical tone (to which Mr. Jones rightly draws attention) and the belief in political expediency are a reflex of Chaucer's personality, not a dimension of the literary *persona* of the Knight.' Theseus is 'less the "typical Italian tyrant" than ... a "lord and governour" ... someone who has to make sure that social order is kept.'
- Review by David Aers, *SAC* 4(1982), 169–75: 'The first effect of [Jones'] approach ... is to obscure [the] powerful critique of all militarism and glorification of war, a critique superbly embodied in the writing about the temple of Mars ... He asserts that the horror Chaucer conjures up is a *perverted* vision which distorts what the poet Chaucer wanted us to think of as the "splendour of the battlefield." Nothing could be more mistaken' (pp 174–5).
- Review by John M. Fyler, *YES* 12(1982), 235–6: Although Jones' reading of the *KnT* shares the sceptical viewpoint of many readings of the past twenty years, it must finally be seen as 'extreme' and 'perverse' (p 236). Jones' *KnT* is so heavily ironic that the corrective vision of the *MilT* is rendered meaningless.

982 Jordan, Robert M. 'The Question of Genre: Five Chaucerian Romances.' In *Chaucer at Albany*. Ed. Rossell Hope Robbins. New York: Burt Franklin, 1975. Pp 77–103.

Jordan describes some elements of design in addition to those cited by Frost **684** and Muscatine **726** . Parts I and II, centering on the rivalry of Palamon and Arcite, are characterized by a 'formalized succession of pairings' (p 91) with abrupt transitions. This pattern is echoed in the balanced descriptions of the temples in Part III, while a complementary pattern is introduced in the brilliant compression of the action of the tournament into fifty lines. In one sense, the tournament is a 'small jewel in the ceremonial setting' (p 92); in another, it is a complex and various action which does not end until Arcite's death. This last pattern, 'a sequence of diversified and individuated rhetorical elements,' (p 93), is repeated in the last 300 lines, which treat Egeus' words, preparations for the funeral, the pyre, Theseus' oration, and the brief resolution of the plot. Jordan then reiterates his general conclusion on Chaucerian romance in **97**.

983 Justman, Stewart. '"Auctoritee" and the *Knight's Tale*.' *MLQ* 39(1978), 3–14.
The operations of authority in the *KnT* conflict with the Boethian definition of authority as an invariable, formally binding guarantor of certainty, exempt from all contingency (pp 4–5). Theseus' decrees are always provisional, not final, and his style of governing displays not a rational mixture of pity with justice, but a self-contradictory process of wrathful pronouncement followed by annulment (p 7). Even Saturn makes only a temporary and provisional peace between Mars and Venus (p 8). Theseus' final speech is entangled in political motives and in time. The Boethian idea of authority is itself implicated in the Tale's ironic criticism because Chaucer shows that human experience does not uniformly produce cases that correspond to pre-existing exemplars (pp 12–3). Egeus' role is typical: his advice is introduced only to be superseded by Theseus' philosophy (p 13). See **1099**.

984 Kean, Patricia. 'The Knight's Tale.' *Chaucer and the Making of English Poetry*. Volume 2. London: Routledge & Kegan Paul, 1972. Pp 1–52.
The *KnT* is a morality play (p 3) whose theme is 'the effects on human life of disorder and unreason opposed to an order which extends from the most minor aspects of life up to [the] unmoved first mover' (p 5). Theseus, 'associated with Jupiter and acting like a beneficent providence,' contrasts with the two princes, who submit themselves to the influence of the lesser gods (p 9). Arcite's and Palamon's philosophic speeches (I.1251–67 and 1303–33) have an ironic relationship to their sources in Boethius, where the arguments 'either carry the reverse meaning or are only used to be contradicted' (p 14). The *demande* (1347–54) distances us from the princes' point of view, reinforcing the Tale's philosophical perspective. The passage on 'destinee' (1663–72) links Theseus with Destiny but does not identify him with it. Theseus uses 'disorderly, individualistic love' to establish 'a general state of peace and order' (p 20); but the tournament and the depiction of disasters in the temples also show Theseus' achievement to be subject to 'all the anomalies which belong to the world of change' (p 24). The temple descriptions reinforce the lovers' point of view: we are led to appreciate the reality of tragedies like Arcite's. At the same time, a more complete view of the planets shows their influence, as in the Children of the Planets tradition, to

be part of a providential design (p 26). Kean discusses Saturn's role at length (pp 28–34), noting Chaucer's use of his traditional associations with wisdom, time, and theory. The 'activity of Saturn as a composer of strife and a bringer of order out of disorder, achieved in combination with Jupiter' is the 'grete effect' of the poem and especially of the fourth part (p 33). Arcite's death-bed speech presents Palamon as ennobled by love, stresses the unifying aspect of love, and prepares for Theseus' speech by its appeal to Jupiter. Chaucer refused to describe the flight of Arcite's soul for several reasons, including a reluctance to describe a celestial end for a man who died as the result of irrational passion, or to mitigate the pain of Arcite's end. Arcite's 'despairing protests' (2777–9) do not state the theme of the poem; but they 'build up the tension which it is the function of the "grete effect" to resolve' (p 38). Kean outlines six steps in the philosophical portion of Theseus' speech (I.2987–3040), culminating in the idea of an ascent to the unity and perfection of the First Mover. Yet the references to rebellion and forced submission allow 'the painful, bewildered and fundamentally pessimistic viewpoint' to be heard again. 'Philosophy speaks a tranquil last word, [but] we are not allowed to forget the difficulty of applying her tenets in an actual world of contradictory and contradicting beings' (pp 47–8). See pp 59 and 70 on narrative structure, and pp 94–6 on the *KnT* and *MilT*: like the *PF*, they provide 'insight into the way in which Nature crams the world full of differing creatures'; this is the moral, rather than any 'heavy-handed comment' on the impracticalities of heroical love (pp 95–6).

- Review by Morton W. Bloomfield, *MÆ* 43(1974), 193–5: The discussion of the *KnT* is one of the stronger parts of Kean's book; John Scotus Eriugena is not likely to have been a Chaucerian source (I, pp 74–5) for the chain of love, however (p 194).

985 Kellogg, Alfred L. and Robert C. Cox. 'Chaucer's May 3 and Its Contexts.' *Chaucer, Langland, Arthur: Essays in Middle English Literature*. New Brunswick, New Jersey: Rutgers University Press, 1972. Pp 155–98.

Chaucer uses May 3 three times in his works (*TC* II.50–6; *KnT* I.1462–8; *NPT* VII.3187–90), always with the suggestion of ill-fortune. The month had ambivalent significance from ancient times, but the day may have had a negative significance for Chaucer as a date associated with the Treaty of Bretigny (1360) which ended the disastrous English campaign in which Chaucer was captured (pp 157–61). In the *KnT* (pp 164–80), May 3 is the date of Palamon's happy escape from prison and of his unhappy confrontation with Arcite in the grove. As the major characters converge on the grove, the power of destiny is demonstrated as it will be again in the tournament (pp 167–9). The sudden death of the tournament's victor presents a new problem, for Theseus: are the gods just (pp 172–3)? From their privileged position, readers can see that destiny is a plan that awards to Palamon, Arcite, and Emily the self-fulfillment that each most desires. This is especially true of Arcite, a man of war who prays for victory, a courtly lover whose 'love' is merely conventional (pp 174–6). Theseus' speech has an hour-glass shape. The doctrine of the First Mover gives it a solid base, but 'consolation is nipped thin at the waist' as Theseus insists on the universality of death (p 178). Nevertheless, he affirms life and the non-rational belief that perfect joy can arise out of sorrow, recognizing the need 'to assert human values in a world where nothing seems more evident than the total disregard of them' (p 180). See **1079**.

986 Kelly, Henry Ansgar. 'The Genoese Saint Valentine and Chaucer's Third of May.' *Chaucer Newsletter* 1.ii(1979), 6–10.
Chaucer may have associated the love of Palamon and Arcite for Emily with May 3 because he thought it was Saint Valentine's Day. The Genoese Saint Valentine, first bishop of that city, died on May 3 and his feastday was May 2.

987 Kiernan, Kevin S. 'The Art of the Descending Catalogue, and a Fresh Look at Alisoun.' *ChauR* 10(1975), 1–16.
Kiernan surveys the uses of the conventional description of the beautiful woman proceeding from head to toe, as recommended by Geoffrey de Vinsauf. 'The description of Emily [I.1048–55] is a particularly effective use of implication because it sets the reader up for a catalogue ('for to devyse'), and a standard one at that (golden hair ...) but the reader must decide for himself whether Emily is a woman or goddess. Chaucer's restraint here compounds, for the reader, the ambiguity of Arcite's and Palamon's reaction' (p 7). The Miller's description of Alisoun represents a humorous use of the convention (p 14).

988 Knight, Stephen. '*The Knight's Tale*.' *The Poetry of the Canterbury Tales*. 1973. See **473**. Pp 19–29.
A mixture of briskness and formality in the opening section establishes the presence of the 'noble but military Knight' (p 19–20). Other effects are essentially Chaucer's, eg, the way style supports Theseus' grandeur and prowess (pp 20–1). Long formal sequences, such as the description of Emilye, are the most obvious stylistic device; a plain, blunt style, as in Palamon and Arcite's uses of animal imagery, reveals the darker side of chivalry (pp 23–4). In the

descriptions of the temples, the two styles are set side by side, posing the question of how the two aspects of life are related (pp 24–6). The brusque style used to describe Arcite's death is juxtaposed with the magnificence of his funeral (pp 26–7). His death-bed speech, 'the "highest" piece of poetry in the whole poem,' demonstrates his nobility, and affirms the possibility of triumph over disorder through self-sacrifice (pp 27–8). Theseus' final speech is in style and content 'a type of synthesis' meant to motivate us to think about the issues in the light of all aspects of the poem (p 28).

989 —— 'The Knight's Tale.' *Rhyming Craftily: Meaning in Chaucer's Poetry.* Sydney: Angus and Robertson, 1973. Pp 98–160.
Chaucer develops a stylistic difference between the two princes (pp 101–24). Palamon's style depends on extended syntax and ornate diction; Arcite's, on brief phrases and homely comparisons. 'Palamon is more elevated than his rival, and the elevation points towards a greater nobility of character; he controls a greater eloquence just as he sees further than Arcite in terms of love and of the heavens' (p 111). The narrator's manner of describing the actions of Palamon and Arcite parallels the princes' individual styles. As tragic hero Arcite is allowed an unaccustomed eloquence in his death-bed speech. Lines 2778–9 mould together formal cadences and colloquial patterns of speech: 'the placing of the word "Allone" itself proclaims the masterful confidence of the great poet' (p 124). Theseus (pp 124–36) does not exhibit a special prosodic style. His speech in the grove has a 'dual note, of noble fluency and clear-sighted common-sense' suggesting 'the complex significance that Theseus has' (p 129). The three styles of his final speech (pp 131–6) embrace through 'poetic reminiscence' much of the subject matter of the poem: the precise intellectual style of the opening (2994–3015) recalls Palamon and Arcite's early laments; a plain lucid style characterizes the list of illustrations; an elevated style in lines 3027–33 recalls earlier discussions of death. The theme of the speech is human limitation, and its syntax makes plain 'the plodding nature of man's attempt to cope with his puzzling world' [citing 3041–9] (p 135). The narrator's style (pp 136–45), as seen in passages that end with a clipped comment, suggests that he is 'alienated from his elaborate tale and the high passions that inform it' (p 138). The 'plain man's view' of Arcite's love (I.1528–39) climaxes this opening stage (p 139). A new stage appears in the more elevated treatment of love in the speech 'O Cupide, out of alle charitee!' (1623 f). The depth of the narrator's involvement, as seen in his comment on 'destinee' (1663–72), helps to create 'the rising emotional pitch of the middle section' of the

Tale (p 142). The two styles alternate in later sections, the detached tone in the comments on Arcite's death (2809–16), and the more engaged style in the *occupatio* on the funeral rites. The narrator is 'not an organic personality, but the tool of the author ... [and his] varying style is an excellent key to his varying function' (p 145). 'Set-Pieces' (pp 145–59): The descriptions in the temples display appropriate characterizations of the gods and echoes of the styles of Palamon and Arcite. Saturn's self-description does not establish a character distinct from Mars. The balance of the portraits of Lygurge and Emetrius arises in part from their common style. In the preparations for the tournament, and the tournament scene itself, Chaucer makes subtle use of alliteration prior to his more emphatic use of it in 2608–11. The style of the *KnT* 'often works to sharpen the meaning of the poem and even, at its subtlest, to imply meaning before it is made explicit' (p 159).

- Review by D.S. Brewer, *RES* 27(1976), 55–7: In this valuable book, characterized by a quantity of detail and a lack of generalization that make it slow reading, Knight's interpretation of Theseus 'subtly alters, and ... improves, the now usual reading of the poem as an exercise in balanced symmetry' (p 55).

990 Kohl, Stephan. *Wissenschaft und Dichtung bei Chaucer: Dargestellt Lauptsächlich am Beispiel der Medizin.* Frankfurt: Akademische Verlagsgesellschaft, 1973. Esp. pp 291–308.

Following the neglect of medical lore in his early love visions, Chaucer gave significant attention to the 'loveris maladye' (I.1373) as a real disease in *KnT* and *TC*. The detailed description of the physical symptoms of Arcite's love-sickness indicates that his love for Emelye is the more fleshly, Palamon's the more spiritual. Medical lore is used to suggest a Christian judgment of moral deficiency in Arcite. Ideal love is represented by Theseus' friendship with Perotheus.

991 — '*The Kingis Quair* and Lydgate's *Siege of Thebes* as Imitations of Chaucer's *Knight's Tale*.' *FCS* 2(1979), 119–34.

Kohl contrasts the *KnT* with the fifteenth-century works on three points (pp 119–28). In the *KnT* Palamon and Arcite are subject to a Fortune which cannot be resisted or influenced by human behavior; in *KQ* [c 1404] and *STh* [c 1420–2] Fortune is seen as distributing rewards for virtuous behavior and punishments for sinful behavior. In the *KnT* the tournament is an accepted means of revealing destiny's decrees; in the *STh*, war is to be avoided because it makes men subject to Fortune, and in the *KQ*, rash actions are to be avoided in favor of steadfast purpose. In the *KnT* love is a cosmic force; in the *STh* it is a political order that can be manipulated by man, and in the *KQ*, it is a particular field of human experience, not a universal law. In the later works, 'the concept of an active and prudent line of conduct has replaced the educational ideal of philosophical resignation' advocated in the *Consol* and *KnT* (p 130).

992 Kuhn, Sherman M. 'The Language of Some Fifteenth-Century Chaucerians: A Study of Manuscript Variants in the *Canterbury Tales*.' *SMC* 4(1974), 472–82.
According to the *Corpus of Variants* of the Manly-Rickert edition **42**, 27 mss read *hevenly* for *hevenishly* in I.1055. Chaucer may first have written *hevenly*, a 'safe conventionalism,' and later substituted *hevenishly*, a 'bold innovation' apparently of his own coinage (p 475).

993 Lambert, Mark. 'Troilus, Books I–III: A Criseydan Reading.' In *Essays on Troilus and Criseyde*. Ed. Mary Salu. Woodbridge, Suffolk: D.S. Brewer; Totowa, New Jersey: Rowman & Littlefield, 1979, pp 105–25.
Criseyde and Theseus share an 'unheroic attitude,' what Burrow **929** calls 'the sober acceptance of things as they are' (p 123). This may be the view most congenial to Chaucer. Still 'it is ultimately the hyperbolists and radicals [like Troilus and Palamon] who turn out to be right ... Chaucer is ... a poet of the unheroic who knows (or suspects) the heroes are finally correct' (pp 124–5).

994 Lawler, Traugott. *The One and the Many in the Canterbury Tales*. Hamden, Conn.: Archon, 1980.
Ch 1, 'Introduction': The diversity of opinion in the Athenians' comments on the two retinues of knights (I.2513–21) contrasts with the authority suggested by Theseus' appearance at the window (2528–32) and with the harmonious vision of Theseus' final speech. These scenes illustrate the pervasive concern with diversity and unity in the *CT* and Chaucer's higher valuation of unity (pp 11–15). Ch 4, 'Experience and Authority' (pp 83–108): The first conjunction in the *CT* of the words *experience* (diversity) and *auctoritee* (unity) occurs in Theseus' final speech (I.3000–2). The uncertain tone indicates that Theseus' first purpose is to 'reestablish order and joy in himself' (p 87). Theseus is a widely experienced man who learns in the course of the story. In the grove he consults both 'reasonable maxims' and 'personal memory' in deciding not to execute Palamon and Arcite (p 89). After the death of Arcite, Theseus must combine 'Egeus's breadth of knowledge with Palamon's and Arcite's youthful ability to suffer new experience with private pain' (p 90). While Egeus's advice has the 'flatness' of an 'auctoritee' (p 90), Theseus' final speech has 'a pulse of individuality' because it 'originates in particular experience' (p 91). Its message is the unity of all things in relation to death and

their divine origin (pp 91–2). The making of the marriage does not contradict Theseus' perception of corruptibility, since Theseus is 'making virtue of necessity all through the final scene ... He imitates Jupiter, but in a chastened, not an arrogant, spirit' (p 93). The *KnT* is 'an experiential tale which leads to an authoritative statement,' revealing how deeply interdependent the two sources of knowledge are. The *MilT* parodies the *KnT* partly by working from general or proverbial statements to experience (pp 95–6). Ch. 7, 'Closure': The *KnT* has a 'figural' relation to the *ParsT*, which fills out its vision (p 169).

995 Leyerle, John. 'The Heart and the Chain.' In *The Learned and the Lewed: Studies in Chaucer and Medieval Literature*. Ed. Larry D. Benson. Cambridge, Mass.: Harvard University Press, 1974. Pp 113–45.
The 'nucleus' of the *KnT* is bonds, both literal and metaphorical (pp 118–21). Theseus and Saturn impose forms of bondage on others, contributing to the portrayal of a human condition with a 'dark side': 'the choice seems to be between freedom and anarchy on the one hand and bondage and order on the other' (p 121). The tale is 'notably lacking in humour,' which Chaucer associates with disruptions of order (p 121). There are over fifty occurrences of the word *prisoun* and related terms such as *cage*, *cheyn*, *dongeon*, *fettre*, *laas*, and *tour* (p 121). Holes provide the nucleus of the parodic *MilT* (pp 122–3).

996 Magoun, Francis P., Jr. 'Two Chaucer Items.' *NM* 78(1977), 46.
While Modern French '*les etres de la maison*' refers to the kitchen, larder, scullery, or butler's pantry, Old French '*estres*' referred to the entire interior of a building, as in I.1971.

997 Manzalaoui, Mahmoud. 'Chaucer and Science.' In *Writers and Their Background*. 1974. See **149**, pp 224–61.
The gods of the *KnT* are 'basically planetary,' but depicted by reference to classical mythology and history. The prayers present a form of pagan worship which never existed, but which Chaucer may have believed authentic. They present the inward reality of the three protagonists, who are otherwise only flat characters (p 246). Emetrius and Lygurge are also psychologically and astrologically significant, with Lygurge, the Saturnian warrior, supporting Venus' champion to balance the otherwise greater force of Mars. The 'determinism and one-trackedness' of the gods distinguishes them from the Boethian providence to which Theseus appeals in his final speech (p 247).

998 McCall, John P. *Chaucer among the Gods*. 1979. See **138**.
The *KnT*, the only one of Chaucer's works to be governed by an allegorical myth, is dominated by its theater (pp 63–4). The opening events anticipate the allegory of the theater: Creon is ruled by Martian irascibility; the Amazons show Diana's insensitive restraint; Theseus is an androgynous figure of Martian and Venerian elements, whose occasional rashness shows that he has not yet attained the ideal moral development he emulates (pp 66–8). The temples define natural instincts that, unchecked, can lead to ruin, but the theater as a whole represents the balanced development of personality (pp 68–72). The narrative works out the implications of the allegory; Palamon and Arcite, for example, fall in love in ways that are respectively Venerian and Martian. Yet, Palamon, Arcite, and Emelye all prove to be 'more generous, more human, and more complicated than any single abstract notion' (p 75) as is demonstrated in their prayers. Before and during the tournament, Theseus represents Jovian justice directing will (pp 77–8); Saturn introduces ill luck and represents the prudence needed to guide intellect in interpreting it (pp 78–80). Egeus articulates Saturnian wisdom and Theseus acts on it in arranging the funeral rites; Theseus' final speech goes beyond Egeus' by stressing life, of which death is a natural part (pp 80–2). The Aristotelian morality represented by the gods, in which the concupiscible appetite, the irascible appetite, the will, and the intellect are governed, respectively, by temperance, fortitude, justice and prudence is also reflected in the Tale's four-part structure: Part I is concerned with love and Venus; Part II, with aggression and Mars; Part III, with justice and Jupiter; and Part IV, with Saturn and prudence (pp 84–5). The *KnT* presents 'a composite image of the chivalric ideal' appropriate to the Knight, and shows Chaucer '*adding allegory* to a historical romance as though his overall goal was to create a blend in which the letter and the spirit [of the text] are one and the same thing' (p 86). See also pp 87–93: Chaucer treats place more as a topos or idea than as a location. In the *KnT* he associates Scythia with barbarity, Thebes with unrestrained aggression and lust, and Athens with philosophical wisdom and mercy.

999 McCann, Garth A. 'Chaucer's First Three Tales: Unity in Trinity.' *Bulletin of the Rocky Mountain Modern Language Association* 27(1973), 10–6.
Critics exaggerate both the generic differences between the *KnT* and the *MilT* and *RvT* and the likenesses of the three tales as treatments of cupidity. The tales show 'a relationship of careful symmetry': 'in the Knight's Tale we see love in terms of feeling, but not of

fulfillment; in the Miller's Tale we see it in both emotion and action; and in the Reeve's Tale we see love devoid of mental attraction, but replete with physical satisfaction' (p 10). In the *KnT* (pp 11–3), love is psychological not physical and 'negative and ironic' (p 10). The princes are frustrated by several barriers to fulfillment: 'prison, conflict, banishment, social rank, fear of death, Theseus, and chivalric propriety' (p 12). The *MilT* 'stands fairly equidistant' between the *KnT* and the *RvT* (p 15): Nicholas' passionate, though not noble, love for Alisoun and his intricate plan to overcome admittedly less serious obstacles ally him with the princes; his speed and carnality ally him with the clerks. Absalom suffers from frustrated love, like the princes, although his courtship is only a parody of theirs; once cured of his infatuation, he is motivated by revenge, and resembles the clerks.

1000 McCobb, Lilian M. 'The English *Partonope of Blois*, Its French Source, and Chaucer's *Knight's Tale*.' *ChauR* 11(1977), 369–72.
The mss of the English *Partonope* cannot help determine the relationship of Chaucer's description of the tournament (I.2601–16) to *Partonope* 11128–45 because the latter passage appears in only one ms from the late fifteenth-century. Study of the French *Partenopeu* (c. 1180–5) shows that the English translator followed his source closely almost everywhere except in this passage. The translator clearly borrowed from Chaucer, rather than Chaucer from him as R. Smith **761** suggests. Smith's alternative suggestion, that the translated passage is a late interpolation under Chaucerian influence, must be rejected, for the Chaucerian text has been adapted and fully integrated into the translation rather than taken over wholesale as it would be by an interpolator; cf. Parr **736**.

1001 Mehl, Dieter. *Geoffrey Chaucer*. 1973. See **478**. Pp 158–62 and 172–6.
Chaucer focuses his Tale on the conflict between Palamon and Arcite but does not individualize the two knights, with the result that the Tale seems 'almost like a puzzle or prize question' [citing I.1347–54] (pp 159–60). The solution arranged by the gods has the 'neatness of a comic denoument' (p 160), but Chaucer, by omitting Arcite's apotheosis as in the *Tes*, leaves it up to the reader to assess the knights' fates. Theseus' advice to submit to necessity is a 'deliberate simplification' (p 161) on Chaucer's part, meant to expose the complexity of the issues. The 'impressive intellectual scope' of the Tale carries it beyond the confines of traditional romance (p 161). An 'unresolved tension' exists between the balanced structure, suggestive of universal harmony, and the actions of the gods, personifying an arbitrary fate, but the chivalric life itself is not attacked (p 162). The

likenesses between the *KnT* and *MilT* are striking: in style, in the recourse to general reflections (which brings the fabliau closer to romance), and in the use of the conventions of courtly love (which are approached with contrasting attitudes but not mocked) (pp 172–4).

1002 Metlitzki, Dorothee. *The Matter of Araby in Medieval England*. New Haven: Yale University Press, 1977.
Metlitzki reviews the reception in England of the Hippocratic, Galenic, and Arabic tradition of the heart as the seat of the soul. Chaucer 'unmistakably placed the spirit in the heart' (p 73, citing I.2765). The name *Arcite* takes its origin from *Akrites*, 'the Byzantine designation of knights who were defenders against Muslim incursions' (p 145). Chaucer took the name from the *Tes*, and Boccaccio may have encountered the name in his study of Greek.

1003 Milne, Fred L. 'Dryden's "Palamon and Arcite": Its Merits and Flaws as a Translation of Chaucer's "Knight's Tale".' *Meta: Journal des Traducteurs* 23(1978), 200–10.
Dryden improved upon Chaucer's work without violating its sense by reducing the divisions from four to three, centered on the prison, the grove, and the tournament. He relied more heavily on the closed couplet, thus tightening the relationship of idea and versification; he reinforced the motif of three's, especially in Arcite's funeral rites, and he strengthened the emphasis on love. Dryden violated Chaucer's sense by representing Arcite as a disloyal knight corrupted by love, as seen in Arcite's response on first seeing Emily (*Pal*, I.277–9; cf I.1118), in Palamon's description of himself and Arcite to Theseus in the grove (*Pal*, II.276–93; cf I.1724–35), and in Arcite's remorseful death-bed speech (*Pal*, III.806–19; cf I.2777–85). Dryden obscures Chaucer's emphasis on fate as the determinant of events.

1004 Miskimin, Alice. 'The Illustrated Eighteenth-Century Chaucer.' 1979. See **479**.
In the late eighteenth century, 'the sharp, bawdy satirist prized by Pope and Gay has become almost invisible, and a tender, melancholy poet has been discovered' (p 41). In Stothard's design for the *KnT* in Bell's *CT*, a 'postmedieval Emily bending over her roses under Palamon's jail window ... resembles [J.B.] Mortimer's romantic Eve among her flowers [in Bell's *Milton*]' (p 46).

1005 Muscatine, Charles. *Poetry and Crisis in the Age of Chaucer*. Notre Dame: University of Notre Dame Press, 1972.
The *KnT* is a 'statement of ultimate belief in royal government and in the higher order of which it is a copy' and the Tale's position in the *CT* 'shows how deeply [Chaucer's] own sympathies – or his sense

of respect — were ultimately bound up with [the royal] ethos' (p 126). The Tale's meaning is touched by irony through its incorporation into the *CT*. Its assignment to the Knight 'fixes its class orientation and suggests a certain nostalgia,' and the parodies of it by the Miller and Reeve, while they 'come nowhere near damaging it ... do not leave it the same' (p 126). Pathos is Chaucer's alternative to irony (pp 128–9). Arcite's death-bed questions expose us to 'a pathos as deep as human doubt can go' and 'the whole of this rich poem devotes itself to finding an acceptable answer' (p 133–4).

1006 Nelson, Joseph Edward. 'Chaucer's *Knight's Tale*: A Vision of a Secular Ideal of Chivalry.' University of Kansas Dissertation, 1979. See also *DAI* 41(1980), 242A.

An optimistic tradition with roots in Augustine and Boethius suggested the possibility of constructing a nearly ideal secular order. Thinkers such as John of Salisbury and Guillaume de Conches tried to found this order on chivalry by reinterpreting the knight as a public man and governor; by the time of Lull **197**, the constructive role of the knight could be assumed. Courtly love, by contrast, directed chivalric ideals to merely personal ends and was thus antithetical to public secular ideals. In *PF*, *TC*, and the *KnT* (pp 104–24), Chaucer used the opposition of chivalric and courtly to express his concern for secular stability. Theseus is the model of chivalry; Emelye, in the garden scene, introduces the solipsism of courtly love. The tournament is designed to settle personal and political issues while maintaining both honor and order; the limits of such chivalric devices are suggested by Theseus' defeat by the less worthy gods. Arcite's death-bed questions are answered in part by his own reconciliation of chivalry and love in his recommendation of Palamon.

1007 Neumann, Fritz-Wilhelm. 'Zeremonie, Gestalt und Wirklichkeit: Anmerkungen zur Phänomenologie der *Knight's Tale*.' In *Literarische Ansichten der Wirklichkeit: Studien zur Wirklichkeitkonstitution in englishsprachiger Literatur: To Honour Johannes Kleinstück*. Frankfurt: Lang, 1980.

An archetypal approach emphasizing the theater and the Tale's astrology. The architecture of the structure represents both the psyche and the world, and the opposition of sun and moon represents the male and female principles. The romance genre is hospitable to and here synthesizes the patriarchal and matriarchal values, as well as the truths of mythology and theology. The plot reveals both the maturation of the individual soul and the achievement of a vision of cosmic harmony. The destructive energy symbolized by the wolf (I.2047–8) can be sublimated only through sacrifice into culture-creating power, represented by Palamon 'the gentil man' (2797) (p 48).

1008 Norton-Smith, John. 'The Canterbury Tales.' *Geoffrey Chaucer.* London and Boston: Routledge and Kegan Paul, 1974. Pp 79–159.
Theseus' final speech 'contains the whole meaning or message of the narrative process' (p 123). 'Theseus expresses his concern that our universe should be whole, perfect and intelligible. His formal address embodies that intelligibility and invites us to apply this wisdom to the process of the total poem' (p 125). The interpretations of Muscatine **726** and Brooks and Fowler **807** are unmedieval. Muscatine establishes an unintelligible Bergsonian world of flux and disorder; Brooks and Fowler unfold a static Spinozan universe where will and appetite are unreal (p 127). Brooks' and Fowler's assumption that the planetary deities have unlimited power and knowledge conflicts with the neo-Platonic philosophy of Theseus' speech, which asserts that the perfection of the Primum Mobile grows less as it moves further away from its source. The planetary deities are among these lesser perfections; they have no knowledge of a higher power or of its intentions. The essential difference between Palamon and Arcite lies in their relation to the neo-Platonic principle that links macrocosm and microcosm, mind and matter, natural and positive law. In his speech justifying his right to Emelye (*KnT* 304–28; I.1162–86), Arcite denies this principle, and commits himself to 'a single act of anarchic appetitiveness' (p 133). He chooses Mars, a god of discord, as his patron and Saturn, the god of disorder, determines his fate. Astrology is used merely to suggest how the neo-Platonic principles are worked out in the physical realm. See **1120R**.

1009 Olson, Paul A. 'Chaucer's Epic Statement and the Political Milieu of the Late Fourteenth Century.' *Mediaevalia* 5(1979), 61–87.
The *KnT* combines history and fable in a manner medieval commentators believed to be typical of epic in order to present 'a mirror and *mythos* for men, particularly knights' (pp 61–5). Chaucer's *mythos* resembles the positions taken by the peace party in the 1390s, notably the members of the Order of the Passion of Jesus Christ (cf **198**, **199**). Theseus is an ideal exemplar both as a peacemaker and as a philosopher-king. The problem of his society is selfish passion exacerbated by the influence of the planets. The significance of the *KnT* as epic lies in the way it shows historical events as existing simultaneously in time and 'as a design *known before* as a pattern in the mind of God,' thereby defining the hero's freedom (p 71). While the other characters misinterpret oracles, Theseus correctly interprets events, most notably Arcita's death, which Theseus sees as having

perfected Arcita. While Palamon and Arcita define joy and sorrow in relation to winning and losing something desireable, Theseus defines them in relation to how a person responds to Nature's cycles. Theseus acts as a free, rational man who controls his stars. The exception is the hart episode, 'a special destiny willed ... by God himself who sends the hart to control the anointed ruler and lead him to dissidents in the realm' (p 75). The Tale is appropriate to a Knight who fought in battles approved by promoters of the Order of the Passion. The *MilT* is an 'anti-*Knight's Tale*' in which there is no Theseus, only a Nicholas, to guide events (pp 76–7). As a mirror for its times, the *KnT* reflects the desirability of peace between England and France, the need for reconciliation of political factions at home, the need for a new chivalric discipline, and, in the contrast offered by the *MilT*, the need for responsible lords to control rebelling peasants.

1010 Owen, Charles A., Jr. 'The First Day's Storytelling.' *Pilgrimage and Storytelling*. 1977. See **482**. Pp 87–111.
An expanded version of **732**. Theseus is an effective, responsible ruler who is sometimes guilty of excess and unable wholly to control events (pp 88–90, 94–5). The comment on destiny (I.1663–73) proves that Theseus is not a representative of divine power: rather he finally sees that the 'sighte above' has determined events better than he could have. Arcite's death-bed reconciliation with Palamon is more important than his laments; the gentleness of the Knight is reflected in Arcite's recommendation of Palamon to Emelye (pp 95–6). The Miller knows that the prominent role he assigns to Alisoun exposes a weakness in the *KnT*: Emily has little to do and what she does do is either ludicrous, to the Miller at least, or purely conventional (p 100). The order of the tales in Fragment A arises from the diverse purposes and qualities of Host, Knight, Miller, Reeve, Cook, and poet. The forms that experience takes are not determined by any individual, but, Chaucer hints, by the 'sighte above' (p 111).

1011 Palmer, David Andrew. 'Chaucer and the Nature of Chivalric Ideas.' 1977. See **483**.
Theseus defends social order just as the Knight of the *GP* defends the church; Arcite and Palamon, like the Squire, subvert knightly duties. The *KnT* 'sets all secular power, of which knighthood is the emblem, in a transcendental perspective.'

1012 Pichaske, David R. 'Knight's Tale.' *The Movement of the 'Canterbury Tales.'* 1977. See **485**. Pp 27–36.
In the *KnT* men's lives are almost entirely controlled by capricious and unknowable destinal forces, and 'he survives who best rolls with

the punches' (p 29). The human and divine spheres show a 'deterministic disorder' and are peopled by inconsistent and frustrated agents (p 30). The 'final irony' of the Tale is that 'Theseus should find himself so much like the gods at the very moment he is frustrated by the gods' while simultaneously 'the gods should find themselves so mortal, so confused, so frustrated ... by the working out of events, by their own squabble, by accident and chance' (p 33). Arcite (I.1251–60) and Palamon (1313–4) see life more clearly than does Theseus in his final speech, and yet neither the malevolent order they envision nor Theseus' benevolent order actually exists (pp 33–5). In the face of the Tale's disorder, Ruggiers' 'Boethian test case' (**752**) collapses and the harmony of Robertson's emblematic marriage (**879**) is shown to be specious (pp 34–5).

1013 Raffel, Burton. 'Chaucer's Knight as Don Quijote.' 1976. See **487**.
The twentieth century does not think as highly of the *KnT* as Dryden did (pp 1–2), but the Tale's 'crudities' are intentional, designed to communicate a critique of knightliness (p 5). The Tale contains two 'blocks' of material: Block A, the love interest, and Block B, traditional knightly attitudes and the romances that embodied them (p 5). The *KnT* is not a satire but contains parodistic elements, (pp 5–8), such as the use of alliteration in the description of the tournament (I.2605–14); the 'deliciously balanced' couplet in which the women lament Arcite's death (2835–6); and the *occupatio* describing the funeral (2929–64). Frost **684** is wrong to take Egeus' clichés seriously; Huppé's comic analysis (**844**), is more appropriate, although his thesis that the Knight intends to instruct the Squire must be rejected (p 8). The Knight's awkward management of the narrative indicates his, and Chaucer's, 'gently divergent stance' toward chivalry, an attitude reminiscent of *SGGK* and *Don Quijote*.

1014 Reidy, John. 'The Education of Chaucer's Duke Theseus.' In *The Epic in Medieval Society: Aesthetic and Moral Values*. Ed. Harald Scholler. Tübingen: Max Niemeyer, 1977. Pp 391–408.
Reidy moderates between Webb's critique of Theseus (**779**) and the approving interpretations of Frost **684**, Muscatine **725**, and Huppé **844**. Theseus is 'a consistent character, not ignobly harsh at first ... whose conduct is governed by what was accepted as an honorable military code, but whom the events of the poem ... led to a deeper understanding ... and to a philosophical articulation of his new insight in Boethian terms' (p 394). Drawing on Keen's *Laws of War* (**190**), Reidy evaluates three of Theseus' acts and finds them largely justified: his undertaking the war against Thebes, the destruction of Thebes, the imprisonment of Palamon and Arcite. Still, 'Chaucer makes it

plain that, though honorable, the military mind ... [is] not enough for a ruler' (p 403). Theseus is 'a follower of *Fortuna*, not a spokesman for Providence; he enjoys good fortune, in contrast to the two lovers, but he is equally blind to the true nature of the case. Palamon and Arcite cannot solve the problem of evil and Providence; Theseus is unaware of it' (p 403). The tournament is an expression of his pride, and to call it, as Huppé does, a 'design for peace in a world of confusion,' 'is indeed to approach the language of 1984' (p 403). When Theseus' plan fails, he enters 'the initial state of Boethian distress' but in his famous Boethian speech he shows 'that he has absorbed his lesson well; ... the path of wisdom is to accept what Fortune brings ... and make the best of it' (p 404). The 'emotional imbalance' of the poem (Salter **883**) 'will seem less pronounced' if we see that Theseus and not Jupiter is responsible for much of the evil. Chaucer may have been weary of war in the early years of Richard's reign when he wrote *Mel*, but he wrote the *KnT* in the same period, showing that 'he knew that military power, however harsh in practice, was the *conditio sine qua non* of a kingdom' (p 408). 'Neither Chaucer himself nor the knightly narrator of the Tale ever criticizes Theseus adversely for the crimes of which Webb and others accuse him. The orderly, ceremonial, dignified life-style which Muscatine finds in the *KnT* is not possible without the sub-stratum of armed might. Theseus must be educated to go beyond it, but cannot do without it. Such is Chaucer's more practical, more mature view of the ideal ruler – one who possesses power, and develops a philosophical mind the better to wield it' (p 408).

1015 Reiss, Edmund. 'Chaucer's Parodies of Love.' In *Chaucer The Love Poet*. Ed. Jerome Mitchell and William Provost. Athens: University of Georgia Press, 1973. Pp 27–44.

In the *KnT* 'worldly desire leads man to death' (p 39). Only when love leads to marriage can it bring happiness. Still, the marriage of Palamon and Emelye is ambiguous, even though this ending fits the 'comic view' the Knight later expresses to the Monk. Marriage itself poses problems and the inadequacy of the Knight's treatment allows his tale to be burlesqued in the *MilT* (p 40).

1016 Riddell, James A. 'The Reliability of Early English Dictionaries.' *YES* 4(1974), 1–4.

In the glossary of Speght's edition (1598), 'geere' (I.1372), spelled 'gyre,' was defined as 'a trance'; 'queynte geres' (I.1531), spelled 'quaint gyres,' was defined as 'strange fits.' These definitions were incorporated into seventeenth-century dictionaries and into the *NED* under 'gyre.' But 'gyre' was never so used and is only a dictionary word.

1017 Robinson, Ian. *Chaucer's Prosody: A Study of the Middle English Verse Tradition*. Cambridge: Cambridge University Press, 1971.
Robinson describes the meter of the *CT* as 'balanced pentameter' (p 51), which includes the half-line structure of alliterative verse (p 154). As illustration, he prints a portion of Theseus' final speech (I.2994–3034) with the half-line punctuation of the Hengwrt manuscript **69** (p 156), followed by the same passage as it appears in F.N. Robinson's edition **39**, where the editor 'has pushed the verse away from the vividness it owes to the half-line movement' (p 158). In the Hengwrt version, he highlights lines 3031–2 with their repetition of *som* and 'dignity of ... tragic emotion' (p 160).

1018 — 'The tragic Canterbury tale.' *Chaucer and the English Tradition*. Cambridge: Cambridge University Press, 1972. Pp 108–46.
Robinson attempts to define a Chaucerian 'tragic grand style' by reference to the 'visionary force' of Mars' temple and to the 'sombre dignity' of Theseus' final speech (pp 110–2). The *KnT* does express the nature of the noble life (Muscatine **726**) but it also criticizes that life. The description of Emelye in the garden does not present a 'clear visualization' of her (Speirs **767**), but rather a knightly idea of woman, which is presented neutrally by Chaucer (pp 115–6). More directly critical is Chaucer's treatment of Theseus' war against Thebes, which shows 'the connection in Theseus between the order of the noble life and bloody chaos' (p 120). Yet the Tale vindicates Theseus, as can be seen by comparing him with Palamon and Arcite, 'men who are fatally determined to make the worst of things' (p 121). The proper questions about them have to do not with likenesses and differences but with whether they are right to love as they do and to complain of the injustice of the gods (p 124). For them courtliness fails to make sense of life; Theseus uses courtly life creatively to organize their love, even though the civilization represented by the tournament is 'not much removed from barbarity' (p 126). The gods make the Tale tragic and turn it into an Arnoldian 'criticism of life' (p 127). Theseus works out a *modus vivendi* with Mars, Venus, and Diana, an essential part of constructing the noble life in the midst of the human condition (p 133). By omitting Saturn, whose function is to destory significance, from his pantheon, Theseus permitted the overturning of his own justice, but his later incorporation of Saturn, subject to Jupiter, into the courtly life, is his greatest triumph. Salter's objection to the illogicality of Theseus' speech (**883**) is irrelevant since the contradiction between the 'fair chain of love' and

the 'foule prison of this lyf' lies 'in the nature of the world' (p 138). Theseus' consideration of mortality reaffirms the Tale's concern with human life as a whole, not just courtly life. Theseus answers Spearing's question (**888**), 'how to go on living in a world ruled by Saturn,' when he says that wisdom is "To maken vertu of necessitee / And take it weel that we may nat eschue."' To Spearing's question, what grace of Jupiter's is displayed in the Tale, we may say that 'the capacity to "take it for the best" is the grace of Jupiter' (p 142). These lines also show Chaucer's final trust in Theseus and the military aristocracy. 'He doesn't want the philosophers to be kings' (p 144). The *KnT* cannot be called 'a tragedy' but it does move beyond itself (cf Speirs **767**) into a seriousness that deserves the adjective 'tragic' (p 146).

1019 Roney, Lois Yvonne. 'Scholastic Philosophies in Chaucer's *Knight's Tale*.' *DAI* 39(1979), 5498A. University of Wisconsin-Madison Dissertation, 1978. Director: Jerome Taylor.
The Tale's chief subject is 'universal human nature, as it was debated in later medieval philosophy.' The descriptions of the temples and of Lygurge and Emetreus appeal to different faculties, such as the senses, judgment, affections, intellect. Arcite is associated with intellect and reflects the theory of the Aristotelian-Thomists: he believes in natural law, emphasizes causation, and experiences freedom as a choice of means. Palamon is associated with will and reflects the theory of Scotus and Ockham: he believes in positive law, emphasizes affection, and experiences freedom as a choice of final goal. Theseus is Boethian 'practical man': combining intellect and will, he probes the hidden causes of things and thereby expands his freedom.

1020 Ross, Thomas W. *Chaucer's Bawdy*. New York: Dutton, 1972.
Treats in alphabetical order over 300 words that may be used by Chaucer in a bawdy sense. See entries for: *ars-metrike* (I.1898); *cokkow* (1810), *Diana* (2282–8), *die* (2243), *juste* (2486), *maydenhed* (2329), *place* (2399), *priketh* (1043), *queynte* (1531, 2333–7), *venerie* (2308), *Venus* (1918–66), and *verde* (1387).

1021 Rowe, Donald W. *O Love, O Charite!: Contraries Harmonized in Chaucer's 'Troilus'*. Carbondale: Southern Illinois University Press, 1976.
The *KnT* 'pervasively pictures life in terms of contraries' that are united, transformed into each other, or at war. The theater is 'an image of contraries unharmonized' in the macrocosm and the microcosm; humans appear to be puppets in the warfare of the gods, and both Theseus and Saturn, a maleficent principle, seek to establish

order through death (pp 30–2). Part IV of the Tale 'corrects' the vision of Part III by introducing the principle of cosmic hierarchy associated with Jove, and by showing the characters capable of rational free choice in response to Arcite's injury (p 33). The marriage is an 'archetypal image in the *concordia discors* tradition of love's power to bind together contraries into a harmonious order' (p 33–4).

1022 Rowland, Beryl. *Blind Beasts*. 1971. See **488**.
Rowland discusses these animals referred to in the *KnT*: the lion, tiger, and boar (pp 21–22, 48–9, 78–9); griffin (pp 46–8); kite (pp 51–2); sow (pp 74–5); cuckoo and hare (pp 94–5 and see **880**); wolf (pp 108–110); horses (pp 121–2); sheep (pp 143–4); alaunts (pp 155–6) and other dogs (p 161). The exclusion of animals from the plan of salvation, mentioned by Arcite (I.1315–21), is discussed on p 20.

1023 — *Birds with Human Souls: A Guide to Bird Symbolism*. Knoxville: University of Tennessee Press, 1978.
Pertinent to the *KnT* are the entries for 'Cuckoo' (pp 38–41; cf I.1810, 1930) and 'Lark' (pp 97–101; cf I.1491).

1024 Rudat, Wolfgang E.H. 'Chaucer's Mercury and Arcite: The *Aeneid* and the World of the *Knight's Tale*.' *Neophil* 64(1980), 307–19. Rpt in *The Mutual Commerce*: *Masters of Classical Allusion in English and American Literature*. Heidelberg: Carl Winter, 1985. Pp 37–48.
Citing five specific links between the *KnT* and the *Aen* (pp 307–9), Rudat argues for an ironic relationship between the two works. Arcite lacks Aeneas' *sapientia* and *pietas*, and the world of the *KnT* lacks moral order, as indicated by the 'allusive switches' among the gods: Saturn for Jupiter, Venus for Juno, Mercury for Pluto, Fortune for Fate (pp 308, 310–1, 313). Lines I.2680–2 echo a misogynistic statement by Mercury in *Aen* IV.569–70. By their allusion to Mercury's earlier speech, they foreshadow Arcite's death and anticipate an act Emily has yet to commit in accepting Palamon. They identify Emily as a subject of Fortune and implicitly commend her submission to Fortune, in which she is unlike Dido. Mercury, not Fortune or woman, is the true personification of instability (p 313), and all the gods are like him, as seen in the similarity between Saturn's speech to Venus (2668–70; Rudat cites 2667–9) and Mercury's speech (p 311–5). Arcite remains uxorious throughout; Palamon takes his place as the Aeneus-figure, their 'exchangeability' mirroring that of the gods and the reality of a world ruled by chance (pp 215–6). Their labor for love, unlike Aeneas' labor, has no fruitful outcome (pp 216–7). The 'Virgilian Jupiter' that Theseus invokes in

his final speech is out of place in the *KnT* where Jupiter 'has ... no message to relate' and has been replaced more truly by Mercury than by Saturn (p 318).

1025 Ruff, Joseph Russell. 'Occupatio and the Meaning of *The Knight's Tale*.' 'Occupatio in the Poetry of Chaucer.' University of Pittsburgh Dissertation, 1971. Pp 79–106. See also *DAI* 32(1971), 3328A.

An abbreviating device occurs on the average of once every 75 lines, and *occupatio*, once every 300 lines. These interruptions disrupt rhetorical balance, undermining Muscatine's view (**726**) that the Tale centers on a rhetorically reinforced theme of order. While the structure of the theater is symmetrical, its rhetoric is chaotic, with the narrator interrupting six times in 200 lines (I.1995–2028). The forty-seven-line *occupatio* concerned with Arcite's funeral centers on the pyre; but the narrator's purpose is to distract himself from Arcite's death-bed questions and from the death by concentrating on the material elements of the ceremony, and this distraction is a form of disorder. The Knight's use of *occupatio* to avoid misery is consonant with his interruption of the *MkT*, and confirms Salter's identification of his two voices (**883**). The Knight's uncertainty may also be Chaucer's, as Salter suggests.

1026 Ruggiers, Paul G. 'Notes towards a Theory of Tragedy in Chaucer.' *ChauR* 8(1973), 89–99.

Arcite's death-bed questions represent, like the *MkT*, the possibility that life is absurd. The *KnT* belongs to a group of works in which Chaucer 'seems always to be searching for a way to dissolve the knot of unrelieved suffering ... he prefers the affects of romance to those of tragedy, lightening the tone, providing touches of comic irony, salvaging his heroes and heroines, or where he cannot ... making them richly deserve the fate that befalls them' (p 95). This 'radically modified tragic experience' (p 95) arises from Chaucer's choice of love as a tragic subject (after the example of the *Filos* and *Tes*) and from the tendency of his Christian culture 'to make tragedy merely one episode in a larger pattern of the reconciliation of man to God' (p 95). Theseus' final speech exemplifies Chaucer's typical emphasis on 'a rational design ... to which each man must accommodate himself' (p 96).

1027 Rutledge, Sheryl P. 'Chaucer's Zodiac of Tales.' *Costerus* 9(1973), 117–43.

The *KnT* is linked to the sign of Gemini — associated with male twins, the month of May, falls from horses, death in youth, and inheritance from friends — and with the god Mercury — associated with deceit, illness, sworn brotherhood, and eloquence (pp 121–3).

1028 Satow, Tsutomu. 'Architectonic Symmetry of the Structure – *Knight's Tale*.' *Sentence and Solaas: Thematic Development and Narrative Technique in the Canterbury Tales*. Tokyo: Kobundo, 1979. Pp 28–49.
Satow reviews the plot of the *KnT*, emphasizing its structural balance and medieval pageantry.

1029 Schaefer, Ursula. 'Die *Knight's Tale*: Auf dem Weg zu einem neuen Ritterbild zwischen Ideal und Pragmatik.' *Höfisch-ritterliche Dichtung und sozial-historische Realität; Literatur-soziologische Studien zum Verhältnis von Adelsstruktur, Ritterideal und Dichtung bei Geoffrey Chaucer.* Neue Studien zur Anglistik und Amerikanistik, 10. Frankfurt: Peter Lang; Bern: Herbert Lang, 1977. Pp 338–65.
In England a pragmatic spirit contested the chivalric ideal imported with the Norman conquest. The discrepancy between that older ideal, preserved in literature, and the realities of fourteenth-century English knighthood is a major subject of Chaucer's poetry. Theseus achieves a perfect balance of the idealistic and the pragmatic. Palamon and Arcite represent the older ideal in some of its more absurd tendencies. Their love for Emily is irrational and narcissistic and does not inspire them to noble deeds; their response to frustration is self-defeating fatalism. The images in the temples of Mars and Venus reveal the negative side of the old ideals of love and war as seen from a pragmatic point of view. Theseus has succeeded in both love and war and knows their imperfections. He is the symbol of order and yet a subject of Fortune. He sets limits to his own power through the exercise of mercy and pity, and accepts the limits imposed by Fortune while retaining the will to act. His final speech displays his understanding of the world's order, his superiority to Palamon and Arcite, and the nature of the compromise he has forged between the old idealism and the new pragmatism.

1030 Scheps, Walter. '"Up roos oure Hoost, and was oure aller cok": Harry Bailly's Tale-Telling Competition.' *ChauR* 10(1975), 113–28.
In trying to determine to which of the tales the Host would have awarded the prize, Scheps considers the *KnT* and *SqT* together. The *KnT* emphasizes the military side of romance; the *SqT*, the love interest. Although Harry does not commend any specific aspect of the *KnT*, he would probably have favored the *KnT* because of the Knight's rank (pp 121–2). The *KnT* is one of five finalists for the prize, which Scheps concludes Harry would have awarded to the *NPT*.

1031 — 'Chaucer's Theseus and the *Knight's Tale*.' *LeedsSE* 9(1976–7), 19–34.
Schep examines first the antecedent 'Tradition of Theseus' (pp 20–3). In his 'Life of Theseus' and his 'Comparison of Theseus and

Romulus,' Plutarch presents 'a morally ambivalent figure' (p 20), who combines intelligence, courage, and magnanimity with arrogance, foolhardiness, and passion. Plutarch implies that the roles of hero and ruler are incompatible, and that Theseus is unwilling to adopt the 'mesure' appropriate to the latter. Ovid's *Met* and *Heroides* present the vicious Theseus; Statius' *Theb* presents the victorious Theseus; and Boccaccio follows Statius (pp 21–3). Thus the tradition has three aspects, not just one; see Webb **779** and D.W. Robertson **879** (p 23). Second, Scheps examines 'Chaucer's Theseus' in *Anel*, *HF*, and *LGW* (pp 23–5). The juxtaposition of Theseus, conqueror of 'Femenye' (22–48) with false Arcite in *Anel* suggests an ironic treatment (p 24). In *HF* (405–26) Theseus is a faithless lover for whom Chaucer offers no excuse (p 25); in *Ariadne* he is a 'thoroughgoing villain' (p 25). Third, Scheps examines 'Theseus in the *Knight's Tale*' (pp 25–30), emphasizing the prison motif. In imprisoning Palamon and Arcite, Theseus acts like the maleficent Saturn, and though he tries to associate himself with the beneficent Jupiter, his inability to settle the love dispute except by a tournament returns the initiative to Saturn (pp 27–9). Chaucer may not have known Plutarch's work, but he creates, out of materials from Ovid, Statius, and Boccaccio, a lord of Plutarchian ambivalence with 'the potential for either productive or destructive action ... symbolized by Jupiter and Saturn respectively' (p 29).

1032 Scott, Arthur F. *Who's Who in Chaucer*. London: Elm Tree, 1974.
The list of characters for the *KnT* contains 45 names. [Lygurge is missing.]

1033 Silvia, Daniel S. 'Some Fifteenth-Century Manuscripts of the *Canterbury Tales*.' In *Chaucer and Middle Studies in Honour of Rossell Hope Robbins*. Ed. Beryl Rowland. London: Allen & Unwin, 1974. Pp 153–63.
Sixteen mss can be regarded as anthologies of Canterbury tales rather than incomplete versions of the whole work. In these mss only three 'courtly' tales (*KnT*, *MLT*, *ClT*) and six 'moral' tales (*PrT*, *SNT*, *MkT*, *Mel*, *ParsT*, *Ret*) appear, with the *KnT* appearing once (in MS Longleat 257). 'None of the fabliaux were so anthologized ... it can be inferred that no one viewed any of the fabliaux as appropriate companions, literally or allegorically, for the explicitly moral pieces' (p 157).

1034 Spearing, A. C. *Criticism and Medieval Poetry*. 2nd ed. London: Edward Arnold; New York: Barnes & Noble, 1972.
The *KnT* was an important influence on Henryson's *Testament of Cresseid*. Arcite's death-bed speech was a source for Cresseid's last

will and testament, and 'in both poems ... [metaphysical] forces are terrifying and either vengeful or callous, and there is a striking and pathetic contrast between the planet gods and the helpless human beings' (p 175). This mythology cannot be reconciled with traditional Christian theology, though it has some similarities to Ockhamist skepticism (pp 175–6).

1035 Stevens, John. *Medieval Romance*. 1973. See **103**.
The *KnT* is a 'social romance' whose purpose is to 'solemnize and celebrate the courtly way of life in its ideal totality' (p 66). The characters symbolize loving (Palamon), fighting (Arcite), beauty (Emilye), and – somewhat unusually in a medieval romance – good rulership (Theseus). Muscatine's 'masterly study' (**726**) (p 67) is important for its exploration of disorder (represented best by Saturn's speech to Venus) in relation to order (represented best by Theseus' final speech). In *TC* Chaucer uses Boethian philosophy to set divine order 'over and against human love even at its highest,' but Theseus' Boethian speech 'does not diminish but enhance[s] the value of this life' (p 69). The *KnT* 'finally transcends "social romance" and celebrates in tones unusually solemn and sombre the essential dignity of man'; but the man it so celebrates is the product of courtly culture (p 70).

1036 Storm, Melvin G., Jr. 'The Knight's Tale.' 'Chaucer's Poetic Treatment of the Figure of Mars.' University of Illinois at Urbana-Champaign Dissertation, 1973. Pp 55–95. See also *DAI*, 34(1973), 742A.
Palamon and Arcite can be distinguished only by their respective dedications to Venus and Mars and the interpretive traditions associated with these gods. Both knights are morally reprehensible, but Arcite is of the greater interest as a failed Martian man who is contrasted with Theseus, Chaucer's study of the successful Martian man. Though repeatedly freed by Theseus, Arcite shows himself fettered by chains of lust. His two-fold error lies in pursuing a goal unsuitable for a warrior and then acting inappropriately in his new role as lover by seeking victory instead of possession of the woman. Theseus has learned to correct both Martian and Venerian excesses. In different ways he overcomes Creon's ire, his own ire, and Palamon's and Arcite's. In conquering the Amazons, he establishes the ascendancy of male rationality over female indulgence, thus defeating the mythic prediction that the Martial figure will be taken captive by Venus.

1037 Strohm, Paul. 'Some Generic Distinctions in the *Canterbury Tales*.' *MP* 68(1971), 321–8.

Chaucer uses certain terms to distinguish degrees and kinds of fictionality; eg, *storie* refers to 'narratives with true or exceptionally venerable plots,' *tale*, to 'narratives with invented plots.' The Knight refers to a *storie* (I.1463–4) or *stories* (859) as his source, but calls his narrative a *tale* (2966). His references to abbreviation and selection indicate a shift in emphasis from preserving a *storie* to creating a *tale* for its own sake (p 325).

1038 Tatelbaum, Linda. 'Venus' *Citole* and the Restoration of Harmony in Chaucer's *Knight's Tale*.' *NM* 74(1973), 649–64.
Venus' role as goddess of cosmic harmony is hinted at by Chaucer's replacement of her traditional shell by a 'citole,' symbol of proportion (pp 652–3). Palamon prays to her in her benign aspect, and her conflict with Mars represents a traditional *concordia-discors* strife (pp 653–8). The love and proportion which the good Venus represents are the very values that underlie the Boethian concept of order (pp 659–63). Venus' triumph over Mars anticipates Palamon's later appreciation of universal order, achieved with the aid of Theseus' Boethian speech (pp 663–4).

1039 Taylor, Ann M. 'Epic Descent in the *Knight's Tale*.' *Classical Folia* 30(1976), 40–56.
For Mercury's appearance to Arcite (I.1381–98), Taylor reviews the sources proposed by Lounsbury (**594**, II: 382), Shannon (**624**, p 303), Skeat (**625**, V: 70), Wilkins (**786**, p 522), and Hoffman (**837**, pp 62–3), and adds two possibilities: *Aen* IV.239–559 and *Theb* I.303–7 (pp 40–3). Another real source is the theme of epic descent, whose features are: 'the hesitation of the hero, the frightening appearance of the visitor ... the command to stir into action ... for the fulfillment of a greater destiny, the sudden awakening ... and the immediate resolution to obey the orders' (p 44). Arcite is ironically unlike Aeneas and tragically like Eteocles (pp 45–9), and this scene shows his decision to be both fated and free (pp 50–52). The theme of descent predicts disaster, for the divine messengers typically appear in disguise, speak deceitfully, are unsympathetic to love, and lead the hero into great conflicts (pp 52–6).

1040 Thompson, Ann. *Shakespeare's Chaucer: A Study in Literary Origins*. Liverpool: Liverpool University Press; New York: Barnes & Noble, 1978.
Thompson aims to establish beyond doubt a significant Shakespearean debt to Chaucer (p 14). Ch 2 comments on R. Edwardes' *Palamon and Arcite* (1566) and on an anonymous play by the same name (1594), citing evidence that Edwardes' play was received enthusiastically (pp 29–30). Ch 3 treats the relationship of *MND* to the *KnT*

(pp 88–92), reviewing debts to Chaucer already identified by critics and citing some close verbal borrowings and the likeness of Shakespeare's Theseus to Chaucer's. Thompson emphasizes Shakespeare's 'variations on a number of themes' (p 91), particularly the effects he achieved by adding a second heroine and making both heroines more active than Emelye. Ch 5 (pp 166–215) offers detailed analyses of Chaucer's influence on *TNK*. Act I, for example, is a 'loose adaptation' of the *KnT* (p 183) in which Shakespeare 'hints at the complexity of the relationship between love and war' (p 178), explores the theme of friendship and the 'discrepancy between intention and action' (p 178), and develops the 'meditative tendency of Theseus earlier than his source' (p 179). Taking over in Act II.ii, Fletcher follows the *KnT* more closely and yet more superficially, speeding up the action, ignoring the Boethian themes of Palamon and Arcite's early speeches in favor of a 'narrower, more personal outlook' for his characters (p 185), and emphasizing pathos, as in Palamon's farewell to the window through which he has observed Emily (II.ii.276–80). The character of Emily is developed inconsistently, Shakespeare preserving Chaucer's depiction of a heroine who vows never to 'love any that's called man" (I.iii.84–5) while Fletcher's Emily (II.ii) is sympathetic to men and capable of sexual innuendo. Shakespeare's work shows 'an attempt to express and elaborate Chaucer's complex attitude and philosophy' (p 214), emphasizing the destructive aspects of sexual love and the helplessness of human beings before external forces.

- Review by G.C. Britton, *N&Q* (1980), 184–6: The discussion of the *TNK* is particularly illuminating for the light it throws on the differences between Fletcher and Shakespeare as adapters of Chaucer (p 185).

1041 Thompson, Charlotte Barclay. 'The Old Testament of Babylon: A Rereading of Chaucer's *Knight's Tale*.' *DAI* 40(1980), 4612–13A. Princeton University Dissertation, 1979.

The *KnT* is at once a pagan analogue of the Old Testament and a prefiguration of the New Testament and of all Christian history. By veiling the biblical element in pagan dress, Chaucer creates a 'complex literary enigma' whose explication involves the reader in an 'intellectual agon.' 'Figurative materials ... provide for a final reading which is virtually the inverse of the tale's literal sense.' For example, Theseus represents all leaders, both Christ and Caesar.

1042 Thundy, Zacharias. 'Chaucer's Quest for Wisdom in *The Canterbury Tales*.' *NM* 77(1976), 582–98.

The quest for wisdom, a synthesis of reason and revelation, is a structural principle of the *CT*. The *KnT* explores 'the scope and limits of human reason' (p 585). The speeches of Arcite (I.1255–8, 2765–79, and 2776–9) and Palamon (1303–27) show that 'there is a fatal gap between human hopes and the arbitrary ways of the world ... The calamitous influence of the gods confirms the general pessimism voiced by most of the characters' (p 586). Theseus' speech, with its emphasis on death, presents a largely pagan world view (p 587). Although there is order, creation, joy, and celebration in the *KnT*, Chaucer implies that 'there is no satisfactory rational answer to the problems of necessity, suffering, and death' (p 588). By demonstrating the inadequacy of human wisdom, the *KnT* transcends it. The *Mel*, a mid-point in the quest, uses both classical writers and the Bible. The *ParsT* presents revelation directly, but the synthesis of reason and revelation 'is primarily accomplished in the poet's own thinking' (p 593).

1043 Tripp, Raymond P., Jr. 'The *Knight's Tale* and the Limitations of Language (The Bountries Which Words Are).' *Rendezvous* 6(1971), 23–8.

The consolations offered for Arcite's death serve to dramatize the limitations of language and thus paradoxically to express Arcite's tragic isolation more effectively than would otherwise be possible. The characters frequently remark on the limitations of human knowledge and language, preparing us for the inadequacy of Egeus' and Theseus' speeches. In *BD* Chaucer had concluded that 'an *unqualified compassion*' is the appropriate response to grief, not intellection or theological argument (p 27). In the *KnT* Chaucer intends the 'offensive gratuitousness' of the consolatory speeches to 'outrage the sensitive reader' and to evoke a more appropriate response than any contained explicitly in the Tale, where Arcite finds no one willing 'to give all for grief' (p 27).

1044 —— 'The *Knight's Tale*.' *Beyond Canterbury: Chaucer, Humanism, and Literature*. Church Stretton, Shropshire: Onny Press, 1977. Pp 151–208.

Tripp ties his reading of the *KnT* to a critique of humanism, an '*emotionally inflated, man-centered, phenomenally oriented relativism*' (p 60). Theseus is an 'epic relic who has not yet learned to distinguish external, military battles from internal, psychological ones' (p 157). The episodic narrative reflects the humanistic emphasis on the individual's isolation and freedom, and thus on chance as opposed to inner causes and teleology (pp 164–8). The heart of Tripp's analysis is his insistence on 'Internalization as the Real Difference between

Palamon and Arcite' (pp 173–84). For Palamon, 'love is desire and procreation, fate is the law of the gods, society a thing to be accepted at face value and used, and the gods beings to be propitiated'; for Arcite, 'love is something unconstrained and unconstrainable, an internal as well as an external force, fate as much man's doing as anybody's, society a thing really no more knowable or usable than fate itself, and the gods, as something like deified emotions, creatures, not to be bought off, but to be appealed to in sympathy. All told, Palamon is an archaic and Arcite a modern man' (pp 183–4). Thus the *KnT*, 'like other pieces of humanist literature, is about *self*' (p 184), and Emelye 'must be a clean mirror for the humanist self' (p 184). Theseus' final speech fails to console because it is 'an easy answer to the mystery of self' (p 199). The speech parodies Boethius and communicates '*the tragedy of the humanist condition*, the tragedy of what it feels like to be a modern self caught in the fascinating yet fatal imperatives of this (now) unknowable process called life' (p 204).

- Review by Alan T. Gaylord, *SAC* 2(1980), 211–8: Tripp's reading of the *KnT* is 'a triumph of tendentiousness' (p 216). His hermeneutics 'are turgidly and obscurely expressed, and presented with such a mixture of arrogance and defensiveness that one is instinctively moved to dissent, even when — as in the attack on hypermodern criticism — he is quite probably correct' (p 217).

1045 Tristram, Philippa. *Figures of Life and Death in Medieval English Literature*. London: Paul Elek, 1976.

Chaucer uses the motif of the Three Ages of Man to examine human life in a deterministic universe. Old Age, represented by Egeus and Saturn, is disabled by cynicism; Youth, represented by Palamon, Arcite, and Emily, Venus, Mars, and Diana, is disabled by dreams of the future. Only Middle Age, represented by Theseus, is able to exercise with dignity the sole freedom human beings have — the freedom to accommodate themselves to whatever Fortune sends (pp 88–91). The *KnT* is an early work emphasizing a human subjection to events which Chaucer later challenged in *TC* (pp 137–8).

1046 Turner, Frederick. 'A Structuralist Analysis of the "Knight's Tale".' *ChauR* 8(1974), 279–96.

The *KnT* has a single world view embodied in the 'syntax' of its plot, which includes binary oppositions (Venus and Mars, Mars and Saturn); triads incorporating the principle of hierarchy (eg, Theseus [apex], Palamon, Arcite); quadratic frames (the Tale's four-part structure and various combinations of human and divine characters); and a circular, unifying structure (the movement from wedding and funeral at the beginning to similar rites at the end, the theater, the concept of Providence). Mythically, the Tale deals with various hindrances to and perversions of the norm of marriage, and their defeat: incest (Theseus and Emelye); infertility (Emelye); unisexual friendship (Palamon and Arcite). The movement from *KnT* to *MilT* shows 'a shift from the Levi-Straussian conception of irregular mating as a structural form in society, to a dynamic Freudian conception in which the young men of the tribe deprive their "father" of his woman' (p 293). See **1099**.

1047 Turner, Robert K., Jr. '*The Two Noble Kinsmen* and Speght's Chaucer.' *N&Q* 27[225](1980), 175–6.
In *TNK* Shakespeare and Fletcher's 'hard-haired' (IV.ii.104) seems indebted to 'of yron" in Speght's 1602 rendering of *KnT* I.2165.

1048 Twycross, Meg. *The Medieval Anadyomene: A Study of Chaucer's Mythography*. Medium Aevum Monographs, New Series, I. Oxford: Blackwell, 1972.
The source of Chaucer's description of Venus (I.1955–66) is almost certainly the Paris version of Bersuire's *Ovidius moralizatus*. The *Libellus de Imaginibus Deorum* (c 1400?) should be eliminated on grounds of date and because one of its supposedly distinctive features, the specification that Venus holds her shell (cf I.1959) in her *right* hand, has been found in mss of the Paris version. See Steadman **768**, Wilkins **786**, Quinn **1048**. Chaucer's 'citole' is probably indebted to Bersuire's second moralization of the goddess where her shell is identified as a 'cithara' (pp 1–14). Chaucer's substitution of the 'citole" for the shell is part of a development in which the late Roman Venus, a goddess of fertility, became the medieval goddess of sensuality (pp 18–45). Against D.W. Robertson's interpretation of Chaucer's Venus as representing concupiscence (**879**), Twycross suggests that in specifying the 'citole' Chaucer may have intended to pun on the goddess' title, 'Venus Cytherea'; or to provide an additional classicizing touch for what he meant to be an authentically ancient portrait of the goddess; or to provide a visual reminder of the astrological tradition of interpretation of the goddess; or to portray Venus as elegantly feminine (pp 46–70, esp 67–70).

1049 Van, Thomas A. 'Imprisoning and Ensnarement in *Troilus* and *The Knight's Tale*.' *PLL* 7(1971), 3–12.
In the *KnT* (pp 9–12), there are literal prisons, and prisons of circumstance and of the self. Palamon and Arcite are 'human prototypes' much like Troilus (p 9), whom 'Eros holds ... in a portable prison' (p 10). Theseus is not, like Pandarus, a priest of love, but 'a foreman of social and psychological order' whose works

nevertheless crumble before 'the flux which controls all' (p 11). Theseus' final speech, however, offers a resolution comparable to Troilus' vision from the eighth sphere by showing that all the snares are necessary concomitants of a corruptible world. The two works invite sympathy for their human subjects but also imply that 'the only binding which matters in the scheme of salvation is fashioned by human choice' (p 12).

1050 — 'Theseus and the "Right Way" of the *Knight's Tale.*' *Studies in the Literary Imagination* 4(1971), 83–100.
The psychological goals of the *KnT* are similar to those of the *Consol* – to understand both Fortune and the self (pp 85–6). At first Theseus looks upon the world 'as an accommodating extension of himself' (p 87): he is irritated by the disturbance of his homecoming, and his treatment of Thebes and his prisoners may be extreme, as indicated by changes from the *Tes* (pp 87–9). Palamon and Arcite resemble their captor in their anger and haste, but unlike Theseus they believe that 'the universe is consciously aligned against them' (pp 89–90). The duel, a more brutal replay of their earlier quarrel, represents the low point of the first half of the story (pp 91–2). The narrator's comment on love and lordship (I.1623–7) reflects critically on Theseus as well as the princes, and Theseus enters the grove representing 'an uncertain mixture of hope and menace' (p 92). Chaucer develops his anger beyond that shown by Teseo (p 93), yet Theseus ultimately sees 'the universality of the situation' (p 94) and 'his own past incarnate' in the princes (p 95). He plans the tournament as 'a symbolic encounter which will reconcile the two knights to the indifferent ways of Fortune' (p 95). In building a theater, as Teseo does not, Theseus designs a structure that reflects, in the oratories, 'the internal human predicament' centered on eros and violence, and in the tournament itself, 'the uncertainty of the outer world' (p 96). Theseus cannot control Fortune, as the fatal accident shows (p 97), but he does bring order to the individual and peace to society through the marriage (p 98). His virtues stand out when he is compared to cold Saturn. In the first half of the story Theseus 'is not a perfect mirror of the stoic ideal of emotional containment' (p 99); but after the forgiveness scene in the grove, he comes to epitomize a Boethian 'ryghte weie,' 'a regimen for the prudent public man ... the highest achievement of a rational nature unaided by revelation' (p 100). See **887**.

1051 Watson, Christopher. 'Chaucer's Knight and His Tale.' *CR* 22(1980), 56–64.

Watson stresses the importance of the Knight as narrator, presenting a list of 'apparently artless contrasts among [the] narrative details and authorial comments' of the Tale (p 56). The Knight's remarks on Arcite's soul, for example, 'suggest an unease felt instinctively rather than considered ... The final dismissive note, the urge to get back to the more manageable affairs of the living, is also characteristic' (p 58). The glory of battle, to which the Knight is attracted, is qualified by the savagery of the pillagers, familiar to such a veteran. The Knight responds to the tournament with enthusiasm, even for its bloodiness, and yet is equally enthusiastic about the restraints Theseus imposes. The line 'Ne how Arcite is brent to asshen colde' (2957) is unemphatically inserted in the midst of three 'ne how' lines in the Knight's longest *occupatio*, its placement at odds with its thematic importance. 'It is as if the Knight, almost absent-mindedly, has done his own imaginative interment of the departed hero ... The point that, however splendid we may be in life, we are of little interest after death, is one the Knight is hardly likely to make explicitly' (p 62). The Knight is, like Theseus, an 'enlightened pragmatist' (p 62). Theseus' final speech represents 'the practical settling of affairs ... by firm direction from the one whose will must be obeyed' (pp 62–3). His attempt to explain events as the providence of Jupiter is contradicted by the demonstrably greater power of Saturn, just as the Knight's characterization of destiny as the executor of God's providence (1663–5) is qualified by his other less decisive formulas (1074, 1465–6). The *KnT* does not solve the philosophical questions addressed by the *Consol* but it 'expands our understanding of such matters by its imaginative and exploratory power; and especially through the presence of the Knight as narrator and commentator, seeking and affirming ordering principles, yet being open to a range of unruly evidence' (p 64).

1052 Weissman, Hope Phyllis. 'Antifeminism and Chaucer's Characterizations of Women.' In *Geoffrey Chaucer*. 1975. See **131**. Pp 93–110. Chaucer was aware of Boccaccio's ambivalent treatment of his women characters in the *Tes*: eg, allowing Emilia, in her first appearance in the garden, a playful freedom and then attacking her as a tease. Chaucer avoids this 'authorial self-deception' (p 98) by granting Emily neither rhetorical nor psychological freedom. The description of her person is incorporated into descriptions of the season. She is not a character but 'an emblematic realization of the central impulse of the courtly life' (p 99). Emily's ignorance of the princes' interest in her leaves her 'virtually without psychological dimension' (p 99), a condition confirmed by Theseus' tacit acceptance of the premise of the heroes' conflict over her when he substitutes a tournament for a duel. Chaucer allows Emily one appearance as a psychological being: Emilia's 'sophisticated familiarity' in addressing Diana becomes Emily's 'expression of personal terror' (p 100). Emily's subsequent subjugation is dramatized by her falling in love with the winner of the tournament, her swooning at Arcite's funeral, and her marrying Palamon, all 'to order' (p 101). The Miller's Alison is also a prisoner, 'compulsorily fulfilling the expectations of her husband's fabliau mind' (p 102). Chaucer's characterizations of Emily and Alison may be 'his definitive statements on the courtly and bourgeois images of women' (p 103).

1053 — 'One Way to End A Chaucer Course.' *Chaucer Newsletter* 2.ii(1980), 3–7.
Weissman compares the tales of Fragment A [I] with the January and February miniatures of the *Très Riches Heures* of the Limbourg brothers. In the January miniature the Duke of Berry is presented as a god, and a commissioned tapestry of a tournament-war displays his military power. In the *KnT* Theseus is arrayed like a god (2529), and attempts to control a tournament. But his purpose is frustrated, and the 'overripe' rhetoric of the most celebratory passages suggests 'a horror of the void' (p 5). Since the *CT*, unlike the *Très Riches Heures*, was not a commissioned work, Chaucer was free to project a critique of aristocratic ideology. The February miniature, like the *MilT*, uses lower-class experience to define the limits of the aristocratic world (p 6).

1054 Wetherbee, Winthrop. 'Some Intellectual Themes in Chaucer's Poetry.' In *Geoffrey Chaucer: A Collection of Original Articles*. Ed. George D. Economou. New York: McGraw-Hill, 1975. Pp 75–91.
The *KnT* dramatizes a synthesis of the philosophical values Chaucer had drawn from Bernardus Silvestris, Alain de Lille, Macrobius, Martianus Capella, Boethius, and Jean de Meun. This synthesis is offered 'as a prelude to the testing of these values in the lives and attitudes of the Canterbury pilgrims (p 84). The Tale raises questions about the relation of humans to greater powers and juxtaposes philosophical optimism with despair and terror (pp 84–5).

1055 Whitbread, L. 'Six Chaucer Notes.' *NM* 79(1978), 41–3.
The description of the planet Mars as red (I.1747) has astronomical authority, as in Firmicus Maternus' *Mathesis*, III.1 (fourth century) (p 42).

1056 Whitlark, James S. 'Chaucer and the Pagan Gods.' *AnM* 18(1977), 65–75.

Throughout Chaucer's works, much imagery suggests 'the idolatrous and demonic ambience of classical mythology' (p 65). In the *KnT* acts of idolatry function as 'signposts of the characters' sinful folly' (p 69). Palamon commits idolatry in identifying Emelye with Venus, and Arcite, in following Mercury's command. The gods fulfill their worshippers' base appetites and kill Arcite by a diabolical means. Human beings take revenge on the gods when they drive out the forest gods. Chaucer's point seems to be 'the similarity of extreme carnal passion and the worship of a "mawmet"' (p 69).

1057 Windeatt, Barry. 'Gesture in Chaucer.' *M&H* 9(1979), 143–61.
Windeatt examines instances in which Chaucer introduces gestures not found in his sources. As in the scene where Emelye exchanges a glance with the victorious Arcite, Chaucer recurs again and again to eyes, faces, and acts of looking, although he also frequently uses kneeling, fainting, weeping and embracing (p 143). Two scenes in the *KnT* are typical in their suggestion of 'the refinement of the inner life' (p 159). Chaucer strengthens the force of Theseus' response to the Theban women by having him dismount and embrace them; in the scene in the grove, the poet provides a measure of the feelings of both Theseus and the ladies by having them fall on their knees before him.

1058 Witlieb, Bernard L. 'Chaucer and a French Story of Thebes.' *ELN* 11(1973), 5–9.
The *Ovide Moralisé* is a possible source for Chaucer's treatment of the battle for Thebes in the *KnT* (I.981–1000) and *TC* (V.1485–1510). It is the only medieval account that mentions Theseus' refusal to accept ransom and his personal involvement in tearing down the walls.

1059 Wright, M.J. 'Comic Perspective in Two Middle English Poems.' *Parergon* 18(1977), 3–16.
Wright relates the *Pearl* and the *KnT* to the attitude of *contemptus mundi*, which sees the world and its goods as trivial, and to the literary mode of divine comedy, a vision of the world as having a value that is transcended but not contradicted by a heavenly perspective. The *KnT* presents a 'secular analogue' to divine comedy by treating Palamon's and Arcite's experiences comically from Theseus' broader secular viewpoint. Theseus is amused by the knights' love but does not dismiss it as meaningless; rather he incorporates it within a larger social order. Theseus' point of view is itself incomplete but the otherworldly perspective beyond his is not incorporated into the poem (pp 9–14).

1060 Yamanaka, Toshio. 'Theseus in *The Knight's Tale.*' *Sophia English Studies* 4(1979), 11–22.
[In Japanese; not seen] 'The keywords to determine Theseus's roles in [the] *KnT* are "lord," "governour," "conquerour," "hunter," "servant," and "judge" (*SAC* 5[1983], p 244).

1061 Yots, Michael. 'Chaucer's *Shipman's Tale.*' *Expl* 36, iv(1978), 23–4.
Commenting on the image of the bird who is happy to see the dawn in B^2.1240–1 [VII.50–1], Yots cites other uses of the image as in A[I].2437, *CYT* (G[VIII].1342), and *TC* (V.425). 'In each instance ... a character associated with the fowl is deceived ... Arcite leaves the temple of Mars satisfied with his fair-seeming omen of victory' (p 23).

1062 Zacher, Christian K. *Curiosity and Pilgrimage*. 1976. See **494**.
By asserting 'order in the face of disorder,' through an emphasis on brotherly bonds and Theseus' rule, the *KnT* 'acts as a corrective to the instability of pilgrimage life' in the *GP* (p 101). But marriage, which symbolizes social order in the *KnT*, becomes material for a joke in the other tales of Fragment I (pp 102–3). The world of the *KnT*, ruled by 'male, supernatural, and rational forces,' contrasts with the world of the *WBT*, ruled by 'feminine power, the cunning of empirical knowledge, and sensual experience' (p 105). The *KnT, Mel*, and *ParsT* articulate the norms of order; the *KnT* and *Mel* present social harmony and the *ParsT*, spiritual community (pp 126–7).

1981-1985

1063 Alexander, Michael. *Notes on The Knight's Tale*. Beirut: York Press; Harlow, Essex: Longmans, 1981.
A study guide (97 pp) offering an introduction to Chaucer, a detailed summary of the *KnT*, a twenty-seven-page commentary, study hints, and brief bibliography. [Not seen]

1064 Allen, Judson Boyce and Theresa Anne Moritz. *A Distinction of Stories: The Medieval Unity of Chaucer's Fair Chain of Narratives for Canterbury*. Columbus: Ohio State University Press, 1981.
From medieval commentaries on Ovid's *Met*, the authors derive four categories – of natural, magical, moral, and spiritual change – for describing the unity of the *CT* as a collection of *exempla* offering a normative definition of human society. As the opening tale, the *KnT* incorporates all four categories (pp 24–31). Part 1 presents the natural order. Theseus, a model ruler reminiscent of Trajan (p 25), establishes order in his family, his city, and himself; Emelye, representative of Amazonian independence, and Palamon and Arcite, representatives of Theban discord, are principles of disorder. Part 2

shows the disruptive magic of the god of love (I.1788) as Arcite undergoes a change in appearance, women's advice is followed (in the grove), disguises and deceptions abound, and animal imagery proliferates: 'this is the most disorderly section of the whole tale' (p 28). Part 3 is moral in that the prayers and the descriptions of the temples reveal the worldliness of the characters. References to Samson (I.2466 and 2415–7) show that Arcite suffers because of 'a commitment to carnality' (pp 28–9). Part 4 is spiritual in that it reveals the limitations of human efforts and provides a correct interpretation of events as disposed by Providence and fortune. The *KnT* offers 'a moderately hopeful definition of human experience' (p 30). As the first member of 'The Natural Group' (Fragment I) (pp 119–36), the *KnT* introduces the theme of justice. In the heavens Saturn represents a virtuous but imperfect, because non-Christian, order. On the earth the central situation of the *KnT* is ramified in the other tales of the Fragment: 'a man in authority takes into his house potentially disruptive forces, trusting to his own presence and power to keep order' (p 124). The story of the adultery of Mars and Venus (I.2385–7) represents the ever-present dangers to marriage, and thus to social order, that are restrained in the *KnT* but set loose in the other tales (pp 125–7).

- Review by Theodore A. Stroud, *MP* (1982), 177–80: The authors' claim that the four parts of the *KnT* both conform to the four-fold *distinctio* they have drawn from Ovid and adumbrate the development of the Canterbury collection as a whole is unconvincing. They cite no other framed collection in which the opening narrative is so used (p 178).
- Review by John C. Hirsch, *MAE* 53(1984), 123–5: It could be objected that the contents of the Tale's four parts are not as distinct as the authors claim; but their main point is still sound: 'that the unity of the tale proceeds from a consideration of subject and parts, not from organic forms, or from theme' (p. 124).

1065 Ames, Ruth M. *God's Plenty*. 1984. See **123**.
Chaucer treats Palamon's questions about the gods sympathetically (pp 233–4). The Knight is an optimist who believes in a destiny subordinated to divine providence and thinks his story has a happy ending (pp 234–5). Theseus' final speech 'sounds rather like Ben Franklin; it is Lady Philosophy adapted for Theseus by the Knight conceived by Chaucer' (p 236). Chaucer does not satirize his characters but presents 'shades of personality' (p 236). And see brief comments on the Knight and love (pp 137–8).

1066 Andersen, Wallis May. 'Canterbury Tales "Rhetors": The Knight.' *FCS* 10(1984), 1–14.
The Knight is an intrusive, pretentious, inept storyteller 'torn between the opposite impulses of brevity and amplification' (p 4). His uses of *occupatio* are sometimes inappropriate: eg, his unintentionally humorous description of Arcite's pyre, his indecorous treatment of Emily's rites (pp 6–7). He combines brevity formulae with amplification, as in the digressions on the theater and the temples (pp 8–11), and introduces inappropriate detail, eg, the undignified reference to the wood gods (pp 11–2). The Knight intends to introduce concern with rhetorical skill into the storytelling contest; Chaucer intends to show that rhetoric can be dramatic, characterizing its user, as well as ornamental (pp 12–3).

1067 Benson, Larry D. 'The "Queynte" Punnings of Chaucer's Critics.' *Studies in the Age of Chaucer: Proceedings, No. 1, 1984: Reconstructing Chaucer*. Ed. Paul Strohm and Thomas J. Heffernan. Knoxville, Tennessee: New Chaucer Society, 1985. Pp 23–47.
The four uses of 'queynte' in I.2333–7 are an example of *adnominatio*, not of punning used to suggest carnality, as in Bolton **803**.

1068 Bishop, Ian. 'Chaucer and the Rhetoric of Consolation.' *MAE* 52(1983), 38–50.
Egeus employs the commonplaces of consolation at their face value; Theseus manipulates them for the purposes of dialectic. Egeus has lost his relish for life and prefers the 'simplicities of religion' to the 'ingenuities of philosophy' (p 43). Theseus uses the topics in I.3017–66 to persuade Palamon and Emelye to act. His speech does not represent Chaucer's solution of metaphysical questions: it is comparable to Ulysses' speech on degree in Shakespeare's *Troilus and Cressida*: a politician's way of meeting a particular situation. Since the marriage satisfies dynastic considerations, the desire for a romantic ending, and Arcite's dying wish, the speech should not be regarded with cynicism (p 44).

1069 Blake, N. F. 'Chaucer's Text and the Web of Words.' In *New Perspectives in Chaucer Criticism*. Ed. Donald M. Rose. Norman, Oklahoma: Pilgrim Books, 1981. Pp 223–40.
In most modern editions, I.1337 reads 'The somer passeth, and the nyghtes longe' (where 'sonne' in Ellesmere has been emended). Blake defends the Hengwrt reading (see **69** and **71**), 'The somer and the nyghtes longe,' as explaining better the sense of 'doublewise' in 1338, and as revealing something about Chaucer's approach to meter, 'which is more adventurous or possibly more careless than we have hitherto allowed' (pp 224–6). Introducing 'passeth' also makes the

time reference more specific, while Chaucer is generally less specific, especially in romances (pp 226–7).

1070 Boitani, Piero. *English Medieval Narrative in the Thirteenth and Fourteenth Centuries*. 1982. See **90**.
Boitani cites the *KnT* in discussing the conflicts between the ecclesiastical and courtly branches of official culture and between official and unofficial culture: eg, the Parson would presumably condemn the *KnT* (pp 247–9). In discussing the literary and philosophical qualities of the *CT*, as contrasted with the historical and secular emphases of Bocaccio's *Dec*, Boitani cites the fabulous history and geography of the *KnT* and the Tale's focus on a dialectic of ideas rather than on conflict among human agents (pp 252–5).

1071 — 'Style, Iconography and Narrative: the Lesson of the *Teseida*.' In *Chaucer and the Italian Trecento*. See **74**. Pp 185–99.
This essay deals mainly with Chaucer's uses of the *Tes*, from *HF* through *Anel*, *PF*, *TC*, and *KnT* (pp 194–9). Drawing on (**992**), Boitani discusses ways in which Chaucer found inspiration in the *Tes* and yet departed from its practice – in plot, character, attitude toward the classical past, and style.

1072 Bowers, John M. '*The Tale of Beryn* and *The Siege of Thebes*: Alternate Ideas of *The Canterbury Tales*.' *SAC* 7(1985), 23–50.
The overlapping of the end of the *STh* with the beginning of the *KnT* creates a circular structure parallel to what Lydgate conceived as the round trip of the Canterbury pilgrimage and to Lydgate's conception of history as cyclic repetition. Lydgate valued the history and 'ernest' of the *KnT* over the fiction and 'game' of the *GP* (pp 38–50).

1073 Boyd, Heather. 'Fragment A of the "Canterbury Tales": Character, Figure, and Trope.' *ESA* 26(1983), 77–97.
In the *KnT* three kinds of *occupationes* are used to communicate Chartrian concerns with man's relationship to the universe. The first kind (I.875–77, 885) reminds us that the story is part of a larger world over which the narrator must exert control (pp 83–4). The second characterizes the Knight and is illustrated by his remarks on Emelye's rites (2284–8) and Arcite's soul (2809–11) and by Arcite's death-bed questions. The Knight cannot resist speculation although he agrees with the Miller that one should not question 'Goddes privetee' (pp 84–5). The third kind of *occupatio* (1895, 2197–206) frames extended descriptions of the disorder (the temples) and the order (tournament, feasting) of man's life, and, with the *occupatio* used in describing Arcite's funeral, suggests the balance of joy and sorrow found in the *CT* as a whole, as in the contrast of *KnT* and *MilT* (pp 85–7). *Anaphora* is associated with Emelye, a symbol of

bounty and order (pp 88–9). The central figure of the *MilT* is *adnominatio*, word-play or parody (p 90). The bitter satire of the *RvT* is evident in its handling of animal imagery (pp 94–5).

1074 Brewer, Derek S. 'A Philosophical Romance: *The Knight's Tale.*' *An Introduction to Chaucer*. London and New York: Longmans, 1984. Pp 106–14.
Brewer comments briefly on the relation of the *KnT* to the *Tes* (pp 106–7) and provides a plot summary of the Tale (pp 108–11) with an extended discussion of the identity of the story-teller (pp 112–4). Brewer rejects the idea of a speaker separate from the poet, especially when this idea involves a characterization of the Tale as 'an ironical liberal pacifist joke' (p 113). Neither is the speaker to be taken as the Knight of the *GP* since the Tale was written first and, on the evidence of I.1201, not systematically revised for the *CT*.

1075 Burnley, J.D. *A Guide to Chaucer's Language*. 1983. See **498**.
References to the *KnT* can be located through the Index of Words. For example, the entry for A[I].2783–95 leads to a discussion of Arcite's dependence on the rhetorical tradition in his praise of Palamon (pp 170–1). the entry for *prisoun* leads to an explanation of legal meanings of 'horrible and strong prisoun' (I.1451) – 'detention aggravated by reduced rations and the deprivation of other comforts' (p 160) – and of perpetual imprisonment – in effect, a death sentence (p 161).

1076 Burrow, J. A. 'Chaucer's *Knight's Tale* and the Three Ages of Man.' In *Essays on Medieval Literature*. Oxford: Clarendon, 1984. Pp 27–48. Rpt in *Medieval and Pseudo-Medieval Literature*. Ed. Piero Boitani and Anna Torti. Tübingen: Narr, 1984; Cambridge: Brewer, 1984. Pp 91–108.
Like Neuse **871**, Burrow sees the *KnT* as representing the three ages of man, an idea associated with death in the homiletic tradition and with good kingship in the secular tradition (pp 27–30). Here time has 'a purely ethical significance' and thus Brooks and Fowler's argument (**807**) for character development is unconvincing, while their attempt to impose patterns of four ages and seven ages leads to unnecessary complications (pp 31–2). Palamon and Arcite represent the venereal and martial interests appropriate to noble youth; the story 'strenuously resists' attempts to find important distinctions between them (p 34). Emily represents the bashfulness appropriate to a youthful phase (p 35). The middle-aged Theseus feels sympathetic detachment toward love and fights only in public, not private, causes. His middle-age is characterized by magnanimity, the passion and generosity appropriate to a great prince (pp 38–9). In

his final speech 'he speaks neither as a grave philosopher nor as a romantic idealist ... [but] as a lord and governor, whose business it is to make the best of difficult and painful situations' (p 40). Theseus is Jovian but more effective than Jove, while Egeus is Saturnian but less effective than Saturn (pp 41–2). These 'asymmetries between the orders' (p 45) arise from imbalances within each. Egeus' aged wisdom, timid and skeptical, is not allowed to prevail in the human sphere (pp 42–4), and Venus, Mars, and Saturn are all ambivalent figures (pp 44–5), having powers of misfortune greater than Jupiter's power for good. The pattern reflects the Knight's point of view as an older man and father: 'the Knight's vision of "middle age" requires that it should be confronted by a universe of *hostile* circumstances' (p 47).

1077 Chamberlain, David. 'Musical Signs and Symbols in Chaucer: Convention and Originality.' In *Signs and Symbols in Chaucer's Poetry*. Ed. John P. Hermann and John J. Burke, Jr. Alabama: University of Alabama Press, 1981. Pp 43–80.

The *KnT* has a musical frame (p 46). The melody associated with wisdom and marriage appears in the opening (I.865–73) and at the end (3097). 'Antithetical concupiscent music' is provided by the songs of Palamon and Arcite, Venus' temple, and the scenes of feasting (p 72, and *passim*).

1078 Chaskalson, L. '"What is this world? What asketh men to have?": Examined Life in the *Knight's Tale.*' *Unisa Medieval Studies* (Pretoria, 1983), 90–118.

[Not seen] 'The pagan outlook of Theseus's world is contrasted to the Christian view of the pilgrim Knight' (*SAC* 9[1987], item 133, pp 310–11.)

1079 Clark, George. 'Chaucer's Third and Fourth of May.' *Revue d'Université d'Ottawa* 52(1982), 257–65.

Clark corrects Manly (**605a**, note to I.1463) and Kellogg and Cox **985** on the date of Palamon's meeting with Arcite: it is May 4, not May 3. Composite moon-books or *lunaria* represent the third day of the lunar month as a perilous day, and the fourth as an auspicious day.

1080 Clasby, Eugene. 'Medieval Ideas of Order: Selections from Four Basic Texts.' In *1983 NEH Institute Resource Book for the Teaching of Medieval Civilization*. Ed. Howell Chickering. Amherst, Ma.: Five Colleges, Inc., 1984. Pp 230–2.

Clasby links *KnT* 1967–3108 with excerpts from Augustine's *Confessions*, the *Consol*, and Dante's *Paradiso* to explain the medieval concept of the physical universe as an expression of a supernatural order.

1081 Collins, Marie. 'Love, Nature and Law in the Poetry of Gower and Chaucer.' In *Court and Poet: Selected Proceedings of the Third Congress of the International Courtly Literature Society (Liverpool 1980)*. Ed. Glyn S. Burgess. Liverpool: Francis Cairns, 1981. Pp 113–28.
Arcite's argument on love and law (I.164–9) is discussed in this analysis of how the metaphorical laws of love and 'Kind' differ from the eternal laws of Nature and from positive law. 'Arcite shows a perverted intensification of his quasi-rational powers' in his appeal to law, 'which should remind him of right reason' (p 118).

1082 Cooper, Helen. 'The Girl with Two Lovers: Four Canterbury Tales.' In *Medieval Studies for J.A.W. Bennett, Aetatis Suae LXX*. Ed. P.L. Heyworth. Oxford: Oxford University Press, 1981. Pp 65–79.
Cooper studies two pairings of romance and fabliau, *KnT* and *MilT*, *MerT* and *FranT*. In the *KnT* the aim is marriage; in the others, adultery. Powerful gods determine the outcome in the *KnT*; debased gods, in the *MerT* (pp 67–8). The garden of the *KnT* suggests Emily's unattainableness; in the *MerT* and *FranT* the gardens are settings for adultery. Emily is identified with May, a symbolic season, while in the *MerT* the phrase 'fresshe May' is sarcastic. In the *MilT* Alison is associated with imagery of the farmyard and the lower senses of taste and smell; Emily is described in courtly imagery and by reference to the higher senses of sight and hearing (p 71). The *KnT*, which 'often sets problems, norms of ideal behaviour or ideal artistry, on which the rest of the tales play variations' (p 72), establishes the symbolic significance of marriage. Both the political treaty and the wedding, placed at the end, 'become an affirmation of faith in the providential ordering of the world' (p 72). In the other tales marriage comes at the beginning, throwing the emphasis not on symbolic order but on human relationships. Here, as in other respects, the *MilT* is 'splendidly devoid of significance' (p 74). The *MerT* may originally have been assigned to the Monk, who is contrasted with the Knight in the *GP* (Kaske **373**). If the Monk had followed the Knight (I.3118–9) with what is now the *MerT*, it would have 'sabotaged' the *KnT*; the *MilT* 'sends up the Knight's Tale without destroying it' (p 77).

1083 — 'An Opening: The Knight's Tale.' *The Structure of the Canterbury Tales*. 1983. See **499**. Pp 91–107.
The *KnT* is Palamon's romance and Arcite's tragedy (pp 91–4). Its symmetrical structure is comparable to that of *SGGK* (pp 93–7); at the center stand the three temples (pp 97–9), representing 'the literal truth of life in the world' (p 97). The 200 lines of Theseus' final speech attempt to answer the image of disorder presided over by cruel and capricious gods in the preceding 2000 lines (p 100).

Because the answer is withheld until the end, the earlier complaints of Palamon and Arcite become not just projections of character but statements of universal import (pp 100–2). Theseus' emphasis on faith and necessity stresses endurance rather than action to a degree unusual in romance, but his slightly greater emphasis on pragmatic solutions brings the work closer to the romance perspective (p 103). He turns Egeus' tragic 'thurghfare ful of wo' (I.2847) into 'something more like a quest' (104). The Tale's attention to extremes of joy and sorrow is mirrored in its use of questions and of high and low styles (pp 105–6). The notoriously flippant passages expose the relativity of the romance perspective (pp 106–7); the *KnT* 'does not pretend to give a definitive view of the world and those who live in it' (p 107). And see pp 110–6: As tragedy challenges the romance of the *KnT* from within, so fabliau challenges it from without in the *MilT*. An analysis of Emily and Alisoun, the various lovers, the uses of the supernatural, and stylistic features leads to the conclusion that if the *MilT* has any deep meaning 'it can only emerge in relation to the Knight's Tale: there is nothing at all in the story in isolation' (p 116). Also see 'The girl with two lovers,' pp 227–30 (cf **1082**).

- Review by Bernard O'Donoghue, *TLS*, May 18, 1984, 555: 'The encyclopedia of genres is the warp of Cooper's book, and her woof is the thematic resurfacing of large questions first raised in *The Knight's Tale*: Providence and unjust suffering, true and false felicity, and so on. These ... remain of the nature of *demandes d'amour*, unanswerable quandaries, for Chaucer's protagonists.'

1084 David, Alfred. 'Recylcing *Anelida and Arcite*: Chaucer as a Source for Chaucer.' *Studies in the Age of Chaucer: Proceedings, No. 1, 1984: Reconstructing Chaucer*. Ed. Paul Strohm and Thomas J. Heffernan. Knoxville, Tennessee: New Chaucer Society, 1985. Pp 105–15.
David constructs a history of I.1761 — 'For pitee renneth soone in gentil herte.' Citing antecedents of the line in *TC* 3.5, 3.904 and 3.947, he arranges the uses of the line itself in this chronological sequence: *KnT*, *LGW* F.503, *SqT* V.479, *MerT* IV.1986 (pp 106–9).

1085 Doederlein, Sue Warrick. '*Ut Pictura Poesis:* Dryden's *Aeneis* and *Palamon and Arcite*.' *CL* 33(1981), 56–66.
Dryden made extensive changes to Chaucer, whom he found 'most deficient' in pictorialism (p 162). 'He paints colors and emblems, slows the motion to a half, experiments with lighting, uses facial expressions as a sign of inward emotion, and paints landscapes and scenes' (p 162). Doederlein cites Dryden's treatments of Emelye in the garden, Palamon in his prison, Arcite's maying, the marriage of Palamon and Emelye, Arcite's banner, the list of trees, and the three

temples. 'Chaucer entered the late seventeenth century as a contemporary English gentleman, schooled in the "sister arts"' (p 166).

1086 Donaldson, E. Talbot. 'Gallic Flies in Chaucer's English Word Web.' In *New Perspectives in Chaucer Criticism*. Ed. Donald M. Rose. Norman, Oklahoma: Pilgrim Books, 1981, pp 193–202.
The use of the definite article in 'The destinee,' (I.1663) may reflect French influence and may suggest that destiny is 'a tangible, real presence' to the Knight (p 196).

1087 — 'Arcite's Injury.' In *Middle English Studies Presented to Norman Davis in Honour of his Seventieth Birthday*. Ed. Douglas Gray and E.G. Stanley. Oxford: Clarendon Press, 1983. Pp 65–7.
Arcite was not pitched to the ground on his head but 'thrust' (*pighte*) against the saddle-bow (*pomel*) (I.2689). '*Of his heed*' ('off his head') probably refers to the horse's head.

1088 — *The Swan at the Well: Shakespeare Reading Chaucer*. New Haven: Yale University Press, 1985.
The optimism of *MND* is shaded by a cynicism derived in part from the *KnT* (pp 30–49). Both works depict in different degrees the irresponsibility of lovers, leaders, and cosmic forces. For example, Theseus' notorious history in love is given more emphasis by Shakespeare; and his lovers are even more murderous toward each other than Chaucer's and more antagonistic toward women. Shakespeare transfers the theme of friendship to his lively heroines, whose constancy to the men is blind (pp 38–41). Titania and Oberon derive in part from the gods of the *KnT* and Oberon especially is motivated by malice (pp 42–9). The happy ending is not undermined but its rareness is implied (p 49). For *TNK* (pp 50–73) Shakespeare 'plundered the paintings on the temple walls' of the *KnT* (p 53), but attributed their horrors to humans rather than gods. Edwards' emphasis on the importance of Venus in the play (**823**) is just, but all of the major characters except Emilia are horrifically Martian. Shakespeare makes both princes destructively egotistical, yet Shakespeare's Emilia is a still more admirable character then Chaucer's (pp 56–65), and Shakespeare transfers to her (as in V.iii.139–44) the poignant despair that Chaucer grants to Arcite (I.2777) (pp 72–3). Shakespeare's Theseus is a harsher figure than Chaucer's, whose final address to the gods (V.iv.131–6) is inappropriate to a plot that focuses on human cruelty (pp 68–72).

1089 Eade, J.C. *The Forgotten Sky*. 1984. See **145**.
Eade comments on the positions of the temples in Theseus' theater and on the hours in which Palamon, Emelye, and Arcite pray to the gods (pp 120–2). In early May the configuration of the zodiac at

sunrise would correlate Scorpio with Mars on the western horizon, Taurus with Venus on the eastern, Cancer with the moon on the northern, and Capricorn with Saturn in the south.

1090 Edsall, Donna Marie. 'Chaucer and the Chivalric Tradition.' 1981. See **500**.
Theseus is briefly discussed as a king comparable to Edward III (pp 80–6); as a knight whose superior education allows him to make a speech that re-establishes order (p 119); and as a knight who follows contemporary practice in refusing a ransom and arranging a woman's marriage (pp 130–4).

1091 Engle, Lars David. 'Character in Poetic Narrative: Action and Individual in Chaucer and Milton.' Yale University Dissertation, 1983. *DAI* 45(1984), 525A.
In a chapter on the *KnT*, Theseus' employment of idealistic rhetoric is said to be 'canny and self-interested, bespeaking considerable self-awareness'; he is not a static or merely conventional character.

1092 Ferster, Judith. 'Interpretation in the *Knight's Tale*.' *Chaucer on Interpretation*. Cambridge: Cambridge University Press, 1985. Pp 23–45.
Seen through the lens of modern hermeneutics, the *KnT* explores the paradoxical relations of isolation and fellowship, compassion and self-interest, especially as these are revealed in acts of interpretation of two kinds: good-faith attempts to understand the other and projective interpretations growing out of ignorance or manipulation (pp 23–4). This approach shows both those critics who celebrate the order in the world of the Tale (eg, Muscatine **726** and Elbow **942**) and those who attack it (eg, Salter **883**, Aers **904**, Jones **981**) to be partially right (pp 23–4). Opposed readings of Theseus' behavior in the grove as compassionate (Elbow) or as selfish (Aers) express the Tale's paradox: that 'the possibility of knowing or feeling with another is fragile and inextricably linked with selfishness' (p 31). Theseus forgives the knights for a variety of reasons ranging from 'gentil' compassion, to a desire for power (pp 31–3). Similarly, 'the First Mover speech is not an attempt to describe the design *of* the world but an indication of Theseus' design *on* the world' (p 35), especially his intention to dominate Thebes through Emily (pp 33–5). The paradox of isolation and relatedness is summed up in Arcite's death when the 'icon of the isolated self' (p 36) 'performs the most generous action in the tale' (p 38). Moral evaluation is not made easier by consulting the results rather than the motives of action, as seen in the ambiguity of the marriage Theseus arranges for Palamon and Emily (pp 40–2). In his *Ret*, Chaucer supplies what is missing

in Theseus' final speech, a sense of the provisional nature of one's depiction of the world (pp 43–5).

1093 Fleming, John V. 'Chaucer and Erasmus on the Pilgrimage to Canterbury: An Iconographical Speculation.' In *The Popular Literature of Medieval England*. Ed. Thomas J. Heffernan. Tennessee Studies in Literature, Volume 28. Knoxville: University of Tennessee Press, 1985. Pp 148–66.
Approaching the *CT* through the subject of relics, Fleming defines Palamon's 'affeccioun of hoolynesse' (I.1158) for Emelye as an instance of *latria* or adoration where only *dulia* or pious veneration is appropriate (pp 157–9).

1094 Freiwald, Leah Zeva. 'Venus in the *Knight's Tale*: Alle the Circumstaunces of Love.' 'Chaucer's Use of Classical Mythology: The Myths in the Context of the Medieval Audience.' University of California-Berkeley Dissertation, 1983, pp 116–72. Director: Charles Muscatine. See also *DAI* 44(1984), 2467–8A.
After making a useful survey of scholarship on Chaucer and mythography (pp 1–34), Freiwald argues that in the *KnT* Venus is 'both larger than lust, less than celestial ... she is for the most part the astrological Venus, modified by her mythological roots and by her medieval associations in courtly poetry' (p 118). In the first two parts of the Tale, principally through the depiction of Emelye, Chaucer presents the courtly characteristics of Venus – charm, elegance, beauty, love of pleasure – although Arcite's sufferings in the grove suggest her darker effects (pp 119–35). In Part 3 Venus' statue blends a number of traditions in an ambiguous manner, but the citole (discussed at length, pp 139–47) highlights her astrological connection with courtly music. The wall paintings 'illustrate the difficulty of achieving mastery over this goddess' (p 153). Chaucer's Venus is concerned only with earthly matters; her followers are beautiful but imperfect. Neither the goddess of cosmic harmony nor the goddess of lechery appears here (p 156). Because the astrological Venus includes noble and base 'circumstaunces' of human experience, it helps to express Chaucer's central concern with attempts to shape human life to an ideal courtly vision (pp 159–65).

1095 Garrison, James D. 'The Universe of Dryden's *Fables*.' *Studies in English Literature* 21(1981), 409–23.
Dryden elaborates a hierarchically ordered universe in Theseus' funeral oration. A hierarchy in the four elements and in various life forms supports the idea of virtue descending from divine perfection, and Dryden adds a couplet (III.1076–7) on a corresponding hierarchy of souls – vegetative, sentient, and rational – within humans (pp

411–2). Bivalent fire imagery structures the work. Dryden accentuates Chaucer's contrasts between the fire of Arcite's love and the fire of his funeral pyre (p 415) and between Creon's impious refusal of funeral rites to his enemies and Theseus' personal attention to Arcite's rites (pp 416–7). In *Pal* 'actions motivated by metaphoric fires of erotic desire or outraged vengeance are transformed into ceremonial fires of festival or funeral' (p 417).

1096 Green, Richard Firth. 'Arcite at Court.' *ELN* 18(1981), 251–7.
Arcite's career at court (I.1408–48) expands the related passages in the *Tes* (IV.22, 23, 49, 59). Chaucer's inspiration cannot have been autobiographical, since he was never a page and served as a squire not of Edward III's chamber but of his household. Pages occupied such a lowly position that Arcite's first employment must be regarded as 'a dramatic act of self-abnegation' emphasizing his 'subservience to the power of love' (p 254). His promotion to Theseus' squire would have seemed 'meteoric' (p 255). Perhaps Chaucer used it as 'a means of idealizing an Athenian court which recognized and rewarded true merit, and by implication of commenting upon the venality and opportunism of court life in his own day' (p 257).

1097 Hagel, Günter. *The Canterbury Tales*. 1982. See **72**.
The *KnT* depicts the noble life, as Muscatine **726** explains, but Theseus is not an ideal knight. He is repeatedly shown to be irrationally impulsive, as in his attack on Creon and his building of the extraordinary theater. Nor can he adequately explain Arcite's death; his final speech leaves many questions unanswered, a situation reflecting the pervasive Boethian influence. Nevertheless, aristocratic society reasserts its authority at the end by bringing irrational love within the bounds of marriage.

1098 Hallissy, Margaret. 'Poison and Infection in Chaucer's Knight's and Canon's Yeoman's Tales.' *Essays in Arts and Sciences* 10(1981), 31–40.
Arcite is poisoned by the sight of Emelye, and stricken with infection by Saturn, the patron of poison and pestilence. Poison provides an analogue for fate, and Emelye is also its victim (pp 33–9).

1099 Harder, Bernhard D. 'Fortune's Chain of Love: Chaucer's Irony in Theseus' Marriage Counselling.' *University of Windsor Review* 18(1984), 47–52.
Theseus' final speech is not authentically Boethian, as claimed by F.N. Robinson **751**, D.W. Robertson **879**, Justman **983**, and others. Theseus relies on experience (I.3001), rather than inward sight (*Consol* Bk III.met.ii) (47–8), and attributes to the chain of love the effects of Fortune (pp 48–9). Robertson and Turner **1046** fail to

distinguish Theseus, who refers to pagan gods, from the Knight, who refers to the Christian god (pp 49–50). Coghill's translation **46** also imports the Christian God into Theseus' speech. Theseus cites only Palamon's service as a reason for the marriage that the Knight sees as based on a love transcending Fortune (pp 51–2). A Boethian ending is provided by the Knight, not Theseus.

1100 Harrison, Joseph. '"Tears for Passing Things": The Temple of Diana in the Knight's Tale.' *PQ* 63(1984), 108–16.
Diana's temple emphasizes mutability, as indicated by its myths of transformation and emblem of the moon, and represents human contact with incomprehensible divine powers (pp 108–10). The narrative 'I' injects a 'note of sympathy' into the Knight's account, and a sense of the sacred is conveyed by his hesitancy about describing Emelye's rites (pp 111–2). The prediction of Emelye's child-bearing suggests the human fall into carnality and mutability (p 112). Unlike the other gods, Diana herself appears; yet she is not powerful but herself subject to mutability (pp 112–3). The Prime Mover remains concealed behind Saturn (pp 113–4). Theseus' final speech, 'an apology for mortality,' cannot console us for a world where all we know is mutability (pp 114–5).

1101 Harty, Kevin J. 'The Tale and Its Teller: The Case of Chaucer's Man of Law.' *American Benedictine Review* 34(1983), 361–71.
The *MLT* responds to the 'degenerative movement' in Fragment I as described by Howard **974** partly by commenting on the moral of the *KnT*. The resignation Theseus recommends is appropriate in a world governed by Fortune and pagan gods, but involves a passivity unacceptable to the lawyer-pilgrim (pp 364–5). His Constance is always active in her own defense through prayer, and he acts as her ideal legal advocate (pp 366–8). His dependence on Christ's intervention borders on presumption, however, undercutting his theological position. Thus in neither the *KnT* nor the *MLT* does Chaucer provide a pat answer to the problem of reconciling divine justice with human action (pp 369–71).

1102 Infusino, Mark, and Ynez Violé O'Neill. 'Arcite's Death and the New Surgery in The Knight's Tale.' *Studies in the Age of Chaucer: Proceedings, No. 1, 1984: Reconstructing Chaucer*. Ed. Paul Strohm and Thomas J. Heffernan. Knoxville, Tennessee: New Chaucer Society, 1985. Pp 221–30.
The invisibility of the physicians attending Arcite, the emphasis on bodily organs, and the manner of the attempted healing suggest the 'Modern' school of surgery based in Bologna rather than the 'Ancient' school based in Salerno. Chaucer's introduction of Saturn as a

personification of 'relentless doom' (p 227) is consonant with his emphasis on clinical detail. He makes Arcite's death more painful than it is in the *Tes* and appeals to Providence at the expense of the gods.

1103 Johnson, James D. 'Identifying Chaucer Allusions, 1953–1980: An Annotated Bibliography.' *ChauR* 19 (1985), 62–85.
Besides citing **661, 671, 687, 736, 895, 1040, 1047**, Johnson gives the substance of two, more inaccessible allusions. Sara Coleridge, in a letter of 1834, complained of a lack of Chaucerian pathos in Dryden's *Pal* (pp 70–1, no 28); Owen Wister, in a letter of 1910, remarked on the lark in *KnT* I.1491, Shakespeare's *Cymbeline* II.ii.22–30, and Spenser's *Epithalamion* I.319 (p 82, no 100).

1104 Kelly, Henry Ansgar. 'Chaucer's Arts and Our Arts.' In *New Perspectives in Chaucer Criticism*. Ed. Donald M. Rose. Norman, Oklahoma: Pilgrim Books, 1981. Pp 107–20.
The visual arts were not as prominent in the literary consciousness in Chaucer's day as they have since become. In the descriptions of the temples, the references to sounds indicate that Chaucer did not clearly visualize his material, and the phrase 'saugh I' is 'decisive proof' (pp 114–5).

1105 Kolve, V.A. 'The Knight's Tale and Its Settings.' *Chaucer and the Imagery of Narrative: The First Five Canterbury Tales*. London: Edward Arnold, 1984. Pp 85–157.
In the *KnT* Chaucer develops visual images to invoke hierarchical truths; in the *MilT*, a 'field image' without symbolic significance, and in the *RvT*, imagery to characterize the teller. Fragment A is concluded not by the *CkT*, which Chaucer probably intended to drop, but by the *MLT*, a retraction in which Chaucer uses imagery in the service of religious allegory (pp 4–7). The *KnT* portrays the nobility and limitations of pagan culture through the images of the prison/garden and the theater. 1) The prison/garden initially functions as a house of fortune, each part representing an extreme possibility of experience (pp 86–7). The treatment of these settings by the Master of René of Anjou in a French translation of the *Tes* of c 1455 is here contrasted with Chaucer's. Once Palamon and Arcite fall in love with Emelye, the literal prison becomes a prison of love, as in Froissart's *Prison amoureuse* (pp 88–98). Chaucer uses this figure not to suggest the ethical bondage of carnal love but 'to clarify and celebrate the mysteries [of love] from within' (p 94). Most of the poem is governed by the garden: the princes' authentic passion is set in a world of ceremony and beauty. Yet their imprisonment is more harsh than in the *Tes*. Treatises by Christine de Pisan **175** and

Honoré Bonet **171** and Froissart's account (**183**) of King John's imprisonment indicate that Theseus acted tyrannically in refusing ransom (pp 98–103). The prison is first a *mise-en-scène*, then a secular metaphor for love, and finally a metaphysical image for the world (p 104). 2) By introducing the construction of the theater, by opposing it to the dangerous and lawless wood, and by re-locating and re-designing Boccaccio's temples, Chaucer turns the theater into 'a comprehensive image of human life both rational and impassioned' (p 114). The statues of the gods draw principally on mythology; the paintings, principally on astrology, particularly the tradition of the 'children of the planets,' represented here by illustrations from a German *Hausbuch* of c 1480 (pp 117–24). Chaucer's paintings represent experience in general, not the characters of the three young people. Their choices of gods reflect 'the human difficulty of knowing what to wish for ... and how to frame that wish without invoking disaster' (p 122). Chaucer charts the 'epistemological and teleological darkness' of the Tale by arranging three 'movers' – Jupiter, Saturn, and Theseus – in a hierarchical chain (pp 123–32). Unlike Divine Providence, these figures cannot transcend disorder but only work toward order, often at great cost, as when the funeral rites require the destruction of the wood. Theseus' final speech deals only with the physical world and with assertions, not proofs, of a transcendent order (pp 136–9). Whereas Boethius' literal prison finally vanishes as an illusion, Chaucer's tower becomes the basis for Theseus' metaphor of the world as a prison. Boethius teaches himself to be free of contingencies and demonstrates man's freedom from destiny; the problems of freedom remain unresolved in the *KnT*. Theseus' remarks and Egeus' amount only to 'a medley of what men say on such occasions' (p 147). 'The movement out is pragmatic, not philosophic' (p 138), and the love of Palamon and Emelye is not in any way transcendent (pp 148–9). The *KnT* preserves a clear distinction between Christian and pagan cultures. Its 'distinctive ethos' is a 'refusal to make final choices' (p 153); the *demande* of Part I is implicitly revived at the end by the princes' different fates, and its answer is still uncertain (p 154).

- Review by A.J. Minnis, *TLS*, August 3, 1984, 865: The exclusion of mythographic materials from Kolve's excellent iconographic readings means that Bersuire's *Ovidius moralizatus* is not discussed in relation to the gods in the *KnT*.
- Review by Martin Stevens, *MLQ* 45(1984), 287–91: 'While [Kolve's book] will serve as one of the best introductions, if not *the* best, for students to the reading of Chaucer, it contains few genuine

discoveries to excite more seasoned readers' (p 290). The discussion of settings as emblems of order repeats the point of Halverson's seminal article (**691**). The illustrations 'serve all too often as mere visual confirmation of discoveries that are readily available from a reading of the text proper' (p 290). Art historians may object to the use of materials too removed in time and place [citing the *Hausbuch*].

- Review by J.A. Burrow, *EIC* 35(1985), 76–82: 'The discussion of the *Knight's Tale* is the best I know'; 'full of incidental felicities,' it includes 'rich and suggestive discussion' of the prison and theater images, and 'an excellent account of the poem's pagan world and especially of Duke Theseus' (p 77). Palamon's reference to 'tyrannye' in I.1111 should be taken as a reference to Creon rather than Theseus, however (p 79). Kolve's treatment of the *MLT* is equally excellent, but his claim that it constitutes a palinode for Fragment A is unconvincing (p 81).
- Review by Richard K. Emmerson and Ronald B. Herzman, *SAC* 7(1985), 212–8: The reading of the *KnT* is 'complete but quite traditional' (p 215) and does not establish the prison/garden and theater as dominant narrative images rather than settings for the action. The choice of illustrations often seems inappropriate: eg, illustrations of the *Tes* are of doubtful value since Kolve emphasizes Chaucer's divergences from Boccaccio; an argument by contrast [concerning the *Hausbuch* Luna and Chaucer's Diana] cannot support Kolve's thesis that the symbolic meaning of Chaucer's images in other medieval arts is relevant to the meaning of his narratives (p 217).

1106 Lawton, David. *Chaucer's Narrators*. Woodbridge, Suffolk: D.S. Brewer, 1985.
The narrator of the *KnT* is the 'poet-translator-historian' and not the Knight. The refusal to discuss Arcite's soul (I. 2809–16) shows Chaucer suppressing a part of the *Tes* and reveals nothing about the Knight. The 'I' who describes the temple of Mars (1995–2053) is the narrator, who 'by reflex' assumes the 'role of guide.' The suitability of the *KnT* to the Knight is only 'a literary version of social hierarchy: a matter of decorum' (pp 95–7).

1107 Leach, Eleanor W. 'Morwe of May: A Season of Feminine Ambiguity.' In *Acts of Interpretation: The Text in Its Contexts 700-1600: Essays on Medieval and Renaissance Literature in Honor of E. Talbot Donaldson*. Ed. Mary J. Carruthers and Elizabeth D. Kirk. Norman, Oklahoma: Pilgrim Books, 1982. Pp 299–310.

Extending Donaldson's comment on Emelye and the month of May (**940**), Leach compares her with the character May in the *MerT*. In both cases the month suggests 'a moment of first meeting ... [which] suspends future promise, either ominous or benign' (p 301). The recurrence of May settings in the *KnT* is aligned with social restraint; the movement into June in the *MerT*, with the release of amoral energy (302–3).

1108 Lester, G. A. 'Chaucer's Knight and the Medieval Tournament.' 1982. See **508**.
Lester defends the chivalric character of the tournament against Jones' criticism (**981**) (pp 463–8). 'A strange combination of mêlée and duel to the death' for which there are no historical analogues (p 464), the tournament is nevertheless 'totally regular' with respect to the design of the lists, religious rites, festivities, and Theseus' alterations in the rules. Jones judges the event by the rules for the joust, but it should be evaluated as a mêlée. Theseus is vindicated by the fact that no lives are lost. The overpowering of Palamon and the participation by footmen are typical of a mêlée.

1109 Mandel, Jerome. 'Courtly Love in the *Canterbury Tales*.' *ChauR* 19(1985), 277–89.
Among the *CT* courtly love seems to be taken seriously only in the *KnT*. Yet the rivalry of two men for a lady is not a courtly plot; the woman's feelings are ignored rather than analyzed; the lover who suffers most, loses; and only political expediency brings another lover and the lady together. After *TC* Chaucer did not find courtly love a viable vehicle for serious human concerns.

1110 Mebane, John S. 'Structure, Source, and Meaning in *A Midsummer Night's Dream*.' *TSLL* 24(1982), 255–70. Esp pp 255–62.
Chaucer's Tale deals explicitly, and Shakespeare's play allusively, with 'the problem of reconciling a faith in cosmic order with our experience of life's apparent chaos' (p 256). Chaucer's confidence is based on rational reflection, observation, and common sense; Shakespeare appeals to imagination and intuition. Muscatine's analysis (**726**) of the Tale shows the order behind chaos. The plots of *KnT* and *MND* embody in different ways the principle of *discordia concors*: the fury who seems to create discord in the *KnT* actually is an agent of the gods working toward justice, and the seemingly chaotic recombinations of lovers in *MND* create a pattern of beautiful regularity. Puck's role is similar to Saturn's and Shakespeare's fairies are, like Chaucer's gods, agents of destiny (pp 260–1).

1111 Middleton, Anne. 'War by Other Means: Marriage and Chivalry in Chaucer.' *Studies in the Age of Chaucer: Proceedings, No. 1, 1984:*

Reconstructing Chaucer. Ed. Paul Strohm and Thomas J. Heffernan. Knoxville, Tennessee: New Chaucer Society, 1985. Pp 119–33.
Partly under the influence of the Great War, Huizinga **188** perceived a gap between chivalric reality and its ritual appearances, but the appearances may create and constitute the social truths. The *KnT*, *SqT*, and *FranT* form 'a meditation on the means of representing [chivalry] ... and on chivalric legend and ceremony as the arts of making appearances' (p 119). When crusading, the *raison d'etre* of knighthood, effectively came to an end, 'translations' of prowess had to be invented (p 122). In counsels to princes such as Gower's *In Praise of Peace* (**185**) and Philippe de Mézière's Rule for the Order of the Passion (cf **198**, **199**) and *Livre de la vertu du Sacrement de Mariage*, martial virtue was associated with marital; the patient wife became a model for the chivalrous male distinguished by his self-restraint and command of appearances (pp 122–7). In the *KnT* (pp 128–9) prowess is pushed to the margins, and marriage and spectacle are placed at the center; Theseus is the ideal prince, advised by Saturn, an elderly counselor like Gower or Philippe; the tournament enacts the society's central myth and is Theseus' most effective means of rule. The *SqT* (pp 129–30) defines *gentilesse* as the art of deploying spectacle and magic with empathy and wonder. In the *FranT* (pp 130–33) marvels become monsters; speaking for 'those who counsel rather than command,' the Franklin redefines marriage, patience, and pity as 'horizontal rather than vertical bonds of fidelity' (p 133). The *KnT* is a 'structure of command and assent,' the *FranT*, 'a structure of advice and consent' (p 133).

1112 Minnis, A.J. 'Making Virtue of Necessity: The Noble Pagans of the *Knight's Tale*.' *Chaucer and Pagan Antiquity*. 1982. See **139**. Pp 108–43.
Chaucer condemns paganism explicitly in *TC*, and implicitly in *KnT*. 1, 'The Sources of Character-Types' (pp 109–21): Arcite is a 'Mars-type' (pp 110–3) whose claim to Emelye is an 'act of aggression' leading to anarchy, and whose love is morbidly linked to death. Palamon is a 'Venus-type' (pp 113–6) whose confusion of Emelye with Venus shows 'the makings of a visionary'; because he is pagan, his devotion to Venus cannot end in Christian perfection but only in human love. Emelye is a 'Diana-type' (pp 116–7), as indicated by her preferences for virginity and hunting, by her bathing, and by the danger she occasions for men. Like Jupiter, Theseus has absolute power and shows good humor and wisdom in using it, and brings peace (pp 117–20). These characters are superior to their gods and never exhibit the evils depicted in the temples, a 'focus for Christian

suspicion of pagan religion' (p 121). 2, 'The Shadowy Perfection of Duke Theseus' (pp 121–31): Theseus is a 'paragon of ethical and political virtue' (p 121). In his treatment of the widows, he appears as a Greek Trajan and his prevention of death in the tournament contrasts with the many deaths in the *Tes*. In his final speech, he describes a Boethian conditional necessity in response to which humans may act virtuously, achieving in life a vision that Troilus achieves only in death. But his wisdom is limited by his belief in fame, which Christians saw as a false good. 3, 'The Young Fatalists...' (pp 131–5): Emelye's passivity is motivated by her virtuous pagan fatalism; she has neither the power of a courtly lady nor the freedom and responsibility of Criseyde. Theseus' monotheism and emphasis on conditional necessity contrast with the polytheism and belief in absolute necessity typical of the younger characters. Partly through Palamon and Arcite's suspicion of the god's injustice, Chaucer implies a Christian standard. 4, '... The Ambiguous Oracle' (pp 135–43): The equal worthiness of Palamon and Arcite is essential to Chaucer's demonstration of the cruelty of the gods. He adds the more specific, yet ambiguous, response of Mars to Arcite's prayer, the argument among the gods, and the role of a malevolent Saturn. The references to Saturn's experience and peacemaking (I.2443–52) are ironic and predict Arcite's disaster. Chaucer exposes the unworthiness of the gods and especially of the cowardly Jupiter, who is nothing like the god Theseus, an exemplary philosopher-king, creates in his own image.

- Review by F.N. Diekstra, *ES* 65(1984), 555–69: Although Minnis is aware of the dangers of source determinism, his work does not entirely escape them. He exaggerates the differences between a Venerian Palamon and a Martian Arcite (p 561). His presentation of late medieval attitudes toward paganism is the more valuable part of the book.
- Review by Bernard O'Donoghue, *TLS*. May 18, 1984, 555: Minnis' study of Chaucerian characters in relation to their belief systems rather than to psychological categories helps us better to understand Emelye, Chaucer's use of his sources, and the ending of the *KnT*.

1113 Moritz, Theresa Anne, and Judson Boyce Allen. *A Distinction of Stories*. 1981.
See Allen **1064**.

1114 O'Neill, William. '"L'Allegro," "Il Penseroso," and Some Daybreak Scenes from *The Canterbury Tales*.' *N&Q* 29[227](1982), 494–5.

Milton's description of a dawn shower in *Il Penseroso* (129–30) is indebted to Chaucer's description of daybreak in the *KnT*, I.1491–6), lines also echoed in *Paradise Regained* IV.431–7.

1115 O'Neill, Ynez Viole. 'Arcite's Death.' 1985.
See Infusino **1102**.

1116 Payne, F. Anne. *Chaucer and Menippean Satire*. Madison: University of Wisconsin Press, 1981.
'*Sic et Non*: Discarded Worlds in *The Knight's Tale*' (pp 207–31): The *KnT* is 'a philosophical parody' (p 207). The dialogic structure of Menippean satire is provided by Theseus' contention (as counterpart of Philosophy) with Palamon and Arcite (as counterparts of Boethius); the Menippean parody of privileged texts is provided by the injection of Boethian issues (p 208). A major antithesis opposes Palamon and natural law (associated with matriarchy, the Golden Age and Saturn) to Arcite and positive law (associated with patriarchy, the Iron Age and Jupiter). This distinction is blurred when the princes adopt each other's values in their early arguments and actions, only to return to their original values in their prayers and choices of allies for the tournament. Their differences are not recognized by Emily, Theseus, or the Knight. 'Chaucer evokes profound mythic conflicts and symbols but also, by the means just suggested, discards them' (p 215). Theseus' resolutions are 'pragmatic rather than profound (p 217). He has no true feeling for natural law, and must be prompted by women, whom he merely tolerates. His status as a philosophy-figure is diminished by his role as an imprisoner, and by the existence of divine powers of which he has no knowledge (pp 219–21). The gods, creatures of time with limited knowledge, are unconcerned with humans. 'With a more exalted conception of divinity ... we would move from the Knight's hopeless confusion, to the pragmatic blindness of Theseus, to the freedom of the celestial vision which understands the mutual reliance of one law on the other ... Instead of the movement upward ... we encounter a deliberate parody of the thought that man can rise ever higher' (pp 223–4). The Boethian speeches of the two princes show Palamon to be 'a fatalist whose assumptions are proved wrong by events' and Arcite to be 'a man searching for God, [who] is contradicted by the absence of any image that fulfills his hope' (p 226). The Knight's failure to comment on these different world views 'sets up a sense of constant contradiction, not to say abandonment' (p 229). 'The Knight: Fragments, Silence, Beauty' (pp 232–58): The Knight's abridgement of the *Tes* has the effect of emphasizing 'disconnected moments and tableaux' (p 235). His struggle with the resulting contradictions is illustrated by his

comment on destiny (I.1663–72; pp 235–9). By exaggerating the deterministic element and linking the comment to an event many times more improbable than the example cited by Boethius (Book IV. pr. 6), the Knight deliberately turns the passage into parody. The Knight's use of rhetorical abbreviation, especially *occupatio* (pp 239–45), constitutes a 'continually verbalized silence' (p 240) meant to distract us from the need for explanation. It suggests a pessimist weary of struggle. The rich descriptions (pp 245–51) provide the 'symbols of beauty which ... [are] the Knight's ultimate source of tentative peace' (p 246). He is willing to deal with pain, death, and chaos only when these are transmuted by the artist, as in the temples, or raised above the familiar misery of human experience, as in Arcite's death (p 253). Theseus' final speech (pp 253–8) is a 'theological version of his own activities' (p 256) and the '*great effect*' seems to be 'the Knight's ironic term for man's propensity ... for creating divinity out of his own profane abilities' (p 256). His narrator's search for peace gives Chaucer's work an epic scope exceeding that of the *Tes* (p 258).

- Review by Helen Cooper, *MAE* 52(1983), 134–6: Payne goes astray in presenting Chaucer's characters as having read and reacted to Chaucer's sources, eg, the Knight as having read the *Tes*. It is Chaucer himself who holds all these views in balance, including contrasts among the views expressed by characters within various tales (135).
- Review by Russell A. Peck, *SAC* 5(1983), 187–92: Although Payne tends to make both Boethius and Chaucer too cynical, on the model of Lucan, she performs a service by placing 'nominalistic tendencies' in the two authors within the 'philosophical and mock-philosophical' tradition of Menippean satire (pp 188–90). Her readings of the tales are somewhat insensitive to religious issues: 'there are deep-felt religious positions ... that cannot be resolved through aesthetics or an affirming of beauty or human invention' as in her reading of the *KnT* (p 192).

1117 Pearsall, Derek. 'Romances.' *The Canterbury Tales*. Unwin Critical Library. London: Allen & Unwin, 1985. Pp 114–165; *KnT*, 115–38. Despite a certain congruence between tale and teller, the *KnT* does not reveal the Knight's character. Jones **981** and others attempt to make Chaucer share modern pacifist views, but the poet's attitudes toward chivalric values require 'altogether subtler handling' (p 116). If Chaucer knew Boccaccio's *Chiose*, he probably found them uncongenial, since he was attracted by the opportunity the paganism of the Tale's setting offered for exploring the relation of man and god (pp 117–21). With the aid of Boethius, Chaucer depicts young men growing toward philosophical understanding through suffering, not fools who invite our laughter (cf Robertson **879**) (pp 121–3). Theseus and Aegeus represent still more mature views that are meant to be taken seriously (pp 123–4). In Theseus' final speech, however, Chaucer's attempted 'graft' of Boethius onto Boccaccio is not successful; the weakness of the speech derives not from Theseus' limitations but from the depth of Chaucer's own depiction of the human situation (pp 124–5). Partly through his transformation of the classical gods into planetary influences, Chaucer 'impregnate[s] the story with the hints of a deeper meaning [beyond the celebration of the noble life], at the same time that he eschews allegory completely' (p 128). His treatment of the characters as 'exemplars,' recognized by critics as unlike as Muscatine **726** and Robertson, moves the story in the same direction (p 130); Emelye in particular is 'a cipher,' an agent of larger forces (pp 131–2). Arcita is the noble hero of the *Tes*, but Chaucer makes the two princes equally ignoble, presaging a resolution 'bleakly capricious' (p 134). Yet a more positive conclusion is made possible by Arcite's very responsibility for the initial disorder. Arcite's dying speech, 'a heroic act of penitence' ending with the Tale's most moving line – 'Foryet nat Palamon, the gentil man' (I.2797) – confirms this view (pp 135–6). Arcite's words, to which Theseus' speech is a 'mere epilogue' (p 137), effectively close the action. The Tale's variegated style of narration is characteristically Chaucerian and adapted from the English popular romances (p 138). Pearsall's discussion sifts the criticism in a more detailed way than can be represented here.

1118 Perryman, Judith C. 'The "False Arcite" of Chaucer's *Knight's Tale*.' *Neophil* 68(1984), 121–33.
Chaucer emphasizes Arcite's falseness through three changes from the *Tes*: unlike Boccaccio's Arcita, Arcite breaks an explicit pact with Theseus by returning to Athens; in the *KnT* only Arcite, and not Palamon, makes use of disguise; and Arcite violates the oath of sworn brotherhood introduced by Chaucer (pp 122–6). The distinction between a 'truthful and open' Palamon and a 'faithless and devious' Arcite is supported by Palamon's association with the noble lion and with Destiny and by Arcite's association with the deceitful tiger and with Fortune (pp 126–30). While the princes do not personify Body and Soul (cf Boheemen **919**), Arcite is allied to mutability and Palamon to eternity (pp 130–1). Arcite's falseness is an image of the instability of temporal things and as such explains why he must die.

1119 Reiss, Edmund. 'Chaucer's Thematic Particulars.' In *Signs and Symbols in Chaucer's Poetry*. Ed. John P. Hermann and John J. Burke, Jr. University, Alabama: University of Alabama Press, 1981. Pp 27–42.
Egeus' function is probably humorous, and depends on the audience's knowing that the Aegeus of myth committed suicide out of grief. His words may also be read as contrasting with the true wisdom of Theseus' final speech or as exposing its inadequacy (pp 37–9).

1120 Salter, Elizabeth. 'Chaucer and Boccaccio: *The Knight's Tale.*' *Fourteenth-Century English Poetry: Contexts and Readings*. Oxford: Clarendon Press, 1983. Pp 141–81.
In this posthumously published work, Salter emphasizes Chaucer's transformation of a minor element in the *Tes* into a major theme: the relation of gods and humans. Chaucer's interest in depicting human pain motivated his recourse to the *Consol* for a philosophical resolution of the problem of suffering (pp 149–50). A test case of his success is Palamon's lament (1303–33), drawn from *Consol* Book I.pr.5 and *Tes* III.3. Palamon's anger is unconstrained by the debate structure of the *Consol*, and the narrative supports his view (pp 150–4). Chaucer increases the role of the gods and emphasizes their malice: eg, the beauty, pleasure, and fear associated with Venus in the *Tes* become here only pain and domination (pp 155–7). The use of the phrase 'saugh I' in the temple of Mars shows Chaucer's personal involvement in the theme of human disaster (p 161). The poem's conclusion illustrates 'the outmanoeuvring of human courage and magnanimity by divine ingenuity' (p 169). Arcite's death, attended by no complex philosophical issues, is quickly accepted in the *Tes*; in the *KnT* Arcite must be reconciled to his death and that death must be explained as part of a divine purpose (p 173). But Theseus' final speech (pp 175–9) directs attention away from both human pain and divine strife. The identification of Jupiter with the First Mover fails partly because Jupiter accepted Saturn's intervention (I.2446) (pp 175–6). The Boethian sections of the speech only highlight the bleakness of the story, and the Boethian and Boccaccian portions of the speech are not smoothly unified (pp 176–9). Chaucer's sense of pathos was stronger than his conviction of order, and the cruelties of his gods are never justified. The *KnT* is 'an uneven work ... expressing best not the great orthodoxies of medieval faith, but the stubborn truths of human experience' (p 180). Although Chaucer's over-all intention remains unclear, his re-working of the *Tes* produces 'an experimental poem of some distinction' (p 181).

- Review by Edward Wilson, *RES* 36(1985), 251–3: Arcite's death should not be attributed to the cruelty of the gods. The image of the sword of Damocles (I.2029–30) is, as Norton-Smith suggests (**1008**, p 132, n 71), taken from Macrobius' *Commentary on the Dream of Scipio*, I.x; it indicates that Arcite brings ruin on himself by 'his basic moral and philosophical anarchy' (p 253).

1121 Schless, Howard H. *Chaucer and Dante: A Revaluation*. Norman, Oklahoma: Pilgrim Books, 1984. Pp 171–8.
Schless lists the passages in which Bethel **527** found debts to Dante and dismisses most of them, often on the ground that the thought and expression are commonplace. He admits two: I.1493–4, the description of the sunrise, indebted to *Purg* I.19 f; and I.1663–4, the reference to *destinee*, indebted to *Inf* VII.67–96; with the possible addition of the image of the bleeding twigs in I.2337–40, which may be indebted to *Inf* XIII.40–1 as well as *Tes* 7.92. Based on Schless' dissertation of the same title. *DAI* 16(1956), 1675A. University of Pennsylvania Dissertation, 1956. Director: Albert C. Baugh.

1122 Schweitzer, Edward C. 'Fate and Freedom in *The Knight's Tale*.' *SAC* 3(1981), 13–45.
Schweitzer examines Arcite's death as the key to the Tale's central paradox. First, he summarizes changes to the *Tes* which have the effect of emphasizing fate (pp 13–5). Planetary influences are especially pervasive (p 16), and though Brooks and Fowler **807** and North **873** incorrectly assert that the tournament begins at sunrise, its actual beginning at 9 AM is also astrologically significant (p 17). In London on Tuesday, 5 May 1388, the date North convincingly establishes for the tournament, the sign of Leo, with Saturn in the ascendent, began to rise above the eastern horizon just before 9 AM (pp 18–9). Leo governs the heart, the area of Arcite's injury (p 19). Given the weight of the astrological machinery, and the 'appearance of universal malice' undercuts allusions to the *Consolation* and their promise of cosmic order (p 20). Second, Schweitzer argues for an element of freedom in Arcite's death (pp 21–30), which is 'an emblem of the end of those who persist in loving unreasonably' (p 29). The fury epitomizes both the intervention of cosmic forces and 'the paradox that those cosmic forces determine only what the human protagonists have freely chosen' (pp 29–30). Third, Schweitzer examines the Boethian allusions (pp 30–6) to show that 'the appearance of misfortune and injustice in the world is an illusion that follows from mistaking the nature of the true good' (p 30). Arcite's speech lamenting his release from prison (I.1251–74) shows him to be philosophically ill (pp 31–3) (pp 33–4). His death-bed question is pathetic but not problematical unless we share his mistaken identification of Emelye with the true good (pp 34–5). His prayer to

Mars symbolizes the pursuit of partial goods (p 35). Boethius' explanation of how passions enslave humans parallels the tale's paradoxical treatment of freedom and fate (p 36). Finally, Schweitzer considers the relation of his argument that Arcite's death is just, to Palamon's marriage and to Theseus' final speech (pp 36–45). The marriage is not a 'reward' unjustly given to a man equally as flawed as Arcite since Emelye, as an earthly good, cannot be a reward (pp 36–8). Theseus' speech is un-Boethian, in its emphases on the bottom of the chain of being, and on fate rather than providence (pp 38–42). The Boethian context, however, allows the audience to appreciate the worthlessness of earthly goods, a perspective Chaucer denies to both Arcite and Theseus. The Knight's own incomprehension of the Boethian perspective is dramatized again in his interruption of the *MkT* (pp 44–5).

1123 Shibata, Takeo. 'Kishi no monogatari ni okeru kunshuzo' ['The Image of Lord Theseus in Chaucer's *Knight's Tale*']. *Shuru* 44 (Doshisha University, 1983), 1–22.
[not seen] Reported by Lorrayne Y. Baird-Lange and Hildegard Schnuttgen, *A Bibliography of Chaucer 1974-1985* (Archon Books, 1988), item 1302, p. 134. See also *SAC* 7(1985), item 141, p 313: 'Examines the role of Lord Theseus, who acts as *minister Dei* and governs on the medieval social principle: *utilitas publica prefertur utilitate privatae*.'

1124 Shoaf, R.A. *Dante, Chaucer, and the Currency of the Word: Money, Images, and Reference in Late Medieval Poetry*. Norman, Oklahoma: Pilgrim Books, 1983.
The Knight is 'one of the least passionate and most rigid men whom Chaucer ever imagined' (p 214). In the *KnT* order is stifling, 'soldierly Stoicism' and 'weary wisdom' serve for Christian vision, the highest good is only fame, and passion is treated cynically (p 169).

1125 Siegel, Marsha. 'What the Debate Is and Why it Founders in Fragment A of *The Canterbury Tales*.' *SP* 72(1985), 1–24.
The *KnT* and *MilT* initiate a philosophical debate on epistemology which is short-circuited by the *RvT* and *CkT*. Through its emphasis on psychology and physicality, and through its explanation of such phenomena as Alisoun's shiny forehead, the *MilT* asserts the knowability of a reality that can be manipulated by Nicholas' kind of intelligence (pp. 2–10). The 'far more realistic' *KnT* (p 10) depicts a largely unknowable world governed by a chance which is not beneficent, as is usually the case in romance (pp 11–2). Chaucer suppresses references to causation in the *Tes*, introduces mystery through the forecasts of Mercury and Diana, and dramatizes chance

in the powerful but non-omniscient gods (pp 12–5). In place of intelligence, Theseus's final speech celebrates faith (pp 15–7). In the *RvT* and *CkT* the 'quitting' of Fragment A shifts from tales to tellers, and Chaucer sets the dramatic principle against the thematic principle to suggest the ways subjectivity interferes with the ability to sustain philosophical inquiry (pp 17–20). Through its 'degeneration' (p 20) Fragment A provides an 'impetus to pilgrimage' (cf Westlund **896**) by establishing the problem explored in the middle fragments (pp 20–1, 24).

1126 Sklute, Larry. *Virtue of Necessity: Inclusiveness and Narrative Form in Chaucer's Poetry*. Columbus: Ohio State University Press, 1984.
The *KnT* is more optimistic than *TC* about man's ability to understand and control his own destiny. Chaucer omits the flight of Arcite's soul and give's Arcite his death-bed questions in order to prompt Theseus to reason his way to the meaning of events. Through the idea of the continuation of the species, Theseus answers Arcite's questions and softens the pain of individual mortality (pp 79–81).

1127 Spearing, A. C. 'Chaucerian Authority and Inheritance.' 1983. See **516**.
A comparison of Palamon's questions (I.1303 f) and the plot with Theseus' final speech (pp 189–91) suggests that 'Jupiter, the benevolent father of all things, is a mere idea; the reality ... is Saturn, the cruel father who does not hesitate to destroy his own children' (p 191).

1128 — 'Lydgate's Canterbury Tale: *The Siege of Thebes* and Fifteenth-Century Chaucerianism.' In *Fifteenth-Century Studies: Recent Essays*. Ed. Robert F. Yaeger. Hamden, Conn: Archon, 1984. Pp 333–64.
The relationship of the *STh* to the *KnT* is an example of the type of poetic influence called the 'tessera' or 'link' by Harold Bloom (in *The Anxiety of Influence*, 1972). Lydgate's work completes Chaucer's by treating the earlier part of the Theban legend. Lydgate sometimes creates a 'generally Chaucerian texture' by weaving together Chaucerian fragments, as in his description of Adrastus' army (*STh* 2661–3); at other times he invites comparison with specific passages, as in his imitation of the *occupatio* on Arcite's rites (I.2919–66) in *STh* 4565–4602 (pp 340–1). Lydgate's *descriptiones* (pp 346–50) are closely related to those of the *KnT*: eg, see the juxtaposition of castle and garden in *STh* 2271–80 and *KnT* I.1056–61. He works toward making explicit an implication he found in the *KnT*: 'that the resort to arms as a means of settling political and personal problems must lead to disaster' (p 352). This interpretation is what Bloom calls 'misreading or misprison' since the *KnT* 'presents the aggressive

instinct as being, like the erotic, an inevitable part of human nature, as productive of genuine chivalric splendor, and as capable of being controlled by justice, *pitee*, and brotherly love. Thus, for all its sombreness and its questioning philosophical scope, *The Knight's Tale* can still be thought of as a chivalric romance'; the *STh* cannot be (p 353). Lydgate also 'misread' Chaucer's 'greatest imaginative achievement' in the *KnT*, his attempt to 'reimagine a classical pagan culture in its own terms' (p 355). Lydgate alternately medievalizes, allegorizes, and condemns, producing a work 'fundamentally unChaucerian' in its lack of openness toward that past (p 358). See **1129**.

1129 — 'Renaissance Chaucer *and* Father Chaucer.' *English* 34 (1985), 1–38.
Presents in very brief form aspects of the argument of **87**. On the relation between the Renaissance and the Middle Ages (pp 1–8 here), see **87**; on the *KnT* (pp 32–4), see **1130**; on Lydgate's *STh* (pp 25–35), see **1128**.

1130 — 'Chaucer's Classical Romances.' In *Medieval to Renaissance*. 1985. See **87**. Pp 30–58.
Chaucer's strong sense of historical perspective (cf Bloomfield **207**) was a result of both his own relativism and his contact with Renaissance Italy. Chaucer's chief interest in antiquity was its paganism. In Emelye's rites (I.2273–94) he attempts to imagine a real past culturally different from his present; he does not allegorize, an approach that would have destroyed the difference he meant to evoke (pp 41–3). In introducing Boethian philosophy, he was both pursuing historical accuracy in the Renaissance manner, and exploring, as Minnis **139** shows, a subject of prime interest to late medieval thinkers, the status of virtuous pagans in salvation economy. He viewed his characters much as Petrarch viewed Cicero, as standing on the brink of Christian understanding (pp 43–6). Astrology provided a bridge between the two cultures (pp 46–51). The narrator speaks from a Christian perspective when he refers to a providence beyond the planets (I.1663–5), for there is none in the world of the Tale (p 48). Palamon's speech (I.1303–24) accurately describes the callousness of the gods. Minnis exaggerates the pagan significance of Emelye's subjection to fate; Chaucer means to explore a universal human condition (p 51). Theseus' final speech is, like his well-intentioned attempts to create order, 'self-negating' (pp 51–5). Its two faults are its veering away from arguing for a divine perfection to advising resignation, and its mistaken identification of Jupiter with the First Mover. Chaucer's deliberate creation of a paradoxical situation in which 'the nearer Theseus comes to an optimistic Christian vision,

the more mistaken he is' (p 55) about the world of the Tale suggests that in depicting his characters' limited knowledge, as well as their limited freedom, Chaucer was not depicting pagans alone, as Minnis insists, but all humans (pp 55–7). Yet Theseus, like Arcite on his death-bed, rises above the gods in generosity of spirit (pp 57–8).

1131 Stroud, Theodore A. 'Chaucer's Structural Balancing of *Troilus* and "Knight's Tale".' *AnM* 21(1981), 31–45.
Chaucer saw the *Tes* and *Filos* as 'contrapuntally balanced or opposed' (p 31) and set out to exploit their oppositions in the *KnT* and *TC* as an 'aesthetic game' (p 33). Each of the Chaucerian works 'tends to look like the other viewed in an inverting mirror' (p 34), as instanced by parallels between hyperbolic Palamon and Troilus; between casuistical Arcite and Diomede; between unwilling Emily (p 35), and reluctant Criseyde; between the Knight, who 'hides his feeling behind a mask of professional toughness' (p 39), and the narrator of *TC*, who openly shows his agony and his amusement; and between Theseus and Pandarus, especially in their uses of Boethian ideas (pp 40–41). This 'antithetical balancing' brings the works' moral seriousness into question (p 41). Both Theseus' final speech and the epilogue of *TC* are undermined by their contexts (p 43).

1132 Waith, Eugene M. 'Shakespeare and the Ceremonies of Romance.' In *Shakespeare's Craft*. Ed. Philip M. Highfill, Jr. Carbondale: Southern Illinois University Press, 1982, pp 113–37.
In *TNK* Shakespeare and Fletcher develop in greater detail than does Chaucer in the *KnT* the ceremoniousness of certain scenes: the appeal of the Theban women to Theseus, the matching scene of intercession in the grove, and the prayers to the gods (pp 130–7). These ceremonies confer 'a brilliant visual immediacy' on moments in which the characters choose honor and courtesy (p 137).

1133 Weiss, Alexander. *Chaucer's Native Heritage*. American University Studies, Series IV, Volume 11. New York: Peter Lang, 1985.
The differences between Theseus' final speech, which uses an expository mode to instill a lesson, and Teseo's (*Tes* XII), which uses an analytical mode to make a logical argument, are attributable to Chaucer's dependence on a didactic native tradition passed on through Middle English lyrics. Like Hrothgar's speech on pride in *Beowulf*, Theseus' speech is a sermon with a text, examples, and application. Other native elements include such stylistic features as the use of alliterative phrases and non-alliterative doublets.

1134 Zanoni, Mary-Louise. 'Cosmic Order and Moral Choice in the *Knight's Tale*.' 'Divine Order and Human Freedom in Chaucer's

Poetry and Philosophical Tradition.' Cornell University Dissertation, 1982, pp 7–36. Director: R. E. Kaske. See also *DAI* 42(1982), 5115A. Palamon and Arcite embrace polytheism, a correlative of their status as satirized romance heroes and as persons who seek delusional earthly goods like Emelye. But Aristotle had argued that pagans could attain to monotheism. Theseus realizes this possibility, one appropriate to his status as a king; he is the intellectual and emotional superior of the princes and has at least a dim vision of eternity.

Index

References preceded by a 'p' refer to page numbers for various Headnotes throughout the volume; all other citations are to items in the bibliography. Numbers in boldface indicate authorship or editorship or translation, or the principal entry, such as the facsimile of a manuscript. A boldface number in parentheses indicates a subdivision of the item immediately preceding it. 'R' indicates review entry.

www.ingramcontent.com/pod-product-compliance
Lightning Source LLC
LaVergne TN
LVHW090757070826
844660LV00022B/1015

* 9 7 8 1 4 4 2 6 1 4 8 5 7 *